Fodor's
Vacations in New York State

Previously published as *Fodor's New York State*

Fodor's Travel Publications, Inc.
New York and London

Fodor's Vacations in New York State

Editors: Kathleen McHugh, Denise Nolty
Editorial Contributors: Joseph Bookbinder, Teresa Buckley, Vinod Chhabra, Charles De Motte, Theodore Fischer, Diane Gallo, Diane Galusha, Marian Goldberg, Paul Grondahl, David Laskin, Mark Novak, Peter Oliver, Roswell Park, John Preston, Patricia Tunison Preston, Michele Schachere, Aaron Sugarman, Fred Sullivan, Deborah Williams
Art Director: Fabrizio La Rocca
Cartographer: David Lindroth
Illustrator: Karl Tanner
Cover Photograph: U. Sjostedt/FPG International

Cover Design: Vignelli Associates

Special Sales

Contents

Maps

Foreword

While every care has been taken to assure the accuracy of the information in this guide, the passage of time will always bring change and, consequently, the publisher cannot accept responsibility for errors that may occur.

All prices and opening times quoted here are based on information supplied to us at press time. Hours and admission fees may change, however, and the prudent traveler will avoid inconvenience by calling ahead.

Fodor's wants to hear about your travel experiences, both pleasant and unpleasant. When a hotel or restaurant fails to live up to its billing, let us know and we will investigate the complaint and revise our entries where the facts warrant it.

Send your letters to the editors of Fodor's Travel Publications, 201 E. 50th Street, New York, NY 10022.

Highlights'91 and Fodor's Choice

Highlights '91

*by Aaron
Sugarman*

Tax increases are more often placed in the category of "inevitable" than in that of "news," but a seriously strapped New York State government has approved a **series of new taxes** that can only be called bad news for visitors. As of August 1990, the state began collecting a 5% tax on hotel rooms costing more than $100. Combined with sales and other taxes, the tax rate on hotel rooms is now about 20%, the worst in the country. The so-called "bed tax" costs hotel guests approximately $20 a day for a $100 room, $30 a day for a $150 room.

Other new taxes tack a 5% charge onto the tab for a car rental and a 4% charge on parking garages. Also part of the new tax package is a 4% surcharge on 800 and 900 telephone calls, including those made from a hotel room. Prices on drinks are also likely to rise as increased taxes on alcohol are pushed on consumers.

Budget cuts won't affect improvements being made on the **New York State Thruway.** Over the next two years, 16 rest-stop restaurants will be redesigned in Adirondack rustic style, with fieldstone walls and exposed timber trusses, and food options will be upgraded to include such fast-food favorites as Nathan's hot dogs and Mrs. Fields Cookies.

New York City   Work continues on projects to enhance **Kennedy International** and **LaGuardia airports,** although air travelers are more likely to see detours than improvements this year. New access roads to ease congestion are under construction at both airports, and Kennedy is getting a new heating and air-conditioning system. These projects should take until 1994 to complete, at a price tag of $1.8 billion.

Unfortunately, plans to bring Kennedy into the 21st century—with an I. M. Pei–designed central terminal building and a slick monorail system—have been postponed indefinitely. And the oft-maligned train-to-the-plane subway service between Kennedy and Manhattan (which New Yorkers love to call the "train-to-the-bus-to-the-plane") has been canceled, eliminating the city's only inexpensive transport option.

Robert De Niro has brought a bit of Hollywood to the Hudson, specifically the Lower West Side neighborhood known as TriBeCa, where he has lived for more than 10 years. The **TriBeCa Film Center,** set in a former coffee warehouse on Greenwich Street, houses film companies, casting agencies, and development offices in search of screenplays. Best of all, the ground floor is home to the **TriBeCa Grill,** a sure contender for hot restaurant of the year.

In other restaurant news, a good argument could be made
that the New York version of New Orleans's famous **K-Pauls**
is a better choice than the original. Now that you can get
a table at **44**—the chic little restaurant hidden away in
the hip Royalton hotel—make the trip for the fashionable crowd, the new American cuisine, and most of
all, the Philippe Starck-designed interior. You might
not expect much from a restaurant called **Coffee Shop,**
but the startlingly large crowds that have been lining up on Union Square West know better. The restaurant sets out to recreate the atmosphere of a party in
Rio de Janeiro night after night: Its success is pure New
York.

The city's quixotic campaign to **redevelop the Times Square
area** continues apace, creating a bizarre mixture of corporate America, Broadway, and leftover sleaze. Hotels are a
big part of the plan, and several have opened recently in the
neighborhood. New additions include the 638-room **Hotel
Macklowe,** the 770-room **Holiday Inn Crowne Plaza** (with
the promising Broadway Grill, operated by David
Liederman of David's Cookies fame), the 460-room **Embassy Suites Hotel,** and the 610-room **Paramount,** a renovation
of a former flophouse by the team responsible for the
Royalton hotel and Morgans. Though the Paramount's
rooms are small, they are reasonably priced by New York
standards.

Persistent rumors of a hotel or two for SoHo continue. Developers swear they will open a 101-room property on West
Broadway by early 1992 to be called the **SoHotel.** The
neighborhood offers a pleasing alternative to midtown locations, though resident groups regularly protest hotel development and the traffic it could bring.

To keep up with the ever-expanding inventory of hotel
rooms, several notable older hotels are plowing significant
sums of money into renovations. The **Drake Swissotel** on
Park Avenue is spending $52 million; the **Essex House** and
Ritz Carlton on Central Park South, $60 million and $35 million respectively; the **St. Regis Sheraton** on Fifth Avenue,
$50 million; the **Algonquin** on West 44th Street, $20 million;
and the **Mark Hotel** on East 77th Street, $30 million. Top-
ping them all is Donald Trump's **Plaza Hotel,** in the midst of
a $150 million overhaul.

The **Guggenheim Museum** is closed for an 18-month restoration and expansion that will add a 10-story tower to the
original Frank Lloyd Wright building.

Hudson Valley   Visitors hoping to avoid the madness of New York City's
congested airports have a new option. American Airlines
has introduced service into **Stewart International Airport,**
located near Newburg, about 100 miles south of Albany.
Daily flights connect with American's Chicago and Raleigh/
Durham hubs.

The **Brotherhood Winery** in Washingtonville is experiencing a revival after its 150th anniversary last year. The winery won a silver medal from the International Intervin competition for its Mariage wine and branched out with an unusual ginseng-infused wine called Genghis Khan. Dinners hosted by winemaster Cesar Baeza include a wide sampling of wines; advance reservations are necessary.

The Catskills The **Concord Resort Hotel,** a Catskills classic on Kiamesha Lake, is upgrading its facilities. The project includes converting a section of the hotel into an all-suite facility, adding a computerized reservations system, concierge service, express checkout, and in-room movies.

The Adirondacks A needed, year-round resort has opened in the region. The new **Copperfield Resort** in North Creek is close to Gore Mountain, which provides winter skiing and summer gondola rides to the scenic peak. There is also good white-water rafting in the area, particularly in the spring.

Rochester The **George Eastman House,** built for the founder of the Eastman Kodak Company, has completed a $1.8 million restoration. Using the dozens of photographs Eastman ordered of his home, craftsmen have restored the mansion to its original splendor—from the highly polished finish on the sandstone columns to the marble floors and oriental carpets. The photographic exhibits that were once displayed in the house have been moved to the new **International Museum of Photography,** a $7.8 million building connected to the house. The museum claims to have the world's largest collection of 19th-century photography—600,000 prints in all—plus 3 million movie publicity stills.

Long Island The **hotel scene on Long Island** has expanded considerably over the past few years to accommodate Long Island's 24 million annual visitors, and as of February 1990 there were some 12,000 hotel rooms on the island. Among the newcomers is the Marriott Wind Watch in Hauppauge, the Islandia Hilton in Islandia, and the Radisson in Melville. The Marriott in Uniondale was undergoing an expansion at press time, and a Comfort Suites is being built in Islip.

An ongoing construction project at the junction of Northern and Meadowbrook parkways to alleviate traffic to and from Jones Beach was interrupted briefly in 1990 when a neighboring town protested what they found to be an insufficient Environmental Impact Statement. Construction resumed later in 1990 and is expected to be completed sometime in 1991 or 1992. For now, you'll want to allow some extra time if you plan to drive along these roads, since construction has slowed travel. Roadwork is also being done along the Long Island Expressway in an effort to decrease congestion on this infamous stretch of "parking lot." Service roads are currently being built and expanded along its length, and there is talk of a fourth lane being added sometime in the distant future.

Fodor's Choice

No two people will agree on what makes a perfect vacation, but it's fun and helpful to know what others think. We hope you'll have a chance to experience some of Fodor's Choices yourself while visiting New York State. For detailed information about each entry, refer to the appropriate chapter in this guidebook.

Sights

Niagara Falls seen from the *Maid of the Mist* tour boat

The Statue of Liberty from the ferry headed to Staten Island, and the New York City skyline on the way back (50¢ round-trip)

Boscobel Mansion and its breathtaking view of the Hudson River, Garrison

The art colony at Woodstock

People-watching at Washington Square Park, Greenwich Village, New York City

People-watching at Saratoga during the racing season

The Atlantic Ocean from the lighthouse at Montauk Point, Long Island

Romantic Hideaways

Lily Pond Lane at dusk, East Hampton

Room in the Runaway Inn, Fleischmanns

The Eggery Inn for breakfast, Tannersville

Historic Sites

Ellis Island, New York City

Federal Hall, New York City

Franklin D. Roosevelt National Historic Site, Hyde Park

Fraunces Tavern, New York City

John Jay Homestead, Katonah

Lindenwald, retirement home of Martin Van Buren, Kinderhook

Schuler Mansion State Historic Site, Albany

Stony Point Battlefield Historic Site, Stony Point

Sunnyside, estate of Washington Irving, Tarrytown

Thomas Paine Cottage, New Rochelle

Hotels

Geneva-on-the-Lake, Geneva *(Very Expensive)*

Hotel Athenaeum, Chautauqua Institution, Chautauqua *(Very Expensive)*

The Pierre, New York City *(Very Expensive)*

Algonquin, New York City *(Expensive)*

Nevele Hotel, Ellenville *(Moderate–Expensive)*

1770 House, East Hampton *(Moderate–Expensive)*

Hotel Thayer, West Point *(Moderate–Expensive)*

Auberge des 4 Saisons, Shandaken *(Moderate)*

Hotel Saranac of Paul Smith's College, Saranac Lake *(Moderate)*

Wyndham Hotel, New York City *(Moderate)*

Hotel Iroquois, New York City *(Inexpensive)*

Restaurants

Chapels, Rochester *(Very Expensive)*

L'Auberge Du Cuchon Rouge, Ithaca *(Very Expensive)*

Lutèce, New York City *(Very Expensive)*

Rue Franklin West, Buffalo *(Very Expensive)*

Belhurst Castle, Geneva *(Expensive)*

Chez Sophie, Saratoga Springs *(Expensive)*

The Escoffier at the Culinary Institute of America, Hyde Park *(Expensive)*

The Sagamore, Bolton Landing, Lake George *(Expensive)*

La Marmite, Williston Park *(Moderate–Expensive)*

Le Petit Bistro, Rhinebeck *(Moderate–Expensive)*

Eartha's Kitchen, Saratoga Springs *(Moderate)*

Hickory Grove Inn, Cooperstown *(Moderate)*

Ye Hares 'N Hounds Inn, Bemus Point *(Moderate)*

Cucina Stagionale, New York City *(Inexpensive)*

Hattie's Chicken Shack, Saratoga Springs *(Inexpensive)*

New York

Kawartha Lakes

Ogd

Kingston

Watertown

Toronto

Lake Ontario

Hamilton

Oswego
Fulton

Niagara
Falls
Lockport

Rochester

Syracuse

Buffalo

Batavia

Canandaigua

Geneva
Finger Lakes

Auburn

Lake Erie

Genesee River

Chautauqua

Bath

Watkins
Glen

Ithaca

Jamestown

Olean

Wellsville

Corning

Elmira

Binghamton

PENNSYLVANIA

Scrant
Wilkes-
Barre

Allen

0   60 miles
0   90 km

Harrisburg

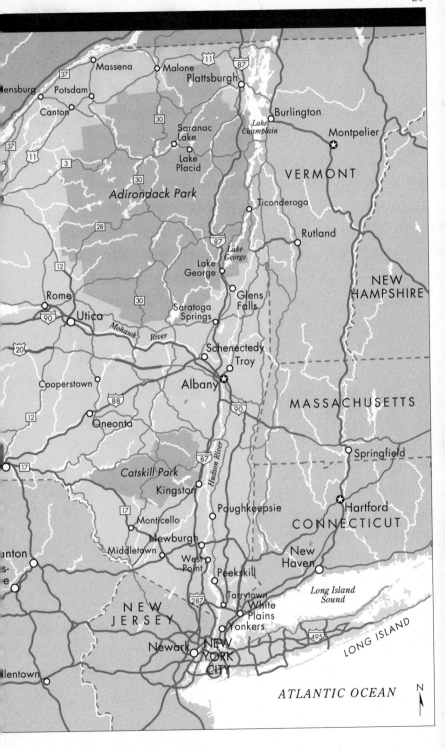

World Time Zones

Numbers below vertical bands relate each zone to Greenwich Mean Time (0 hrs.).
Local times frequently differ from these general indications,
as indicated by light-face numbers on map.

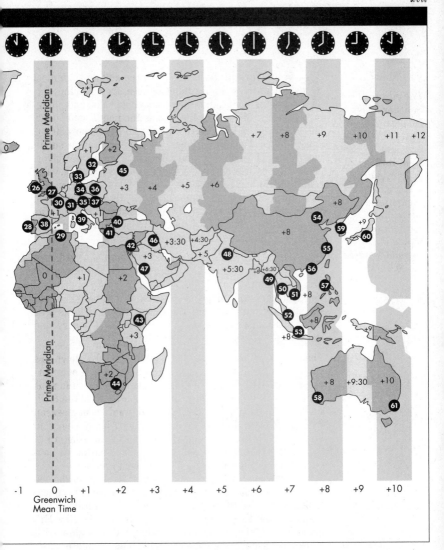

Introduction

by Diane Gallo

The editor of Southern Tier Images, Diane Gallo has written extensively about New York's people, places, history, and events for a variety of national and regional newspapers and magazines.

New York State has more to see and do than most countries. It has miles of oceanfront, rolling forests, mountain ranges, dizzying peaks, and plunging cataracts. More than 4,000 lakes and ponds, and 70,000 miles of rivers and streams course through its almost 50,000 square miles. For promotional purposes the state is subdivided into 11 regions, each with its own distinct flavor. (This regionalization makes for hot political battles.) The regions include New York City, Long Island, Hudson Valley, the Catskills, Capital-Saratoga, the Adirondacks, Thousand Islands-Seaway, Central-Leatherstocking, the Finger Lakes, Niagara Frontier (Niagara Falls-Buffalo area), and Chautauqua-Allegheny.

Despite these divisions, New York's 18 million people are rather cavalier about their geography. To the brash and brassy urbanites, anything not New York City is upstate. For upstaters, anything that's not New York City is downstate. And then there are those in the Adirondacks who think of themselves as living in the North Country and those who . . . you get the idea.

The essence of the Empire State can be distilled down to a single word: diversity. It has four distinct seasons of unsurpassed beauty. Winter snows range from the infamous whiteouts of Buffalo to the storybook snowfalls of the Hudson Valley. In spring, flower festivals herald the new season with azaleas on Long Island, tulips in Albany, lilacs in Rochester, and roses and apple blossoms from Niagara to Montauk. In the summer, playing fields and parks, and rivers and lakes come alive when more than 50 million visitors take advantage of the state's nearly 150 state parks, 35 state historic sites, and a variety of recreational, educational, and cultural facilities. In the fall, the forests and woods of New York match any autumn display the New England countryside might proffer when hillsides glow with scarlet, crimson, and gold, and weekly foliage updates alert the "leaf peepers" to the change in colors.

When Henry Hudson sailed into New York Harbor in 1609, Algonquian Indians came to offer greetings. Dressed in deerskins and ceremonial headfeathers, the Algonquians carried gifts of tobacco, sweet berries, and furs. Although the reception was apparently friendly, the crew's chief mate wrote in the log, "We durst not trust them." This set the tone for later generations of tourists to New York City.

A few years later in 1626, Peter Minuit, the first governor of New Netherland, arrived with orders from the Dutch West India Company to buy Manhattan Island from the Algonquians. With his famous $24 purchase, Minuit struck New

York's first marketing coup and became one of the few white men who ever paid the Indians for anything. The investment paid off. Today Manhattan is the national headquarters for communications and advertising, fashion and sports, banking and finance. The city is also a hub for publishing, shipping, and shopping. And it can rightly be called a world cultural capital: Artists, actors, musicians, writers, poets, conductors, magicians, and craftspeople all work and play here. New York City justifiably needs a list of superlatives to describe it. It has a reputation for being the best and the biggest.

Viewed at night from the World Trade Center, the island of Manhattan spreads out in front of you, with equal parts glitter and greasepaint. From here you can make out Wall Street and the South Street Seaport, SoHo and the East and West villages, Rockefeller Center and Radio City Music Hall, Times Square and the convention center, and Central Park and Lincoln Center. Through the 12-mile length of the island runs the long ribbon of Broadway. Although you can't see them, down there are world-renowned museums of science, nature, film, and ethnic and creative arts; Broadway theaters and off-Broadway showcases; temples of haute cuisine and streets lined with ethnic eateries; and Art-Deco dance palaces and standing-room-only jazz clubs.

Some insist that Manhattan is the only *real* New York, but the purist will argue that the city is incomplete without the four other boroughs—Brooklyn, Queens, the Bronx, and Staten Island. And although many native New Yorkers rarely see more of the city than their own neighborhood, they take the attitude of one visitor who said, "Even if you can't do and see it all, it's nice to know it's all there."

Little has changed since 1644 when one cynical observer noted that 18 languages were spoken in Manhattan and that the city had acquired the "arrogance of Babel." During the late 1800s and early 1900s, Irish, Germans, Italians, Poles, Russians, Romanians, and Eastern European Jews emigrated to America through the Ellis Island processing facility in New York Harbor. Each group brought their varied customs, cultures, and religions, thereby enriching the melting pot of New York City and the nation.

New York City has one of the most diverse populations in the world. The ethnic composition changes so rapidly, it's tough to nail down exactly who is coming from where and when. (In how many places in the world could you find a Peruvian/Chinese bodega?) In addition to the enclaves of Chinatown and Little Italy, there are large Indian and Latin American populations, as well as growing Russian, Korean, and West Indian communities. Dozens of languages rumble from throats like subways from tunnels.

Despite its slick urban reputation, New York State isn't all skyscrapers and city streets: It's farmlands and waterfalls, Long Island potatoes, Finger Lakes wine, and upstate fruit orchards. It's dairy farms (New York is the leading dairy state) and maple syrup (it outproduces Vermont), vineyards (on Long Island and in the Finger Lakes), strawberry fields, and pumpkin patches. The state's agricultural bounty surprises those who haven't ventured outside of New York City or explored beyond Niagara Falls.

Just a 45-minute drive on the Long Island Expressway (if it's not jammed up, as it's likely to be) takes you from Manhattan's crush to one of the world's premier playgrounds. A narrow spurt of land (23 miles at its widest) with 250 miles of accessible coastline, Long Island is the urban dweller's escape from New York. It has superb public parks including Jones Beach, the largest swimming facility in the world. On the island's smooth beaches, one may ignore the world and swim, jog, sunbathe, and clam.

Despite a housing explosion in the past 20 years, Long Island still has a strong appeal. The Hamptons, on its South Shore, offer summer ambience, accentuated by fashionable shopping streets, art galleries, theaters, and restaurants. At Montauk Point, the island's tip, the lighthouse built during Colonial times still flashes its warning beacon to signal home port to the Northeast's largest fleet of charter and party boats. On the North Shore are the beaches and harbors of Long Island Sound, where Great Gatsby châteaus politely elbow for room on the Gold Coast.

If water is a region's lifeblood, then New York is blessed with a great circulatory system. In addition to the Atlantic surf, the state borders on two Great Lakes and has mountain streams and mighty rivers. Of New York's major waterways, the Hudson River is perhaps the most scenic and is often referred to as "America's Rhine."

On the west side of the Hudson are the Palisades and the Catskills; on the east are the Taconic Mountains. The heights of both sides offer splendid views. Seven scenic bridges cross the river, allowing travelers to sample the best of both shores. Passengers aboard Metro-North's Hudson line train have an eye-level view as it wends its way upriver. Just south of dramatic Storm King Mountain is West Point, where young men (now also young women) have been molded into army officers since 1802.

The river towns cluster on the Hudson's banks harboring quaint restaurants, museums, art galleries, antiques shops, marinas, amusement parks, county fairs, 19th-century mansions, and 17th-century manor houses. The landscape chronicles the names of those who contributed to a young nation's rise—Van Cortlandt, Livingston, Paine, Washington, Fulton, Carnegie, Vanderbilt, Harriman, Rockefeller. Although Dutch New Netherland lasted only 55 years, the Dutch legacy lives on in place names like Yonkers, Rensselaer, Tappan Zee, Kill Van Kull, and Peekskill.

History, innovative cuisine, and restored or original Victorian architecture are found north of Poughkeepsie, in the towns of Hyde Park and Rhinebeck. Springwood, the sprawling estate at Hyde Park, was built in 1867 by FDR's father and was not only the president's residence but his birthplace. Both FDR and Eleanor Roosevelt are buried on the grounds. The Italian Renaissance Vanderbilt Mansion, also in Hyde Park, has a magnificent view of the lower Hudson Valley from its backyard. The Culinary Institute of America (affectionately dubbed the CIA), is widely regarded as one of the country's best training grounds for up-and-coming restaurateurs. Students practice every aspect of running a restaurant from preparing the food to inventory at the three on-site restaurants. The small village of Rhinebeck, just north of Hyde Park, contains excellent examples of Victorian architecture. The Rhinebeck Arms, in operation since 1766, is one of the country's oldest inns, having once served George Washington himself.

Throughout the Hudson Valley are state historic sites that recall the courage of the rebel army. (Colonial New Yorkers bore the brunt of the Revolutionary War. About 45,000—or one-fourth of the state's population—took up arms. Nearly one-third of all Revolutionary War battles were fought in New York.) At each turn of the road, you'll follow Washington's trail as he battled, dined, and slept his way through historic moments of the war.

Northwest from the Hudson Valley is the Rip Van Winkle country of the Catskills. Deeply forested and beautiful, this area is where you are urged to slow down and enjoy the scenery. Pick any hill, climb it, and savor the view. Skiing, camping, hiking, rock-climbing, and biking are challenges in this hilly country. But even with all that exercise, your waistline is in danger in a land where the rallying cry is, "Eat, eat."

The Catskills tradition of hospitality started during the 19th-century resort boom, when thousands of holiday travelers came to escape the city's swelter. Those traditions evolved into the posh resort hotels, inns, and guest farms like those in Monticello and Liberty and more modest inns and guest farms, and the area gained the nickname "borscht belt." (The film *Dirty Dancing* took place at such a Catskill resort set in the 1960s.) The borscht-belt quality has softened in recent years with the influx of young, upscale Manhattanites attracted by reasonably priced real estate within driving distance of the city. The old general stores are now gourmet delis that stock the *New York Times* and croissants for their well-heeled customers.

The once-quaint town of Woodstock, in the eastern Catskills, has cashed in on its association with the landmark rock concert of 1969, sharing the name but not the site: Its main drag is lined with T-shirt outlets and shops selling batik, tie-dye, and macrame. Bethel, some 50 miles southwest of Woodstock in Sullivan County, is where the Woodstock Music and Art Fair was moved after promoters had trouble getting permits for Woodstock.

To the north, the Catskills melt into the gentler terrain of the Capital-Saratoga district. Here, near the juncture of the Mohawk and Hudson rivers, lies Albany, the state capital and regional commercial center. The city's rich historic legacy is set within a bustling commercial framework. Despite startling differences in architectural eras, Albany's stylistic juxtaposition achieves a curious harmony. The modern space-age complex of the Empire State Plaza provides a spectacular introduction to the city's center. Against the backdrop of the futuristic government plaza with its landmark "egg" (the Performing Arts Center), stands the State Capitol, Albany's star attraction. This impressive example of Château architecture boasts the "Million Dollar Staircase," a Romanesque version of the Paris Opera's elaborately curved staircase.

Just about a 45-minute drive north is the smaller but no less sophisticated Saratoga Springs. At the turn of the century, Saratoga was *the* place to indulge oneself for the summer season. Saratoga casinos rivaled Las Vegas and Monaco for opulence. Whether visitors came to take the mineral waters or wager on their favorite racehorse, Saratoga offered hedonistic seduction. The town's main street is lined with boutiques, gallerias, hotels, and bistros; and visitors still come for the soothing mineral springs, and the world-class entertainment and cultural programs at the Saratoga Performing Arts Center.

To the north of the Capital-Saratoga district begins the slow rise of the Adirondack range. This vast wilderness area is rugged, timeless, and remote. The Adirondacks were the last region of New York to be explored and surveyed. Of the area's 11,000 square miles, nearly a third is reserved by the state to be held "forever wild."

With 6.2 million acres, the Adirondack State Park is the largest wilderness area west of the Mississippi. There are 42 peaks above 4,000 feet, among them the mile-high Mount Marcy and the east's highest ski slope, Whiteface Mountain. For those less physically inclined, Whiteface Mountain Memorial Highway leads visitors to one of the Adirondack's most spectacular views.

The region's magnificent upland lake district includes Lake Placid, Saranac Lake, Tupper Lake, and Lake George—

Queen of the Lakes. Lake George has a "million dollar beach" and Lake Placid's ski lifts and elevators provide breathtaking excursions—winter and summer. Also prime among Adirondack attractions is the fully restored Fort Ticonderoga, the "Key to a Continent."

The Thousand Islands (the French call them Les Milles Isles) are actually 1,834 islands clustered in a 50-mile stretch of the St. Lawrence River. Curving northwest around the Adirondacks like a mother's protective arm, the Thousand Islands region still preserves vestiges of the romance of 19th-century grand hotels and mansions. Clayton and Alexandria Bay are headquarters for cruises in the area that often take in a tour of Boldt Castle, a 300-room replica of a Rhine castle on Heart Island.

The waters surrounding the Thousand Islands offer some of the best fishing in North America. By local custom, a shore dinner is freshly caught, then panfried by the guide on the nearest island. Every year anglers descend on Pulaski and Oswego for the towns' annual trout and salmon derbies. The St. Lawrence Seaway forms part of the world's longest unfortified international border. The Thousand Islands International Bridge at Alexandria Bay is a tribute to neighborly relations between the United States and Canada.

Surrounding the center of the state is the Leatherstocking region, so named for the leather breeches worn by its New England settlers. Leatherstocking Country's crown jewel is Cooperstown. Set at the foot of Lake Otsego, Cooperstown bills itself as the "village of museums." Most people know it as the home of the National Baseball Hall of Fame and Museum, but Cooperstown is more than a baseball fan's mecca. The Fenimore House, which has an extensive collection of American Folk Art is here, as is the Farmer's Museum and Village Crossroads, a re-creation of 19th-century life featuring craftspeople in authentic settings. The town is also the home of the Glimmerglass Opera.

Throughout the Mohawk Valley-Utica region you'll find such Revolutionary War sites as Oriskany Battlefield, where General Herkimer's men did battle with Chief Joseph Brant's in "the bloodiest battle of the Revolution." Erie Canal Village in Rome marks the spot where the first shovelful of dirt was turned for the 363-mile waterway between Albany and Buffalo. Built between 1817 and 1825, the artery—dubbed "Clinton's Ditch" after promoter De Witt Clinton—was a major pipeline for goods towed on barges by teams of mules. The many museums in the cities all along the canal route preserve the romance and excitement of the 19th-century days of growth and expansion.

Indian legend says that the Great Spirit put down his hand, and water sprang from where his fingers pressed the earth. It's not hard to imagine a master's hand at work in the Finger Lakes. The district has 11 bodies of water, including the five lakes of Cayuga, Owasco, Skaneateles, Otisco, and Seneca. Unimpeachable sources rumor that the trout in Seneca Lake weigh in at as much as 32 pounds. And when you reel in that big one, make sure you've got a bottle of Finger Lakes wine on hand. The region is famous for its wineries. Remember the rule for wine tasting: See, smell, swirl, and sip.

"Spectacular" is not too strong an adjective to describe Niagara Falls. Indians who witnessed the dramatic splitting of the Niagara River called it "thunder of the waters." In any given second, 200,000 cubic feet of water (weighing more than 62 pounds per foot) rush over the lip of the falls, providing the single greatest source of electric power in North America. Don a slicker and take a *Maid of the Mist* tour to the very foot of the cataracts. England's King Edward VII, India's Prime Minister Nehru, and America's own Marilyn Monroe are among the millions who have experienced the deafening roar of Niagara from these boats.

Tucked away in the state's southwest corner is the Chautauqua-Allegheny region. When pioneers and settlers headed west from the terminus of the Erie Canal, they largely ignored the southern region and left it relatively undeveloped and sparsely populated. Those who did settle here suffered the same lack of imagination as did the folks who brought us Main Street. The naming of things in this region is cause for some confusion. "Allegheny," "Cattaraugus," and "Chautauqua" crop up over and over as place names for lakes, rivers, and counties. Chautauqua is a county, a town, a lake, and an institute. Allegheny is a county, a river, and a mountain range. Allegany, with a slightly different spelling, is a county and a state park. Cattaraugus is a county, a town, and a creek.

This westernmost region of New York is a land of small towns and lakes, one Great Lakes shore, and vast forests. Allegheny County alone has 23 almost untouched state forests and 50,000 acres of publicly owned wild woods. Farther west in Chautauqua County is Allegany State Park. With 94.5 square miles (65,000 acres), Allegany is New York's largest state park, as well as one of its most primitive. Wildlife is abundant (beaver, raccoon, deer, black bear, game birds) and the bird-watching, with more than 200 species, is superb. The park also has great fishing, hiking, and camping.

In the years since Henry Hudson first entered New York Harbor, a new world has flourished. Today New York City sets the pace for the nation in economy, cultural activities, and urban living. From its urban centers to its rolling hillsides, New York is a microcosm of America.

1 Essential Information

Before You Go

Visitor Information

Contact the New York State Division of Tourism, (1 Commerce Plaza, Albany, NY 12245, tel. 518/474–4116 or 800/225–5697). Its *I Love NY* booklets are excellent resources on various areas of the state (including NYC). (*See* also Important Addresses and Numbers in each city/area section.)

In the United Kingdom, contact the New York State Tourist Office (2 Cinnamon Row, Plantation Wharf, York Pl., London SW11 3TW, tel. 071/978–5222).

Tour Groups

Although you will have to march to the beat of a tour guide's drum rather than your own, a package tour is likely to save you money on airfare, hotels, and ground transportation while covering a lot of territory. For the more experienced or adventurous traveler, there is a variety of special-interest and independent packages available. Listed below is a sampling of options. Check with your travel agent or the New York State Division of Tourism (tel. 212/827–6250) for additional resources.

When considering a tour, be sure to find out (1) exactly what expenses are included (particularly tips, taxes, side trips, additional meals, and entertainment); (2) ratings of all hotels on the itinerary and the facilities they offer; (3) cancellation policies for both you and the tour operator; and (4) the single supplement if you are traveling alone. Most tour operators request that bookings be made through a travel agent—there is no additional charge for doing so.

General-Interest Tours "Autumn Highlights" from **Globus Gateway/Cosmos** (150 S. Los Robles Ave., Suite 860, Pasadena, CA 91101, tel. 818/449–0919 or 800/556–5454) takes you through some of the state's most scenic spots during the fall foliage season. "Historic East" tours New York; Washington, DC; Virginia; and Pennsylvania. Globus also has a 13-day tour that begins with the state and winds its way up through New England, Ontario, and Quebec.

Casser Tours (46 W. 43rd St., New York, NY 10036, tel. 800/251–1411 or 212/840–6500) has a three-day "Leatherstocking Country Tour" that takes in Cooperstown, Erie Canal Village, the Adirondack Museum, and Fulton Chain of Lakes. Weekend tours to Saratoga and Lake George, the Catskill Mountains, Lake Placid, Lake George, and the Adirondacks are also available.

Talmage Tours (1223 Walnut St., Philadelphia, PA 19107, tel. 215/923–7100) gives you four nights in Lake George, hitting the Adirondack Museum, Lake Placid, and the home of Franklin Roosevelt in Hyde Park.

Domenico Tours (751 Broadway, Bayonne, NJ 07002, tel. 800/554–TOUR) will take you to Niagara Falls and the Thousand Islands or from Niagara Falls through the state en route to Washington, DC.

Special-Interest Tours
History
The National Trust for Historic Preservation (1785 Massachusetts Ave., NW, Washington, DC 20036, tel. 202/673–4138) operates a variety of history tours in New York State.

Music and Art **Dailey-Thorp Travel** (315 W. 57th St., New York, NY 10019, tel. 212/307–1555) performs admirably with its deluxe New York City art, music, and culture programs. Itineraries vary according to available performances.

Nature **Dire Wolf Natural History Tours** (124 Pool Rd., Ithaca, NY 14850, tel. 607/272–7409) organizes informative nature tours exploring New York State's geology, paleontology, plant/wildlife, and Native American culture.

New York Field Office (1736 Western Ave., Albany, NY 12203, tel. 518/869–6959) organizes nature tours through a variety of preserves in New York State.

Package Deals for Independent Travelers

American Fly AAway Vacations (tel. 800/321–2121) offers New York City packages with discounts on hotels and car rentals. Its "Glimpse of Manhattan" includes hotel, sightseeing, and a New York City information package complete with map and discount coupons. **Carlson Travel Group's** "Supercities" tours (7855 Haskell Ave., 3rd floor, Van Nuys, CA 91406, tel. 800/556–5660) has "Theater Weekends." Also check with **United Airlines** (tel. 312/952–4000 or 800/328–6877) and **Continental Airlines** (tel. 800/634–5555) for packages.

Tips for British Travelers

Passports and Visas
You will need a valid 10-year passport (cost £15) to enter the United States. You will not need a visa if you are staying for less than 90 days, have a return ticket, and are flying with a participating airline. There are some exceptions to this, so check with your travel agent or with the United States Embassy (Visa and Immigration Dept., 5 Upper Grosvenor St., London W1A 2JB, tel. 071/499–3443).

Customs
Visitors 21 or over can bring in 200 cigarettes or 50 cigars or three pounds of tobacco; one U.S. quart of alcohol; and duty-free gifts to a value of $100. Be careful not to bring in meat or meat products, seeds, plants, fruits, etc. Avoid illegal drugs of any kind.

Returning to Britain, you may take home (1) 200 cigarettes or 100 cigarillos or 50 cigars or 250 grams of tobacco; (2) two liters of table wine and, in addition (a) one liter of alcohol over 22% by volume (most spirits) or (b) two liters of alcohol under 22% by volume (fortified or sparkling wine); (3) 60 milliliters of perfume and ¼ liter of toilet water; and (4) other goods up to a value of £32.

Insurance
We recommend that you insure yourself against health and motoring mishaps. **Europ Assistance** (252 High St., Croydon, Surrey CR0 1NF, tel. 081/680–1234) is a firm that offers this service.

It is also wise to take out insurance to cover loss of luggage if it isn't already covered by any existing home-owner's policies you may have. Trip-cancellation coverage is another good buy. The **Association of British Insurers** (Aldermary House, Queen St.,

London EC4N 1TT, tel. 071/248–4477) will give comprehensive advice on all aspects of vacation insurance.

Tour Operators   **American Airplan** (Marlborough House, Churchfield Rd., Walton-on-Thames, Surrey KT12 2TJ, tel. 0932/231322) has a seven-day "American Adventure" package that spends five jam-packed days in New York and two in the spectacular surroundings of Niagara Falls. Prices per person begin at £565.

Destination USA (Clitstone House, Hospital Rd., Hounslow TW3 3HT, England, tel. 081/577–1786) offers excellent air tours that include transatlantic airfare, flights between U.S. cities, and all hotel accommodations. Tour prices begin at £729. One popular 14-day tour includes New York, Los Angeles, Las Vegas, and San Francisco for £995.

Jetsave (Jetsave America, Sussex House, London Rd., East Grinstead, Sussex RH19 1LD, tel. 0342/328231) has seven-day vacations in New York, with a choice of hotels. Prices are from £499 per person.

Poundstretcher (Airlink House, Hazelwick Ave., Three Bridges, Crawley, Sussex RH10 1YS, tel. 0293/519–233) offers New York as part of a two- or three-center vacation. Supplement your stay in New York with a stay in Orlando and/or New Orleans, or extend your vacation further with a week in either St. Petersburg or Clearwater. Prices, per person, for nine nights in New York and Orlando are from £779; New York, Orlando, and Clearwater/St. Petersburg for 16 nights from £929; or New York, New Orleans, and Orlando for 14 nights from £1,025.

Airfares   Independent travelers may want to take a cheap flight to any of the major cities in the state and explore from there. APEX round-trip fares from London at press time (July 1990) to New York cost from £399; to Albany from £555; to Buffalo from £559; to Syracuse from £577. If you're flexible, check the small ads of Sunday and daily newspapers for last-minute, low-cost tickets. Round-trip fares to New York can start as low as £199, but check to see if taxes are included in the price quoted.

Electricity   110 volts. You should take along an adapter since American razor and hair-dryer sockets require flat two-pronged plugs.

When to Go

It's not being facetious to say that the tourist season for New York State runs from January through December. The best months for visiting, however, depend on which area of the state you plan to visit and what you wish to do. While some museums and historic sites in the Hudson Valley, the Catskills, and the Adirondacks may be closed for the winter, for instance, there are still enough places to visit, sights to see, and winter sports to enjoy (*see* Festivals and Seasonal Events, below). Many hotels and resorts offer accommodations at lower off-season rates as well as attractive weekend packages. And while New York City can get very hot and humid in the summer, particularly in July and August, that's also the season during which the city is most crowded—not only with tourists but with New Yorkers themselves enjoying a host of street fairs, outdoor concerts, and other activities. For the rest of the state, the weather can be pleasantly warm during the summer. Fall months can be glorious throughout the state; this is a time when the foliage is most colorful in the countryside and cities regain their vitality.

Climate What follows are the average daily maximum and minimum temperatures for major cities in New York State.

Albany	**Jan.**	32F	0C	**May**	70F	21C	**Sept.**	74F	23C
		16	−9		49	9		54	12
	Feb.	32F	0C	**June**	79F	26C	**Oct.**	61F	16C
		16	−9		58	14		43	6
	Mar.	43F	6C	**July**	83F	28C	**Nov.**	47F	8C
		27	−3		63	17		32	0
	Apr.	56F	13C	**Aug.**	81F	27C	**Dec.**	36F	2C
		38	3		61	16		22	−6

Buffalo	**Jan.**	34F	1C	**May**	67F	19C	**Sept.**	72F	22C
		20	−7		47	8		54	12
	Feb.	34F	1C	**June**	77F	25C	**Oct.**	63F	17C
		20	−7		56	13		45	7
	Mar.	43F	6C	**July**	81F	27C	**Nov.**	49F	9C
		27	−3		61	16		34	1
	Apr.	56F	13C	**Aug.**	81F	27C	**Dec.**	36F	2C
		38	3		61	16		23	−5

New York City	**Jan.**	37F	3C	**May**	68F	20C	**Sept.**	79F	26C
		24	−4		53	12		60	16
	Feb.	38F	3C	**June**	77F	25C	**Oct.**	69F	21C
		24	−4		60	16		49	9
	Mar.	45F	7C	**July**	82F	28C	**Nov.**	51F	11C
		30	−1		66	19		37	3
	Apr.	57F	14C	**Aug.**	80F	27C	**Dec.**	41F	5C
		42	6		66	19		29	−2

Current weather information on 750 cities around the world— 450 of them in the United States—can be obtained by calling the **WeatherTrak** information service at 900/370–8728 or 900/575–8728 in TX. A taped message will tell you to dial a three-digit access code for the destination in which you are interested. The code is either the area code (in the United States and Canada) or the first three letters of the foreign city. This system also provides the time in the specified destination, as well as information on road and traffic conditions. The service costs 75¢ for the first minute and 50¢ for every minute thereafter.

Festivals and Seasonal Events

Top seasonal events in New York State include the I Love New York Winter Festival in Hamilton County (in the Adirondacks), the I Love New York Fall Foliage Festival in the Catskills, the New York City Marathon in November, Macy's Thanksgiving Day Parade down Broadway, and the lighting of the Christmas tree at Rockefeller Center. For a complete listing of New York State events, request the "Major Events in New York State" calendar from the **Division of Tourism** (1 Commerce Plaza, Albany, NY 12245, tel. 518/474–4116 or 800/823–4582).

Jan.–Mar.: I Love New York Winter Festival takes place throughout Schenectady County. Festivals include snowmobile races, winter carnivals, ethnic salutes, performing arts, and cross-country and downhill skiing. Tel. 800/962–8007.

Late Jan.: Chinese New Year Celebrations, Chinatown, New York City. Tel. 212/397–8200. **Alpo International Sled Dog Races** are the largest pursed races in North America, with 200 dog teams participating. Tel. 518/891–1990.

Late Jan.–Feb.: Winter Carnival at Lake George includes fourwheel-drive races on ice, sky divers, and a golf tournament. Tel. 518/668–5755.

Late Jan.–early Feb.: Winterfest in Syracuse includes parties, fishing derby, and fireworks. Tel. 315/470–1343.

Mid-Feb.: Westminster Kennel Club Show is a prestigious dogshow event held in Madison Square Garden. 4 Penn Plaza, New York, NY, tel. 212/563–1990.

Mid-Feb.: Winter Carnival at Saranac Lake is one of the oldest in the country. Tel. 518/891–1990.

Mid- to late Feb.: Ice Castle Spectacular in Mayville is centered around ice-harvesting from Chautauqua Lake. Tel. 716/754–4304.

Late Feb.-early Mar.: Empire State Winter Games are Olympic-style competitions held at Lake Placid. Tel. 518/474–8889.

Late Feb.: Competitive Events at Lake Placid include bobsled and luge competitions, ski jumping, and cross-country ski meets. Tel. 518/523–1655.

Mid-Mar.: Big East Basketball Championship Tournament is held at Madison Square Garden in New York City. Tel. 212/563–8114.

Mid- to late Mar.: Northeastern Wildlife Expo in Albany includes a wildlife art show, crafts, wild-game cooking demonstrations at Empire State Plaza. Tel. 518/434–1217.

Apr.: Professional Baseball Season Opens. New York Mets are at Shea Stadium, the New York Yankees are at Yankee Stadium, and AAA (minor league) teams play in Buffalo, Rochester, and Syracuse.

Early May: Hudson River White-Water Derby lures canoeists and kayakers to the upper Hudson River in North Creek. Tel. 518/761–6366.

Late May: Ninth Avenue International Festival is a huge outdoor festival, with one mile of ethnic foods from 37th to 57th streets in New York City. Ninth Avenue Association, 400 W. 50th St., New York, NY 10019. Tel. 212/581–7029.

Late May: General Clinton Canoe Regatta is the longest flatwater race in the country, from Cooperstown to Bainbridge. Tel. 607/746–2281.

Early to mid-June: Belmont Horsefair is carried on around the Belmont Stakes, thoroughbred racing's final Triple Crown event run at Belmont Park. Tel. 718/641–4700.

June–July: The Metropolitan Opera performs free starlit concerts in parks in all five New York City boroughs. Tel. 212/799–3100.

June–Aug.: The Season at Chautauqua Institution in Chautauqua includes workshops, classes, opera, and ballet. Tel. 716/357–6200.

June 10: Belmont Stakes, thoroughbred racing's final Triple Crown event, takes place at Belmont Park in Elmont. Information from the New York Racing Association, Box 90, Jamaica, NY 11417, tel. 718/641–4700.

Mid-June–Labor Day: The New York Shakespeare Festival brings the Bard to the Delacorte Theater in Central Park. Performances are free; tickets are necessary. Tel. 212/861–PAPP.

June–Aug.: The New York Philharmonic's free summer concert series takes place in parks throughout New York City, and in Suffolk, Nassau, and Westchester counties. All begin at 8 PM. Tel. 212/580–8700.

Mid-June: Allentown Art Festival in Buffalo includes 500 outdoor exhibitors. Tel. 518/849–6609.

Late June: Crafts Fair at Rhinebeck is a major show at Dutchess County Fairgrounds. Tel. 914/876–4001.

Early July: Harbor Festival means regattas, fireworks, and parades in New York City. Tel. 212/944–2990.

Mid-July: Empire State Summer Games take place in various locations. Tel. 518/474–8889.

July 23: National Baseball Hall of Fame Induction Ceremonies in Cooperstown. Tel. 607/547–9988.

Aug.–Sept.: New York Renaissance Festival in Tuxedo includes jousts, crafts, and Elizabethan theater. The festivities are on weekends only. Tel. 516/325–1331.

Early Aug.: Flight '90 Air Show in Schenectady features ground displays, aerial acts, and military team flights. Tel. 518/393–3606.

Mid-Aug.: Travers Stakes in Saratoga Springs is the oldest stakes race for three-year-olds at the nation's oldest racetrack. Tel. 718/641–4700.

Late Aug.–early Sept.: Great New York State Fair, in Syracuse, is the oldest state fair in the country. Tel. 315/487–7711.

Sept. and Oct.: I Love New York Catskills Fall Festival takes place during peak foliage season in Ulster, Greene, Sullivan, and Delaware counties. Tel. 800/343–INFO and in NY, 800/882–CATS.

Mid-Sept.: Canal Town Days in Palmyra consists of boat rides on the Erie Canal and a parade. Tel. 315/946–6191.

Mid- to late Sept.: Trout and Salmon Derby represents thousands of dollars in prizes for catches in Lake Ontario and the Niagara River. Tel. 716/439–6064.

Mid-Oct.: Craft Fair at Bear Mountain lures more than 100 exhibitors three weekends in a row. Tel. 914/786–2701.

Early Nov.: New York City Marathon, which winds through all of five boroughs, attracts 22,000 runners and 2 million spectators. For information, contact New York Roadrunners Club, 9 E. 89th St., New York, NY 10028, tel. 212/410–7770.

Nov. 23: Macy's Thanksgiving Day Parade, in New York City, is the world's largest. Tel. 212/560–4670.

Late Nov.: Christmas Parade, in Schenectady the night after Thanksgiving, kicks off the holiday season. Tel. 518/372–5656.

Late Nov.–early Dec.: Festival of Lights in Niagara Falls is a bright and beautiful holiday celebration. Tel. 716/278–8010.

Early Dec.: Christmas Tree Lighting at Rockefeller Center, New York City, is a highlight of the city's holiday season.

Dec. 31: New Year's Eve celebration in Times Square is legendary. Fireworks go off in Central Park.

What to Pack

Pack light because porters and luggage trolleys are hard to find. Luggage allowances on domestic flights vary slightly from one airline to another. Most allow two checked pieces and two carry-ons. In all cases, check-in luggage cannot weigh more than 70 pounds each or be larger than 62 inches (length + width + height). Carry-on luggage cannot be larger than 45 inches (length + width + height) and must fit under the seat or in the overhead luggage compartment. (*See* By Plane in Getting to and around New York State, below.)

What you pack depends largely on where you're headed. New York City is basically informal but has many restaurants that require a jacket and tie. Theaters and nightclubs in New York City range from the slightly dressy on Broadway to extremely casual Off-Broadway and in Greenwich Village. For sightseeing and casual dining, jeans and sneakers are acceptable just about anywhere in the state. Some country inns in the Hudson Valley request that men wear a jacket and tie for evening meals. Bed-and-breakfast establishments are totally informal. New York City can be very cold in the winter, but there's not much snow. Upstate New York has lots of snow, so be prepared. Also be prepared for thunderstorms in the summer throughout the state. The humidity level tends to be high, so leave the plastic raincoats at home.

Cash Machines

Virtually all U.S. banks belong to a network of Automatic Teller Machines (ATMs), which gobble up bank cards and spit out cash 24 hours a day in cities throughout the country. There are some eight major networks in the USA, the largest of which are Cirrus, owned by MasterCard, and Plus, affiliated with Visa. Some banks belong to more than one network. These cards are not issued automatically, you have to ask for them. If your bank doesn't belong to at least one network you should consider moving funds, for ATMs are becoming as essential as check cashing. Cards issued by Visa and MasterCard can also be used in the ATMs, but the fees are usually higher than the fees on bank cards, and there is a daily interest charge on the "loan," even if monthly bills are paid on time. Each network has a toll-free number you can call to locate machines in a given city. The Cirrus number is 800/4–CIRRUS; the Plus number is 800/THE–PLUS. Check with your bank for fees and for the amount of cash you can withdraw on any given day.

Traveling with Film

If your camera is new, shoot and develop a few rolls of film before leaving home. Pack some lens tissue and an extra battery for your built-in light meter. Invest about $10 in a skylight filter and screw it onto the front of your lens. It will protect the lens and also reduce haze.

Film can be harmed in hot weather. If you're driving in summer, don't store film in the glove compartment or on the shelf under the rear window. Put it behind the front seat on the floor, on the side opposite the exhaust pipe.

On a plane trip, never pack unprocessed film in check-in luggage; if your bags get X-rayed, pictures can be ruined. Always carry undeveloped film with you through security and ask to have it inspected by hand. (It helps to isolate your film in a plastic bag, ready for quick inspection.) Inspectors at American airports are required by law to honor requests for hand inspection.

The newer scanning machines used in all U.S. airports are safe for anything from five to 500 scans, depending on the speed of your film. The effects are cumulative; you can put the same roll of film through several scans without worry. After five scans, though, you're asking for trouble.

If your film gets fogged and you want an explanation, send it to the National Association of Photographic Manufacturers, 550 Mamaroneck Ave., Harrison, NY 10528, tel. 914/698–7603. Association experts will try to determine what went wrong. The service is free.

Car Rentals

Where to rent a car in New York State depends largely on your travel plans. A trip covering the Niagara frontier and a couple of upstate cities like Rochester and Syracuse should probably start in Buffalo, since the Greater Buffalo International Airport has the state's best connections outside of New York City. An Adirondack adventure could take advantage of Albany's rental rates, often the state's lowest. New York City has its own pros and cons as a rental location: You might find a better combination of budget rental companies, special deals, and low airfares, but it is also one of the worst places in the nation to drive a car—let alone a recreational vehicle. Almost all national companies have rental offices at the airports in Buffalo, Rochester, Syracuse, Albany, and Binghamton, plus downtown locations. Many also have offices in smaller cities like Jamestown, Elmira, Oneonta, Kingston, Lake Placid, Watertown, and Utica. Major companies with locations statewide include **Avis** (tel. 800/331–1212), **Budget** (tel. 800/527–0700), **Dollar** (tel. 800/421–6868), **Hertz** (tel. 800/654–3131), **National** (tel. 800/328–4567), **Payless** (800/PAY–LESS), and **Thrifty** (tel. 800/367–2727). **American International** (tel. 800/527–0202) and **Rent-A-Wreck** (tel. 800/221–8282) are budget firms with offices around the state, usually offering pickups and drop-offs at local airports.

New York City has the state's highest rates, ranging from $50 to $70 per day at major companies and bottoming out at $35 with local budget firms. Buffalo is about $10 cheaper than that, Syracuse slightly less, and Albany the best deal of all: Even leader Hertz charges less than $40 daily for a subcompact. New York State now requires that basic car-rental rates include collision insurance for all but a deductible of $100. Find out if you must pay for a full tank of gas, whether you use it or not, and ask about promotional, weekend, and 14-day advance reservation rates.

Traveling with Children

Publications   *Family Travel Times* is an 8- to 12-page newsletter published 10 times a year by Travel with Your Children (TWYCH), 80 Eighth Ave., New York, NY 10011, tel. 212/206–0688. Subscription includes access to back issues and twice-weekly opportunities to call in for specific advice.

The Family Travel Guides Catalogue, edited by Carole Meyers and updated annually, is the only catalog that lists and describes current books covering the area of family travel. (Carousel Press, Box 6061, Albany, CA 94706, tel. 415/527–5849. Send $1 for postage and handling.)

Great Vacations with Your Kids: The Complete Guide to Family Vacations in the U.S. by Dorothy Ann Jordon and Marjorie

Adoff Cohen (E.P. Dutton, 2 Park Ave., New York, NY 10016; $9.95) details everything from city and adventure vacations to child-care resources.

The Candy Apple: New York for Kids by Bubbles Fisher (Prentice Hall Press, New York; $12.95) profiles places and things especially suited to children.

ParentGuide (2 Park Ave., New York, NY 10016, tel. 212/213–8840) is a monthly publication with event and resource listings. The subscription cost for one year is $11.90, or send $1.50 for a single issue.

Hotels   New York City hotels that allow children under 13 to stay in their parents' room for free include:

Plaza 50 Suite Hotel (155 E. 50th St., at 3rd Ave., 10022, tel. 212/751–5710); the **Shelburne Murray Hill Hotel** (303 Lexington Ave., at 37th St., 10018, tel. 212/689–5200); and **Southgate Tower Hotel** (371 7th Ave., at 31st St., 10001, tel. 212/563–1800).

The Catskills: **Mohonk Mountain House** (Lake Mohonk, New Paltz, NY 12561, tel. 914/255–1000) has scores of programs, facilities, and activities for children of all ages, as well as convenient two-rooms-connected-by-bath accommodations. **Pinegrove Resort Ranch** (Lower Cherrytown Rd., Kerhonkson, NY 12446, tel. 914/626–7345) has children's programs and activities. **Rocking Horse Ranch** (Highland, NY 12528, tel. 914/691–2927 or 800/437–2624) welcomes families with organized activities, a day camp, and spacious accommodations.

The Adirondacks: **The Sagamore** (Bolton's Landing, NY 12814, tel. 518/644–9400) has children's programs and menus, plus family rates.

Home Exchange   Exchanging homes is a surprisingly low-cost way to enjoy a vacation in another part of the country. **Vacation Exchange Club, Inc.** (12006 111th Ave., Unit 12, Youngstown, AZ 85363, tel. 602/972–2186) specializes in domestic home exchanges. The club publishes one directory in February and a supplement in April. Membership is $24.70 per year, for which you receive one listing. Loan-a-Home (2 Park La., Mount Vernon, NY 10552, tel. 914/664–7640) is popular with academics on sabbatical and businesspeople on temporary assignment. There's no annual membership fee or charge for listing your home, but the cost for a directory and a supplement is $30.

Getting There   On domestic flights, children under two not occupying a seat travel free. Various discounts apply to children 2 to 12 years of age. Regulations about infant travel on airplanes are in the process of being changed. Until they do, however, if you want to be sure your infant is secured in his/her own safety seat, you must buy a separate ticket and bring your own infant car seat. (Check with the airline in advance; certain seats aren't allowed. Or get the booklet "Child/Infant Safety Seats Acceptable for Use in Aircraft" by writing to the Federal Aviation Administration, APA-200, 800 Independence Ave. SW, Washington, DC 20591, tel. 202/267–3479). Some airlines allow babies to travel in their own safety seats at no charge if there's a spare seat available on the plane, otherwise safety seats will be stored and the child will have to be held by a parent. If you opt to hold your baby on your lap, do so with the infant outside the seat belt so he or she won't be crushed in case of a sudden stop.

Also inquire about special children's meals or snacks. See the February 1990 issue of *Family Travel Times* for "TWYCH's Airline Guide," which contains a rundown of the children's services offered by 46 airlines.

Baby-sitting Services Make child-care arrangements with the hotel concierge or housekeeper. New York City agencies: **Babysitter's Guild** (60 E. 42nd St., Suite 902, New York, NY 10017, tel. 212/682–0227) and **Gilbert Child Care Agency** (115 W. 57th St., Suite 3–12, New York, NY 10019, tel. 212/757–7900).

Hints for Disabled Travelers

The Information Center for Individuals with Disabilities (Fort Point Pl., 27–43 Wormwood St., Boston, MA 02210, tel. 617/727 –5540) offers problem-solving assistance and information including lists of travel agents that specialize in tours for the disabled.

Moss Rehabilitation Hospital Travel Information Service (12th St. and Tabor Rd., Philadelphia, PA 19141, tel. 215/329–5715) provides information on tourist sights, transportation, and accommodations in destinations around the world for a small fee.

Mobility International (Box 3551, Eugene, OR 97403, tel. 503/ 343–1284) has information on accommodations, organized study, and the like around the world.

The Society for the Advancement of Travel for the Handicapped (SATH) (26 Court St., Penthouse, Brooklyn, NY 11242, tel. 718/858–5483) offers access information. Annual membership costs $40, or $25 for students and senior travelers. Send a stamped, self-addressed envelope.

Disabled residents of New York State should apply for the **Disabled Access Pass,** which provides free use of state park facilities. Contact Access, State Parks, Albany, NY 12238 or call the Department of Parks and Recreation, tel. 518/474–0456.

Greyhound (tel. 212/971–6363 in NYC) will carry a disabled person and companion for the price of a single fare. **Amtrak** (tel. 800/USA–RAIL) requests 24-hour notice to provide redcap service, special seats, and a 25% discount.

Publications *The Itinerary* (Box 2012, Bayonne, NJ 07002, tel. 201/858–3400) is a bimonthly travel magazine for the disabled.

Access to the World: A Travel Guide for the Handicapped by Louise Weiss. Available from Henry Holt and Co. (Box 30135, Salt Lake City, Utah 84130, tel. 800/247–3912; order number 0805001417).

Hints for Older Travelers

The **American Association of Retired Persons** (AARP, 1909 K St. NW, Washington, DC 20049, tel. 202/662–4850) has two programs for independent travelers: (1) The *Purchase Privilege Program*, which offers discounts on hotels, airfare, car rentals, and sightseeing; and (2) the *AARP Motoring Plan*, which offers emergency aid and trip-routing information for an annual fee of $33.95 per couple. The AARP also arranges group tours, including apartment living in Europe, through **American Express Vacations** (Box 5014, Atlanta, GA 30302, tel. 800/ 282–0800 in GA). Annual dues are $5 per person or per couple.

When using an AARP or other identification card, ask for a reduced hotel rate at the time you make your reservation, not when you check out. At restaurants, show your card to the maître d' before you're seated, since discounts may be limited to certain menus, days, or hours. When renting a car, remember that economy cars, priced at promotional rates, may cost less than cars that are available with your ID card.

Elderhostel (80 Boylston St., Suite 400, Boston, MA 02116, tel. 617/426–7788) is an innovative 16-year-old program for people 60 and older. Participants stay in dorms on some 1,200 campuses around the world. Mornings are devoted to lectures and seminars; afternoons to sightseeing and field trips. The all-inclusive fee for two- to three-week trips, including room, board, tuition, and round-trip transportation, is $1,700–$3,200.

Travel Industry and Disabled Exchange (TIDE, 5435 Donna Ave., Tarzana, CA 91356, tel. 818/368–5648) is an industry-based organization with a $15 per person annual membership fee. Members receive a quarterly newsletter and information on travel agencies and tours.

National Council of Senior Citizens (925 15th St. NW, Washington, DC 20005, tel. 202/347–8800) is a nonprofit advocacy group with some 5,000 local clubs across the country. Annual membership is $12 per person or per couple. Members receive a monthly newspaper with travel information and an ID card for reduced-rate hotels and car rentals.

Mature Outlook (6001 N. Clark St., Chicago, IL 60660, tel. 800/336–6330), a subsidiary of Sears Roebuck & Co., is a travel club for people over 50, with hotel and motel discounts and a bimonthly newsletter. Annual membership is $9.95 per couple. Instant membership is available at participating Holiday Inns or by calling the 24-hour toll-free number.

The Mature Traveler (Box 50820, Reno, NV 89513, tel. 702/786–7419), published and edited by Gene Malott, is a monthly newsletter for the over-50 traveler. The cost of an annual subscription is $23.50.

Golden Age Passport is a free lifetime pass to all parks, monuments, and recreation areas run by the federal government. People over 62 should pick one up in person at any national park that charges admission. A driver's license or other proof of age is required.

Further Reading

For nonfiction about the area, look at Ted Aber's *Adirondack Folks; Niagara*, by Gordon Donaldson; Jack Hope's *A River for the Living: The Hudson and its People; The Catskills from Wilderness to Woodstock*, by Alf Evers; Edmund Wilson's *Upstate: Records and Recollections*.

Or pick up some historical fiction: Walter D. Edmonds's *Drums Along the Mohawk; Butt's Landing*, by Jean Rikhoff; Robert L. Taylor's *Niagara;* Jack Finney's *Time and Again*.

Suspense novels set in New York State include Bernard F. Conners's *Dancehall;* Donald E. Westlake's *Bank Shot;* and Joyce Carol Oates's *Mysteries of Winterthurn*.

Two family sagas set primarily in New York are Irwin Shaw's *Rich Man, Poor Man* and *Beggarman, Thief.*

Other novels set in the state include: *Ragtime*, by E. L. Doctorow; *Bullet Park*, by John Cheever; William Kennedy's Pulitzer Prize-winning *Ironweed;* Bernard Malamud's *Dubin's Lives;* and *A Bloodsmoor Romance*, by Joyce Carol Oates.

The Adirondacks has inspired many works of literature. Still foremost among these is William H.H. Murray's *Adventures in the Wilderness*, published in 1869. This century's books of note include William Chapman White's *Adirondack Country* and Lincoln Bennett's *Ancient Adirondacks*. For a compilation of short essays, there is Paul Jamieson's *Adirondack Reader* by various writers and Jamieson's own collection, *Adirondack Pilgrimage.*

Set in the Saratoga area are *Saga of an Impious Era*, by George Waller, and the lively novel *Saratoga Trunk*, by Edna Ferber.

Thousands of books have been written about or set in New York City, from Washington Irving's *Knickerbocker's History of New York* to the novel *The Bonfire of the Vanities* by Tom Wolfe, a harrowing look at the city today. The manners of early uppercrust New York society are dissected in Henry James's *Washington Square* and Edith Wharton's *House of Mirth*. New York and Long Island during the Roaring '20s are shown in F. Scott Fitzgerald's *The Great Gatsby*. Books describing the New York immigrant experience include *World of Our Fathers* by Irving Howe, *Call It Sleep* by Henry Roth, *The Invisible Man* by Ralph Ellison, and *Manchild in the Promised Land* by Claude Brown. For a behind-the-scenes look into politics and business, read *The Power Broker* by Robert A. Caro, *Mayor* by Mayor Edward I. Koch, and *Trump* by Donald H. Trump (with Tony Schwartz). For a building-by-building guide to the city's architecture, see *AIA Guide to New York City* by Norval White. Other useful guides are *A Guide to New York City Landmarks*, published by the Landmark Preservations Committee, *The Street Book* by Henry Moscow, and *The Movie Lover's Guide to New York* by Richard Alleman.

Getting to and around New York State

By Plane

Most major U.S. airlines schedule regular flights into New York. The major cities are serviced by **American** (tel. 800/433–7300), **Continental** (tel. 800/525–0280), **Delta** (tel. 800/872–7786), **Pan Am** (tel. 800/221–1111), **TWA** (tel. 800/221–2000), **United** (tel. 800/241–6522), and **USAir** (tel. 800/428–4322). Several of these airlines also have flights within the state. Many foreign airlines also fly into the three airports of New York City—LaGuardia, JFK, and Newark International.

Smoking As of late February 1990, smoking is banned on all scheduled routes within the 48 contiguous states; within the states of Hawaii and Alaska; to and from the U.S. Virgin Islands and Puerto Rico; and on flights of under six hours to and from Hawaii and Alaska. The rule applies to the domestic legs of all foreign routes but does not affect international flights.

On a flight where smoking is permitted, you can request a nonsmoking seat during check-in or when you book your ticket. If the airline tells you there are no seats available in the nonsmoking section, insist on one. Department of Transportation regulations require U.S. carriers to find seats for all nonsmokers, provided they meet check-in time restrictions.

Carry-on Luggage New rules have been in effect since January 1, 1988 on U.S. airlines in regard to carry-on luggage. The model for these new rules was agreed to by the airlines in December 1987 and then circulated by the Air Transport Association with the understanding that each airline would present its own version.

Under the model, passengers are limited to two carry-on bags. For a bag you wish to store under the seat, the maximum dimensions are 9″ × 14′ × 22″, a total of 45″. For bags that can be hung in a closet or on a luggage rack, the maximum dimensions are 4″ × 23″ × 45″, a total of 72″. For bags you wish to store in an overhead bin, the maximum dimensions are 10″ × 14″ × 36″, a total of 60″. Your two carryons must each fit one of these sets of dimensions, and any item that exceeds the specified dimensions will generally be rejected as a carryon, and handled as checked baggage. Keep in mind that an airline can adapt these rules to circumstances, so on an especially crowded flight don't be surprised if you are allowed only one carry-on bag.

In addition to the two carryons, the rules list eight items that may also be brought aboard: a handbag (pocketbook or purse), an overcoat or wrap, an umbrella, a camera, a reasonable amount of reading material, an infant bag, and crutches, a cane, braces, or other prosthetic device upon which the passenger is dependent. Infant/child safety seats can also be brought aboard if parents have purchased a ticket for the child or if there is space in the cabin. (Regulations are in the process of being changed, so check with the airline ahead of time.)

Note that these regulations are for U.S. airlines only. Foreign airlines generally allow one piece of carry-on luggage in tourist class, in addition to handbags and bags filled with duty-free goods. Passengers in first and business classes are also allowed to carry on one garment bag. It is best to check with your airline ahead of time to find out the exact rules regarding carry-on luggage.

Checked Luggage U.S. airlines allow passengers to check in two suitcases whose total dimensions (length + width + height) do not exceed 62″ and whose weight does not exceed 70 pounds per bag.

Rules governing foreign airlines vary from one airline to another, so check with your travel agent or the airline itself before you go. All the airlines allow passengers to check in two bags. In general, expect the weight restriction on the two bags to be a maximum of 70 pounds each, and the size restriction on each bag to be 62″ total dimensions.

Lost Luggage Airlines are responsible for lost or damaged property only up to $1,250 per passenger on domestic flights; $9.07 per pound (or $20 per kilo) for checked baggage on international flights; and up to $400 per passenger for unchecked baggage on international flights. If you're carrying valuables, either take them with you on the airplane or purchase additional insurance for lost luggage. Some airlines will issue additional luggage insurance when you check in, but many do not. One that does is American Airlines. Its additional insurance is only for domestic flights or flights to Canada. Rates are $1 for every $100 valuation, with a maximum of $25,000 valuation per passenger. Hand luggage is not included. Insurance for lost, damaged, or stolen luggage is available through travel agents or directly through various insurance companies. Two that issue luggage insurance are **Tele-Trip** (tel. 800/228–9792), a subsidiary of Mutual of Omaha, and **The Travelers Insurance Co.** (tel. 203/277–0111 or 800/243–3174). Tele-Trip operates sales booths at airports and also issues insurance through travel agents. It will insure checked luggage for up to 180 days and for $500 to $3,000 valuation. For one to three days, the rate for a $500 valuation is $8.25; for 180 days, $100. The Travelers Insurance Co. will insure checked or hand luggage for $500 to $2,000 valuation per person, and also for a maximum of 180 days. Rates for one to five days for $500 valuation are $10; for 180 days, $85. For more information, write The Travelers Insurance Co., Ticket and Travel Dept. (1 Tower Sq. Hartford, CT 06183). Both companies offer the same rates on domestic and international flights. Check the travel pages of your Sunday newspaper for the names of other companies that insure luggage. Before you go, itemize the contents of each bag in case you need to file an insurance claim. Be certain to put your address on each piece of luggage, including carry-on bags. If your luggage is stolen and later recovered, the airline must deliver the luggage to your home free of charge.

By Bus

Greyhound offers frequent service throughout the state to and from major cities in the United States and Canada. Regional bus lines (Central New York Coach, Hudson Transit, etc.) offer service between points within the state. Contact your local Greyhound office for information.

For information on specific bus stations, see the individual chapters.

By Train

Amtrak's Empire Corridor Service runs from New York's Grand Central Terminal to upstate New York with stops at Croton-Harmon, Poughkeepsie, Rhinecliff, Hudson, Albany-Rensselaer, Schenectady, Amsterdam, Utica, Rome, Syracuse, Rochester, Buffalo, and Niagara Falls. The Adirondack runs from Grand Central (en route to Montreal) to Croton-Harmon, Poughkeepsie, Rhinecliff, Hudson, Albany-Rensselaer, Schenectady, Saratoga Springs, Fort Edward–Glens Falls, Whitehall, Fort Ticonderoga, Port Henry, Westport, Willsboro, Port Kent, Plattsburgh, and Rouses Point. The Lake Shore Limited, which runs between Grand Central and Chicago, makes stops at Croton-Harmon, Poughkeepsie, Rhinecliff, Hudson, Albany–Rensselaer, Schenectady, Utica, Syracuse, Rochester, and Buffalo.

For information on schedules and fares, tel. 800/USA–RAIL. For information on specific train stations, see the individual chapters.

Metro-North Commuter Railroad (tel. 800/223–6052) trains depart from Grand Central for points along the Hudson Valley into Connecticut on its Harlem, Hudson, New Haven, Port Jervis, and Pascack Valley lines.

By Car

The principal east–west highway in New York is the New York State Thruway from Buffalo and the Pennsylvania border on the west and New York City and the Connecticut border on the east. Several major highways, all accessible from the thruway, run in a north–south direction, including U.S. 87 from Albany to the Canadian border, U.S. 81 from Binghamton to the Thousand Islands, and I–390 from the Pennsylvania border to Rochester.

Wherever you drive in New York, remember to buckle up. It is against the law to drive anywhere in the state without the driver's and the front-seat passenger's seat belts being securely fastened.

The maximum speed limit on state highways is 55 miles per hour, with various lower limits within cities and residential areas. Be sure to watch road signs for these limits and any changes on major highways.

Unless otherwise stated, right turn on red is permitted almost everywhere except in New York City. Parking is an expensive proposition in the Big Apple—and there is very little street parking available. Parking in a "Tow Away Zone" will cost $100 in cash, plus the parking fine and a great deal of aggravation, to get your car back if it is towed.

In upstate regions, snow tires and/or chains may be required during the winter.

Staying in New York

Beaches

The best beaches in New York are found on Long Island's South Shore. The largest and best kept of these is Jones Beach State Park, Wantagh, with changing rooms, picnic grounds, boardwalk, restaurant, cafeterias, and food stands. The 2,400 acres of beaches and parkland also have facilities for outdoor theaters and concerts, miniature golf, and fishing.

Also on Long Island, Captree State Park, at the easternmost tip of Robert Moses State Park, features untamed grassy-duned beaches, with minimal facilities. Fire Island is perhaps the most popular beach area in New York for straight and gay singles. Despite its stunning beaches, however, you might find a day's visit arduous unless you are a guest of a summer resident. The Hamptons, from Westhampton east to Montauk Point, feature still more outstanding beaches with chic towns to explore.

The most famous beach in the outer boroughs of New York City is no doubt Coney Island in Brooklyn. Although the beach is now a mere shadow of its former glory, the water is usually fine and there are changing rooms, restaurants, food stands, and other facilities. The other major beach within the city limits is in the Rockaways—a peninsula that juts out into the Atlantic. Jacob Riis Park in Queens, at the western end of the peninsula, is rated among the cleanest beaches in the city. Now part of the Gateway National Recreation Area, Riis has changing rooms, food stands, some shaded picnic areas, and numerous children's playgrounds and sports facilities. *Note:* Increased enforcement of antidumping laws and environmental pressure lead to cleaner Long Island beaches and very few closures in 1989.

Participant Sports

Biking Practically every city, state, and national park in New York has bicycle trails. In New York City, for instance, Central Park in Manhattan and Prospect Park in Brooklyn have roadways that are closed to cars and reserved for bikers (as well as joggers and walkers) during daylight hours on weekends and often during non-rush hours weekdays. You can find plenty of bike rentals on nearby streets—check the Yellow Pages—or you can rent a bike in Central Park at the Loeb Boathouse near the 72nd Street lake. The New York State Tourism Division (1 Commerce Plaza, New York, NY 12425) publishes a brochure, *I Love NY Outdoors*, which has extensive information on biking and other sports in parks throughout the state.

Fishing The state's 70,000 miles of rivers and streams offer a wide range of fishing opportunities, with maps to each area available from Outdoor Publications (Box 355, Ithaca, NY 14850). The *I Love NY Outdoors* brochure also lists all the regional fishing offices and fishing hotlines throughout the state.

Everyone over age 16 needs a license, available at most sporting-goods stores, to fish in freshwater rivers, lakes, and ponds. No license is needed to fish in deep-sea or coastal waters. Best bet for deep-sea fishing boat excursions is at Sheepshead Bay, Brooklyn.

Hiking Part of the 2,000-mile Appalachian Trail winds through New York State. For hiking details consult Volume 4 of the *Appalachian Trail Guide Series* (Appalachian Trail Conference, Box 807, Harpers Ferry, WV 25425). Also useful is *Hiking Trails in the Northeast* by Thomas A. Henley and Neesa Sweet (Great Lakes Living Press). The *I Love NY Outdoors* brochure also includes some hiking information.

Winter Sports For skiers, the Catskills and the Adirondacks are favorites for downhill, with practically the rest of upstate New York for cross-country. The Catskills resorts also offer snowshoeing and tobogganing, while ice skating is available at rinks throughout the state—even at New York City's Rockefeller Center. Some of the rinks are in state parks and some are privately owned.

State and National Parks

State Parks An extensive state park system exists in New York, with many locations offering outstanding recreational features. An **Empire State Passport,** permitting unlimited free entrance to New York State Parks for one year (Apr. 1–Mar. 31 of the following year) is available for $30 at individual parks by writing to Passport, State Parks, Albany, NY 12238, or by calling the Department of Parks and Recreation at 518/457-7433.

To make hiking, boating, or canoeing reservations, call 518/457-7433.

National Park Gateway National Recreational Area extends through Brooklyn, Queens, Staten Island, and New Jersey. The area includes the Jamaica Bay Wildlife Sanctuary, Jacob Riis Park (*see* Beaches, above), and various facilities for outdoor and indoor festivals, beaches, and parkland.

A **Park Pass** is an annual entrance permit to a specific national park, monument, or historic site that admits the pass holder and any accompanying passengers in a single vehicle. It costs between $10 and $15, depending upon the area, and is valid for one calendar year from January through December.

Dining

In and around the major cities of New York State—especially the Big Apple—it is always best to have reservations at the most popular restaurants. These restaurants, particularly the most expensive ones, fill up rapidly. In New York City and the Hudson Valley, where the best food is to be found, tables may be at a premium during weekends. Prices will be about the same for comparable food and surroundings—$50 and up for first-class nouvelle American or French food.

At the less expensive options, reservations are well advised. We've singled out restaurants in all price ranges worth a special effort to visit, and provided guidelines for costs and what you might expect in the way of atmosphere and ambience as well as food. Inns and resorts offering accommodations as well as meals often represent excellent values. When dining out in New York City, expect to pay an additional 25%–40%.

Ratings

Category	Cost*: Major City	Cost*: Other Areas
Very Expensive	over $60	over $50
Expensive	$40–$60	$30–$50
Moderate	$20–$40	$15–$30
Inexpensive	under $20	under$15

per person, without tax, service, or drinks

Lodging

Wherever you decide to stay in New York, it's always best to reserve ahead. Booking may not be a problem in every corner of the state, but you don't want to be caught at dusk searching for a place to stay, particularly in New York City.

Hotels In addition to the major chains—Hilton, Holiday Inn, Hyatt, Marriott, Sheraton—the state has many independent luxury hotels and resorts that offer just about the best of everything, from cuisine to recreation.

Motels All the motel chains are represented in the state—from strictly budget places to those with the same amenities found in hotels. Rates may differ markedly from one area to another, even within the chains.

Lodges Popular around the ski areas, lodges offer a dormitorylike atmosphere, common meals (often buffet style), and relatively inexpensive accommodations.

Catskills Resorts Truly unique New York State, the Catskills resorts are cities unto themselves, where you probably won't need to leave the grounds: Meals are all-you-can-eat extravaganzas; sports range from golf to tobogganing; and singles weekends are regular attractions (some resorts even have resident matchmakers). Prices at the resorts reflect this all-inclusive nature, but for those who take advantage of the entertainment and activities available, they can be a bargain.

Ratings

Category	Cost*: Major City	Cost*: Other Areas
Very Expensive	over $125	over $100
Expensive	$100–$125	$80–$100
Moderate	$80–$100	$45–$80
Inexpensive	under $80	under $45

per room, double occupancy, without taxes

Bed-and-Breakfasts B&Bs offer room in the owner's home, with breakfast usually included. Each area of the state has its own B&B association, which can be contacted through the local chamber of commerce or the area telephone book.

Camping and RV Facilities Most state parks have campsites as reflected in the *I Love NY Outdoors* brochure. Sites at state parks can be reserved ahead by writing to State Parks (Albany, NY 12238) or by calling the New York State campground reservation number at 800/456–CAMP. However, only a small number of campsites, as well as cabins, are available for reservation; most are first-come, first-served. There are numerous private campgrounds throughout the state, including some belonging to the KOA chain (Kampgrounds of America, Box 30558, Billings, MT 59114). The AAA also publishes annual camping directories for the state that are free to members. Be forewarned: There are neither campgrounds nor trailer parks near New York City. Bringing an RV to Manhattan is a mistake; few garages will accept them, and street parking is hard to find.

Credit Cards

The following credit card abbreviations are used in this book: AE, American Express; CB, Carte Blanche; DC, Diners Club; MC, MasterCard; V, Visa.

2 Portraits of New York State

The Heritage of the Hudson

by Carl Carmer

Hudson Valley historian Carl Carmer is the author of The Hudson *and* Songs of the Rivers of America.

Writing about the romantic Hudson River is a welcome task since it can begin at home. From the eight-sided, many-windowed cupola which surmounts my eight-sided house, I can behold not only the wide stream moving massively toward the sea but many a century-old dwelling which was planned long ago by people who thought it would be a credit to its neighborhood and a reminder of their period's dedication to beauty.

A little to the east I can see without the aid of binoculars the turrets of the Beltzhoover Castle (now known as the Halsey Castle) and I know that a rippling lake lies beside it—a lake that bears upon its surface the slow white swans that every visitor feels are essential to so beautiful a dwelling.

If I look south, I see the old home of Colonel James Hamilton, son of Alexander, and I must again wonder what motives led to the wild and untrue legend that the colonel built the house in which I stand as a convenient dwelling for his son's mistress.

As I look to the Hudson, I see projecting into its waters from the far side the long railroad pier which gave the little town of Piermont its name. History tells me that Daniel Webster once sat in a rocking chair on the floor of an open flatcar and was borne away by the first train of the just-completed New York and Erie Railroad toward a magnificent dinner in Fredonia, New York, on the banks of Lake Erie. The new railroad was not allowed to come farther than the middle of the river; hence the pier that would allow the new line to transfer all New York City–bound cargo to riverboats for the rest of the journey.

As for my northern view I can only say that, as soon as the War for Independence ended, building a house on the banks of the Hudson became an indication of status and many an ambitious and well-to-do citizen of New York City took advantage of the opportunity for becoming highly respected by his contemporaries.

If a good friend visited me on the east bank of the Hudson, I would take him first to look at the big yellow house called Nuit and tell him that its very name suggests the hours of evening when shadow supplants a western glory. I would make him aware that the cobbles which he treads toward the entrance had been shipped across an ocean from the streets of Marseilles and had a history of their own long before they had left the shores of France to glint under a stretch of American sunset.

From this home onward my guest and I would travel north to pass other homes or sites of vanished houses romantically named. Netherwood, Locust Grove, Windcliff, Ellerslie, Leacote, Tivoli, Rose Hill are only a few of the names that give evidence of the poetic fancies of their owners.

Broadway is the river road on the east side of the Hudson—the same Broadway that all America knows, it runs all the way from New York City to Albany. It passes the top of Main Street in Irvington and, as it does, the summer traveler may look down through a long, leafy tunnel to a splatter of shining Hudson water. Running parallel to that green-lined tube lies another, named Sunnyside Lane, which leads down to the charming and whimsical cottage that housed Washington Irving in his latter days. Restored to the exact image it presented when America's first world-famous author was its occupant, the house still looks as if it were wearing a cocked hat, as Irving said it did.

No restoration in the nation makes its guests feel more at home, perhaps because it continues to exist in the more august company of castles and mansions that grace the countryside. As it sits in delightful modesty beside the great river, I believe that it conveys more successfully than any other restored dwelling in America the character, the sly humor, the imaginative fancy of the man who chose to live in it. Somehow it creates a *neighborhood* in which at dusk the Hamiltons await, as they often did, the arrival at their home (now next door to my own) of the town's quite unpretentious author living a half mile away. Sometimes Irving would bring with him one of his own houseguests, such as the renowned Swedish spinster-writer Fredrika Bremer, who was so elated when her host did not fall asleep before the dessert, as he usually did, that she must record the fact in her diary.

The staff of the Sunnyside Restoration has been so successful in its researches that many of the homely day-by-day practices, routines, and habits which assume significance only when attributed to a great man are revealed. The sensitive visitor of today grieves with the long-dead Irving when he comes upon the gravestones of his dogs, or rejoices with him when he finds that shaving after midnight provides a temporary relief from the torture of sleeplessness. It is no wonder then that the writer's warm humanity seems to lie concentrated within the old Dutch house and the simple pattern of his living out his remaining years.

When Irving died in 1859, just after completing his biography of Columbus, ours was not the only nation that was in tears. England and Spain—particularly Spain—have mourned him until today. And many an American ignores the current revolt of the uncompromisingly literary against oversentimentality when he stands before the simple grave at Sleepy Hollow Cemetery and reads the first lines of Longfellow's tribute:

> *Here lies the gentle humorist, who died*
> *In the bright Indian Summer of his fame.*
> *A simple stone with but a date and name*
> *Marks his secluded resting place beside*
> *The river that he loved and glorified.*

Irving, one of the most famous men of letters, was also interested in art, for the river stirs every facet of the creative instinct. Were he alive today, he would be rejoicing over the current interest in the paintings of his contemporaries. When he was young, he had considered becoming an artist as a life-work, and his enthusiasm for art never left him. The fact that he sometimes chose the pen name of Geoffrey Crayon indicated his feeling for and knowledge of the products which he was given every opportunity to praise.

A new and spontaneous spirit rose among hills and groves through which the Hudson passed. The landscapes offered by the river were superior in their beauty to any that might be admired in Europe, said the sensitive Thomas Cole, and he set out to prove his statement. A believer in the close relationships of the arts, he took his flute with him and sought rocky ravines, the channels whitened by splashing waters which inevitably ran through steep tributaries to invade the level surface of the three-mile-wide Tappan Zee. Having found a scene that moved him, the young painter let his flute speak for him and, once it had spoken, began to imitate with his brushes and colors that part of the divine creator's universe he had chosen for a painting.

The immeasurable expanses of an untamed land challenged Thomas Cole and his artist colleagues, and they all were accepting the challenge. On enormous canvases for the most part, they set about impressing potential patrons and purchasers. They believed that their products were meticulously accurate as to subject matter. They also were encouraged by the fact that they *and* the possible purchaser were convinced that a good picture cannot fail of having a praiseworthy "moral effect." On a highly artistic plane they were evangelists.

It has long been my contention that landscape has a special influence on those who inhabit it—not merely in economic ways, as the wheat or cotton spring from the earth, not in geographic ways, as rivers and mountains become boundaries to be crossed, but in spiritual and psychic ways. The look and feel of a land communicate not easily described messages to those who are sensitive enough to receive them. Perhaps because rivers in their courses offer poetic parallels to human life, people are inclined to attribute to them influences that strongly affect their lives.

In 1609 the Great River of the Mountains (as the Elizabethan explorer Captain Henry Hudson called it) had long awaited the inevitable dramas for which it would serve as a setting. Upon entering the wide stream, Hudson's crew were aware of the backdrop. Its banks, they said, "were so pleasant with grass and flowers—and goodly trees—as ever we had seen." They were more deeply concerned, however, as are most explorers, with their own roles on the great stage which encompassed them. The fortnight of sunlit September days during which the dusky natives sang choruses of welcome, and their ship drew near the blue mountains to the north, held no omen of the climatic day years later when the treacherous keeper of their log—old Robert Juet—would set their captain adrift in the arctic sea.

No change of backdrop would be necessary for ensuing acts. As might have been expected, then, characters and plot would supersede place. Early depictions of life along the river would therefore be more concerned with those stalwarts who lived it than with the river valley itself.

The Dutchmen who came from the Netherlands to the river were audacious adventurers, eager for profits in beaver and wildcat pelts obtainable in the valley woods. Their prosperity was immediate and the patterns of their living had little time to change from those they already knew. Portraits, showing the distinction of their wives and their own qualities as successful merchants and landholders, were symbols of high status. Painters were soon competing for commissions. Called "limners" by our frontier society, not many of the newly developed artists indulged in the subtleties of their professional European prototypes. They emphasized, rather, the obvious. The result was a group of boldly realistic portraits. The stamp of major characteristics was realized in them more directly than it would have been by more sophisticated painters. The carrying of this method further might have resulted (as it did in Washington Irving's amusing word portraits of Dutch dignitaries) in caricature. Hence the work of the "patroon painters" (so-called because their work was commissioned by the privileged Dutch patroons, or landowners, of the period) was not so important a contribution to American art as it was to American history. It might be noted in this connection that consciousness of place had already begun to grow, for Hudson River scenic backgrounds became both symbols and decorations in some of the limners' portraits.

Though, as always in time of war, the portraits of heroes assume authority, the fact that the Hudson River was of the greatest strategic importance and the realization that its beauty was overwhelming drew the attention of all who looked upon it. Even the British officer sent under a flag of truce by General John Burgoyne to offer surrender of his army at Saratoga discoursed for the first ten minutes of his visit on the colors of mid-October foliage in the Hudson Valley.

So compelling was the Hudson's beauty that it was regarded as a special gift of God. Painters, awed by the "divine architecture" they beheld in the mountains, hollows, and waters of its valley, chose to convey what God had said to them through these media of the "sublime subject" in terms of canvas and paint. They paid tribute to the blue stream and its bluer mountains with a conscientious and disciplined artistry which resulted in skills never before obtained by American artists. Not long after the mid-19th century they were designated as the "Hudson River School." Proud that they had won for themselves this unique distinction, they sought to express wild natural glories with ever larger canvases. On these they exulted in meticulous representations of foreground plants, of middle-ground waters, of distant peaks rising beyond both into mist-strewn heavens. Having nearly exhausted Hudson River scenes, they used their techniques on other subjects —the less dramatic, elm-punctuated slopes of the Genesee, the greater challenge of Niagara's plunging waters.

As art directions changed in the last quarter of the century, American landscape gave way to canvases depicting Americana—genre paintings, representations of life in the almost measureless gray city at the big stream's wide mouth. The river retired into its mists. Artists, stimulated by metropolitan vigor and excitement, began, to the stunned surprise of the public, to paint ashcans, dreary tenements, and drearier saloons.

As if fleeing from the cruel realism of these sights, other painters sought release in a dream world where juxtaposition of unrelated objects was a commonplace; but even there their surrealism produced little hope or joy. River water continued, however, to flow by their doors, and the incredible river itself offered so varied and glittering a pile of incongruous and challenging materials that an age of empirical and highly individualistic experiment began.

It still continues. Always, as in our past, the tidal waters of the river-that-flows-two-ways fill the brain with images so intimate that on occasion the artist must become interpreter as well as creator, and the viewer is often entranced by the strange language the paintbrushes speak. The lively minds that exist among the inhabitants of the river-girt City of Greater New York leave few avenues of artistic endeavor untraveled.

Adirondack Country

To Begin With

by William
Chapman White

A former New
York City
newspaper
columnist,
William
Chapman White
summered in
Saranac Lake, in
the Adirondacks,
for many years.
He is the author
of Adirondack
Country.

It depends on what sort of day October 2, 1536, was. It may have been one of those high autumn days, so common in the northland, with infinite blue sky above, with clear air that brings distant horizons near. If so, the first white man ever to see the Adirondack Mountains of northern New York was the French explorer Jacques Cartier.

On that day, in the full flaming of autumn, he came to the Indian village that was to be the site of Montreal. The Indians led him up the high hills behind the mud flats. He saw the river below and the level woods that stretched away unbroken to the south. On the horizon, 70 miles off, were mountains, not one solid range but a broad sea of hills, intensely blue under the October sun. Cartier may have asked questions about them, for at some time he learned that to the south was "an unexplored region of lakes, of mountains, and delightful plains."

Three generations of Indians lived and died by the St. Lawrence before another white man looked on those hills. In July 1609, Samuel de Champlain, who had been in Canada for a year trying to revive the French settlement, explored that land to the south. With a small group of Europeans and Indians he moved slowly down the Sorel River to the mouth of a lake and saw "a number of beautiful islands filled with fine woods and prairies." He named the lake after himself. As he continued down its west side he noticed high mountains on the east and to the south.

He saw no people, although his guides told him that the country was inhabited by Indians. Champlain found that out for himself a few days later as his group came near the head of the lake. Here they met a band of Iroquois; when Iroquois and Canadian Indians met a fight always followed. In this fight Champlain used his arquebus loaded with four balls. His one shot instantly killed two Iroquois. That shot, in the shadow of the Adirondacks, changed American history. The Iroquois never forgot it. Forever after, they hated the French with the special hatred usually reserved for the Canadian Indians.

By odd coincidence, less than two months after Champlain first saw the Adirondacks at close range, another European, Henry Hudson, came near them. In September 1609, he sailed up the Hudson to stop above Albany where the rolling country hints at the blue hills to the north.

After Champlain's passage, the waters of Lake Champlain and Lake George just below it, which set the eastern boundary of the Adirondack country, were red with blood for the next 170 years. Blood of red men and white stained the pine duff on the forest floor by those lakes. A few Jesuit missionaries trod the Lake Champlain–Lake George route to constant torture from their Indian captors. Trappers from Montreal and from Fort Orange, later Albany, traveled the region. While a few men did settle on the fringes of the region in the middle of the 18th century, most of the history of that period is military history, of fighting between French and British and later British and American rebels for control of the lake route north and south.

Although the southern boundary of the Adirondack country is only 200 miles north of Manhattan and less than 50 miles north of Albany, it was not explored in any detail until the 1830s. Explorers had gone into the Northwest Territory as far as the Pacific before anyone even climbed Mount Marcy, the highest of the Adirondack peaks. The sources of the Columbia River were known 60 years before the northernmost source of the Hudson was finally located. The mountains were not named "the Adirondacks" until 1837. Less than 40 years later men were saying sadly that the Adirondack country, bristling with newly built summer hotels, was hunted out, timbered out, overrun with people, and ruined. When the country did develop—between 1840 and 1880—it developed fast.

Today almost every part has been trodden at one time or another by hikers, hunters, and visitors. Instead of being impassable, no spot today is more than 10 miles from a road of some sort. The Adirondack country can be crossed by car, north to south or east to west, in three hours. Approximately a rectangle, it contains 5,000 square miles, which is roughly the size of Connecticut . . . .

Mountains, Lakes, Rivers

The Adirondack country is a varied land. Seen from the air, a series of high peaks at the center, most irregularly placed, run off almost to sea level on all sides. In 40 miles the land drops from 5,344 feet above sea level on Mount Marcy to 100 feet at the shores of Lake Champlain. Not all the region is mountain and lake, however. As the land slopes down from the higher altitudes in the northeast and the northwest, it levels off for a time into rolling country and broad plateaus.

To people who know the Alps or the Rockies the idea of calling the Adirondacks "mountains" may seem ridiculous; the city of Denver is higher than any Adirondack peak. They are not jagged brute rocks piercing the sky, with summits almost always cloud-wrapped. On clear days the round top of Marcy can be seen from 30 miles away. Almost all the Adirondack peaks have these rounded tops, worn by storm and time. . . .

While more than 100 peaks are higher than 3,500 feet above sea level, many seem only like giant bumps, for they take off from a plateau of 1,500 feet or more. The 46 that are more than 4,000 feet high represent the "high peaks." Almost all are crowded together in an area of 50 square miles, and topped by the summit of Marcy.

The many mountains have some things in common. Some have abrupt rocky slides, often rising out of lakes; these precipices may not be thousands of feet high, but even one 500 feet high, rising sheer, is quite a sight. As a group, the mountains have little topsoil on them. Trees grow, but little farming has ever been done on their flanks. Another feature is the number of lakes found close to the mountains. The belief that between two mountains there must be a valley is not always true in the Adirondacks; likely as not, a lake is there instead. Finally, the interconnections of the various ranges are such that a man can climb up and down many peaks, one after the other, without coming down to the 2,500 foot level. . . .

The Adirondack people use their lakes, rivers, and woods, but, except for small boys on small peaks, they do not go in much for scaling the hills. No arrowheads or other relics have ever been found on mountaintops to show that the Indians climbed the peaks. Few pioneers did any mountain climbing; life was tough enough without that. Climbing as sport began after the announcement in 1837 that Marcy was the highest point in the state. Today it is the outsiders and the vacationists who do most of it. Thanks to the magnificent system of trails built by the Department of Conservation working with the Adirondack Mountain Club, climbing is more popular than ever today. Trails lead up most of the better-known peaks; along many of the paths are state-built lean-tos where hikers can spend the night. One favorite mountain hike is along the 135-mile trail from Lake Placid to Northville.

The existence of a marked trail does not mean therefore that the way is easy going. Climbing can be arduous, particularly on the more than 20 peaks over 4,000 feet that are still without trails. Those skilled enough to try unmarked ascents find exciting climbing on the many steep cliffs and precipices. The more daring, using regular Alpine equipment, try them each summer. In many places the rocks have been worn so smooth by slides that they offer few cracks for the pitons, the metal points which climbers use. In recent years winter climbing on snowshoes or skis has become popular. . . .

A view from any Adirondack height, even a lowly hill, or the view from an airplane over the region shows the second distinctive feature of the landscape: the tremendous number of lakes. The Adirondack country has more than 1,345 of them named, and more nameless. In the southwest quarter many are connected by inlets and outlets so that canoe trips of 100 miles can be made at will, broken only by a few portages of less than two miles each; at these carries today the Conservation Department thoughtfully provides wheeled boat carriers. In the famous Fulton Chain, known to many children who have been summer campers and made a long canoe trip on these waters as the high spot of the summer, eight lakes are strung together like beads on a necklace.

Elsewhere the lakes are beside mountains, between mountains, and, in some cases, on mountains. The highest lake is Tear-of-the-Clouds, 4,400 feet high on the side of Marcy and the most northerly source of the Hudson. Many lakes are dotted with small tree-clad islands. Lake George has more than 200. Lower Saranac Lake has 50. Some few lakes have white sandy beaches but most are tree-girt to the waterline. . . .

. . . Lake Champlain is not usually counted as an Adirondack lake. If it were it would far surpass all of them in size and depth, for it is 107 miles long and 12 miles wide at its widest, with a depth of 400 feet at one place. The largest lake fully within the Blue Line is Lake George, 30 miles long. Next in order are Long Lake and Indian Lake.

The Adirondack lakes are of various sorts. Most have clear, clean water, spring-fed, with rocky shores. Because of their springs the water of the lakes is cold in summer, although it may sometimes reach 70° in a few places. In winter the lakes are covered with ice, sometimes 20 inches deep. At the bottom their winter temperature is a uniform 38°. Some of the smaller lakes are surrounded by swamp and mud and are almost impossible to get at on foot in summer. Some were scooped out by glaciers and are small, neat ponds. Many, such as Long Lake, are the result of glacial widening of riverbeds, and are often long with narrow places; at some points Long Lake, 15 miles in length, is only 100 yards wide. Some of the lakes, like Cranberry and Flower in Saranac Lake village, are the result of damming a river or have been increased in size by such damming.

The naming of the lakes was as haphazard and unimaginative as the naming of the mountains. In a few cases Indian names were abandoned, as when some settler gave the name of Long Lake to what the Indians had called "Linden Sea." Early surveyors and settlers tagged on the first and handiest name which came to mind, with the result that there were many duplications, since so many of the lakes look round, muddy, or clear, and have duck and otter on them. The word "pond" is used quite as often as "lake." No one knows at what point of decreasing size a lake becomes a pond.

In the long list of Adirondack lakes, in addition to the well-known ones, are Single Shanty, Terror, Goose, Wild Goose, Whortleberry, Hog, Artist, Squaw, Poor, Big Slim, Little Slim, and three just plain Slim ponds. To confound visitors and natives, there are two Antediluvian ponds, 20 Long ponds, 10 East ponds, 16 Clear ponds, 20 Mud ponds, six

Mud lakes, seven Spring ponds, 10 Round ponds, 10 Duck ponds, 12 Otter ponds, along with one Pepper Box Pond and one Queer Lake. . . .

Seen casually, one Adirondack lake may look like another. No one man knows them all. To pick out the loveliest is impossible. From the highway on a hill at the south, Lake George is a magnificent sight. Blue Mountain Lake, with its many islands, the deep forest by its shore, its clear blue water reflecting the mountains nearby, is often called the loveliest lake of the lot—an opinion immediately challenged and hooted at by anyone who knows some other lake a little better.

Any Adirondack native will defend the right to call eminences of 5,400 feet "mountains," no matter what Colorado or Alpine people may say. He is not quite so sure that some of the streams deserve the name of "river." He has no doubt about the Hudson, rising on the side of Marcy, or the Raquette, the Saranac, the Oswegatchie, the Grass, and the Black, but he is uncertain about the other 20 and more "rivers," the Cold, the Bog, the Chazy, the Jordan, the Opalescent, the Chub, or the Cedar. At their mouths some of these streams may approach the common idea of river. Elsewhere they may often be only small mountain streams easily jumped by a deer and even by a hunter in pursuit.

These rivers carry much less water now than in years past. Many a 19th-century story of adventure in the Adirondacks tells of pleasant boat trips down a number of the rivers; few people would try them today. The larger rivers and many of the small ones carried log runs in the spring that would be impossible on most of them today. That steadily decreasing volume of water has been noted in all Adirondack history. It is not a recent phenomenon but appeared after the first heavy lumbering.

The Hudson is the best known of the Adirondack rivers. Its northernmost source is more than 4,000 feet up on Marcy, in Lake Tear-of-the-Clouds. By the time the Hudson reaches Manhattan it is a sophisticated river, changing its mood many times. Below Luzerne, where the Adirondack foothills yield to rolling fields, it is broad and placid. At Glens Falls, out of the Adirondacks, it is a turbulent rapids and waterfall. At Troy it is dirty and bedraggled, showing no sign of the clear, green, mountain-water source whence it came. At Haverstraw it is a broad inland sea.

But up in the Adirondacks where it comes tumbling out of the mountains it is a gracious little stream that races over rounded pebbles and is all of 10 feet wide. The children of the miners who work at Tahawus below Marcy cross back and forth, first carefully rolling up their jeans. The river that flows so majestically by the Palisades and on to its deep sea gorge may be the weary river of the poet at its mouth, but it is fresh and young up where it begins. There it reflects the tamarack and the pine, and bears the little toy boats of the children. Far south it will reflect skyscrapers and carry ocean liners. It is still the same water, some of it, that has come gushing out of the ancient rocks of the Adirondacks.

More than any other stream, the Hudson helped to move the forest riches out to the mills. It carried lumber drives as early as 1813. During the mid-century most of the rivers of the Adirondacks were declared "public highways" for log driving by the state and log drivers were at work along them. Where rivers ran into lakes and then out into river again, the logs had to be floated through the lake in large booms to prevent them from piling up on shores. Today, shortage of water and scarcity of trained labor has made log driving forever a part of the Adirondack past. Trucks move the logs out of the woods faster, if less picturesquely.

The Adirondacks mark the water divide of the state. The same meadow on the shoulder of Marcy sends water south to the Hudson and north in the Ausable, which flows on to Lake Champlain and so to the St. Lawrence. This favorite two-pronged river of fishermen drops some 4,000 feet in covering its 50 miles. Near its mouth it runs through a chasm advertised 60 years ago as one of the natural wonders of the world, a miniature Grand Canyon, 150 feet high at some places and two miles long. Set conveniently by one of the main Adirondack highways, Ausable Chasm is still a tourist objective of the region. . . .

Each river has its own charms, although little traffic of any sort, even canoes, passes over them these days. The Raquette is the most meandering of rivers, coming out of Blue Mountain Lake through Long Lake. It flows 172 miles on to the St. Lawrence to cover a distance of perhaps 80 miles as the crow flies, and was once a favorite route for trips into the wilderness. Flowing south from Fulton Chain, the Moose connects more than 100 bodies of water, large and small. The Black River, flowing west out of the woods, has provided power and riches for the area around Watertown. The Oswegatchie, the Saint Regis, and the Schroon were all lumbermen's rivers in their day. Trout fishermen wade them in spring. The rest of the year the only sound along them is the rush of their own water, south to the Atlantic, north to the St. Lawrence. . . .

The Woods

Mountains and lakes may mark the region as unusual, but it is the woods, above all, that make the Adirondacks. They bring the summer people. They provide all or part of the income of many a family. For years it was believed that odors and chemicals borne on the air from the woods played an important part in curing the sick who came and found their health restored.

The Adirondack woods are not isolated patches but the ever-present covering of the country. Now and then roads may run through a stretch of open country, but woods soon come to their sides, even on main roads. Driving them in spring and summer is like driving through green canyons. In many places, particularly on state land where the underbrush is never cleared, the woods seem impenetrable even a few feet back from the road. Woods frame almost every lakeshore. . . .

With a variation in altitude from almost sea level at Lake Champlain to more than 5,000 feet on the high peaks, the Adirondack country has distinct forest zones. Red oak will grow in the lowland but not in the higher country. Balsam, tamarack, ash, cedar, and yellow birch are trees of the 1,500- to 2,000-foot plateau. Spruce and hemlock grow on the sides of the higher peaks where hardwoods disappear and the evergreens are eventually stunted. The top of Marcy is slightly above timberline; just below it dwarf balsams grow short and crooked but with as many as a hundred rings of growth, while on the peak is a genuine arctic or Alpine zone and many a rare plant. The southern border of the park also marks a dividing line in plant life. Poison ivy does not grow above it. The dogwood, so common to the south, dies in the Adirondack winter. The white pine does not do well below that line. . . .

Two characteristics mark the Adirondack woods. The first is the change in tree species. Because of changes in climate or for some other reason, in recent years the second growth has been largely hardwood, thus reducing the percentage of evergreens. After fires, inferior trees such as cherry and poplar are the first to come back and thrive; birches appear next, and beech, but other trees may not show for decades. While most of the woods seem thick and heavily grown, a large part, perhaps as much as 50%, has little or no timber worth the name. Except on the highest peaks, little is completely bare, but much is scrub growth, with many a meadow or sparsely grown clearing appearing in unexpected places. On the other hand, where lumbermen have worked on their own land or on leased land, fair second growth may show from "mamma trees," maples and spruces which have reseeded themselves. Parts of the Adirondacks that were cleared land 70 years ago are heavily and usefully wooded today. Such reforested farmland explains why, in places where trees are 60 years old and more, a hiker comes on a lone gnarly apple tree or even a lilac bush in the middle of deep woods. Nearby, usually, are the traces of the foundations of a house. But many parts of the woods still show in slash and vanished water resources where the 19th-century lumberman passed.

The second distinctive characteristic is the rich growth on the floor of the woods. Where no fires have destroyed the deposits of centuries, spring flowers are abundant, beginning with trilliums and lady's slippers. Ground pine is plentiful, along with partridge berry. Two years after storm damage or lumbering make a clearing, the open place can be a thick raspberry bramble. Ferns and mosses are abundant: 43 of the 60 varieties of ferns found in the state grow in the Adirondacks.

Of the various trees of the Adirondack woods, the tall white pine stands out as best loved and most prized. The Adirondack woods have other native pines, red and pitch, but the white pines tower over them as the symbol of the North Woods. Once they stood seven feet through at the base. Eight oxen had to be hitched up to budge one 13-foot log. A few old white pines still stand, either saved miraculously on state land or overlooked by the lumbermen.

The white pine often appears in early Adirondack history. In the 18th century the French cut suitable trees for ships' masts and spars. They were floated to Montreal, then shipped to France for the royal navy. The British were just as busy in the woods around Ticonderoga. Both the British and French ships that fought at Trafalgar may have had masts, spars, and planking from the Adirondack hills. The British continued to buy Adirondack pine after the Revolution and had it shipped to them down the Hudson, then by sailing vessel from New York. White-pine boards, sledded from the Lake George region to Albany and down the Hudson, were shipped to Europe and even to the West Indies in the early part of the 19th century. Adirondack white pine helped to build many an Early American building in the seaboard cities.

By 1800 much of the great white pine along the shores of Lake Champlain was gone. By 1850 the great trees had been cut throughout the region and the amount of white pine taken from the woods fell off sharply. The thousands of feet timbered later came from second- and even third-growth trees. Today the state sets out millions of white-pine seedlings in an effort to return to the Adirondack country the glory of the dignified tree. Most of the seeds are handpicked from parent trees, but some are collected from hoards gathered by squirrels. Wherever the white pine grows in the woods, it is subject to a blight called Blister Rust. This mysterious spore disease, which must have wild currants or gooseberries nearby for part of its development, is kept under control. Many a taxpayer's dollar goes to pay for men to tramp the woods and weed out the wild currant.

As the white pine disappeared, the red spruce took its place as the backbone of the woods and of the lumber industry. Some were giants in the early days. The average tree was 80 feet tall, with a diameter of 18 inches and a ring count of 175 to 200 years. Sixty years ago one spruce was found near Lake Meacham in the northwest quarter that was 41 inches in diameter and overtowered the forest. It was later cut down for pulpwood.

The spruce entered into politics as the white pine never did. It was the decision of a pliant governor to let all spruce above a certain size on the forest preserve be lumbered that dramatized the need to protect the preserve, and brought about the "forever wild" amendment to the state constitution in 1894.

The most serious attack on the spruce was not the work of men who wanted it for lumber; it was, in fact, lightly timbered until the thick pine was gone, and even then only the largest trees were taken. The real attack came after 1867, when it was found that the long spruce fibers were by far the best raw material for paper pulp. Thereafter, the take was merciless and heavy. . . .

The spruces darken as winter comes and give the hills their black-green look, but two other trees add their coloring at other times. Maples fire the hills in autumn, birches set them shining in summer or winter. Of the four kinds of maples, the hard maple is the most useful for lumber and sugar. The favorite birch of the woods is the canoe or paper birch, a dead-white chalky tree with black streaks on its bark which punctuates the lake shores and stands on the distant hills like an exclamation mark. The yellow birch, no less striking with its golden bark, is the favorite tree for furniture making and other commercial uses.

These and another score of species, from ash to ironwood and balsam, make up the Adirondack woods as they stretch from Poke O'Moonshine in the northeast to the shores of West Canada Creek in the southwest. They clothe the valleys, hills, and swamps. They give the land its color, through the greens of spring, the fire reds of autumn, and the blackness of winter.

3 New York City

Introduction

Whatever you're looking for in a big-city vacation, you'll find in New York.

The city has history: You can trace the life of the early Dutch settlers, canny traders who, unconstrained by religious strictures of fellow colonists in Massachusetts and Pennsylvania, gave the city its enterprising soul. You can see the spot where George Washington was sworn in as first U.S. president, the grave of Alexander Hamilton, and the restored site of America's greatest 19th-century seaport.

The city has architecture: "New York" and "skyline" are virtually a single word. But along with a succession of buildings that, in their time, ranked as the world's tallest structures (the Flatiron, Woolworth, Chrysler, and Empire State buildings, and the World Trade Center Towers), New York retains many handsome residential reminders of its Colonial and Victorian past. Contemporary architectural treasures range from the bizarre (Guggenheim Museum) to the sublime (Trump Tower) to the perplexingly postmodern (AT&T Building).

No one has to make a case for New York's performing arts. In show-biz terms, the Big Apple is top banana. A New York street by the name of Broadway is an international adjective for theater. The Metropolitan Opera, New York Philharmonic, and New York City Ballet are national companies. Their greatness is nurtured by the talent of hundreds of non-Broadway theaters, musical ensembles, and dance troupes—all performing nightly in New York. The city remains the world center of jazz, rock, and dance music attuned to every generation.

New York has a full complement of professional sports organizations: two baseball teams (Mets and Yankees), two football teams (Giants and Jets), two basketball teams (Knicks and New Jersey Nets), and three hockey teams (Rangers, Islanders, New Jersey Devils). It's easy to find a boxing or wrestling match. And horse races, both thoroughbred and standardbred, are off and running almost every day of the year at one of the four area tracks.

Perhaps because New York lacks the outdoor endowments of other locales, the city places a stronger emphasis on the joys of the table. New York has 17,000 restaurants, some world-famous institutions, others the "in" spots of the day, neighborhood standbys, or back-street discoveries.

Even though the island of Manhattan has largely become a river-to-river high-rent district, its ethnic neighborhoods thrive. Little Italy, Chinatown, and other pockets of ethnicity are not theme parks but vibrant, ever-changing areas that remain magnets for Old Country settlers.

Some New York attractions occupy a class by themselves. The Statue of Liberty, the Brooklyn Bridge, the Empire State Building, Times Square, and Central Park may be situated in New York City, but all belong to the world.

Above and beyond the laundry list of sights and activities, New York has an undefinable aura that exists nowhere else. It's a kind of energy level that has something to do with being in the big league, where everybody's watching and keeping score.

Part of the big-league mentality derives from the kind of industries headquartered here. New York has Wall Street, the financial center of the world. It contains the corporate headquarters of major TV networks, most national magazines, book publishers, and news-gathering organizations. The largest advertising agencies and public relations firms are here. New York also has the fashion industry and the United Nations. A lot goes on here, and a lot of people are around to tell about it.

Walking down a New York street, you might pass Henry Kissinger (with a bodyguard or two). You could go into a restaurant and get a table across from Robert DeNiro. You are very likely to turn a corner and see a feature film or TV series being filmed. And even if you don't see someone you recognize, you always feel that you just *might*. Paraphrasing a slogan coined for The Plaza hotel, you get the feeling that "nothing unimportant ever happens in New York," and it lends an edge to everything that goes on.

You may already have heard that New York can be an expensive place in which to live or to visit. New York hotels are among the country's most costly, and the price ranges of Manhattan restaurants seem to be a couple of levels above those one finds elsewhere in the country. Movie tickets, museum admissions, clothing, drinks, incidentals—many things cost more here. Yet there are shopping bargains in New York; those things that New York produces, such as books, can often be found at much lower prices here than in the other 49 states.

And there is crime, which can occur in the most unexpected places. The person who appears to have an accident at the exit door of a bus is in reality a pickpocket who will flee with your wallet or purse if you attempt to give aid. The individual who approaches you with a complicated story about having "found" money or other valuables is playing a confidence game and hopes to get something from you. Violent crime can occur anywhere, at any hour, and the only reasonable precautions anyone can take are to keep jewelry and valuables out of sight on the street and to walk generally on the main thoroughfares, with the crowds. Women should never hang a purse on a chair in a restaurant or on a hook in a rest-room stall.

New Yorkers themselves often appear to be brusque, haughty, cold, even rude in their manner. This is largely a defensive attitude that residents develop, consciously or not, to cope with living so closely with so many other people. When you encounter rudeness, don't take it personally; it's just that individual's way of behaving. And when you have the opportunity to talk for a bit with New Yorkers, you'll find that they usually warm to you and will often go out of their way to be accommodating.

Many are the tales of visitors lost on the subway who are shepherded to safety by a Good Samaritan from Canarsie. Strangers constantly come forward to mediate disputes between out-of-towners and cab drivers. Ask New Yorkers for simple directions and they're likely to tell you a lot more than you need to know. New Yorkers can be as down-to-earth as people anywhere. Yet they can also be brash, opinionated, impatient, smug, self-important, and, in a peculiar way, maddeningly provincial. As O. Henry wrote, "What else can you expect from a town that's shut off from the world by the ocean on one side and New Jersey on the other?"

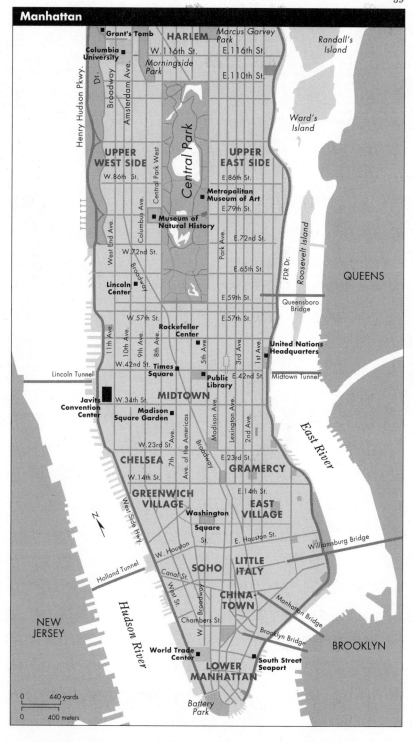

Manhattan

Grant's Tomb

Columbia University

HARLEM

Marcus Garvey Park

W.116th St.

E.116th St.

Morningside Park

E.110th St.

Randall's Island

Henry Hudson Pkwy.

Dr.

Broadway

Amsterdam Ave.

UPPER WEST SIDE

W.86th St.

Central Park West

Central Park

Ward's Island

UPPER EAST SIDE

E.86th St.

Metropolitan Museum of Art

E.79th St.

West End Ave.

Columbus Ave.

Museum of Natural History

Park Ave.

E.72nd St.

W.72nd St.

Broadway

E.65th St.

FDR Dr.

Roosevelt Island

Lincoln Center

E.59th St.

Queensboro Bridge

QUEENS

11th Ave.

10th Ave.

9th Ave.

8th Ave.

W.57th St.

Rockefeller Center

E.57th St.

5th Ave.

3rd Ave.

1st Ave.

United Nations Headquarters

Lincoln Tunnel

W.42nd St.

Times Square

Public Library

E.42nd St.

Midtown Tunnel

Javits Convention Center

W.34th St.

MIDTOWN

Madison Square Garden

Madison Ave.

Lexington Ave.

2nd Ave.

W.23rd St.

7th Ave.

Ave. of the Americas

Broadway

E.23rd St.

East River

CHELSEA

W.14th St.

GRAMERCY

GREENWICH VILLAGE

E.14th St.

West Side Hwy.

Washington Square

EAST VILLAGE

W. Houston St.

E. Houston St.

Williamsburg Bridge

Holland Tunnel

Canal St.

SOHO

West St.

Broadway

LITTLE ITALY

CHINA-TOWN

Manhattan Bridge

Chambers St.

W.

Brooklyn Bridge

NEW JERSEY

Hudson River

World Trade Center

South Street Seaport

BROOKLYN

LOWER MANHATTAN

Battery Park

0   440 yards
0   400 meters

Manhattan Subways

86th St Bway ① ② ③ ⑨

86th St Central Park W

86th St Lexington Ave ④ ⑤ ⑥

81st St Museum of Natural History

79th St Bway

77th St Lexington Ave

CENTRAL PARK

72nd St Bway

Roosevelt Island

66th St/Bway Lincoln Center

68th St Lexington Ave

Ⓐ Ⓑ Ⓒ Ⓓ

Ⓑ Ⓠ

63rd St Lexington Ave

TRAMWAY

Ⓡ Ⓝ

59th St Columbus Circle

5th Ave 60th St

59th St Lexington Ave

Queensboro Bridge

QUEENS

50th St 8th Ave

Ⓓ

5th Ave

Lexington Ave/53rd St.

23rd St Ely Ave

42nd St 8th Ave

57th St/Bway

50th St/7th Ave

Lexington Ave 52nd St.

Ⓔ Ⓕ

Ⓢ

Ⓓ Ⓕ

Vernon Blvd Jackson Ave ⑦

Times Sq

5th Ave 42nd St

Grand Central

Queens-Midtown Tunnel

Lincoln Tunnel

Penn Station

34th St Herald Sq

34th St 8th Ave

28th St

33rd St Park Ave S

23rd St 8th Ave

Ⓑ Ⓓ Ⓕ Ⓠ

Ⓡ Ⓝ

④ ⑤ ⑥

28th St Park Ave S

Ⓐ Ⓒ Ⓔ

① ② ③

23rd St Park Ave S

14th St 8th Ave

Ⓛ

18th St

6th Ave

3rd Ave

Ⓛ

14th St Union Sq

1st Ave

8th St/Astor Pl

Christopher St Sheridan Sq

W 4th St

Bleecker St Lafayette St

Ⓜ Ⓙ Ⓩ

Houston St Varick St

Prince

Spring

2 Ave/E Houston St

Williamsburg Br.

Holland Tunnel

Spring

Delancey St/Essex St

Delancey St/Spring St

Grand/Christie

E. B'way

Canal St Varick St

Canal Bway

Manhattan Bridge

Ⓕ BROOKLYN

Franklin St Varick St.

Ⓓ Ⓑ Ⓠ

York St

Chambers St

City Hall Bway

Chambers St Varick St

Brooklyn Bridge

Fulton

Park Pl

Fulton

Cortland St World Trade Center

Ⓐ Ⓒ

High St

Clark

Broad/Wall

② ③

Subway Lines

━━━━ BMT

───── IND

▪▪▪▪▪ IRT

Rector St Greenwich St

Rector/Trinity Pl

Ⓜ Ⓝ Ⓡ

Borough Hall

South Ferry

Whitehall

④ ⑤

Jay St Borough Hall

Brooklyn Battery Tunnel

America's greatest metropolis presents the visitor with a superfluity of opportunity. You can't do it all; you don't have the time, and nobody has the money. So you will have to make decisions, and the big one will probably be whether you see what New York does best or you do the things that you like best. On the whole, that's a great choice to have.

Essential Information

Arriving and Departing

By Plane Virtually every major U.S. and foreign airline serves one or
The Airlines more of New York's three airports: *LaGuardia Airport, John F. Kennedy International Airport,* and *Newark International Airport.*

When choosing a flight, be sure to distinguish among (a) *nonstop flights*—no stops or changes or aircraft; (b) *direct flights*—one or more stops but no charge of aircraft; (c) *connecting flights*—at least one change of aircraft and possibly several stops as well.

Airlines serving the New York area include: America West (tel. 800/247–5692), American (tel. 800/433–7300), Braniff (tel. 800/272–6433), Continental (tel. 800/525–0280), Delta (tel. 800/221–1212), Midway (tel. 800/621–5700), Northwest (tel. 800/225–2525), Pan Am (tel. 800/442–5896), TWA (tel. 800/221–2000), United (tel. 800/241–6522), and USAir (tel. 800/428–4322).

As of late February 1990, smoking is banned on all routes within the 48 contiguous states; within the states of Hawaii and Alaska; to and from the U.S. Virgin Islands and Puerto Rico; and on flights of under six hours to and from Hawaii and Alaska. The rule applies to the domestic legs of all foreign routes but does not apply to international flights.

On a flight where smoking is permitted, you can request a nonsmoking seat during check-in or when you book your ticket. If you are told that there are no seats available in the nonsmoking section, insist on one: Department of Transportation regulations require carriers to find seats for all nonsmokers, provided they meet check-in time restrictions.

From Airports to **LaGuardia Airport** is in the borough of Queens, eight miles
Center City northeast of midtown Manhattan. Taxis cost $12–$18 plus toll (up to $2.50) and take 20–40 minutes. Group taxi rides to Manhattan are available at taxi dispatch lines just outside the baggage-claim areas during most travel hours (no service Saturdays or holidays). Group fares range from $7 to $9 per person (plus share of tolls), depending on your destination. Call 718/784–4343 for more information.

Carey Airport Express (tel. 718/632–0500) buses depart for Manhattan every 20–30 minutes from 6:45 AM to midnight. It's a 20–30 minute ride to 42nd Street and Park Avenue, directly opposite Grand Central Terminal. A shuttle bus runs from here to the New York Hilton, Sheraton City Squire, and Marriott Marquis hotels. To other midtown hotels, it's a short cab ride. The bus fare is $7.50; pay the driver. The **Gray Line Air Shuttle Minibus** (tel. 212/581–3929) serves major Manhattan hotels direct to and from the airport. The fare is $10 per person; make arrangements at the ground transportation center or use the courtesy phone.

John F. Kennedy International Airport (JFK) is in the borough of Queens, 15 miles southeast of midtown. Taxis cost $24–$30 plus tolls (up to $2) and take 35–60 minutes.

Carey Airport Express (tel. 718/632–0500) buses depart for Manhattan from all JFK terminals every 20–30 minutes, 6 AM to midnight. The ride takes about one hour to 42nd Street and Park Avenue (Grand Central Terminal). A shuttle bus runs from there to the New York Hilton, Sheraton City Squire, and Marriott Marquis hotels; it's a short cab ride to other midtown hotels. The bus fare is $9.50; pay the driver. The **Gray Line Air Shuttle Minibus** (tel. 212/581–3929) serves major Manhattan hotels directly from the airport; the cost is $13 per person. Make arrangements at the ground transportation counter or use the courtesy phone.

The **JFK Express** is a special subway service from the Howard Beach station near JFK Airport to downtown Brooklyn, lower Manhattan, Greenwich Village, and Midtown, terminating at 57th Street and Sixth Avenue. Shuttle buses from JFK terminals to the Howard Beach station depart every 20 minutes from 6:06 AM to 12:56 AM. The ride to the 57th Street terminus takes 50 minutes. Trains have luggage space and plenty of transit police. The fare is $6.50, including connection to the entire subway system; pay on the train. (To reach JFK, you pay $1 to enter the subway system and an additional $5.50 on board the train.)

Newark International Airport is in Newark, New Jersey, 16 miles southwest of Midtown. Taxis cost $28–$30 plus tolls ($3) and take 20–45 minutes. "Share and Save" group rates are available for up to four passengers between 8 AM and midnight; make arrangements with the taxi dispatcher.

NJ Transit Airport Express buses (tel. 201/460–8444) depart every 15–30 minutes for the Port Authority Terminal, at 42nd Street and Eighth Avenue. From there it's a short cab ride to midtown hotels. The ride takes 30–45 minutes. The fare is $7; buy your ticket inside the terminal. The **Olympia Airport Express Bus** to the World Trade Center and Grand Central Terminal departs every 20 minutes from 6 AM to midnight. The travel time to the World Trade Center is 20 minutes; to Grand Central, 35 minutes. The fare is $6; pay the driver. **Newark Airport/NYC Minibus** departs for major Manhattan hotels about every 30 minutes, but schedules vary according to passenger demand. The fare is $15; make arrangements at the ground transportation counter.

By Car The **Lincoln Tunnel** (I–495), **Holland Tunnel**, and **George Washington Bridge** (I–95) connect to the New Jersey Turnpike system and points west. The Lincoln Tunnel leads to midtown Manhattan, the Holland Tunnel to lower Manhattan, the George Washington Bridge to northern Manhattan. Each of the three arteries requires a toll ($3 for cars) eastbound into New York, but no toll westbound.

From Long Island, the **Midtown Tunnel** (I–495) and **Triborough Bridge** (I–278) are the most direct arteries to Manhattan. Both require tolls ($2.50 for cars) in both directions.

From upstate New York, the city is accessible via the **New York (Dewey) Thruway** (I–87) (toll) and the **Major Deegan Expressway** (I–87) through the Bronx and across the **Triborough Bridge** (toll).

From New England, the **Connecticut Turnpike** (I–95) connects to the **New England Thruway** (I–95) (toll), the **Bruckner Expressway** (I–278), and the **Triborough Bridge** (toll) to upper Manhattan.

Be forewarned: Driving within Manhattan can be a nightmare of gridlocked streets and predatory fellow motorists. Free parking is almost impossible to find in Midtown, and parking lots are exorbitant—$16 for three hours is not unusual in midtown lots—all over town. If you do drive, don't plan to use your car much for driving within Manhattan.

By Train **Amtrak** (tel. 800/872–7245) offers frequent service within the Northeast Corridor, between Boston and Washington. Trains arrive and depart from Pennsylvania Station (31st to 33rd Sts., between Seventh and Eighth Aves.). Amtrak trains also serve Penn Station from the Southeast, Midwest, and Far West.

Amtrak service from Montreal and upstate New York and the Lake Shore Limited from Chicago both use Grand Central Terminal (42nd St. and Park Ave.).

Metro-North Commuter Railroad (tel. 212/532–4900) serves Grand Central from the northern suburbs and Connecticut as far east as New Haven. The **Long Island Railroad** (tel. 718/217–5477) has service from all over Long Island to Penn Station. Also at Penn Station, **New Jersey Transit** (tel. 201/460–8444) offers frequent service from the north and central regions of the state.

By Bus All long-haul and commuter bus lines feed into the **Port Authority Terminal,** a mammoth multi-level structure that occupies a nearly two-square-block area between 40th and 42nd streets and Eighth and Ninth avenues. Though it's recently modernized and fairly clean, the large number of vagrants make the terminal an uncomfortable place to spend much time. Especially on night arrivals, plan to move swiftly through the terminal.

For information on any service into or out of the Port Authority Terminal, call 212/564–8484. Some of the individual bus lines serving New York include **Greyhound-Trailways** (consult local information for a number in your area), **Adirondack** and **Pine Hill Trailways** from upstate New York (tel. 914/339–4230); **Bonanza Bus Lines** from New England (tel. 401/331–7500); **Martz Trailways** from northeastern Pennsylvania (tel. 717/821–3838); **Peter Pan Bus Lines** from New England (tel. 413/781–2900); and **Vermont Transit** from New England (tel. 802/862–9671).

Important Addresses and Numbers

Tourist Information The **New York Convention and Visitors Bureau** at Columbus Circle (58th St. and Eighth Ave.) provides a wealth of free information, including brochures, subway and bus maps, listings of hotels and weekend hotel packages, and discount coupons for Broadway shows. Drop in or, better yet, contact them before you arrive. *2 Columbus Circle, New York, NY 10019, tel. 212/ 397–8222. Open weekdays 9–6. Closed holidays.*

Emergencies	911 for **police, fire,** or **ambulance** in an emergency.
Doctor	**Doctors On Call, 24-hour house-call service** at 212/737–2333. Near Midtown, 24-hour emergency rooms are open at **St. Luke's–Roosevelt Hospital** (458 W. 59th St., tel. 212/523–4000) and **St. Vincent's Hospital** (Seventh Ave. and 11th St., tel. 212/790–7000).
Dentist	The **Dental Emergency Service** (212/679–3966; after 8 PM, tel. 212/679–4172) will make a referral.
24-Hour Pharmacy	**Kaufman's Pharmacy** (Lexington Ave. and 50th St., tel. 212/755–2266).

Getting Around

New York is a city of neighborhoods best explored at a leisurely pace, up close, and by foot. But New York neighborhoods are big, and you'll need some motorized means of travel between them.

By Subway   The 300-mile subway system is the fastest and cheapest way to get around the city. It operates 24 hours a day and, especially within Manhattan, serves most of the places you'll want to visit. The New York subway also deserves many of the negative aspects of its image. Even though new graffiti-proof, air-conditioned cars predominate now, many trains are crowded, dirty, noisy, somewhat unreliable, and occasionally unsafe. Unsavory characters lurk in the stations, and panhandlers, who are noisy but usually harmless, work their way through the cars. Don't write off the subway—it really is colorful, and millions ride it every day without incident—but stay alert at all times.

The subway costs $1.15, with reduced fares for the disabled and senior citizens at all hours. You must use a token to enter. They are sold at token booths that are *usually* open at each station. It's advisable to stock up on tokens since the token booth may not be open and, if open, may have a long line. You can also use tokens on city buses. A token permits unlimited transfers within the subway system.

Free subway maps are given out at token booths upon request. They are often out of stock, so ask at several booths until you find one. Maps are also posted in subway cars but are seldom found on platforms. Make sure you refer to an up-to-date map; lengthy repair programs often cause reroutings that last long enough for new "temporary" maps to be printed.

For route information, ask the token clerk or a transit policeman. And don't hesitate to ask directions from any knowledgeable-looking fellow rider: Once New Yorkers realize you're harmless, they bend over backward to help. For 24-hour information, call 718/330–1234. (Calls from the 212 area code to 718, and vice versa, cost the local rate, 25¢ from pay phones.)

A few words on safety: Most of the stops in Midtown are crowded with riders all hours of the day or night. Stay among those crowds—there's safety in numbers. Don't wander off to a deserted section of the platform, and don't enter empty or nearly empty cars. At off-peak hours, try to ride in the same car as the conductor; it will stop near a line of light bulbs above the edge of the platform. Follow the crowd until you reach the comparative safety of the street.

By Bus Most buses follow easy-to-understand routes along the Manhattan grid. Routes go up or down the north-south avenues, east and west on the major two-way crosstown streets. Most bus routes operate 24 hours, but service is infrequent late at night. Buses are great for sightseeing, but traffic jams—a potential threat at any time or place in Manhattan—can make rides maddeningly slow.

Bus fare is $1.15 in change only (no pennies) or a subway token. When you get on the bus you can get a free transfer good for one change to an intersecting route. Legal transfer points are listed on the back of the transfer. Transfers have time limits of at least two hours, often longer. You cannot use the transfer to enter the subway system.

Each of the five boroughs of New York has a separate bus map, and they are scarcer than hen's teeth. They are occasionally available in subway token booths and never available on buses. Your best bets are the Convention and Visitors Bureau at Columbus Circle or the information kiosks in Grand Central Terminal and Penn Station.

By Taxi Taxis are usually easy to hail on the street or from a line in front of major hotels. Taxis cost $1.50 for the first ⅛ mile, 25¢ for each ⅛ mile thereafter, and 25¢ for each minute not in motion. A 50¢ surcharge is added to rides begun between 8 PM and 6 AM. There is no charge for extra passengers. Taxi drivers also expect a 15% tip. Barring performance above and beyond the call of duty, don't feel obliged to give them more.

To avoid unhappy taxi experiences, be sure to have a general idea of where you want to go. Some cab drivers are dishonest; some are ignorant; some can barely understand English. In any case, if you don't have any idea of the proper route, you may be taken for a long and costly ride.

New York taxis are mile-for-mile less expensive than in many places, and in some instances taxis can be a bargain. A short trip for two or more people may cost less than the combined bus or subway fare.

Jogging The principal area for jogging is Central Park, a runner's paradise from dawn till sundown. A 1.59 mile soft surface track rings the Reservoir (Fifth Ave. and 90th St.). For information on group runs, call the **Road Runners Club** (tel. 212/860–4455).

Bicycling You can rent bikes in Central Park from **AAA Bikes in Central Park,** located beside the Loeb Boathouse parallel to 72nd Street (tel. 212/861–4137). Outside but near the park, you can rent bikes from **Metro Bicycles** (1311 Lexington Ave. at 88th St., tel. 212/427–4450); **Bicycles Plus** (204 E. 85th St., tel. 212/794–2201), and **Gene's Bicycles** (242 E. 79th St., tel. 212/249–9218).

Guided Tours

Orientation Tours The most pleasant way to get a crash orientation to Manhattan is aboard a **Circle Line Cruise.** Once you've finished the three-hour 35-mile circumnavigation of Manhattan, you'll have a good idea of where things are and what you want to see next. Narrations are as interesting and individualized as the guides—often moonlighting actors—who deliver them. *Pier 83, west end of*

42nd St., tel. 212/563–3200. Fare: $15 adults, $7.50 children under 12. Operates daily, early Mar.–Dec.

At South Street Seaport's Pier 16 you can take two- or three-hour voyages to New York's past aboard the iron cargo schooner, *Pioneer* (tel. 212/669–9416). You can take 90-minute tours of New York Harbor aboard the sidewheeler *Andrew Fletcher* or the re-created steamboat *DeWitt Clinton*.

For a shorter excursion, the **TNT Express,** a new hydroliner, will show you the island of Manhattan in only an hour. *Pier 11, south of South Street Seaport, tel. 212/244–4770. Fare: $15 adults, $13 senior citizens, $8 children under 12, under 5 free. Boats depart Mon.–Sat. noon and 2 PM.*

The Gray Line (900 Eighth Ave. at 53rd St., tel. 212/397–2600) offers a number of different city bus tours, plus cruises and day trips to Brooklyn and Atlantic City. **Short Line Tours** (166 W. 46th St., tel. 212/354–5122) offers a number of tour options. **Manhattan Sightseeing Bus Tours** (150 W. 49th St., tel. 212/869 –5005) has 10 different tours.

Island Helicopter (Heliport at E. 34th St. and East River, tel. 212/683–4575) offers a number of flyover options, from $38 (for 16 miles) to $89 (for more than 75 miles). From the west side, **Manhattan Helicopter Tours** (heliport at W. 30th St. and Hudson River, tel. 212/247–8687) has tours from $35 to $144.

Special-Interest Tours   **Backstage on Broadway** (tel. 212/575–8065) takes you behind the scenes of a Broadway show and lets you mingle with show people. Reservations are mandatory. **Art Tours of Manhattan** (tel. 609/921–2647) provides an inside view of museum and gallery exhibits. **Gallery Passports** (tel. 212/288–3578) admits you to artists' studios and lofts and other art attractions near Manhattan. **Soho Art Experience** (tel. 212/219–0810) offers tours of Soho's architecture, galleries, shops, and artists' lofts. **Doorway to Design** (tel. 212/221–1111) tours fashion and interior design showrooms, as well as artists' private studios. **Harlem Your Way!** (tel. 212/690–1687) offers daily walking tours and Sunday gospel trips to one of the most exciting areas of the city.

Walking Tours   **Sidewalks of New York** (33 Alan Terr., Suite #2, Jersey City, NJ 07306, tel. 212/517–0201) hits the streets from various thematic angles—Historic Church Tours, Ye Old Tavern Tours, Celebrity Home Tours, Final Resting Places of the Rich and Famous Tours. Tours are offered on weekends, both days and evenings, year-round. Tours last 2–2½ hours and cost $15; no reservations are required. **Adventure on a Shoestring** (300 W. 53rd St., New York, NY 10019, tel. 212/265–2663) is a 27-year-old organization that explores unique New York neighborhoods. Tours are scheduled periodically, $5 per person. **The Municipal Art Society** (tel. 212/935–3960) operates a series of bus and walking tours. The **Urban Park Rangers** (tel. 212/397–3080) offers weekend walks and workshops, most of them free, in city parks. The **92nd Street YMHA** (tel. 212/996–1105) always has something special to offer on weekends.

The most comprehensive listing of tours offered during a particular week is published in the "Other Events" section of *New York* magazine.

Self-Guided Walking Tours   The **New York Convention and Visitors Bureau** provides three pamphlets that cover historical and cultural points of interest in Manhattan and Brooklyn: the "I Love New York Visitors

Guide and Map," "42nd Street–River to River," and "Brooklyn on Tour." The materials are available at the bureau's information center (2 Columbus Circle, tel. 212/397–8222).

The **Municipal Art Society of New York** has prepared a comprehensive "Juror's Guide to Lower Manhattan: Five Walking Tours" for the benefit of jurors who are often required to kill a lot of time while serving in downtown courthouses. Along with an explanation of the New York jury system, the pamphlet includes tours of Lower Manhattan and Wall Street; City Hall District; Chinatown and Little Italy; South Street Seaport; and TriBeCa. Jurors get copies free; nonjurors can purchase copies at Urban Center Books (457 Madison at 51st St., New York, NY 10022, tel. 212/935–3595).

A free "Walking Tour of Rockefeller Center" pamphlet is available from the information desk in the lobby of the RCA Building (30 Rockefeller Plaza).

Exploring New York City

Visitors finding their way around the city soon discover that Manhattan has a Jekyll-and-Hyde personality. Rational Dr. Jekyll dwells above 14th Street, where the streets form a regular grid pattern. Avenues run north (uptown) and south (downtown). Streets run east and west (crosstown). The exceptions are Broadway, a diagonal from 14th to 79th streets, and the thoroughfares along the Hudson and East rivers.

Fifth Avenue (originally Middle Road) is the baseline: Street addresses begin at Fifth Avenue and increase in regular increments. East of Fifth, the addresses 1–99 E. are between Fifth and Park avenues; 100–199 E. between Park and Third avenues; 200–299 E. between Third and Second avenues; and so on. West of Fifth Avenue, the addresses 1–99 W. are between Fifth and Sixth avenues; 100–199 W. between Sixth and Seventh avenues; 200–299 W. between Seventh and Eighth avenues; and so on. Above 59th Street, West Side addresses begin at Central Park West, an extension of Eighth Avenue.

Avenue addresses are much less regular. The building numbers begin wherever the avenue begins, and they increase by irregular increments. An address at 552 Third Avenue, for example, will not be at the same cross street as (or necessarily anywhere near) 552 Second Avenue or 552 Lexington Avenue. Avenue addresses given in this book (and in many other listings) include both the number and the nearest cross street, for example, "303 Lexington Avenue at 37th Street." When you don't know the nearest cross street, you can calculate the location of an avenue address by referring to the formulas in the Manhattan Address Locator (*see* below).

Below 14th Street, Manhattan streets reflect the disordered personality of Mr. Hyde. They are either diagonals aligned with present or long-gone shorelines or the twisting descendants of an ancient cow path. Below 14th Street you will encounter such anomalous situations as the intersection of West 4th Street and West 11th Street, the misunderstandings caused by the proximate and roughly parallel Greenwich Street and Greenwich Avenue, the transformation of Leroy Street into St. Luke's Place for one block before reverting to

Manhattan Address Locator

To locate avenue addresses, take the address, cancel the last figure, divide by 2, add or subtract the key number below. The answer is the nearest numbered cross street, approximately. To find addresses on numbered cross streets, remember that numbers increase east or west from 5th Ave., which runs north–south.

Ave. A... *add 3*

Ave. B...*add 3*

Ave. C...*add 3*

Ave. D...*add 3*

1st Ave....*add 3*

2nd Ave....*add 3*

3rd Ave....*add 10*

4th Ave.... *add 8*

5th Ave.

Up to 200...*add 13*

Up to 400...*add 16*

Up to 600...*add 18*

Up to 775...*add 20*

From 775 to 1286... *cancel last figure and subt. 18*

Ave. of the Americas...*subt. 12*

7th Ave....*add 12*

Above 110th St... *add 20*

8th Ave....*add 9*

9th Ave....*add 13*

10th Ave....*add 14*

Amsterdam Ave. ...*add 59*

Audubon Ave. ...*add 165*

Broadway (23–192 Sts.)...*subt. 30*

Columbus Ave. ...*add 60*

Convent Ave....*add 127*

Central Park West... *divide house number by 10 and add 60*

Edgecombe Ave. ...*add 134*

Ft. Washington Ave. ...*add 158*

Lenox Ave......*add 110*

Lexington Ave....*add 22*

Madison Ave....*add 27*

Manhattan Ave. ...*add 100*

Park Ave....*add 34*

Park Ave. South ...*add 8*

Pleasant Ave....*add 101*

Riverside Drive... *divide house number by 10 and add 72 up to 165 Street*

St. Nicholas Ave. ...*add 110*

Wadsworth Ave. ...*add 173*

West End Ave. ...*add 59*

York Ave....*add 4*

Leroy, and the general confusion engendered by East Broadway, West Broadway, and just plain Broadway.

Logic won't help you below 14th Street; only a good street map and good directions will.

You may also be confused by the way New Yorkers use "uptown" and "downtown." These terms refer both to locations and to directions. Uptown means north of wherever you are at the moment; downtown means south. Yet uptown and downtown are also geographical areas of the city. Unfortunately, there is no consensus about where these areas are: "Downtown" may mean anyplace from the tip of Lower Manhattan through Chelsea; it depends on the orientation of the speaker.

A similar situation exists with "East Side" and "West Side." Someone may characterize a location as being "on the East Side," meaning somewhere east of Fifth Avenue. A hotel described as being "on the West Side" may be located on West 42nd Street. But when many New Yorkers speak of the East Side or the West Side, they have in mind the respective areas above 59th Street (the southern boundary of Central Park), on either side of the park. Admittedly, the usage is not precise; you should be prepared for misunderstandings.

Tour 1: Midtown: Rockefeller Center

Numbers in the margin correspond with points of interest on the Midtown Manhattan map.

❶ The heart of midtown Manhattan is **Rockefeller Center,** a complex of 19 buildings occupying nearly 22 acres of prime real estate between Fifth and Seventh avenues and 47th and 52nd streets. Built during the Great Depression of the 1930s by John D. Rockefeller, Jr., this city-within-a-city is the capital of the communications industry, with the headquarters for a TV network (NBC), major publishing companies (Time Inc., McGraw-Hill, Simon & Schuster, Warner Brothers), and the world's largest news-gathering organization, the Associated Press. It is an international center housing the consulates of many foreign nations, the U.S. passport office, and ticket offices for numerous airlines. Most human needs—restaurants, shoe repair, doctors, barbers, banks, post office, bookstores, clothing, variety stores—can be accommodated within the center, and all parts of the complex are linked by underground passageways.

Begin a tour at the ice rink on **Lower Plaza** along a little street called Rockefeller Plaza between 49th and 50th streets. Crowned by a gold-leaf statue of Prometheus stealing the sacred fire for mankind, this famous New York attraction is an ice rink from late September through April and an outdoor cafe the rest of the year. The site of a huge Christmas tree and caroling concerts during December, Lower Plaza is surrounded by the flags of all the members of the United Nations. Incidentally, those "Private Street, No Parking" signs along Rockefeller Plaza aren't jokes: This really is a private street that must be closed to both cars and pedestrians one day a year to maintain its private status.

Just east of Lower Plaza are the **Channel Gardens,** a promenade with six pools surrounded by flower beds filled with seasonal plantings, conceived by artists, floral designers, and sculptors

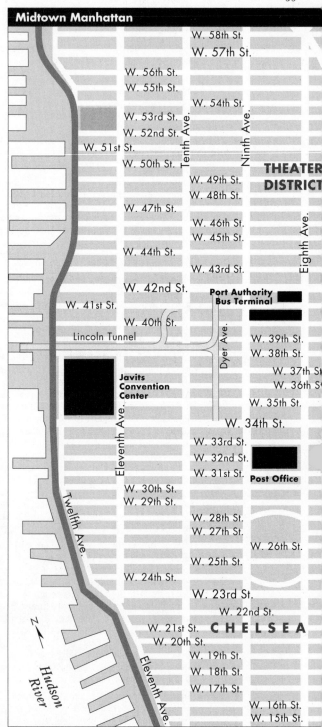

A & S Plaza, **21**
American Craft Museum, **3**
AT&T Bldg., **6**
Bryant Park Half-Price Tickets, **12**
Chrysler Building, **15**
Church of the Transfiguration, **24**
Daily News Building, **16**
Empire State Building, **22**
Ford Foundation Building, **17**
Gramercy Park, **27**
Grand Central Terminal, **14**
Macy's, **20**
Madison Square, **25**
Madison Square Garden, **19**
Marble Collegiate Church, **23**
Museum of Broadcasting, **5**
Museum of Modern Art, **4**
New York Public Library, **13**
Penn Station, **19**
Place des Antiquaires, **8**
Rockefeller Center, **1**
St. Patrick's Cathedral, **2**
Sutton Place, **9**
Theodore Roosevelt Birthplace, **26**
Times Square, **10**
TKTS Booth, **11**
Trump Tower, **7**
Union Square, **28**
United Nations Headquarters, **18**

E. 58th St.

E. 57th St.

Carnegie Hall

E. 56th St.

E. 55th St.

E. 54th St.

E. 53rd St.

E. 52nd St.

E. 51st St.

E. 50th St.

Radio City Music Hall

E. 49th St.

E. 48th St.

E. 47th St.

E. 46th St.

E. 45th St.

E. 44th St.

E. 43rd St.

Times Square

E. 42nd St.

E. 41st St.

Bryant Park

E. 40th St.

E. 39th St.

E. 38th St.

Broadway

E. 37th St.

E. 36th St.

MURRAY HILL

Queens Midtown Tunnel

E. 35th St.

Madison Ave.

Park Ave.

Third Ave.

Vanderbilt Ave.

Tudor City Pl.

East River

Sutton Pl.

Fifth Ave.

Seventh Ave.

E. 34th St.

E. 33rd St.

Herald Square

E. 32nd St.

E. 31st St.

E. 30th St.

E. 29th St.

Ave. of the Americas

E. 28th St.

E. 27th St.

E. 26th St.

E. 25th St.

E. 24th St.

Park Ave. S.

Lexington Ave.

Second Ave.

First Ave.

Madison Square

E. 23rd St.

E. 22nd St.

E. 21st St.

Gramercy Park

E. 20th St.

E. 19th St.

Irving Pl.

E. 18th St.

E. 17th St.

0 ___ 880 yards

0 ___ 800 yards

Union Square

E. 16th St.

E. 15th St.

Stuyvesant Square

—10 shows a season. They are called Channel Gardens because they separate the British building (to the north) and the French building (to the south). The French building contains the **Librairie de France,** which sells French-language books, periodicals, and records; its surprisingly large basement contains a Spanish bookstore and dictionary store.

A huge statue of Atlas supporting the world stands sentry before the **International Building** on Fifth Avenue between 50th and 51st streets. With a lobby inspired by ancient Greece and fitted with Grecian marble from the island of Tenos, the building houses foreign consulates, international airlines, and a passport office from which lines of applicants overflow into Fifth Avenue throughout the summer.

2 Across Fifth Avenue stands the Gothic-style **St. Patrick's,** the Roman Catholic cathedral of New York. Dedicated to the patron saint of the Irish—then and now one of New York's principal ethnic groups—the white marble and stone structure was begun in 1858, consecrated in 1879, and completed in 1906. Among the statues in the alcoves around the nave is a striking modern rendering of the American saint, Mother Seton.

One of Rockefeller Center's main attractions is the **RCA Building,** the 70-story tower that occupies the block bounded by Rockefeller Plaza, Avenue of the Americas (which New Yorkers call Sixth Avenue), and 49th and 50th streets. The building is headquarters for NBC. One way to see what goes on up there is to request free tickets to the NBC shows that are produced in New York—currently *Late Night with David Letterman, Saturday Night Live,* and *Donahue*—by writing NBC Tickets, 30 Rockefeller Plaza, New York, NY 10112. (Unfortunately, the first two shows are usually booked solid for more than a year in advance, *Donahue* for about six months.) Or you might take a tour of the NBC studios: One leaves every 15 minutes, 9:30–4, Monday through Saturday, and Sundays during the summer; Thursdays 9:30–8 (cost: $7). And you can buy a T-shirt, ashtray, frisbee, or other paraphernalia bearing logos from your favorite programs at a boutique in the magnificent black granite lobby. Look up at the ceiling mural above the Rockefeller Plaza entrance: The figure seems to be facing you no matter where you stand.

Those who are intent on seeing network TV should look around Rockefeller Center for pages distributing tickets to screenings of TV shows contemplated for broadcast by NBC (tel. 212/664–7174), CBS (tel. 212/975–2476), and ABC (212/887–3537). On some weekdays, pages stand on the sidewalks buttonholing passersby for screenings that normally begin within an hour or two.

Escalators in the RCA Building will take you to the marbled catacombs that connect the various components of Rockefeller Center. A lot goes on down under: There are restaurants in all price ranges, from the chic American Festival Café, alongside the skating rink, to McDonald's; the Rockefeller Center Museum; a post office and clean public washrooms (both scarce in Midtown); and just about every kind of store. To find your way around, consult the strategically placed directories or obtain the free "Shops and Services Guide" at the RCA Building reception desk. *Center,* a free quarterly magazine containing articles about Rockefeller Center, a calendar of events, and capsule descriptions of the restaurants, is available in the lobbies of most of the buildings.

Across 50th Street from the RCA Building is America's largest indoor theater, the 6,000-seat **Radio City Music Hall.** Home of the fabulous Rockettes chorus line (which actually started out in St. Louis in 1925), Radio City was built as a movie theater with live shows; today it produces concerts, Christmas and Easter extravaganzas, awards presentations, and other special events. When there's no show you can tour the premises for $6 (tel. 212/632–4041).

Components of the Rockefeller Center community along Sixth Avenue include the 51-story **McGraw-Hill Building** (Sixth Ave. between 48th and 49th Sts.). Its lower plaza contains a 50-foot steel sun triangle that points to the seasonal positions of the sun at noon, and a pool that demonstrates the relative size of the planets.

Time Out   For supercasual eating when the weather is good, the **Sixth Avenue food vendors** near Rockefeller Center offer the best selection in the city. Most à la "cart" diners eschew the hot dog as being too pedestrian when they can just as easily have tacos, falafel, souvlaki, tempura, Indian curry, Afghani kofta kebabs, or Caribbean beef jerky. Locations change periodically, so look around until you find what you like. Food carts are licensed and inspected by the Department of Health. And the price is right; no dish is more than $5, and most cost much less. For seating, perch on the benches and low walls in the plazas beside the massive Sixth Avenue office towers.

Heading east again, 53rd Street between Sixth and Fifth avenues is a mini Museum Row. The **American Craft Museum** spotlights the work of contemporary American and overseas craftspersons working in clay, glass, fiber, wood, metal, paper. *40 W. 53rd St., tel. 212/956–3535. Admission: $3.50 adults, $1.50 students and senior citizens. Open Tues. 10–8; Wed.– Sun. 10–5.*

The **Museum of Modern Art** (MOMA) is a bright and airy four-story structure built around a secluded sculpture garden. All the important movements of modern art are represented here. After only a quick look-see, you'll be able to drop terms like Cubism, Surrealism, Abstract Expressionism, Minimalism, and Postmodernism as though you've known them all your life. Some of the world's most famous paintings are hung on the second floor: Van Gogh's *Starry Night,* Picasso's *Les Demoiselles d'Avignon,* Matisse's *Dance.* The superstars of American art appear on the third floor: Andrew Wyeth, Andy Warhol, Jackson Pollock, Frank Stella, Mark Rothko—to name a few. Don't miss the classic office furniture and Paris subway bench in the fourth-floor Architecture and Design Collection. Afternoon and evening film showings, mostly foreign films and classics, are free with the price of admission; tickets are distributed in the lobby, and on some days they go fast. Programs change daily; call 212/708–9500 for a schedule. *11 W. 53rd St., tel. 212/708 –9500. Admission: $6 adults, $3.50 students, $3 senior citizens; children under 16 free. Pay what you wish Thurs. 5–9. Open daily 11–6; Thurs. 11–9; closed Wed.*

The **Museum of Broadcasting** presents special screenings, usually retrospectives of the work of a particular radio or TV star or of an era in broadcasting history. The museum also offers its stupendous collection of more than 25,000 TV shows, 10,000 commercials, and 15,000 radio programs for individual screening. *23 W. 53rd St., tel. 212/752–7684. Suggested contribution: $4 adults, $3 students, $2 senior citizens and children under 13. Open Tues. noon–8; Wed.–Sat. noon–5.*

Tour 2: Midtown: Fifth Avenue

The stretch of Fifth Avenue between Rockefeller Center and 57th Street glitters with world-famous shops. The list begins with **Saks Fifth Avenue** (Fifth Ave. and 50th St.), the flagship of the national chain. Another big-name store is **Gucci**— actually two Guccis, on adjacent corners of Fifth Avenue and 54th Street. **Bijan** (699 Fifth Ave.) sells wildly expensive men's Continental clothing—by appointment only. Health warnings and no-smoking ordinances notwithstanding, **Nat Sherman** (711 Fifth Ave.) continues to market his own brands of cigarettes, cigars, and smoking accessories from his clubby shop.

Steuben Glass occupies a ground-floor showroom of a green-glass tower at Fifth Avenue and 56th Street. Across the street, **Harry Winston** (718 Fifth Ave.) has fabulous jewelry but does not encourage browsers. **Tiffany & Co.** (727 Fifth Ave., at 57th St.) is less intimidating and perhaps somewhat less expensive than you may fear.

Take a serenity break in **St. Thomas's Church** (Fifth Ave. at 53rd St.), an Episcopal institution that has occupied the site since 1911. The impressive huge stone reredos behind the altar holds the statues of more than 50 apostles, saints, martyrs, missionaries, and church figures. Upon entering, look to the far right to see enameled discs representing the branches of the armed forces and carved busts of four U.S. military chiefs-of-staff.

A block east, on Madison Avenue and 55th Street, you can pop into the post-deregulation home of Ma Bell in the new **AT&T World Headquarters.** Unlike the sterile ice-cube-tray buildings of Sixth Avenue, AT&T's rose granite columns, its regilded statue of the winged *Golden Boy* in the lobby, and its peculiar Chippendale roof have earned it its sobriquet as the first postmodern skyscraper. An adjacent structure houses the **AT&T InfoQuest Center,** a postmodern museum of communications technology. Entrants receive an access card on which they encode their names and then use to operate displays on lightwave communication, microelectronics, and computer software. Displays are neither terribly technical nor (on behalf of AT&T) zealously self-serving. Some exhibits, such as those where you program your own music video and rearrange a scrambled picture of your face, are downright entertaining. *Madison Ave. and 56th St., tel. 212/605–5555. Admission free. Open Wed.–Sun. 10–6; Tues. 10–9.*

Cross 56th Street to the **IBM Building,** with its fragrant and inviting public atrium (*see* Off the Beaten Track, below). A passage connects it to its next-door neighbor, but you'll do better to walk around the corner and encounter **Trump Tower** through the grand Fifth Avenue entrance. Trump Tower is an exclusive 68-story, dark-glass apartment house. What's open to the public is a six-story shopping atrium paneled in pinkish-orange marble and trimmed with high-gloss brass. A fountain cascades against one wall, drowning out the clamor of the city. In further contrast to the real world, every inch of Trump Tower is kept gleamingly shined, and security is omnipresent but discreet. Shops are chic and tony, among them Cartier, Bucellati, and Abercrombie & Fitch, and the public restrooms in the basement are invitingly clean and spacious.

Time Out The intimate front bar at **Jean Lafitte** (68 W. 58th St., tel. 212/751–2323) is an unusually relaxed place for this busy area of New York. While waiting for a table at this pleasant French bistro, sip your drink and leisurely take in your surroundings.

Tour 3: Midtown: 57th Street

Don't consider hunting for bargains in the exclusive shops and galleries of 57th Street. A recent survey determined that merchants here paid the world's highest ground-floor retail rents: $425 per square foot, edging out Tokyo's Ginza ($400) and Fifth Avenue between 52nd and 58th streets ($375). In general, the high costs are passed along to the consumer.

Occupying the span of Fifth Avenue between 57th Street and the Plaza Hotel, **Bergdorf Goodman** contains designer boutiques and a surprisingly complete men's department. **Van Cleef & Arpels** jewelers is located within Bergdorf's 57th Street corner.

Buy the classic trenchcoat with the distinctive plaid lining straight from the source, at no savings whatsoever, at **Burberry's Ltd.** (9 E. 57th St.). **Hermès** (11 E. 57th St.) is a small, dignified, and intermittently chic Paris leather shop.

Louis Vuitton (51 E. 57th St.) stamps its familiar "LV" monogram on its luggage, which it produced first for the ocean-liner crowd and later for the jet set. Best known now for the catalog through which it distributes gizmos for people who can afford anything, **Hammacher Schlemmer** (147 E. 57th St.), founded in 1848, has stood at this spot since 1926.

In two sleekly Art Deco subterranean levels, the recently
(8) opened **Place des Antiquaires** (125 E. 57th St.) is an ultra-high-class shopping mall where several dozen of the city's top art and antiques dealers operate out of plate-glass stalls. Some shops have specialties: **Lune** sells almost nothing but antique fans. You may find the prices out of your league but, as anywhere, it costs nothing to look.

When you've had your fill of shopping, walk to 58th Street and
(9) head east across **Sutton Place** until you can go no farther. There you will find the romantic spot overlooking the East River and the Queensboro (or 59th Street) Bridge where Woody Allen and Diane Keaton talked the night away in *Manhattan*. Cinema trivia buffs please note that no bench presently occupies the precise spot where Woody and Diane sat; however, several benches in Sutton Place Park, a small terrace several steps below, afford a comparable view.

Tour 4: Midtown: 42nd Street

Crossroads of the World, Great White Way, the New Year's Eve
(10) Capital of America, **Times Square** remains one of New York's

principal energy centers. Like most New York City "squares," Times Square is a triangle, this one formed by Broadway, Seventh Avenue, and 42nd Street. The square itself is occupied by the former Times Tower, now simply **One Times Square Plaza.** On its roof, workmen still lower the 200-pound New Year's Eve ball down the flagpole by hand, just as they have since 1908.

11 At Duffy Square, on 47th Street between Broadway and Seventh Avenue, the **TKTS booth** of the Theater Development Fund sells half-price (plus $1.50 per ticket service charge) day-of-performance tickets to Broadway and Off-Broadway shows. Signboards on the front of the booth list the shows available that day, and the offerings fluctuate greatly. Some nights (or matinees) it seems that almost every show in town is up for grabs; at other times there may be nothing but a few long-running hits and some sleepers. The lines may look long, but they move surprisingly fast. TKTS accepts only cash or traveler's checks. *Tel. 212/354–5800. Open 10–2 for Wed. and Sat. matinees; 3–8 for evening performances; noon–8 for Sun. matinee and evening shows. TKTS booths are open earlier in the day at 2 World Trade Center and in front of Borough Hall in Brooklyn.*

Most Broadway theaters are located on the streets west of Broadway from 52nd Street to 44th Street. The offices of *The New York Times* (229 W. 43rd St.), the institution that gave the area its name, occupy much of the block between Seventh and Eighth avenues.

42nd Street is the title of a long-running musical (and an earlier movie) that evokes the glamour and excitement of the New York stage. Today a group of thriving Off-Broadway playhouses west of Ninth Avenue are the only live theater on 42nd Street; the block between Seventh and Eighth avenues that was once the heart of the theater district is now a disreputable strip of porno shops, movie houses, and loiterers, all marking time while the city assembles the pieces of a redevelopment project that will transform the area. The most prominent vestige of the now legendary 42nd Street is the **New Amsterdam** (214 W. 42nd St.), a designated landmark that opened in 1903. Today the New Amsterdam is "dark," but in its prime the opulent facility, with a second, rooftop theater, showcased the likes of Eddie Cantor, Will Rogers, Fanny Brice, and the Ziegfeld Girls.

Heading east on 42nd Street, you'll pass **Hotaling's News** (142 W. 42nd St., tel. 212/840–1868), where the front compartment of the bustling little shop carries more than 220 daily newspapers from throughout the USA, the publications generally only a day or two old. The rear section stocks current newspapers, magazines, and foreign language books from more than 40 countries.

Bryant Park and the New York Public Library occupy the entire block bounded by 42nd Street, Fifth Avenue, 40th Street, and Sixth Avenue. Named for the poet and editor William Cullen Bryant (1794–1878), Bryant Park was the site of America's first World's Fair, the Crystal Palace Exhibition of 1853–1854. In recent years, new landscaping and tightened security have reclaimed what had come to be a hangout for undesirables. The long-term future of the park is still in question.

12 Inside the park, along 42nd Street, **Bryant Park Half-Price Tickets** sells same-day tickets for music and dance performances throughout the city. Like theater TKTS, they go for half-price, plus $1.50 per ticket service charge, cash or traveler's checks only. *Open Tues., Thurs., Fri. noon–2 and 3–7; Wed. and Sat. 11–2 and 3–7; Sun. noon–6; tel. 212/382–2323 for daily listings.*

Time Out A cafeteria on the 18th floor of the **City University Graduate Center** provides a serene setting for a reasonably priced repast, from a snack or salad-bar salad to a full meal. *33 W. 42nd St., tel. 212/642–2013. Open weekdays 10–8.*

A ground-level passage through the building, connecting 42nd and 43rd streets, often contains art exhibits: Walk through it and behold the offices of *The New Yorker* magazine at 25 W. 43rd Street.

13 The central research building of the **New York Public Library** is one of the largest research libraries in the world. Ascend the sweeping staircase between the two crouching Tennessee marble lions—dubbed "Patience" and "Fortitude" by former Mayor Fiorello LaGuardia, who visited the facility to "read between the lions"—and you enter a distinguished achievement of Beaux Arts design (note the triple bronze front doors), an art gallery, and a museum. The research hub of the 85-branch New York Public Library system, the main building displays a Gilbert Stuart portrait of George Washington, Charles Dickens's desk, and Jefferson's own handwritten copy of the Declaration of Independence. Periodic exhibitions focus on literary matters. Free one-hour tours, each as different as the library volunteer who leads it, are given Monday through Saturday at 11 AM and 2 PM. *Tel. 212/930–0800. Open Mon.–Wed. 10–9, Thurs.–Sat. 10–6.*

14 Continue east on 42nd Street to **Grand Central Terminal** (never "station," since all runs begin or end here). Constructed between 1903 and 1913, this Manhattan landmark was originally designed by a Minnesota architectural firm and later gussied up with Beaux Arts ornamentation. Make sure you notice the three huge windows separated by columns, and the Beaux Arts clock and sculpture on the facade above 42nd Street. The 12-story ceiling of the cavernous Main Concourse displays the constellations of the Zodiac. *Tel. 212/935–3960. Free tours Wed. at 12:30 PM.*

Two facilities of note stand at adjacent corners of Park Avenue and 42nd Street, directly opposite Grand Central. On the southwest corner, the **Whitney Museum of American Art at Philip Morris** (120 Park Ave.) occupies the ground floor of the Philip Morris Building. Each year this free branch of the Whitney (*see* Tour 7: Upper East Side, above) presents five successive exhibitions of 20th-century painting and sculpture. An espresso bar and seating areas make it a much more agreeable place to rest and reconnoiter than anywhere in Grand Central.

The second floor of the building on the southeast corner of 42nd Street and Park Avenue houses ticket counters for most major U.S. airlines. Buses to three New York airports depart from just outside the Park Avenue entrance. Around the corner is the main office of the **Bowery Bank** (110 E. 42nd St.), whose massive arches and 70-foot-high marble columns give it the grand presence of a medieval castle.

Ask New Yorkers to name their favorite skyscraper, and the
response you'll hear most often will be the **Chrysler Building** at
42nd Street and Lexington Avenue. The Chrysler Corporation
itself is long gone, yet the graceful shaft that culminates in a
stainless steel point still captivates the eye and the imagination. The building has no observation deck, but you can exam-
ine the elegant dark lobby faced with African marble and
covered with a ceiling mural that honors transportation and human endeavor.

Time Out   The **Automat** at the southeast corner of Third Avenue and 42nd
Street is the last survivor of the world's first fast-food chain.
Patrons use coins or tokens to extract dishes—baked beans and
macaroni and cheese are perennial favorites—from glass-
fronted cubbyholes, and they crank their coffee out of fish-head
spouts. Authentic automat facilities are confined to one wall (a
cafeteria, sandwich bar, and bakery occupy most of the space),
but the sleek contours of Art Deco styling prevail throughout.

New York's biggest-selling newspaper is produced in the **Daily
News Building** (220 E. 42nd St.), an Art Deco tower designed
with brown-brick spandrels and windows to make it seem lofti-
er than its 37 stories. The lobby features a revolving illuminated globe, 12 feet in diameter. The floor is a gigantic compass
on which bronze lines indicate air mileage from principal world
cities to New York. A small gallery displays *News* photos.

The **Ford Foundation Building** (320 E. 43rd St.) encloses a 12-
story, one-third acre greenhouse. With a terraced garden, a
still pool, and a couple dozen full-grown trees as centerpieces,
the Ford garden is open to the public—for tranquillity, not for
picnics—weekdays from 9 to 5.

Climb the steps along 42nd Street between First and Second
avenues to enter **Tudor City,** a self-contained complex of a doz-
en buildings in the Tudor Gothic style, featuring half-
timbering and lots of stained glass. Constructed between 1925
and 1928, the apartments of this residential enclave originally
had no east-side windows, lest the tenants be forced to gaze at
the slaughterhouses, breweries, and glue factories then located along the East River.

Walk north across the overpass above 42nd Street and turn east
on 43rd Street until the street ends in a terrace overlooking the
United Nations Headquarters. The terrace stands at the head
of the Sharansky Steps (for Natan, formerly Anatoly, the Soviet dissident), which run along the Isaiah Wall (inscribed, "They
Shall Beat Their Swords Into Plowshares"), and overlooks
Ralph J. Bunche Park (for the black American former UN un-
dersecretary) and Raoul Wallenberg Walk (for the Swedish dip-
lomat and World War II hero).

The **United Nations Headquarters** complex occupies a lushly
landscaped riverside tract along First Avenue between 42nd
and 48th streets. A line of flagpoles with banners representing
the current roster of 159 member nations stands before the
striking 550-foot slab of the Secretariat Building. The interior
corridors overflow with imaginatively diverse artwork donated
by member nations. Free tickets to most sessions are available
on a first-come, first-served basis 15 minutes before sessions
begin; pick them up in the General Assembly lobby. Visitors
can take early luncheon in the Delegates Dining Room or eat

anytime in a public coffee shop. *Tel. 212/963–7539. One-hour tours leave the General Assembly lobby every 20 minutes, daily 9:15–4:45. Admission: $5.50 adults, $3.50 students, children under 5 not permitted.*

Tour 5: Midtown: South of 42nd Street

The gateway to the city for Amtrak passengers and commuters from New Jersey and Long Island, **Penn Station** is a convenient place to begin a tour of lower Midtown. However, it is not in itself a particularly felicitous spot. Unattractive, unsavory, and underground, it serves as an embarrassing reminder of the grand old Penn Station that fell to the wrecking ball in 1963. (If you arrive in New York at Penn Station, do not under any circumstances surrender your baggage to the characters hovering about its many exits: They are not porters; their business is extortion and theft.)

Madison Square Garden (tel. 212/563–8300), here in its fourth incarnation, is located directly above **Penn Station.** Home of the New York Knickerbockers (pro basketball) and the New York Rangers (pro hockey), the Garden lights up almost every night with dog and cat shows, college basketball, wrestling, rock concerts, circuses, and other events and expositions; boxing takes place in the smaller Felt Forum. One of the last remaining bowling alleys in Manhattan, the 48-lane Madison Square Garden Bowling Center, is located just above the ticket office.

Head north from Penn Station on Seventh Avenue, and you enter New York's tumultuous **Garment District:** Street signs declare the stretch of Seventh Avenue between 31st and 41st streets "Fashion Avenue." The Garment District teems with warehouses, workshops, and showrooms that manufacture and finish mostly women's and children's clothing. On weekdays the streets are crowded with trucks and the sidewalks swarm with daredevil deliverymen hauling garment racks between factories and subcontractors.

Perhaps to inspire the garment dealers, **Macy's,** the world's largest department store under one roof, occupies the entire block bounded by Broadway, Seventh Avenue, and 34th and 35th streets. Made world-famous by *Miracle on 34th Street* and as the destination of the Thanksgiving Day parade, Macy's is still good for a few surprises: At the gourmet food shop in The Cellar, someone is usually distributing free samples of something good to eat (lower level). Other popular spots are the New York, New York souvenir boutique (first floor); the Metropolitan Museum gift shop (mezzanine); and Center Stage Recording Studio, where you can record yourself singing over the instrumental tracks of your favorite hits (fourth floor).

With the demise of the New York Gimbels, one of the few other major retail enterprises on Herald Square is **Herald Center** (Sixth Ave. and 34th St.), a vertical shopping mall reputedly owned by the footloose Imelda Marcos. Each level of the streamlined center bears the name of a New York neighborhood (SoHo, Greenwich Village, etc.); most stores are high-toned branches of national chains (Ann Taylor, Ylang-Ylang, Caswell-Massey).

㉑ A block south of Macy's you'll find the nine-story **A&S Plaza** (33rd St. and Sixth Ave.) in the old Gimbel's location. The 120 shops and restaurants found here are anchored by the Abraham & Straus department store.

㉒ The **Empire State Building** may no longer be the world's tallest, but it is certainly the world's best-loved skyscraper. The Art Deco playground for King Kong opened in 1931 after only about a year of construction. More than 15,000 people work in the building, and more than 2.5 million people a year visit the 86th-floor and 102nd-floor observatories. At night the top 30 stories are illuminated with colors appropriate to the season (red and green around Christmas; orange and brown for Halloween). *Fifth Ave. and 34th St., tel. 212/736–3100. Admission: $3.50 adults, $1.75 children under 12. Open daily 9:30–midnight.*

㉓ Continue south on Fifth Avenue to 29th Street and the **Marble Collegiate Church** (1854), a marble-fronted structure built for the Reformed Protestant Dutch Congregation first organized in 1628 by Peter Minuit, the canny Dutchman who bought Manhattan from the Indians for $24. In modern times the church was the pulpit for Dr. Norman Vincent Peale (*The Power of Positive Thinking*), its pastor from 1932 to 1984.

㉔ Go east on 29th Street to the **Church of the Transfiguration** (1 E. 29th St.), which is much better known as the Little Church Around the Corner. Set back in a shrub-filled New York version of an old English churchyard, it won its memorable appellation in 1870 when other area churches refused to bury an actor and colleague of the well-known thespian Joseph Jefferson. Jefferson was directed to the "little church around the corner" that did that sort of thing, and the Episcopal institution has welcomed literary and show-biz types ever since.

㉕ Bordered by Fifth Avenue, Broadway, Madison Avenue, 23rd and 26th streets, **Madison Square** was the site (circa 1845) of New York's first baseball games. Though recently rehabilitated with modern sculpture, new benches, and a playground, the most interesting aspects of Madison Square are found along its perimeter.

The block at 26th Street and Madison Avenue, now occupied by the ornate **New York Life Insurance Building,** was the site of the second (1890–1925) Madison Square Garden. The old Garden was designed by the architect and playboy Stanford White, who was shot on the Garden roof by Harry K. Thaw, the jealous husband of the actress Evelyn Nesbit. This lurid episode was more or less accurately depicted in the movie *Ragtime*, scenes of which were filmed on the then-cobblestoned street in front of the **Appellate Division of the State Supreme Court** (Madison Ave. and 25th St.). The roof balustrade of this imposing, white-marble Corinthian structure depicts great lawmakers of the past: Moses, Justinian, Confucius, and others. **The Metropolitan Life Insurance Tower** (Madison Ave. between 23rd and 24th Sts.) re-creates the campanile of St. Mark's in Venice.

The Renaissance-style **Flatiron Building** occupies the triangular lot formed by Broadway, Fifth Avenue, and 23rd Street. Soon after the three-sided 20-story skyscraper was built in 1902, it became a symbol of New York on the rise. Now it lends its name to the Flatiron District that lies to the south, an area of photographers' studios, residential lofts, and advertising agencies.

Continue down Broadway and turn east on 20th Street to the **26** **Theodore Roosevelt Birthplace,** a reconstructed Victorian brownstone where Teddy lived until he was 15 years old. Before becoming President, Roosevelt was New York City police commissioner and the governor of New York State. The house contains Victorian period rooms and Roosevelt memorabilia; a selection of videos about the namesake of the teddy bear are shown on request. *28 E. 20th St., tel. 212/260–1616. Admission: $1. Open Wed.–Sun. 9–5.*

Next door to Roosevelt's home is an interesting shop called **Darts Unlimited, Limited** (30 E. 20th St.), which sells nothing but professional English darts, dartboards, patches, and other dart accessories.

Time Out **Miss Kim's** typifies a kind of dining establishment unique to Manhattan. At this combination grocery store, salad bar, and cafeteria, you obtain your food from a huge 50-item salad table, sandwich bar, steam table with hot foods, pastry counter, or directly from the shelves. Countermen serve hot drinks (including espresso); you take cold drinks (including beer) straight from the cooler. After you weigh and pay, you can either take your meal out or climb to seats on a mezzanine. Similar places exist all over town. *270 Park Ave. S. Open 24 hrs.*

Just east of Park Avenue South, between 20th and 21st streets, **27** lies **Gramercy Park,** a picture-perfect city park complete with flower beds, bird feeders, sundials, cozy benches, and a statue of the actor Edwin Booth portraying Hamlet. It stays nice because it's surrounded by a locked cast-iron fence and only residents of the property around the park possess keys. Laid out in 1831 according to a design inspired by London's residential squares, Gramercy Park is surrounded by interesting structures.

Begin at the northeast corner and head clockwise. The white terra-cotta apartment building at 36 Gramercy Park East is guarded by concrete knights in tarnished armor. The turreted redbrick building at 34 Gramercy Park East was one of the city's first apartment houses. The austere gray Friends Meeting House at 28 Gramercy Park South has lately become The Brotherhood Synagogue.

Mrs. Stuyvesant Fish, a society doyenne remembered as the fearless iconoclast who reduced the time of formal dinner parties from several hours to 50 minutes, resided at No. 19. Edwin Booth lived at No. 16, now an affiliation of show-biz people called The Players Club. The site of the **National Arts Club** (15 Gramercy Park South) was the home of Samuel Tilden, a governor of New York and the Democratic presidential candidate who in 1876 received more votes than Rutherford B. Hayes, who won the presidency.

28 Return to Park Avenue South and continue south to **Union Square,** the area between Park and Broadway, 14th and 17th streets. During the early part of the century, Union Square was a popular patch of green and the site of political demonstrations. Over the years it deteriorated into a habitat of drug dealers and kindred undesirables; until a massive renewal program in the 1980s transformed it into one of the city's most attractive miniparks.

If possible, visit Union Square on greenmarket days (Wednesday, Friday, Saturday), when farmers from all over the Northeast bring their goods to the big town. Farmers, including some Pennsylvania Dutch and latter-day hippies, sell their own produce, homemade baked goods, cheeses, cider, New York State wines, even fish and meat. If the prices aren't much lower than those in stores, the quality and freshness are much greater. When the weather allows, the benches of Union Square make a great site for a city-style picnic.

Tour 6: Upper West Side

Numbers in the margin correspond with points of interest on the Upper West Side map.

Diversity may be the quality that best characterizes the Upper West Side. A once-fashionable district that had become a multiethnic neighborhood of families and intellectuals, the Upper West Side now attracts young professionals who can afford to live anywhere. Lincoln Center is the cultural anchor, Columbus Avenue the newly fashionable boutique and restaurant strip. Many of the old residents decry the changes that have befallen the neighborhood, but then contentiousness is another characteristic of the Upper West Side.

1 The West Side story begins at **Columbus Circle,** where a statue of Christopher himself crowns a stately pillar at the intersection of Broadway, Eighth Avenue, Central Park West, and Central Park South. Columbus Circle is a good place to begin any tour of New York, for it is the location of the **New York Convention and Visitors Bureau.** Count on the bureau for brochures; bus and subway maps; hotel, restaurant, and shopping guides; a seasonal calendar of events; free TV-show tickets and discounts for Broadway shows; and sound advice. The New York City Department of Cultural Affairs operates an art gallery on the second floor. *2 Columbus Circle, tel. 212/397–8222. Open weekdays 9–6.*

Central Park West Walk north from Columbus Circle along Central Park West and you quickly reach the haunted apartment house of the film *Ghostbusters* (55 Central Park West at 66th St.). Just inside the park, at 67th Street, is **Tavern on the Green,** a landmark spot for romantic indoor and outdoor dining. The stretch of Central Park roadway between the restaurant and the verdant Sheep Meadow is the finish line for the New York Marathon (the first Sunday in November). It's also the start and finish of a five-mile "fun run" that begins on the stroke of the New Year.

2 The stately **Dakota** presides at the corner of Central Park West and 72nd Street. One of the first fashionable West Side apartment buildings, this powerful, relatively squat structure is now better known as the place where *Rosemary's Baby* was filmed and John Lennon was shot. Directly across Central Park West, a hilly stretch of parkland has been designated **Strawberry Fields** in Lennon's memory. A black-and-white-tile mosaic containing the word "Imagine," another Lennon song title, is embedded in one of the paths.

3 The city's oldest museum, the **New-York Historical Society,** preserves what was unique about the city's past, including the

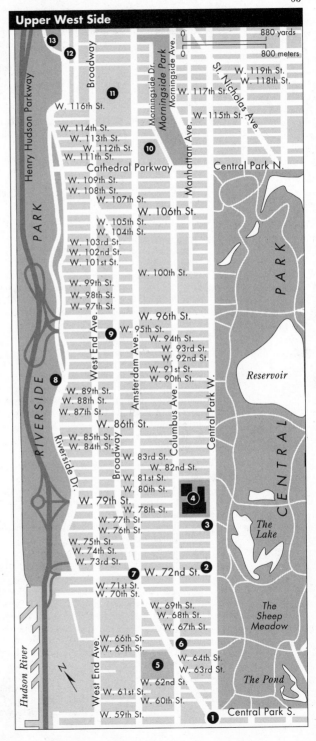

Upper West Side

American Museum of Natural History, **4**

Cathedral of St. John the Divine, **10**

Columbia University, **11**

Columbus Circle, **1**

The Dakota, **2**

Grant's Tomb, **13**

Hayden Planetarium, **4**

Lincoln Center, **5**

Museum of American Folk Art, **6**

New York Historical Society, **3**

Riverside Church, **12**

Soldiers and Sailors Monument, **8**

Symphony Space, **9**

Verdi Square, **7**

0   880 yards

0   800 meters

Broadway

Henry Hudson Parkway

PARK

W. 119th St.

W. 118th St.

W. 117th St.

W. 116th St.

W. 115th St.

W. 114th St.

W. 113th St.

W. 112th St.

W. 111th St.

Cathedral Parkway

W. 109th St.

W. 108th St.

W. 107th St.

W. 106th St.

W. 105th St.

W. 104th St.

W. 103rd St.

W. 102nd St.

W. 101st St.

W. 100th St.

W. 99th St.

W. 98th St.

W. 97th St.

W. 96th St.

W. 95th St.

W. 94th St.

W. 93rd St.

W. 92nd St.

W. 91st St.

W. 90th St.

W. 89th St.

W. 88th St.

W. 87th St.

W. 86th St.

W. 85th St.

W. 84th St.

W. 83rd St.

W. 82nd St.

W. 81st St.

W. 80th St.

W. 79th St.

W. 78th St.

W. 77th St.

W. 76th St.

W. 75th St.

W. 74th St.

W. 73rd St.

W. 72nd St.

W. 71st St.

W. 70th St.

W. 69th St.

W. 68th St.

W. 67th St.

W. 66th St.

W. 65th St.

W. 64th St.

W. 63rd St.

W. 62nd St.

W. 61st St.

W. 60th St.

W. 59th St.

Central Park N.

Morningside Dr.

Morningside Park

Morningside Ave.

St. Nicholas Ave.

Manhattan Ave.

West End Ave.

Amsterdam Ave.

Columbus Ave.

Central Park W.

Broadway

Riverside Dr.

RIVERSIDE PARK

Hudson River

West End Ave.

Reservoir

CENTRAL PARK

The Lake

The Sheep Meadow

The Pond

Central Park S.

quaint hyphen in New-York. Along with changing exhibits of American history and art, the museum displays original Audubon watercolors, Early American toys, Tiffany lamps, antique vehicles, and Hudson River School landscapes. There is an important research library on the second floor. *170 Central Park West at 77th St., tel. 212/873–3400. Admission: $3 adults, $2 senior citizens, $1 children under 12; pay what you wish Tues. Open Tues.–Sun. 10–5.*

4 The **American Museum of Natural History,** the adjacent **Hayden Planetarium,** and the surrounding grounds take up a four-block tract bounded by Central Park West, Columbus Avenue, and 77th and 81st streets. With a collection of more than 36 million items, the museum certainly has something for every taste, from a 94-foot blue whale to the 563-carat Star of India sapphire. The Naturemax Theater projects films on a giant screen. The Hayden Planetarium (on 81st Street) has two stories of exhibits, and the Sky Shows are projected on 22 wraparound screens. The rock Laser Shows draw crowds of teenagers on Friday and Saturday nights. *Museum: tel. 212/ 769–5100. Suggested contribution: $4 adults, $2 children. Open daily 10–5:45, Wed., Fri., Sat. 10–9. Planetarium: tel. 212/769–5920. Admission: $4 adults; $3 senior citizens, members, and students; $2 children; $6 for laser show. Open weekdays 12:30–4:45, Sat. 10–6, Sun. noon–6. Naturemax Theater admission: $4–$6 adults, $2–$3 children.*

Upper Broadway Another Upper West Side trail angles diagonally from Columbus Circle up Broadway. At the world headquarters of the **American Bible Society** (1865 Broadway at 61st St.), you ascend a ruby-red carpet to a little-known second-floor museum that has temporary exhibits of the society's worldwide Bible-distributing activities and permanent displays of Helen Keller's 10-volume Braille Bible, a replica of the original Gutenberg press, and a Torah (Jewish scriptures) from China. An adjunct to Lincoln Center, **The Ballet Shop** (1887 Broadway at 62nd St.) sells books and records, photos, paraphernalia, and mementos.

5 Covering an eight-block area west of Broadway between 62nd and 66th streets, **Lincoln Center** is an architecturally unified development that encompasses New York's major-league performing arts institutions. Built during the 1960s to supplant a rundown urban ghetto, the complex can at one time seat nearly 15,000 spectators for performances of classical music, opera, ballet, drama, and film.

Lincoln Center consists of eight distinct units. **Avery Fisher Hall,** named after the founder of Fisher Radio, hosts the New York Philharmonic Orchestra. The Metropolitan Opera and American Ballet Theatre perform at the **Metropolitan Opera House.** The **New York State Theater** is home to the New York City Ballet and the New York City Opera. The **Guggenheim Bandshell,** south of the Met, has free open-air concerts in summer. A single structure devoted to drama includes the **Vivian Beaumont** and **Mitzi E. Newhouse** theaters. The **Library and Museum of the Performing Arts** maintains an extensive collection of records, scores, and books on music, theater, and dance. Across 65th Street lies the world-renowned **Juilliard School,** which houses **Alice Tully Hall,** home of the Chamber Music Society of Lincoln Center, the Film Society of Lincoln Center, and the New York Film Center.

Visitors can wander freely through the lobbies of all buildings and relax in Damrosch Park or beside Lincoln Center's fountains; an outdoor cafe operates throughout the summer. The best free indoor attractions are found in the Performing Arts Library, where visitors can listen to a collection of 42,000 records and tapes or check out any of four galleries. A one-hour guided "Take-the-Tour" covers all the grand theaters. *Tel. 212/877–1800, ext. 512, for schedule. Admission: $6.25 adults, $5.25 students and senior citizens, $3.50 children.*

Tickets for Lincoln Center events are costly and, because many performances sell out to season subscribers, sometimes impossible to obtain at box offices or through ticket services. Some tickets are usually available just outside the theater during the half-hour before the performance, someone's companion(s) having been unable to make it. Occasionally there are scalpers, and although it's illegal in New York to sell tickets for more than a specified amount above the printed price, such commerce transpires more or less openly before every performance.

Across the busy intersection from Lincoln Center, the long-orphaned **Museum of American Folk Art** has found a new home at Columbus Avenue and 66th Street. Its collection includes primitive paintings, quilts, carvings, dolls, trade signs, painted wooden carousel horses, and a giant Indian-chief copper weathervane. *2 Lincoln Sq., tel. 212/977–7298. Admission free. Open daily 9–9.*

One of the busiest spots on the Upper West Side is the intersection of Broadway, Amsterdam Avenue, and 72nd Street. Officially, the area south of 72nd Street is Sherman Square (for the Union Civil War general, William Tecumseh) and the area north of 72nd Street is **Verdi Square** (for the Italian composer, Giuseppe). Until about a decade ago, Verdi Square was an addicts' hangout known informally as Needle Park. The Upper West Side in general and this intersection in particular have improved considerably in recent years, and real estate values have had a dramatic upsurge.

The subway kiosk on the island south of 72nd Street is an official city landmark, a structure with rounded neo-Dutch moldings that was the first express station north of 42nd Street. Occupying the southeast corner of Amsterdam Avenue and 72nd Street is **Gray's Papaya**, a New York quasi-institution that pairs the sacred (health-enriching papaya and other natural juices) with the profane (hot dogs, smothered in sauerkraut and onions if desired).

Farther up Broadway are two of New York's great food shrines. The fresh produce in the bountiful but unpretentious **Fairway Market** (2127 Broadway at 74th St.) literally bursts onto the street. Have a look at the handmade signs describing the produce and cheese; they can be as fresh as the merchandise itself. At Broadway and 80th Street, **Zabar's** sells exquisite delicatessen items, prepared foods, gourmet groceries, coffees, and cheeses. A mezzanine level has cookware, dishes, and small appliances. The prices are competitive.

When the **Ansonia Hotel** opened at Broadway and 73rd Street in 1904, its white facade, fairy-castle turrets, and new soundproof partitions attracted show people and writers to a hitherto unfashionable area. Now an apartment building, the

Ansonia has provided temporary homes for Florenz Ziegfeld, Mischa Elman, Theodore Dreiser, and the great Babe Ruth.

For a quick off-Broadway experience, walk two blocks west to **(8)** the **Soldiers and Sailors Monument** at Riverside Drive and 89th Street. The monument commemorates Civil War casualties; the environs afford a refreshing view of Riverside Park, the lazy Hudson River, and the New Jersey shore.

Pomander Walk is an attractive slice of Old England wedged between 94th and 95th streets, between Broadway and West End Avenue. The charming enclave was inspired by the stage sets of an American version of a British play of 1911, *Pomander Walk*. Walk in—or peep through the gate if it's locked—and see Tudor houses, window boxes, and neatly trimmed hedges. **(9)** Around the corner, **Symphony Space**, a not-for-profit, community-sponsored center for the performing arts, presents a regular schedule of low-priced (free–$20) classical, international, and contemporary concerts, readings, and assorted marathons (Mozart, James Joyce, Cole Porter). *2537 Broadway at 95th St., tel. 212/864–5400.*

(10) The **Cathedral of St. John the Divine,** one block east of Broadway, is New York's major Episcopal church and the largest Gothic cathedral in the world (St. Peter's Basilica in Rome is the only larger church of any kind). The vast 600-foot nave can seat 5,000 worshipers. Small, uniquely outfitted chapels border the nave, and a "Biblical Garden" contains herbs and flowers mentioned in the Bible. It's still perhaps 100 years from completion, and master craftsmen are instructing neighborhood youth in the traditional methods of stonecutting and carving. Along with Sunday services (8, 9, and 11 AM, and 7 PM), the cathedral operates community outreach programs and presents nonreligious (classical, folk, winter solstice) concerts. *Amsterdam Ave. and 112th St., tel. 212/316–7400. Tours Mon.–Sat. 11, Sun. 12:45.*

(11) The main campus of **Columbia University** (founded 1754), a large and wealthy private institution, occupies an area bounded by 114th and 121st streets, Broadway, and Amsterdam Avenue. Enter from either direction on 116th Street: The buildings so effectively wall off the city that it's easy to believe you've been transported to a more rustic Ivy League campus. The central campus has the rotunda-topped Low Memorial Library to the north and the massive Butler Library to the south. A cafe on the southwest corner of the quad has indoor and outdoor tables perfectly situated for student-watching.

East of the Columbia campus and a short block farther east of Amsterdam Avenue, Morningside Drive runs along a ridge that lies above the incline of Morningside Park and affords an impressive view of the low-rise buildings of Harlem that stretch across the city.

(12) **Riverside Church** (Riverside Dr. and 122nd St., tel. 212/222–5900) is nondenominational, interracial, international, extremely political, and socially conscious. It is a massive structure with a 356-foot observation tower (admission: $1) and a 74-bell carillon, the largest in the world, whose bells range in weight from 10 pounds to 20 tons. Along with regular Sunday services (10:45 AM), community events, concerts, and dance and theater programs abound. A reasonably priced, reasonably good cafeteria operates on weekdays and Sundays.

Across Riverside Drive, in Riverside Park, stands the General Grant National Memorial Monument, commonly known as **⑬** **Grant's Tomb,** where the Civil War general and two-term president and his wife rest. In addition to the sarcophagi, the white granite mausoleum contains photographs and Grant memorabilia. *Riverside Dr. and 122nd St., tel. 212/666–1640. Admission free. Open Wed.–Sun. 9–4:30.*

Tour 7: Upper East Side

Numbers in the margin correspond with points of interest on the Upper East Side map.

The Upper East Side is the area east of Central Park between 60th and 96th streets. Long the city's most expensive and desirable residential area, the Upper East Side is the home of old money, new money, foreign money—any kind of money will do. From Fifth Avenue mansions and the smart town houses of the East 60s and 70s to the high-rise corridors of First and Second avenues, this area, more than any other, epitomizes what many people think of as the Manhattan style.

Begin a tour of the Upper East Side at the Plaza. That can mean **❶** either **Grand Army Plaza,** an open space along Fifth Avenue between 58th and 60th streets, or the world-famous hotel at the western border of that space. Shaped like the token for a hotel in Monopoly, the **Plaza Hotel** is a registered historical landmark that has been in fashion for upper-crust transients, charity balls, coming-out parties, and romantic rendezvous since 1907.

Grand Army Plaza is flanked by an equestrian statue of William Tecumseh Sherman on the north and the Pulitzer (of Pulitzer Prize fame) Fountain to the south. Appropriately enough for this ritzy area, the fountain is crowned by a female figure representing Abundance. When the fountain is dry (as it is much of the time), its rims become perches for sunbathers and the clients of food vendors who station themselves along the perimeter of the plaza.

Grand Army Plaza, or any intersection along Central Park South, is the place to look for horse-drawn carriage rides through the park. Like motorized taxi drivers, hansom drivers are independent operators, and the quality of your ride will depend much on their disposition. Carriages operate all year, except in extremely hot or cold weather, and blankets are provided when it's cool. The city sets the official rates ($34 for the first half hour, $10 for each additional 15 minutes), but drivers will often try to get more. Be sure to agree on a price in advance.

Adjacent to Grand Army Plaza stands the **General Motors Building,** an imposing 50-story Georgia marble tower. One section of the main floor lobby displays a dozen or so shining new GM vehicles. The other part of the lobby has recently become the flagship of the legendary **F.A.O. Schwarz** toy store. Bigger than it looks from outside, the toy-o-rama extends up and around the south side of the GM building, all the way over to the Madison Avenue side. A vast selection, good lighting, and gorgeous displays make this a pleasant place to shop—and somewhat compensate for the lofty price tags. The store contains a Hair Parlour for teenage cuts and a Two-Minute Shop where

Central Park Zoo, **5**
Frick Collection, **7**
Grand Army Plaza, **1**
Great Lawn, **4**
Guggenheim
Museum, **11**
International Center
of Photography, **14**
Jewish Museum, **13**
Loeb Boathouse, **3**
Metropolitan Museum
of Art, **10**
El Museo del
Barrio, **16**
Museum of the City of
New York, **15**
National Academy of
Design, **12**
Ralph Lauren, **8**
Temple Emanu-El, **6**
Whitney Museum, **9**
Wollman Rink, **2**

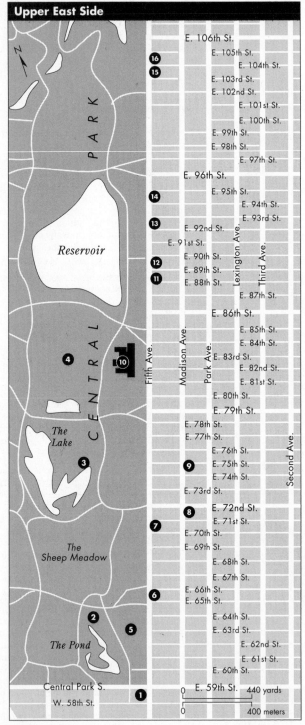

Upper East Side

E. 106th St.
E. 105th St.
E. 104th St.
E. 103rd St.
E. 102nd St.
E. 101st St.
E. 100th St.
E. 99th St.
E. 98th St.
E. 97th St.
E. 96th St.
E. 95th St.
E. 94th St.
E. 93rd St.
E. 92nd St.
E. 91st St.
E. 90th St.
E. 89th St.
E. 88th St.
E. 87th St.
E. 86th St.
E. 85th St.
E. 84th St.
E. 83rd St.
E. 82nd St.
E. 81st St.
E. 80th St.
E. 79th St.
E. 78th St.
E. 77th St.
E. 76th St.
E. 75th St.
E. 74th St.
E. 73rd St.
E. 72nd St.
E. 71st St.
E. 70th St.
E. 69th St.
E. 68th St.
E. 67th St.
E. 66th St.
E. 65th St.
E. 64th St.
E. 63rd St.
E. 62nd St.
E. 61st St.
E. 60th St.
E. 59th St.

Central Park S.
W. 58th St.

Reservoir

*The
Lake*

*The
Sheep Meadow*

The Pond

CENTRAL   PARK

Fifth Ave.
Madison Ave.
Park Ave.
Lexington Ave.
Third Ave.
Second Ave.

0   440 yards
0   400 meters

people pressed for time can choose from a selection of wrapped and ready toys.

Central Park Central Park is the 843-acre space bounded by 59th Street and 110th Street, Fifth Avenue and Central Park West (Eighth Avenue). Spared from the schemes of real estate developers by a *New York Evening Post* campaign that began in 1850, Central Park was designed by Frederick Law Olmsted and Calvert Vaux and constructed by a crew of 3,000 mainly Irish workmen and 400 horses.

Today Central Park hosts just about any activity a city dweller might engage in out of doors: jogging, cycling, horseback riding, softball, ice skating, croquet, tennis, bird-watching, boating, chess, checkers, theater, concerts, skateboarding, and break dancing. Central Park is reasonably safe during the day and—in populous areas—at night. *Tel. 212/397–3156 for general information, 212/360–1333 for a recorded message on city park events, 212/397–3080 for information on weekend walks and talks led by Urban Park Rangers. Bus tours are offered on Tues. and Thurs.*

East Drive is the road that runs north through Central Park from Grand Army Plaza; like West Drive, the southbound artery in the western precincts of the park, it is closed to automobiles on weekends and during some hours on weekdays. Strolling north along East Drive, you soon pass the buildings of the newly renovated Central Park Zoo, which must be entered from the Fifth Avenue side, at 64th Street.

❷ Beyond the zoo, East Drive takes you past the **Wollman Rink** (tel. 212/517–4800), an ice-skating rink that has become a symbol of contemporary urban life. Fruitless and costly attempts by the city to repair the deteriorated facility had kept the rink closed for years, until the builder Donald Trump adopted the project and quickly completed it. In the minds of New Yorkers, the Wollman Rink represents municipal incompetence conquered by the efficiency of private enterprise.

East Drive loops around to **The Mall,** a broad walkway lined with stately elms and busts of famous men. Here one is likely to witness whatever new craze has come along, from the latest dance to some trendy Oriental athletic discipline. The Mall leads to the **Bandshell,** site of summer concerts, speeches, and performance art. A bit farther north, the handsome, newly renovated **Bethesda Fountain** and the graceful iron bridge often model for "Sunday in New York" postcard pictures.

❸ At the **Loeb Boathouse** you can rent a rowboat to cruise the lake or a bike for a spin around the park. You can also buy a fast-food snack or a sit-down lunch. North of the lake is the Ramble, a wooded, hilly area scored by twisting paths, where bird-watchers gather early in the morning, especially during the migratory seasons.

As East Drive moves into the 80s, it passes between the sprawling Metropolitan Museum of Art (on the right) and the eastern
❹ edge of the **Great Lawn** (about 50 yards to the left). The athletic fields of the Great Lawn are busy most summer evenings and on weekends, and its wide expanse has accommodated tens of thousands of people for megaconcerts by Luciano Pavarotti, Diana Ross, Simon and Garfunkel, and others. Should you see a few hundred people picnicking on the ground in an orderly for-

mation that extends around the oval edge of the lawn, you'll know it's summer and there's a performance that night at the nearby **Delacorte Theater** of the New York Shakespeare Festival. *Tel. 212/598–7100. Admission free. Tickets distributed at 6:15 PM for the performance at 8 PM.*

Fifth Avenue Upper Fifth Avenue was settled during the last decade of the 19th century by millionaire migrants from the 34th Street area, the Astors, the Carnegies, the Vanderbilts, and the Whitneys, who moved into palatial stone mansions overlooking newly fashionable Central Park. Few of the residential mansions remain. Some were supplanted by high-rise apartments, others were transformed into museums or foundation headquarters. The west side of Fifth Avenue is one of the few city walks where intersections will not constantly interrupt your stroll.

Fifth Avenue above Grand Army Plaza begins on a literary note, with **open-air bookstalls** operated (when the weather is reasonably clement) by the Strand and Rogers & Cogswell bookstores. The stalls sell new and used books, New York maps and reference material, cassette tapes, and postcards. The best buys are the half-price "reviewers copies" of lightly used recent hardcover books and brand new trade paperbacks.

A few blocks north, at 64th Street, the **Arsenal Building** stands before the entrance to New York City's newest attraction, the **❺** 5.5-acre **Central Park Zoo.** Reopened in August 1988 following a five-year, $35 million renovation, the wildlife showcase recreates a series of habitats that include polar, temperate, and tropical climate zones in which animals roam at will. Visitors look on from various vantage points in each habitat and can even watch the animals' underwater activities. Polar bears and penguins are among the attractions; there are no elephants here. Admission to the adjacent children's zoo is granted to adults only when accompanied by a child. *Central Park at E. 64th St., tel. 212/439–6500. Admission: $1 adults, 25¢ children 3–12, 50¢ senior citizens. Open Apr.–Oct., weekdays 10–5 (May–Sept., Tues. 10–8) weekends and holidays 10–5:30; Nov.–Mar., daily 10–5.*

❻ With seats for 2,500 worshippers, **Temple Emanu-El** (1929) is the world's largest Reform Jewish synagogue. Built in 1929 of limestone, it is covered with mosaics and designed in the Romanesque style with Byzantine influences; the building features Moorish and art-deco ornamentation. *Fifth Ave. and 65th St., tel. 212/744–1400. Services Mon.–Thurs. 5:30 PM; Fri. 5:15 PM; Sat. 10:30 AM. Guided group tours by appointment only.*

❼ The **Frick Collection** is housed in the mansion built by the Pittsburgh coke and steel baron Henry Clay Frick. It was designed to display his private collection of art, and a bona fide masterpiece graces almost every room: Renoir's *Mother and Children*, Rembrandt's *Self-Portrait*, Fragonard's *The Progress of Love*, and distinguished works by Bellini, Vermeer, Titian, El Greco, Turner, Whistler, and Gainsborough. Even the rest area is a masterpiece: a tranquil indoor court with a fountain and glass ceiling. *1 E. 70th St., tel. 212/288–0700. Admission: $3 adults, $1.50 students and senior citizens. Open Tues.–Sat. 10–6, Sun. 1–6.*

The Madison Mile Just before World War I, the railroad tracks down the center of Park Avenue were covered with a roadway, and Park Avenue, like Fifth Avenue, became a distinguished residential thoroughfare. Between the two avenues, the low-rise brownstones of Madison Avenue, which had started out as a commercial universe serving the grand mansions of Fifth Avenue, remain unchanged.

The connotation of "Madison Avenue" has undergone a major change in recent years. New Yorkers no longer readily associate the words (or the place) with the advertising business, much of which has fled Madison Avenue in the East 40s and 50s for less costly downtown real estate. Madison Avenue, in particular the Madison Mile between 59th and 79th streets, is now the home of high chic: The lower stories of Madison Avenue's brownstones house many of the world's major fashion designers, patrician art galleries, and unique specialty stores. For the most part, these shops are small, intimate, expensive, and almost invariably closed on Sunday.

Heading uptown and working both sides of the street, you come to **The Gazebo** (660 Madison Ave.) with country-style home furnishings such as quilts, pottery, wicker work, and rag rugs. **The Coach Store** (710 Madison Ave.) devotes two floors to fine leather. **M. J. Knoud** (716 Madison Ave.) purveys hunting and polo saddles and accessories, jockey silks, and other equine-themed clothing and gear.

As opulent as the boudoirs for which its wares are destined, **La Lingerie** (792 Madison Ave.) features high-priced nightgowns, dressing gowns, embroidered shawls, and other intimate apparel. At the same address, **Sonia Rykiel** sells expensive high-fashion garments in styles that won't go out of style next month.

Once owned by the former New York Yankees manager, **Billy Martin's Western Wear** (812 Madison Ave.) features urbane renderings of city-slicker saddlebags, cowboy shirts, suede jackets, Indian-style silver, beaded jewelry, and snakeskin-brimmed baseball caps for all the major league teams. A familiar name in European high fashion, **Giorgio Armani** (815 Madison Ave.) is a "soft-tech" setting for men's and women's clothing in Armani-made and licensed lines. One of the first Madison Mile designer boutiques, **St. Laurent Rive-Gauche** (855 Madison Ave.) is a somewhat haughty place to shop for women's fashions, accessories, and cosmetics.

❽ By far the most spectacular store on Madison Mile, **Ralph Lauren** (867 Madison Ave.) hardly seems like a store at all. In fact, it's the landmark Rhinelander Mansion replete with walnut fittings, Oriental carpets, family portraits, and all that high-style preppie clothing that seems to be lying around waiting to be put away. The atmosphere surpasses unintimidating; it's actually inviting. Be sure to visit the fourth-floor home furnishings section, where merchandise is arrayed in to-the-manor-born dream suites.

One Night Stand (905 Madison Ave., tel. 212/772–7720) *rents* designer ball gowns and cocktail dresses; call for an appointment. **Antiquarian** (948 Madison Ave.) is a small gallery that specializes in fine ancient art.

Time Out   In a neighborhood where reasonably priced eating spots are scarce, **Soup Burg** (922 Madison Ave.) is a clean, well-lighted coffee shop that dishes up burgers and soup, salads, all sorts of sandwiches, and breakfast (featuring homemade oatmeal) any time of day.

---

9 The **Whitney Museum of American Art** is a gray granite vault separated from Madison Avenue materialism by a dry moat. An outgrowth of a gallery that began in the studio of the sculptor and collector Gertrude Vanderbilt Whitney, the museum is devoted exclusively to 20th-century American work, from naturalism and impressionism to pop art, abstractionism, and whatever comes next. *945 Madison Ave. at 75th St., tel. 212/ 570-3676. Admission: $4.50 adults, $2.50 senior citizens; free for students with school I.D. and children at all times and for everyone Tues. 6–8. Open Tues. 1–8, Wed.–Sat. 11–5, Sun. noon–6.*

Just off Madison is the so-called **Gucci Townhouse** (16 E. 76th St.), the former Gucci family mansion, which in 1988 sold for $7 million, at the time the most ever paid for a New York town house.

Continue north on Madison to the **Frank E. Campbell Funeral Chapel** (1076 Madison Ave. at 81st St.), *the* place for fashionable funerals since 1898. The somber chocolate-color edifice has seen massive funeral events for Rudolph Valentino (1926) and Judy Garland (1969) and more recent ceremonies for Robert Kennedy, John Lennon, and Rita Hayworth. Across the street you may recognize P.S. 6 as Justin Henry's school in *Kramer v. Kramer.*

Museum Mile   Museum Mile is a strip of cultural institutions located on or near Fifth Avenue between 82nd and 104th streets. Although the structures themselves and their contents represent a broad spectrum of subjects and styles, most of them have at least two things in common: They are closed Monday, and they allow free admission on Tuesday evening.

10 The **Metropolitan Museum of Art** has valid evidence for billing itself "New York's number one tourist attraction." This is the largest art museum in the Western Hemisphere (1.6 million square feet), and its permanent collection of 3.3 million works of art includes items from prehistoric to modern times from all areas of the world. Its 19 curatorial departments include the world's most comprehensive collection of American art, and its holdings of European art are unequaled outside Europe. The museum also has one of the world's best collections of ancient Greek, Roman, and Egyptian art.

Within this "city of art," we tend to prefer the old neighborhoods. The small chamber lined with reliefs from the Northwest Palace of the Assyrian King Assurnasirpal II (BC 882–859) replicates the serene atmosphere of an undiscovered tomb. The Astor Court Chinese garden reproduces a Ming Dynasty (1368–1644) scholar's courtyard with water splashing over artfully positioned rocks. The magnificent Temple of Dendur (circa BC 15) was transplanted from Egypt to a huge gallery with a wall of windows looking onto Central Park.

Walking tours and lectures are free with your admission contribution. Tours covering various sections of the museum begin about every 15 minutes on weekdays, less frequently on weekends. They depart from the Tour Board in the Great Hall (main entrance), but you may attach yourself to any group you encounter along the way. Lectures, which are often related to temporary exhibits, are given on Sunday, Tuesday, and Friday. *Fifth Ave. at 82nd St., tel. 212/535–7710. Suggested contribution: $5 adults, $2.50 senior citizens and students, children free. Open Fri. and Sat. 9:30–8:45, Tues.–Thurs. and Sun. 9:30–5:15.*

⑪ Frank Lloyd Wright's **Guggenheim Museum** is a six-story spiral rotunda through which you wind down past mobiles, stabiles, and other exemplars of modern art. Displays alternate new artists and modern masters; the permanent collection includes more than 20 Picassos. A newly expanded and fully restored Guggenheim is scheduled to reopen in the fall of 1991 after being closed for a half-year. A new tower and expanded gallery space will display the newly acquired Panza Collection of minimalist art, among other works. *1071 Fifth Ave. at 89th St., tel. 212/360–3500. Admission: $4.50 adults, $2.50 students and senior citizens, free Tues. 5–7:45. Open Tues. 11–7:45, Wed.–Sun. 11–4:45.*

⑫ Housed in a stately 19th-century mansion, the exhibits of **The National Academy of Design** usually focus on comparatively unsung artists of Europe and America. *1083 Fifth Ave. at 89th St., tel. 212/369–4880. Admission: $2.50 adults, $2 senior citizens and students, free Tues. 5–8. Open Tues. noon–8, Wed.–Sun. noon–5.*

A former residence of the industrialist and philanthropist Andrew Carnegie now houses the **Cooper-Hewitt Museum,** officially the Smithsonian Institution's National Museum of Design. Exhibitions, which change regularly, focus on an aspect of contemporary or historical design. Major holdings include: drawings, prints, textiles, furniture, metalwork, ceramics, glass, woodwork, and wall coverings. *2 E. 91st St., tel. 212/860–6868. Admission: $3 adults, $1.50 senior citizens and students, free Tues. 5–9. Open Tues. 10–9, Wed.–Sat. 10–5, Sun. noon–5.*

Time Out **Jackson Hole** (Madison Ave. at 91st St.) is a cheerful spot that serves the great American hamburger, sandwiches, omelets, chicken, and salads. Ski posters evoke the mood of the eponymous Wyoming resort. Prices are reasonable; beer and wine are available.

⑬ The largest collection of Jewish ceremonial objects in the Western Hemisphere is usually housed in the **Jewish Museum.** The museum is closed for renovation for 1991–1992, during which time it will present its exhibitions at the New York Historical Society (*see* Tour 6: Upper West Side, above). *1109 Fifth Ave. at 92nd St., tel. 212/860–1889.*

⑭ Located in a landmark mansion at the corner of Fifth Avenue and 94th Street, the **International Center of Photography** (ICP) generally focuses its exhibits on the work of a single prominent photographer or one photographic genre (portraits, architecture, etc.). The bookstore carries an impressive array of photography-oriented books, prints, and postcards; courses and special programs are offered throughout the year. *1130 Fifth Ave., tel. 212/860–1777. Admission: $3 adults, $1 senior citizens, $1.50 students, $1 children under 12, free Tues. 5–8. Open Tues. noon–8, Wed.–Fri. noon–5, Sat.–Sun. 11–6.*

⑮ The **Museum of the City of New York** makes the history of the Big Apple—from the Dutch settlers of Nieuw Amsterdam to yesterday's headlines—come to life with period rooms, dioramas, slide shows, and clever displays of memorabilia. Weekend programs appeal especially to children. *Fifth Ave. at 103rd St., tel. 212/534-1672. Suggested contribution: $3 adults, $1.50 students and senior citizens, $1 children. Open Tues.-Sat. 10-5; Sun. and legal holidays, 1-5.*

⑯ The final stop on Museum Mile, **El Museo del Barrio,** concentrates on Latin culture in general, with a particular emphasis on Puerto Rican art. The permanent collection includes numerous pre-Columbian artifacts. *1230 Fifth Ave. at 104th St., tel. 212/831-7272. Suggested contribution: $2. Open Wed.-Sun. 11-5.*

Tour 8: Greenwich Village

Numbers in the margin correspond with points of interest on the Greenwich Village map.

Writers and artists have converged on Greenwich Village for generations. In the 19th century the writers Henry James, Edgar Allan Poe, Mark Twain, Walt Whitman, and Stephen Crane lived and worked in the area. The turn of the century brought O. Henry, Edith Wharton, Theodore Dreiser, and Hart Crane. During the 1920s and 1930s, John Dos Passos, Norman Rockwell, Sinclair Lewis, Eugene O'Neill, Edward Hopper, and Edna St. Vincent Millay resided in its row houses and frequented its speakeasies.

During the late 1940s and early 1950s, Village cultural life was dominated by the abstract expressionist painters Franz Kline, Jackson Pollock, Mark Rothko, and Willem de Kooning and the beat writers Jack Kerouac, Allen Ginsberg, and Lawrence Ferlinghetti. A later wave brought the folk musicians and poets of the 1960s, led by Bob Dylan and Peter, Paul, and Mary.

As in much of Manhattan, high rents have priced all but the most affluent out of the Greenwich Village housing market. Today the Village—New Yorkers almost invariably speak of it simply as "the Village"—is inhabited principally by affluent professionals, students, and others aspiring to blend the flavor of small-town life with the bright lights of the big city.

Begin a tour of Greenwich Village at Washington Arch in
① **Washington Square** at the foot of Fifth Avenue. Designed by Stanford White, Washington Arch was built in 1892 to commemorate the 100th anniversary of George Washington's presidential inauguration and was originally placed about a half-block north of its present location. The permanent arch was built in 1906 and the statues—*Washington at War* on the left, *Washington at Peace* on the right—were added in 1913. The body builder Charles Atlas modeled for *Peace.*

Washington Square started out as a cemetery, principally for yellow fever victims, and an estimated 10,000-22,000 bodies lie below. In the early 1800s it was a parade ground and the site of public executions; bodies dangled from a conspicuous Hanging Elm at the northwest corner of the Square. Later it became the focus of a fashionable residential neighborhood and the center of outdoor activity.

By the early 1980s, Washington Square had deteriorated into a tawdry place only a drug dealer could love. Then community activism motivated a police crackdown that sent the drug traffic elsewhere and made Washington Square comfortable again for Frisbee players, street musicians, skateboarders, jugglers, stand-up comics, sitters, strollers, and the twice-a-year art fair.

Most of the buildings bordering Washington Square belong to New York University. "The Row" of federal town houses along Washington Square North, between Fifth Avenue and University Place, serves as faculty housing. The house at **20 Washington Square North** is the oldest building (1820) on the block. You can tell it was built before 1830 by the Flemish bond brickwork —alternate bricks inserted with the smaller surface facing out. Before 1830, builders thought that this was the only way to build walls that would stand.

Turn north on MacDougal Street and walk a half-block to **MacDougal Alley,** a private (fenced with locked gate) cobblestone street where stables and carriage houses have been converted into charming homes adorned with gas lamps.

Eighth Street, the main commercial strip of the Village, is not the "real" Greenwich Village but a collection of fast-food purveyors, poster and record shops, and glitzy clothing stores whose customers are chiefly the "bridge and tunnel people"—a disparaging term that Manhattan dwellers assign to those who come to the city from the other boroughs or the suburbs.

Time Out Don't miss **Patisserie Lanciani** (271 W. 4th St., between W. 11th and Perry Sts., tel. 212/929–0739), a tiny black-and-white café where writers gain inspiration as they sample the freshly baked pastries and excellent coffee.

For a more authentic village atmosphere, go north on Sixth Avenue to **Balducci's** (Sixth Ave. and 9th St.), a full-service gourmet department store that sprouted from the vegetable stand of the late Louis Balducci, Sr. Along with more than 80 Italian cheeses and 50 kinds of bread, this family-owned enterprise features imported Italian specialties and a prodigious selection of fresh seafood.

Directly opposite, the triangle formed by West 10th Street, Sixth Avenue, and Greenwich Avenue originally held a greenmarket, a jail, and the magnificent courthouse that is now the **Jefferson Market Library.** Critics termed the courthouse's hodgepodge of styles Venetian, Victorian, or Italian; Villagers, noting the alternating wide bands of red brick and narrow strips of granite, dubbed it Lean Bacon style. Over the years the structure has housed a number of government agencies (public works, civil defense, census bureau, police academy) but was on the verge of demolition when public-spirited citizens saved it and turned it into a public library in 1967. Note the fountain at the corner of West 10th Street and Sixth Avenue and the seal of the City of New York on the east front; on the inside, look at the handsome interior doorways and climb the graceful circular stairway.

Take Christopher Street, which veers off from the southern end of the library triangle, a few steps to **Gay Street.** A bending lane lined with small row houses circa 1810, Gay Street was

Greenwich Village and the East Village

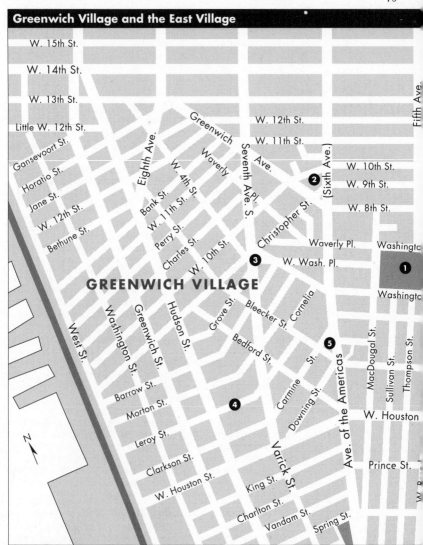

W. 15th St.
W. 14th St.
W. 13th St.
Little W. 12th St.
Gansevoort St.
Horatio St.
Jane St.
W. 12th St.
Bethune St.
Eighth Ave.
Greenwich Ave.
W. 4th St.
Waverly
Bank St.
W. 11th St.
Perry St.
Charles St.
W. 10th St.
Seventh Ave. S.
(Sixth Ave.)
W. 12th St.
W. 11th St.
W. 10th St.
W. 9th St.
W. 8th St.
Fifth Ave.
Christopher St.
Waverly Pl.
W. Wash. Pl.
Washington
Washington

GREENWICH VILLAGE

West St.
Washington St.
Greenwich St.
Hudson St.
Grove St.
Bleecker St.
Cornelia
Bedford St.
Barrow St.
Morton St.
Leroy St.
Clarkson St.
W. Houston St.
Carmine St.
Downing St.
Varick St.
King St.
Charlton St.
Vandam St.
Spring St.
Ave. of the Americas
MacDougal St.
Sullivan St.
Thompson St.
W. Houston
Prince St.

N

Father Demo Square, **5**	St. Luke's Place, **4**
Jefferson Market Library, **2**	St. Mark's Church-in-the-Bowery, **7**
Public Theater, **6**	St. Marks Place, **8**
	Sheridan Square, **3**
	Tompkins Square, **9**
	Washington Square, **1**

Union Square

E. 15th St.

E. 14th St.

Broadway

Fourth Ave.

E. 13th St.

E. 12th St.

Third Ave.

Second Ave.

E. 11th St.

7

E. 10th St.

E. 9th St.

Tompkins Square

University Pl.

Astor Pl.

Fourth Ave.

St. Marks Pl.

8

First Ave.

9

E. 7th St.

Sq. N.

Greene St.

Mercer St.

6

E. 6th St.

E. 5th St.

EAST VILLAGE

Sq. S.

NYU

W. 3rd St.

Broadway

St.

Gt. Jones St.

E. 4th St.

E. 3rd St.

E. 2nd St.

Ave. A

Ave. B

Lafayette

The Bowery

E. 1st St.

Bleecker St.

St.

E. Houston St.

Clinton St.

Wooster St.

Greene St.

Mercer St.

Crosby St.

Baxter St.

Mulberry St.

Mott St.

Elizabeth St.

Chrystie St.

Forsyth St.

Eldridge St.

Stanton St.

Rivington St.

Allen St.

Orchard St.

Ludlow St.

Essex St.

Norfolk St.

Suffolk St.

Spring St.

Delancey St.

0   440 yards

0   400 meters

originally a black neighborhood and later a strip of speakeasies. Ruth McKinney lived and wrote *My Sister Eileen* in the basement of No. 14, and Howdy Doody was designed in the basement of No. 12.

Go west on Christopher past the **Lion's Head** (59 Christopher St.), a longtime hangout for literati.

❸ At **Sheridan Square,** Christopher Street becomes the heart of New York's gay community and the location of many intriguing boutiques.

West of Seventh Avenue, the Village turns into a picture-book town of twisting, tree-lined streets, quaint houses, and tiny restaurants. Follow Grove Street from Sheridan Square past the boyhood home of the poet Hart Crane (45 Grove St.) to the house at the corner of Grove and Bedford streets. This building merits notice as one of the few clapboard structures in the Village; wood construction was banned as a fire hazard in 1822, the year it was built. The house has served many functions; it housed a brothel during the Civil War.

Grove Street curves before the iron gate of **Grove Court,** an enclave of brick-fronted town houses of the middle 1800s. Built originally as apartments for employees at neighborhood hotels, Grove Court was called Mixed Ale Alley because of the residents' propensity to pool beverages brought from work. It now houses a more affluent crowd: A town house there recently sold for $3 million.

Time Out	Where Christopher meets Grove Street and Waverly Place, **Pierre's** (170 Waverly Pl., tel. 212/929–7194) is everyone's favorite little French corner bistro. The sumptuous couscous and the profiterole are two specialties. Music may include guitar or piano played during dinner at this relaxed, friendly place.

The building at 77 Bedford Street is the oldest house in the Village (1799), yet the place next door has a greater claim to fame. Not only was 75½ Bedford the residence (at different times) of Edna St. Vincent Millay and John Barrymore, it is also New York's narrowest house. Just 9½ feet wide, the lot was an alley until rising real estate prices inspired the construction.

Heading west on Commerce Street, you soon reach the **Cherry Lane Theater,** one of the original Off-Broadway houses and the site of American premieres of works by O'Neill, Beckett, Ionesco, and Albee. Across the street stand two identical brick houses separated by a garden. Popularly known as the **Twin Sisters,** the houses were built (according to legend) by a sea captain for two daughters who loathed each other. Historical record insists they were built by a milkman who needed the two houses and an open courtyard for his work.

Barrow and Hudson streets meet at the corner of a block owned by **St. Luke's-in-the-Fields,** a simple country church whose grounds are made available to church members and neighborhood residents for gardening space.

❹ Head south on Hudson Street to **St. Luke's Place,** a row of classic town houses of the 1860s, shaded by graceful ginkgo trees. Mayor Jimmy Walker lived at No. 6. The lampposts are "mayor's lamps," which were sometimes placed in front of the residences of New York mayors. Theodore Dreiser wrote *An*

American Tragedy at No. 16. No. 12 is the residence of the Huxtable family depicted in the credits of *The Cosby Show*— but the Huxtables purportedly live in Brooklyn. Before 1890 the playground on the south side of St. Luke's Place was a graveyard where, according to legend, the dauphin of France, the lost son of Louis XVI and Marie Antoinette, is interred.

Across Seventh Avenue, St. Luke's Place becomes Leroy Street, which terminates in an old Italian neighborhood at Bleecker Street. Amazingly unchanged amid all the Village gentrification, Bleecker between Sixth and Seventh avenues abounds with fragrant Italian bakeries (**Zitos**, 259 Bleecker St.), butcher shops (**Ottomanelli's**, 285 Bleecker St.), pastry shops, fish stores, vegetable markets, pizza stands, and restaurants. The activity here focuses on **Father Demo Square** (Bleecker St. and Sixth Ave.), once a cluster of pushcarts and now the site of the **Church of Our Lady of Pompeii**, where Mother Cabrini, the first American saint, often prayed.

Across Sixth Avenue lies the stretch of Bleecker Street depicted in songs by Bob Dylan and other folk singers of the 1960s. Standing in the shadow of New York University, the area around the intersection of Bleecker and MacDougal streets attracts a young crowd to its cafes, bars, jazz clubs, coffeehouses, pizza stands, Off-Broadway theaters (**Provincetown Playhouse, Minetta Lane Theater**), cabarets (**Village Gate**), fast-food stands, and unpretentious restaurants.

Continuing north on MacDougal, you pass two houses (127 MacDougal St. and 129 MacDougal St.) once owned by Aaron Burr, who held much of the land that became Greenwich Village. At the end of the block, you've returned to Washington Square.

Tour 9: The East Village

The gritty tenements of the East Village—an area bounded by 14th Street on the north, Fourth Avenue or the Bowery on the west, Houston Street on the south, and the East River— provided inexpensive living places for artists, writers, and actors until very recently. Now the East Village is as costly a place to live as anywhere else south of 96th Street. Yet, in a way, the area has the best of both worlds. The new residents have been accompanied by new restaurants, shops, and galleries, while the old East Villagers maintain the fascinating trappings of the counterculture.

To explore the East Village, begin at the intersection of East 8th Street, Fourth Avenue, and Astor Place. Works of modern sculpture occupy two traffic islands in the square: One island contains *Alamo*, a massive black cube sculpted by Bernard Rosenthal; another island bears an ornate Beaux Arts subway entrance that provides access to the uptown No. 6 trains. Weather permitting, the sidewalks on the southern edge of Astor Place become a makeshift flea market.

On one corner of the intersection stands **Astor Wine and Spirits** (12 Astor Pl.), one of New York's most comprehensive and attractive liquor stores. It has good prices on imports, even better deals on house brands. (New York State has unexpectedly restrictive liquor control laws: Liquor and wine can be sold only in liquor stores, which can sell *only* liquor and wine—no beer, soda, ice, or glasses—and must close on Sunday.)

Continue west on Astor Place to **Astor Place Hair Designers** (2 Astor Pl.), where lines stretch out to the sidewalk awaiting service by four levels of barbers. Choose your cut from Polaroid snapshots in the window—maybe a Village Cut, a Guido, or a Li'l Tony. It costs only $10 for men and $12 for ladies, and it's open every day.

Returning to Fourth Avenue and heading south on Lafayette Street, you quickly come upon **Colonnade Row.** These run-down row houses of 1833, fronted by marble Corinthian columns, were once inhabited by John Jacob Astor and Cornelius Vanderbilt.

In 1854 Astor opened the city's first free library in the imposing structure directly across the street. That building now houses a significant New York institution, the New York Shakespeare Festival's **Public Theater.** The Public's six playhouses (and a cinema) present plays from abroad, some classic theater, and challenging new work by young American writers. *A Chorus Line* had its first performances here. The New York Shakespeare Festival is in the midst of a six-year Shakespeare marathon that, for the first time in America, will present all 37 plays consecutively. *425 Lafayette St., tel. 212/598–7150. Theater tickets: $10–$20 for regular performances, $30 for Shakespeare marathon productions. Some half-price tickets for most performances available at 6 PM (matinees, 1 PM); the line forms 1–2 hrs earlier.*

Cooper Square takes its name from Peter Cooper, an industrialist who in 1859 founded a college to provide a forum for public opinion and free technical education for the working class. The brownstone **Cooper Union Foundation Building** at Astor Place and Fourth Avenue was the first structure to be supported by steel railroad rails—rolled in Cooper's own plant. Cooper Union still offers tuition-free education and an active public-affairs program. A basement art gallery presents changing exhibits on history and design.

Old New York joke: Q. How do you get to Carnegie Hall? A. Practice, practice, practice. Variation on old New York joke: Q. How do you get to Carnegie Hall? A. Go to the **Carl Fischer Music Store** (62 Cooper Sq., tel. 212/677–1148), select from the infinitude of sheet music, confer with the knowledgeable staff, mingle with the other musicians hanging out, and practice, practice, practice.

You will probably find **McSorley's Old Ale House** (15 E. 7th St.), one of several claimants to the distinction of being New York's oldest bar, crammed with college types enticed by McSorley's own brands of ale. It opened in 1854 and did not admit women until 1970.

Surma, The Ukrainian Shop (11 E. 7th St.) reminds you that the East Village is essentially a Ukrainian neighborhood of onion-domed churches, butcher shops, bakeries, and restaurants serving hearty Middle European fare. What does a Ukrainian shop carry? Ukrainian books, magazines, and cassette tapes; greeting cards; musical instruments; colorful painted eggs and Surma's own brand of egg coloring; honey; and an exhaustive selection of peasant blouses.

Stuyvesant Street veers away from St. Marks Place and Third Avenue at an angle and runs through what was once Governor Peter Stuyvesant's "bouwerie," or farm. The street ends before **St. Mark's Church-in-the-Bowery,** a fieldstone country church of 1799 appended with a Greek Revival steeple and cast-iron front porch. Stuyvesant and Commodore Perry are buried in the cemetery beside the city's oldest continually used church, which has hosted much countercultural activity over the years. In the 1920s a forward-thinking pastor injected the Episcopalian ritual with American Indian chants, Greek folk dancing, and Eastern mantras. During the hippie era, St. Mark's welcomed avant-garde poets and playwrights. Today, dancers, poets, and performance artists cavort in the main sanctuary, where pews have been removed to accommodate them.

Second Avenue borders the church on the east, a thoroughfare that in the early part of this century was known as the Yiddish Rialto. Between Houston and 14th streets, eight theaters presented Yiddish-language productions of musicals, revues, and heart-wrenching melodramas. Today the theaters are gone; all that remains are Hollywood-style stars (Stars of David, that is) embedded in the sidewalk in front of the **Second Avenue Deli** (Second Ave. and 10th St.) to commemorate the Yiddish stage luminaries.

Time Out For some of the best Italian pastries in the city, try **Veniero Pasticerria** (342 E. 11th St., near 1st Ave., tel. 212/674–7264) a lively café that has rows and rows of incredibly fresh cannolis, fruit tarts, cheesecakes, and other desserts on display. If you can't get in, try **Derobertis Pastry Shop** (176 1st Ave., tel. 212/674–7137) across the street; it's a more subdued neighborhood hangout.

The intersection of Second Avenue and **St. Marks Place** (the name given to 8th Street in the East Village) is the hub of the "hip" East Village. During the 1950s Allen Ginsberg and Jack Kerouac lived and wrote in the area; the 1960s brought Bill Graham's Fillmore East, the Electric Circus, and hallucinogenic drugs to these blocks. The black-clad, pink-haired or shaven-headed punks followed, and many of them remain today. St. Marks Place between Second and Third avenues is a counterculture bazaar lined with vegetarian restaurants, jewelry stalls, leather shops, haircutters, and stores selling books, posters, and weird clothing. If you want to find a souvenir that will shock Aunt Minnie, this is the place to look. The East Village manages to get all the new styles first; the trend that *Time* magazine will discover in six months is parading St. Marks Place today.

East of Second Avenue, the area becomes more arty. **Theater 80** (80 St. Marks Pl., tel. 212/254–7400), one of New York's few remaining revival movie houses, shows a different double feature almost daily (same show Friday and Saturday); the fare includes American and foreign classics, relatively recent films, and cult classics.

P.S. 122 (150 First Ave. at 9th St., tel. 212/477–5288) is a former public school building transformed into a complex of spaces for avant-garde entertainment. Shocking, often crude, and frequently unpredictable, P.S. 122 happenings translate the spirit of the street into performance art. Prices are low, rarely more than $10, except for occasional benefit performances.

9 Far East Village activities focus on **Tompkins Square,** the park bordered by avenues A and B and 7th and 10th streets. Although the square itself could use a facelift, the restored brownstones along 10th Street are evidence that Tompkins Square is already smartly gentrified.

Not long ago, the outer limits of the East Village were a hotbed of avant-garde activity. More than two dozen art galleries, with names like Gracie Mansion and P.P.O.W., featured work that was often startling, innovative, or political. The art dealers, however, have either gone out of business or moved to more mainstream (and spacious) locations in SoHo or other parts of the Village.

Time Out **Jerry's 103** (103 Second Ave., at Sixth St., tel. 212/777–4120) stays open until 4 AM four days a week, and until 5 AM on Fri. and Sat. Its reasonably priced menu (pizzas, pastas, salads, and seafood) and informal atmosphere make it popular at all hours, especially with young artists.

Tour 10: SoHo

Numbers in the margin correspond with points of interest on the SoHo, Little Italy, and Chinatown map.

Twenty years ago, SoHo (the district South of Houston Street, bounded by Broadway, Canal Street, and Sixth Avenue) had just about been left for dead. In 1962 a City Club of New York study called this area of small 19th-century factories and warehouses "the wasteland of New York City" and "commercial slum number one." Numerous industrial fires had earned it the nickname Hell's Hundred Acres.

Two factors changed the perception and the fate of SoHo. One was the discovery that the hot hundred contained the world's greatest concentration of cast-iron buildings. The architectural rage between 1860 and 1890, cast-iron buildings did not require massive walls to bear the weight of the upper stories. Lighter and less expensive than stone, they were produced from standardized molds to mimic any architectural style: Italianate, Victorian Gothic, and neo-Greek can be seen today in SoHo. By eliminating loadbearing walls, cast-iron buildings gained interior space and made possible larger windows. Many subsequent nonmetallic buildings attempted to copy the graceful cast-iron design; how can you tell true cast-iron buildings from the counterfeits? Hold a magnet against the suspect and see whether it sticks.

The other factor of the SoHo renaissance was the influx of artists attracted to the large, cheap, well-lighted spaces that cast-iron buildings provided. At first it was illegal for artists to live in their lofts; then, during the 1970s, the municipal zoning laws were changed to permit residence. However, as the tide of artists and galleries and quaint cafes made this convenient neighborhood a more attractive residential area, the rising rents forced out all but the most successful artists.

Today, SoHo offers architecture and art, highstyle shopping, and plenty of intriguing places to eat and drink. West Broadway (which runs parallel to and four blocks west of Broadway) is SoHo's main drag and the location of many shops and galleries. Saturday is the big day for gallery-hopping, and it's when the sidewalks of SoHo turn into a strolling fashion show of today's wildest styles.

South on West Broadway from Houston Street (pronounced "How-ston"), **Circle Gallery** (468 West Broadway) spotlights a number of artists at a time and sells posters and jewelry. **Suzanne Bartsch** (456A West Broadway) is a semi-Oriental setting for British-designed clothing. **Victoria Falls** (451 West Broadway) sells authentic antique and reproduced women's clothing, including fine lingerie and handknit sweaters.

❶ **420 West Broadway** is one address that houses several galleries: **Leo Castelli Gallery** displays the big names of modern art; **Sonnabend Gallery** has important American and European artists; the **49th Parallel** features Canadian artists; and **Charles Cowles Gallery** has fine painting, sculpture, and photography. Several showrooms in the **Mary Boone Gallery** (417 West Broadway) display what's hot in contemporary art.

It's hard to overlook **Think Big** (390 West Broadway), a shop that features elephantine versions of sporting goods, items commonly found in the home, and souvenirs. Next door, **D. F. Sanders & Co.** (386 West Broadway) markets contemporary furnishings and housewares that look stylish enough to make housework seem like fun. The **O.K. Harris Gallery** (383 West Broadway) is known for works of photorealism and unusual sculpture.

Time Out   Head west to find the long-awaited **TriBeCa Grill** (375 Greenwich St., tel. 212/941–3900). It's located on the first floor of the old Martinson Coffee Building, which now houses actor Robert De Niro's **Tribeca Film Center,** a movie production complex. The Grill specializes in fresh grilled fish, sumptuous salads, and charcuterie. And that's the old Maxwell Plum's bar in the middle of the restaurant.

SoHo's finest cast-iron architecture lies east of West Broadway. Head east on Broome Street and cross Wooster Street, which is paved with Belgian blocks, a smoother successor to the traditional cobblestone. The **Gunther Building,** with its gracefully curving window panes, stands at the southwest corner of Broome and Greene streets. Go north on Greene to –72–76, the so-called **King of Greene Street,** a five-story, Renaissance-style, cast-iron building with a magnificent projecting porch of Corinthian columns. Today the King (now painted yellow) houses art galleries plus **The Second Coming,** a department store of "vintage"—too old for "secondhand," not old enough for "antique"—women's and men's clothing, furniture, and other curiosities. The **Queen of Greene Street** (28–30 Greene St.) is a Second Empire cast-iron structure with a huge mansard roof but no retail enterprises.

Continue east on Broome Street to the corner of Broome and Broadway to see a classic of the cast-iron genre, the 1857 ❷ **Haughwout Building** (488 Broadway). Inspired by a Venetian palace, this five-story blackened Parthenon of Cast Iron contained the world's first commercial passenger elevator, a steam-powered device invented by Elisha Graves Otis. For a closer look at the tin ceilings and interior columns, and perhaps

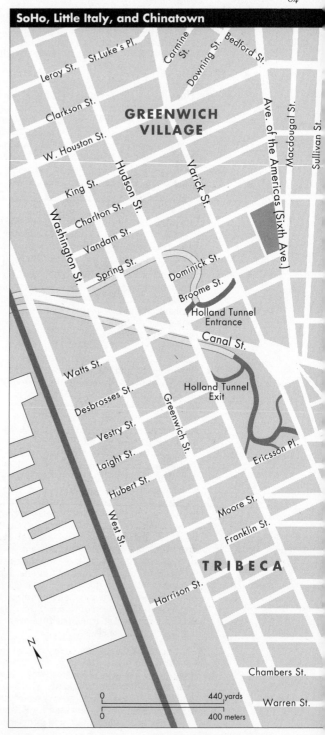

SoHo, Little Italy, and Chinatown

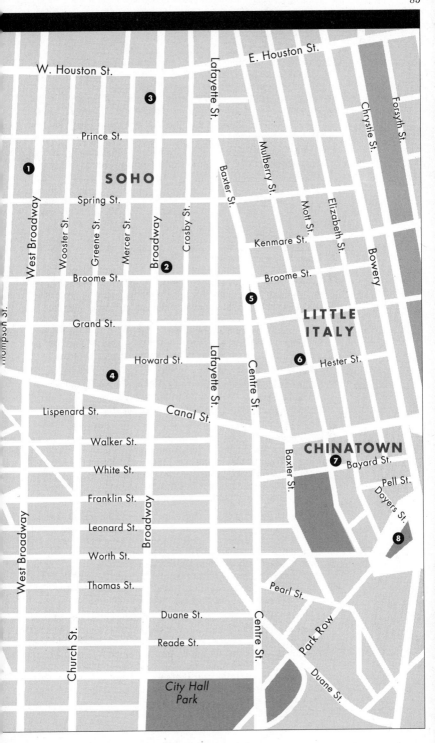

a bargain on linens or underwear, step inside the **SoHo Mill Outlet** on the ground floor.

The Broome-Broadway intersection is a few blocks from
❸ SoHo's two unusual museums. The **New Museum of Contemporary Art** shows experimental, often radically innovative work by unrecognized artists. It will display nothing more than 10 years old. *583 Broadway between Houston and Prince Sts., tel. 212/219–1355. Suggested admission: $2.50 adults, $1.50 students, senior citizens, and artists. Open Wed.–Sun. noon–6; Fri.–Sat. noon–8.*

❹ **The Museum of Holography** has a permanent exhibit on the history of holograms, three-dimensional photographs created by laser beams. This combination science show and art gallery projects a film on holography and has three changing exhibits a year. The gift shop has a terrific selection of 3-D art and souvenirs. *11 Mercer St. (near Canal St.), tel. 212/925–0581. Admission: $3.50 adults, $2.50 students, children, and senior citizens. Open Tues.–Sun. 11–7.*

Tour 11: Little Italy

Where are the cops when you need them? Certainly not in the former **police headquarters building,** a magnificent 1909 Renaissance palazzo that occupies the entire block bounded by Grand, Centre, and Broome streets and Centre Market Place. The police moved to new quarters in 1973, and the stately domed edifice has been converted into a luxury co-op project
❺ aptly called the **Police Building,** where apartments range in price from $338,500 to $1,746,000.

Walk one block east to Grand and Mulberry streets, and you enter Little Italy. Look south on Mulberry Street at the tenement buildings with fire escapes projecting over the sidewalks:

Most of these buildings are of the late 19th-century New York tenement style known as railroad flats, five-story buildings on 25-foot by 90-foot lots. The rooms in each apartment are arranged in a straight line, like railroad cars, with no hallway on either side. The style was predominant in the densely populated lower Manhattan until 1901, when the city passed an ordinance requiring air shafts in the interior of buildings.

Mulberry Street has long been the heart of Little Italy, and at this point it's virtually the entire body. In 1932 an estimated 98% of the residents of the area were of Italian birth or heritage; since then the growth and expansion of Chinatown has encroached on the Italian neighborhood to such an extent that the merchants and community leaders of the Little Italy Restoration Association (LIRA) negotiated a truce in which the Chinese agreed to let Mulberry remain an all-Italian street.

Today Mulberry Street between Broome and Canal consists entirely of restaurants, cafes, bakeries, imported food shops, and souvenir stores. Some restaurants and cafes display high-tech Eurodesign; others seem dedicated to remaining precisely as their old customers remember them. How can you find the restaurant that's right for you? Perhaps by choosing the place that displays photos of the celebrity you like best: Sinatra, Cher, Dom DeLuise, Mayor Koch.

Former residents keep returning to Little Italy's venerable institutions. At the corner of Mulberry and Grand, **E. Rossi & Co.** (established 1902) is an antiquated little shop that sells housewares, espresso makers, embroidered religious postcards, and jocular Italian T-shirts. Down the street is **Ferrara's** (195 Grand St.), a nearly 100-year-old pastry shop that ships its creations—cannoli, peasant pie, Italian rum cake—all over the world.

6 **Umberto's Clam House** (129 Mulberry St., tel. 212/431–7545), where mobster Joey Gallo munched his last scungili in 1973, occupies the northwest corner of Mulberry and Hester streets. Quite peaceable now, Umberto's specializes in fresh shellfish in a spicy tomato sauce. At 247 Mulberry Street, you may get the urge to check out the doorway of the **Ravenite Social Club,** where reputed mobster John Gotti and his pals have been known to hang out. Turn onto Hester Street to visit yet another Little Italy institution, **Puglia** (189 Hester St., tel. 212/966–6006), partly disguised as a restaurant where guests sit at long communal tables, sing along with house entertainers, and enjoy moderately priced southern Italian specialties with quantities of homemade wine.

Around the corner on Baxter Street stands the **San Gennaro Church** (officially, Most Precious Blood Church, National Shrine of San Gennaro), which sponsors Little Italy's annual keynote event, the Feast of San Gennaro. When it happens each September, the streets become a bright and turbulent Italian kitchen.

Tour 12: Chinatown

In theory, Little Italy and Chinatown are divided by Canal Street, the bustling artery that links the Holland Tunnel (to New Jersey) and the Manhattan Bridge (to Brooklyn). However, in recent years Chinatown has gained an influx of immigrants from the People's Republic of China, Taiwan, and especially Hong Kong. Anticipating the return of the British colony to PRC domination in 1997, Hong Kong residents consider Chinatown real estate a safe repository for capital. Consequently, Chinatown has expanded beyond its traditional borders into Little Italy to the north and the formerly Jewish Lower East Side to the east.

Canal Street itself abounds with crowded markets bursting with mounds of fresh seafood and strangely shaped vegetables in extraterrestrial shades of green. Food shops proudly display their wares; if America's motto is "a chicken in every pot," then Chinatown's must be "a roast duck in every window."

The slightly less frantic **Kam Man** (200 Canal St.), a duplex supermarket, has fresh and canned imported groceries, herbs, and the sort of dinnerware and furniture familiar to patrons of Chinese restaurants. Choose from 100 kinds of noodles or such delicacies as dried starch and fresh chicken feet.

Mott Street is the principal business street of the neighborhood. Narrow and twisting; crammed with souvenir shops and restaurants in funky, pagoda-style buildings; crowded with pedestrians at all hours of the day or night, Mott Street looks the way you might expect Chinatown to look. Within the few dense blocks of Chinatown, hundreds of restaurants serve every imaginable type of Chinese cuisine, from simple fast-food noodles or dumplings to sumptuous Hunan, Szechuan, Cantonese, Mandarin, and Shanghai feasts. It may be hard to choose among them, but two things you can know for sure: (1) Every New Yorker thinks he or she knows the absolute flat-out best, and (2) at 8 PM on Saturday, don't be surprised if you have to wait in line to get into any one of them.

In the midst of the Mott Street hubbub stands the **Church of the Transfiguration** (Mott and Mosco Sts.). An imposing Georgian structure built in 1801 as the Zion Episcopal Church, it is now a Chinese Catholic church that delivers mass in Cantonese and Mandarin.

❼ The **New York Chinatown History Project** (70 Mulberry St., between Bayard and Canal Sts., tel. 212/619–4785) shows interactive photographic exhibits on Asian-American labor history. It also has become a resource library and bookstore and offers a walking tour of Chinatown.

Double back to Pell Street, a narrow lane of wall-to-wall restaurants whose neon signs stretch halfway across the thoroughfare. Turn onto **Doyers Street,** a twisty little byway whose storefronts house an extraordinary density of barber shops and the excellent **Viet-Nam Restaurant** (*see* Dining, below). Duck into Wing Fat, a new multilevel shopping mall that serpentines its way up, around, and out to Chatham Square.

❽ **Chatham Square** is the furthest thing from a square; it's more of a labyrinth, where 10 converging streets create pandemonium for autos and a nightmare for pedestrians. A Chinese arch honoring Chinese casualties in American wars stands on an island in the eye of the storm.

Two remnants of Chinatown's pre-Chinese past stand near Chatham Square. Walk down St. James Place to the **First Shearith Israel** graveyard, the first Jewish cemetery in the United States. When consecrated in 1656, the area was considered outside the city. Walk a half-block farther, turn left on James Street, and you'll see **St. James Church,** a stately 1837 Greek Revival edifice where Al Smith (the former New York governor and a Democratic presidential candidate) served as altar boy.

Go back past Chatham Square and up the Bowery to **Confucius Plaza,** the open area monitored by a statue of Confucius and a high-rise apartment complex named for him. America's oldest drugstore, Olliffe's Apothecary, once occupied an adjacent building at 6 Bowery; now it's the Abacus Federal Savings Bank. At 18 Bowery, corner of Pell Street, stands one of Manhattan's oldest homes, a Federal and Georgian structure built in 1785 by the meat wholesaler Edward Mooney.

Head up the Bowery toward the grand arch and colonnade entrance to the Manhattan Bridge, and you'll soon return to Canal Street. The corner of Bowery and Canal was once the center of New York's diamond district. Many jewelry dealers have moved uptown (to 47th Street between Fifth and Sixth avenues), but a substantial number of jewelers still occupy shops on the Bowery and the north side of Canal. The selection is pretty good, and you shouldn't expect to pay the first price you are quoted.

Tour 13: Lower Manhattan

Numbers in the margin correspond with points of interest on the Lower Manhattan map.

Lower Manhattan is relatively small in area yet dense with attractions. The New Amsterdam colony was established here by the Dutch in 1625, and the first capital of the United States was located in the area. Wall Street is here, which means the New York and American stock exchanges plus innumerable banks and other financial institutions. Boats depart for Staten Island, the Statue of Liberty, and on ferry and excursion routes; the waterfront also inspired the South Street Seaport Museum project.

West Side Our West Side and East Side tours of lower Manhattan both be-
   ❶ gin outside the **Staten Island Ferry Terminal** at the southern-
most tip of Manhattan. For subway riders, that's just outside the South Ferry station on the No. 1 line.

The **Staten Island Ferry** is still the best deal in town. The 20-to-30-minute ride across New York harbor provides great views of the Manhattan skyline, the Statue of Liberty, the Verrazano Narrows Bridge, and the Jersey coast, and it costs only 50¢ *round-trip*. A word of advice: While commuters love the ferry service's swift new low-slung craft, the boats ride low in the water and have no outside deck space. If one of the low-riders is next in line, you might be happier if you missed the boat and waited for one of the higher, more open old-timers.

To the west of South Ferry lies **Battery Park,** a verdant landfill loaded with monuments and sculpture at Manhattan's green toe. The **East Coast Memorial,** a statue of a fierce eagle, presides over eight granite slabs on which are inscribed the names of U.S. servicemen who died in World War II.

The steps of the East Coast Memorial afford a fine view of the main features of **New York Harbor:** From left to right, **Governor's Island,** a Coast Guard installation; hilly **Staten Island** in the distance; the **Statue of Liberty** on Liberty Island; **Ellis Island,** gateway to the New World for generations of immigrants; and the old railway terminal in **Liberty Park,** on the mainland in Jersey City, New Jersey.

Farther along, you'll see a romantic **statue of Giovanni da Verrazano,** the Florentine merchant who piloted the ship that first sighted New York and its harbor in 1524. From here the Verrazano Narrows Bridge between Brooklyn and Staten Island, the world's longest suspension bridge, is visible beyond Governor's Island.

❷ **Castle Clinton** may have gone through more changes than any other public building. Built in 1811 as a defense for New York Harbor, the circular brick fortress was constructed on an island 200 feet from shore. In 1824 it became Castle Garden, an entertainment and concert facility that reached its high point in 1850 when more than 6,000 people (the capacity of Radio City Music Hall) attended the U.S. debut of the "Swedish Nightingale," Jenny Lind. After landfill had connected it to the city, Castle Clinton became, in succession, an immigrant processing center, an aquarium, and now a restored fort, museum, and ticket office for the Statue of Liberty.

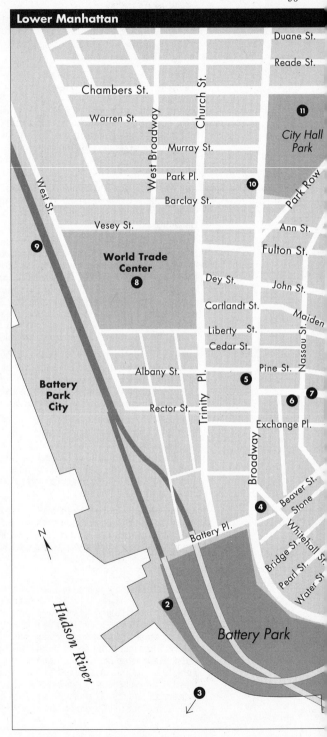

Lower Manhattan

Duane St.

Reade St.

Chambers St.

Warren St.

Church St.

City Hall
Park

Murray St.

West Broadway

Park Pl.

Barclay St.

Park Row

Vesey St.

Ann St.

West St.

Fulton St.

**World Trade
Center**

Dey St.

John St.

Cortlandt St.

Maiden

Liberty St.

Nassau St.

Cedar St.

Albany St.

Pine St.

**Battery
Park
City**

Trinity Pl.

Rector St.

Exchange Pl.

Broadway

Beaver St.

Stone

Battery Pl.

Whitehall St.

Bridge St.

Pearl St.

Water St.

N

Hudson River

Battery Park

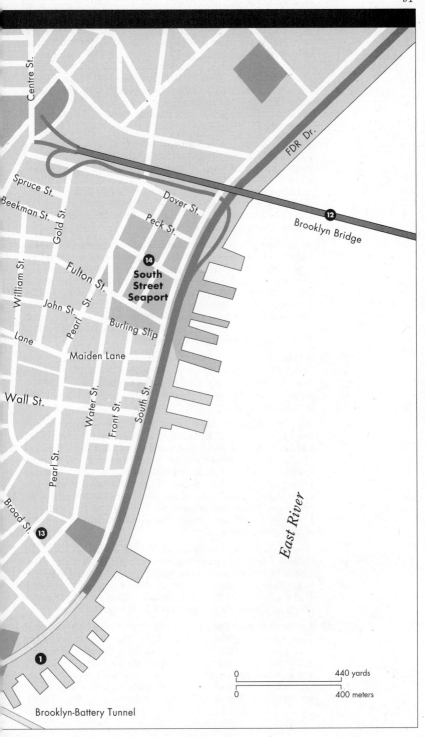

Centre St.

FDR Dr.

Spruce St.

Beekman St.

Gold St.

Dover St.

Peck St.

William St.

Fulton St.

14
**South
Street
Seaport**

Brooklyn Bridge **12**

John St.

Pearl St.

Burling Slip

Lane

Maiden Lane

Wall St.

Water St.

Front St.

South St.

East River

Pearl St.

Broad St.

13

1

0   440 yards

0   400 meters

Brooklyn-Battery Tunnel

Castle Clinton is also to be the departure point for ferries to **Ellis Island,** set to open this year after a $140 million restoration, the largest-ever U.S. project of its kind (the fundraising drive was headed by Chrysler Corporation chairman Lee Iacocca). Now a national monument, Ellis Island was once a federal immigration facility that processed 17 million men, women, and children between 1892 and 1954—the ancestors of more than 40% of the Americans living today. *Tel. 212/883–1986. Admission prices and opening times not available at press time.*

❸ The popularity of the **Statue of Liberty** surged following its 100th birthday restoration in 1986. After arriving on Liberty Island, you can take an elevator 10 stories to the top of the pedestal. The strong of heart and limb can climb another 12 stories to the crown. Currently you may have to wait in line for up to three hours for the privilege. *Tel. 212/363–3200. Round-trip fare: $3.25 adults, $1.50 children. Daily departures on the hour 9–5; extended hours in summer.*

At the end of a broad mall outside the landward entrance to Castle Clinton stands the **Netherlands Memorial,** a quaint flagpole depicting the bead exchange that established Fort Amsterdam in 1626. Inscriptions describe the event in English and Dutch. Across State Street is the facade of the imposing **U.S. Customs House,** adorned by a double row of statuary. The lower statues depict each of the continents; the upper row represents the major trading cities of the world (the woman to the left of the central shield stands for Lisbon).

❹ **Bowling Green** is an oval greensward that in 1733 became New York's first public park. On July 9, 1776, a few hours after citizens learned about the signing of the Declaration of Independence, rioters toppled a statue of King George III that had occupied the spot for years.

Broadway begins beside Bowling Green and continues north all the way to Albany. **25 Broadway** used to be headquarters of the Cunard steamship line. The ground floor is now one of the most spectacular post offices you'll ever see, a cathedral of gracious travel with sea gods and mermaids romping across the vaulted ceiling and walls, frescoes depicting great vessels of yore, and richly detailed wall maps of the seven seas. To the left of the vestibule, in a charming niche with an inviting fireplace, is a Philatelic Exhibition Center that displays and purveys commemorative stamps.

George Washington really did sleep at **39 Broadway,** not in the office building now occupying the site, but in the McComb Mansion, which functioned as the second presidential residence between February 23 and August 30, 1790, when it overlooked the Hudson River. The first presidential residence was at 3 Cherry Street, which would now be under the Brooklyn Bridge.

❺ Jet-black **Trinity Church** (Broadway and Wall St.) was New York's first Anglican Parish (1646). The present structure (1846) ranked as the city's tallest building for most of the last half of the 19th century. Alexander Hamilton is buried beneath a huge white pyramid in Trinity's south-side graveyard; Robert Fulton, the inventor of the steamboat, lies nearby. *Tours weekdays at 2; free 30- to 40-min concerts, Tues. 12:45.*

Arguably the most famous thoroughfare in the world, **Wall
Street** was where stock traders used to conduct business along
the sidewalks or at tables beneath a sheltering buttonwood
❻ tree. Wall Street's principal facility today is the **New York
Stock Exchange,** which has its august Corinthian main entrance around the corner on Broad Street. Enter at 20 Broad
Street and, after what may be a lengthy wait, take an elevator
to the third-floor visitor center. A self-guided tour, informative slide shows, video displays, and guides may help you interpret the chaos that seems to be transpiring down on the trading
floor. *Tel. 212/656–5167. Open weekdays 9:20–3:30. Free tickets available at 20 Broad St. at 9:30.*

In building only a two-story investment bank at the corner of
Wall and Broad Streets, J. P. Morgan was thumbing his nose at
Wall Street real estate values. Now **Morgan Guaranty Trust,**
the building bears pockmarks near the fourth window on the
Wall Street side, created when a bomb in a pushcart exploded
in 1920.

A regal statue of George Washington stands at the spot where
he was sworn in as the first U.S. president in 1789. The Federal
Hall of that day was demolished when the capital moved to Phil-
❼ adelphia. The current **Federal Hall National Memorial** is a
stately period structure containing exhibits on New York and
Wall Street.

Walk through Federal Hall, past the gift shop, and turn right
onto Pine Street. You soon reach a plaza around the 65-story
Chase Manhattan Bank Building. The perimeter of Chase Plaza
has become an impromptu flea market for merchandise and fast
food, and the interior holds a striking Dubuffet sculpture,
Trees.

Kitty-corner from the Chase Building, **Louise Nevelson Plaza**
occupies the triangle formed by William Street, Liberty
Street, and Maiden Lane. The plaza contains benches and four
black welded-steel abstract Nevelson sculptures, three middle-
size pieces, and one huge 70-footer. Sit in the plaza and contemplate the **Federal Reserve Bank** directly across the street. This
is a bank that looks like a bank ought to look: gray, solid, imposing, absolutely impregnable—and it had better be, for its
vaults reputedly contain a quarter of the world's gold reserves.

Across Maiden Lane from the Fed, take an escalator down to
the **Whitney Museum of American Art, Downtown at Federal
Plaza,** a free museum that displays 20th-century American art.

❽ Continue west on Maiden Lane to the **World Trade Center,** a 16-
acre complex that contains New York's two tallest buildings, a
hotel, a shopping center, a huge main plaza, and, somewhat in-
congruously, a farmers' market on Tuesday and Thursday in a
parking area along Church Street. The Observation Deck is located on the 107th floor of 2 World Trade Center, yet the ride
up takes only 58 seconds. The view is potentially 55 miles, but
signs at the ticket window (Admission: $3.50 adults, $1.75 children) disclose how far you can see that day and whether the
outdoor deck is open. You get the same view with a costly meal
at **Windows on the World** atop 1 World Trade Center; prices are
somewhat lower for breakfast or for drinks and "grazing" at the
Hors d'Oeuvrerie at Windows on the World (tel. 212/938–1111).
The TKTS booth (half-price Broadway and Off-Broadway
shows) in the mezzanine of 2 World Trade Center is open

Monday–Saturday 11–5:30, earlier than the Times Square location, and has shorter lines.

The rock and soil excavated for the World Trade Center begat **Battery Park City,** a hundred new acres of Manhattan reached by a pedestrian overpass above West Street on the western border of the center. Battery Park City is a complete neighborhood built from scratch. It has office buildings (including the offices of *The Wall Street Journal*), high-rise apartment houses, low-rise old-looking town houses, and a modest selection of shops. Gazing at the Hudson from the placid riverside promenade, you may find it difficult to believe that the New York Stock Exchange lies less than a half-mile away.

9 Battery Park City is also home to the **World Financial Center,** a mammoth granite-and-glass commercial complex designed by architect Cesar Pelli. Inside the four-tower structure is a melange of 30 upscale shops (including Ann Taylor, Barneys New York, Mark Cross, and Godiva Chocolatier), and a palatial public space called the Winter Garden. The room, adorned by a vaulted-glass roof, an immense stairway, and 16 palm trees (carefully transplanted from Borrigo Springs, California), hosts an array of performances through the center's Arts and Events program.

Across Church Street from the World Trade Center stands **St. Paul's Chapel** (Broadway and Fulton St.), the second-oldest structure (1766) in Manhattan and the only surviving example of Colonial architecture. St. Paul's displays George Washington's pew and is open throughout the day for prayer, rest, and meditation.

10 Head north on Broadway to the so-called Cathedral of Commerce, the ornate **Woolworth Building** (Park Pl. and Broadway). Once the world's tallest building at 792 feet, this agglomeration of architectural styles still houses the Woolworth corporate offices. Gargoyles set into arches in the lobby ceiling represent old man Woolworth pinching his pennies and the architect Cass Gilbert contemplating a model of his creation.

Park Row, the street across City Hall Park from the Woolworth Building, was known as Newspaper Row from the mid-19th century to the early 20th century, when most of the city's 20 or so daily papers had offices there. Now the city is down to four dailies, and Park Row is an undistinguished commercial strip. In its day, triangular **City Hall Park** hosted hangings, riots, meetings, and demonstrations; much of the time now it accommodates brown-baggers and pigeon feeders.

11 **City Hall,** built between 1803 and 1811, is unexpectedly elegant, sedate, graceful, small-scale, and charming. Its exterior columns reflect the classical influence of Greece and Rome, and the handsome cast-iron cupola is crowned with the statue of lady Justice. The major interior feature is a sweeping marble double staircase. The wood-paneled City Council Chamber in the east wing is small and clubby; the Board of Estimate chamber to the west has Colonial paintings and seating in the church pew manner. Were it not for the metal detectors through which all visitors must pass, you'd think this was a county courthouse in rural Virginia rather than the epicenter of the nation's biggest metropolis.

🔟 Directly east of City Hall is the **Brooklyn Bridge,** New York's oldest and best known span. When built in 1883 it was the world's longest suspension bridge and, like so many others in turn, the tallest structure in the city. Now its graceful stone towers no longer seem so awesome. It hasn't been sold to a gullible out-of-towner for years.

Walking across the Brooklyn Bridge is a peak New York experience. The distance is just over a mile, and thousands of commuters make the trip on foot whenever the weather allows. Located in the center of the span, the walkway passes beneath the towers and through the filigree. On the Brooklyn side the span bisects the expansive Watchtower complex operated by the Jehovah's Witnesses. Take the first exit to Brooklyn Heights, a charming neighborhood of brownstones, and head back toward the river to the Promenade for an exciting view of Lower Manhattan.

East Side Directly north of South Ferry stands the **Shrine of St. Elizabeth Ann Seton** (7–8 State St.). The red brick Federal-style town house was built in 1783 as the home of the wealthy Watson family, and Mother Seton dwelled and gave birth to her fifth child in what is now the rectory. Mother Seton went on to found the Sisters of Charity, the first American order of nuns, and in 1975 became the first American-born saint. Masses are held daily.

East of the shrine, State Street becomes Water Street and passes **New York Plaza,** a complex of high-tech office towers linked by an underground concourse. Turn left on Broad Street and you quickly reach **Fraunces Tavern,** a combination restaurant, bar, and museum that occupies a Colonial (brick exterior, cream-colored portico and balcony) tavern built in 1719 and restored in 1907. Best remembered as the site of George Washington's farewell address to his officers celebrating the British evacuation of New York in 1783, Fraunces Tavern contains two fully furnished period rooms and other displays of 18th- and 19th-century American history. *Broad and Pearl Sts., tel. 212/ 425–1778. Suggested contribution: $2.50 adults, $1 students, senior citizens, and children, free Thurs. Restaurant open weekdays. Museum open June–Sept., weekdays 10–4; Oct.– May, weekdays 10–4, Sun. noon–5.*

Continuing up Broad Street and turning right on South William Street, you enter an area of curving streets (the routes of old New Amsterdam cowpaths) and low-rise houses that still look much as they did in the 19th century. **Delmonico's,** at the rounded corner of South William and Beaver streets, opened in 1888. The haute cuisine and one of America's first female cashiers made it the place to go at the turn of the century. Head east on William Street to **Hanover Square,** a quiet tree-lined plaza that stood on the waterfront when the East River reached Pearl Street. The pirate Captain Kidd lived in the neighborhood, and the brownstone **India House** (1837) used to house the New York Cotton Exchange.

🔟 Go one block east to Water Street and turn north to the **South Street Seaport Museum,** part of an 11-block historic district that encompasses shopping centers, historic ships, cruise boats, a multimedia presentation, art galleries, and innumerable places to eat. In spirit linked more closely to other Rouse Corporation waterfront developments in Boston and Baltimore boats, a multimedia presentation, art galleries, and innumerable places to eat. In spirit linked more closely to other Rouse Corporation waterfront developments in Boston and Baltimore than to the rest of Manhattan, the project still has a lot of appeal.

Schermerhorn Row (2–18 Fulton St.), a series of early 1800s Georgian and Federal-style warehouses, is the Seaport's architectural centerpiece. The ground floors are occupied by shops and bars. The cobblestone street is closed to traffic and, on Friday evening during summer, young professionals from the Financial District stand shoulder-to-shoulder at cocktail hour. Markets have occupied the **Fulton Market Building** site across the way since 1822. Now the rebuilt structure contains shops, restaurants, even a fish stall. The 15 restored buildings in **Museum Block,** across Front Street, include Bowne & Co., a reconstructed working 19th-century print shop, and the Museum Shops along twisting Cannon's Walk.

Cross South Street to Pier 16 to view the historic ships: the second-largest sailing ship in existence, *Peking;* the full-rigged *Wavertree;* and the lightship *Ambrose. Admission to ships, galleries, walking tours, Maritime Crafts Center, films, and other Seaport events: $5 adults, $4 senior citizens, $3 students, $2 children. Open daily 10–5, longer hours in summer.*

Pier 16 is the departure point for the 90-minute **Seaport Harbor Line Cruise** (tel. 212/385–0791). The fare is $12 adults, $6 children. Notice how two large cargo containers used on modern-day freighters are transformed into a toy shop and a cafe.

Time Out   Pier 17 is a massive dockside shopping mall. If you're hungry, skip the overpriced seafood joints and head for the fast-food stalls on the third-floor **Promenade Food Court.** Cuisine is nonchain eclectic: Third Avenue Deli, Pizza on the Pier, Wok & Roll, the Yorkville Packing House for meat, the Salad Bowl for veggies, Bergen's Beer & Wine Garden (10 brews on tap). What's really spectacular is the view of the East River, Brooklyn Bridge, and Brooklyn Heights from the well-spaced tables in a glass-wall atrium. Seating is on an outdoor deck when weather permits.

As your nose may already have surmised, the blocks along South Street north of the museum complex still house a working fish market. Although the city has tried to relocate the hundreds of fishmongers of the **Fulton Fish Market** in the South Bronx, the area remains a beehive. Get up early (or stay up late) if you want to see it: The action begins around midnight and ends by 8 AM.

Continue north to Peck Slip where, on the wall of a building on the north side of the street, you'll see a 90-foot trompe l'oeil mural by Richard Haas showing how that view of the Brooklyn Bridge might have looked 100 years ago. Across the street stands an ornate co-op apartment that used to be **Meyer's Hotel,** where in 1883 Annie Oakley threw a wild rooftop party to celebrate the opening of the Brooklyn Bridge.

Off the Beaten Track

Public Spaces Public spaces go a long way toward making New York a more livable—and visitable—city. Public spaces are created when, in return for receiving a zoning variance, the builders of new office towers agree to design and maintain a portion of the interior space for public use. As such, public spaces perform roles formerly played by public parks and hotel lobbies: They provide clean, safe, physically attractive areas where you can sit, relax, read a newspaper, peruse your guidebook, and watch the world go by. You're welcome to stay as long as you like, and you don't have to spend a dime.

Many of the buildings that have public spaces have turned them into showplaces. And while each indoor park is unique, most of them have features in common. They provide places to sit, such as benches, ledges, and chairs with tables; they have greenery, from potted plants to towering trees; they have fountains or waterfalls to muffle the sounds of the city. Many have snack bars, working telephones, and what can be very difficult to find elsewhere in Manhattan, clean public washrooms.

Buildings with public spaces identify themselves with a logo of a leafy tree over a checkered grid. Public spaces are usually open during the day, and many stay open late into the evening. The following public spaces are listed from Lower Manhattan up.

Continental Insurance Building (180 Maiden La. at Front St.). A modernist atrium just two blocks south of the South Street Seaport Museum. Benches surround copious foliage amid an ultramodern structure that appears to be made of Tinker Toys.

ChemCourt (272 Park Ave. between 47th and 48th Sts.). The Chemical Bank Building provides benches around plantings of exotic shrubs, all helpfully labeled in English and Latin. A glass roof lets the sunshine into the ground floor of the 50-story silver-gray tower.

Olympic Place (645 Fifth Ave., enter on 50th or 51st St.). A splendid space directly opposite St. Patrick's Cathedral and Rockefeller Center, on the ground floor of the brown-tinted Olympic Tower shop, office, and apartment complex. A wall of water drowns out exterior noise. Space includes a Japanese restaurant, a snack bar serving take-out sandwiches and pastries, washrooms, and phones.

Park Avenue Plaza (55 E. 52nd St. between Park and Madison Aves., enter on 52nd or 53rd St.). Conspicuous signs proclaim: "All seating available to public and no purchase of food or beverage required." Nonetheless, most of the tables are covered with tablecloths and table settings for an indoor café, and only a half-dozen tables and chairs at each end of the café are in fact available to the public.

875 Third Avenue (between 52nd and 53rd Sts.). Tables and chairs are on the mezzanine and basement floors. Basement seating is surrounded by an array of fast-food establishments: pizza, bagels, muffins, Chinese buffet, deli, salad bar. The basement also connects with the 53rd Street subway station (E, F lines).

The Market at Citicorp Center (Lexington Ave. and 53rd St.). The distinctive skyscraper whose roof slopes at a 45-degree angle has a thriving three-level atrium lined with restaurants, fast-food stores, and shops. Seating is at tables and chairs and along ledges. The center of the space frequently displays art exhibits or hosts free concerts and movies. Citicorp Center also encompasses the stunning Church of St. Peter's, a Lutheran institution that sold the land the building stands upon and now presents Off-Broadway plays and jazz concerts. Washrooms are on the lower level.

IBM Garden Plaza (56th St. and Madison Ave.). This most spectacular of public spaces has been carved out of the ground floors of the green-granite IBM building. Fully grown bamboo trees rise to the heavens, and seasonal flowers fill the air with fresh scents. The south wall and ceiling are all glass. Seating is available at comfortable chairs and marble tables and on benches beside the plantings. Sandwiches and pastries are sold at a charming round kiosk. The New York Botanical Garden operates a gift shop here, and the free **IBM Gallery of Science and Art** is located off the main lobby. Free concerts Wednesday at 12:30. The atrium connects to Trump Tower, which has phones and washrooms on its lower level.

499 Park Avenue (enter on 59th St.). This is one of the smaller public spaces, and the tinted black windows make it easy to miss. The atrium offers hard benches and a little calmness a block away from Bloomingdale's.

Other Attractions   **The Cloisters.** Perched atop a wooded hill near Manhattan's northernmost tip, the Cloisters houses part of the Metropolitan Museum of Art's medieval collection in the style of a medieval monastery. Five cloisters connected by colonnaded walks transport you back 700 years. The view of the Hudson and the New Jersey Palisades enhances the experience. The No. 4 "Cloisters-Fort Tryon Park" bus provides a lengthy but scenic ride up there; catch it along Madison Avenue. You can also take the A subway to the 190th Street station. *Fort Tryon Park, tel. 212/923–3700. Suggested admission: $5 adults, $2.50 senior citizens and students, children free. Open Nov.–Mar., Tues.–Sun. 9:30–5:15 and 9:15–4:45.*

General Theological Seminary (Ninth Ave. and 21st St.). This Episcopal institution opened in 1826 on a full city block contributed by Clement "Twas the night before Christmas" Moore. A secluded Victorian quadrangle enclave of shady trees surrounded by proud ecclesiastical buildings, it is a pleasant refuge from workaday life. A 10-year restoration project is under way.

Roosevelt Island Aerial Tramway (Second Ave. and 60th St.). The high-wire ride to Roosevelt Island, a residential complex in the East River, looks like an oversize Fisher-Price toy. It is a slightly terrifying fun ride that gives you a great view of the city. The one-way fare is $1.25.

Playground at Sixth Avenue and Third Street. Want to see where the NBA hoop stars of tomorrow learn their moves? Check out this patch of Greenwich Village asphalt where city-style basketball is played afternoon and evening in all but the very coldest weather.

Sniffen Court (36th St. between Lexington and Third Aves.). Here is an easy-to-miss cul-de-sac of 19th-century brick stables that were converted into town houses. Equal parts old London and New Orleans, Sniffen Court was for many years the home of the sculptor Malvina Hoffman.

East 90th Street Entrance to Central Park. At this open-air singles hangout for athletes, joggers congregate in the evening to chat, trade training tips, and occasionally run off together.

Paley Park (3 E. 53rd St.). Beside the Museum of Broadcasting, this was the first of New York's "pocket parks" inserted among the high-rise behemoths. A waterfall muffles street noise; a snack bar is open when weather permits.

McGraw-Hill Park (Sixth Ave. between 48th and 49th Sts.). The pocket park behind the McGraw-Hill Building has a stunning walk-through wall of water. Head west on 48th Street to Seventh Avenue, and you'll pass a half-block of stores that sell musical instruments.

Croquet and Lawn Bowling (Central Park, off Central Park West and 69th St.). Clad in spiffy white linen, the croquet players face off on this well-manicured patch of green almost every day of spring and summer.

Conservatory Pond (Central Park, off Fifth Ave. and 74th St.). Radio-controlled model armadas hold miniregattas every Saturday from April through November.

Duane Park (Duane and Hudson Sts.). Surrounded by striking 19th-century masonry buildings, this little triangle in the TriBeCa neighborhood is becoming one of the city's most fashionable addresses. Formerly the center of the dairy industry, horse-drawn egg wagons delivered here until 1954.

Staple Street (west of Hudson St. between Harrison and Duane Sts.). Named for the staple products unloaded here, this narrow alley was where ships in transit through New Amsterdam sold cargo they didn't want to pay duty on. An overhead passage connected sections of the former New York Hospital House of Relief.

Gansevoort Market (around Gansevoort and Greenwich Sts.). Otherwise undistinguished warehouse buildings each morning become the meat market for the city's retailers and restaurants. Racks of carcasses make a fascinating, though not necessarily a very pretty, sight. Action peaks on weekdays 5 AM–9 AM.

Ladies' Mile (Sixth Ave. between 18th and 22nd Sts.). Toward the end of the 19th century, the grand buildings on both sides of the street housed the city's finest department stores, including Simpson-Crawford, O'Neill's, Altman's, and Cammeyers. Trimmed with classical features but now fallen into disrepair, the vast Siegel-Cooper store occupied two-thirds of the block between Fifth and Sixth avenues.

Police Academy Museum (235 E. 20th St., tel. 212/477–9753). Here you can see an emergency procedures display, bizarre weapons, and the latest developments in law-enforcement technology. *235 E. 20th St., tel. 212/477–9753. Admission free. Open weekdays 9–3.*

Shopping

In general, major department stores and other shops are open every day and keep late hours on Thursday. Many of the upper-crust shops along Upper Fifth Avenue and the Madison Mile close on Sunday. Stores in such nightlife areas as SoHo and Columbus Avenue are usually open in the evenings. The bargain shops along Orchard Street on the Lower East Side are closed on Saturday.

Most of the department stores accept their own charge cards and American Express. Macy's and Alexander's accept Visa and MasterCard. Most smaller stores accept major credit cards. Paying by personal check is sometimes permitted but seldom encouraged. Sales tax in New York City is 8¼%.

Shopping Districts

Upper Fifth Avenue. Fifth Avenue from 49th to 58th streets, and 57th Street between Sixth and Third avenues, contains many of the most famous stores in the world, among them Saks Fifth Avenue, Bergdorf Goodman, Henri Bendel, Tiffany & Co., Cartier, and the exclusive shops in Trump Tower.

Herald Square. The area extending from Herald Square (Sixth Ave. and 34th St.) along 34th Street and up Fifth Avenue to 40th Street includes several major stores (Macy's, A&S, Lord & Taylor) and a host of lower-price clothing stores.

Madison Mile. The 20-block span along Madison Avenue between 59th and 79th streets consists of mainly low-rise brownstone buildings housing the exclusive boutiques of American and overseas designers.

SoHo. Along West Broadway between Houston ("How-ston") and Canal Streets you'll find galleries, boutiques, avant-garde housewares shops, and shops that defy categorization.

Columbus Avenue. This shopping area between 66th and 86th streets features far-out European and down-home preppie fashions, some antiques and vintage stores, and outlets for adult toys.

Lower East Side. The intersection of Orchard and Delancey streets is the axis of bargains on women's and men's fashions, children's clothing, shoes, accessories, linens. Closed on Saturday; mobbed on Sunday.

South Street Seaport. This historic district's cobbled streets are home to such nationally known retailers as **Ann Taylor, Laura Ashley, Caswell-Massey,** and **Sharper Image,** plus such one-of-a-kind shops as **Hats in the Belfry** and the **Strand** bookstore.

World Financial Center. This elegant new complex in Battery Park City offers a few dozen upscale shops. Most are open on Sundays, when there are often concerts in the glass-domed Wintergarden.

Department Stores

A&S (33rd St. and Sixth Ave., tel. 212/594–8500). The old Gimbel's, a block south of Macy's, lives again as home to A&S

Plaza, whose 120 shops and restaurants on nine floors are anchored by Abraham & Straus, well established in the outer boroughs.

Alexander's (Lexington Ave. and 58th St., tel. 212/593–0880). New York's least-expensive full-service department store may surprise you. The men's department features high quality attractive imports; women's sections reward sharp-eyed shoppers.

Barneys New York (106 Seventh Ave. at 17th St., tel. 212/929–9000). Famous for its menswear, this retailer has become the place to see what's hot in women's clothing and linens as well. Prices are high, but so are quality and style.

Henri Bendel (10 W. 57th St., tel. 212/247–1100). A specialty store made up of many classy boutiques. Prices are not necessarily stratospheric.

Bergdorf Goodman (754 Fifth Ave. at 57th St., tel. 212/753–7300). A chic and very New York place to shop for women's designer clothes; the men's department is underrated.

Bloomingdale's (59th St. and Lexington Ave., tel. 212/705–2000). The quintessence of New York style—busy, noisy, crowded, and thoroughly up-to-date.

Lord & Taylor (424 Fifth Ave. at 38th St., tel. 212/391–3344). Not flashy but a relatively uncrowded establishment that emphasizes well-made clothing by American designers.

Macy's (34th St. and Broadway, tel. 212/695–4440). The country's largest retail store occupies 10 stories (nine above ground, one below) and an entire block. Always comprehensive and competitive, Macy's has become quite fashionable as well.

Saks Fifth Avenue (611 Fifth Ave. at 50th St., tel. 212/753–4000). The flagship store of a nationwide chain has an outstanding selection of women's and men's designer outfits.

Flea Markets

Annex Antiques and Flea Market (Sixth Ave. and 25th St.; open weekends 9–5) consists mostly of antiques dealers selling furniture, vintage clothing, books, and jewelry. Admission is charged. The **I.S. 44 Flea Market** (Columbus Ave. and 77th St.; open Sun. 10–6) overflows with clothing, jewelry, books, and collectibles.

Specialty Shops

Antiques **American Hurrah** (766 Madison Ave., between 65th and 66th Sts., 3rd floor, tel. 212/535–1930). One of the country's premier dealers in Americana.
Didier Aaron (32 E. 67th St., tel. 212/988–5248). This esteemed gallery specializes in superb 18th- and 19th-century furniture and paintings.
Israel Sack (15 E. 57th St., tel. 212/753–6562). Widely held to be one of the best places to find 18th-century American furniture.
Manhattan Art & Antiques Center (1050 2nd Ave., between 55th and 56th Sts., tel. 212/355–4400). More than 100 dealers stock three floors with antiques from around the world.

Shopping Uptown

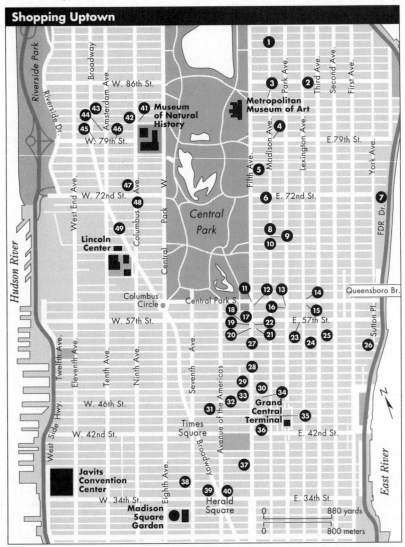

Shopping Downtown

Madison Square Garden

W. 31st St.
E. 31st St.
W. 23rd St.
E. 23rd St.
Madison Square
Gramercy Park
Stuyvesant Square
Union Square
W. 14th St.
E. 14th St.
Greenwich Ave.
Tompkins Square
8th St.
Washington Square
Astor Pl.
E. 4th St.
Bleecker St.
W. Houston St.
E. Houston St.
Spring St.
Delancey St.
Grand St.
Canal St.
Canal St.
Manhattan Bridge
Chambers St.
Brooklyn Bridge
Fulton St.

Eleventh Ave.
Tenth Ave.
Ninth Ave.
Eighth Ave.
Seventh Ave.
Avenue of the Americas (Sixth Ave.)
Fifth Ave.
Park Ave. S.
Lexington Ave.
Third Ave.
Second Ave.
First Ave.
Ave. A
Ave. B
Ave. C
Twelfth Ave.
Greenwich Ave.
W. 4th St.
Christopher St.
Greenwich St.
Washington St.
West St.
Hudson St.
Varick St.
University Pl.
Irving Pl.
4th Ave.
Lafayette St.
Bowery
Orchard St.
W. Broadway
Broadway
Centre St.
Church St.
Park Row
Pearl St.
E. Broadway
West Side Hwy.

East River
FDR Dr.
Hudson River

N

50 51 52 53 54 55 56 57 58 59 60 61 62 63 64 65 66 67 68 69 70 71 72 73 74

0   1 mile
0   1 km

Macy's, **39**
Manhattan Art & Antiques Center, **25**
Michael's Resale, **4**
Ms., Miss, or Mrs., **38**
New York Bound Book Shop, **29**
Newel Art Galleries, **26**
Patricia Field, **58**

Paul Stuart, **35**
Penny Whistle, **1, 41, 67**
Place des Antiquaires, **23**
Polo/Ralph Lauren, **6**
Rizzoli, **18, 62**

Saint Laurie, Ltd., **52**
Saks Fifth Avenue, **30**
Sotheby's, **7**
Strand Book Store, **55**
Syms, **73**
T. Anthony, **16**
Tiffany & Co., **21**
Tower Records, **49, 60**
A la Vieille Russie, **11**

William Doyle Galleries, **2**
Wolfman-Gold & Good Co., **64**
Ylang Ylang, **8, 20**
Zabar's, **45**
Zona, **63**

Newel Art Galleries (425 E. 53rd St., tel. 212/758–1970). This huge, eclectic gallery is a favorite among local designers.
Place des Antiquaires (125 E. 57th St., tel. 212/758–2900). Two elegant subterranean levels of high-ticket antiques and art dealers.

Auctions **Christie's** (502 Park Ave. at 59th St., tel. 212/546–1000). Fine art at suitably fine prices.
Lubin Galleries (30 W. 26th St., tel. 212/924–3777). Reasonably priced furniture and antiques.
Sotheby's (1334 York Ave. at 72nd St., tel. 212/606–7409). Check out the Arcade at this famous house, where well-priced also-rans go on the block.
William Doyle Galleries (175 E. 87th St., tel. 212/427–2730). The charismatic William Doyle is at the helm of a major force on the New York auction scene.

Books **Barnes & Noble** (105 Fifth Ave. at 18th St., tel. 212/807–0099). The world's largest bookstore.
Gotham Book Mart (41 W. 47th St., tel. 212/719–4448). A browser's paradise of books on literature and the performing arts.
Rizzoli (31 W. 57th St., tel. 212/759–2424; and two other locations). This elegant shop specializes in the arts.
Strand Book Store (828 Broadway at 12th St., tel. 212/473–1452). A Greenwich Village institution with a vast selection of new and used books.

Cameras, **47th Street Photo** (67 W. 47th St., 115 W. 45th St., and 116 Nas-
Electronics sau St., tel. 212/398–1410). No hand-holding but great deals.

Food **Zabar's** (2245 Broadway at 80th St., tel. 212/787–2000). From jams, cheeses, spices, and smoked fish to a superb selection of kitchenwares, this store has long been a favorite with New York foodies.

Home Decor **Conran's** (Citicorp Center, Third Ave. and 54th St., tel. 212/371–2225; 2248 Broadway at 81st St., tel. 212/873–9250; and 2 Astor Pl., tel. 212/505–1515). This is the store that furnishes those cunningly chic Manhattan apartments.
D. F. Sanders (386 West Broadway, tel. 212/925–9040; and 952 Madison Ave. at 75th St., tel. 212/879–6161). The slickest of Eurostyle high-tech housewares.
Wolfman-Gold & Good Company (116 Greene St., tel. 212/431–1888; 142 E. 72nd St., tel. 212/288–0404). A trendsetter in tableware.
Zona (97 Greene St., tel. 212/925–6750). Handmade work from the Southwest.

Jewelry Every store is a jewelry shop in the **Diamond District** (47th St. between Fifth and Sixth Aves.). Shop around—and be ready to haggle.
À la Vieille Russie (781 Fifth Ave. at 59th St., tel. 212/752–1727). Fabulous antique pieces from Imperial Russia.
Fortunoff (681 Fifth Ave. at 54th St., tel. 212/758–6660). A flashy discount jeweler.
Tiffany & Co. (727 Fifth Ave. at 57th St., tel. 212/755–8000). A venerable institution with prices ranging from out-of-sight to affordable.
Ylang-Ylang (806 Madison Ave. at 67th St., tel. 212/879–7028; 4 W. 57th St., tel. 212/247–3580; and Herald Center, 34th St. and Broadway, tel. 212/279–1428). Outrageous styles of costume jewelry at more or less affordable prices.

Leather and Luggage   **Crouch & Fitzgerald** (400 Madison Ave. at 48th St., tel. 212/755–5888). An excellent source for good luggage and handbags, in business since 1839.
T. Anthony (480 Park Ave. at 58th St., tel. 212/750–9797). Exquisitely crafted suitcases and totes.

Discount   **Fine & Klein** (119 Orchard St., tel. 212/674–6720). One of Orchard Street's most illustrious discounters.

Menswear   **Brooks Brothers** (346 Madison Ave. at 44th St., tel. 212/682–8800). An institution in American menswear, with conservative styles and quality tailoring.
Paul Stuart (Madison Ave. at 45th St., tel. 212/682–0320). At this celebrated, pricy store, the look is traditional without being stodgy.
Saint Laurie, Ltd. (897 Broadway, between 19th and 20th Sts., tel. 212/473–0100). Traditional suits made on the premises at this family-run establishment sell for less than they would uptown.

Discount   **Syms** (45 Park Pl., tel. 212/791–1199). Designer labels at bargain basement prices. They also have women's clothing.

Records and Tapes   **Bleecker Bob's Golden Oldies** (118 W. 3rd St., tel. 212/475–9677). A Greenwich Village spot with all the good old rock.
Footlight Records (113 E. 12th St., tel. 212/533–1572). New York's largest selection of old musical and movie soundtracks.
Jazz Record Center (135 W. 29th St., 12th floor, tel. 212/594–9880). The city's only jazz-record specialist.
Tower Records (692 Broadway at 4th St., tel. 212/505–1500; 1965 Broadway at 67th St., tel. 212/496–2500). A huge selection, with bargain prices, and videotapes galore.

Souvenirs of New York City   City souvenirs are widely available, but for something more unusual in tie tacks and T-shirts, try the city-run **Citybooks** (61 Chambers St., tel. 212/669–8245), or stop in at the **New York Bound Bookshop** (50 Rockefeller Plaza, tel. 212/245–8503) for old or rare New York books and prints.

Toys   **F.A.O. Schwarz** (Fifth Ave. and 58th St., tel. 212/644–9400). A cathedral of childhood delights—with similarly lofty prices.
The Last Wound-Up (290 Columbus Ave., between 73rd and 74th Sts., tel. 212/787–3388; 889 Broadway at 19th St., tel. 212/529–4197). This place offers a mind-boggling selection of wind-up toys.
Penny Whistle (1283 Madison Ave. at 91st St., tel. 212/369–3868; 448 Columbus Ave. at 81st St., tel. 212/873–9090; 132 Spring St., tel. 212/925–2088). Upper East Side, Upper West Side, and SoHo locations for high-tone selection of European and American novelties.

Women's Clothing   **Canal Jean** (504 Broadway, between Spring and Broome Sts., tel. 212/226–1130). The look in this cavernous store is casual funk.
Charivari (2315 Broadway between 83rd and 84th Sts., tel. 212/873–1424). High style, at prices to match, with branches all over the West Side.
Harriet Love (412 W. Broadway, between Prince and Spring Sts., tel. 212/966–2280). If you're looking for vintage clothing, look no further.
Patricia Field (10 E. Eighth St., tel. 212/254–1699). The place to acquire the "downtown" look.
Polo/Ralph Lauren (867 Madison Ave. at 72nd St., tel. 212/606–

2100). All the essentials for the Ralph Lauren wardrobe can be found in this turn-of-the-century town house.

Discount **Forman's** (82 Orchard St., tel. 212/228–2500). An unexpectedly attractive mainstay of the Lower East Side.
Ms., Miss, or Mrs.—A Division of Ben Farber Inc. (462 Seventh Ave. at 35th St., tel. 212/736–0557). A Garment District establishment with new designer fashions at 40%–60% off.

Discount Shoes Discounters dot Reade Street between Church and West Broadway, including **Anbar** (93 Reade St., tel. 212/227–0253).

Resale Shops To pick up top-of-the-line designs at secondhand prices, try **Encore** (1132 Madison Ave. between 84th and 85th Sts., upstairs, tel. 212/879–2850) and **Michael's Resale** (1041 Madison Ave. between 79th and 80th Sts., tel. 212/737–7273).

Dining

Name any country, name any city or province in any country, and New York will probably have a *selection* of restaurants specializing in the cuisine of that area.

New York restaurants are expensive, yet savvy diners learn how to keep their costs within reason. Since most restaurants post menus in their front windows or lobbies, at least you will have a general idea of what you're getting into. But they don't post drink prices, and these can be high: $2.50 and up for a beer or a glass of wine; $3 and up for mixed drinks (some places charge *considerably* more). To run up your drink bill, many restaurants will ask you to wait in the bar until your table is ready. This occurs even when you have arrived on time and can see plenty of empty tables. While you may have to wait, you don't have to buy a drink.

One way to save money and still experience a top-echelon restaurant is to go there for lunch rather than dinner. It may also be easier to get lunch reservations on short notice.

Be sure to make a reservation when you intend to patronize a first-class restaurant. Be sure to make a reservation for *any* restaurant on a weekend, especially on Saturday night, when the only places that aren't filled up are the places you can live without. To limit no-show diners, many of the most popular restaurants insist that patrons reconfirm on the day of their reservation. Some restaurants will accept a reservation only if you supply a credit card number.

What follows is a selective list of New York restaurants serving a variety of cuisines in all price ranges in neighborhoods throughout Manhattan. As the list can by no means be comprehensive, some of the city's classic restaurants have not been included. In their place, however, you'll find some lesser-known eateries that are frequented by locals. The most highly recommended restaurants in each price category are indicated by a star ★ .

Category	Cost*
Very Expensive	over $60
Expensive	$30–$60

Moderate	$20–$30
Inexpensive	under $20

per person without tax (8¼%), service, or drinks

American–Continental

Very Expensive
★
Four Seasons. Menus and decor shift with the seasons in this class act. The bright and spacious Pool Room has a marble pool, changing floral displays, paintings by Picasso, Miró, and Rauschenberg. It's the rosewood Grill Room, however, where movers and shakers rendezvous for Power Lunches. Both settings have wide open spaces, impeccable service—and very high prices. An imaginative and unpredictable menu puts an Oriental spin on traditional American and French cuisine. Duck au poivre and tuna steak are reliable choices. The Spa Cuisine menu appeals to weight-watchers; lower-priced pre- and post-theater menus (5–6:15 and 10–11:15) please wallet-watchers. *The Seagram Building, 99 E. 52nd St., tel. 212/754–9494. Reservations required, in advance for weekends. Jacket required. AE, CB, DC, MC, V. Closed Sat. lunch and Sun.*

Expensive
The Coach House. Opened in the late 1940s, this genteel West Village dining spot serving traditional American cuisine seems lost in another long-ago, slower paced time period, with its wood-shuttered windows, charming equestrian-themed oil paintings, rose-colored tablecloths, and copper pots. Red banquettes along brick and wood-paneled walls and fresh flowers in ceramic jugs around the room add to the homey, old-fashioned atmosphere. Begin your meal with the mouth-watering cornsticks, cold eggplant Provençale, deviled crab cake, or black bean soup madeira. Meat and fish entrées are well-prepared, especially roast ribs of beef, rack of spring lamb, and fish poached in boullion; vegetables and potatoes, however, receive a more lackluster presentation. The hearty desserts include an excellent apple tart with fresh whipped cream and the Coach House chocolate ice-cream cake. Although you'll probably spend a pleasant evening here, you may find this place disappointing, especially if you're seeking exceptional or more exciting fare. *110 Waverly Pl. (near Ave. of the Americas), tel. 212/777–0303. Reservations required weekends. Jacket required. AE, CB, DC, MC, V. Closed Mon.*

Gotham Bar and Grill. A place with a name like Gotham better be huge, crowded, the quintessence of sophistication—and that's what this is. Owned by a former New York City commissioner, the Gotham Bar and Grill has a postmodern decor with tall columns, high ceilings decked with parachute shades, a pink-marble bar, and a striking pink-green-black color scheme. The menu is eclectic and surprising: Try duck roast carpaccio or roasted quail salad. *12 E. 12th St., tel. 212/620–4020. Reservations advised. Dress: casual. AE, CB, DC, MC, V. No lunch weekends.*

Odeon. A converted Art Deco cafeteria in the TriBeCa neighborhood south of SoHo and north of the Financial District, it's a lively place where everyone can feel at home. The menu mingles French brasserie-style dishes with purely American fare. Steak and *frites* or fettuccine in shrimp are always good choices. *145 West Broadway at Thomas St., tel. 212/233–0507. Reservations advised. Dress: casual. AE, DC, MC, V. No lunch Sat.*

Dining Uptown

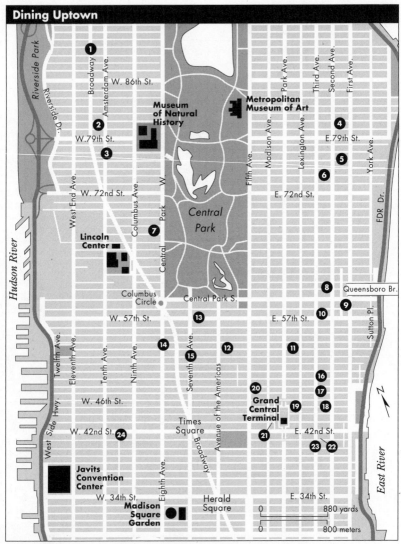

Alcala, **3**
Amsterdam's Bar and Rotisserie, **2**
Arizona 206, **8**
Bangkok Cuisine, **14**
Café des Artistes, **7**
Chez Josephine, **24**
China Grill, **12**
Dawat, **10**
Docks, **1**, **23**
Extra! Extra!, **22**

Four Seasons, **11**
Grand Central Oyster Bar, **21**
Hatsuhana, **19**, **20**
J.G. Melon, **6**
Le Bernardin, **14**
Lutèce, **16**
Pig Heaven, **4**
Rosa Mexicana, **9**

Russian Tea Room, **13**
Smith & Wollensky, **17**
Sparks Steak House, **18**
Vasata, **5**

Dining Downtown

Acme Bar and
Grill, **32**

The Ballroom, **25**

Benito's II, **35**

Coach House, **31**

Gotham Bar &
Grill, **28**

Indochine, **30**

Il Cortile, **36**

Katz's
Delicatessen, **33**

La Colombe D'Or, **26**

Odeon, **39**

Omen, **34**

Silver Palace, **37**

Siracusa , **29**

Tommy Tang's, **40**

Union Square
Café, **27**

Wong Kee, **38**

Expensive **Union Square Café.** A young, monied crowd frequents this site,
★ mere feet from the greenery of renovated Union Square.
Light-wood floors and cream-colored walls splashed with
Chagallesque murals lend a bit of airiness to the awkward layout of the three dining areas. Grilled baby eggplant with
shittake mushrooms or terrine of pheasant with hazelnuts
make excellent starters, but don't overindulge in either the appetizers or the country-style bread—you'll want to leave plenty of room for the main course and later for dessert. Executive
chef Michael Romano uses nouvelle touches in such entrées as
rabbit with garlic-seared artichokes in a white wine sauce and
lemon-pepper duck with honey mustard, but unlike nouvelle,
the portions are generous. Recommendable desserts include
the warm banana tart or chocolate-stuffed soufflé cupcake with
espresso chocolate sauce. *21 E. 16th St., tel. 212/243-4020.
Reservations advised. Dress: casual but neat. AE, DC, MC, V.
Closed Sun.*

Inexpensive **Amsterdam's Bar & Rotisserie.** The name tells most of the story: It's basically a bar on the Upper West Side's Amsterdam
Avenue where most of the food is prepared on an open rotisserie. Low prices for roasted poultry (chicken and duck are tops)
and beef dishes accompanied by a vegetable and an ambitious
house salad elicit standing-room crowds late into the night.
Fish dishes are also good and homemade ketchup graces every
table. *428 Amsterdam Ave. between 80th and 81st Sts., tel. 212/
874-1377. No reservations. Dress: casual. AE, CB, DC, MC,
V.*

J.G. Melon. This is the ideal place for a relaxing and casual
meal. A real "neighborhood" pub, with locations on both the
East and West sides, Melon's consistently makes people feel at
home. Decorated with countless paintings, and prints of (what
else?) melons, the bar/restaurant is a good spot in which to
meet people or have a laid-back American meal. The burgers
and club sandwiches are always a good choice, accompanied by
crispy cottage fries. *1291 3rd Ave. (at 74th St.), tel. 212/744-
0585; 340 Amsterdam Ave., tel. 212/877-2220. No reservations. Dress: casual. No credit cards.*

Cajun

Moderate **Acme Bar and Grill.** From the outside, you might mistake this
restaurant for a warehouse and never discover the narrow,
noisy dining area opening up to a bar behind its large metal
doors. This is not the place for delicate dining—from its mismatched chairs with ripped upholstery and wood tables bearing vintage hot-sauce ads to its ample portions of down-home
southern cooking, there's nothing pretentious about a meal
here. The kitchen serves up plenty of seafood, including plump
fried oysters and farm-raised catfish, but it also produces delicious corn fritters, a wonderful Cajun peanut soup, Cajun
chicken, and an incredibly rich chocolate mud pie as part of its
repertoire. The dishes arriving at your table are not very
spicy, but the bottles of hot sauces lining the exposed-brick
walls should serve to satisfy the most avid heat enthusiast. *9
Great Jones St. (near Broadway), tel. 212/420-1934. No reservations. Dress: casual. No credit cards.*

Chinese

Note: Chinese food is a staple of the New York diet. Most restaurants serve interchangeable menus that combine dishes from various areas of China and use a star or red lettering to indicate spicy dishes. With few exceptions the food is good and truly inexpensive (less than $10 per person). Chinese restaurants typically offer low-priced lunch specials—soup, egg roll, main dish, tea—for between $3.50 and $5. Restaurants listed here offer something more than the typical neighborhood Chinese place. You can't go wrong, either, with any busy restaurant in Chinatown—the area bordered by Canal Street on the north, and the Bowery on the east.

Pig Heaven. This popular Upper East Side restaurant is gimmicky to the max. A cutout pig greets you with the menu; wallboards are painted a shocking pig pink; tea is served in pigsnout mugs. Yet the food is serious. Pork dominates the menu, with about 20 nightly specials available. Try Cantonese-style suckling pig or minced pork sautéed with corn, peppers, and pine nuts. Patience may be called for when big crowds slow up the mostly non-Oriental service staff. *1540 Second Ave. at 80th St., tel. 212/744-4333. Reservations required. Dress: casual. AE, DC.*

Inexpensive **Silver Palace.** The draw here on weekends is dim sum, a parade of dishes wheeled around the banquet-size second-floor dining room on carts that stop at each table for diners to sample from at random. The steamed dumplings contain tasty fillings (the shrimp is particularly good), and the fried dumplings are light and delicately flavored. From the exotic (curried squid) to the familiar (barbecued beef on a stick), there's something here to please everybody. Portions are small, but you'll fill up fast. The tables are large, and no chair goes unused for long, so you'll probably join a meal that's already in progress. *50–52 Bowery, tel. 212/964-1204. Reservations not accepted for dim sum. Dress: casual. AE, DC, MC, V (no cards accepted before 6 PM). Dim sum served weekends 8–4 only.*

Wong Kee Restaurant. Diners gather behind the columned, brushed metal facade for the renowned barbecued pork, or the spiced beef chow fun (wide rice noodles), or maybe the sweet and pungent chicken (a refinement of sweet-and-sour), all highlights on this menu. Wong Kee's hallmark is the reliability of its low-priced, high-quality Cantonese fare, made with fresh ingredients and served in ample portions. Service is swift, and expect a short wait for a table on weekends. Take-out is also available, and nearly irresistible. *113 Mott St. (north of Canal St.), tel. 212/966-1160. No reservations. Dress: casual. BYOB. No credit cards.*

Czechoslovakian

Moderate **Vašata.** A cozy Czech restaurant that has been serving hearty food since 1952. Vašata is a survivor in a neighborhood once full of East European places. Except for a few touches of American '50s decor, this place has the look of a homey Old World wine cellar—lanterns and colorful ceramic dishes decorate pale-yellow brick walls. It's still very popular with émigrés, who come for the goulash, schnitzel, roast duck, dumplings, and genuine Pilsner Urquell beer. You'll feel pleasantly stuffed by the end of the meal, but whatever you do, don't leave without sampling the *palačinky*, delicate dessert crepes with fruit or chocolate filling, doused in orange liqueur and flambéed at the table. *339 E. 75th St. (near 1st Ave.), tel. 212/988–7166. Reservations advised. Dress: casual. AE, CB, DC, MC, V. No lunch Tues.–Sat. Closed Mon.*

Deli

Inexpensive **Katz's Delicatessen.** This Kosher-style New York delicatessen in the heart of the Lower East Side can get a bit chaotic at times. There is a method to the madness, however: grab a ticket when you enter, give it to the counterman as you shout your order, and hold on to it to pay the bill when you leave. You might recognize your surroundings—walls and ceilings hung with war memorabilia and hanging salamis—from the film *When Harry Met Sally*. The noise level can be a bit much, but so are the portions, so come hungry. Classics from knishes, pastrami, and brisket to the neighborhood's famous pickles—are all here, and if you like corned beef, it's a must. *205 E. Houston St. (near Orchard St.), tel. 212/254–2246. No reservations. Dress: casual. AE ($50 minimum).*

French

Very Expensive ★ **Lutèce.** There isn't anyone who doesn't adore Lutèce, a temple of classic French gastronomy for over 25 years. The intimate and understated midtown town house has seating around an enclosed garden or in two more formal upstairs chambers. The regular menu is varied and specials change daily; grilled trout and pheasant are always fine choices. The impeccable service is invariably attentive and helpful, to first-time and hundredth-time diners alike. *249 E. 50th St., tel. 212/752–2225. Reservations required 2 weeks or more in advance. Jacket and tie required. AE, CB, DC, MC, V. No lunch Sat.; closed Sun., Mon., and Aug.*

Expensive **Café des Artistes.** A romantic and extremely popular Lincoln Center area institution. Murals of nudes cavorting in a sylvan glade and sparkling mirrors transport you far from the madding Manhattan crowd. Food is country French with *confit* of duck and lamb with *flageolet* beans recommended specialties. The place crowds up with West Side locals and out-of-towners. *1 W. 67th St. at Central Park West, tel. 212/877–3500. Reservations required. Jacket required at dinner. AE, CB, DC, MC, V.*

Moderate **Chez Josephine.** The reincarnation of a former massage parlor on West 42nd Street into a 1920s era bistro is Jean-Claude Baker's tribute to his second mother, Josephine Baker. Mr. Baker is in the process of writing a biography of Josephine, so his knowledge of the age is extensive. After installing the long, narrow space with what he considers to be the most important element—a piano and singer—he has added red-velvet drapes, ceiling fans, and murals and posters of Ms. Baker. Though he says "I'm no soup seller," Mr. Baker does a creditable job in the food department also. Entrées such as rack of lamb marinated in juniper berries on a bed of *pomme purée* and carrots, and veal scaloppine with warm potato salad and diced tomatoes, not to mention the thick accent of the waitress, give the impression of dining in a somewhat funky Montmarte bistro. And the West 42nd Street location appeals to the pre- and posttheater crowd.

414 W. 42nd St. (west of Ninth Ave.), tel. 212/594–1925. Reservations advised. Dress: casual. AE, MC, V. Closed Sun.

★ **La Colombe D'Or.** Pots of geraniums by the front door, lace curtains at the windows, and interior walls of rough white plaster and exposed brick set a cozy bistro atmosphere, carried out by friendly, unfawning service. The food, however, goes well beyond standard bistro fare, with creative combinations such as sea scallops and yellow tomatoes with tarragon, grilled salmon with chanterelle mushrooms and lettuce, or a surprisingly succulent calves' liver with carrots and grilled sweet onions. Each plate is arranged as beautifully as a still life. The wine list is long, decidedly French, and well priced. *134 E. 26th St. (near Lexington Ave.), tel. 212/689–0666. Reservations required. Dress: casual. AE, DC, MC, V. Closed Sun.*

Indian

Moderate **Dawat.** A sophisticated note is struck at once by softly lit, simple decor, colored in peach and aqua and accented by gleaming copper serving dishes. Classic Indian food, following the recipes of actress-author Madhur Jaffrey, carries out the promise with savory and often spicy dishes, including several vegetarian specialties and robust breads. Try the tandoori mixed grill, baked in its clay oven, the *rogan josh* (baby goat in cardamom sauce), or the *farasvi bhaji* (green beans in coconut). Lunch specials are an excellent value. *210 E. 58th St. (near 3rd Ave.), tel. 212/355–7555. Reservations advised. Dress: casual. AE, CD, DC, MC, V.*

Italian

Moderate–Expensive
★ **Il Cortile.** This classy establishment is one of the brightest spots in the sea of restaurants for which Little Italy is famous. Dark colors and exposed brick set a warm, intimate tone in the front dining room (try for a table by the window), while the back rooms of the restaurant are brightened by a skylight and an abundance of greenery. An efficient, personable staff is happy to assist you with the menu, printed in Italian. Dishes are well prepared and presented—try the simple *Scaloppine di Vitello al Cognac* (tender slices of veal smothered in mushrooms and a cognac gravy) or any of the fresh seafood dishes. Desserts here do not live up to the standard set by the earlier courses, and diners would do better to venture into one of the neighborhood's numerous pastry shops for dessert and espresso. *125 Mulberry St. (near Hester St.), tel. 212/226–6060. Reservations advised. Dress: casual. AE, CB, DC, MC, V.*

Moderate **Siracusa.** A rather eclectic decor—clean-lined Art Deco combined with Italian folk art—sets the tone for this charming Italian eatery, where country-style Sicilian recipes are geared toward sophisticated palates. The entrées consist of a variety of fresh pastas with different sauces; an excellent angel-hair pasta with capers, anchovies, olives, and sun-dried tomatoes in oil and garlic is among the choices. The desserts are what really stand out here, however; if you don't feel like coming for a meal, stop by the *gelateria* next door and enjoy such flavors as ricotta, cappuccino, or chocolate—all made on the premises and wonderfully creamy. *65 4th Ave. (near 10th St.), tel. 212/254–1940. Reservations advised. Dress: casual. AE. Closed Sun.*

Inexpensive **Benito's II.** A window display of figurines and a photographic mural of the Italian coast welcome you into this one-room dining spot in the heart of Little Italy. Adding to the feel of intimacy are several personable waiters who will answer all your questions about the menu and converse in Italian if you wish. They arrange for eclectic appetizers of hot and cold antipasto, including vegetables with fresh garlic, baked clams, and superb breaded squares of mozzarella cheese. For the most part, the cuisine is Old World Italian, but several selections may surprise you; those with an adventurous palate can order the octopus polipo, prepared in a spicy tomato sauce with plenty of garlic. An itinerant and animated guitar player occassionally makes an appearance, serenading tables with Italian ballads. *163 Mulberry St. (near Grand St.), tel. 212/226–9012. Reservations advised. Dress: casual. No credit cards.*

Japanese

Expensive **Hatsuhana.** The authenticity of Hatsuhana's two bright and cheerful Midtown locations is verified by conspicuous contingents of visiting Japanese businessmen. They come for ultrafresh sushi and sashimi, which are best enjoyed close up at the sushi bar. Other recommended items include bite-size Japanese fried crabs, ungreasy Japanese fried chicken, and any of the grilled fish teriyaki. *17 E. 48th St., tel. 212/355–3345; 237 Park Ave. at 46th St., tel. 212/661–3400. Reservations required. Jacket and tie advised. AE, MC, V. Closed weekends.*

Moderate **Omen.** Old brick, hardwood floors, timber ceilings, and Oriental lanterns give this SoHo ex-store the relaxing ambience of a Japanese country inn. *Omen* is the name of an opening dish almost everybody orders. It's a dark hot broth served with halfcooked exotic vegetables, sesame seeds, and noodles that you add to the soup. Other favorites include a boned chicken dish called *sansho*, scallops and blanched spinach, and avocado with shrimp in miso sauce. *113 Thompson St. between Spring and Prince Sts., tel. 212/925–8923. Reservations advised. Dress: casual. AE, DC. Closed Mon.*

Mexican

Expensive **Arizona 206.** The ambience of the American Southwest is captured a block away from Bloomingdale's: stark white plaster walls, wood-burning fireplace, raw timber trimming, and piped-in Willie Nelson records. Spicy New Wave Mexican cuisine stresses chili peppers, and the brief menu (by chef Marilyn Frobuchino) offers nothing ordinary, only the likes of green chili paella for two; grilled salmon steak with *poblano* corn pudding; and pistachio-crusted tenderloin of rabbit with *mole poblano* sauce. Desserts are just as unusual, and the service staff is downright perky. *206 E. 60th St., tel. 212/838–0440. Reservations advised. Dress: casual. AE, CB, DC, MC, V. No lunch Sun.*

Moderate **★** **Rosa Mexicano.** This is a crowded midtown hangout for young professionals. Serious dining takes place amid subdued pink stucco walls and lush horticulture. Two standard Mexican items are exceptional here: chunky *guacamole* prepared at your table and margaritas blended with pomegranate. Grilled versions of shell steak, chicken, and snapper; pork *carnitas;* and skinned breast of duck are other noncombustible house specialties. *1063 First Ave., tel. 212/753-7407. Reservations advised. Dress: casual. AE, CB, DC, MC, V.*

Mixed Menu

Moderate **China Grill.** This stark restaurant, located in the CBS building, has endured in atmosphere and quality since its opening in 1987. The sleek room is orange and slate gray with huge kite-like lights on the 40-foot ceiling, and although spacious, it tends to get noisy quickly. Described as being French-American with oriental accents, the menu is an assortment of grilled dishes, with an emphasis on fish. Start the meal with the Peking duck salad, which is minced to perfection and served in a tangerine and orange sauce. The entrées are served on over-sized plates with portions to match. The grilled dry aged Szechuan beef with shredded potatoes and the grilled golden squab make a nice combination. On the side, and not to be missed is the crispy spinach, which literally melts in your mouth. To top off the meal indulge in the dark and white chocolate in a bed of freshly whipped cream and fresh fruit—sure to delight everyone at the table. *60 W. 53rd St. (off 6th Ave.) tel. 212/333-7788. Reservations advised. Jacket advised. AE, CB, DC, MC, V. Closed lunch Sat. and Sun.*

Inexpensive **Extra! Extra!** Black and white walls peppered with giant newsprint seem appropriate for this fun spot, located in the Daily News building. Life-size comic strip cutouts look on as diners feast on pasta (in full or half portions), salads, sandwiches, pizzas, and a full range of Tex-Mex dishes, all served with creative flair. The grilled vegetable appetizer includes such unusual choices as eggplant and leeks, while the beef fajitas are served with healthy portions of meat and fillings with warm fresh-flour tortillas. It's an especially lively locale for lunch. Friday nights feature a comedy improv group. *767 2nd Ave. (at 41st St.), tel. 212/490-2900. Reservations advised. Dress: casual. AE, CB, DC, MC, V. Closed Sun. Cover charge Fri. evenings for comedy group.*

Russian

Expensive **Russian Tea Room.** Russian food is probably the last reason to eat here. Located beside Carnegie Hall, the Russian Tea Room is a major New York scene loaded with media people, their agents, and kindred would-be deal cutters. (Dustin Hoffman lunched here with his agent in *Tootsie.*) It's also filled with local commoners and out-of-towners, some of whom get exiled to the celebrityless second-floor—"Siberia." Best menu choices are hot or cold borscht, *karsky shashlik* (lamb with kidneys), and a selection of red and black caviars rolled into tender *blini* (pancakes). *150 W. 57th St., tel. 212/265-0947. Reservations advised. Jacket required at dinner. AE, CB, DC, MC, V.*

Seafood

Very Expensive **Le Bernardin.** The New York branch of an illustrious Paris seafood establishment occupies the ground floor of the midtown
★ Equitable Assurance Tower; the elegant corporate decor was reportedly inspired by the Equitable boardroom. The all-seafood menu teems with rare treasures. For starters, try black bass flecked with coriander or sea urchins baked in their

shell. Go on to lobster in pasta or any of the fresh, artfully arranged fillets. *155 W. 51st St., tel. 212/489–1515. Reservations required. Jacket and tie required. AE, CB, DC, MC, V. Closed Sun.*

Moderate–Expensive **Docks.** The fresh fish in this natty Upper West Side bistro serves as a delicious reminder that New York is, after all, a seaport. Classy and unpretentious, Docks has earned a loyal clientele at both this and its east side location (633 Third Ave. at 40th St.). The crab cakes here are the best in town, and all frying is done with a light touch, with seasonings that enhance—not overpower—the fish's flavor. Whether grilled or broiled, the salmon and tuna dishes are excellent, and the shellfish is consistently pleasing. There is an extensive selection of beers, and the wine list is tailored to complement seafood. Try to leave room for the chocolate mud cake or the Key lime pie. *2427 Broadway (at 90th St.), tel. 212/724–5588. Reservations necessary. Dress: casual. AE, DC, MC, V.*

Grand Central Oyster Bar. Down in the catacombs beneath Grand Central Terminal, the Oyster Bar has a reputation for serving ultrafresh seafood. The vast main room has a vaulted tile ceiling, and lots of noise and tumult. Solos may prefer to sit at the wide white counter. By contrast, the wood-paneled Saloon feels downright clubby. More than a dozen varieties of oysters may be on hand. Pan-roasted shellfish, a kind of stew, is a house specialty. Broiled fillets change with the daily catch. *Lower level Grand Central Terminal, 42nd St. and Vanderbilt Ave., tel. 212/490–6650. Reservations advised, required for lunch. Dress: casual. AE, CB, DC, MC, V. Closed Sat. and Sun.*

Spanish

Moderate–Expensive **The Ballroom.** Located in Chelsea a few blocks from Penn Station, this is the place to sample tapas, Spanish appetizers that quickly accumulate into a full meal. Some like their tapas hot—grilled eggplant, stuffed squid, baked fennel, sauteed shiitake mushrooms, baby lamb chops. Others prefer them cold—octopus in oil, bay scallops, *chorizos* (sausage) with peppers, chicken with tomato. The spacious, palmy setting focuses on a huge mural of local painters and art dealers. A popular cabaret theater occupies a separate room. *253 W. 28th St., tel. 212/244–3005. Reservations advised. Dress: casual. AE, CB, DC, MC, V. Closed Mon. No dinner Sun.*

Moderate **Alcala.** Visit this Spanish restaurant and tapas bar for the tranquil atmosphere and the varied menu. The large, exposed brick-walled room gives diners an opportunity to relax over a wide variety of seafood, fish, chicken, and beef dishes. Appetizers such as fried calamari and cream of cauliflower soup far surpass the entrées. Try the cinnamon ice cream for dessert. *349 Amsterdam Ave. (near 76th St.), tel. 212/769–9600. Reservations advised. Dress: casual. AE, CB, DC, MC, V.*

Steaks

Expensive **Smith & Wollensky.** This midtown steak house opened only 12 years ago, but plank floors, bent-wood chairs, and walls decked with classic sporting prints make it look like it's been here forever. Steak is the forte of this establishment, big blackened sirloins and filets mignon with a pepper sauce. Huge lobsters, veal chops, and terrific onion rings round out the menu. *201 E. 49th St., tel. 212/753–1530. Reservations advised. Jacket advised. AE, CB, DC, MC, V.*

Sparks Steak House. Steaks and male camaraderie are the specialties of this midtown restaurant. The tender prime sirloin is the most popular selection. Filets are unusually juicy and flavorful; lobsters cruise the three- to five-pound range. Although most of the ex-athlete-size customers seem to go for beer or whiskey, Sparks boasts an award-winning wine list. *210 E. 46th St., tel. 212/687–4855. Reservations required. Jacket and tie advised. AE, CB, DC, MC, V. Closed Sun.*

Thai

Moderate   **Tommy Tang.** This exuberant TriBeCa Thai restaurant, set in a
★   bright, high-ceilinged long room with Art Deco-ish decor of turquoise and beige, has mellowed a bit since it opened in 1986, but all for the better—the black tables covered with white linen now have more space between them, and the background music is no longer loud. Yet the high spirits remain, helped enormously by the delightfully efficient, white-smocked staff. The place draws a mixed crowd of professionals, artists, and local residents who continue to return for the consistently fine food—a pleasure to behold and prepared with delicate or zesty seasonings, depending on your tastes; if possible, come with a group so you can sample a range of dishes on the imaginative menu. For starters, try the tuna spring roll or "naked" shrimp, grilled and spiced with roasted curry paste, mint, and lime juice. Entrées include the luscious Malaysian clams, sautéed with Thai basil and garlic; the ever-popular boneless Original Tommy Duck with fresh vegetables; and dependable noodle dishes. Desserts, such as Key lime cheesecake, can be refreshingly adventurous. *323 Greenwich St. (near Reade St.), tel. 212/334–9190. Reservations advised. Dress: casual chic. AE, CB, DC, MC, V. Closed Sat. lunch and Sun.*

Inexpensive   **Bangkok Cuisine.** New York's oldest Thai restaurant operates out of an Orientalized storefront just north of the Theater District. Some of the spicy specialties include *tod mun pla* (deep-fried fish patties dipped in a sweet sauce), *pad thai* (an exciting noodle dish), and whole fish dinners. A small knife indicates superhot dishes—and here that warning means something. *885 Eighth Ave. at 53rd St., tel. 212/581–6370. Reservations advised. Dress: casual. AE, CB, MC, V. No lunch Sun.*

Vietnamese

Expensive   **Indochine.** On the ground floor of landmark East Village town houses, the scene here mingles downtown artists with displaced French colonialists. The space is large and airy, decorated with palm leaves and tropical murals. The menu offers exotically spiced Vietnamese and Cambodian specialties. *Rouleau de printemps* (spring roll) is the standard appetizer; stuffed boneless chicken wings or steamed fish in coconut milk make excellent entrees. *430 Lafayette St. between Astor Pl. and E. 4th St., tel. 212/505–5111. Reservations advised. Dress: casual. AE, DC, MC, V. No lunch.*

Lodging

by Jane Hershey

A New York-based freelance writer whose work has appeared in Good Housekeeping, US, *and* Elle, *Jane Hershey is a contributing travel editor for* Hollywood *magazine, and a long-time contributor to various Fodor's guides.*

If any single element of your trip to New York City is going to cost you a lot of money, it'll be your hotel bill. Real estate is at a premium here, and labor costs are high, so hoteliers start out with a lot of expenses to cover. And there are enough well-heeled visitors to support competition at the premium end of the spectrum, which is where the profits are. Considering the healthy occupancy rate, market forces are not likely to drive current prices down. We have noted a few budget properties, but on the sliding scale of Manhattan prices even our "Inexpensive" category includes hotels that run as high as $160 for one night's stay in a double room.

Once you've accepted that you must pay the going price, though, you'll have plenty of choices. In general, Manhattan hotels don't measure up to those in other U.S. cities in terms of room size, parking, or outside landscaping. But, this being a sophisticated city, New York hotels usually compensate with fastidious service, sprucely maintained properties, and restaurants that hold their own in a city of very knowledgeable diners.

Basic rules of decorum and dress are observed at the better hotels. With few exceptions, jackets (and frequently ties) are required in formal dining and bar areas after 5 or 6 PM. Bare feet or beach sandals are not allowed, and an overall sloppy appearance won't encourage good service.

Most Manhattan hotels are in the midtown area, so we have categorized them by price range rather than location. Exact prices could be misleading: Properties change their so-called "rack rates" seasonally, and most hotels offer weekend packages that include such tempting extras as complimentary meals, drinks, or tickets to events. Your travel agent may have brochures about such packages; also look for advertisements in travel magazines or the Sunday travel sections of major newspapers such as the *New York Times,* the *Washington Post,* or the *Los Angeles Times.*

Price categories are as follows:

Category	Cost*
Very Expensive	over $260
Expensive	$200–$260
Moderate	$160–$200
Inexpensive	under $160

*All prices are for an above-standard double room, excluding 13¼% city and state sales tax and $2 occupancy tax. (Note: At press time, the city was planning to raise hotel taxes by an additional 5%.)

Highly recommended lodgings in each price category are indicated by a star ★. Though not *every* acceptable hotel has been included, enough ground has been covered to help you find a good match.

Aberdeen, **27**

Algonquin, **22**

Beekman Tower, **14**

Best Western
Woodward, **10**

Carlyle, **3**

Chatwal Inn, **21**

Chatwal Inn on
Park, **28**

Days Inn, **18**

Dumont Plaza, **25**

Hotel Edison, **19**

Hotel Empire, **6**

Hotel Elysée, **11**

Mark, **2**

N.Y. Int'l Youth
Hostel, **1**

Pierre, **7**

The Plaza, **8**

Quality Inn, **20**

Ramada Inn, **17**

Roger Smith
Winthrop, **16**

Royalton, **23**

Shelburne, **24**

Sloane House
YMCA, **26**

Southgate Tower, **29**

Summit, **12**

Surrey Hotel, **4**

Vanderbilt YMCA, **15**

Waldorf-Astoria, **13**

West Side YMCA, **5**

Wyndham, **9**

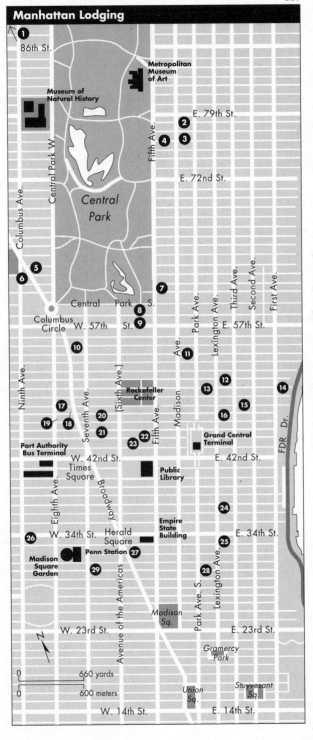

Manhattan Lodging

Very Expensive

The Carlyle. Located in one of the city's finest residential areas, this beautifully appointed traditional hotel is considered one of New York's finest. The mood is English manor house; larger rooms and suites, many of them decorated by the famous interior designer Mark Hampton, have terraces, pantries, and antique furnishings. Baths, though more subdued than others in town, are marbled and chock-full of de rigueur amenities such as hair dryers, fine toiletries, and makeup mirrors. Most visitors have heard about the famous Café Carlyle, where performers such as Bobby Short and George Shearing entertain throughout the year. But the hotel also contains the charming Bemelman's Bar, with whimsical animal murals on the walls and live piano music at night, and the formal Carlyle Restaurant, with French cuisine and old-fashioned courtly service. *35 E. 76th St. (at Madison Ave.), 10021, tel. 212/744-1600. 185 rooms. Facilities: restaurant, café, bar, lounge, fitness center, VCRs and stereos, kitchenettes and pantries in larger units, meeting rooms. AE, CB, DC, MC, V.*

★ **The Pierre.** Ever since its opening at the height of the Depression, the Pierre has symbolized dignified elegance. One might expect haughtiness along with the creamy, oriental-carpeted halls and bright chandeliers, but you won't find that here: The staff has a sense of fun about working in these posh surroundings. Rooms, most of which have been recently refurbished, are traditionally decorated in soft florals with quilted bedspreads. Bathrooms have recently been upgraded and are generously stocked with Four Seasons' amenities. Café Pierre, under the direction of executive chef Franz Klampfer, can hold its own against many of the city's best spots; the Bar features low-key jazz piano in the evenings, and formal afternoon tea is served under the blue cherubim-filled dome of the Rotunda. *5th Ave. at 61st St., 10021, tel. 212/838-8000 or 800/332-3442. 204 rooms. Facilities: restaurant, bar, tearoom, meeting rooms, manned elevators, packing service upon request, hand-laundry service. AE, CB, DC, MC, V.*

The Plaza. When real-estate developer and casino operator Donald Trump purchased this National Historic Landmark in 1988, locals shuddered a bit but so far, misgivings have been unfounded. Although this former haunt of F. Scott Fitzgerald, George M. Cohan, Frank Lloyd Wright, and the Beatles is going through growing pains, it's ready to receive a relatively demanding public. New color schemes are in burgundy or teal blue; fresh, floral-patterned quilted spreads grace the large beds. Furnishings, though still "hotel-like" in most units, are of high quality. Bathrooms, even those not yet fully redone, have fluffy new towels and Chanel toiletries. One real advantage here is the size of guest rooms—only a handful of other classic properties can offer similar spaciousness in nearly all accommodations. Food-and-beverage service has made major strides, and current executive chef Kerry Simon (formerly of Lafayette and Lutèce) will certainly earn plaudits here. The last word was that Trader Vic's bar—renowned for its elaborate exotic drinks—will stay open, although the space formerly occupied by its restaurant might be converted into a health club. *5th Ave. at 59th St., 10019, tel. 212/759-3000 or 800/228-3000. 807 rooms. Facilities: 2 restaurants, 2 bars, café, art gallery,* *handicapped-guest rooms, meeting rooms, packing service upon request, large concierge staff. AE, CB, DC, MC, V.*

Expensive

The Mark. Just one block north of the Carlyle (*see* Very Expensive, above), the former Madison Avenue Hotel has recently been completely redone by its new owner, Rafael Hotels. Even the least expensive rooms have high-quality TVs and VCRs, and its bathrooms feature Art Deco tiles or marble, deep tubs, *and* separate stall showers. Most rooms have pantries, too. Color schemes are warm to reflect the neoclassical Italian motif. There is an elegant restaurant and lounge called Mark's, which features the cuisine of chef Philippe Boulot. The staff seems committed and professional. *25 E. 77th St., 10021, tel. 212/744–4300 or 800/THE–MARK. 185 rooms. Facilities: restaurant, café, lounge, meeting rooms, VIP suites with terraces. AE, CB, DC, MC, V.*

The Royalton. Former Studio 54 disco kings Ian Schrager and the late Steve Rubell, in their quest for a second career as New York hotel moguls, completely rehabilitated this once-shabby property directly across from the Algonquin (*see* Moderate, below). The Royalton, with its witty "art moderne" design by French decorator Philippe Starck, has a plush but slightly spooky atmosphere: The halls are narrow and dark, as are some of the strangely shaped rooms. Still, the beds and other furnishings are quite comfy, and the bathrooms are decidedly fun —they all have either oversize slate shower stalls or giant circular tubs (a few have both). Toiletries are elegant, and so is the service. The restaurant, Restaurant 44, has finally been granted a liquor license, and it's worth noting that this is the only place on hotel premises where guests can purchase liquor. *44 W. 44th St., 10036, tel. 212/869–4400 or 800/635–9013. 205 rooms. Facilities: restaurant with bar, meeting rooms, game and library areas, VCRs, stereos. AE, CB, DC, MC, V.*

The Waldorf-Astoria. Along with the Plaza (*see* Very Expensive, above), this art deco masterpiece personifies New York at its most lavish and powerful. Hilton, its owner, has spent a fortune on refurbishing both public areas and guest rooms. Original murals and mosaics, elaborate plaster ornamentation, fine old-wood walls and doors—all look fresh and new. In the guest rooms, some of which start at the low end of this category, there are new bedspreads, carpets, and other signs of upgrading. Bathrooms throughout are old but beautifully kept up and rather spacious by today's standards. There has been a move to modernize the menu at Peacock Alley, where Waldorf salad first made news. Famous guest chefs are adding innovative touches, some of which fortunately stick. Service in the dining areas, however, can be pokey and rude, especially outside of regular meal times. The hotel's richly tinted, hushed lobby serves as an interior centerpoint of city life; it's nice to see the rest of the place looking proud, too. *301 Park Ave., 10022, tel. 212/355–3000 or 800/HILTONS. 1,692 rooms. Facilities: 3 restaurants, coffee shop, tearoom, lounge, ballroom, meeting rooms. AE, CB, DC, MC, V.*

Moderate

The Algonquin. While this landmark property's English-drawing-room atmosphere and burnished-wood lobby are being kept intact, its working parts (the plumbing, for instance) are being improved under new Japanese owners. Management is also redecorating, restoring the old mahogany doors and trim, improving the telephone service, and creating a conference and business area. This much-beloved hotel, where the Round Table group of writers and wits once met for lunch, still shelters many a celebrity, particularly literary types visiting nearby publishing houses or the *New Yorker* magazine offices across the street. Bathrooms and sleeping quarters retain Victorian-style fixtures and furnishings, only now there are larger, firmer beds, modern TVs, VCRs (upon request), computerized phones, and Caswell-Massey toiletries. Personal service, especially for repeat customers, continues to be excellent. *59 W. 44th St., 10036, tel. 212/840–6800 or 800/548–0345. 165 rooms. Facilities: restaurant, 2 lounges, meeting rooms, complimentary parking on weekends, business center. AE, CB, DC, MC, V.*

Hotel Elysée. This relatively small hotel, on a prime block between Madison and Park avenues, has a rather offbeat atmosphere with a 1950s feel. Rooms have a slightly lived-in charm; all of them have names instead of numbers. Bathrooms are currently being renovated. Among the surprising amenities for the price are VCRs. The friendly desk staff is happy to help with standard requests. *60 E. 54th St., 10022, tel. 212/753–1066. 110 rooms. Facilities: restaurant, lounge, art gallery, concierge. AE, CB, DC, MC, V.*

Loews Summit, *see* the Summit, below.

★ **Manhattan Suites East.** Here's a group of good-value properties for the traveler who likes to combine full hotel service with independent pied-à-terre living. These nine midtown hotels have different characters and varying prices, though all fall within the Moderate category. The four best are the **Beekman Tower** (3 Mitchell Pl.), near the United Nations and on the edge of a trendy East Side residential area; the **Dumont Plaza** (150 E. 34th St.), especially convenient for convention goers with its location on a direct bus line to the Javits Center; the **Surrey Hotel** (20 E. 76th St.), in the neighborhood of Madison Avenue art galleries and designer boutiques; and the **Southgate Tower** (371 7th Ave.), the most attractive and secure place to sleep within close range of Madison Square Garden and Penn Station. Except for the modern style at the Dumont, all have traditional guest-room decor; the Surrey's rooms border on the truly elegant. Most accommodations have pantries, and larger units have dining areas with full-size tables. The Beekman, Surrey, Shelburne, and Dumont Plaza have restaurants and room service. The Dumont, Southgate, and Shelburne have on-premises fitness centers. Other hotels in this group tend to be more residential, except for the full-service **Shelburne** (303 Lexington Ave.); many top corporations use them as interim lodgings for newly relocated executives. The older hotels in the group do have some disappointing rooms, but overall these properties are outstanding for the price, considering their convenience, location, and space. Their weekend package rates are hard to beat. *Sales office, 505 E. 75th St., 10001, tel. 212/772–2900 or 800/ME–SUITE. AE, CB, DC, MC, V.*

★ **The Roger Smith Winthrop.** Don't be put off by the dusty, faded lobby—the hotel is in the process of a gradual redecoration, and its public areas are being completely overhauled. The guest rooms upstairs are clean, well decorated, and spacious, and special units on the ninth floor have small but luxurious marble baths with Jacuzzis. All rooms have pantries, and there's a complimentary Continental breakfast on weekends. A dingy coffee shop downstairs was recently turned into a full restaurant and a tea lounge. *501 Lexington Ave., 10017, tel. 212/755–1400 or 800/241–3848. 200 rooms. Facilities: restaurant, meeting room. AE, CB, DC, MC, V.*

The Summit. Loews' moderate-price New York property has an impersonal style, but most of its regulars—business travelers —don't mind because the hotel generally runs quite well. Rooms, most of them recently refurbished, are standard fare. Downstairs you'll find Maude's, one of those loud after-work gathering places with good buffets and drinks. Loews takes care of its properties, so the Summit can more than hold its own with some of its neighbors. *Lexington Ave. (at 51st St.), 10022, tel. 212/752–7000. 766 rooms. Facilities: restaurant, lounge, meeting rooms, fitness center. AE, CB, DC, MC, V.*

Inexpensive

Chatwal Inns. The six Chatwal properties, located mostly in the Broadway midtown area, provide clean, attractively designed rooms at reasonable prices. Don't be put off by the rather dingy facades of some of the hotels—rooms at all six locations are immaculate and, though somewhat small, have all the basic amenities travelers have come to expect, including bathroom toiletries, telephones, and TVs. All guests receive a complimentary continental breakfast and some of the larger properties have on-premises full-service restaurants as well. Only time will tell if the Chatwal's good standards will be kept up, but right now, this is a budget-minded New York visitor's best bet. *Aberdeen (17 W. 32nd), Chatwal Inn (132 W. 45th), Chatwal Inn on Park (429 Park Ave. S.), Days Inn (234 W. 48th), Best Western Woodward (210 W. 55th), and Quality Inn (157 W. 47th); Tel. 800/826–4667, or 800/621–4667 in Canada. Facilities: restaurants, small meeting rooms, lounges, depending on the property. AE, CB, DC, MC, V.*

Hotel Edison. A popular budget stop for tour groups from here and abroad, this offbeat old hotel has a sense of weatherbeaten style in its art deco lobby. A gruesome murder scene for *The Godfather* was shot in what is now Sophia's restaurant, and the pink plaster coffee shop has become a hot place to eavesdrop on show-business gossip thanks to such celebrity regulars as Jackie Mason. Guest rooms are brighter and fresher than the dark corridors seem to hint. There's no room service, but this part of the theater district has so many restaurants and delis that it doesn't matter much. *228 W. 47th St., 10036, tel. 212/840 –5000. 1,000 rooms. Facilities: restaurant, coffee shop, bar. AE, CB, DC, MC, V.*

★ **Hotel Empire.** This old hotel recently changed ownership, so it's a matter of time before one knows what's what, but since the new owner is media mogul John Kluge, the Empire should only gain in luster. The lobby is warm and inviting; halls are decorated in soft gray with elegant lamps. Rooms and suites are a bit like small boxes, but nicely furnished; bathrooms are immaculate if on the small side. The restaurant is new, and the neighborhood is loaded with all-hours dining options. For the money, you'll be hard-pressed to find a cleaner, more conveniently located hotel. *Broadway (at 63rd St.), 10023, tel. 212/ 265–7400, 800/221–6509, or 800/223–9868. 368 rooms. Facilities: restaurant, coffee shop. AE, CB, DC, MC, V.*

New York International Youth Hostel. American Youth Hostels recently opened this ambitious facility on Manhattan's Upper West Side. Here, in a renovated 19th-century Gothic-style building, you'll find dormitory accommodations at rock-bottom prices. In addition, the hostel will eventually be equipped with conference areas, kitchens, dining rooms, a retail travel store, a public restaurant, and an Off-Off Broadway theater. Only a few of the large "family" units have private baths; rooms hold up to six beds; and guests must bring their own sheets. All ages are welcome, but there is a limit of one week per stay. Each guest is responsible for minor housekeeping chores, as well as other services that in other properties would be performed by hotel employees. Although the immediate neighborhood is still a bit rough, the location is convenient to Columbia University, Harlem, and new stores and eating spots on upper Broadway and Columbus and Amsterdam avenues. This is a welcome alternative for the self-sufficient traveler. At press time, the hostel was going through an early shakedown period, so call in advance about exact prices and available amenities. *891 Amsterdam Ave., 10025, tel. 212/932–2300. 90 rooms. Planned facilities: dining area, patio, kitchen, self-service laundry, travel service desk, theater, public restaurant, conference rooms for nonprofit groups. AE, CB, DC, MC, V.*

Ramada Inn. Another of Loews' budget properties, this motel-style building has an outdoor rooftop swimming pool and lounge area with snack bar. Rooms and suites were recently upgraded. Daily garage rates are reasonable. This is a good bet for theater-bound families during the summer months. *48th St. and 8th Ave., 10019, tel. 212/581–7000 or 800/2–RAMADA. 366 rooms. Facilities: restaurant, lounge, pool, meeting room. AE, CB, DC, MC, V.*

Vanderbilt YMCA. Of the various Manhattan Ys offering accommodations, this is the best as far as location and facilities are concerned. Although rooms hold up to four people, they are little more than dormitory-style cells—even with only one or two beds to a room, you may feel crowded. Each room does have a late-model TV, however. There are no private baths; communal showers and toilets are worn but clean. Guests are provided with basics such as towels and soap. Besides the low price, this Y offers instant free membership to its on-premises pool, gym, running track, exercise rooms, and sauna. An informal cafeteria and a friendly hospitality desk encourage travelers to mix with one another. The Turtle Bay neighborhood is safe, convenient, and interesting (the United Nations is a few short blocks away). Other YMCAs in town include the 561-room **West Side Y** (5 W. 63rd St., 10023, tel. 212/787–4400), which may be hard to get into but is in the desirable Lincoln Center area; and the 1,490-room **Sloane House YMCA** (356 W. 34th St., 10001, tel. 212/760–5860), which is in a gritty and somewhat unsafe neighborhood. *224 E. 47th St., 10017, tel. 212/755–2410. 430 rooms. Facilities: cafeteria, meeting rooms, self-service laundry, gift shop, luggage storage, pool, fitness center. No credit cards.*

★ **The Wyndham.** This genteel treasure sits across from The Plaza and adjacent to the Helmsley Park Lane. The savvy, independent traveler who cares more about gracious rooms and a friendly atmosphere than about imposing lobbies and hand-to-mouth service might well choose this spot over its neighbors. Owner and general manager John Mados keeps prices down by not offering room service or fancy amenities; what he does provide is some of the prettiest and most spacious accommodations in Manhattan. Even the least expensive double room has fresh floral-print bedspreads, comfortable chairs, and decorator wall coverings. A slight drawback is the old-fashioned, white-tile bathrooms. Suites (all of which come with pantries) start as low as $160 per night; they are painted in sunny shades and fitted with antique furniture, tasteful Chinese rugs, and an eclectic mix of everything else. The small lobby is unusually secure—a doorman controls the "in" buzzer 24 hours a day. This hotel is a favorite of stars such as Carol Burnett and media personalities Leonard Maltin and Barbara Walters. *42 W. 58th St., 10019, tel. 212/753–3500. 201 rooms. Facilities: restaurant. AE, CB, DC, MC, V.*

Bed-and-Breakfasts

Hundreds of rooms are available on a bed-and-breakfast basis in Manhattan and the outer boroughs, principally Brooklyn. B&Bs almost always cost well below $100 a night; some singles are available for under $50.

New York B&Bs, however, are not the quaint old mansions you find in other localities. They fall into two categories: (1) *Hosted apartments*, a bedroom in an apartment where the host is present; (2) *unhosted apartments*, entire apartments that are temporarily vacant. The unhosted option is scarcer and somewhat more expensive.

Along with saving money, B&Bs permit you to mingle with New Yorkers and stay in "real" neighborhoods rather than in tourist enclaves. The disadvantages are that accommodations, amenities, service, and privacy fall far short of what you get in hotels. Sometimes you really do get breakfast and sometimes you don't. And you usually can't pay by credit card.

Here are a few reservation agencies that book B&B accommodations in and near Manhattan. There is no fee for the service, but they advise you to make reservations as far in advance as possible. It's a good idea to find out something about the city before you contact them, and then to request accommodations in a neighborhood that you prefer.

Bed and Breakfast Network of New York (134 W. 32nd St., Suite 602, 10001, tel. 212/645–8134).
City Lights Bed and Breakfast, Ltd. (Box 20355, Cherokee Station, 10028, tel. 212/737–7049).
New World Bed and Breakfast (150 5th Ave., Suite 711, 10011, tel. 212/675–5600 or 800/443–3800).
Urban Ventures (306 W. 38th St., 10018, tel. 212/594–5650).

The Arts

Full listings of weekly entertainment and cultural events appear in *New York* magazine; they include capsule summaries of Broadway, Off-Broadway, and Off-Off-Broadway shows and concerts, performance times, and ticket prices. The Arts & Leisure section of the Sunday *New York Times* lists and describes events but provides no service information. The Theater Directory in the daily *New York Times* advertises ticket information for Broadway and Off-Broadway shows. Listings of arts events appear weekly in *The New Yorker* and *Village Voice.*

Theater

New York theater is the benchmark for quality and variety. At the height of the season, theatergoers might see anything from full-scale star-studded Broadway musicals to intimate, locally developed dramas. at nearly 40 Broadway theaters, three dozen Off-Broadway theaters, and 200 Off-Off-Broadway houses. Generally, Broadway productions are the most extravagant and expensive, while the more daring, if less polished, shows are found Off and Off-Off Broadway. Production costs aside, provocative theater can be found anywhere in this city.

Broadway theaters are located in the Theater District, most of which lies between Broadway and Eighth Avenue, from 43rd to 52nd streets. Some of these theaters are small gems, comfortable and luxurious yet intimate enough to make the audience feel part of the show. The newer, larger theaters are no less luxurious. All performers work under an Actors Equity contract that guarantees them a basic minimum salary. Ticket prices range from $22.50 to as much as $100, depending on the show, the time of performance, and the location of the seat. Generally, plays are less expensive than musicals; and matinees (Wednesday, Saturday, and sometimes Sunday) and weeknight performances cost less than shows on Friday and Saturday nights. Most Broadway theaters are "dark" (closed) on Monday, although some are dark on other days.

Off-Broadway theater has professional performers but generally less elaborate productions. The theaters are located all over town. Many can be found along Theater Row, a strip of 42nd Street between Ninth and Tenth avenues; others are located in Greenwich Village, and some are on the Upper West Side. Ticket prices range from $10 to $30, with most falling into the $20–$25 range.

Off-Off-Broadway theater is alternative theater. Performers and production staff may be professionals, but they get little or no salary. Although you won't find lavish sets and plush seating, plays can be highly professional—with performances of everything from Shakespeare to mixed-media performance art. Off-Off-Broadway houses are located in all kinds of spaces —lofts, church basements, converted storefronts—all over town. Tickets rarely exceed $15, and you can phone ahead for reservations. The *Village Voice* contains the most comprehensive Off-Off-Broadway listings.

It's easy to buy tickets for Broadway and Off-Broadway shows; you can do it even before you reach New York. All Broadway show tickets are available by phone from either **Tele-Charge** (tel. 212/239–6200) or **Ticketron** (tel. 212/246–0102). You pay the price of the tickets plus a surcharge to a major credit card and pick them up at the box office before the show. Both of these services operate 24 hours a day, seven days a week. Similar arrangements are available for Off-Broadway through **HIT –TIX** (tel. 212/564–8038), **Ticketmaster** (tel. 212/307–7171), or individual theaters.

In New York, you can buy Broadway tickets at the box offices, which are open most of the day and evening. Tickets for many

Off-Broadway shows are available at **Ticket Central** (416 W. 42nd St., tel. 212/279–4200). Tickets for the hottest shows in town—of late *The Phantom of the Opera* and *Les Misérables*— may be available only through ticket brokers. Brokers in New York can sell the ticket for full price plus a *legal* surcharge of $2.50 per ticket; consequently, many operate out of New Jersey, where such limits don't apply. Look them up in the Manhattan Yellow Pages under "Ticket Sales—Entertainment & Sports."

For discounts of nearly 50% on Broadway and Off-Broadway shows, you can try your luck at **TKTS** (tel. 212/354–5800). This nonprofit service sells day-of-performance tickets for half the regular price, plus a $1.50 per ticket service charge ($2 for tickets over $50). Supply is erratic. Sometimes it seems that every show in town appears on the display board just outside the ticket window. At other times only long-running hits and little-known sleepers are available.

The main TKTS booth is located in the Theater District on Duffy Square, a triangle formed by Broadway, Seventh Avenue, and 47th Street. It's open from 3 to 8 PM daily for evening performances, 10 to 2 for Wednesday and Saturday matinees, and noon to 8 for Sunday matinee and evening performances. A TKTS booth at 2 World Trade Center opens earlier in the day and generally has shorter lines. Its hours are weekdays from 11 to 5:30, Saturday from 11:30 to 3:30. Matinee and Sunday tickets are sold the day before the performance; Off-Broadway tickets are sold 11 AM to 1 PM for evening performances only. Another TKTS booth in front of Borough Hall in Brooklyn (tel. 718/625–5015) operates Tuesday–Friday 11–5:30 and Saturday 11–3:30 for evening performances only. Matinee and Sunday tickets are available the day before the performance; Off-Broadway tickets are sold only until 1 PM. TKTS accepts only cash or traveler's checks—no checks or credit cards.

The Duffy Square lines are long but congenial, with street entertainers galore and envoys from some of the shows trying to lure you out of line with no-wait discounts. It may be worth a trip to the World Trade Center or Brooklyn TKTS so you can save the waiting time and plan the remainder of the afternoon around your evening at the theater.

Concerts

Much of New York's serious music scene clusters around the magnificent concert halls and theaters of Lincoln Center (Broadway and 65th St., tel. 212/877–2011). **Avery Fisher Hall** (tel. 212/874–2424) is the home of the New York Philharmonic Orchestra, the American Philharmonic, the Mostly Mozart festival, and visiting orchestras and soloists. Smaller **Alice Tully Hall** (tel. 212/362–1911), in the Juilliard School of Music building, features chamber music and jazz performances. Although most tickets are sold on a subscription basis, individual seats may be available at the box office in advance or through Centercharge (tel. 212/874–6770).

Since 1891, playing **Carnegie Hall** (154 W. 57th St., tel. 212/247 –7800) has epitomized a musician's ascent to the big time. Now it presents visiting orchestras, recitals, chamber music, and pop concerts. The **Weill Recital Hall** features lesser-known artists at lower prices. Student/senior rush tickets are available from 6 PM on performance nights. Public tours are given on Tuesday and Thursday; call 212/247–7800 for information.

Merkin Concert Hall (129 W. 67th St., tel. 212/362–8719) is a reasonably priced stop on the concert circuit. Though threatened with gentrification-motivated demolition, **Symphony Space** (2537 Broadway at 95th St., tel. 212/864–5400) continues to present an eclectic program of concerts, literary readings, dance, and drama at painless (free–$35) prices. The **Metropolitan Museum of Art** (1000 Fifth Ave., tel. 212/570–3949) hosts a concert series in its 708-seat Grace Rainey Rogers auditorium. The **92nd Street Y** (1395 Lexington Ave., tel. 212/996–1100) offers chamber music and recitals by top-name musicians.

Concerts are also performed regularly at churches, colleges, museums, recital halls, lofts, parks, and other spaces throughout the city. To find out when and where, consult the Music and Dance section of *New York* magazine, the Sunday *New York Times* Arts & Leisure section, or listings in the *New Yorker*.

A TKTS-like operation called **Bryant Park Music and Dance Ticket Booth** sells discount day-of-performance tickets for music and dance concerts all over the city—including Lincoln Center and Carnegie Hall. Tickets cost half the regular price plus a $1.50 service charge. *42nd St. just east of Sixth Ave., tel. 212/382–2323. Open Tues., Thurs., Fri., noon–2, 3–7; Wed. & Sat. 11–2, 3–7; Sun. noon–6. Cash or traveler's checks only.*

Opera

The **Metropolitan Opera House** (Broadway and 65th St., tel. 212/362–6000), at Lincoln Center, is a sublime setting for mostly classic operas performed by world-class stars. Tickets can be expensive—up to $90—and hard to get, but low-price standing-room tickets may be available.

New York City Opera (Broadway and 65th St., tel. 212/870–5570), at the State Theater, Lincoln Center, is a first-class opera company with lower ticket prices—under $50—and an innovative and unpredictable schedule.

Other New York opera companies include the **Amato Opera Theatre** (319 Bowery, tel. 212/228–8200), a downtown showcase for young performers. **New York Gilbert and Sullivan Players** (251 W. 91st St., Apt. 4C, tel. 212/769–1000) perform G & S classics at Christmas time, **Opera Ebony** (2109 Broadway, Suite 1418, tel. 212/690–4100) is an all black company performing major and minor classics, and at **Repertorio Español** (138 E. 27th St., tel. 212/889–2850), performers sing in Spanish. Check *New York* magazine or the *New York Times* for current productions.

Dance

The **American Ballet Theatre** (Broadway and 65th St., tel. 212/362–6000), formerly under the direction of Mikhail Baryshnikov, is the resident company of the Metropolitan Opera House in Lincoln Center. ABT is noted for its lyrical renditions of story ballets during the spring (May–June) season. Ticket prices start low, around $8 for standing room, and rise to over $50.

The renowned **New York City Ballet** (Broadway and 65th St., tel. 212/496–0600), a resident of Lincoln Center's New York State Theater, reached world-class prominence under the direction of George Balanchine. The largest dance organization in the Western World (107 dancers) performs a spring season in May and June, and a winter program from November through February. Tickets range from $8 to $46.

A Moorish-style former Masonic temple, **City Center** (131 W. 55th St., tel. 212/581–7907) hosts innovative dance companies like the Harlem Dance Theater, the Paul Taylor Company, and the Joffrey Ballet. The **Joyce Theater** (175 Eighth Ave., tel. 212/242–0800) is an Art Deco former movie house with a contemporary fall and spring season; it is also the New York home of the Eliot Feld dance company. Nearby, the **Dance Theater Workshop** (219 W. 19th St., tel. 212/691–6500) is a second-floor performance space that highlights the work of avant-garde dancers and choreographers. The 127-year-old **Brooklyn Academy of Music** (BAM; 30 Lafayette Ave., Brooklyn, tel. 718/636–4100) presents programs of ballet and modern dance, and a futuristic Next Wave Festival each fall.

Weekly listings of ballet, modern, and folk dance performances can be found in *New York* magazine and the Arts and Leisure section of the Sunday *New York Times*. Half-price day-of-performance tickets are available at **Bryant Park Music and Dance Discount Ticket Booth** (*see* Concerts, above for details).

Film

Few cities rival New York's selection of films. Along with all the first-run Hollywood features, an incomparable selection of foreign films, classics, documentaries, and experimental works are playing all over town. The daily *New York Daily News* and *New York Newsday*, the Friday *New York Times*, and the weekly (available Wednesday) *Village Voice* publish schedules and show times for Manhattan movies. *New York* magazine and the *New Yorker* publish programs and capsule reviews but no schedules.

The vast majority of Manhattan theaters are first-run houses. Most charge $7.50 a ticket for adults at all times; some offer off-peak discounts for children and senior citizens. Even though New York has recently lost some of its venerable revival houses (the Thalia, the Regency), many remaining theaters still feature revivals, classics, and off-beat films.

The **Film Forum 2** (209 W. Houston St., tel. 212/431–1590) in SoHo features contemporary foreign films, documentaries, and other unusual work. The **Thalia Soho** (15 Vandam St., tel. 212/675–0498) has six weekly double-feature revivals and retrospectives. The **Bleecker Street Cinemas** (144 Bleecker St., tel. 212/674–2560) in Greenwich Village have foreign and American favorites, often double features. **Cinema Village** (22 E. 12th St., tel. 212/924–3363) changes its programs of double-feature revivals three times a week. **Theatre 80 St. Mark's** (80 St. Marks Pl., tel. 212/254–7400) in the East Village has different double-feature revival programs nearly every day. The **Public Theater** (425 Lafayette St., tel. 212/598–7171) concentrates on retrospectives and documentaries.

Museum of the Moving Image (36–01 35th Ave., Astoria, tel. 718/784–0077) is found at the historic Kaufman Astoria Studios. The museum presents over 700 programs annually, including major artist-oriented retrospectives, Hollywood classics, experimental videos, and TV documentaries.

The **Museum of Modern Art** (11 W. 53rd St., tel. 212/708–9490) shows film classics every day in two theaters; movies are free with museum admission. The **Collective for Living Cinema** (41 White St., tel. 212/505–5181) in TriBeCa has an ambitious, constantly changing program of experimental films.

Some foreign cultural institutions show films in their respective languages, with subtitles. They include the **French Institute-Alliance Française** (22 E. 60th St., tel. 212/355–6100); the German **Goethe House** (1014 Fifth Ave., tel. 212/972–3960); and **Japan House** (333 E. 47th St., tel. 212/832–1155).

Nightlife

Cabaret

The Ballroom. A Chelsea tapas (Spanish appetizers) bar with top-name cabaret acts and outrageous revues. *253 W. 28th St., tel. 212/244–3005.*

Broadway Baby. A piano bar featuring performing waiters and waitresses. *407 Amsterdam Ave. at 79th St., tel. 212/724–6868.*

Catch A Rising Star. Continuous comedy by performers on their way up—or down. *1487 First Ave. near 78th St., tel. 212/794–1906.*

Don't Tell Mama. Lively piano bar up front with no cover or minimum and chancey "open mike" policy. Cabaret performers work the back room. *343 W. 46th St., tel. 212/757–0788.*

The Duplex. A bilevel Village club with torch singers and hot comics. *61 Christopher St., tel. 212/255–5438. Shows at 8, 10, and midnight Fri. and Sat.*

Danny's Skylight Room (346 W. 46th St., tel. 212/265–8130). Danny's is housed in the Grand Sea Palace, a fixture on Restaurant Row. You'll find the entertainment to be a little bit of everything rather eclectic here, from jazz musicians and crooners to pianists and monologuists. **Eighty–eight's** (228 W. 10th St., tel. 212/924–0088). Come to hear the best tunes from Broadway in inventively assembled programs.

Jan Wallman's. Hot restaurant-cabaret on the ground floor of the Hotel Iroquois features jazz-oriented singers and players. *49 W. 44th St., tel. 212/764–8930.*

The Original Improvisation. New York's original comedy showcase where all the big-name yucksters (Rodney Dangerfield, Richard Pryor, Robert Klein) earned their first giggles. *358 W. 44th St., tel. 212/765–8268.*

Steve McGraw's. West Side showroom presents scathingly irreverent satirical revues and cabaret shows. *158 W. 72nd St., tel. 212/595–7400.*

Jazz Clubs

Most jazz clubs have substantial cover charges and a drink minimum for table service. You can usually save one or both of these charges by sitting at or standing around the bar.

In Greenwich Village, the **Village Vanguard** (178 Seventh Ave. S, tel. 212/255–4037) is a basement joint that has ridden the crest of every new wave in jazz for over 50 years. The **Village Gate** (160 Bleecker St., tel. 212/475–5120) can present different jazz-related acts and shows simultaneously in three places. No cover on the Village Gate terrace. Go to **Sweet Basil** (88 Seventh Ave. S near Bleecker St., tel. 212/242–1785) for a roomful of jazz memorabilia and top-name groups. The East Village's **Dan Lynch Bar and Restaurant** (221 Second Ave., tel. 212/677–0911) is full of jazz surprises, especially on Sunday afternoons.

The Blue Note (131 W. Third St., tel. 212/475–8592) is a new incarnation of a legendary jazz club. Smoky and crowded, **Bradley's** (70 University Pl., tel. 212/228–6440) is a low-key place that spotlights piano-and-bass combos. **The Knitting Factory** (47 E. Houston St., tel. 212/219–3055), a hot new place on the frontier of SoHo, features avant-garde groups. **Upstairs at Greene Street** (105 Greene St., tel. 212/925–2415) is a restaurant converted from a three-story parking garage. Greene Street spent a long time looking for its niche, but it seems to have found it with free jazz and an ultracool setting.

Farther uptown, **Angry Squire** (217 Seventh Ave. near 23rd St., tel. 212/242–9066) is a Chelsea neighborhood pub with contemporary sounds from small groups. At cozy **Fat Tuesday's** (190 Third Ave. at 17th St., tel. 212/533–7902), two sets are played every night of the week in an intimate basement, and there's a popular restaurant/bar upstairs. **Michael's Pub** (211 E. 55th St., tel. 212/758–2272) has mainstream jazz, top vocalists, jazz-based revues—and Woody Allen's Dixieland band most Mondays.

On the Upper West Side, go to **Mikell's** (760 Columbus Ave. at 97th St., tel. 212/864–8832) for a variety of jazz-influenced sounds.

Pop and Rock Clubs

The *Village Voice* carries the best listings of who's playing where on the pop and rock scene.

In Greenwich Village, folk headliners usually dominate the bill at **The Bottom Line** (15 W. Fourth St. off Mercer St., tel. 212/228–7880). Past performers include everyone from Stevie Wonder to Suzanne Vega. For over 25 years **The Bitter End** (147 Bleecker St., tel. 212/673–7030) has been giving a break to folk, rock, jazz, comedy, and country acts. Everyone goes to the **Cat Club** (76 E. 13th St., tel. 212/505–0090) for dancing. Heavy metal presides, though occasional swing nights vary the tempo. A low-key Irish pub, the **Eagle Tavern** (355 W. 14th St., tel. 212/924–0275) presents traditional Irish music, with bluegrass and comedy thrown in for variety.

CBGB & OMFUG (315 Bowery, tel. 212/982–4052) still blasts eardrums with the hard rock sound of heavy metal.

Nightlife Uptown

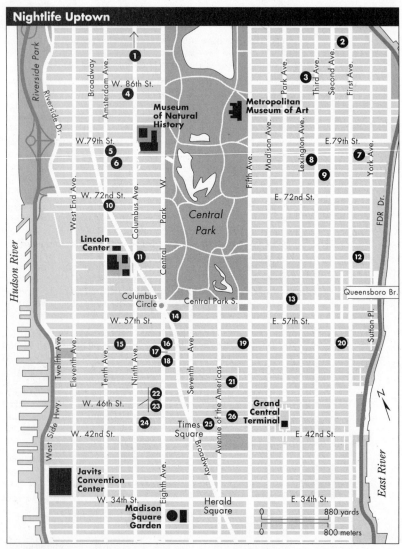

Broadway Baby, **5**
Catch a Rising Star, **7**
Corso, **3**
Danny's Skylight Room, **23**
Don't Tell Mama, **22**
The Ginger Man, **11**
Hard Rock Cafe, **14**
The Original Improvisation, **24**
J.G. Melon, **6, 9**
Jan Wallman's, **26**

Jim McMullen's, **8**
Lone Star Roadhouse, **17**
Lucy's Restaurant, **4**
Michael's Pub, **20**
Mikell's, **1**
Rainbow Room, **21**

The Red Zone, **15**
Regines, **13**
The Ritz, **16**
Roseland, **18**
Shout!, **25**
Steve McGraw's, **10**
The Surf Club, **2**
T.G.I. Friday's, **12**
Top of the Sixes, **19**

Nightlife Downtown

Angry Squire, **28**
The Ballroom, **27**
The Bitter End, **51**
Blue Note, **47**
Bottom Line, **46**
Bradley's, **37**
Café Society, **30**
Cat Club, **39**

CBGB & OMFUG, **49**
Cedar Tavern, **38**
Club Paradise, **44**
Dan Lynch Bar and Restaurant, **41**
Downtown Beirut I, **42**
The Duplex, **45**
Eagle Tavern, **33**
Ear Inn, **54**
Fat Tuesday's, **31**

Knitting Factory, **52**
Mars, **34**
McSorley's Old Ale House, **43**
Palladium, **40**
Pete's Tavern, **32**

S.O.B.'s, **53**
South Street Seaport, **56**
Stringfellow's, **29**
Sweet Basil, **48**
Upstairs at Greene Street, **55**
Village Gate, **50**
Village Vanguard, **36**
White Horse Tavern, **35**

Farther uptown, dance at **The Ritz** (254 W. 54th St., tel. 212/ 541–8900), a restored Art Deco ballroom that hosts the newest rock groups. **The Lone Star Roadhouse** (240 W. 52nd St., tel. 212/245–2950) offers big names in country swing and big city blues.

Latin Clubs

Latin rhythms fill the air at **Corso** (205 E. 86th St., tel. 212/534–4964), an institution on the Latin scene. **S.O.B.'s** (Sounds of Brazil) (204 Varick St., tel. 212/243–4940) is a sophisticated tropical setting for south-of-the-border music. **Club Paradise** (15 Waverly Pl., tel. 212/533–3048), billed as the "hottest tropical bar on the island," lives up to its reputation with top tropical bands nightly.

Discos and Dance Clubs

While club-hopping don't miss New York's largest, the **Palladium** (126 E. 14th St., tel. 212/473–7171). Practically an institution by now with Club MTV, this place is to the club scene what Macy's is to shopping. Occupying an old meat-packing warehouse, **Mars** (10th Ave. at 13th St., tel. 212/691–6262) was redone à la early urban decay; take your pick among five levels. The door staff is *very* particular. **The Red Zone** (440 W. 54th St., tel. 212/582–2222), a 14,000-square-foot discotheque, features huge movie screens where images of water-lapped beaches and the Wild West are projected. At **The Surf Club** (416 E. 91st St., tel. 212/410–1360), the East Side upper crust lets down its hair (though managing even in the heat of the moment to remain impeccably coiffed).

For "touch dancing" the way they used to do it, 70-year-old **Roseland** (239 W. 52nd St., tel. 212/247–0200) has two orchestras Thursday through Sunday nights and matinees from 2:30 PM. Whoosh through the revolving door at **Café Society** (915 Broadway, tel. 212/529–8282) to find soaring ceilings, pink art deco decor, a long, inviting bar, and dinner and dancing. The quixotic entrepreneur who owns Café Society also runs Society Billiards next door. At elegant **Regines** (502 Park Ave. at 59th St., tel. 212/826–0990) an expensive dinner buys access to the disco floor—or you can eat elsewhere and pay a cover charge. Most spectacular of all, the newly remodeled **Rainbow Room** atop the 65-floor RCA Building (30 Rockefeller Center, tel. 212/ 632–5100) gives you a dance floor straight out of the Hollywood classics.

Bars for Singles (Under 30)

Downtown, there's no dearth of drinking opportunities at **South Street Seaport** (Water and Fulton Sts., tel. 212/732–7678). Bars at this major New York attraction include Fluties, Roeblings, Jeremy's, the Fulton Street Café, and McDuffy's Irish Coffee House, to name a few. On warm Friday evenings the Seaport takes on the appearance of an Ivy League homecoming/college mixer, where Wall street-types raise a glass with young professionals from around the city. The **Ear Inn** (326 Spring St. near Greenwich St., tel. 212/226–9060) boasts an archetypal juke box and regular poetry readings. Young people throng to **McSorley's Old Ale House** (15 E. 7th St., tel. 212/473–9148), one of the oldest and most crowded bars in the city. **Downtown Beirut I** (156 First Ave., tel. 212/777–9011) is an off-beat East Village hangout that attracts artists and student types. Occasionally, live music is played by local rock bands.

Farther uptown, lines are usually waiting outside the **Hard Rock Café** (221 W. 57th St., tel. 212/489–6565), a shrine to rock 'n' roll. The nine-to-five crowd unwinds to '50s and '60s tunes at **Shout!** (124 W. 43rd St., tel. 212/869–2088). On the Upper East Side, **T.G.I. Friday's** (1152 First Ave. at 63rd St., tel. 212/832–8512) has a long tradition as a congenial gathering place. On the Upper West Side, young crowds congregate at **Lucy's Restaurant** (503 Columbus Ave., tel. 212/787–3009).

Clubs and Bars for Singles (Over 30)

Three traditional Greenwich Village literary hangouts continue to attract local regulars and curious visitors. **Pete's Tavern** (129 E. 18th St., tel. 212/473–7676), a crowded, friendly saloon, is famous as the place where O. Henry wrote "The Gift of the Magi." The **White Horse Tavern** (567 Hudson St. and 11th St., tel. 212/243–9260), which figures prominently in the legend and lore of Dylan Thomas, now has outdoor seating during summer. The **Cedar Tavern** (82 University Pl., tel. 212/243–9355) was a haunt of beatnik writers and abstract expressionist painters.

Farther uptown, **Stringfellows** (35 E. 21st St., tel. 212/254–2444), an upscale bar, restaurant, and dance club, stays hopping with British and American sounds until the wee, wee hours. **Jim McMullen's** (1341 Third Ave., tel. 212/861–4700) is a young, upscale, Upper East Side watering hole with a large, busy bar decked with bouquets of fresh flowers. The **Ginger Man** (51 W. 64th St., tel. 212/399–2358) is a reliable Lincoln Center area establishment which offers a seemingly endless warren of rooms, handsome Tiffany lamps, and famous faces from nearby ABC–TV. On the 39th floor of 666 Fifth Avenue, **Top of the Sixes** (tel. 212/757–6662) offers 360-degree views to a large cocktail-hour crowd. East Side, West Side, the **J. G. Melon** establishments (1291 Third Ave. at 74th St., tel. 212/650–1310; and 340 Amsterdam Ave. at 76th St., tel. 212/877–2220) are comfortable, low-pressure places where you can meet people.

4 Long Island

Introduction

At 1,682 square miles, Long Island is not only the largest island on America's East Coast but the most varied. From west to east, Long Island shades from suburban sprawl to farmland and vineyards punctuated by historic seaside villages. It has what is arguably the nation's finest stretch of white-sand beach as well as one of our most congested highways—the notorious Long Island Expressway. There is the Long Island of the rich, who for generations have retreated to the princely estates of the North Shore's Gold Coast; the Long Island of the famous, who flock to the string of South Shore villages known collectively as the Hamptons; and the Long Island of hard-working commuters who journey each day from their "bedroom communities" to their Manhattan offices or to one of the many Long Island office parks. In addition to superb beaches, nature has given Long Island innumerable natural harbors, excellent soil, and a fascinating geology; man has given it a long and distinguished history, beautiful old homes, and, more recently, wonderful places in which to eat and to stay.

Although two of New York City's boroughs, Brooklyn and Queens, occupy Long Island's western section, the *real* Long Island—known to residents simply as the Island—begins only when one leaves the city behind and crosses into Nassau County (Brooklyn and Queens are described in the New York City chapter of this book). East of Nassau is the more rural Suffolk County, with its two "forks," north and south, extending far into the Atlantic Ocean. From the Nassau/Queens border to its eastern terminus at Montauk Point, Long Island is 103 miles long and from 12 to 20 miles wide. Together, Nassau and Suffolk counties have nearly 3 million residents, making Long Island more populous than 19 states.

On Long Island, the north/south distinction applies not only to the "forks" of the East End but to the North and South shores that run the length of the island. Jagged in its coastal outline and gentle in topography, the North Shore is lapped by Long Island Sound, which F. Scott Fitzgerald called "the most domesticated body of salt water in the Western hemisphere." The considerably less domesticated Atlantic Ocean sends its rollers onto the white-sand beaches that fringe the South Shore. Many of these beaches, including Jones Beach, Fire Island, and Westhampton Beach, are actually long, narrow barrier islands that wind and tide have thrown up as a kind of sandy protection to Long Island's South Shore.

Long Island was settled early and quickly, in part because two nations were planting colonies here simultaneously. While the Dutch were pushing eastward from their stronghold on New Amsterdam (today's Manhattan), the English were sailing down from newly settled Connecticut and Massachusetts to set up outposts at Hempstead, East Hampton, Southampton, Southold, and Brookhaven on central and eastern Long Island. By 1650 the two nations brushed up against each other at Oyster Bay, and conflict ensued. Eventually—in 1674—the English took final possession of New Amsterdam, and all of Long Island came under the jurisdiction of the English crown.

Agriculture was the basis of Long Island's early economy, and later—in the 18th and early 19th centuries—whaling brought a brief period of wealth and prominence to places like Sag Harbor and Cold Spring Harbor. After the Civil War, when well-to-do Americans discovered the pleasures of saltwater bathing, the Hamptons were transformed from farming and fishing communities into fashionable summer resorts, and the North Shore became the playground of the Vanderbilts, Whitneys, and Roosevelts. It wasn't until after World War II, when highways were constructed and Americans began owning cars as a matter of course, that vast numbers of the middle class moved out to Long Island, transforming farm fields into new suburbs and shopping centers.

Today the suburbanization of Long Island continues at a dizzying pace as the population of Nassau and Suffolk booms. But amid the sprawl of new houses, old village centers remain intact. Historic sites and museums protect many of the oldest, finest, and most magnificent homes; and new farms growing wine grapes, herbs, sod, and nursery plants have been established on old potato and vegetable farms. Beyond the hubbub of development and traffic, the beaches and the waters of the sound and ocean beckon to swimmers, fishermen, yachtsmen, sunbathers, and beachcombers as they always have. Long Island today is, if anything, more varied, more richly diverse in vacationing possibilities, and more rewarding to the visitor than ever before.

Essential Information

Getting Around

By Plane In addition to John F. Kennedy International Airport and LaGuardia Airport in Queens, Long Island is served by Long Island MacArthur Airport in Ronkonkoma. For airline information at MacArthur Airport, call 516/467–6161.

By Car The best and most convenient way to see Long Island is by car. There are four major east–west thoroughfares that stretch the length of the island. State Route 25A is on the North Shore, the Long Island Expressway passes through the middle of the island, and State Route 27 (Sunrise Highway) and State Route 27A (Merrick Road-Montauk Highway) are on the South Shore. Try to avoid the Long Island Expressway during rush hour, as its reputation as "the world's longest parking lot" is well justified.

Guided Tours

Harran Coachways runs escorted day tours for groups and families to many Long Island points of interest. The tours cost between $35 and $49 and include a restaurant lunch. *30 Mahan St., West Babylon. For registration and schedule information, call 212/840–2120 or 516/491–9100.*

Hampton Express offers escorted day trips to eastern Long Island (the Hamptons, Shelter Island, etc.) from its office on the east side of Manhattan. The trips cost about $25 and include a box lunch, bus transportation, and sightseeing. *242 W. Montauk Hwy., Hampton Bays, tel. 516/874–2400; in New York City, 1429 Third Ave., tel. 212/233–4403.*

Long Island Railroad packages more than a dozen day tours to local attractions, including the Hamptons, the Bridgeport Ferry, a Long Island winery, and a number of spectacular mansions. The tours are offered between May and October, with morning departures from the LIRR terminal at Penn Station in New York City, the Flatbush Avenue Station in Brooklyn, and the Jamaica Station in Queens, and return to these stations in the evening. The price of each tour is approximately $35, which includes rail and tour-bus transportation, all admissions, and—as a rule—lunch. There is a reduced price for children 5–11. *Tel. 718/990–7498.*

Cruises **Okenos Research Foundation** runs research cruises to view whales, dolphins, and sea birds in their natural environment. The four- to six-hour cruise departs daily year-round from Montauk Viking Dock at 10 AM from May 1 through July 10. From July 11 through Labor Day there are two sailings per day, 8:30 AM and 1:30 PM. Reservations are advised. Not recommended for children under 5. Admission is $25 adults, $15 children 13 and under, 10% discount for senior citizens. Group discounts are available. *Box 776, Hampton Bays, 11946, tel. 516/728–4522 or 4523, weekdays 9–5.*

Captree State Park Ferries runs 1½-hour cruises around the Great South Bay every day except Saturday from July 4 through Labor Day at 1 PM. The price is $6 for adults, $5 for senior citizens, $4 for children 12 and under. In addition, from July 4 through mid-September, '60s music is featured for dancing on the *Moonchaser* during its three-hour cruise, sailing on Thursday evenings at 7:30. The cost is $11 per person, and reservations are required. *Captree Island, Babylon, tel. 516/661–5061.*

Fire Island Cruises runs a luncheon excursion to the Fire Island lighthouse every Friday from July through Labor Day for $22.50 per person. It also has Sunday brunch cruises with special menus on Easter, Mother's Day, and Father's Day for $35 per person. Dinner cruises are available for $38 per person every Tuesday and Thursday at 7:30 from late-June through mid-September. *Maple Ave., Bayshore, tel. 516/666–3601.*

Port Jefferson Steamboat Co. offers evening Music Cruises from July 4 through Labor Day. The three-hour cruise leaves at 8 PM on Wednesday and Thursday, 9:30 on Saturday. The price is $12 per person. *102 W. Broadway, Port Jefferson, tel. 516/473–6282.*

Plane and Helicopter Tours **Barts Auto and Aviation Service** runs narrated "flightseeing" tours of Long Island. The cost is $2 per minute for the 10- to 30-minute flights, which run daily 8:30 AM–dusk. No reservations necessary. *Montauk Hwy., East Moriches, tel. 516/878–1125.*

Mid Island Aviation has one- to two-hour flights for up to three passengers at $106 per hour, year-round 8 AM–5 PM. *Tours leave from Brookhaven Airport, Grand Ave., Shirley and MacArthur Airport, Johnson Ave., Ronkonkoma, tel. 516/588–5400.*

American Helicopters sightseeing tours operate daily from MacArthur Airport. The per-hour price is $155 for one passenger, $275 for two passengers, and $595 for three passengers. *Two-day advance reservations required. Tel. 516/981–6555.*

Island Helicopter has charters of Long Island for four–six people available, daily 9–9, beginning at $600 per hour. *Reservations required, tel. 516/228–9355 or 212/925–8807.*

Important Addresses and Numbers

Tourist
Information

Long Island Tourism Association (tel. 516/794–4222). Visitor information centers are located at Eisenhower Park (parking field 6A, East Meadow, open Mon.–Fri. 9–5), Southern State Parkway (between Exits 13 and 14, Valley Stream, open daily 9–5, May–Oct.), and Long Island Expressway (Dix Hills–Deer Park, daily 9:30–4:30, May–Oct.). Most towns also have their own chamber of commerce offices that can supply information on the towns as well as scheduled local events.

Emergencies

Dial 911 for **police** and **ambulance** assistance.

Hospitals

The following hospitals have 24-hour emergency services: **Nassau:** *Long Island Jewish Hospital* (located on the Queens-Nassau border at Lakeville Rd., New Hyde Park, tel. 718/470–7500; physician referral, tel. 718/470–8690); *Huntington Hospital* (270 Park Ave., Huntington, tel. 516/351–1200); *Nassau County Medical Center* (2201 Hempstead Tpke., East Meadow, tel. 516/542–0123). **Suffolk:** *St. Charles Hospital* (200 Belleterre Rd., Port Jefferson, tel. 516/473–2800) and *Southampton Hospital* (240 Meeting House Ln., Southampton, tel. 516/283–2600).

24-hour Pharmacy

Stuart's Pharmacy and Surgical World, 833 N. Broadway, North Massapequa (tel. 516/799–5858).

Exploring Long Island

Orientation

Long Island has plenty to see, but you'll only see traffic from the Long Island Expressway (LIE), which runs smack down the middle of the island from Long Island City in Queens to Riverhead in Suffolk. Largely contributing to that traffic is the fact that most visitors head straight for the Hamptons and points east to Montauk. But if you're more interested in museums, stately mansions, nature preserves, and other attractions the Island has to offer along its North and South shores, take the more leisurely roads that parallel the two coastlines. On the North Shore, your best bet is Route 25A; on the South Shore, follow Route 27 (Sunrise Highway).

A couple of days would be enough to explore all the way east to Orient Point at the tip of the North Fork, swing down to the South Fork, and return westward to New York City along the South Shore. But you can also go for the day or overnight to the Hampton area. There are many lateral roads that connect the North and South shores, so cutting back and forth is also easy. Travelers with less generous schedules can use the LIE to make better time between points of interest. By choosing the most direct route, it is possible to drive from Manhattan to Orient Point in less than four hours—although rush-hour and weekend traffic will slow the trip considerably.

When exploring the South Shore, switch from Route 27 (Sunrise Highway) to nearby Route 27A (Montauk Highway) in the vicinity of Bayshore in southwestern Suffolk County. This can be done by taking Exit 41 south off Route 27 on to the Robert Moses Causeway and then Exit C2 east off that to Route 27A. This route is more direct and avoids congestion.

Long Island Beaches

Numbers in the margin correspond with points of interest on the Long Island Beaches map.

Its beaches are what attract most visitors to Long Island. If you want to see gardens, historic houses, and historic towns, take the tours of the North and South shores that follow this tour.

Long Island's beaches will spoil you for beaches anywhere else. Although the beaches along the North Shore looking toward Connecticut are rocky, nearly the entire 103-mile length of the South Shore is fringed with wide bands of sand. These magnificent beaches are certainly no secret and they do tend to get crowded on summer weekends, but the crowds thin out as you move east and they vanish altogether in the off-season. Crowds also are much smaller at the North Shore beaches on Long Island Sound. Though they lack the drama of pounding surf and endless horizons, the North Shore beaches are ideal for young children because the Sound water is calmer and warmer than the ocean.

Long Island beach connoisseurs know that early autumn is the best time to come. The water stays warm into September and even early October. Recently, there has been some concern about organic and inorganic waste polluting beaches throughout the Northeast. For information on beach emergencies and closings in Nassau, call County Executive Tom Gulotta's 24-hour hotline, 516/535–6000. In Suffolk, there is no 24-hour telephone service, but the Legislature's office will answer questions during business hours, 516/360–4070.

In terms of sheer magnitude and magnificence, no Long Island beach rivals Jones Beach. Yes, the crowds are notoriously large on hot summer weekends. The secret is to come early or late (bring a picnic supper in June or July and watch the moon rise out of the Atlantic as the people drain away) and to avoid the massive central parking lots. Fire Island, reached by causeway or ferry, has 32 miles of beach; you can simply walk away from the crowds, especially along the eight-mile stretch of wilderness at the island's eastern end. To avoid traffic completely, hop aboard the Long Island Railroad (tel. 718/217–LIRR or 516/822–LIRR), which beefs up its summer runs with trains to Freeport and Bayshore that connect with shuttle buses to the beach or ferry. The East Hampton beaches offer some of the best people-watching, and there are unofficial nude beaches at the east end of Smith Point County Park and at Gibson Beach between Sagaponack and Wainscott (just west of East Hampton). The best-known gay beaches are on Fire Island (*see* below), and gays also congregate at East Hampton's Two Mile Hollow Beach.

Many beaches are restricted to Nassau and Suffolk County residents, and such restrictions are rigidly enforced. Luckily, some of the best beaches are open to the public as state parks. Here is the rundown, from west to east, first on the South

Shore and then on the North Shore. If you are interested in camping at one of the park camping areas, you should get a camping permit from the park superintendent or camp supervisor. Lifeguards are on duty only from Memorial Day to Labor Day on South Shore beaches and from the end of June to Labor Day on North Shore beaches; beach refreshment stands follow the same schedule.

South Shore **Jones Beach State Park:** Five miles of ocean beach surrounded
Beaches by 2,400 acres of parkland, Jones Beach has surf, bay, and pool
❶ bathing; bathhouses; surf, bay, and pier fishing; pitch-and-putt golf courses, outdoor dancing, shuffleboard, paddle tennis, basketball, exercise trails, picnic areas, refreshment stands and a terrific Boardwalk restaurant, extensive boardwalk, and the Jones Beach Marine Theater.

The parking fields situated right on the beach fill up by 9 AM on hot summer weekends, but spots will open up again by 2 or 3 PM. Field 6, at the very end of the beach, has the shortest walk to the ocean and may fill as early as 8 AM. Field 3 and the mammoth fields 4 and 5 are on the other side of the highway from the ocean and require a long, hot walk through cars and tunnel, and bring you to the most crowded part of the beach.

Jones Beach was established by Parks Commissioner Robert Moses in 1929 and has been New York's finest oceanside playground ever since. *Wantagh Pkwy., Wantagh, tel. 516/785–1600. Admission: $4 per car (Memorial Day–Labor Day). Open year-round sunrise–sunset; sunrise–midnight late June–Labor Day for special activities.*

❷ **Robert Moses State Park:** This 1,000-acre state park at the western tip of Fire Island is less than half the size of Jones Beach, but on a peak summer weekend it attracts only about one-fifth as many people, so there is really more beach per person. Though the beach itself is narrower than Jones Beach, you don't have to walk as far from your car to get to the sand. Perhaps because Robert Moses is farther away from the city, the water here is a shade closer to aquamarine than most area beaches.

Robert Moses has a number of parking fields. Field 3 is the smallest and will probably be full by 10 AM on summer weekends. Field 5 is particularly nice because it has a boardwalk, and you can walk from there to the Fire Island lighthouse, which stands inside the adjacent National Seashore.

Facilities include boating, surf fishing, bathhouses, picnic grounds, and a refreshment stand. *Babylon, Robert Moses Causeway, tel. 516/669–0449. Admission: $4 per car Memorial Day–Labor Day. Open year-round sunrise–sunset.*

❸ **Fire Island National Seashore:** Fire Island, 32 miles of protected ocean beach punctuated by 17 summer resort communities, is like a never-never land for grown-ups. Little passenger ferries ply the shallow waters of the Great South Bay with cargoes of vacationers. Since there are no cars or roads, except at the parks at the east and west ends (*see* above and below), everyone walks everywhere on boardwalks or sandy paths. But since the island is nowhere wider than half a mile, there isn't much of anyplace to walk to except from the ocean to the bay and back, with perhaps a side trip to the tennis court or boat slip.

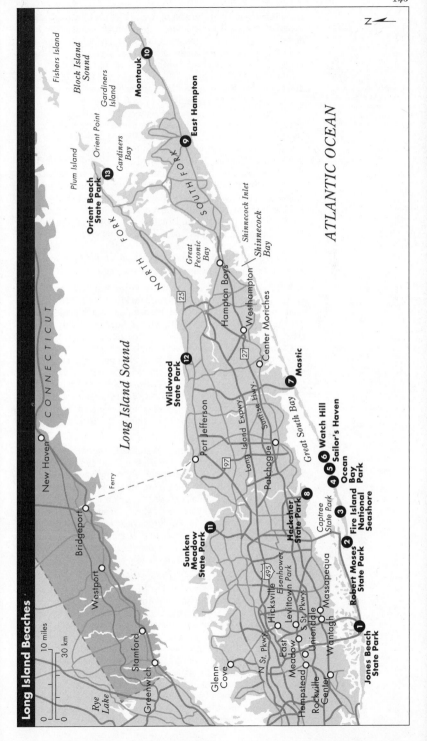

Long Island Beaches

CONNECTICUT

Fishers Island

Block Island Sound

Gardiners Island

Orient Point

Plum Island

Gardiners Bay

● 10 **Montauk**

● 9 **East Hampton**

● 13 **Orient Beach State Park**

NORTH FORK

SOUTH FORK

Long Island Sound

New Haven

Bridgeport

Westport

Stamford

Greenwich

Rye Lake

Ferry

Great Peconic Bay

Shinnecock Inlet

Shinnecock Bay

ATLANTIC OCEAN

Hampton Bays

Westhampton

Center Moriches

[25]

[27]

● 12 **Wildwood State Park**

Port Jefferson

Long Island Expwy

Sunrise Hwy

[97]

Patchogue

● 7 **Mastic**

Great South Bay

● 5 ● 6 **Watch Hill**
Sailor's Haven

● 4 **Ocean Bay Park**

● 3 **Fire Island National Seashore**

● 8 **Heckscher State Park**

Captree State Park

● 11 **Sunken Meadow Park**

[495]

Eisenhower Park

● 2 **Robert Moses State Park**

Glenn Cove

Hicksville

Levittown

N. St. Pkwy

S. St. Pkwy

East Meadow

Hempstead

Uniondale

Rockville Center

Wantagh

Massapequa

● 1 **Jones Beach State Park**

0 miles 10

0 30 km

N

In 1964 the federal government declared Fire Island a National Seashore, thus protecting what open land had not yet fallen to development. The 17 resort communities, many dating from the turn of the century, were allowed to remain and continue to grow within designated confines. Fire Island has two gay communities—flamboyant Cherry Grove and the more discreet and expensive Fire Island Pines; the other communities reflect a wide range of tastes and lifestyles. Ocean Bay Park, Fair Harbor, and Kismet are party meccas for straight singles. Saltaire, Ocean Beach, and Seaview are fairly exclusive and extremely expensive retreats for families. Point O'Woods, Fire Island's oldest and stodgiest community, preserves its dignity behind a six-foot-high fence topped with barbed wire. **Ocean Bay Park** is one of the few communities where you can step off the ferry from **Bay Shore** without being bombarded by town rules and regulations and wander down to the beach without feeling as if you're intruding on a private compound. It also has a decent no-frills hotel and restaurant, both rare on Fire Island. *The Ocean Bay Park and Saltaire ferries leave from Maple Ave., Bay Shore, tel. 516/665–2115 May–Nov. Cost: $9.50 adults round-trip, $5 one-way; $4.75 children round-trip, $2.50 one-way; $4.25 senior citizens one-way only.*

If you're coming to Fire Island to enjoy the beaches *and* observe the barrier island in its natural state, your best bet is to visit one of the National Seashore areas. From **Sayville,** you can get the ferry to **Sailor's Haven,** where there is not only a superb stretch of beach (with lifeguard protection during the summer) but a network of boardwalks through the Sunken Forest, a primeval maritime hardwood forest hidden behind the dunes. On the bay side of Sailor's Haven there is a marina, a visitor center, and a snack bar. *Ferry leaves from River Rd., Sayville, tel. 516/589–8980, May–Nov. Cost: $3.75 adults one-way; $2 children under 12 one-way. For more information, contact the Fire Island National Seashore headquarters in Patchogue, tel. 516/289–4810.*

Farther east down the island at **Watch Hill,** there is another National Seashore visitor center with the same facilities found at Sailor's Haven, as well as camping. To experience the beach in its primitive state, hike east from Watch Hill into the eight-mile wilderness area that extends to Smith Point West. This is New York State's only federally designated wilderness area. *Shuttles available from the Patchogue LIRR station to the ferry, which leaves from West and Division Sts., Patchogue, tel. 516/475–1665, May–Nov. Cost: $4.50 adults, $2.75 children, $4.25 senior citizens and the handicapped.*

You can also approach the wilderness area from the east by driving to the end of the William Floyd Parkway and parking your car in **Mastic** at the **Smith Point County Park.** Technically, this 2,300-acre park belongs to Suffolk County, and the National Seashore (one-quarter mile west) belongs to the federal government—but it's all the same fabulous barrier beach. Smith Point County Park has a food stand open in the summer and a first-come, first-served camping area. The National Seashore beach, known as Smith Point West, has parking only for the disabled, but it's a short walk from the county lot and the beach is much less crowded. There is also a visitor center open 9–5:30, and a short boardwalk that serves as a self-guided nature trail through the fringe of the wilderness. After that you're on your own. *Smith Point County Park and Smith Point West, end of William Floyd Pkwy., Mastic, tel. 516/281–3010. Admission: $3.50 per car weekdays, $4.50 weekends, Memorial Day–Labor Day. Open year-round sunrise–sunset.*

❽ Heckscher State Park: This is a 1,500-acre park on Great South Bay, the shallow body of water that separates Fire Island from the "mainland" of Long Island. The protected bay waters are calmer and warmer than the ocean—and thus safer for young children. This is a popular park for families, who come to picnic, barbecue, and swim. There are three bay beaches, a pool, boat ramp, nature trails, a bathhouse, camping area, picnic grounds, refreshment stand, cross-country skiing, and hiking trails. *Heckscher State Pkwy., East Islip, tel. 516/581–2100. Admission: $3 per car Memorial Day–June, $4 per car July–Labor Day. Open year-round, sunrise–sunset.*

❾ East Hampton Village and Town Beaches: East Hampton has lovely white-sand beaches overlooked by beautiful, large summer homes, but only *Main Beach* at the end of Ocean Avenue is open to the general public without a permit. Consequently, the beaches attract different types of people here as opposed to, say, Jones Beach. Parking costs $10 per day. In order to park at the other East Hampton village beaches—*Georgica Beach* at the end of Apaquogue Road (family-oriented), *Wiborg Beach* on Highway Behind the Pond, *Egypt* at the end of Old Beach Lane, and *Two Mile Hollow* at the end of Two Mile Hollow Road (popular with gays)—nonresidents must get a season permit from the East Hampton Village Hall at 27 Main St. (tel. 516/324–4150, open weekdays, 9–4) or at Main Beach. The cost is $100 for the season, mid-May through September. Out of season, no permit is necessary to park at the village beaches.

There are also eight restricted beaches controlled by the Town of East Hampton. The ocean beaches are *Indian Wells* and *Atlantic Avenue* in Amagansett (east of East Hampton), and *Kirk Park* and *Ditch Plains* in Montauk; the bay beaches are *Maidstone Park* in East Hampton, *East Lake Drive* and *South Lake Drive* in Montauk, and *Albert's Landing* in Amagansett. Nonresidents can get a season sticker to park at these beaches for $100 at the East Hampton Town Hall, which is at 159 Pantigo Rd.—on Montauk Highway—between East Hampton and Amagansett (tel. 516/324–4143, open weekdays 9–4). Before Memorial Day and after Labor Day, town beaches are open and free to everyone.

❿ Hither Hills State Park: An oceanfront park at **Montauk** with beaches, bathhouse, surf fishing, oceanfront camping, picnic area, refreshment stand, hiking, central shower building, playground, and store (open in summer only). Hither Hills is the only official public beach in Montauk where you can park without a town permit. (There is an unofficial beach just over the dunes from the IGA supermarket at the west end of Montauk village.) *Rte. 217, Montauk, tel. 516/668–2493. Admission: $3.50 per car. Open daily sunrise–sunset, first week of Apr.– mid-Oct. Call 800/456–CAMP for reservations and information on this and all New York State-operated campgrounds.*

North Shore Beaches **Sunken Meadow State Park:** One of the most popular North Shore public beaches, this 1,230-acre state park attracts as **⓫** many as 40,000 people on peak summer weekends. On Sunday the four parking lots may fill up in the morning, so if the weather is hot, try to come on Saturday instead. This is a park for families, who come for the 5,000-foot sound beaches and the lovely wooded picnic and barbecue areas.

Other facilities include a boardwalk, bathhouses, three golf courses, hiking trails, and refreshment stands. *Kings Park, Rte. 25A, north end of Sagtikos Pkwy., tel. 516/269–4333. Admission: $4 per car Memorial Day–Labor Day. Open weekends 6–sunset, weekdays 7–sunset.*

⑫ Wildwood State Park: The big attractions at this lovely 737-acre park are the 1⅜ miles of beach on the sound and the 10 miles of hiking trails through the woods (good for cross-country skiing in the winter). There is also a woodland campground with 320 campsites. The younger, wilder crowd tends to congregate in the most remote section of the campground, and families in the areas nearer the parking lots. Wildwood is most crowded on summer Sundays, when the 500-car lot may fill up by 1 or 2 PM; on Saturdays parking spots are available all day. Other facilities include a bathhouse, central shower building, picnic area, two refreshment stands, a baseball field, and basketball courts. *Hulse Landing Rd., Wading River, Rte. 25A, tel. 516/ 929–4314. Admission: $2.50 per car Memorial Day–third week of June, $3.50 per car third week of June–Labor Day. Open year-round, sunrise–sunset.*

⑬ Orient Beach State Park: This 357-acre park has magnificent views in protected Gardiner's Bay at the eastern tip of the North Fork. Orient Beach is a favorite with bird-watchers and nature lovers who come to observe the osprey and wander in and out of the coves that comprise 10 miles of natural beach or collect shells. On weekends the parking lot can fill up, particularly on beautiful Sundays. Facilities include a bathhouse, fishing, hiking, picnic area, refreshment stand, and horseshoe court. *Rte. 25, Orient, tel. 516/323–2440. Admission: $3 per car Memorial Day–July 3; $4 per car July 4–Labor Day.*

The North Shore

Numbers in the margin correspond with points of interest on the Long Island map.

As you enter Nassau County on Route 25A, you'll cut across the bases of two large peninsulas, Great Neck and Port Washington, the West Egg and East Egg of Fitzgerald's *Great Gatsby*.
❶ Slightly east is **Roslyn,** home to Long Island's largest art museum, the **Nassau County Museum of Art,** located on 145 acres of grass, wild berries, trees, and ponds. Formerly the Frick country home, the building was donated to Childs Frick by his father as a wedding present. With two floors, including 10 galleries, a gift shop, and an art bookshop, the museum displays a variety of changing exhibitions; the grounds include public sculptures. Both the grounds and the museum are open year-round and admission is free, but a donation is suggested. Call before planning a trip to make sure they are not between exhibitions. *Tel. 516/484–9337. Grounds open daily 9–5; museum open Tues.–Sun. 11–5. Café open for lunch.*

Farther east, 25A opens out into the horse country of Old Brookville and Upper Brookville. A short drive north from
❷ there on winding country roads will bring you to **Oyster Bay** and the **Planting Fields Arboretum,** 150 acres of immaculately

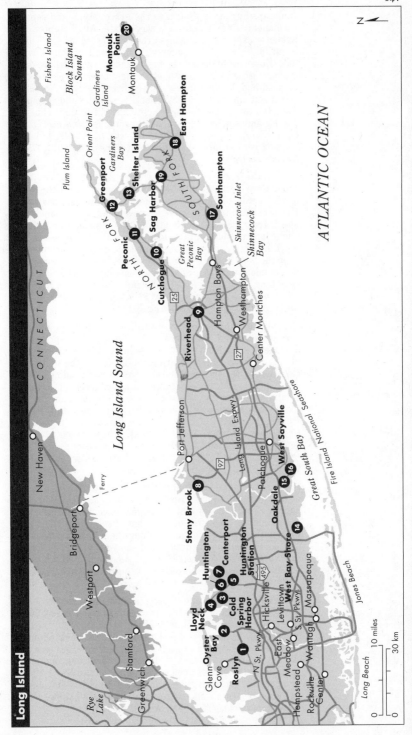

Long Island

N

Fishers Island

Block Island Sound

CONNECTICUT

New Haven

Long Island Sound

Stamford

Greenwich

Rye Lake

Westport

Bridgeport

Ferry

Orient Point

Plum Island

Gardiners Island

Montauk Point

⓴

Montauk

East Hampton

Gardiners Bay

Shelter Island

Greenport

⑫

⑬

Sag Harbor

⑱

⑲ Southampton

NORTH FORK

Peconic

⑪

Cutchogue

⑩

SOUTH FORK

⑰

Shinnecock Inlet

Great Peconic Bay

Shinnecock Bay

25

Riverhead

⑨

Hampton Bays

Westhampton

ATLANTIC OCEAN

Port Jefferson

27

Center Moriches

Long Island Expwy.

97

Stony Brook

⑧

Patchogue

West Sayville

⑮ ⑯

Oakdale

Huntington

Centerport

④ ③ ⑥⑦

⑤

Lloyd Neck

Cold Spring Harbor

Huntington Station

495

Glenn Cove

Oyster Bay

②

West Bay Shore

⑭

Great South Bay

Fire Island National Seashore

Roslyn

①

Hicksville

Levittown

East Meadow

N. St. Pkwy.

S. St. Pkwy.

Wantagh

Massapequa

Hempstead

Rockville Center

Jones Beach

Long Beach

0   10 miles

0   30 km

landscaped grounds that have the grace, style, and sense of permanence of an English country estate. At the center of an immense expanse of flawless green woods stands **Coe Hall,** a beautiful Tudor-style manor with imported antique furnishings. Botanical highlights include stands of rhododendrons and azaleas, greenhouses with stunning flowering plants from tropical and desert climes, and the five-acre synoptic garden (arranged alphabetically by scientific name). Guided tours of Coe Hall are available May–September, Tuesday–Thursday 1–4 PM and year-round by appointment. *Planting Fields Rd., Oyster Bay, 2 mi. north of Rte. 25A, tel. 516/922–9200. Admission: $3 per car, May 1–Labor Day. Open daily 10–5. Closed Christmas Day.*

East of the very posh town of Oyster Bay, a small peninsula called Cove Neck juts into Long Island Sound, and in the center of this peninsula stands **Sagamore Hill,** the summer White House of President Theodore Roosevelt and his permanent residence from 1887 until his death in 1919. The rambling, 23-room Victorian mansion contains many original furnishings, including T.R.'s big-game hunting trophies and gifts from rulers all over the world. The grounds comprise 88 acres of woodlands and manicured grass, and there is an apple orchard and pet cemetery. *Cove Neck Rd., Oyster Bay, 1 mi north of Rte. 25A, tel. 516/922–4447. Admission: $1 adults; children under 16 and senior citizens free. Open daily 9:30–5.*

From the grounds of Sagamore Hill you can take a guided nature walk through the woods to the beach at Cold Spring Harbor; then get back in your car and follow 25A to the Main Street of this historic village. During its heyday in the mid-1800s, ❸ **Cold Spring Harbor** was home port to a fleet of whaling vessels, and today the **Cold Spring Harbor Whaling Museum** offers a fascinating glimpse into this exciting era. The museum contains four rooms of whaling memorabilia, including a fully rigged whaling boat. *Rte. 25A opposite the Turkey La. intersection, Cold Spring Harbor, tel. 516/367–3418. Admission: $2 adults, $1.50 senior citizens, $1 children 6–16. Children under 6 free. Open daily 11–5 Memorial Day–Labor Day; Sept.–May, Tues.–Sun. 11–5.*

If you're interested in what fish look like before they're served at one of Long Island's restaurants, stop at the **Cold Spring Harbor Fish Hatchery and Aquarium.** Since it was established in 1883, more than 15 billion fish have been raised here. Children will enjoy viewing and feeding the numerous species of fish, amphibians, and turtles on display here. *Rte. 25A, Cold Spring Harbor, tel. 516/692–6768. Admission: $2 adults, $1 children 5–12 and adults over 65. Children under 5 free. Open daily 10–5.*

❹ **Caumsett State Park,** one of Long Island's finest natural areas, occupies the bulk of the broad peninsula known as **Lloyd Neck.** Originally the estate of Marshall Field III, Caumsett, the Indian name for the area, is 1,500 unspoiled acres of cliffs, meadows, and woodlands; a two-mile hiking trail emerges on a long stretch of primeval beach on Long Island Sound, one of the very few wild beaches open to the public on the North Shore. The park permits surf fishing and cross-country skiing and offers guided nature walks by reservation. *West Neck Rd., Lloyd Neck, 2 mi north of Rte. 25A, tel. 516/423–1770. Admission: $3 per car May–Sept., free Oct.–Apr. Open daily 8–4:30.*

From Lloyd Neck, return to 25A, proceed a very short way east, and then head south on Route 110 through Huntington and **Huntington Station** to the **Walt Whitman House,** the only New York State historic site on Long Island. Huntington Station has changed beyond recognition since Whitman's day, but the farmhouse where the poet spent his childhood has been preserved. Built by Whitman's father in 1810, the house contains a good collection of 19th-century furnishings as well as some fascinating Whitman memorabilia. There is also a library, a video show, and changing exhibitions relating to the poet's life. *246 Old Walt Whitman Rd., Huntington Station, tel. 516/427–5240. Admission free. Open Wed.–Fri. 1–4, weekends 10–4. Closed holidays. Guided tours and picnic facilities available.*

Continue south along Route 110, crossing over the Northern State Parkway. At Old Country Road head west to Round Swamp Road. Follow signs south to the **Old Bethpage Village Restoration.** On its 200 acres are a blacksmith, a general store, and a country inn with barrels of spices, and sarsaparilla (root beer) on tap. Tour the historic homes. *Round Swamp Rd., Bethpage, tel. 516/420–5280 or 516/420–5281. Admission: $4 adults, $2 children, $1 discount for residents of Nassau County. Open daily 10–4 in winter, 10–5 spring–fall.*

Return north to 25A and **Huntington** to reach another important Long Island cultural landmark, the **Heckscher Museum** in Heckscher Town Park. The museum has a particularly rich collection of 19th-century landscape paintings, and there are changing exhibits relevant to Long Island. The museum staff offers guided tours, and the museum's grounds include picnic areas. *Rte. 25A and Prime Ave., Huntington, tel. 516/351–3250. Suggested donation: $1 adults, 50¢ children under 12 and senior citizens. Open Tues.–Fri. 10–5, weekends 1–5.*

Long Island has been a playground and retreat for the rich for well over 100 years, and there is no better place to see just how different the rich really are than the **Vanderbilt Mansion** in **Centerport,** just a few miles east of the Heckscher Museum on 25A. The 24-room mansion is built in an ornate, Spanish-revival style, and has three impeccably manicured formal gardens. The Vanderbilt Museum houses 17,000 marine and wildlife specimens, and the nearby Vanderbilt Planetarium puts on a fantastic show of more than 11,000 stars in its modern sky theater. The planetarium's 16-inch telescope is available to the public for sky viewings on clear evenings. Call 516/262–STAR for planetarium information, charges, and show times. *Little Neck Rd., Centerport, 1 mi north of Rte. 25A, tel. 516/262–7888. Admission: $5 adults, $4 students and senior citizens, $2 children under 12. Open Tues.–Sat. 10–4, Sun. and holidays 12–5. Closed Thanksgiving, Christmas, New Year's Day.*

From Centerport, follow Route 25A east as it parallels the contours of Smithtown Bay. A few minutes' drive will take you to the **Museums at Stony Brook,** a fascinating group of buildings and exhibits that focus on 19th-century America and give an excellent portrait of the history and art of this epoch. Of particular interest are the internationally famous Carriage Museum, which displays more than 60 horse-drawn vehicles, and the History Museum, which holds changing exhibits of period clothing, historic textiles and toys, and a collection of decoys. The complex also features an art museum (housing the works of William Sidney Mount and other 19th-century Long Island art-

ists), a blacksmith shop, and a restored 19th-century schoolhouse. *1208 Rte. 25A, Stony Brook, tel. 516/751–0066. Admission: $4 adults, $3 senior citizens, $2.75 students, $2 children
6–12, children under 6 free. Open Wed.–Sat. 10–5, Sun. 12–5.
Closed Thanksgiving, Christmas Eve and Day, New Year's
Day.*

Continue east along Route 25A, a hilly, winding, tree-lined
road that opens into **Port Jefferson** harbor. Leave your car in
the parking lot behind Main Street to explore the waterfront
and its many unique crafts and antiques shops. Walk to Prospect Street and visit the **Mather House Museum** with its collection of 19th-century costumes, shell crafts, Indian art, model
boats, and antique furnishings. Admission includes a tour of a
restored pre-Civil War home, a country barn, and an earth
garden. *Tel. 516/473–2665. Open Memorial Day–Labor Day,
weekends 1–4 PM; July and Aug., Tues. and Wed. 1–4 PM. Donation: $1 adults.*

To complete your tour of the North Shore, continue east on
Route 25A until it turns into the rural Sound Avenue just past
Wading River Station. Sound Avenue in turn becomes State
Route 48, the main road through the North Fork, which
branches off from the main body of Long Island east of
❾ Riverhead. This is beautiful farm country, with fields stretching off to the horizon, well-kept, picturesque farmhouses, and
many roadside farm stands open during the summer and early
autumn. Briermere Farm has homemade fruit and berry pies,
Berezny's Farm Stand has superior vegetables and flowers,
and Young's Orchard is the place to stop for apples. All are on
Sound Avenue, just east of Roanoke Avenue. In the past 15
years, the North Fork has emerged as an exciting new wine district; there are now 12 wineries and 30 commercial vineyards
❿ ⓫ scattered around **Cutchogue** and **Peconic.** The area is one of
New York State's sunniest spots, and the climate is very similar
to that of the Bordeaux wine-producing region of France.
Among the most popular vineyards are **Pindar** and **Hargrave.**
While Hargrave is the oldest, in operation since 1973, Pindar,
in existence since 1979, has turned nearly 300 acres of former
potato farms into a thriving vineyard. Tours are offered daily
every half hour year-round, 11–6, concluding with a wine tasting. Long Island wineries produce a variety of wines, but their
specialties tend to be cabernet sauvignon and Chardonnay. In
addition, in the fall of 1985, Pindar produced the first Long Island champagne. *Hargrave is located on Rte. 48 in Cutchogue,
tel. 516/734–5111. Pindar is on Rte. 25 in Peconic, just south of
Rte. 48, tel. 516/734–6200.* For further information about other
Long Island vineyards and wineries, call the Long Island
Grape Growers Association at 516/727–6464.

After touring the Hargrave Vineyard, cut south to State Route
25 and drive east through the historic towns of Cutchogue and
⓬ Southold, through the old fishing village of **Greenport,** which
has a pretty Main Street with quaint shops and a picturesque
harbor, and finally east to Orient Beach State Park at the tip of
the North Fork. (*See* North Shore Beaches, above.)

While in Greenport, you might want to take the 10-minute car
⓭ and passenger ferry over to **Shelter Island,** a beautiful and historic island nestled between the North and South forks. Now
primarily a summer resort and boating center, Shelter Island
was among the first sections of Long Island to be settled by the

English. Points of interest include the **Havens House** on Route
114, built in 1743; the **Victorian-era cottages** and **Union Chapel**
on Shelter Island Heights near the North Ferry dock; the
Manhanset Chapel on Route 114, built in 1890; and the
mansions along Shore Drive in Dering Harbor. The entire
southeast section of the island is the 2,000-acre Mashomack Nature Preserve, with 12 miles of wild shoreline. There is also a
ferry to Shelter Island from the town of North Haven on the
South Fork, and you can use the island as a scenic stepping-
stone to pass from one fork to the other. North Ferry leaves
from Route 114 off Route 25 in Greenport. Call 516/749–0139
for fares and schedule. South Ferry leaves from Route 114 in
North Haven, three miles north of Sag Harbor (*see* below). Call
516/749–1200 for fares and schedule.

Although it is possible to tour the North Shore in one day, you
may want to take refuge for the night in Greenport. Or you can
stretch out the tour a day or two longer, stopping off at one of
the hotels in Cold Spring Harbor, Huntington, or Stony Brook.
(*See* Lodging, below, for each of these towns.)

The South Shore

Begin your tour of the South Shore 50 miles from Manhattan to
⑭ visit the **West Bay Shore** and **Sagtikos Manor,** one of the finest
Colonial homes in America. The British used it as a headquarters during the Revolutionary War; in 1790, after the defeated
British cleared out, George Washington slept here during his
tour of Long Island. The nearly 300-year-old house contains
original furniture, family memorabilia, and Native-American
artifacts. *Rte. 27A, West Bay Shore, tel. 516/661–8348 (call
weekdays 10–noon only). Admission: $2.50 adults, 50¢ chil-
dren. Open July and Aug., Wed., Thurs., and Sun. 1–4; by appointment only during Sept.*

A short drive east of West Bay Shore on Route 27A takes you to
⑮ **Oakdale** and one of the great estates of the South Shore, the
690-acre **Bayard-Cutting Arboretum.** The noble Tudor-style
mansion, the former residence of the Cutting family, serves as
a natural history museum featuring an extensive collection of
mounted birds and Native American artifacts, but it is the
grounds that lures most visitors. There are five self-guided nature walks you can take to see a wide variety of trees, shrubs,
and flowers. *466 Montauk Hwy. (Rte. 27A), Oakdale, tel. 516/
581–1002. Admission: $3 per car, walk-ins free. Open May–
Oct., Wed.–Sun. 10–5:30; Nov.–Apr., Wed.–Sun. 10–4:30.*

⑯ **West Sayville,** a few miles east of Oakdale, is the site of the wonderful **Suffolk Marine Museum,** fittingly situated overlooking
Great South Bay. The small-craft collection includes oyster
vessels, South Bay sailboats, and ice scooters. Also noteworthy
is the exhibit on the U.S. Life Saving Service, fore-runner of
the Coast Guard. *Rte. 27A, West Sayville, tel. 516/567–1733.
Admission free (there is a charge for special exhibits). Open
Wed.–Sat. 10–3, Sun. noon–4.*

⑰ Proceeding east from West Sayville, you'll reach **Southampton**
and the **Parrish Art Museum,** which features 19th- and 20th-
century American paintings and prints, a superbly chosen collection of Renaissance works, and a variety of regularly changing visiting exhibitions. Rare trees imported from all over the
world offset the many fine works of art in the well-tended sculp-

ture garden. A one-hour guided tour is available. *25 Jobs La.,
Southampton, tel. 516/283–2118. Suggested donation: $2.
Open Mon. and Thurs.–Sat. 10–5, Sun. 1–5. Also open Tues.
10–5 mid-June–mid-Sept. Closed Feb.*

Southampton is in the heart of the Hamptons, a string of seaside villages that the East Coast upper crust "discovered" in
the late 19th century and transformed into elegant summer resorts. At the pinnacle of fashion and fame is **East Hampton,**
which, despite the hordes of celebrities and tourists who descend each summer, retains the grace and dignity of its Colonial heritage. If you are driving east along the Montauk
Highway, you'll enter East Hampton on its elm-shaded Main
Street, where the town's classic white Presbyterian Church
(built in 1860), and stately old homes and inns (*see* Lodging, below) stand shoulder to shoulder with trendy shops and galleries. Main Street also has the **Guild Hall,** the town's center of
culture, with changing art exhibits and a year-round program
of community theater.

East Hampton is not a drive-through town; to really see it,
leave your car in the large village parking lot in the commercial
district, behind the playground and tennis courts (turn left
from Main Street onto Newtown Lane, left again on Race Lane
and right on Gingerbread Lane). This is the only place in town
where you can park free all day (village streets have one- or
two-hour parking limits). The most beautiful walk in the village
is around the Town Pond between Main Street and James Lane,
where in the space of a few blocks you'll pass **Home Sweet
Home,** the 1680 saltbox gem commemorated in John Howard
Payne's song and now a museum, and its twin built the same
year, the **Mulford Farm,** also a house museum with period furniture. You will also pass one of the town's much-photographed
and much-painted windmills—Pantigo Mill. The other mill,
Hook Mill, is at the north end of Main Street at the edge of the
North End Burying Ground. *Home Sweet Home, 14 James La.,
tel. 516/324–0713. Admission: $1.50 adults, $1 children. Open
Mon.–Sat. 10–4, Sun. 2–4. Closed Thanksgiving, Christmas,
New Year's Day, and Feb. The Mulford Farm, 10 James La.,
tel. 516/324–6869. Admission: $2 adults, $1.50 senior citizens,
$1 children under 12. Open July–Labor Day, Tues.–Sun. 1–5;
Sept., weekends 1–5; by appointment only at other times.*

Follow James Lane until it runs into Ocean Avenue, and then go
right onto Lily Pond Lane. The rambling, shingle-style houses
on Lily Pond Lane, which parallels the ocean just a block away,
may look like large, elegant, well-tended inns, but in fact they
are private mansions, most of them dating from the turn of the
century. Ocean Avenue, Lily Pond Lane, Egypt Lane, and Two
Mile Hollow Road all dead-end at the ocean, but you need parking permits to park your car at the lots (*see* South Shore
Beaches, above). Newtown Lane will take you back to your car
at the playground. Before you leave, you may want to browse in
the shops and boutiques along Main Street and Newton Lane.

Sag Harbor, which is on the north shore of the South Fork, is a
quick drive from East Hampton through some of the finest,
richest farm country on the island. This quaint and quiet waterside village was an important whaling center from 1775 to 1871.
The town today looks much as it did in the 1870s, with the stately homes of whaling merchants lining Main Street. Leave your
car in the lot between Main Street and Meadow Street and

stroll down the back lanes. Main Street terminates in the 1,000-foot Long Wharf (circa 1820), where there's a nice harbor view. Return to Main Street and walk past the American Hotel (built in 1825), then head left down Washington Street to Division Street, where you'll find the Old Umbrella House, a hip-roofed home built before 1790 and the Georgian-style Sleight houses. A right turn onto Union Street brings you to the Whaler's Church. Built in 1844 in the style of an Egyptian temple, the church is one of the few examples of Egyptian Revival architecture in the United States. Other historic houses of worship include the **Old Methodist Church,** on Madison Street opposite Sage Street, and the **Elizabeth Street Synagogue,** built in the 1880s.

Union Street takes you back to Main Street and the **Sag Harbor Whaling Museum,** the town's best-known attraction and one of the most interesting museums on the island. You enter the collections, appropriately enough, through the jawbones of a right whale. Featured attractions include logbooks, harpoons, and scrimshaw. *Garden and Main Sts., Sag Harbor, tel. 516/ 725-0770. Admission: $2 adults, $1.50 senior citizens, 75¢ children 6–12. Open daily Memorial Day–Sept., Mon.–Sat. 10–5, Sun. 1–5.*

Across the street is the Italianate Hannibal French mansion, built in the 1860s. On nearby Garden Street is New York State's first **Custom House,** which dates from 1789. The building, which also served as a post office into the 19th century, has been restored and contains some lovely antique furnishings. *Garden St., Sag Harbor, tel. 516/941-9444. Admission: $1.50 adults, $1 children, 75¢ senior citizens. Open June–Sept., Tues.–Sun. 10–5; May and Oct., Fri.–Sun. 10–5.*

If you're visiting during the summer, make a trip to the **Sag Harbor Fire Department Museum.** Built in 1834, this building was home to New York State's first fire department. Exhibits include trophies and antique fire equipment, and tours are available by appointment. *Corner of Sage and Church Sts., Sag Harbor, tel. 516/725-4135. Admission: $1 adults, 50¢ children. Open July 4–Labor Day, Thurs.–Tues. noon–4 PM.*

20 Return to State Route 27 and proceed through the village of Montauk to Long Island's eastern extremity at **Montauk Point.** The 109-foot **Lighthouse** at Montauk Point State Park was built in 1797 by order of President George Washington. There is a small museum housed in the old keeper's quarters, and you can now climb up to the top of the tower for a fantastic view of the East End, the distant shore of Connecticut, and Block Island off the coast of Rhode Island. *Rte. 27, Montauk, tel. 516/668-2544. Admission: $2 adults, 75¢ children 6–12, children under 6 free. Open May–Columbus Day, daily 11–6; Columbus Day–Nov., weekends 10–4:30.*

What to See and Do with Children

New York State Fish Hatchery and Aquarium (*see* Exploring Long Island, above).

Lewin Farms, on Route 48 in Wading River (tel. 516/929-4327), is one of the largest u-pick farms on Long Island. From June through December you can pick strawberries, melons, nectarines, peaches, corn, cucumbers, peas, peppers, squash, tomatoes, and apples, among other fruits and vegetables. Strawberry season is extremely popular. Generally you pay only 50¢–$1 per quart, and there is no charge for strawberries you eat while you pick. The New York State Department of Agriculture's free "Guide to Farm Fresh Food" lists all farms that allow you to pick your own with the dates and fruits and vegetables available (tel. 516/727–3580). Additional information can also be obtained from the Riverhead Chamber of Commerce (tel. 516/ 727–7600).

Long Island Game Farm. Children of all ages can cuddle and bottle-feed baby animals and hand-feed deer. There is a 20-minute wild-tiger show, a 10-minute elephant show, and an authentic 1860s train that takes you around the farm to see zebras, llamas, monkeys, camels, bears, buffalos, peacocks, and many other animals. There are also amusement rides, picnic areas, and snack bars. *Exit 70 of the Long Island Expressway to Chapman Blvd., Manorville, tel. 516/878–6644. Admission: $8.45 adults, $5.95 children 2–11 and senior citizens; children under 2 free. Open mid-Apr.–mid-Oct. daily 9–6.*

Animal Farm. Similar to the game farm, this facility has hundreds of animals to pet and feed, as well as an antique auto museum, a puppet theater, kiddie rides, and a picnic area. *184A Wading River Rd. (Exit 69 on the Long Island Expressway), Manorville, tel. 516/878–1785. Admission: $6 adults, $4 children 2–12 and senior citizens; children under 2 free. Open Apr.–Oct., daily 10–5.*

Off the Beaten Track

For a unique view of Long Island, you can learn to parachute and make your first jump on the same day. Call **Skydive Long Island** (tel. 516/878–JUMP) Thursday–Monday, April–November. Rates are from $185 to $210, and you must be 18 or over.

Shopping

Long Island offers a rich variety of shopping opportunities. The island is known for its shopping malls, the largest of which is the **Roosevelt Field Mall** (tel. 516/742–8000) in Garden City, with 185 stores. Branches of many New York City department stores, including Bloomingdale's, Saks Fifth Avenue, and Lord & Taylor are also located in Garden City (on Franklin Avenue). Manhasset's "Miracle Mile" along Route 25A has such fashionable stores as Bonwit Teller, Brooks Brothers, Lord & Taylor, and Polo/Ralph Lauren.

If you're looking for bargains, visit the **Flea Market at Roosevelt Raceway** (tel. 516/222–1530) on Old Country Road, Westbury, which claims to be the largest flea market in the country (2,000-plus vendors). It is open year-round on Sundays 9–5 ($2 per car, $1 per walk-in) and on Wednesdays from April to December 9–4 ($1.50 per car, 50¢ per walk-in).

The Hamptons are the place for shoppers looking for the most stylish, trendy (and expensive) clothing, artwork, leather goods, rugs, and antiques. Many shops and boutiques can be found along East Hampton's Main Street. (*See* The South Shore, above.)

Participant Sports

Surf fishing, golf, hiking, horseback riding, roller skating, and cross-country skiing are popular activities at many of the state parks on Long Island. Call the Long Island Tourism Association (tel. 516/794–4222) or the individual state parks (*see* Long Island Beaches, above) for more information.

Boating The sailing, yachting, and deep-sea fishing possibilities on Long Island's waters are nearly limitless. For information about boat rentals, contact one of the organizations below.

Captree Boatmen's Association. The association has a combined fleet of 34 open- and charter-fishing boats with courteous crews. *Captree State Park, Box 5372, Babylon 11707, tel. 516/ 669–6464.*

Great South Bay Charters, Ltd. Yacht charters are available on a daily or weekly basis. *5510 Merrick Rd. (Rte. 27A), Massapequa 11758, tel. 516/799–5968.*

Oyster Bay Sailing School. This 10-year-old sailing school offers weekend classes and three–five day vacation packages—including "Learn to Sail," "Coastal Cruising," and "Barefoot Cruising"—at their two locations in Oyster Bay and Port Jefferson. *Box 447, West End Ave., Oyster Bay 11771, tel. 516/624–7900. Open Apr.–Oct., daily 8:30 AM–6 PM.*

Long Island Sportfishing Network. This is a booking and information service for all of Long Island. *Box 2008, Calverton 11933, tel. 516/369–0879 (after 3 PM).*

Spectator Sports

Car Racing General stock-car racing from late April–mid-September. *Riverhead Raceway, Riverhead, tel. 516/727–0010.*

Hockey The New York Islanders of the NHL play at the Nassau Veterans Memorial Coliseum on Hempstead Turnpike in Uniondale. For ticket information call 516/794–4100, but keep in mind that Islander tickets may be difficult to obtain.

Dining and Lodging

Dining When you mention Long Island food, most people tend to think of duckling, clams, and potatoes—but nowadays Long Island restaurants run the gamut from fast-food chains through pizzerias and family-style eateries to ethnic restaurants and elegant country inns.

Not surprisingly, Long Island draws on the bounty of its surrounding waters, especially on the East End, where commercial fishing remains a vital industry. The catch of the day at Montauk or Greenport may feature swordfish, halibut, flounder, bluefish, or shrimp. Many island restaurants reflect the area's large Italian-American population, either in their menus, their ownership, or both. The East End has long historic ties to New England, so don't be surprised to find such typically New England specialties as clam and corn chowder, clam pie, turkey, and lobster on the menus of restaurants out here. If the idea of dining near the water appeals to you, Long Island will reward you with many memorable meals with a view.

Category	Cost*
Very Expensive	over $60
Expensive	$40–$60
Moderate	$20–$40
Inexpensive	under $20

per person without tax, service, or drinks

Lodging Not long ago, lodging on Long Island meant dreary guest houses, cozy bungalow colonies, or a few long-established and rather stodgy hotels—but recent years have brought all of the major motel chains to Long Island, as well as a resurgence in hotel construction. If you're spending the night on the island now, you should have little trouble finding accommodations to suit your itinerary and your budget. One of the more outstanding island lodgings, the Garden City Hotel opposite the Long Island Railroad station in Garden City, sets the standard for luxury on Long Island. A landmark for over 100 years, the hotel was razed a decade ago and replaced by an even posher, more stylish incarnation.

For those who prefer the bed-and-breakfast route, most local chambers of commerce, particularly on the East End, can provide information on B&Bs in their towns.

Category	Cost*
Very Expensive	over $120
Expensive	$90–$120
Moderate	$50–$90
Inexpensive	under $50

The price categories reflect prices during the "season" (Memorial Day–Labor Day). Off-season prices are considerably lower. These prices are for a double room and do not include tax or gratuities.

Highly recommended restaurants and accommodations are indicated by a star ★.

Amagansett

Dining **Gordon's.** This airy, modern, and welcoming restaurant is a longtime favorite with the locals and popular with summer people. The best entrees are veal chops with brown sauce and mushrooms, Long Island duckling with apricot brandy sauce and wild rice, and scampi. This is not a flashy, ostentatious restaurant, but rather a simple and comfortable place to relax over very good food. *Main St., tel. 516/267–3010. Jacket required for dinner. Reservations essential for summer weekends. AE, DC, MC, V. Closed for lunch July and Aug. Closed Mon.; Sun.; and Mon. after Columbus Day; and Jan. and Feb. Expensive.*

Inn at Napeague. Nautical is the decor at this restaurant to match the fresh seafood served, including mako shark caught off the shores of Long Island. Besides the seafood specialties— bouillabaise, broiled swordfish, lobster fradiavolo—the inn serves Continental meat dishes such as beef Wellington. Special attention is given families; children's portions are available. *Montauk Hwy., tel. 516/267–3332. Dress: casual. Reservations advised. AE. Closed early Nov.–end of Apr. Moderate.*

Lodging **Sea Crest.** These full efficiency apartments are located on 500
★ feet of oceanfront, putting them several notches above the ordinary motel fare. The rooms are air-conditioned and have private balconies/patios. You have your choice of poolside or more expensive oceanside rooms. *Drawer X, 11930, tel. 516/267–3159 or 800/SEA-DAYS. 74 rooms with bath. Facilities: barbecue grills, heated pool, tennis. MC, V. Open Apr.–Nov. Very Expensive.*

★ **Windward Shores.** If you're looking for elegance with an oceanside setting, you'll find it year-round in one of the modern suites of this luxury resort motel. The suites have sun decks or patios, ceiling fans, skylights, and spiral staircases, and the tan-and-beige color scheme makes the rooms look like an extension of the sand dunes right outside the picture windows. The 400 feet of ocean beach is private. *Box L, 11930, tel. 516/267–8600. 45 rooms with bath. Facilities: heated freshwater pool, tennis. No credit cards. Very Expensive.*

Sun Haven Motel. The rooms are clean and modern, with kitchenettes and ceiling fans, and the ocean is right at your doorstep. *Box BE, Montauk Hwy., 11930, tel. 516/267–3448. 48 rooms with bath. Facilities: heated pool, Chinese restaurant, sauna, tennis. AE, MC, V. Open late May–mid-Oct. Moderate–Very Expensive.*

East Hampton

Dining **The Palm at the Huntting Inn.** The Palm (with two branches in New York City and another East Hampton location at the Hedges Inn) is a power restaurant. It attracts a powerful crowd of high-profile New York Upper East Siders who come here on weekends to see and be seen and to treat themselves to the lavish portions of steak and lobster for which the Palm has become famous. The New York–cut sirloins, 16-ounce filet mignons, and three-pound (and up) lobsters may not be the most delicate fare, but they are prepared carefully and served sumptuously. If you're not in the mood for beefsteak, you can choose a fish steak such as tuna, swordfish, or salmon; among the better pasta offerings are linguine with red or white clam sauce. What the Palm lacks in imagination, it more than makes up for in the generosity of the portions. Dessert may be unthinkable after three pounds of lobster or a pound of beef, but if you can contemplate a sweet, try the Key lime pie or pecan pie. The room is done in dark wood and brass fixtures, and there is a screened-in porch with ceiling fans. The lively lounge area features a guitar player on weekends. The Hedges location is quieter, more intimate, and less flashy, but the food is the same. *94 Main St., tel. 516/324–0410. Reservations for parties of four or more only. Dinner. AE, DC, MC, V. Very Expensive.*

The Laundry. Formerly a commercial laundry, this place is now one of the most chi-chi restaurants in an increasingly chi-chi town. It is also one of the few East End restaurants that stay open year-round. If you're looking for East Hampton celebrities, you'll find them here (one of the restaurant's owners is Hollywood superagent Sam Cohen). American grill food is served in a simple, no-frills dining room that retains the brick wall and high-pitched ceiling from the old wash-and-fold days. Grilled seafood is the specialty of the house, and seafood entrees vary with the season. The smash-hit dessert is black-and-white chocolate mousse for two. The restaurant is great fun, and after midnight there is a lively bar scene for singles. The lounge has a pit area with a fireplace roaring in the cooler months. *31 Race La., tel. 516/324–3199. No reservations. AE, DC, MC, V. No lunch. Closed Mon. Moderate.*

The Buttery. This quaint indoor/outdoor cafe is open for breakfast, lunch, and early dinner. The light, airy room is decorated with art from a local gallery and opens onto a porch filled with umbrella-topped tables. The restaurant's head baker is English, and he oversees the on-premises production of top-notch breads, muffins, pies, and cakes. His influence is reflected in their popular English breakfast: kippers and scones. The restaurant does a brisk morning business, when local folk and weekend visitors stop in to read their newspapers over cups of coffee and fresh muffins. *66 Newtown La., tel. 516/324–3725. Reservations accepted. No credit cards. Inexpensive.*

Lodging   **Huntting Inn.** Each room at the Huntting, built in 1699 and run as an inn since 1751, is different, but all are furnished with floral chintz wall coverings, chaise-longue sofas, fluffy comforters, brass and wrought-iron beds, and fresh flowers; all are air-conditioned. The highly regarded Palm Restaurant is on its premises (*see* Dining, above). *94 Main St., 11937, tel. 516/324–0410. 26 rooms with bath. Facilities: bar, fishing, horseback riding, restaurant, tennis privileges. AE, DC, MC, V. Open late Mar.–Dec. Expensive–Very Expensive.*

Bassett House Inn. This 12-unit inn is noted for its friendly, home-style feel. Fireplaces and whirlpool tubs are available in some rooms, and there is a common living room/dining area where a full breakfast is included. *128 Montauk Hwy., Box 1426, 11937, tel. 516/324–6127. Facilities: backyard with barbecue, beach. AE, MC, V. Moderate–Very Expensive.*

1770 House. This Early American village house has been tastefully converted into a gem of a small hotel. Rooms are furnished with antiques from the owner's collection, which includes a number of superb old grandfather and mantel clocks. There is a pretty little garden right outside the front door and a fine restaurant known for its Continental cuisine and candlelight dinners. *143 Main St., 11937, tel. 516/324–1770. 12 rooms with bath. Facilities: golf and tennis nearby. CB, DC, MC, V. Moderate–Very Expensive.*

★   **Maidstone Arms.** This historic inn, founded in 1850, is the coziest and most comfortable in town. It also has one of the best locations—right across from the town pond, a pristine park surrounded by East Hampton's oldest streets and most beautiful homes. The rooms are air-conditioned and Continental breakfast is included. The inn's dining room features French country cooking (*see* Dining, above). *207 Main St., 11937, tel. 516/324–5006. 16 rooms and 3 cottages with bath. Facilities: bar, restaurant. AE, MC, V. Moderate–Expensive.*

Freeport

Dining   **Trudy B.** Situated right on the Hudson Canal, this Continental restaurant features fresh fish and lobster, as well as hefty meat dishes. The dining room is modern and stylish with lots of cedar wood, glass, and brass, and there is a stone fireplace. You can also dine overlooking the canal in a glassed-in greenhouse. If you're really hungry try the "Hudson Canal"—half a lobster, clams, scallops, squid, and shrimp in marinara sauce, served over linguine. The best dessert is the homemade puff pastry filled with ice cream and covered with chocolate sauce and whipped cream. Friday and Saturday 9 PM–1 AM, enjoy live '50s & '60s music; there is a $5 cover charge without dinner. *255 Hudson Ave., tel. 516/546–5555. Reservations advised for Fri. or Sat. night. AE, CB, DC, MC, V. Closed Mon.–Tues. Moderate.*

Garden City

Lodging **Garden City Hotel.** Until it was razed a decade ago, this hotel
★ had been a landmark of tradition and impeccable standards for more than a century. The all new Garden City Hotel is more luxurious, more sophisticated, and even more expensive than the original. This is a world-class hotel, the most opulent on Long Island, and the rival of the finest Manhattan has to offer. Air-conditioned rooms are furnished with fine furniture and oversize beds, and there is 24-hour room service. Special rates for senior citizens and facilities for the disabled are available. *45 Seventh St., 11530, tel. 516/747–3000 or 800/547–0400 outside New York. 280 rooms with bath. Facilities: shopping arcade, bar, health club, nightclub, golf nearby, indoor pool, beauty salon, lounge, 2 restaurants. AE, CB, MC, V. Expensive.*

Glen Head

Dining **Pappagallos.** The northern Italian cooking here makes this one
★ of the best restaurants on the North Shore. Under the striking modern chandeliers that hang from the high ceiling, you can feast on seafood, the pasta of the day prepared at your table, or such dishes as steak Rossini, filet mignon on toast served with truffles and topped with a rich wine sauce flavored with imported mushrooms. The dessert cart is also a knockout. *716 Glen Cove Ave., tel. 516/676–3400. Jacket and tie required. Reservations advised for dinner. AE, CB, DC, MC, V. Closed Sat., Sun. No lunch, Mon. Moderate.*

Greenport

Dining **Claudio's.** A Greenport landmark for well over 120 years, Claudio's is the oldest family-owned restaurant in the United States. This is the place where waterside dining began. The two large dining rooms, decorated with artifacts from the J-boats that raced in the America's Cup during the 1930s, face the harbor through large picture windows. Local seafood is the specialty. The one fancy touch here is the 35-foot-long marble and mahogany bar with huge mirrors behind it. Claudio's, which also has a marina, is popular with yachtsmen in the summer. If you're coming from Shelter Island, you can walk here from the north ferry. *Foot of Main St. on the harbor, tel. 516/477–0627. Dress: informal. Reservations accepted. Lunch, dinner. MC, V. Closed mid-Nov.–mid-Apr.; closed Tues. mid-Apr.–May, Sept.–mid-Nov. Moderate.*

Lodging **Silver Sands Motel.** At this motel, you have Greenport at your backyard and 1,000 feet of private Peconic Bay beach in your front yard. There are a variety of rooms and cottages (some with kitchenettes); refrigerators, complimentary Continental breakfasts and, except for the cottages, daily maid service. *Box 285, Silvermere Rd., 11944, tel. 516/477–0011. 40 rooms with bath. Facilities: fishing, sailing, pool, waterskiing. Special rates during the off-season. AE, CB, DC, MC, V. Moderate– Expensive.*

Townsend Manor Inn. This charming, historic inn, built in 1835, combines the best of country style with the convenience of a waterside location just one-half mile beyond downtown Greenport. There are single rooms, suites, and apartments, all air-conditioned. The decor is Colonial, but each room is furnished differently. An inviting family-type hotel, it is especially popular with yachtsmen because it has its own full-service transient marina. Wineries, beaches, and Greenport shops are nearby. *714 Main St., 11944, tel. 516/477–2000. 23 rooms with bath. Facilities: bar, marina, restaurant, swimming pool, with golf, fishing, and tennis nearby. AE, CB, DC, MC, V. Moderate–Expensive.*

Greenvale

Dining **Dar Tiffany.** Appearances notwithstanding—the gray-stone building looks more like a space-age fortress than a restaurant, and the inside is heavy on chrome, mirrors, and neon—this is a traditional steak and seafood house. The crowd is stylish. The extensive wine list features more than 140 varieties, and don't leave without sampling the homemade ice cream. *44 Glen Cove Rd., just north of Rte. 25A, tel. 516/625–0444. Dress: informal. Reservations advised. Lunch weekdays, dinner daily. AE, CB, DC, MC, V. Expensive.*

Hampton Bay

Lodging **Hampton Maid.** The Hampton Maid is a decided cut above the standard American motel. Air-conditioned rooms are furnished with brass and antiques, and their private patios/balconies overlook Shinnecock Bay. Two units are located in a reproduction of an old windmill. The five acres of grounds are meticulously landscaped. Rooms have refrigerators. *Box 713, 11946, tel. 516/728–4166. 30 rooms with bath. Facilities: antiques shop, meeting rooms, playground, picnic tables, pool. AE, MC, V. Closed Nov.–Mar. Expensive.*

Hauppauge

Lodging **Wind Watch.** Situated in the middle of Long Island just off the LIE, this full-service Marriott hotel and golf club is a convenient halfway point between Manhattan and the East End. Amenities include a concierge floor, complimentary breakfast, and an honor bar with complimentary hors d'oeuvres. *1717 Vanderbilt Motor Pkwy., 11788, tel. 516/232–9800. 362 rooms, 6 suites. Facilities: 4 restaurants, 18-hole golf course, indoor and outdoor pools, whirlpool, sauna, health club, 2 tennis courts, gift shop, laundry and dry-cleaning service, conference rooms. AE, DC, MC, V. Very Expensive.*

Huntington

Dining **Fabio's.** This intimate, romantic restaurant offers cuisines of both Brazil and northern Italy. A highly recommended Brazilian dish is Peixada, a fish soup brimming with lobster, shrimp, scallops, and clams. Italian cooking is deliciously represented by the black and white ravioli filled with lobster and served with a lobster tail. A piano bar and weekend samba player enhance the appeal of this popular, sophisticated place. *62 Stewart Ave., tel. 516/549-7074. Dress: informal. Reservations advised for weekend dinners. AE, MC, V. Closed Sat. and Sun. lunch. Moderate.*

Jericho

Dining **Milleridge Inn.** Basic, old-fashioned American food is served here in a historic, Colonial mansion, complete with fireplaces and antiques. Specialties include prime rib of beef and jumbo mushrooms stuffed with shrimp and crabmeat. Milleridge features a couple of low-calorie entrees for either lunch or dinner. Children will enjoy a visit to the replica of a Colonial village just outside; it has eight shops, including a bakery where the inn's bread is baked. The inn is appropriately decorated for every holiday, and carolers are a highlight of the Christmas season. *Hicksville Rd., tel. 516/931-2201. Jacket required. Reservations advised. Lunch, dinner and Sun. brunch, 11:30-2:30. AE, CB, DC, MC, V. Closed Christmas. Inexpensive.*

Melville

Lodging **Royce Carlin Hotel.** This midisland hotel, a blend of casual elegance and lush decor, has 305 spacious guest rooms and suites. *598 Broadhollow Rd., 11747, tel. 516/845-1000. Facilities: 2 restaurants, piano lounge, disco, indoor pool with waterfall, fitness center, health spa, outdoor pool, lighted tennis courts, ballroom, meeting rooms. AE, MC, V. Very Expensive.*

Merrick

Dining **The Chinatown Seafood Restaurant.** Szechuan and Cantonese
★ dishes presented with style and priced reasonably make this a truly superior Chinese restaurant. A host of attentive waiters are ready to bring you such specialties as the Seafood Basket, a deliciously crunchy, deep-fried Taro basket filled with lobster, crabmeat, scallops, and Chinese vegetables. *2222 Merrick Rd. (Rte. 27A), tel. 516/546-0671. Dress: informal. Reservations advised for large groups on weekends. Lunch, dinner. AE, CB, DC, MC, V. Inexpensive.*

Montauk

Dining **Gosman's.** This classy fish restaurant, jam-packed in the summer, has a spectacular location at the entrance to Montauk harbor, indoor and outdoor dining, and the freshest possible fish (Gosman's is also a wholesale and retail fish supplier). It's also huge—it seats 400 between its indoor dining room, done in a low-key nautical style, two deck dining areas, and patio on the water—and hugely popular. Since reservations aren't taken, you may have to wait some time to be seated and served in peak season. Spend the time browsing through the numerous art, gift, and clothing shops, located in the Gosman's Dock complex. Try the broiled fluke, which is not available at many places outside Montauk, or the broiled tuna. Good choices for dessert are chocolate torte, pecan chocolate pie, and lime pie. *West Lake Dr., tel. 516/668-5330. Dress: casual but proper (no jogging shorts). No reservations. No credit cards. Open noon-10 PM. Closed mid-Oct.-Mar. Moderate.*

Lodging **Gurney's Inn Resort and Spa.** Long popular for its fabulous loca-
★ tion high on a bluff overlooking 1,000 feet of private ocean beach, Gurney's has become even more famous in recent years for its health and beauty spa, which features the use of seawater and sea plants. The large, luxurious rooms all have ocean views. The indoor pool is nearly Olympic-size and has heated salt water. Guests have the choice of a modified or full American meal plan; the ocean-view restaurant has a huge dining room and delicious Continental cuisine. *Old Montauk Hwy., 11954, tel. 516/668-2345. 125 rooms with bath. Facilities: bar, health club, barber, drugstore, beauty shop, meeting rooms, recreation room, indoor pool, restaurant, golf and tennis privileges, and extensive spa facilities, 5 including Roman bath, whirlpool, mud baths, and massage. AE, DC, MC, V. Very Expensive.*

Driftwood. These deluxe studios, junior one-bedroom apartments, or 2½-room suites feature daily maid and baby-sitting services. The executive studios have private patios overlooking the water. All 52 units have refrigerators. *Box S, Montauk 11954, tel. 516/668-5744. Facilities: pool, beach, tennis, playground, shuffleboard, ping-pong, volleyball. No credit cards. Closed Oct.-Apr. Moderate-Very Expensive.*

★ **Shepherds Neck Inn.** This country inn gives you a real feel for the simple, unpretentious seagoing style that sets Montauk apart from the trendier Hamptons to the west. Located right in the village, it has five acres of quiet grounds and spacious rooms. All rooms have color TVs and cable, and all are air-conditioned. Guests choose between two meal plans: Bed & Breakfast or Modified American (breakfast and dinner). The kitchen features seafood and locally grown vegetables. Golf, beaches, and boats are nearby. *Second House Rd., Box 639, 11954, tel. 516/668-2105. 70 rooms with bath. Facilities: 2 conference rooms available with AV and VCR equipment, movie room with nightly features, horseback riding and fishing nearby, restaurant, bar, heated pool, tennis. MC, V. Moderate-Expensive.*

Northport

Dining **Australian Country Inn and Gardens.** The owners of this restaurant have tried hard to re-create a little bit of "Down Under" in the midst of Northport. Waiters and waitresses wear bush clothing, and the Australian beer comes in whopping 25-ounce cans. The downstairs dining rooms feature an adventurous menu, and the bar area is casual and relaxing. Specialties include Golden Mountain Lambatty (loin lamb chops with peaches and brandy cream sauce) and Sydney Steamboat (lobster tails with shrimps, clams, crab legs, and Pacific Pearl mussels brewed in butter, garlic, scallions, parsley and pimentos). *1036 Salonga Rd. (Rte. 25A), tel. 516/754-4400. Dress: infor-*

mal. Reservations advised for weekend dinners. AE, DC, MC, V. Closed Sat. lunch. Inexpensive.

Oyster Bay

Dining **Canterbury Ales.** Although you can still order such traditional fare as shepherd's pie or brown stew, the kitchen of this publike establishment has of late moved away from the English theme and turned to seafood. The oyster bar, one of the most extensive on Long Island, features oysters from Oyster Bay. (No relation to the Canterbury Ales at 314 New York Ave. in Huntington, tel. 516/549–4404.) *46 Audrey Ave., tel. 516/922–3614. Dress: informal. AE, CB, DC, MC, V. Inexpensive.*

Port Jefferson

Dining and Lodging ★ **Danfords Inn at Bayles Dock.** This exquisite English-style country inn, directly overlooking Long Island Sound, has all the amenities of a well-run modern hotel. The rooms are tastefully furnished with antiques or reproductions and first-class paintings from the owner's collection. Tennis courts and swimming are within walking distance. The inn's restaurant serves gourmet cooking in a dining room with a spectacular view of Port Jefferson Harbor. The sautéed filet of sole in pecan butter sauce and the jumbo shrimp wrapped in bacon and Swiss cheese are excellent. *25 East Broadway, 11777, tel. 516/928–5200. 86 rooms and suites with bath. Facilities: 75-slip transient marina, exercise room, conference rooms, FAX machine. Restaurant: reservations advised; dress: informal. AE, CB, DC, MC, V. Expensive–Very Expensive.*

Dining **Savories.** Delicate French lace window curtains are a clue to the cuisine of this northern Italian/French restaurant in the heart of Port Jefferson Village. House specialties include shrimp cognac and beef chanterelle. The Theatre III dinner/theater package ($31.95 per person) includes theater ticket, soup or salad, main course, dessert, coffee or tea. Call in advance as tickets sell out quickly. *318 Wynne La., tel. 516/331–4747. Jacket advised at dinner. Reservations advised. AE, DC, MC, V. Expensive.*

Quogue

Lodging **The Inn at Quogue.** This is a quaint 200-year-old inn with 15 rooms, 12 with private bath, TV, and telephone. Two cottages are also available. *Quogue St., 11959, tel. 516/653–6560. Facilities: restaurant, piano bar, and access to beach, golf, and shops. Closed Nov.–Apr. Expensive–Very Expensive.*

Roslyn

Dining **Il Villagio.** This restaurant offers a touch of Continental sophistication in the heart of picturesque Old Roslyn village. Specialties include *Dentice Al Rosmarinio* (red snapper with white-wine sauce), *Crevettes aux Roquefort* (large shrimp and Roquefort cheese), and *osso buco* (braised veal shanks). Valet parking is available. *1446 Old Northern Blvd., tel. 516/484–9550. Jacket required. Reservations advised for weekends. AE, MC, V. Moderate.*
George Washington Manor. Though George Washington did not

sleep here, he did have breakfast in this 1740 Colonial mansion, now an elegant restaurant. The spacious, antiques-filled interior is divided into nine dining rooms. The kitchen does quite well with Yankee pot roast served with potato pancakes, Norwegian salmon, fried scallops, and prime rib on Saturday nights. Black forest layer cake heads the dessert list. *1305 Old Northern Blvd., tel. 516/621–1200. Jacket and tie recommended. Reservations advised for weekend dinners and Sunday brunch. AE, CB, DC, MC, V. Inexpensive–Moderate.*

Sag Harbor

Dining **American Hotel Restaurant.** This historic bed & breakfast is exceptionally noted for its fine French country restaurant, which spreads through two dining rooms. Its renowned wine list includes 600 varieties ranging in price from $18 to $3,000 a bottle. *Main St., 11963, tel. 516/725–3535. No credit cards. No lunch weekdays. Very Expensive.*

Lodging **Baron's Cove Inn.** This newly renovated motel has its own marina. The air-conditioned rooms have kitchenettes and color TVs and some have private patios/balconies with water views. *West Water St., 11963, tel. 516/725–2100. 66 rooms with bath. Facilities: fishing, golf, horseback riding, nearby marina, pool, room service, tennis, restaurant, meeting rooms. AE, MC, V. Open year-round. Moderate–Very Expensive.*

St. James

Dining **Mirabelle.** As soon as you're seated, complimentary pâté or
★ salmon-mousse tidbits are brought to the table. This is the first of the many fine touches that make a meal at this sophisticated but unpretentious French chef–owned restaurant so special. Among the entrees, rack of lamb and boned duck with glazed sauce show off the chef's strengths. And don't leave without sampling the ginger-almond tart. The elegant French-country atmosphere perfectly complements the food. *404 N. Country Rd. (Rte. 25A), tel. 516/584–5999. Dress: informal. Reservations advised. AE, CB, DC, MC, V. Closed Mon. Dinner only weekends. Moderate.*

Shelter Island

Lodging **Ram's Head Inn.** The Ram's Head has the most picturesque location on Shelter Island and makes the most of it. An attractive, shingle-style building, it sits atop a gentle hill with acres of lawn sloping down to the calm waters of Coecles Harbor. The rooms are small but comfortable, with flowery wallpaper and maple furniture. The inn also has a fine restaurant featuring Continental cuisine, with such offerings as Long Island duckling, rack of lamb, and saffron shrimp. *Shelter Island Heights, 11965, tel. 516/749–0811. 18 rooms, 4 with private bath. Facilities: swimming, boating, tennis, restaurant. MC, V. Closed Nov.–Apr. Expensive.*
★ **Shelter Island Resort.** This is a friendly, family-run resort on a gentle bluff overlooking Shelter Island Sound. The resort's 750 feet of private beachfront is ideal for swimming: The water is warm and gentle, the sand soft and white. The comfortable air-conditioned rooms have large private sun decks with chaise longues and umbrellas. The charming Victorian district known

as Shelter Island Heights is a short walk away. A modified American meal plan (breakfast, dinner) is available. *Box AO, Shore Rd., 11965, tel. 516/749–2001. 20 rooms with bath. Facilities: bicycles, barbecue grill, paddleboats, fishing, meeting room, restaurant, golf and tennis privileges. AE, DC, MC, V. Moderate–Very Expensive.*

Southampton

Dining **Old Post House Restaurant.** Housed in the Post House Inn, this elegant French-American restaurant exudes the subtle, unobtrusive atmosphere of a historic manor. Built in 1684, it is the second-oldest building in South Hampton. Specials include rack of lamb with lentils and rosemary, and grilled tuna, and the service is excellent. *136 Main St., 11968, tel. 516/283–9696. Reservations required. DC, MC, V. Very Expensive.*

Lobster Inn. As you might suspect from the name, this is a seafood restaurant specializing in lobster—steamed and simply served with fresh lemon and melted butter. Fresh fish of the day and the bizarrely named Splat (Steamed Shellfish Platter for Two) also are available. *162 Inlet Rd., eastern end of Rte. 27, tel. 516/283–9828. Dress: informal. No reservations. AE, MC, V. Expensive.*

Driver's Seat. Manhattan Yuppies love this warm and rustic restaurant, and others find it appealing, too. Winter guests like its fireplace-heated, 100-seat dining room, and summer visitors prefer its cheerful, umbrella-shaded patio. The cuisine is basic American (steaks, burgers, and chops), with the emphasis on local fishes (tuna, mako shark, and weakfish) caught in season. There are two bars for the thirsty. *62 Jobs La., tel. 516/283–6606. Dress: casual. No reservations. AE, DC, MC, V. Inexpensive.*

Lodging **Southampton Inn.** This is not a country inn but a deluxe miniresort with comfortable accommodations, tennis courts, a pool, and a health spa. The shops of Southampton are a short walk away, and the beach is just a mile and a half down the road. There is a good restaurant featuring standard American fare, live entertainment and dancing on weekends, and room service. Special rates for senior citizens and facilities for the handicapped are available. *Hill St. at First Neck La., 11968, tel. 516/283–6500. 90 rooms with bath. Facilities: bar, health club, fishing, golf privileges, game room, meeting rooms, recreation room, pool, restaurant, tennis, catering services. AE, CB, DC, MC, V. Very Expensive.*

South Hampton Resorts at Watch Hill. This family-style motel offers large suites that include living room, kitchen, and bedroom with two double beds. The rooms are clean and modern, and each has a patio or terrace overlooking Peconic Bay. Continental breakfasts are included on Sundays during the summer season. *County Rd. 39, 11968, tel. 516/283–6100. 38 rooms with bath. Facilities: fishing, golf privileges, horseback riding, meeting rooms, pool, tennis. AE, MC, V. Moderate–Very Expensive.*

Stony Brook

Dining **Three Village Inn.** This is the perfect setting for traditional
★ American fare: a lovely old Colonial homestead set back on attractive grounds overlooking Stony Brook Harbor. Recom-

mended entrees include Long Island duck with Grand Marnier
(orange-flavored liqueur) sauce, New England lobster pie, and
filet mignon stuffed with oysters. *150 Main St., tel. 516/751–
0555. Jacket required. Reservations strongly advised. Breakfast, lunch, dinner. AE, MC, V. Inexpensive–Moderate.*

Westbury

Lodging **Island Inn.** This is a large, modern, well-run motel with many of
the amenities of a hotel, including a beauty salon. Located near
some of the major shopping centers, the Island Inn offers a
wide selection of rooms, all air-conditioned and newly renovated. As motel rooms go, these are fairly plush. Special
touches include free newspaper, color TV with in-room movies,
and valet service. There is also a restaurant, live entertainment, and dancing. Pets are permitted. Senior-citizen and
some weekend rates are available. *Old Country Rd., 11590, tel.
516/228–9500. 204 rooms with bath. Facilities: bar, barber,
beauty shop, gift shop, convention and meeting rooms, banquet
rooms, pool, restaurant. AE, CB, DC, MC, V. Expensive–
Very Expensive.*

Williston Park

Dining **La Marmite.** Casually elegant, this French and northern Ital-
 ★   ian restaurant in an old farmhouse is one of the best on the island. The four dining rooms, seating a total of 200 people, are
decorated in a pleasing country style, and the service is impeccable. Some of the more memorable dishes include rack of lamb,
lobster fricassee, and beef Wellington with spinach and mushrooms. For dessert, there's *gâteau St. Honoré*, cheesecake, or
delicate fruit tarts. *234 Hillside Ave., tel. 516/746–1243. Jackets required. Reservations strongly advised. AE, CB, DC, MC,
V. Closed Sun., lunch Sat. Moderate.*

The Arts

Culturally, New York City casts a long shadow over Long Island. Nonetheless, the island has a wide variety of its own cultural offerings, including professional theater, music concerts,
dance programs, and appearances by big-name entertainers.
In addition to the places listed below, check the Friday edition
of *Newsday*, the Long Island newspaper, which has a weekend
supplement containing an abundance of information about
Long Island arts, and the new magazine *Long Island Monthly*.

Theater

Airport Playhouse. This is a small, local playhouse not too far
from MacArthur Airport. Tickets are $9–12. *Nickerbocker
Ave., Bohemia, tel. 516/589–7588.*
Arena Players Repertory Company of Long Island. This is the
island's oldest professional repertory company; plays are presented throughout the year. *296 Rte. 109, East Farmingdale,
tel. 516/293–0674.*
Broadhollow Theatre. Broadway hits are the specialty of this
professional cast and staff. *229 Rte. 110, Farmingdale, tel. 516/
752–1400.*

John Drew Theatre. This is part of **Guild Hall** in East Hampton (tel. 516/324–1850).

Long Island Stage. As the island's only professional resident theater, this company presents major plays year-round. *Hays Theatre, Rockville Centre, tel. 516/546–4600.*

Studio Theatre. The professional cast and staff here also mounts Broadway hits. *141 S. Wellwood Ave., Lindenhurst, tel. 516/226–1833.*

Theatre Three Productions. This nonprofit professional company offers productions throughout the year. *412 Main St., Port Jefferson, tel. 516/928–9202.*

Music

Jones Beach Marine Theatre. Major contemporary pop artists are booked for live concerts here during summer months. *Jones Beach, Wantagh, tel. 516/221–1000.*

Long Island Philharmonic. This orchestra performs classical contemporary music at the Tilles Center at C. W. Post College and Hauppauge High School, and gives free outdoor concerts in the summer. *For schedule and ticket information, tel. 516/293–2222.*

Nassau Coliseum. Major rock and pop concerts are scheduled here periodically throughout the year. *Hempstead Tpke., Uniondale, tel. 516/796–9300.*

Nassau Symphony Orchestra. Performances are given at the Hofstra University playhouse throughout the year. *For schedule and ticket information, tel. 516/877–2718.*

Westbury Music Fair. Live concerts and shows here feature major names in entertainment. *Brush Hollow Rd., Westbury, tel. 516/333–0533.*

Dance **North Shore Dance Theater.** Free performances of contemporary dance programs are scheduled in summer. *Heckscher Park, Prime Ave. and Rte. 25A, Huntington, tel. 516/271–8442.*

Cinema **New Community Cinema.** This film-theater, specializing in superior American and international cinema, brings the best of New York City film culture to Long Island. Silent film series are often accompanied by live piano music, and film directors and producers are frequently on hand to discuss their films. New Community Cinema is a nonprofit educational organization housed in a converted elementary school. *423 Park Ave., just south of Rte. 25A, Huntington, tel. 516/423–7610 weekdays 10–6; 516/423–7653 after 7 weeknights and all day weekends. Admission: $5 for nonmembers, $3 for members and senior citizens Sun.–Thurs., $2.50 for children.*

Visual Art In addition to the art museums mentioned earlier, the following are worth noting:

East End Arts Council. Exhibits include works by East End artists. *133 E. Main St., Riverhead, tel. 516/727–0900. Open weekdays 10–5.*

East Hampton Center for Contemporary Art. Exhibits by contemporary artists from Long Island and New York City fill 850 square feet of gallery space. *16R Newton La., East Hampton, tel. 516/324–8939. Open mid-Apr.–Christmas, daily except Tues. and Wed. 11–7. Open Sat. during Feb. for children's programs.*

Elaine Benson Gallery. Established in 1965, the Benson is the oldest and most successful gallery on Long Island. In six theme-oriented group shows held from May to September, the gallery exhibits painting, sculpture, photography, and crafts by both established and lesser known Hamptons artists. *Montauk Hwy., Bridgehampton, tel. 516/537–3233. Open mid-May–mid-Sept., Thurs.–Tues. 12–6.*

Emily Lowe Art Gallery. Exhibits at this Hofstra University gallery include a variety of art from different periods. *Hempstead Tpke., Hempstead, tel. 516/560–5672. Open Tues. 10–9, Wed.–Fri. 10–5, weekends 1–5. Admission free.*

Fine Arts Museum of Long Island. Exhibitions of work by Long Island and New York–area artists. *295 Fulton Ave., Hempstead, tel. 516/481–5700. Open Wed.–Sat. 10–4:30, Sun. noon–4:30.*

Firehouse Gallery. Month-long exhibits in a variety of media are featured at this Nassau Community College Campus gallery. *Stuart Ave., Garden City, tel. 516/222–7165. Admission free. Open Mon.–Thurs. 11:30–4 and Tues. 7–10 PM. Closed July and Aug.*

Staller Center for the Arts. Located on the campus of SUNY-Stony Brook, this fine arts center has performances of music and theater as well as an expansive gallery exhibiting first-rate contemporary art. *Nicholls Rd., Stony Brook, tel. 516/632–7240. For performances call 516/632–7230. Admission free. Gallery hours are Tues.–Sat. noon–4; also open evenings before some performances.*

Nightlife

Long Island is a hot place for singles and young couples. Clubs feature the loudest in music and the fanciest in video display, and there are big, glitzy discos. For current club information, call 516/540–NITE; about $2 per call. Intimate jazz joints attract an older, mellower clientele. In recent years, comedy clubs have joined the other forms of nighttime entertainment on Long Island. The humor tends to be what they call adult, and the crowds are diverse in age. Check *Newsday* for information.

Discos & Nightclubs

Bay Street. This is one of the few East End clubs that stay open year-round. There's live music on Saturdays. Call for a performance schedule. *Long Wharf, Sag Harbor, tel. 516/725–2297. Open from 9, music at 11.*

Chevy's Bel Air Cafe. This swinging nostalgia club features danceable hits from the '50s through the '80s. *135 Sunrise Hwy., West Islip, tel. 516/422–5278.*

Decisions. Open seven days, offering lunch as well as great evening dance entertainment. Weekly music theme nights include Wednesday Sing-A-Long, Thursday New Wave, Friday House Music, Saturday Classic, and Sunday Light Rock. *170 Old Country Rd., Carle Pl., tel. 516/248–5130.*

Long Island Exchange. From happy hour on, this is one of the hottest clubs on the island. *598 Broad Hollow Rd., Melville, tel. 516/845–1000.*

Malibu Night Club. This big dance club draws a young, energetic crowd with New Wave and Top-40 hits. The room is big and classy, with multiple video displays. *Lido Blvd., Lido Beach, tel. 516/432–1600. Open 9:30 PM–3 AM Tues., Fri., Sat.*

Oak Beach Inn. There's jazz upstairs, disco downstairs, deli-style food, and live bands that play Top-40 dance music on weekends. The crowd ranges from 21 to 60. *Ocean Pkwy., Oak Beach, tel. 516/587–0097. Open 7 days midnight–4 AM.*

Park Bench. In addition to lunch and dinner Tuesday–Sunday, there's dancing 9 PM–4 AM. *Rte. 25A, Stony Brook, across from LIRR station, tel. 516/751–9734. No lunch on Mon.*

Stephen Talkhouse. Rock, blues, and folk music is performed in an intimate coffeehouse atmosphere. There is a full bar, and southern-style BBQ. *Main St., Amagansett, tel. 516/267–3117. Open from 5 PM with music most days during the summer, Thurs.–Sat. in the winter.*

Jazz

Sonny's. There's jazz seven nights a week at this intimate club, where the walls are covered with photographs of performers. There's no food; drinks only. *3603 Merrick Rd., Seaford, tel. 516/826–0973. Open from 2 PM; music 9 PM–1 Sun.–Thurs. and 9:30 PM–2 AM Fri. and Sat.*

Comedy Clubs

Brokerage Comedy. This small homey club features comedy shows on weekends, and rock, funk, and blues bands during the week. There's a full bar and pub food. *2797 Merrick Rd. and Bellmore Ave., Bellmore, tel. 516/785–8655. Open Mon.–Sat. 8 PM–2 AM.*

Chuckles. The fanciest comedy club on the island, this place has a nightclub atmosphere and features a full restaurant. *159 Jericho Tpke., Mineola, tel. 516/746–2770. Open Wed.–Sat. with shows at 9 Wed.–Thurs., 9 and 11:30 Fri., and 8, 10, and 12:30 Sat.*

East Side Comedy. The atmosphere is warm and cozy, and there's a full restaurant and bar. *326 West Jericho Tpke., Huntington, tel. 516/271–6061. Open Tues.–Sun. with shows at 9 Tues.–Thurs. and Sun., 9 and 11:30 Fri., and 7, 9:30, and midnight Sat.*

Governor's Comedy Shops. This casual place attracts a crowd ranging in age from 18 to 70. There's a pub-style menu and full bar. *90A Division Ave., Levittown, tel. 516/731–3358. Open Thurs.–Sun. with shows at 9 Thurs. and Sun., 9 and midnight Fri. and Sat.*

Laff's Comedy Club. Live stand-up comics entertain enthusiastic South Fork crowds here. *Montauk Hwy., Hampton Bays, tel. 516/728–LAFF. Show 9:30 Sat.*

5 Hudson Valley

Introduction

The Hudson River, in the stretch that links the fresh waters of Troy, Schenectady, and Albany to the salt waters of the Atlantic, is one of the busiest and most beautiful waterways in America. Beginning just above New York City and stretching 140 miles north to the state capital in Albany, the surrounding lands—lush and rich on both sides of the river—comprise the Hudson Valley.

If the number of Revolutionary War battle sites in the valley are testimony to the strategic importance of the river, the dozens of stately mansions on magnificent estates affirm the scenic attraction of the region. Indeed, the landscape's natural beauty—dramatic palisades, pine-scented forests, cool mountain lakes and streams—inspired an entire art movement, the Hudson River School, in the 19th century.

This is also a rich agricultural region, where visitors can visit scores of orchards, vineyards, and farm markets along country roads.

The Hudson Valley's proximity to Manhattan makes it a viable destination for day trips, but the numerous country inns, bed-and-breakfast lodgings, and resorts make longer, more leisurely journeys especially attractive.

Among the region's most important attractions are magnificently restored mansions such as Boscobel in Garrison, Washington Irving's home near Tarrytown, and Franklin Delano Roosevelt's home at Hyde Park; the U.S. Military Academy at West Point; Bear Mountain State Park; and the state capital in Albany.

The Hudson Valley tour begins just over the New York City line at Yonkers in Westchester County.

Essential Information

Getting Around

By Plane Hudson Valley can be reached conveniently by major airlines with flights into LaGuardia, John F. Kennedy, Stewart International, Albany, and Newark (NJ) airports, or with local service to Dutchess County Airport in Poughkeepsie and Westchester County Airport in White Plains.

By Train **Amtrak** (tel. 800/872–7245) provides rail service from New York City to Hudson, Rhinecliff, Rensselaer (Albany), and points west and north of Poughkeepsie.
Metro-North Commuter Railroad (tel. 212/532–4900 or 800/638–7646, or 800/METRO–INFO) trains leave Grand Central Terminal at Park Ave. and 42nd St. in Manhattan for Poughkeepsie, Brewster, Dover Plains, and other upstate points.
New Jersey Transit (tel. 800/522–5624 or 800/772–2222) trains leave from Hoboken, NJ, for points in Rockland and Orange counties.

By Bus **Adirondack and Pine Hill Trailways** (tel. 914/339–4230) has daily service between Port Authority Bus Terminal, 41st Street and Eighth Avenue, New York City, and New Paltz, Kingston,

Albany, and other Hudson Valley towns. Charter and package tours are available.

Leprechaun Lines & Tours (tel. 914/565–7900 or 914/896–4600) offers daily service to New York City and Atlantic City. Charter and package tours are available.

Flight Catcher (tel. 800/533–3298) has daily van service between the Hudson Valley and New York–area airports.

Shortline Bus (tel. 212/736–4700 or 800/631–8405) also has daily service between Port Authority Bus Terminal, area airports, and Hudson Valley communities. Charter and package tours are available.

Important Addresses and Numbers

Tourist Information All of the following tourist information offices are open weekdays 9–5:

Albany County Convention & Visitors Bureau, Inc., 52 South Pearl St., Albany 12207, tel. 518/434–1217 or 800/622–8464.

Columbia County Chamber of Commerce, 401 State St., Hudson 12534, tel. 518/828–3375 or 800/777–9247.

Dutchess County Tourism Promotion Agency, 46 Albany Post Rd., Box 2025, Hyde Park 12538, tel. 914/229–0033 or 800/445–3131 (in N.Y.S.) and 800/343–7007.

Greene County Promotion Department, Exit 21, N.Y.S. Thruway, Box 527, Catskill 12414, tel. 518/943–3223 or 800/542–2414.

Hudson River Valley Association, McCabe Carriage House, 42 Catharine St., Poughkeepsie 12601, tel. 914/452–4910 or 800/232–4782.

Office of General Services, Empire State Plaza, Visitor Assistance, Concourse Room 106, Empire State Plaza, Albany 12242, tel. 518/474–2418.

Orange County Tourism, 124 Main St., Goshen 10924, tel. 914/294–5151, ext. 1770 or 800/7C–TOUR.

Putnam County Tourism, 76 Main St., Cold Spring-on-Hudson 10516, tel. 914/265–3066.

Rockland County Tourism Board, One Blue Hill Plaza, Pearl River 10965, tel. 914/735–7040.

Ulster County Public Information, County Office Bldg., Box 1800, Kingston 12401, tel. 914/331–9300 or 800/DIAL–UCO.

Westchester Tourism Council, 148 Martine Ave., White Plains 10610, tel. 914/285–2941.

State Police Departments **Columbia:** tel. 518/851–3111
Dutchess: tel. 914/876–4033
Greene: tel. 518/622–8600
Orange: tel. 914/562–1133
Putnam: tel. 914/279–6161
Rockland: tel. 914/353–1100
Ulster: tel. 914/338–1702

Emergencies
County Fire Control and Ambulance **Columbia:** tel. 518/828–4114
Dutchess: tel. 914/471–1427
Greene: tel. 518/943–2424
Orange: tel. 914/294–6106
Putnam: tel. 914/225–4300
Rockland: tel. 914/354–8300
Ulster: tel. 914/338–1440
Westchester: tel. 914/225–4300

Hospitals **Dutchess:** *Northern Dutchess Hospital*, Rhinebeck (tel. 914/ 867–3001); *St. Francis Hospital*, Poughkeepsie (tel. 914/471– 2000); *Vassar Hospital*, Poughkeepsie (tel. 914/454–8500). **Greene:** *Albany Medical Center*, Albany (tel. 518/445–3125). **Orange:** *Arden Hill Hospital*, Goshen (tel. 914/294–5441). **Putnam:** *Putnam Hospital Center*, Carmel (tel. 914/279–5711). **Rockland:** *Nyack Hospital*, Nyack (tel. 914/358–6200); *Good Samaritan Hospital*, Suffern (tel. 914/357–3300). **Ulster:** *Kingston Hospital*, Kingston (tel. 914/331–3131); *Benedictine Hospital*, Kingston (tel. 914/338–5590); *Ellenville Hospital*, Ellenville (tel. 914/647–6400). **Westchester:** *White Plains Hospital*, White Plains (tel. 914/ 681–0600); *Westchester Medical Center*, Valhalla (tel. 914/ 285–7000).

Guided Tours

Special-Interest Tours **Annandale Tours** (Box 90, Wappingers Falls 12590, tel. 914/ 896–0456) specializes in themed tours for individuals or groups showcasing the history of the Hudson Valley. **Aristocrat Tours, Inc.** (Box 3038, Poughkeepsie 12603, tel. 914/ 452–2130) provides complete tour packages for groups of 30 or more. **Discover Our Valley Sightseeing** (Box 3038, Poughkeepsie 12603, tel. 914/452–5840) offers group and individual tours, including accommodations and meals. **Grayline Transportation** (900 Eighth Ave., New York 10019, tel. 212/397–2600) has summer tours to West Point, Wed. and Sat., July–Oct. **The Green Scene Guided Tours** (Box 486, Palenville 12463, tel. 518/678–5689) designs guided tours to order. **West Point Tours** (Box 268, Highland Falls 10928, tel. 914/446– 4724) offers guided tours of the U.S. Military Academy for groups and individuals.

Hudson River Cruises **Dutch Apple Cruises, Inc.** (1668 Julianne Dr., Castleton 12033, tel. 518/463–0220), offers daily trips from Albany, with or without meals and entertainment. Moonlight cruising and private charters also available. May–Oct. **Hudson Highland Cruises & Tours, Inc.** (Box 265, Highland Falls 10928, tel. 914/446–7171). *M/V Commander* sails from West Point, West Haverstraw, and Peekskill. Daytime sightseeing cruises with historic narrations; private charters available. May–Oct. **Hudson River Cruises** (Box 333, Rifton 12471, tel. 914/255– 6515). Narrated cruises from Kingston and West Point aboard *M/V Rip Van Winkle*. Mini- and evening cruises and private charters. May–Oct. **Hudson River Day Line** (Pier 81, west end of 42nd St., New York 10036, tel. 212/279–5151). Monthly mini-cruises to Bear Mountain and West Point from Manhattan. **Hudson Rondout Cruises** (1 Rondout Landing, Kingston 12401, tel. 914/338–6280). Lighthouse cruises, charters, and dinner cruises from Kingston's Rondout waterfront. May–Oct. **Riverboat Tours** (310 Mill St., Poughkeepsie 12601, tel. 914/ 473–5211). Sightseeing, dinner, brunch cruises, and private charters from Poughkeepsie. May–Oct. **Shearwater Cruises and Sailing School** (RD 2, Box 329, Rhinebeck 12572, tel. 914/876–7350). Self-captained charters,

two-hour sailing tours, and sailing lessons from Norrie Point
Marina. May–Oct.

Exploring the Hudson Valley

*Numbers in the margin correspond with points of interest on
the Hudson Valley map.*

Westchester and Rockland Counties

❶ Located in the magnificent 1876 Trevor Mansion overlooking
the Hudson in **Yonkers,** the collections of the **Hudson River Museum**
include impressive paintings from the Hudson River
School of artists, such as Jasper Cropsey and Albert Bierstadt.
Many of the art, history, and science exhibits focus on the work
of local artists. Furnishings of the Victorian era and personal
objects of the Trevor family, including huge Persian carpets,
are shown in the main building where the family lived. Also
part of the museum is the Andrus Planetarium, which offers
simulated space travel as well as an awesome look at the stars.
The museum hosts a series of chamber music concerts Oct.–
Apr. *511 Warburton Ave. (off Rte. 9), Yonkers, tel. 914/963–
4550. Admission: $2 adults, $1 children under 12 and senior
citizens. Admission to the planetarium: $3 adults, $1.50 children under 12 and senior citizens. Open Wed.–Sat. 10–5, Sun.
noon–5 (later hours on Thurs. in summer).*

Less than a mile south on Warburton Avenue is the **Philipse
Manor Hall State Historic Site,** a history and art museum in a
mansion once owned by the wealthy proprietors of the manor of
Philipsburg. The loyalist Philipse family lost its mansion and
vast landholdings during the American Revolution. The house,
a fine example of 18th-century Georgian architecture, has ornate interiors, including a rare Rococo-style ceiling and contains an extraordinary collection of portraits of American
presidents. *Warburton Ave. and Dock St., Yonkers, tel. 914/
965–4027. Admission free. Open late-May–late-Oct., Wed.–
Sun. noon–5.*

❷ Head north on Route 9 several miles to **Tarrytown** and follow
signs to **Sunnyside.** The romantic estate on the banks of the
Hudson belonged to Washington Irving. The author of *The Legend of Sleepy Hollow* and *Rip Van Winkle* purchased the home
in 1835. The 17 rooms, including Irving's library, contain many
of his original furnishings. A stream flows through the landscape from a pond Irving called his "little Mediterranean."
Sunnyside is a Registered National Historic Landmark and one
of several Historic Hudson Valley Restorations. Tours and special events are organized, and picnicking is encouraged. *Rte. 9,
Tarrytown, tel. 914/631–8200. Admission: $5 adults, $4.50
senior citizens, $3 students. Open Apr.–Oct., daily 10–5; Mar.
and Nov.–Dec., Wed.–Mon. 10–4; and Jan.–Feb., weekends
10–4.*

Heading north of Tarrytown, follow signs on Route 9 to **Lyndhurst,** a castlelike Gothic Revival home set on a bluff overlooking the Hudson. Designed in 1838 by Alexander Jackson Davis,
Lyndhurst has had a noteworthy list of occupants—from former New York City mayor William Paulding to merchant

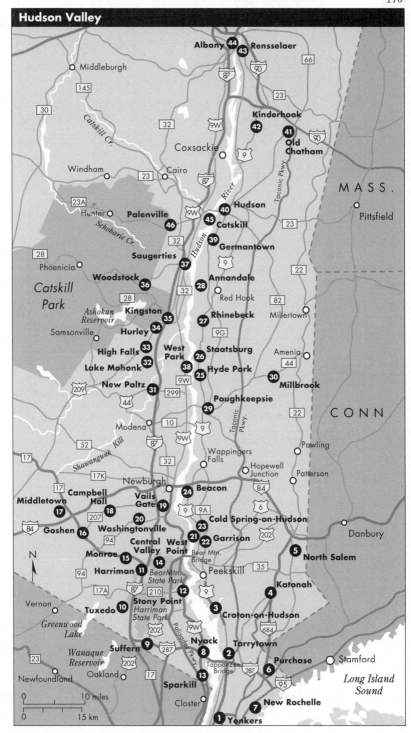

Hudson Valley

Albany 44 43 Rensselaer
87 90
66
Middleburgh
145
30 Catskill Cr.
32 9W Kinderhook 42
Coxsackie 41 81
Old
9 Chatham
Windham 87
Cairo M A S S.
23
River Pittsfield
23A Hudson
Hunter 9W 40
Palenville 45 Catskill
Schoharie Cr. 46 23
32 39 Germantown
28 Saugerties 37 9
Phoenicia Woodstock 28 Annandale
Catskill 36 32 28
Park Red Hook 82
Ashokan Kingston Millertown
Reservoir 35 Rhinebeck
Samsonville Hurley 34 27 Amenia
High Falls 33 9G 44
Lake Mohonk 32 West Staatsburg 30 Millbrook
Park
New Paltz 38 Hyde Park C O N N
209 31 26 25
299 9W
Modena 30
10
52 9 Taconic Pkwy. Pawling 22
Shawangunk Kill 87 Poughkeepsie
32 29
17 17K Wappingers
Newburgh Falls
Hopewell Patterson
Campbell 24 Beacon Junction
Middletown Vails
17 Hall 9 9A
18 Gate 84
Goshen 17 19 Cold Spring-on-Hudson 6
84 16 Washingtonville 23 Danbury
20 21 22 Garrison
Central West 202
Monroe Valley Point 5 North Salem
15 14 Bear Mtn.
Harriman 11 Bridge 35
17A 87 BearMtn. Peekskill Katonah
State Park 12 9 4
Vernon 210
Tuxedo 10 Stony Point 3 Croton-on-Hudson
Greenwood Harriman 684
Lake State Park 202
9W
23 Suffern 9 Nyack
Newfoundland 287 8 Tarrytown
Oakland 17 13 2 Purchase Stamford
Wanaque Sparkill Tappan Zee 6 95
Reservoir Bridge Long Island
Closter 7 New Rochelle Sound
0 10 miles 1 Yonkers
0 15 km

George Merritt and railroad magnate Jay Gould. The house is filled with an impressive collection of decorative Victorian furniture and art, and the 67-acre estate includes sweeping lawns and lovely gardens. *635 S. Broadway, Tarrytown, tel. 914/631-0046. Admission: $5 adults, $4 senior citizens, $3 students. Open May–Oct. and Dec., Tues.–Sun. 10–5; Jan.–Apr. and Nov., Sat.–Sun. 10–5.*

Farther north on Route 9 is another Historic Hudson Valley Restoration, the **Philipsburg Manor Upper Mills,** an 18th-century Dutch Colonial site that served as a trading center and the country home of the wealthy merchant Frederik Philipse. This 90,000-acre estate was the center of a bustling commercial empire that included milling and trading operations. Tours visit the stone manor house, a gristmill still run by water power (you can purchase at the gift shop the flour that's ground here), and the farm's animals and gardens. *Rte. 9, North Tarrytown, tel. 914/631–8200. Admission: $5 adults, $4.50 senior citizens, $3 students. Open Mar., Sat.–Sun. 10–5; Apr.–Dec., daily (except Tues.) 10–5.*

❸ Continue north on Route 9 to **Croton-on-Hudson** for yet another of the Historic Hudson Valley Restorations, **Van Cortlandt Manor.** This estate, home of a wealthy and prominent family that supported the American Revolution, shows life along the Hudson when the nation was young. Generals Lafayette and Washington were guests in this house, which is known today for its elegant antique furnishings and well-kept 18th-century gardens and orchards. *Rte. 9, Croton-on-Hudson, tel. 914/631–8200. Admission: $5 adults, $4.50 senior citizens, $3 students. Open Mar., Sat.–Sun. 10–5; Apr.–Dec., daily (except Tues.) 10–5.*

❹ Continue north on Route 9, then take Route 35 east 10 miles to the intersection at Route 22, in **Katonah,** to visit the **John Jay Homestead.** Jay was appointed by George Washington as the first chief justice of the United States and was co-author with John Adams of the "Federalist Papers." Jay also co-authored, with Benjamin Franklin and John Adams, the Treaty of Paris, which ended the Revolution. He was elected to two terms as governor of New York. He retired to this Westchester farmhouse in 1801 after three decades of public service and lived here until his death in 1829. The homestead remained in the Jay family until 1953, when the property was sold to the state. It is well stocked with furnishings and antiques. Sixty acres of the original 900-acre farm are part of this State Historic Site encompassing the homestead, gardens, and meadows. *Rte. 22, Katonah, tel. 914/232–5651. Admission free. Tours every half-hour; last tour begins at 4. Open late-May–Labor Day, Wed.–Sat. 10–5, Sun. 1–5; Sept.–Oct., Wed.–Sun. noon–5; Nov.–Dec., Sat.–Sun. noon–5. Closed Jan.–Mar. Grounds open year-round.*

Take Route 22 north for three miles to Girdle Ridge Road and the **Caramoor Center for Music & The Arts,** set on 117 acres of the estate built in the 1930s by Walter Tower Rosen to house his collection of fine art from Europe and the Orient. Caramoor is the setting for an acclaimed summer music festival. Operas and concerts are presented in the Venetian Theater, an outdoor showcase built around 15th-century Venetian columns, while smaller chamber concerts take place in the Spanish Courtyard. The House Museum displays period rooms from European palaces and hundreds of pieces of Oriental fine and decorative art. *Girdle Ridge Rd., Katonah, tel. 914/232–5035. Admission: $4 adults, $2 children under 12. Open May–Nov., Thurs. and Sat. 11–4 and Sun. 1–4; Nov.–May by appointment only.*

Leave Route 22 at Route 121 to connect with Route 116, which takes you east into **North Salem. The Hammond Museum and Oriental Stroll Gardens,** off Route 116, was created by Natalie Hammond and contains 15 small garden landscapes and a waterfall. The museum and the art collection represent a devotion to humanity, justice, and wisdom. *Deveau Rd., North Salem, tel. 914/669–5033. Admission: $3 adults, $2 senior citizens, $1 children under 12. Open Wed.–Sun. 11–5; museum, May–Dec. and gardens, May–Oct.*

❺ Westchester's only winery, **North Salem Vineyard,** can be reached from Exit 8 off I-684. Follow Hardscrabble Road for 2½ miles until you see signs for the vineyard, a small private winery that produces three wines and opens its facilities for tours, wine tasting, and picnicking. A basket lunch and wine can be purchased here. *RR 2, Hardscrabble Rd., North Salem, tel. 914/669–5518. Admission free. Open daily June–Oct., weekends Nov.–May.*

Return to I-684 and head south, taking the exit for the State ❻ University at **Purchase.** The **Neuberger Museum** on this campus has a fine collection of 20th-century American and European as well as African art and Greek pottery. Outdoor sculpture is displayed throughout the 500-acre campus. *Anderson Hill Rd., Purchase, tel. 914/251–6133. Suggested donation: $2 adults. Open Tues.–Fri. 10–4, weekends 11–5.*

❼ On Route 1, head south to the city of **New Rochelle** and the **Thomas Paine Cottage.** In 1784, one year after the end of the American Revolution, New York State granted Thomas Paine 300 acres of land as a reward for his vigorous written campaign during the Revolutionary War to incite Americans to defeat the British. The patriot, famous for his statement, "These are the times that try men's souls," lived in this little house until his death in 1809. The Thomas Paine Cottage was built in 1793 and originally stood atop a hill, but it was relocated to its current site. The author of *Common Sense* had lived frugally, leaving behind few possessions relating to his personal life. However, the artifacts that are shown in the cottage are typical of the Colonial period of New Rochelle and its Huguenot settlers. There are several authentic Franklin stoves, presented to Paine by Ben Franklin himself, and handmade quilts, including a Star of Bethlehem quilt. *983 North Ave., New Rochelle, tel. 914/632–5376. Suggested donation: $3 adults, $1 senior citizens and children under 12. Open Fri.–Sun. 2–5 or by appointment. Closed Nov.–Apr.*

Head back to I-287 and go west straight onto the Tappan Zee ❽ Bridge. Take the **Nyack** exit for that quaint village in Rockland County. The Dutch originally farmed this region, but when the steamboats arrived Nyack became a shipping and boatbuilding center. The town is now an antiques and arts center, and the village sponsors many special events and street fairs. Take a walking tour to see Nyack's architectural history in its public library, the Couch Court, the Presbyterian Church, the Tappan Zee Theatre, the Reformed Church, and the Congregation of the Sons of Israel; along with numerous shops, galleries, and antiques shops. *For more information and walking-tour maps, contact The Friends of the Nyacks, Box 384, Nyack 10960, tel. 914/353–0586, or Chamber of Commerce of the Nyacks, Box 677, Nyack 10960, tel. 914/353–2221. Most stores closed Mon.*

The Rockland Community College is also a focal point of this town. Frequent programs of interest to the public are presented throughout the year. *For more information, contact the college's Cultural Events Office, 914/356–4650.*

While in Nyack, be sure to visit the **Edward Hopper House,** also known as the Hopper House Art Center. This was the birthplace and home of the American realist painter from 1882 until his death in 1967. Several of his paintings, featuring local landmarks, are on display. Hopper posters, books, and postcards are available for purchase. Exhibits by outstanding local artists are held year-round. Concerts and special events are held in the gardens. *82 North Broadway, tel. 914/358–0774. Suggested contribution: $1. Open Sat. and Sun. 1–5.*

9 Take Route 287 west to **Suffern,** a town known for its local produce farms and roadside stands. One of the most popular for pick-your-own fruits and vegetables is Van Ripers Farm. *121 College Rd., Suffern, tel. 914/352–0770. Open May–Dec., daily 9–5 or longer.*

10 Go west on Route 17 to **Tuxedo** and into Sterling Forest, located just off Route 17 on Route 17A. **Sterling Forest** is beautiful to visit anytime of the year, but it is especially enjoyable during the summer months when the **New York Renaissance Festival** is held on weekends. There are productions of Shakespearean plays by Equity actors, as well as jugglers, mimes, musicians, jousts on horseback, and plenty of food and drink. *Rte. 17A, Tuxedo, tel. 914/351–5171. Admission: $12.50 adults, $5 children under 12. Open Aug.–mid-Sept., weekends 11–6.*

11 Take Route 17 and follow signs for Route 210 onto the Palisades Interstate Parkway until you reach the entrances for **Harriman** and **Bear Mountain State Parks,** the most famous parks of the vast Palisades Interstate system. The two parks share 54,000 acres and both offer plenty of outdoor activity year-round. Facilities exist for boating, roller skating, picnicking, swimming, hiking, and fishing, and there are rest rooms, a bookshop, and a restaurant. At the Trailside Museum in Bear Mountain Park, exhibits and programs describe Native American history as well as the natural history of the area. Children can enjoy the zoo, beaver lodge, and reptile house. A drive, bike ride, or even a hike along the Seven Lakes Drive, and especially Lake Welch Drive, can be breathtaking in the fall and winter. Paddleboats and rowboats can be rented on the lakes. In January and February professional ski-jumping competitions and a juried crafts fair are held in the park, and in December there is a Christmas festival. *Entrance off the Palisades Interstate Pkwy., tel. 914/ 786–2701. Admission free; parking $3 May–Sept. Open daily dawn to dusk.*

12 Route 9W south will take you to the **Stony Point Battlefield Historic Site,** where George Washington demonstrated that American troops could stand up to superior British forces in the Hudson Highlands. In July 1779 General "Mad" Anthony Wayne led the elite Corps of Light Infantry in a daring midnight raid against the British. The British fortifications in the battlefield are still standing. At the museum, a slide show depicts the events that led up to the battle, and there are memorabilia explaining the tactics and strategies that led to the American victory. *Park Rd., off Rte. 9W, Stony Point, tel. 914/ 786–2521. Admission free. Open late-Apr.–Oct. 31, Wed.–Sat. 8:30–5 and Sun. 9–4:30.*

⓭ Head back on Route 9W south to **Sparkill** and the **Piermont Marsh and Tallman State Park,** a nature preserve covering more than 1,000 acres of tidal marsh, mountains, and rivers, considered to be some of the most important fish-breeding areas along the Hudson. Wildflowers abound, and bird-watching is a year-round possibility throughout portions of the marsh. There are man-made ponds, home to many varieties of reptiles and amphibians. *Rte. 9W, north of Palisades Interstate Pkwy., Exit 4, Sparkill, tel. 914/359–0544. Tallman Park cost: $3 per vehicle; Piermont Marsh, free. Open 8 AM–dusk summer, 8 AM–4:30 weekdays, 8AM–7:30 holidays and weekends remainder of year.*

Orange and Putnam Counties

Take the New York State Thruway north to Harriman Exit 16
⓮ and proceed to the junction of Route 17 for the town of **Central Valley. Woodbury Commons,** a group of world-famous factory outlets set in a charming Colonial shopping village here offers good values on clothing, shoes, jewelry, gifts, and household items. There is also a racetrack in the area. *Information booth in the Restaurant Court, tel. 914/928–6840. Open May–Dec., Mon.–Wed. and Sat. 10–6, Thurs. and Fri. 10–9, Sun. 11–5; Jan.–Apr., Mon.–Sat. 10–6, Sun. 11–5.*

⓯ Three miles west on Route 17 is the town of **Monroe** and **Museum Village,** where the daily life of preindustrial America has been re-created. There are more than 35 buildings on the site, including a blacksmith's shop where artisans hammer and pound hot metal into door latches and horseshoes. Visit the potter's workshop and see butter churned and mugs shaped on the wheel. *Museum Village Rd., Monroe, tel. 914/782–8247. Admission: $5 adults, $4 senior citizens, $3 children under 15. Open May–Dec., Wed.–Fri. 10–5, weekends noon–5; shorter weekday hours after Labor Day.*

Back on Route 17, head west to its intersection with Route
⓰ 17M, which leads to the village of **Goshen.** Noah Webster of dictionary fame was born in this 275-year-old rural town, as was Ulysses S. Grant. In the center of town is the **Trotting Horse Museum,** or Hall of Fame of the Trotter. Housed in a former stable are more than 100 Early American oil paintings and lithographs depicting the sport of harness racing. The museum contains a huge collection of Currier and Ives prints and famous racing silks, and a Hall of Immortals where dozens of small, lifelike statues recall great trotters. Restored stalls have full-size replicas of horses and their equipment. *240 Main St., Goshen, tel. 914/294–6330. Admission: $1.50 adults, 50¢ children. Open Mon.–Sat. 10–5, Sun. noon–5.*

Continue west on Route 17 a few miles and you will reach the
⓱ junction with Routes 84 and 6 and the town of **Middletown.** This is the locale for the **Orange County Fair,** one of the oldest county fairs in New York State, in July or August. Started as a smalltime agricultural display in 1818, the fair has expanded

immensely since then. It is now an extravaganza featuring farm animals, exhibits, races, and top-name entertainment, lots of food booths, and thrilling rides. There are also Native American shows, stock-car races, and petting zoos. *County Fairgrounds, Middletown, tel. 914/343–4826. Admission: $6 adults, $2.50 children under 12.*

⓲ You can also take Route 207 north from Goshen to **Campbell Hall** to visit a 1769 family farm and stone farmhouse, the **Hill-Hold Historic Farm Museum.** The land of this 300,000-acre estate was once owned by William Bull, an English stonemason. His son, Thomas, built Hill-Hold. This large, Georgian-style mansion, still owned by the Bull family, has elegant wood- and-stonework, barrel-backed cupboards, paneling, and deep-silled windows. Rooms have original furnishings in the Chippendale style. On the working farm, sheep, cows, chickens, and geese are raised. Guided tours are available. *Rte. 416, Campbell Hall, tel. 914/294–7661. Admission: $2.50 adults, $1.50 children. Open mid-Apr.–mid-Oct., Wed.–Sun. 10–4:30.*

⓳ Return to Route 207 and head east to Route 300 south to **Vails Gate.** In this village stands **Knox's Headquarters State Historic Site.** The stone house, built in 1754, was owned by John Ellison. But during the American Revolution it was occupied by Continental officers, including Major-General Henry Knox, chief of the artillery. The house served as headquarters for other Colonial heroes as well, among them Generals Horatio Gates and Nathanael Greene. It has been restored with camp beds and folding desks of the period. *Forge Hill Rd. and Rte. 94, Vails Gate, tel. 914/561–5498. Admission free. Open early Apr.–late-Oct., Wed.–Sat. 10–5 and Sun. 1–5; also open Memorial Day, Independence Day, and Labor Day.*

Where Route 300 intersects with Route 32 in Vails Gate is the **New Windsor Cantonment State Historic Site,** the last camp of Washington's army. Featured are exhibits, artillery displays, a blacksmith's shop, and military demonstrations. More than 10,000 soldiers, cooks, blacksmiths, and other camp followers constructed the log cabins, outbuildings, and the meeting hall where Washington quelled a mutiny by his troops, who resented the slow payment of wages and pensions. At the orientation center, a slide show illustrates the history of the area and the difficulties faced by the leaders and the troops. *Rtes. 300 and 32, Temple Hill Rd., Vails Gate, tel. 914/561–1765. Admission free. Open Apr.–Oct., Wed.–Sat. 10–5, Sun. 1–5.*

⓴ Take Route 94 east to **Washingtonville.** Continue, following the signs for America's oldest winery, **Brotherhood.** More than 150 years old, the winery offers guided tours of its cavernous underground cellars. Tours end in a wine tasting at which hors d'oeuvres and a selection of pastries, cheeses, strudels, and quiches are also sold. *Rte. 208, 35 North St., Washingtonville, tel. 914/496–9101. Admission: $3 adults, children under 21 free. Winery outlet open daily 11–6. Tours May–Oct., daily 11–6; Jan.–Apr. and Nov.–Dec., weekends noon–5.*

㉑ You can visit America's oldest and most distinguished military academy, **West Point,** by taking Route 94 west to Route 9W and then south. Situated on the bluffs overlooking the Hudson River, West Point has been the training ground for U.S. Army officers since 1802. Distinguished graduates include Robert E. Lee, Ulysses S. Grant, and Douglas MacArthur. There is a visitor center that shows an orientation movie. A museum at Thayer Hall houses one of the world's foremost collections of military memorabilia and equipment. Uniforms, weapons, field equipment, flags, and American military art are on display. There are also new galleries depicting the history of West Point. On the grounds there are memorials, cannons, and restored forts, such as Fort Putnam. *Rte. 9W, West Point, tel. 914/938–2638 or 914/938–5261. Admission free, but tours cost $3 adults, $2 children under 12. Visitor center open daily except major holidays 9–4:45; museum open daily 10:30–4:15.*

Constitution Island, a small island off the east shore of the Hudson, is separated from the mainland by marshes and can only be reached via a boat ride that leaves from West Point. The island played a critical role in General George Washington's strategy to keep the British naval traffic out of the Hudson River. During the Revolutionary War, the island had switched hands from American to British and then back to American. The British ships were stopped by an enormous iron chain that was stretched across the river from West Point to the island.

When the war ended in 1783, the barracks were decommissioned and the island returned to civilian control. However, the fort structure remains intact. Part of the present tour of the island includes a visit to the home of Susan and Anna Warner, sisters and prolific writers who wrote under pseudonyms. The house has 15 rooms, all furnished in Victorian style. *Boats leave West Point's South Dock, Peekskill, tel. 914/446–8676. Cost: $5 adults, $4 senior citizens and students, $2 children under 5. Advance reservations required. Tours depart Wed. and Thurs. 1 and 2 PM.*

㉒ Take the Bear Mountain Bridge across the Hudson and head north on 9D to Garrison. The **Garrison Art Center** is housed in a turn-of-the-century building facing the Hudson River, opposite the Garrison train station. The center's programs include an annual arts and crafts fair in August, as well as changing exhibits. Spring and fall auctions are held on the premises. *Garrison's Landing, Garrison, tel. 914/424–3960. Admission to the center is free, but a $2 donation is usually requested for the annual fair. Open weekdays 10–5, weekends noon–5. Closed mid-Dec.–Mar.*

The **Hudson Valley Information Center & Gift Gallery** features gifts, mementos, hiking maps, postcards, travel guides and brochures, books, and even paintings—all dedicated to the Hudson Valley region. It's a good place to get oriented. *76 Main St., tel. 914/265–3060. Open Wed.–Mon. 9–5.*

Take Route 9D south to Garrison to visit **Boscobel,** an early 19th-century mansion that has been fully restored and furnished with the decorative arts of the Federal period (1800–1820), including elegant carpets, fine porcelains, and hand-carved furniture. Standing on a bluff surrounded by beautiful gardens with thousands of flowers that bloom in the spring, Boscobel affords a breathtaking view of the Hudson River. Concerts are held on the lawn throughout the summer. In the fall, apples from Boscobel's orchards go on sale. *Rte. 9D, Garrison, tel. 914/265–3638. Admission: $5 adults, $4 senior citizens, $2.50 children under 14. Open Apr.–Oct. 9:30–5; Mar., Nov., and Dec. 9:30–4. Closed Tues.*

㉓ Cold Spring-on-Hudson, across from West Point, on the east side of the Hudson River, is a small 19th-century village in the heart of the Hudson Highlands. You can stroll in its quiet streets and visit its antiques and crafts shops on your own, or join a guided walking tour of the historic district. *76 Main St., or write Box 71, Cold Spring-on-Hudson 10516, tel. 914/265–3066. Donations accepted. Tours May–Nov., Sun. 2 PM.*

㉔ About 12 miles north on Route 9D in the town of **Beacon** is the **Madam Brett Homestead,** a Dutch dwelling built in 1709 and visited by Washington, Lafayette, and Baron von Steuben (technically in Dutchess County, but a fitting last stop on this circuit). The furnishings reflect the lifestyles of the seven generations of the Brett family through 1954, when the Daughters of the American Revolution purchased the house. The 28,000-acre estate and gristmill were used to store military supplies during the Revolutionary War. There is original period furniture, Canton china, paintings, and a formal garden. The homestead is on the National Register of Historic Places. *50 Van Nydeck Ave., Beacon, tel. 914/831–6533. Admission: $2 adults, $1 children 13–18, 50¢ children under 12. Open May–Oct., weekends 1–4.*

A short distance away, **Howland Center,** a community arts center, is housed in an 1872 building designed by American architect Richard Morris Hunt. The center has a gallery for exhibits on art and history, a performance hall for concerts, dramatic productions, and dance, and a lecture hall. *477 Main St., Beacon, tel. 914/831–4988. Donations accepted. Gallery hours: Wed. and Sun. 1–5 and by appointment. Call for performance schedule.*

Ulster and Dutchess Counties

㉕ An appropriate place to begin touring the great estates of these two counties is **Hyde Park** and the **Franklin Delano Roosevelt National Historic Site.** The library and museum contain collections of manuscripts and personal documents displaying FDR's extensive career. Family photographs, gifts he received as president of the United States, his desk from the Oval Office, items dating from the period of his service in the U.S. Navy, letters, speeches, state documents, and official correspondence are on display. The large Roosevelt family house contains original furnishings. The rose gardens surrounding the gravesites of both Franklin and Eleanor Roosevelt are serene. The library is open only for research. *Rte. 9, Hyde Park, tel. 914/229–9115. Admission: $3.50 adults, senior citizens over 62, school groups, and children under 12 free. Open Apr.–Oct., daily 9–5; Nov.–Mar., Thurs.–Mon. 9–5, except major holidays.*

The only historic site in the nation devoted to a first lady is the **Eleanor Roosevelt National Historic Site** at nearby Val-Kill. Amid 172 acres of woods, the restored home of Eleanor Roosevelt is open for guided tours. Begin your visit by viewing the film biography, "First Lady of the World," followed by a tour of the Val-Kill cottage where Eleanor Roosevelt lived from 1945 to 1962. *249 Albany Post Rd. (R.R. 9), Hyde Park, tel. 914/229–9115. Admission free. Open May–Oct., daily 9–5; Nov.–Dec., Mar.–Apr., weekends 10–4. Closed Jan.–Feb.*

Two miles north of the Roosevelt historic sites along the river is the 54-room **Vanderbilt Mansion,** the former spring and fall home of Frederick and Louise Vanderbilt. Built in 1896–98, it is a splendid example of the Beaux Arts style of architecture and a fitting symbol of the Gilded Age. The decor includes elaborate gold-leaf trim, mahogany paneling, and many original furnishings such as marble mantels, throne-type chairs, Venetian lanterns, beaded crystal chandeliers, Persian rugs, Flemish tapestries, and hand-painted silk lampshades. The grounds offer panoramic views of the Hudson and acres of gardens. *Rte. 9, Hyde Park, tel. 914/229–9115. Admission: $2 adults; senior citizens over 62 and children 16 and under free. Open Apr.– Oct., daily 9–6; Nov.–Mar., Thurs.–Mon. 9–5 except major holidays.*

A short distance away on Route 9 in Hyde Park is the most respected cooking school in the United States, **The Culinary Institute of America (CIA),** founded in 1946. Located on a 75-acre campus overlooking the Hudson River, the institute is home to 1,850 students enrolled in a 21-month culinary arts program and more than 300 faculty and staff members. More than 90 chefs and instructors from 18 countries conduct courses in the fundamentals of cooking, charcuterie, American, Oriental, and international cuisines, with related courses in wines, table service, purchasing, stewarding, beverage control, and food-service science.

The facilities include 18 commercially equipped production kitchens, five bakeshops, two food-preparation and demonstration auditoriums, a food and sanitation laboratory, a nutrition center, meat room, 26,000-volume library, four residence halls, and eight instructional dining rooms—including four student-staffed restaurants that are open to the public by reservation (*see* Dining, below).

Tours of the campus, designed primarily for prospective students, are conducted by appointment only, on Wednesdays when the school is in session, at 9:15 and 2:30. Tours are also available, by appointment, to small groups who have made reservations to dine at one of the school's restaurants; the cost for group tours is $2 per person.

After dining or taking a tour, visitors are free to visit the Culinary Institute's bookstore and browse through the hundreds of titles that are of interest to both amateur and professional cooks. The shop is also a good source for kitchen accessories and baking aids. *For more information, contact The CIA, Rte. 9, Hyde Park 12538, tel. 914/471–6608. Bookstore open weekdays 10–7:45, Sat. 11:30–3:45.*

Northern Tour Head north on Route 9 for five miles to the town of **Staatsburg** ㉖ and follow signs for **The Mills Mansion,** the opulent country estate of Ogden and Ruth Livingston Mills. There are original furnishings of the Louis XV and Louis XVI periods. Flemish tapestries and Oriental porcelains embellish the oversize rooms of this mansion, which has panoramic views of the Hudson River valley and the vast manicured acreage bordering the shoreline. Guided tours are available and hiking, picnicking, and cross-country skiing are encouraged. Special lawn concerts and workshops are held during the summer. *Old Post Rd., Staatsburg, tel. 914/889–4100. Admission free. Open May– Labor Day, Wed.–Sat. 10–5 and Sun. 1–5; Labor Day–Oct.,*

Wed.–Sat. noon–5 and Sun. 1–5. Also special tours at
Christmastime; call for schedule.

Continue north on Route 9 for three miles and enter one of the
27 oldest villages in the country, **Rhinebeck. The Beekman Arms**
(1766), located here, is purported to be the oldest inn in America and was a meeting place for such famous people as George
Washington and Franklin Roosevelt. Founded in 1688 and incorporated as a village in 1834, Rhinebeck contains a state historic district called White's Corner that has the town's second-
oldest church, the Dutch Reformed, built in 1802. Also in the
area is the town post office, a Roosevelt-era WPA project that
looks like a Dutch farmhouse. The district's Victorian-style
buildings are charming, as are the antiques shops, boutiques,
and galleries that line the streets of the village center.

On Route 9 continue north for one mile and you will encounter
the **Dutchess County Fairgrounds.** If you are lucky or smart
enough to plan to be in the area during the second or third week
of August, you can experience the Dutchess County Fair—the
biggest and best in New York State—which has operated at the
site every year since 1845, except during World War II. The
event, created to promote agriculture in the area, lives up to its
goals, exhibiting hundreds of different animals in the livestock
shows, various kinds of food, an outdoor horse-racing track,
plus an "old-fashioned" village. The Rhinebeck Crafts Fair is
held at the fairgrounds in the month of June and two large antique fairs, one on Memorial Day weekend and one during the
Columbus Day weekend, draw dealers and buyers from all over
the county. *Rte. 9, Rhinebeck, tel. 914/876–4001. Admission:*
$5 adults, children under 12 free. Parking: $1. Open May–Oct.

The **Old Rhinebeck Aerodrome** is three miles outside Rhinebeck Village—just follow the signs on Route 9. This museum
has one of the largest collections of antique airplanes dating
from 1900 through 1937. Many of these historic wonders are
still flown in weekend air shows. Adventurous visitors can experience barn-storming rides in open-cockpit biplanes, such as
a 1929 New Standard D-25, which carries up to four passengers. These 15-minute flights cost $20 per person. Rides book
up early, so call first thing in the morning. *42 Stone Church*
Rd., Rhinebeck, tel. 914/758–8610. Admission weekdays: $3
adults, $1 children under 10; weekends (includes an airshow):
$8 adults, $4 children under 10. Open mid-May–mid-Oct., dai-
ly 10–5; air shows at 2:30 weekends.

Continue north on Route 9 to **Red Hook,** a village with many
Federal- and Victorian-style homes and a number of fine antiques and crafts shops. A slight detour north of the village
leads to one of the county's largest pick-your-own farms. Follow
Rte. 9 for three miles, then turn left at Pitcher Lane for the
Greig Farm Market, *tel. 914/758–1234. Open May–Dec., daily*
8–6. In the center of the village, turn left at the traffic light
onto Route 199 and continue in a westward direction for approximately three miles to Route 9G. Turn right (north) and go
28 three miles to **Annandale.** Take a left on Annandale Road and
follow the signs to **Montgomery Place,** the Hudson Valley's
newest great home to open its doors to the public. Situated on a
400-acre estate on the banks of the Hudson, Montgomery Place
is a 23-room classical-revival mansion built in 1802–05 by Janet
Livingston Montgomery, widow of the Revolutionary War hero
General Richard Montgomery. The interior, which is in the

process of being restored, holds two centuries worth of family memorabilia as well as exquisite French china, chandeliers, leatherbound books, hand-carved furniture, ancestral portraits, and kitchen utensils. Tours are conducted regularly by uniformed docents. In addition, the sign-posted grounds offer views of the Hudson River and the Catskill Mountains, walking trails, gardens, woodlands, waterfalls, and an orchard of 5,000 fruit trees. (You can pick your own fruit in the autumn.) *Annandale-on-Hudson, tel. 914/758–5461. Admission: $5 adults, $4.50 senior citizens, $3 students under 18, children under 6 free. Open Apr.–Oct., daily 10–5 (except Tues.); Nov., Dec., and Mar., weekends only 10–5. Closed Jan.–Feb.*

Southern Tour **Poughkeepsie,** in the heart of Dutchess, New York's original
㉙ county, was founded in 1683. The Dutchess County Historical Society houses its collection in the **Clinton House** and the nearby **Glebe House,** two 18th-century buildings that served New York's fledgling government when it operated here in 1777. Three centuries of Hudson Valley history are documented by manuscripts, books, maps, photographs, art objects, and furnishings on display in these two historic houses. *Corner of Main and North White Sts., Poughkeepsie, tel. 914/471–1630. Admission to Clinton House free. Open Mon.–Fri. 9–3. Admission to Glebe House by appointment only; a donation is requested.*

Just down the road on Main Street in the Old City Hall is the **Mid Hudson Arts and Science Center (MASC),** a multiarts service organization that organizes exhibitions and art shows throughout the year. The main floor contains two showcase galleries and the offices of the Summergroup Cooperative, a professional visual-arts group that maintains a small gallery in the rear. The second floor is used by local theater and performing-arts groups. *228 Main St., Poughkeepsie, tel. 914/471–1155. Donation: $1. Open Tues.–Fri. 11–4, Sat. noon–4 and by appointment. Galleries closed Aug.*

Taking a slight detour, two miles south of Poughkeepsie on Route 9 is Locust Grove, the home of Samuel F. B. Morse, the inventor of the telegraph. A National Historic Landmark, the house was designed by Alexander Jackson Davis and is a classic example of mid-19th-century Italian villa-style architecture. It sits on a bluff overlooking the Hudson amid 150 acres of gardens and woodland. Memorabilia on display—in addition to a model of Morse's original telegraph—includes an extensive collection of furniture, china, and art. *Admission: $4 adults, $3.50 senior citizens, $1 children 7–16. Open late-May–late-Sept., Wed.– Sun. 10–4; Oct., Sat.–Sun. 10–4; Nov.–Dec., Apr.–May by appointment. Closed Jan.–Mar.*

Returning to the heart of Poughkeepsie, Main Street intersects with Route 44/55 right off the Mid-Hudson Bridge. Head three miles west on Route 44 to Raymond Avenue and turn south to reach the **Vassar College Art Gallery.** Matthew Vassar not only broke new ground when he founded Vassar as a women's college in 1861, but he also was the first to include an art gallery and museum as part of an American college. The gallery owns 8,000 works of art, many of them Hudson River landscapes. There are also prints by Rembrandt and Whistler. After visiting the art museum, stop at the chapel to see the rare Tiffany glass windows. *Raymond Ave., Poughkeepsie, tel. 914/437–5235 or*

914/437–5241. Admission free. Open Wed.–Sat. 10–5, Sun. noon–5.

30 Return to Route 44 and head east for 10 miles to the town of **Millbrook,** proceed 2½ miles past the town of South Millbrook and turn left on Tyrrel Road for **Innisfree Garden.** In this Oriental garden, designed in 1930 by Walter Beck, harmony and placement are valued above color or species. Beck spent more than 22 years shaping the landscape to encompass streams, waterfalls, terraces, and rock walls. *Tyrrell Rd., Millbrook, tel. 914/677–8000. Admission: $2 weekends, free weekdays. Open May–Oct., Wed.–Fri. 10–4, weekends 11–5.*

Back in the town of Millbrook, turn left on Route 44A, the Sharon Turnpike. The **Mary Flagler Cary Arboretum** is headquartered in a redbrick building on the left, one mile north of Route 44. The Arboretum contains more than 1,900 acres of nature trails and plant collections, special horticultural displays, guided ecology walks, a greenhouse, and nursery. The **Institute of Ecosystem Studies,** which is a division of The New York Botanical Garden, is also located at the arboretum. *Rte. 44, Millbrook, tel. 914/677–5359. Admission free; obtain an access permit at the Gifford House. Open year-round Mon.–Sat. 9–4, Sun. 1–4, with extended hours in summer. Closed major holidays.*

On Route 44, head east eight miles to Route 83, turn left and follow signs 5.5 miles to **Amenia** and the award-winning winery, **Cascade Mountain Vineyards.** There are daily tours of the winery and the vineyards, plus wine tastings. A restaurant on the grounds serves lunch (12–3) daily in summer, weekends during the rest of the year, and dinner by reservation on Saturday nights. *Flint Hill Rd., Amenia, 914/373–9021. Admission free. Open daily 10–6.*

Alternatively, from Route 44, proceed west to Taconic Parkway. Travel one mile north to the Salt Point exit and follow the signs to **Clinton Vineyards** at **Clinton Corners.** Situated on a 100-acre farm, this winery produces the dry Seyval Blanc found in the top restaurants of the area, and Seyval Naturel, the Hudson Valley's first sparkling wine made in the French style of *méthode champenoise. Schultzville Rd., Clinton Corners, tel. 914/266–5372. Admission free. Tours and tastings, weekends 9–5 and by appointment.*

31 Take routes 22 and 55 back into Poughkeepsie and over the Mid-Hudson Bridge. Follow signs off the bridge for the New York State Thruway, the first right after the bridge. Stay on this road (Route 9W) until you reach the intersection for Route 299 and follow Route 299 into **New Paltz.**

New Paltz offers a chance to see life as it was more than three centuries ago when the French Huguenots settled the area and founded the town in 1678. The **Huguenot Street Stone Houses** constitute some of the oldest streets in America with their original houses. A walking tour begins at an orientation center and visits six houses and a church where visitors can view a large collection of local artifacts, indigenous furniture, costumes, and portraits. The short tour takes 1½ hours, the long tour is three hours. All the buildings are owned and maintained by the Huguenot Historical Society. *18 Brodhead Ave., Box 339, New Paltz, tel. 914/255–1660. Admission: $5 adults, $4* *senior citizens, $2 children under 12. Open Memorial Day–late-Sept., Wed.–Sun. 10–4.*

㉜ Take Route 299 six miles west of New Paltz over the Walkill River into **Lake Mohonk** and then follow signs for the **Mohonk Mountain House,** a resort located high above the Hudson River valley on several thousand unspoiled acres of the Shawangunk Mountains. Built in 1869, Mohonk is furnished with Victorian furniture and ornaments, and has oak paneling and floors. The resort has a trout-stocked lake, and its gardens have won international awards. The mountains are ideal for hikers, bird-watchers, golfers, ice skaters, horseback riders, and cross-country skiers. Day visitors are welcome for afternoon hikes or a visit to the skytop observation tower. *Mohonk Mountain House, Lake Mohonk, New Paltz 12561, tel. 914/255–1000. Admission to grounds: $7 weekends and $5 weekdays for adults, $4 weekends and $3 weekdays for children under 12. Open year-round, 7 AM–sunset.*

Five miles south of the turn for Mohonk Mountain House, via Libertyville Road, is **Rivendell Vineyards** at **Chateau Georges Winery,** one of the Hudson Valley's most acclaimed wineries. The selection includes award-winning Chardonnays and blush wines as well as cabernet sauvignon and unusual dessert wines. Facilities include a tasting room with panoramic views of the vineyards and farmlands, a gift shop, and picnic tables. *714 Albany Post Rd., New Paltz, tel. 914/255–0892. Admission free. Open for tours and tastings May–Sept., daily 10–6; call in advance for off-season hours.*

㉝ In the middle of the village, take Route 32 to Route 213 and go west into the town of **High Falls.** Turn right on Mohonk Road to visit the **Delaware and Hudson Canal Museum.** The museum commemorates the system of channels that was developed during the critical coal shortage brought on by the War of 1812. Channels, locks, and structures that facilitated the transportation of coal on the Delaware River from the mountains of Pennsylvania to New York City are displayed here. The D&H Canal Historical Society has restored and preserved five locks in the vicinity. They can be visited via a system of hiking trails. At the museum ask for a copy of the self-guided 45-minute walk and see the excellent collection of stonework, snubbing posts, weirs, locks, and loading ships. *Mohonk Rd., High Falls, tel. 914/687–9311. Admission: $1 adults, 50¢ children. Open Memorial Day–Labor Day, Mon., Wed.–Sat. 11–5, Sun. 1–5; May, Sept.–Oct., Sat. 11–5 and Sun. 1–5.*

㉞ Back on Route 213, head west to Route 209, then north for a very scenic drive to **Hurley.** This village was established in 1651 by the Dutch and French Huguenot settlers who built wooden homes along the Esopus Creek. After a short war with the Esopus Indians that resulted in the burning of most of the settlement, the homes were replaced with the **Hurley Stone Houses,** of which 25 are still standing. Hurley has the largest group of stone houses remaining in the country. Hurley was also the birthplace of the former-slave-turned-abolitionist Sojourner Truth, the temporary seat of New York's capital in 1777, and the Jan Van Deusen House. A free brochure, available at the library, banks, and most shops, describes the homes. Once a year, on the second Saturday of July, the homes are open for tours. A festival is held in mid-August to celebrate the local sweet corn industry. *For more information, write*

Hurley Heritage Society, c/o Reformed Church of Hurley, Box 300, Hurley 12443, tel. 914/338–2283. The annual house tours begin at 11 AM. Cost: $8.

35 Route 209 north leads into **Kingston.** At the traffic circle take the second exit for Broadway. At the end of Broadway, make a right at the traffic light and follow the road to Clinton Avenue and the **Kingston Urban Cultural Park Visitors' Center.** Designated by New York State to preserve and develop urban settings with special historic and cultural interest, the center offers orientation displays on the entire Kingston area. Directions for self-guided walking tours are available, and guided tours can be arranged by appointment. *308 Clinton Ave., Kingston 12401, tel. 914/331–9506. Admission free. Open Mon. and Wed.–Sat. 11–5, Sun. 1–5, with shorter hours in off-season.*

From the center you can walk to the **Senate House,** the meeting place of the first New York State Senate, in Kingston's historic stockade district. The state government had relocated upstate when it was forced to leave New York City during the Revolution. The house where the Senate meetings took place was built by a 17th-century Dutch settler, Wessel Ten Broeck. Tours of the historic house include an old kitchen with a huge stone fireplace and the meeting room in which the state constitution was created. There is also a museum building with 18th- and 19th-century paintings by Hudson Valley artists. One room of the museum contains works of Kingston native John Vanderlyn, considered to be one of the finest American painters of the 19th century. *312 Fair St., Kingston, tel. 914/338–2786. Admission free. Open Apr.–Dec., Wed.–Sat. 10–5 and Sun. 1–5; Jan.–Mar., Sat. 10–5 and Sun. 1–5.*

Take Broadway downtown to the **Hudson River Maritime Center** and **Rondout Landing** in the Rondout historic district. The port at the Rondout Landing was once a bustling area of boat-yards and rigged lofts. The center opened in 1980 to preserve the heritage of the river. It comprises a visitor center, museum, several restored buildings, historic vessels, an exhibit hall displaying marine art, and a huge boat shop and rigging loft. Craftspeople restore boats at the river's banks. The 1898 steam tug, *Mathilda,* is docked here, and tours of the Kingston Lighthouse leave from the landing. Several special weekend festivals are held throughout the year, and there are art galleries and restaurants in the area. *1 Rondout Landing, Kingston, tel. 914/ 338–0071. Museum admission: $2.50 adults, $2 senior citizens, $1 children 6–12. Museum open May–Oct., Mon., Wed.–Fri. 11–5, weekends 10–5.*

36 Back at the traffic circle, take Route 28 west 10 miles to the celebrated artist colony, **Woodstock.** Make a right turn onto Route 375 and follow it a few miles until it ends, then make a left onto route 212 into the heart of the 200-year-old town. Woodstock has a long tradition of attracting creative people. In 1969, a music concert, actually held 50 miles away in Sullivan County, made Woodstock a rock-music legend. All the town's art galleries, theaters, unique shops, boutiques, and restaurants are easily reached by walking (*note:* parking is a problem on the main thoroughfare). The town has become somewhat commercial, but the people-watching alone is interesting. *For more information, contact the Woodstock Chamber of Commerce, Box 36, Woodstock 12498, tel. 914/679–6234. In the summer*

months, an information booth is staffed on the main thorough-
fare, Mill Hill Rd., at the intersection of Rtes. 212 and 375.
Thurs.–Mon. 11:30–5, and on weekends during the rest of the
year.

㊲ Take Route 212 east 10 miles to a village that hangs a sign outside welcoming people: "Welcome to Friendly **Saugerties.**" This
quaint village is much less expensive and crowded than Woodstock; it has a small but attractive town park by the water and
good shops and restaurants.

㊳ Take Route 9W south from Saugerties a few miles to **West Park,**
where 170 acres of woodland, nature trails, and ponds comprise
the **John Burroughs Nature Sanctuary.** The 19th-century nature observer and writer who led and influenced environmental conservation movements lived in a cabin known as
Slabsides, where he created some of his finest writing and illustrations. The grounds are open throughout the year. *Bur-*
roughs Dr., off Floyd Ackert Rd., West Park 12493, tel. 914/384–
6320. Admission free. Open house for Slabsides is the third Sat.
of May and first Sat. of Oct., 11–4; or by appointment.

Albany, Columbia, and Greene Counties

㊴ A good place to start exploring the upper region of the Hudson
Valley is **Germantown** with a visit to **Clermont,** an estate that
was home to seven generations of prominent Livingston families between 1728 and 1962. The historic house, gardens, and
estate grounds have been restored to their 1930s appearance,
and the setting offers magnificent views of the Hudson River.
Special celebrations, including a sheep-shearing festival, a croquet day, a pumpkin festival, and a Hudson River steamboat
festival, are held here throughout the year. *Off Rte. 9G, Ger-*
mantown, tel. 518/537–4240. Admission free. The mansion is
open May–Oct., Wed.–Sat. 10–5, Sun. 1–5. The grounds are
open year-round, 8:30–sunset.

㊵ Take Route 9G north on a scenic ride to **Hudson** to view the
Moorish-style castle created by artist Frederic Church, the
foremost painter of the 19th-century Hudson River School.
Church and his wife, Isabel, returned from Europe and the
Middle East to build **Olana,** or "our place on high." Picturesque
grounds surrounding the villa offer panoramic vistas of the
Hudson River valley. The 37-room mansion features hand-
painted tiles on the roof, turrets, and garden paths; rich Per-
sian rugs; and hundreds of pieces of pottery and china as well as
Egyptian wall paintings. *Rte. 9G, Hudson, tel. 518/828–0135.*
Admission: $1 adults, 50¢ children under 12. Reservations rec-
ommended. Open Memorial Day–Labor Day, Wed.–Sat. 10–4,
Sun. 1–4; Sept.–Oct., Wed.–Sat. 12–4, Sun. 1–4.

㊶ Take Route 66 north to Chatham and then northeast for a scenic drive to **Old Chatham.** Here you'll find **The Shaker Museum,**
dedicated to members of the sect of English men and women
who immigrated to America in the late 18th century in order to
practice their communal religion. Called "Shakers" because
they danced and moved during worship services, the group established settlements throughout the new country. The Shakers were known for being industrious, thrifty, and plain—
attributes that are reflected in the artifacts and objects on display: chairs, seed packets, tin milk pails, brooms, clothing,
cloaks, and another Shaker enterprise—pharmaceuticals.

Shaker Museum Rd., Old Chatham, tel. 518/794–9100. Admission: $6 adults, $5 senior citizens, $3 children 8–17, children under 8 free. Open May–Oct., daily 10–5.

42 Take Route 13 heading west to Route 28 to **Kinderhook** for a visit to **Lindenwald,** the retirement home of Martin Van Buren, the eighth president of the United States. Van Buren was born in Kinderhook and returned here to purchase Lindenwald in 1839. The Federal-style house was built in 1797, and the mansion has been restored to reflect the original furnishings and architecture, complete with shutters, double chimneys, and arched windows. Today it is a National Historic Site. The house contains a fine collection of Van Buren memorabilia. *Rte. 9H, Kinderhook, tel. 518/758–9689. Admission: $1 adults, senior citizens over 62 and children under 12 free. Open May–Oct., daily 9–4:30; Nov., Tues.–Sun. hours vary.*

Also in Kinderhook is the **James Vanderpoel House,** an 1820 Federal-period house of the former prominent attorney, assemblyman, and judge. On display are early 19th-century furniture and decorative arts, including a fine selection of paintings by local artists that depict Columbia County life. *16 Broad St., Kinderhook, tel. 518/758–1627. Admission: $2 adults, $1.25 senior citizens and children 12–18; children under 12 free. Open Memorial Day–Labor Day, Tues.–Sat. 11–5, Sun. 1–5.*

Columbia County Museum and Library is a complex established by the Columbia County Historical Society to interpret the 300-year history of the county. There is a gallery offering changing exhibits of paintings, costumes, photographs, and artifacts illuminating the county's cultural and historic heritage. *5 Albany Ave., Kinderhook, tel. 518/758–9265. Admission free. Open year-round, weekdays 10–4, weekends 1–5.*

Route 9J runs along the Hudson west of Kinderhook 15 miles to **43** **Rensselaer,** where you can visit the **Crailo State Historic Site.** This museum, located in a house built by Hendrick Van Rensselaer in 1704, features the rich heritage of the Dutch in the upper Hudson River valley. Exhibits detail such aspects of Dutch lifestyles as a cellar kitchen, herb garden, and riverside park. *9½ Riverside Ave., Rensselaer, tel. 518/463–8738. Admission free. Open Apr.–Nov., Wed.–Sat. 10–5 and Sun. 1–5, with shorter hours at other times.*

44 From Rensselaer, take Route 90 directly into **Albany.** Make your first stop the **Albany Visitor Center** at the Albany Urban Cultural Park. In addition to the information services available, there is a hands-on exhibit about the history of Albany, as well as walking and driving tours for adults and children. *Corner of Broadway and N. Pearl St., 25 Quakenbush Sq., Albany, tel. 518/434–5132. Hours change with the seasons; call for current hours.*

At the **Empire State Plaza** adjacent to the historic State Capitol, a half-mile concourse displays modern art and sculpture and an exciting architectural blend of government, business, and cultural buildings. There is an outdoor plaza, a skating rink, restaurants, and a 42nd-floor Observation Gallery. On site is the **New York State Museum** with life-size exhibits recreating the natural and cultural history of New York. There are also changing fine-arts exhibitions and special education and science exhibits for children. The adjacent **New York State Capitol** is one of the great examples of late-19th-century American public architecture. Built over a 33-year period, it combines the designs of five architects. Free guided tours of the Capitol, including the Million Dollar Staircase and the Legislative and Executive Chambers, are conducted daily on the hour, except holidays. *For information, contact Visitor Assistance NYSOGS, Concourse Level, Empire State Plaza, Albany 12242, tel. 518/474–2418. Admission free. Open daily 9–4.*

Centrally located in the city is the **Schuyler Mansion State Historic Site,** the 18th-century Georgian mansion of Philip Schuyler, a noted general of the American Revolution, who entertained George Washington and Benjamin Franklin at the estate. The elegant drawing room in which his daughter Elizabeth married Alexander Hamilton is part of the guided tour. *32 Catherine St., Albany, tel. 518/434–0834. Admission free. Open Apr.–Dec., Wed.–Sat. 10–5, Sun. 1–5; days and times vary Jan.–Mar.; call to check.*

Take either the New York State Thruway south to Exit 21, or for a more scenic ride, take Route 9W south into the 150-year-old town of **Catskill,** which has long served as a stop for ships and sailors working on the Hudson River. There are walking tours that offer such interesting bits of history as the Palmer-Willsey Ice House, one of the few surviving 19th-century commercial ice houses; the Catskill Inn, erected in 1797, and the Catskill Public Library, all combining 19th-century architectural styles. *For information, contact Greene County Promotion, NYS Thruway Exit 21, Catskill 12414, tel. 518/943–3223 or 800/542–2414. Open daily 9–5, with extended hours in summer.*

Right outside of Catskill in the small town of Lawrenceville is the **Catskill Game Farm,** one of the country's oldest and best-known game farms, which was built in 1933. Visitors can explore a zoological park that houses such rare and exotic animals as lions, tigers, monkeys, elephants, and giant tortoises. There is a nursery for the baby animals and a petting zoo where you can feed tame deer and goats by hand. Trained bears, elephants, and dancing chickens also perform. *Located off Rte. 32 on Game Farm Rd., Catskill, tel. 518/678–9595. Admission: $10 adults, $6 children 4–12; children under 4 free. Open Apr. 15–Oct. 31, daily 9–6.*

Head south on Route 32, then west onto the Rip Van Winkle Trail, or Route 23A, to **Palenville.** The Interarts Festival—World's Fair of the Arts, combining theater performances, dance, art classes, jazz, Dixieland shows, circus arts, magicians, and mimes—is scheduled throughout the summer months. *Woodstock Ave., off Rtes. 23A and 32A, Palenville, tel. 518/678–3332. Admission: $12 adults, $6 senior citizens and children under 12. Open July–Sept.*

Off the Beaten Track

Westchester County The **Museum of Cartoon Art,** about a mile northeast of Rye, was founded in 1974 by Mort Walker, the creator of Beetle Bailey. It is dedicated to the acquisition, preservation, and exhibition of all forms of cartoon art, including comic strips and comic books, book illustrations, caricatures, and animation. There are ongoing and special exhibits and film and video programs. Visitors can buy original cartoon art from the museum's gallery, as well as less expensive items from the gift shop. *Comly*

Ave., Rye Brook, tel. 914/939–0234. Admission: $3 adults, $2 students and senior citizens, $1 children 5–12. Open Tues.– Fri. 10–4, Sun. 1–5.

Near the Philipsburg Manor in North Tarrytown is the **Old Dutch Church of Sleepy Hollow,** one of the oldest churches in the Hudson Valley. Made famous in Washington Irving's *Legend of Sleepy Hollow,* the church is the only remaining example of 17th-century Dutch religious architecture in the United States. Stone walls surround furnishings typical of 17th- and 18th-century Netherlands. The grave of Washington Irving, a National Historic Landmark, is located on the grounds. *Rte. 9, North Tarrytown, tel. 914/631–1123 or write Friends of the Old Dutch Burying Ground, 35 South Broadway, Tarrytown 10591. Admission free.*

Orange County The **Storm King Arts Center** at Mountainville is an outdoor park and home to over 130 large-scale contemporary sculptures by American and European artists, all displayed in a sylvan setting on 400 hilly acres. There is also an enclosed château-style museum containing rotating sculpture exhibits. *Old Pleasant Hill Rd., Mountainville, tel. 914/534–3115. Admission: $5 adults, $3 students and senior citizens. Open Apr.–Nov., daily (except Tues.) noon–5:30.*

Rensselaer County The **Junior Museum** offers everything from constellation shows in a Sky Dome Theater to reproductions of log cabins built during the 1800s. In addition, there are natural-science exhibits that include honeybees in a hive, live reptiles, and both salt- and freshwater aquariums. The main gallery of the museum features hands-on, interactive art, history, and science exhibits that change annually. *282 Fifth Ave., Troy, tel. 518/235– 2120. Admission: $2, including shows. Open Sat.–Wed. 1–5.*

Ulster County Unusual, different, and unique are the words for **Opus 40,** "The Quarryman's Museum," described in its own pamphlet as a "monumental environmental sculpture rising out of an abandoned bluestone quarry." An artistic landscape, it is totally the work of sculptor Harvey Fite. The structure covers more than six acres and is made of more than 100 tons of finely fitted bluestone. Fite took more than 37 years to construct it. On the grounds is a museum built to house Fite's collection of quarryman tools and artifacts. Opus 40 is accessible by car from Exit 20, off the NYS Thruway, and Route 9W; follow signs to Opus 40. *7480 Fite Rd., Saugerties, tel. 914/246–3400. Admission: $3 adults, $2 students and senior citizens. Open May–Oct., Fri.– Sun. noon–5.*

In an area undergoing artistic resurgence, the town of Rosendale is home to several antiques shops and art galleries. Leader among these artistic adventurers is the **Women's Studio Workshop,** which features photography, paintings, prints, woodwork, and sculpture shows by women artists. Head south on Route 32 from Kingston and turn right onto Route 213 in Rosendale. From there follow signs to the WSW at the Binnewater Arts Center. *Binnewater La., Rosendale, tel. 914/ 658–9133. Gallery open Tues.–Fri. 10–5, Sat. 12–4.*

Participant Sports

Fishing

The Hudson River valley provides a wealth of fishing opportunities. The river is affected by the tides from the federal dam at Troy, south to the Atlantic Ocean, providing an immense diversity of habitat and species.

Saltwater intrusion varies with the seasons; in the springtime, the saltwater line may be as far south as Yonkers, but in the fall and winter, salt water has been found as far north as Hyde Park. Because of this, the Hudson River estuary contains a remarkable variety of fish, most notably American shad, fished at low, slack tide from mid-April to early June, and striped bass, from June through November. Other species that are available, at various times, are black bass, small-mouth and large-mouth bass, and sturgeon. In addition, the lakes, ponds, and streams of the valley yield trout, pike, pickerel, and perch.

Almost everyone over 16 years old must have a license to fish in fresh waters, although no license is presently required for Hudson River fishing. For information on licenses, permits, or restrictions, as well as fishing hot spots and charts, contact the *New York State Department of Environmental Conservation (DEC), 21 S. Putt Corners Rd., New Paltz, NY 12561, tel. 914/ 255-5453; 50 Wolf Rd., Albany, NY 12233, tel. 518/457-3521; or Stony Kill Farm, Rte. 9D, Wappingers Falls, NY 12590, tel. 914/831-8780. Licenses can also be obtained at town and county clerks' offices, bait shops, and some sporting-goods stores.*

Golf

The fertile green hills and dales of the Hudson Valley make good golfing turf. In fact, this eight-county region has more than 50 golf courses that welcome visiting players. Lists and descriptions of the courses can be obtained by contacting the individual county tourist offices or area chambers of commerce.

Although many of the fairways are inland, there is one club that not only offers a golfing challenge, but also provides spectacular views of both the Hudson River and the distant Catskill Mountains—the 18-hole **Dinsmore Golf Course**. *Rte. 9, Staatsburg, tel. 914/889-4751. Open Apr.–Nov., daily.*

Two other outstanding, though not as scenic, courses are the 27-hole **Beekman Country Club** (Hopewell Junction, tel. 914/ 226-7700), open daily April through November; and the **James Baird State Park Golf Course** (Pleasant Valley, tel. 914/452- 1489), an 18-hole championship course located off the Taconic State Parkway, open daily mid-April through mid-November.

Winter Sports

Cross-country and downhill **skiing** are popular sports at a number of Hudson Valley locations, such as **Bear Mountain State Park** at Bear Mountain, **Rockefeller State Park Preserve** at North Tarrytown, the **Mills-Norrie State Park** at Staatsburg, the **Clermont State Historic Site** at Germantown, and **Olana State Historic Site** at Hudson.

In addition, **ice skating** is available at some park locations, as are **ice fishing, ice boat sailing,** and **snowmobiling.** For up-to-date information, contact the **Hudson River Valley Association** (McCabe Carriage House, 42 Catharine St., Poughkeepsie 12601, tel. 914/452–4910 or 800/232–4782).

Two downhill skiing areas—the **Catskill Mountains** and the **Berkshires**—are also easily accessible from the Hudson Valley.

Dining

Highly recommended restaurants are indicated by a star ★.

Category	Cost*
Expensive	over $40
Moderate	$20–$40
Inexpensive	under $20

*per person without tax (7¼% to 8¼%), service, or drinks

Westchester and Rockland Counties

Ardsley   **Cantina.** Set in a beautiful, 100-year-old stone building overlooking Woodlands Lake, this restaurant's specialties are Mexican food and fresh fish; outdoor dining is featured in the summer months. *Saw Mill River Pkwy., tel. 914/693–6565. Dress: casual to neat. Reservations suggested. AE, MC, V. Moderate.*

Ship's Galley. This family-owned and -operated restaurant specializes in seafood dishes, including trout, red snapper, salmon, bouillabaisse, and zuppa di pesce. The pasta is homemade and delicious. *5 Village Green, Rte. 9A, tel. 914/693–4878. Dress: casual. Reservations suggested. AE, DC, MC, V. Dinner only weekends and June–Aug. Inexpensive.*

Chappaqua   **Crabtree's Kittle House.** A 200-year-old country house is the setting for this delightful restaurant, run by Dick and John Crabtree. The menu features American and Continental cuisines, with such dishes as shrimps Madagascar, roast duckling, rack of lamb, veal medallions, and daily seafood specials. *11 Kittle Rd. off Rte. 117, tel. 914/666–8044. Jacket or neat attire required. Reservations suggested. AE, CB, DC, MC, V. Dinner only Sat. Expensive.*

Congers   **Bully Boy Chop House.** Specializing in steaks, chops, and seafood with an English touch, this restaurant is renowned for its prime ribs, rack of lamb, English pies, and Yorkshire pudding. There are seven dining rooms, some of which overlook a lovely pond with ducks. Other rooms are quite elegant, with plush red carpeting. Homemade scones are served with butter and honey. *117 Rte. 303, tel. 914/268–6555. Dress: casual. Reservations suggested. AE, MC, V. Dinner only weekends. Moderate.*

Romolo's. Veal dishes are the specialty here. Try the veal Verbena or scaloppine with white asparagus, prosciutto, and fresh mozzarella in wine sauce. If you prefer steak, order the filet mignon Zingara, sautéed in marsala wine with cream, ham, and mushrooms. The atmosphere is warm and friendly, a true Italian family restaurant. *Rte. 303 and Tremont Ave., tel. 914/268–*

3770/9855. Dress: casual. Reservations suggested. AE, CB, DC, MC, V. Closed Mon., dinner only weekends. Moderate.

Dobbs Ferry **The Chart House.** This is a contemporary restaurant with magnificent views of the Palisades, the Tappan Zee Bridge, and the New York City skyline. The all-American specialties include prime ribs, thick steaks, and an enormous selection of seafood. Mud pie is the preferred dessert. *High St., tel. 914/693–4131. Dress: casual chic. No reservations. AE, CB, DC, MC, V. Dinner and Sun. brunch only. Moderate.*

Hartsdale **Auberge Arenteuil.** Set in a former 1920s speakeasy, this French restaurant is hidden high up in a wooded area overlooking Central Avenue. Specialties include lobster bisque, chicken with tarragon or raspberry vinegar, and veal with wild mushrooms. *42 Healy Ave., tel. 914/948–0597. Dress: casual. Reservations suggested. AE, MC, V. Closed Mon., dinner only weekends. Expensive.*

Hawthorne **Gasho of Japan.** Housed in a 400-year-old farmhouse, this Japanese restaurant is surrounded by three acres of lush Oriental gardens. The menu includes hibachi steak, chicken, and seafood prepared at individual tables. *2 Saw Mill River Rd., tel. 914/592–5900. Also located on Rte. 32, Central Valley in Orange County, tel. 914/928–2387. Proper attire required. Reservations suggested. AE, CB, DC, MC, V. Moderate.*

Montrose **India House Restaurant.** Lots of greenery surrounds this restaurant decorated to resemble a colorful tent. Dining rooms are covered with antique Indian tapestries. The specialties are Tandoori lamb, chicken, or shrimp. The vegetarian entrees are also excellent and can be prepared mild, spicy, or hot. *199 Albany Post Rd., tel. 914/736–0005. Dress: casual. Reservations accepted for parties of 5 or more. AE. Closed Tues., dinner only. Moderate.*

Mt. Kisco **La Camelia.** Located in a 140-year-old restored clapboard house on the north side of town, this restaurant combines an old-world ambience with a mostly Spanish menu. Specialties include paella Valenciana with saffron rice, grilled shrimp in lobster sauce, and a variety of tempting tapas. *234 N. Bedford Rd., tel. 914/666–2466. Dress: neat attire. Reservations suggested, especially on weekends. AE, CB, DC, MC, V. Closed Mon., dinner only weekends. Moderate.*

North Salem **Auberge Maxime.** A restored country inn is the setting for this
★ classic French restaurant. There is a fixed price for five-course dinners. Specialties include duck prepared with various sauces and hot or cold soufflés. *Rte. 116, tel. 914/669–5450. Jackets required. Reservations suggested. AE, MC, V. Closed Wed., dinner only Sat. Expensive.*

Piermont **The Turning Point.** This is a great place to relax and listen to live music, Wednesday–Sunday. Dinner specialties include poached salmon with tarragon and sautéed mushrooms, and there are always several vegetarian choices on the menu, along with 15 herbal teas and 20 types of beer. Sunday brunch features buttermilk pancakes, vegetarian omelets, or French toast. *468 Piermont Ave., tel. 914/359–1089. Dress: casual. Reservations suggested. AE, CB, DC, MC, V. Brunch only Sun. Moderate.*

Pound Ridge **The Inn at Pound Ridge.** Four American presidents have dined at this restaurant within the past 40 years. The original building dates to 1883. Specialties include prime rib, rack of lamb, roast duckling, and fresh seafood. *Rte. 137, tel. 914/764–5779. Jacket requested. Reservations suggested. AE, CB, DC, MC, V. Closed Tues., dinner only weekends. Moderate.*

Port Chester **The Oasis.** International art covers the walls of this trendy enclave, which features an outdoor garden patio in summer. The eclectic menu features new American versions of breast of duck, stuffed veal, grilled swordfish, and a variety of pastas. *23 N. Main St., tel. 914/939–7220. Dress: casual. Reservations suggested. AE, MC, V. Lunch weekdays, dinner Tues.–Sun. Moderate.*

Rye Brook **Mallard's at Arrowwood.** Reminiscent of a late 19th-century
★ gentlemen's club, this restaurant is rich with mahogany wainscoting, sterling-silver wall sconces, etched mirrors, and wildlife paintings. The American menu offers such choices as hickory-roasted duckling, blackened tenderloin of beef, poached striped bass, and lobster and scallop ravioli. *Anderson Hill Rd., tel. 914/939–5500. Jacket required. Reservations required. AE, CB, DC, MC, V. Closed Sun. and Mon., dinner only Sat. Expensive.*

Scarsdale **Il Cigno.** Owned and operated by the DePietro family for many years, this restaurant features grilled wild mushrooms, duck ravioli, fresh fennel, endive salad, and filet mignon with walnuts and Gorgonzola. *1505 Weaver St., tel. 914/472–8484. Jackets preferred. Reservations suggested. AE, CB, DC, MC, V. Closed Mon. and 2 wks in July. Moderate.*

South Salem **Le Chateau.** Set on a 32-acre estate with a lake, gardens, and
★ woodland, this elegant restaurant—in a Tudor mansion built by J. P. Morgan in 1907—has a turn-of-the-century ambience and a classic French menu. Entrees include rack of lamb, Muscovy duck in cherry port sauce, and venison with white raisins and green peppercorns. Cocktails are served on the terrace in the summer. *Rte. 35 at junction of Rte. 123, tel. 914/533–6631. Jacket required. Reservations required. AE, CB, DC, MC, V. Lunch Tues.–Fri., dinner Tues.–Sun. Expensive.*

Spring Valley **La Capannina.** The name of this restaurant means "little house
★ in the country" and gives a clue to its setting—an 18th-century Dutch home in the historic Haring Homestead. It is nestled amid seven acres of gardens with a duck pond and waterfall. The menu is mostly French and Italian, and daily blackboard specials often include rack of lamb, duckling, calves' liver, or sweetbreads; for dessert, with a little advance notice, you can enjoy crepes suzette, cherries jubilee, or sabayon. *606 S. Pascack Rd., tel. 914/735–7476. Jacket required. Reservations accepted. AE, CB, DC, MC, V. Closed Sun.; dinner only Sat., lunch only Mon. Expensive.*

Tappan **Giulio's.** Fine northern Italian cuisine is served in this 100-year-old Victorian house, which features romantic candlelight settings at dinner and a strolling vocalist or guitarist on Friday evenings. The *Valdostana Vitelle,* or veal stuffed with prosciutto and cheese in a champagne sauce, and the scampi Giulio, or jumbo shrimp sautéed with fresh mushrooms, are the house specialties. *154 Washington St., tel. 914/359–3657. Jacket preferred. Reservations recommended. AE, CB, DC, MC, V. No lunch weekends. Moderate.*

Tarrytown **Horsefeathers.** Dark-paneled walls and an antique bar distinguish this restaurant, which features great hamburgers and steaks, barbecued baby-back ribs, overstuffed sandwiches, and rich New England clam chowder. The atmosphere is casual and comfortable. *94 N. Broadway, tel. 914/631–6606. Dress: casual. Reservations accepted for parties of 5 or more. AE, MC, V. Closed Sun. Moderate.*

Tuckahoe **Salerno's.** For more than 20 years, this family-run restaurant has been "the place" in lower Westchester for prime beef, lamb, and fresh seafood, as well as pastas and Italian specialties. *100 Main St., tel. 914/793–1557. Dress: casual. No reservations. MC, V. Dinner only. Closed Mon., 1 wk in Feb., and last 2 wks of Aug. Moderate–Expensive.*

Valley Cottage **Cottage Cafe.** This family-run seafood restaurant serves such dishes as seafood Fra Diavolo, which is a combination of mussels, clams, scallops, shrimp, and pasta. All desserts are made on the premises; try the chocolate cheesecake, peanut butter pie, or Swiss chocolate layer cake. *2 Lake Ridge Plaza, Rte. 303, tel. 914/268–3993. Dress: casual. Reservations suggested on weekends. AE, CB, DC, MC, V. Dinner only weekends. Moderate.*

White Plains **Quarropas.** The name means "white swamp," which was the original name for White Plains. The dining room contains a collection of antique American packing-crate labels and food ads. Specialties include ravioli filled with shrimp, crab, and escarole, and for dessert walnut strudel. *478 Mamaroneck Ave., tel. 914/684–0414. Dress: informal. Reservations required on weekends, appreciated on weekdays. AE, CB, DC, MC, V. Closed Mon., dinner only Sat. Moderate.*

Orange and Putnam Counties

Cold Spring **Plumbush Inn.** Dating to 1867, this lovely inn is furnished in an
★ opulent Victorian style. It offers dining by candlelight amid a decor of rose-patterned wallpaper, dark oak paneling, paintings by local artists, and the warmth of wood-burning fireplaces. In summer there is also outdoor dining on a porch overlooking the gardens. The menu ranges from fresh seafood and veal to Swiss specialties, with both fixed-price and à la carte services. The inn also has three guest rooms with bath upstairs if you want to plan an overnight. *Rte. 9D, tel. 914/265–3904. Jacket required in evening. Reservations suggested. AE, CB, DC, MC, V. Closed Mon. and Tues. Expensive.*

Breakneck Lodge. A restaurant for more than 50 years, this cozy Old World Swiss-Tudor lodge overlooks the Hudson River and Storm King Mountain. The menu features fresh seafood, beef, veal, and game, plus Austrian, Swiss, and German dishes. *Rte. 9D, Old River Rd., tel. 914/265–9669. Dress: neatly casual. Reservations suggested, especially on weekends. AE, DC, MC, V. Moderate.*

Dockside Harbor. Hard by the banks of the Hudson, this restaurant is at its best on the lazy, hazy days of summer. Depending on the weather, you can choose either indoor or outdoor dining, with varying riverside views. There is also music on the lawn each Sunday afternoon. The menu focuses primarily on seafood, steaks, and chops. *1 North St., tel. 914/265–3503. Dress: casual. Reservations suggested. AE, MC, V. Hours vary, check in advance. Moderate.*

Cornwall-on-Hudson **Painter's Tavern.** In the center of the village on the Square, this Art Deco restaurant has a splendid display of paintings by local artists. The decor also features memorabilia and antiques from the area. The ever-changing chalkboard menu is equally eclectic, with a medley of regional and international selections, such as Cajun shrimp, chili and Mexican chicken, blackened steak, seafood diablo over pasta, surf and turf, scallops Dijonaise, as well as burgers, salads, and steaks. Most dishes owe their special flavors to an herb garden behind the restaurant. *Rte. 218, tel. 914/534–2109. Dress: casual. Reservations suggested for weekends. AE, CB, DC, MC, V. Moderate.*

Garrison **The Bird and Bottle Inn.** Established in 1761, this spot was once
★ a major stagecoach stop along the route from New York to Albany. Today it has three dining rooms, all with wood-burning fireplaces. The Colonial ambience is enhanced by candlelit table settings, antiques, old prints, beamed ceilings, and wideplank floors. The menu choices include roast pheasant, rack of lamb, salmon Wellington, and fillet of sole poached in wine; and be sure to sample the special pumpkin bread. Desserts are also very tempting, from butter pecan soufflés to chocolate rum tortes. Open for dinner only and Sunday brunch, all meals are five courses and fixed-price. *Old Albany Post Rd. (Rte. 9) at Nelson's Corners Rd., tel. 914/424–3000. Jacket required. Reservations advised. AE, DC, MC, V. Closed Mon., Tues. Expensive.*

★ **Xavier's at Garrison.** This elegant French restaurant sits in a country setting, surrounded by the Highland Golf Course. Fresh flowers, crystal, and silver adorn each table, and on weekends there is background music by a harpist or pianist. In the summer, outdoor dining is also available on a covered terrace overlooking the putting greens. The menu changes often, but top entrees are grilled quail over pasta, medallions of rabbit with white grapes, and grilled Norwegian salmon basted with honey and Chinese mustard. *Rte. 9D, tel. 914/424–4228. Jacket required. Reservations required. No credit cards. Closed Mon., dinner only Tues.–Sat. Expensive.*

New Windsor **Brewster House.** A registered landmark, this Colonial-era fieldstone inn dates to 1762, and the decor features the original beams, floors, and doors. House specialties include lobster, barbecued shrimp, smoked fish, and pasta. There is also a raw bar, and piano entertainment on weekends. *Temple Hill Rd., tel. 914/561–1762 or 914/562–2018. Dress: casual. Reservations suggested. AE, CB, DC, MC, V. Closed Mon., dinner only weekends. Moderate.*

Patterson **L'Auberge Bretonne.** This is a cozy French restaurant with a dining room enhanced by wood-beamed ceilings and large windows overlooking the foothills of the Berkshires. The menu changes constantly, but specialties often include breast of duck with a honey-mustard sauce, roast saddle of lamb in a puff pastry, and sea scallops Veronique. *Rte. 22, tel. 914/878–6782. Dress: neatly casual. Reservations required for weekends. AE, CB, DC, MC, V. Closed Wed. Expensive.*

Sugar Loaf **Barnsider Tavern.** This restaurant offers a choice of dining settings, including a rustic taproom with hand-wrought beams, country furnishings, and a glass-enclosed patio that overlooks the Sugar Loaf crafts community. During the winter months there is always a warming fire in the hearth. The menu is fairly simple, with steaks, burgers, quiches, chili, soups, and salads.

Kings Hwy., tel. 914/469–9810. Dress: casual. No credit cards. Moderate.

Warwick   **Warwick Inn.** Owned and operated by the Wilson family for a quarter of a century, this 165-year-old home contains original moldings, fireplaces, and furnishings. The menu offers a variety of seafood, from baked stuffed shrimp to broiled swordfish, as well as prime ribs and fresh turkey. *36 Oakland Ave., tel.914/986–3666. Dress: casual. Reservations suggested. AE, MC, V. Closed Mon. and Tues., dinner only. Expensive.*

Dutchess and Ulster Counties

High Falls   **DePuy Canal House.** Dating to 1797 and originally a tavern, ★ this stone house is now the domain of John Novi, a chef ranked by a leading national magazine as "the father of American nouvelle cuisine." The menu, which offers fixed-price, three- or seven-course dinners, changes weekly; it features such dishes as rabbit pâté with pine nuts or poached sole with salmon and red-pepper mousse, as well as fresh fruits with goat cheese from nearby farms. An à la carte menu is also available. The wine cellar boasts more than 100 different wines from the Hudson Valley. *Rte. 213, tel. 914/687–7700. Dress: neatly casual. Reservations required. AE, MC, V. Closed Mon.–Wed.; dinner only Thurs.–Sat., dinner and brunch Sun. Expensive.*

Highland   **Mariner's Harbor.** This restaurant overlooks the Hudson, with indoor and outdoor seating. It is popular with visiting celebrities such as Phil Rizzuto. Specialties are lobster, seafood combination platters, and steaks. *45 River Rd., tel. 914/691–6011. Dress: casual. No reservations. AE, CB, DC, MC, V. Lunch and dinner, Tues.–Sun. Moderate.*

Hopewell Junction   **Le Chambord.** You'll find this award-winning French restaurant ★ northeast of Fishkill, in southern Dutchess County less than a mile east of the Taconic Parkway. It is housed in a restored 1863 Georgian-Colonial home that is furnished with fine paintings and antiques. The menu focuses on inventive dishes such as bay scallops with mushrooms and escargot, breast of chicken Provençale, beef Stroganoff with fettuccine, salmon with truffles, chateaubriand with béarnaise, and seafood with fine herb sauces. *2075 Rte. 52 at Carpenter Rd., 12533, tel. 914/ 221–1941. Jacket recommended. Reservations recommended. AE, DC, MC, V. Dinner only weekends. Expensive.*

Hyde Park   **The Culinary Institute of America,** or CIA (*see* Exploring the Hudson River Valley, above), located on Route 9, has four restaurants for public dining. *Tel. 914/471–6608 weekdays 9–5. Jacket and reservations are required for each venue. AE, DC, MC, V. All are closed on school holidays and the first 3 wks of July.*

★   **The Escoffier.** This award-winning restaurant is the domain of students in their final semester at the school who practice the preparation and serving of classical haute cuisine. The menus are fixed-price or à la carte and the standards are impeccable— so much so, in fact, that the restaurant is often fully booked a month or more in advance, especially for weekends. *Closed Sun., Mon. Expensive.*

American Bounty. The focus here is on an à la carte service of American regional fare, including such southern specialties as crawfish pie or shrimp etoufée and midwestern game dishes. *Closed Sun., Mon. Moderate–Expensive.*

Caterina de Medici. Regional Italian cuisine—both modern and traditional—is the focus here at the smallest of the CIA's four dining rooms, so space is very limited and the menu is fixed-price. *Lunch: one seating at 11:30, dinner: one seating at 6. Closed weekends. Moderate–Expensive.*

St. Andrew's Cafe. This is the most informal of the four CIA restaurants, offering à la carte service of well-balanced meals prepared according to sound nutritional guidelines. *Closed weekends. Moderate.*

Kingston **Armadillo Bar and Grill.** Located in the historic Rondout district, this relaxed restaurant serves mostly southwestern and Mexican cuisine. Specialties include fresh grilled seafood, shrimp-stuffed jalapeños, *fajita* steaks, and frozen margaritas. There is both outdoor and indoor dining, depending upon the season. *97 Abeel St., tel. 914/339–1550. Dress: casual. Reservations suggested for 6 or more (on weekends, smaller parties should phone 45 minutes in advance to check availability). AE, DC, MC, V. Closed Mon., dinner only weekends. Moderate.*

Hillside Manor. Situated south of the city along the west bank of the Hudson, this is a favorite spot for fine northern Italian cuisine as well as great views. Specialties include veal dishes, salmon with dry vermouth and chives, fresh pastas, and such local dishes as Hudson Valley shad roe. Live entertainment is featured on Friday and Saturday nights. *240 Boulevard (Rte. 32), tel. 914/331–4386. Dress: Jacket preferred. Reservations recommended. AE, CB, DC, MC, V. Dinner only, Tues.–Sat. Moderate–Expensive.*

★ **Skytop Steak and Seafood House.** Panoramic views of the Hudson Valley are part of the attraction at this hilltop restaurant, located a quarter-mile from Exit 19 of the New York State Thruway. The menu features steaks and meats grilled over a charcoal pit, fresh seafood, including lobsters from a tank, and an all-you-can-eat salad bar. There is live entertainment Tuesday through Saturday. *Rte. 28, tel. 914/338–6161. Dress: casual. AE, CB, DC, MC, V. Dinner only. Moderate.*

Millerton **Simmon's Way Village Inn.** The dining room of this charming
★ mid-19th-century inn is reason enough to head inland toward the Connecticut border. The decor is bright and airy, with a skylit vaulted ceiling, pastel linens, leafy plants, and light woods. The menu, prepared by a Culinary Institute–trained chef, changes seasonally but often includes such dishes as shad roe with crayfish sauce, rack of lamb encrusted with herbed breadcrumbs, baked sole with lime beurre blanc, salmon en papillote with white-wine and brandy sauce, rock Cornish hen à l'orange, or linguine primavera. This is a nonsmoking dining room. *Main St. (Rte. 44), tel. 518/789–6235. Dress: neatly casual. Reservations recommended. AE, MC, V. Dinner only Wed.–Sun., brunch Sun. Moderate–Expensive.*

Poughkeepsie **Caesar's Ristorante.** As might be expected, the Caesar salads at this fine, northern Italian restaurant are exceptional, as is the antipasto. There are also many fine pasta, beef, chicken, and veal dishes on the menu. You'll find this restaurant in the heart of the historic district, directly under the Poughkeepsie Railroad Bridge. *2 Delafield St., tel. 914/471–4857. Dress: casual. Reservations not accepted. AE, CB, DC, MC, V. Dinner only. Moderate.*

John L's. Located in an early 1800s farmhouse about three miles east of the city, this restaurant has a warm and rustic atmosphere and a contemporary menu of mesquite-grilled fish, baby-back rib, steak, prime rib, and seafood. There is also a salad bar. *522 Dutchess Tpke. (Rte. 44), tel. 914/471–6660. Dress: casual. Reservations accepted except on Fri. and Sat. AE, DC, MC, V. Dinner only. Moderate.*

River Station. "Down by the riverside" dining is the theme of this informal restaurant overlooking the Hudson. You can enjoy river views either from the inside dining room or the outdoor deck. Specialties include seafood, veal, steak, and pasta. *25 Main St., tel. 914/452–9207. Dress: casual. Reservations not accepted on weekends. MC, V. Moderate.*

Red Hook **Greene & Bresler Ltd.** This contemporary shopfront restaurant in the heart of town serves creative American and European cuisines, with such dishes as apple-smoked turkey and brie, smoked fish, charcoal-grilled fillet of beef, Norwegian salmon, pastas, and a wide variety of colorful salads. In summer, tables are set up on an outside deck. *29 W. Market St., tel. 914/758–5992. Dress: casual. Reservations suggested. AE, MC, V. Lunch and dinner daily in summer, with reduced schedule at other times. Moderate.*

McCaffrey's Cottage. Situated in a quiet, tree-shaded setting two miles north of town, this country-style restaurant specializes in well-aged steaks and fresh seafood prepared to order and accompanied by unlimited helpings from the salad bar. Weekends often feature live Irish music. *Rte. 9, tel. 914/758–8782. Dress: neatly casual. Reservations suggested for weekends. MC, V. Dinner daily. Moderate.*

Savoy. Located across from the entrance to Bard College and northwest of town, this relatively new restaurant features a blend of American and Continental cuisines, with such dishes as steak au poivre, veal champignon, and sautéed sweetbreads, as well as fillet of salmon, lobster, and (on weekends) prime rib. *Rte. 9G, tel. 914/876–1200. Dress: neatly casual. Reservations suggested. AE, DC, MC, V. Closed Mon., dinner only. Moderate.*

Rhinebeck **The Beekman Arms.** This historic spot, renowned as one of the
★ nation's oldest hotels (*see* Lodging, below), presents a choice of four different dining rooms, starting with the **1776 Tap Room,** which was the original bar and restaurant in Colonial days. It still has the 20-foot wooden benches from George Washington's day, as well as walls covered with old prints, deeds, maps, muskets, mugs, sabers, powder horns, and corncob pipes. At the south end of the Tap Room is the candlelit **Wine Cellar,** a cozy blend of old barrels, beams, and brick, with booth-style seating. The adjacent **Pewter Room** has a warm country-inn atmosphere, with a handsome corner cupboard, chiming clocks, and prints on the walls. The fourth dining area is the conservatory-style **Greenhouse,** brimming with flower boxes and hanging plants. It faces the front lawn of the hotel and looks out onto Rhinebeck's main thoroughfare. No matter where you sit, however, the menu is the same, with emphasis on American regional fare. Entrees include pan roast of shrimp and scallops, blackened salmon fillet, grilled apricot-ginger chicken, and pork medallions with Husdon Valley apples. *4 Mill St. (Rte. 9), tel. 914/876–7077. Dress: neatly casual. Reservations suggested. AE, DC, MC, V. Moderate–Expensive.*

★ **Le Petit Bistro.** Situated in the heart of Rhinebeck less than a block from the Beekman Arms, this is a small and intimate restaurant with a French ambience, artfully prepared food, and enthusiastic service. It is run by Yvonne and Jean-Paul Croizer, previously associated with the catering department of Air France and leading restaurants in New York City and the Hudson Valley. Featured dishes include duck with fruits, Dover sole, seafood crepes, coquilles St. Jacques, coq au vin, steak au poivre, and sautéed softshell crab in season. Desserts range from feather-light meringues to velvety fondues or *crème brûlées*. The crusty breads and rich ice creams are made locally. *8 E. Market St., tel. 914/876–7400. Dress: neatly casual. Reservations suggested. AE, CB, DC, MC, V. Closed Tues. and Wed., dinner only. Moderate–Expensive.*

Chez Marcel. Located less than two miles north of Rhinebeck, this French country inn is the domain of Renee and Marcel Disch (formerly of Chez Renee in Manhattan). Everything is cooked to order, and the menu includes such choices as sole *bonne femme*, chicken almondine, veal *cordon bleu*, and a delicately seasoned rack of lamb. *Rte. 9, tel. 914/876–8189. Dress: neatly casual. Reservations suggested. AE, DC. Closed Mon., dinner only. Moderate.*

Mariko's. This is an authentic Japanese restaurant, specializing in "Tokyo nouvelle cuisine." The menu includes a full selection of sushi and sashimi, as well as yakitori, tempura, sukiyaki, and teriyaki entrees. Some unique dishes include softshell-crab tempura, vegetarian tofu delight, and "sushi 101," an introductory seven-piece assortment of sushi. Mariko's is located two miles north of Rhinebeck, one mile past the intersection of routes 9 and 9G. *Rte. 9, tel. 914/876–1234. Dress: neatly casual. Reservations suggested. MC, V. Closed Tues., dinner only. Moderate.*

Fox Hollow Inn. Freshly made pasta and other Italian dishes are the specialties at this rustic restaurant, located in a converted country inn about two miles south of the village. Owned and operated by the LaRocca family for 35 years, this spot is also known for steaks, shellfish, and thick cuts of prime ribs. *Rte. 9, tel. 914/876–4696. Dress: casual. Reservations usually not necessary, except weekends. MC, V. Closed Tues. Moderate–Inexpensive.*

Foster's Coach House. The site of this restaurant-pub was once the home of a Revolutionary War drillmaster who so loved his horse that he gave the animal a proper funeral when it died. You'll not only see hitching posts on the sidewalk outside and horse prints and racing scenes on the walls within, but you can also sit at a table in a horse stall or place a call from a phone booth fashioned from a horse-drawn carriage. The atmosphere is informal and the menu concentrates on burgers, steaks, and salads. It's in the heart of town, one block north of the Beekman Arms and adjacent to Upstate Films. *22 Montgomery St., tel. 914/876–8052. Dress: casual. No credit cards. Reservations not accepted. Closed Mon. Inexpensive.*

Schemmy's. For a light snack, lunch, or coffee, don't miss this old-fashioned ice-cream parlor (with a wrought-iron ice-cream cone hanging over the front door). Situated in the center of the village, it is a real Rhinebeck institution that used to be Schermerhorn's Drug Store. You'll see a wall lined with original medicine drawers, apothecary jars, and other local memorabilia. The menu features sandwiches, burgers, quiches, soups, salads, and homemade ice cream in assorted flavors. *19 E. Market St., tel. 914/876–6215. Dress: casual. No credit cards. Open daily 7 AM–5 PM. Inexpensive.*

Woodstock   **The Artist's Grill.** Located just over two miles east of town (toward Saugerties), this charming restaurant is housed in a restored 150-year-old farmhouse. The menu emphasizes French country cuisine and fresh seafood. *Rte. 212, tel. 914/679–5977. Dress: casual. Reservations suggested. AE, DC, MC, V. Dinner only, nightly June–Sept., Wed.–Sun. rest of year. Moderate.*

The Seasons. Newly opened in 1990, this restaurant combines lovely views of the countryside with a Continental/Italian menu. Specialties include veal picatta, roast lamb with rosemary sauce, and seafood pasta. All vegetables and herbs are grown in the adjacent garden. *Route 212, tel. 914/246–0500. Dress: neatly casual. Reservations recommended. AE, CB, DC, MC, V. Closed Tues.–Wed., dinner only. Moderate–Expensive.*

Albany, Columbia, and Greene Counties

Albany   **L'Auberge.** Situated in a historic building that once housed the ★ ticket office of the Hudson River Dayliner (circa 1907), the decor of this restaurant is a blend of rustic dark woods and romantic pink fabrics and fixtures. Proprietor Nicole Plisson, a native of the Loire Valley and a former cooking-school instructor, strives to maintain a distinctive menu, including such specialties as Muscovy duck, goat-cheese ravioli, ragout of snails, roast quail, scallop mousse, loin of veal, and French pastries. *Located just south of the state university at the foot of State St. hill, 2 blocks from the new Knickerbocker Arena. 351 Broadway, tel. 518/465–1111. Jacket preferred. Reservations suggested. AE, CB, DC, MC, V. Closed Sun., dinner only Sat. Expensive.*

Jack's Oyster House. Claiming to be Albany's oldest restaurant, this revered spot has been in the same family for more than 75 years. The decor reflects the history of the capital, with old pictures, dark oak trim, and assorted memorabilia. The menu beckons diners "with a hungry appetite," offering bountiful dishes, with emphasis on seafood (from oyster stew to Boston scrod), steaks, and chops. *42–44 State St., tel. 518/465–8854. Dress: casual. Reservations suggested. AE, CB, DC, MC, V. Moderate–Expensive.*

Coco's. This is a fun restaurant, known for its vast choice of giant drinks (often served with balloons attached) and for its four carousel-style salad bars. The menu ranges from ribs and burgers to duck, veal, seafood, pastas, and steaks. *1470 Western Ave., tel. 518/456–0297. Dress: casual. Reservations suggested for 5 or more. AE, DC, MC, V. Moderate.*

Lombardo's. This restaurant has been an Albany institution for more than 70 years. Known for its attractive wall murals, tile floors, and well-prepared Italian dishes, its specialties include all kinds of pastas, veal dishes, steaks, and seafood. *121 Madison Ave., tel. 518/462–9180. Dress: casual. Reservations not accepted. AE, DC, MC, V. Closed Mon. and Tues. Moderate.*

★ **Ogden's.** Located on the ground floor of a 1903 brick and limestone building, this restaurant has a unique decor incorporating the original oak interior, tall arched windows, and lots of leafy plants. In the summer, you can dine alfresco on an adjoining patio overlooking the Empire State Plaza. The menu focuses on Continental cuisine, with such dishes as veal with morels, roast duckling, tournedos Rossini, and Dover sole. *42 Howard St., tel. 518/463–6605. Dress: neatly casual. Reserva-*

tions suggested. AE, CB, DC, MC, V. Closed Sun., dinner only Sat. Moderate.

Quakenbush House. A few steps from the Palace Theater, this restaurant is housed in one of Albany's oldest buildings, notable for its latticed windows and textured handmade brick. The menu emphasizes veal, chicken, and seafood dishes. There is classical guitar music on Friday and Saturday nights. *Quakenbush Sq. at Clinton Ave. and Broadway, tel. 518/465–0909. Dress: casual. Reservations suggested. AE, CB, DC, MC, V. Closed Sun., dinner only Sat. Moderate.*

Yono's. Located in historic Robinson Square, this restaurant offers dining in a trilevel brownstone. The menu combines Continental and Indonesian cuisines, with noodle dishes, *satays*, and eggrolls, as well as seafood and meats. *289 Hamilton St., tel. 518/436–7747. Dress: casual. Reservations required. AE, DC, MC, V. Closed Sun., dinner only Mon. and Sat. Moderate.*

Catskill **La Rive.** An old farmhouse serves as the setting for this delightful country restaurant, off routes 23A and 47. You can feast on traditional French cuisine in the house or on an enclosed porch; the price of the entree includes a full five-course dinner (hors d'oeuvres, soup, main course, fruit and cheese, and dessert). Main courses include such classics as steak au poivre, fillet of beef bordelaise, sole almondine, salmon béarnaise, and roast duckling. *Old King's Rd., tel. 518/943–4888. Dress: casual. Reservations required. MC, V. Closed Mon., dinner only. Closed Thanksgiving–early May. Moderate–Expensive.*

Hillsdale **L'Hostellerie Bressane.** Transplanted from the Rhone Valley,
★ Jean and Madeleine Morel have graciously transformed an 18th-century Hudson Valley home into a French country inn. There are three cozy dining rooms, with brick walls, wood paneling, open fireplaces, and tables meticulously set with white linens, fine china and flatware, and fresh flowers and candles. The entrees, all artfully presented with colorful arrays of seasonal vegetables, include local trout, veal chop, roast duck, fillet of beef, rack of lamb, braised chicken breast, and poached king salmon. For dessert, the hot soufflés are hard to resist. *Rtes. 23 and 22, 518/325–3412. Jacket suggested. Reservations suggested. No credit cards. Closed Mon. and Tues., dinner only. Expensive.*

Kinderhook **Old Dutch Inn.** Set in the heart of the village and overlooking the green, this restaurant provides a look at Columbia County of yesteryear. The decor includes country-style furnishings, a brick hearth, and a wood stove. Featured dishes include marinated lamb roast and grilled seafood. *8 Broad St., tel. 518/758–1676. Dress: casual. Reservations suggested. CB, MC, V. Closed Mon. Moderate.*

Lodging

Highly recommended properties are indicated by a star ★.

Category	Cost*
Very Expensive	over $150
Expensive	$100–$150

Moderate	$60–$100
Inexpensive	under $60

*per room, double occupancy, without tax

Westchester and Rockland Counties

Pearl River
★ **Pearl River Hilton.** This five-story château-style hotel sits amid 17 acres of countryside, adjacent to the Blue Hill golf course. Much of the decor is French provincial in style, with pastel tones, floral fabrics, and light woods. A variety of reduced-rate weekend packages are available. *500 Veterans Memorial Dr., 10965, tel. 914/735–9000 or 800–HILTONS. 150 rooms with bath. Facilities: restaurant, piano lounge, indoor pool, whirlpool, 2 saunas, exercise room. AE, CB, DC, MC, V. Expensive–Very Expensive.*

Rye Brook
★ **Arrowwood.** One of the area's foremost executive conference centers, this hotel is situated in a country-club setting on 114 wooded acres, including a three-acre pond, across from the Pepsico Sculpture Gardens. *Anderson Hill Rd., 10573, tel. 914/939–5500 or 800/633–6569. 276 rooms with bath. Facilities: 3 restaurants, indoor and outdoor pools, 2 indoor and 2 outdoor tennis courts, racquetball, gym, squash, sauna, paddle tennis, jogging trails, 9-hole golf course, bicycling, cross-country skiing, and sledding. AE, CB, DC, MC, V. Very Expensive.*

Rye Town Hilton. Nestled amid 50 wooded acres, this rambling contemporary inn provides deluxe lodgings in a relaxed setting less than 35 minutes from Manhattan. *699 Westchester Ave., 10573, tel. 914/939–6300 or 800/HILTONS. 440 rooms with bath. Facilities: restaurant, coffee shop, 2 lounges, indoor and outdoor pools, whirlpool, 3 lighted tennis courts, gym, sauna, game room, hair salon, florist. AE, CB, DC, MC, V. Expensive–Very Expensive.*

Suffern
Executive Park Hotel. Formerly a Holiday Inn, this modern hotel is situated just off the New York State Thruway at Airmont, Exit 14B, close to Bear Mountain State Park as well as within 20 miles of West Point, shopping centers, and area wineries. *3 Executive Blvd., 10901, tel. 914/357–4800. 243 rooms with bath. Facilities: cable TV, 2 restaurants, lounge, indoor pool and recreation center/gym, 2 tennis courts, putting green, game room. AE, CB, DC, MC, V. Moderate.*

Wellesley Inn. Like most members of this chain, this property is conveniently situated and provides clean and comfortable accommodations with no frills. Free Continental breakfast. *17 N. Airmont Rd., Exit 14B, NYS Thruway, 10901, tel. 914/368–1900 or 800/654–2000. 97 rooms with bath. AE, DC, MC, V. Inexpensive–Moderate.*

Tarrytown
Tarrytown Hilton. In a 10-acre garden setting, this multi-winged low-rise hotel makes an ideal base for exploring the Sleepy Hollow region. Although the architecture is modern, there are cozy touches in the public rooms, such as beamed ceilings, wood-paneled walls, wood-burning fireplaces, Oriental rugs, antique furnishings, and crystal chandeliers, and most of the guest rooms have individual patios or terraces. *455 S. Broadway, 10591, tel. 914/631–5700 or 800/HILTONS. 249 rooms with bath. Facilities: restaurant, coffee shop, entertainment lounge, indoor and outdoor pools, 2 tennis courts, exer-*

cise room, jogging trail, airport shuttle, baby-sitter service. AE, CB, DC, MC, V. Expensive–Very Expensive.

Westchester Marriott. This modern 11-story hotel is close to the NYS Thruway and other major thoroughfares and is a favorite with business travelers. *670 White Plains Rd., 10591, tel. 914/ 631–2200 or 800/228–9290. 444 rooms with bath. Facilities: 2 restaurants, 2 lounges, nightclub, indoor/outdoor pool, sauna, whirlpool, universal gym, gift shop; nearby are golf, tennis, jogging trails. AE, CB, DC, MC, V. Expensive–Very Expensive.*

White Plains
★

Stouffer Westchester. Although the furnishings are deluxe and modern, the real charm of this hotel is its location—on a wooded 26-acre estate, originally known as Red Oaks and previously owned by noted architect John Carrere, codesigner of the New York Public Library. *80 W. Red Oak La., 10604, tel. 914/694–5400 or 800–HOTELS–1. 364 rooms with bath. Facilities: 2 restaurants, lounge, indoor pool, 2 tennis courts, whirlpool, exercise room, paddleball court, illuminated jogging trail. AE, DC, MC, V. Expensive–Very Expensive.*

Holiday Inn Crowne Plaza. A modern 12-story complex, this hotel is in the heart of the city, within walking distance of major department stores. *66 Hale Ave., 10601, tel. 914/682–0050 or 800/2–CROWNE. 400 rooms. Facilities: 2 restaurants, lounge with nightly entertainment, indoor pool, whirlpool, sauna, exercise room, free enclosed parking, airport and train shuttle, gift shop. AE, CB, DC, MC, V. Expensive.*

Orange and Putnam Counties

Bear Mountain

Bear Mountain Inn. For more than 50 years, this chalet-style resort has been known for both its bucolic location (in the Bear Mountain State Park on the shores of Hessian Lake) and its warm hospitality. There are rooms in the main inn and units in five different lodges on the opposite side of the lake. A two-night minimum is often imposed on weekends. *Rte. 9W, 10911, tel. 914/786–2731. 60 rooms with bath. Facilities: restaurant, lounge, outdoor pool, picnic grounds, hiking trails, and access to ice skating, ski jumping, sledding, cross-country skiing. AE, MC, V. Moderate–Expensive.*

Cold Spring
★

Hudson House. Formerly known as the Hudson View Inn, this is a restored historic landmark (circa 1831) on the banks of the Hudson River. Several guest rooms have balconies with views of the Hudson, West Point, or the village. The furnishings include antiques and curios such as Shaker-style sconces, lamps made from French wine decanters, and wall decorations fashioned from cookie cutters. Continental breakfast is included. *2 Main St., 10516, tel. 914/265–9355. 13 rooms with bath, 2 with shared bath. Facilities: restaurant, lounge, bicycle rentals. AE, MC, V. Closed Jan. Expensive.*

Pig Hill Inn. This charming bed-and-breakfast home is located three blocks from the banks of the Hudson River. Innkeeper Wendy O'Brien has furnished most of the guest rooms with four-poster beds and antiques, some of which are for sale. Most rooms have either a fireplace or wood stove. *73 Main St., 10516, tel. 914/265–9247. 4 rooms with bath, 4 rooms with shared bath. Full breakfast included, picnic lunches available by request. AE, DC, MC, V. Closed 2 weeks in late Feb. or early Mar. Expensive.*

Olde Post Inn. This restored inn, dating from 1820, offers bed-

and-breakfast in an Old World setting with such modern amenities as air-conditioning. The on-premises stone tavern features jazz entertainment on Friday and Saturday nights. Innkeepers are Barbara and Jim Ryan. *43 Main St., 10516, tel. 914/265–2510. 6 rooms share 2 bathrooms. Facilities: tavern, patio, garden. MC, V. Moderate.*

Fishkill **The Residence Inn by Marriott.** Each guest unit in this all-suite property has a fully equipped kitchen, living room, one or two bedrooms, and a private entrance. Some suites have fireplaces. Continental breakfast is included. *Rte. 9 and I–84, 12524, tel. 914/896–5210 or 800/331–3131. 116 rooms with bath. Facilities: outdoor pool, hot tub, health club. AE, CB, DC, MC, V. Expensive.*

Garrison **The Bird and Bottle Inn.** Dating to 1761, this one-time stage-
★ coach stop on the Albany Post Road is still primarily known for its award-winning restaurant (*see* Dining, above). Overnight accommodations with a Colonial ambience are available on the second floor of the inn and in an adjoining cottage. The guest rooms have four-poster or canopy beds, antique furnishings, and working fireplaces. Breakfast is included. *Old Albany Post Rd. (Rte. 9), Nelson's Corners, 10524, tel. 914/424–3000. 4 rooms with bath. AE, MC, V. Very Expensive.*

Newburgh **Holiday Inn.** Less than two miles east of Stewart Airport at Exit 17 of I–87, this two-story property is a good base for touring West Point, 16 miles away. The decor is modern, and guest rooms surround a central courtyard. *90 Rte. 17K, 10940, tel. 914/564–9020 or 800/HOLIDAY. 121 rooms. Facilities: cable TV, 2 restaurants, lounge, outdoor pool. AE, CB, DC, MC, V. Moderate.*

Ramada Inn. Recently renovated and expanded, this hotel has a rounded futuristic facade. It is convenient (less than three miles from Stewart Airport, 15 miles from West Point, and close to exits for I–87 and I–84), yet it enjoys a serene setting, set back from the main roads on a hillside. About half of the units are suites, with separate sitting rooms and a raspberry-and-pink decor; other rooms are smaller and more traditional in style. *1055 Union Ave. (Rte. 300), 10940, tel. 914/564–4500 or 800/2RAMADA. 165 units. Facilities: cable TV, restaurant, lounge, outdoor pool. AE, CB, DC, MC, V. Moderate–Very Expensive.*

West Point **Hotel Thayer.** On the grounds of the U.S. Military Academy,
★ this stately brick hotel steeped in history and tradition has been welcoming military and civilian guests for more than 60 years. The hotel's public rooms are highlighted by marble floors, iron chandeliers, military portraits, and leather furnishings. The guest rooms have standard appointments, but many have views of the river and the West Point grounds. *Rte. 9W, 10996, tel. 914/446–4731 or 800/247–5047. 197 rooms with bath. Facilities: restaurant, lounge, tennis court. AE, CB, DC, MC, V. Moderate–Expensive.*

Dutchess and Ulster Counties

Amenia **Troutbeck.** Surrounded by the rural farmlands of northeastern Dutchess County, this Tudor-style country inn was built in 1918 on the site of an earlier manor (1790). It sits on a 422-acre estate amid lovely gardens, wooded paths, towering trees, and a stretch of the Wetabuck River. A perfect executive "retreat," it is used for conference groups on weekdays but is open for individual guests from Friday through Sunday. Bedrooms, many with antiques and four-poster beds, are situated in the main house and in an adjacent restored farmhouse. The restaurant is also open to the public on weekends. Overnight rates include three meals. *Leedsville Rd., off Rte. 343, 12501, tel. 914/373–9681. 31 rooms, 26 with bath. Facilities: restaurant, library, indoor and outdoor pools, 2 tennis courts, exercise room, sauna, walking and jogging trails. AE. Very Expensive.*

Highland **Rocking Horse Ranch.** Now in its 33rd year, this lakeside resort is especially appealing to families because of its many outdoor activities. There is a variety of package rates, most of which include all meals and activities; inquire at the time of booking for the deal that most suits your requirements. *Rtes. 44/45, 12528, tel. 914/691–2927, 800/647–2624 in NYS, or 800/437–2624. 120 rooms with bath. Facilities: restaurant, 3 lounges, evening entertainment, horseback riding, waterskiing, indoor and outdoor pools, sauna, 2 tennis courts, fitness room, minigolf, volleyball, handball, softball, rowboats, paddleboats, shuffleboard, archery range, day camp. AE, CB, DC, MC, V. Moderate.*

Hopewell Junction **Le Chambord.** Known primarily as a fine restaurant, this property is fast becoming a choice place lodging. Accommodations are spread between the second floor of the main Georgian Colonial manor building (which also houses a fine French restaurant; *see* Dining, above) and the adjacent Tara Hall, a new Georgian-Victorian building. Guest rooms vary, but most offer period furnishings (some antiques), wingback chairs, fine tapestry fabrics, and original oil paintings. *25 rooms with bath. Facilities: restaurant, bar, lounge. AE, DC, MC, V. Expensive.*

Hyde Park **The Roosevelt Inn.** This relatively new Colonial-style motel is set back from the main road in a tree-shaded setting one mile north of the Franklin D. Roosevelt National Historic Site. *38 Albany Post Rd. (Rte. 9), 12538, tel. 914/229–2443. 25 rooms with bath or shower. Facilities: coffee shop (breakfast only), nearby dining, tennis, golf, and cross-country skiing. AE, MC, V. Closed Jan. and Feb. Moderate.*

Dutch Patroon. This handy, well-kept motel is right on the main north–south route through western Dutchess County. About one quarter of the units have kitchenettes. Complimentary Continental breakfast. *Rte. 9, 12538, tel. 914/229–7141. 33 rooms with bath. Facilities: restaurant, outdoor pool. AE, MC, V. Inexpensive.*

Kingston **Holiday Inn.** Located at Exit 19 of the NYS Thruway, this modern two-story motor hotel is within a few minutes of Kingston's downtown attractions and less than 30 miles from the popular Hunter Mountain ski area. *503 Washington Ave., 12401, tel. 914/338–0400 or 800/HOLIDAY. 212 rooms with bath. Facilities: restaurant, lounge, indoor pool, whirlpool, sauna, putting green, AE, CB, DC, MC, V. Moderate–Expensive.*

Sky Top. This resort off Exit 19 of the NYS Thruway is set on 11 acres high on a hillside, affording lovely views of the mountains and surrounding countryside. There is a Victorian-style lobby, but most of the guest rooms are furnished in contemporary style. Complimentary Continental breakfast is included. *Rte. 28, at Skytop Dr., 12401, tel. 914/331–2900. 72 rooms with bath.*

Facilities: cable TV, outdoor pool, gift shop. AE, CB, DC, MC, V. Moderate–Expensive.

Howard Johnson Lodge. Located within a mile of the New York State Thruway (Exit 19) and two miles from downtown Kingston, this contemporary motel is newly refurbished. *Rte. 28, 12401, tel. 914/338–4200 or 800/654–2000. 118 rooms with bath. Facilities: cable TV, restaurant, lounge, indoor and outdoor pools, sauna. AE, CB, DC, MC, V. Moderate.*

Millerton
★
Simmon's Way Village Inn. Located near the Connecticut border in northeast Dutchess County, this inn is named in honor of E. W. Simmons, a local educator/statesman/lawyer who built the original house (in 1854) from which this inn has evolved. The current innkeepers, Richard and Nancy Carter, have decorated the guest rooms with antiques and furnishings that reflect the house's earlier days; some rooms have private porches, draped canopy beds, sitting areas, or fireplaces. Continental breakfast is included. Summer bookings require a two-night minimum on weekends. *Main St. (Rte. 44), 12546, tel. 518/789–6235. 11 rooms with bath. Facilities: restaurant (see Dining, above), and bar. AE, MC, V. Expensive.*

New Paltz
★
Mohonk Mountain House. Founded as a 10-room inn by Quakers in 1869, Mohonk Mountain House, situated on a lake amid 7,500 acres of land in the heart of the Shawangunk Mountains, has grown into one of the great resorts of the Hudson Valley. Declared a National Landmark in 1986, it is a mostly Victorian-style building, with various wings, turrets, cupolas, and spires. Run by the Smiley family, descendants of the original founders, it maintains some of the traditions (i.e., there is no bar or cocktail lounge, but drinks can be ordered with evening meals). Room prices include three meals and afternoon tea; there is also a variety of package plans ranging from mystery, musical, or cooking weekends to sporting, stargazing, or stress-management programs. The layout includes three verandas lined with rockers; 100 of the guest rooms have working fireplaces, and 200 have balconies. *Lake Mohonk, 12561, tel. 914/255–1000 or 212/233–2244. 281 rooms with bath. Facilities: 3 dining rooms, 6 clay tennis courts, beach, basketball court, fitness center, aerobics classes, croquet, lawn bowling, shuffleboard, softball, volleyball, croquet, 9-hole golf course, horseback riding, 135 miles of hiking trails, nature preserve, cross-country skiing, ice skating, and more. AE, MC, V. Expensive–Very Expensive.*

Poughkeepsie
★
Inn at the Falls. Operating as a bed-and-breakfast, this relatively new inn combines the amenities of a modern hotel with the ambience and personal attention of a country home. Situated in a residential area beside a rushing waterfall about two miles southeast of the city, the inn has an arched courtyard that joins two wings of guest rooms. The public areas are bright and airy, with pastel-toned furnishings, floor-to-ceiling paned windows, brass chandeliers, marble floors, and an abundance of leafy plants. The guest rooms, all accessible by computer-card keys, vary in decor from English-mansion style to American country, Art Deco, or Oriental. Many bedrooms have four-poster, wrought-iron, or canopied beds, brass headboards, armoires, rolltop desks, crystal and china lamps. Continental breakfast, delivered to each guest room on a silver tray, is included. *50 Red Oaks Mill Rd., 12603, tel. 914/462–5770. 22*

rooms and 14 suites, all with private bath. AE, CB, DC, MC. Expensive–Very Expensive.

Radisson Poughkeepsie. Located in the heart of the city, this modern 10-story property is adjacent to the Mid-Hudson Convention Center. Relatively new (opened in 1987), it is the largest full-service hotel in the mid-Hudson Valley. The decor is bright and contemporary, enhanced by expansive views of the river from many of the guest rooms. *40 Civic Center Plaza, 12601, tel. 914/485–5300 or 800/333–3333. 225 rooms with bath. Facilities: cable TV, restaurant, lounge, nightclub, sauna, health club, gift shop, airport shuttle, valet parking and self-park garage. AE, CB, DC, MC, V. Expensive.*

Courtyard by Marriott. Opened in June 1988, this contemporary inn has a homey, plant-filled atmosphere, with guest-room wings grouped around a central courtyard. It is located south of downtown, with easy access to Route 9. *408 South Rd., 12601, tel. 914/485–6336 or 800/321–2211. 149 rooms with bath. Facilities: cable TV, restaurant, lounge, indoor swimming pool, exercise room, whirlpool, game room, nonsmoking rooms. AE, CB, DC, MC, V. Moderate–Expensive.*

Edison Motor Inn. Situated four miles east of the city, this dependable motel has equipped about one-third of its units with kitchenettes, ideal for family travelers. *313 Manchester Rd. (Rte. 55), 12603, tel. 914/454–3080. 138 rooms with bath. Facilities: restaurant, lounge, 2 tennis courts, outdoor pool, shuffleboard, playground. AE, DC, MC, V. Moderate.*

Red Hook   **Gaslight Motel.** Located three miles north of Red Hook and set back from the main road in a tree-shaded setting, Gaslight has a Colonial-style motif and country furnishings; about half of the units have kitchenettes. There are also views of the Catskill Mountains in the distance. *Rte. 9, 12571, tel. 914/758–1571. 12 rooms with bath. Facilities: private gardens, patio, barbecue. MC, V. Inexpensive.*

Hearthstone Motel. This is a basic one-story motel, situated on a hillside about three miles north of the village. The guest rooms have views of the Catskill Mountains to the west. *RD3, Box 51, Rte. 9, 12571, tel. 914/758–1811. 8 rooms with bath. AE, MC, V. Inexpensive.*

Rhinebeck   **Beekman Arms.** One of America's oldest inns (dating to 1766), ★ this hotel has welcomed such historic guests as George Washington, Thomas Jefferson, and Franklin Roosevelt. A variety of accommodations are available, including 13 rooms in the original building (smallish units with authentic squeaky floorboards, braided rugs, and antique furnishings); and four motel-style rooms at the rear of the inn. About a block away, there are seven rooms in Delamater House (circa 1844), a delightful two-story, American Gothic residence furnished with wicker furniture, huge armoires, and Victorian touches. There are also 30 new rooms located behind Delamater in a surrounding courtyard, carriage house, and restored town house; all have air-conditioning and some have working fireplaces. A room at the Delamater House comes with complimentary Continental breakfast. *4 Mill St. (Rte. 9) 12572, tel. 914/876–7077. 54 rooms with bath. Facilities: 4 dining rooms, tavern. AE, DC, MC, V. Expensive for the newer rooms, Moderate for the older sections.*

Village Victorian Inn. Located on a quiet residential street, this two-story Italianate home (circa 1860) is a quintessential bed-and-breakfast inn, with well-tended gardens, white picket fence, and front-porch rockers. The owners, Judy and Richard Kohler, have decorated the interior with area antiques, French Victorian fabrics, and Oriental rugs. Each guest room has a brass or canopy bed (king- or queen-size) adorned with a country quilt or comforter, a ceiling fan, books, and other homey touches. A gourmet breakfast (such as eggs Benedict, pecan French toast, or quiches) is included. *31 Center St., 12572, tel. 914/876–8345. 5 rooms with bath. AE, MC, V. Expensive.*

Rhinebeck Village Inn. Owned and operated by the Behrens family, this one-story motel, about a mile south of the village in a tree-shaded setting, has country-house charm. The spacious guest rooms are very homey, with handcrafted local furnishings and wall hangings. Continental breakfast is included in the room charge. Weekend rates are slightly higher. *Rte. 9, Box 491, 12572, tel. 914/876–7000. 16 rooms with bath. Facilities: cable TV, refrigerators available on request. AE, CB, DC, MC, V. Inexpensive–Moderate.*

Whistlewood Farm. For a more rural ambience, you can enjoy bed-and-breakfast at this 13-acre horse farm, located three miles east of Rhinebeck village, off Route 308. The grounds offer lovely gardens and views of the countryside, and the interior of the house is full of beamed ceilings and antique furnishings. Innkeeper Maggie Myer is well known for her hearty breakfasts (included in the rates) of fresh local fruits, cheese-filled omelets, sour-cream coffee cake, blackberry or apple crumb pie, and blueberry-banana muffins. Rates are slightly higher on weekends. *11 Pells Rd., 12572, tel. 914/876–6838. 3 rooms with private bath, 2 rooms with shared bath. Facilities: pets can be accommodated in house or in adjacent kennels. No credit cards. Moderate–Expensive.*

Albany, Columbia, and Greene Counties

Albany **Albany Hilton.** Situated in the heart of the capital, this modern 15-story property is the leading full-service downtown hotel. It is within walking distance of the Empire State Plaza and the convention center as well as shops and other midcity attractions. *10 Eyck Plaza, State and Lodge Sts., 12207, tel. 518/462–6611. 387 rooms with bath. Facilities: 2 restaurants, 2 lounges, disco, indoor pool, Jacuzzi, valet service, shopping boutiques. AE, CB, DC, MC, V. Expensive.*

★ **Desmond Americana.** Located just outside Albany Airport, this hotel is laid out in a configuration reminiscent of a Colonial village, with various wings surrounding a central courtyard. The decor also carries out an 18th-century theme, with Federal and Queen Anne reproductions, vintage paintings, and wood paneling in the public rooms; and guest units have custom-made furnishings that feature Colonial-style fabrics and colors. *660 Albany Shaker Rd., 12211, tel. 518/869–8100, 800/448–3500 in NYS or 800/235–1210. 324 rooms with bath. Facilities: cable TV, 2 restaurants, lounge, 2 indoor pools, health club, sauna, exercise room, billiards room, game room, gift shop. AE, CB, DC, MC, V. Expensive–Very Expensive.*

★ **Mansion Hill Inn.** Located around the corner from the Executive Mansion, this is Albany's only downtown bed-and-breakfast inn and a preservation award winner from the Historic Albany Foundation. Innkeepers Mary Ellen and Steve Stofelano, Jr. have decorated the rooms with antiques and vintage furnishings. Three of the guest units are suites, with bedroom, living room, study, and kitchenette; and two rooms have rear decks. Rates include a full breakfast. *115 Philip St., 12202, tel. 518/465–2038 or 518/465–2059. 15 rooms with private bath. Facilities: restaurant. AE, DC, MC, V. Moderate–Expensive.*

Canaan **Queechy Lake Motel.** Nestled on Queechy Lake in a quiet, tree-shaded setting, this contemporary two-story lodging in north-eastern Columbia County is close to the Massachusetts border, less than 10 miles from Tanglewood and the Berkshire ski resorts. The guest units are furnished in a country style, but the biggest attraction is the sylvan lake view from each window. Continental breakfast included on weekdays; coffee shop operates on weekends. *Queechy Lake Dr. (Rte. 30), Box 106, 12029, tel. 518/781–4615. 18 rooms with bath. Facilities: outdoor heated pool, lake beach passes provided to guests. MC, V. Moderate.*

Palenville **Hans' County Line Motel.** Situated on Route 32A, this comfortable Alpine-style lodging is in the heart of ski and festival country. Guest units feature all the standard amenities, including air-conditioning. *HCR –1, Box 52, 12463, tel. 518/678–3101. 42 rooms with bath, 5 cabins with bath. Facilities: cable TV, restaurant, heated outdoor pool, game room, playground, complimentary shuttle service to ski slopes and summer festivals. AE, CB, DC, MC, V. Moderate–Expensive.*

Tannersville **The Eggery Inn.** Nestled amid the ridges of the Catskill Mountains at an elevation of 2,200 feet, this rustic inn offers views of Hunter Mountain from every window and from a wraparound porch. Innkeepers Abe and Julie Abramczyk have added lots of country touches, such as a wood-burning Franklin stove, brick hearth, antique player piano, and a handcrafted oak bar. There is a two-night minimum stay on most weekends. *Rte. 16, 12485, tel. 518/589–5363. 13 rooms with bath and one two-bedroom suite with bath. Facilities: cable TV, restaurant (dinner on Sat. only). AE, MC, V. Moderate–Expensive.*

Windham **Albergo Allegria.** A real find in this area, this unusual inn is the
★ result of the joining together of two Victorian homes, replete with gingerbread trim, stained-glass windows, brass fixtures, dried floral arrangements, stenciled walls, and polished wood floors with braided rugs. There are two sitting rooms, both with fireplaces, and a small outdoor patio where breakfast is served in summer (full breakfast is included in the room rates). Innkeeper Lenore Radelich has recently launched a series of year-round seminars on northern Italian cooking for guests. *Rte. 296, 12496, tel. 518/734–5560. 24 rooms with bath (including 1 suite with a double Jacuzzi). MC, V. Moderate–Expensive.*

The Arts

There are a number of excellent multipurpose performing arts centers throughout the Hudson Valley. Their schedules include a variety of shows from concerts by symphony orchestras to pop soloists to road-show theatricals. Here are the most important venues:

Eisenhower Hall Theater (U.S. Military Academy, tel. 914/938–4159). Although this West Point venue is best known for its military-band concerts, many other performances are also scheduled, ranging from full-scale musicals and appearances by pop artists to modern-dance ensembles and classical concerts. General starting time is 8, but afternoon performances are also often scheduled.

The Empire State Performing Arts Center (Madison Ave. and S. Swan St., Albany, tel. 518/473–1061). Drama, dance, and musical events are scheduled year-round in "The Egg," as this huge, curving concrete building in the Empire State Plaza is called. Home to the Empire State Institute for the Performing Arts, it has a 500-seat recital hall and an 886-seat main theater. The season is September to June, with most performances at 8.

The Knickerbocker Arena (51 S. Pearl St., Albany, tel. 518/487–2080). With over 18,000 seats, this is the state capital's newest year-round showplace and a venue for concerts, ice shows, circus performances, sports, and other events.

Mid-Hudson Civic Center (Civic Center Plaza, Poughkeepsie, tel. 914/454–5800). In the heart of the city, this is a multipurpose recreation and entertainment center offering ever-changing programs ranging from rock concerts and comedy shows to movies and country-western shows. Call for the latest schedule.

The Music Hall Theater (13 Main St., Tarrytown, tel. 914/941–1757) offers classical music, dance ensembles, and other musical works for both adult and student audiences. Adult programs are usually at 8, student shows at 2 PM and 3:30 PM.

Dance

Kleinert Arts Center (34 Tinker St., Woodstock, tel. 914/679–2079). You can watch or participate in various types of folk dancing led by John Delson and Myra French. No experience or partners are necessary; regular sessions are held at 7:30 on most summer nights, but call for exact schedule.

Film

Upstate Films (26 Montgomery St., Rhinebeck, tel. 914/876–2515). Located less than two blocks from the landmark Beekman Arms, this repertory movie theater shows international and American classics, art films, and some new or experimental works. The schedule is usually Sunday through Thursday at 7 PM and 9 PM, Friday and Saturday at 7:30 PM and 9:30 PM, with variations possible. The shows are often augmented by comments from guest filmmakers.

Music

Caramoor Center for Music and the Arts (Rte. 22 and Girdle Ridge Rd., Katonah, tel. 914/232–5035). Chamber music recitals and brass concerts are among the many events scheduled during the annual summer-long music festival on this 117-acre estate. Call in advance for the program.

Emelin Theater (Library La., Mamaroneck, tel. 914/698–0098). An ever-changing program of solo instrumentalists, vocalists, and string quartets, as well as bluegrass bands and occasional foreign or classic films. Show time is usually 8:30.

The Music and Art Center of Green County (Jewett Center, Rte. 23A, Jewett, tel. 518/989–6479). This is an ideal place to visit during July and August for chamber music, recitals, and other serious music. Most performances are at 8.

Paramount Theater (19 South St., Middletown, tel. 914/342–6524). This theater showcase concerts and guest artists as well as the Hudson Valley Philharmonic. The curtain is usually at 8, but check for latest schedule.

Ulster Performing Arts Center (601 Broadway, Kingston, tel. 914/339–6088). A frequent showcase for the Hudson Valley Philharmonic on the west side of the river, this arts center also presents solo performances and orchestral concerts by visiting talent. Curtain is usually at 8; call for current schedule.

Theater

The Bardavon 1869 Opera House (35 Market St., Poughkeepsie, tel. 914/473–2072). The pride of the Hudson Valley, this is one of the oldest theaters in the country and is listed on the National Register. It is a year-round venue for all types of theatrical and variety productions, as well as concerts by the Hudson Valley Philharmonic. Curtain is usually at 8, Monday through Saturday.

Capital Repertory Company. Known locally as "Cap Rep," this Albany Equity company presents classic and contemporary drama productions at the 258-seat Market Theatre. *111 N. Pearl St., Box 399, 12201-0399, tel. 518/462–4534. Oct.–May, performances Tues.–Fri. at 8, Sat. at 4:30 and 9, Sun. at 2:30.*

An Evening Dinner Theater. Broadway musical productions are presented year-round at this suburban dinner-theater in Elmsford. *11 Clearbrook Rd., Elmsford, tel. 914/592–2222. Performances Wed.–Sun. at 6, matinees Wed. and Thurs. at 11 AM and Sun. at noon.*

MacHaydn Theater. For more than 20 years, this has been one of New York State's foremost summer-stock playhouses. The program usually features the best of Broadway's musicals. *Rte. 203, Chatham, tel. 518/392–9292. Open late May–end of Sept., Wed.–Fri. at 8, Sat. at 8:30, Sun. at 7; matinees Sat. at 5, Sun. at 2, and every other Wed. at 2.*

Nightlife

Bars and Clubs

Westchester/ Rockland Counties

Backstage Limited (348 Huguenot St., New Rochelle, tel. 914/636–2111). This place offers a dance floor with live band music Wednesday through Saturday.

The Coven Cave (162 Main St., Nyack, tel. 914/358–9829). This spot is known for its live dance music Tuesday through Sunday nights.

Gambits (670 White Plains Rd., Tarrytown, tel. 914/631–2200). There are two dance floors here and DJ music every night, located at the Westchester Marriott Hotel.

O'Donoghue's (66 Main St., Nyack, tel. 914/358–0180). Whether it's St. Pat's Day or not, this is a good place to hear folk and Irish music, with live guest performers on Monday.

J. Parkers (189 E. Post Rd., White Plains, tel. 914/428–3377). A live band plays Top 40 hits here Thursday, Friday, and Saturday nights.

Teddy's (1 Holiday Inn Dr., Mt. Kisco, tel. 914/241–2600). A night club in the Holiday Inn, off Mt. Kisco Avenue and the Sawmill River Parkway, featuring live DJ music Tuesday through Saturday.

Orange/Putnam Counties

Gatsby's (Rte. 17M, Monroe, tel. 914/782-5152). For DJ music try this spot in the K-Mart Plaza, Thursday, Friday, and Saturday nights.

Memory Lane (Rte. 52, Walden, tel. 914/778-9913). Come here on Saturday night for live country-western music or '50s/'60s hits.

Rosebuds (Rte. 9W, New Windsor, tel. 914/565-6588). You'll find a bit of variety here—Top 40 music Thursday through Friday nights and comedy shows on Saturday nights.

Rusty Nail (50 Dunning Rd., Middletown, tel. 914/343-8242). There is usually live entertainment here on weekends.

Dutchess/Ulster Counties

Bertie's. This is the place for continuous DJ music. *9–11 Liberty St., Poughkeepsie, tel. 914/452-2378. Open Wed.–Sat.*

La Fonda Del Sol (Rte. 9, Wappingers Falls, tel. 914/297-5044). This place offers a variety of music styles from blues and jazz to folk rock, often with live performers. There is also a dance floor.

Moogs Farm (Rte. 9 at I-84, Fishkill, tel. 914/896-9975). This is one of the valley's premier venues for country-western music, with live performances most Saturdays.

The New Chateau (Rte. 9W, Port Ewen, tel. 914/338-5000). There is dancing to live bands and DJ music, Friday and Saturday nights, for a crowd that's mostly 25 and older.

P & G's (Main St., New Paltz, tel. 914/255-6161). Popular with college students, this spot offers live music on Friday and Saturday nights.

Rhinebeck Tavern (19–21 W. Market St., Rhinebeck, tel. 914/876-3059). Located opposite the Beekman Arms, this informal spot often features live rock, country-western, and pop music, especially on weekends.

Skytop Lounge (Rte. 28, Kingston, tel. 914/338-6161). This is an ideal spot for panoramic night views and easy-listening music, with dancing on weekends.

Town Crier Cafe. This suburban club offers well-known guest artists performing folk, traditional, contemporary, or classical music. *62 Rte. 22, Pawling, tel. 914/855-1300. Shows or concerts are usually on weekends, though times vary.*

Albany

Cahoots (State and Lodge Sts., tel. 518/462-6611, ext. 285). This classy downtown spot at the Albany Hilton has a DJ most nights.

Fenders. Here you will find live entertainment, Atlantic City cabaret-style. *Holiday Inn, 205 Wolf Rd., tel. 518/458-7250. Live entertainment Mon.–Sat., Sun. dance to "oldies."*

LP's Dance Club (Western Ave. and Quail St., tel. 518/427-0728). Dancing to the music of Top 40 hits is featured here, as well as music videos on a large screen.

Van's Night Cap (177–179 Northern Blvd., tel. 518/463-1787). This club offers a potpourri of live jazz, reggae, Latin music, and disco.

6 The Catskills

Introduction

To early explorers, the Hudson was "the River of the Mountains." Sailing up the Hudson River today, one is struck by their grandeur. Possessing neither the jagged peaks nor the epic dimensions of other mountain ranges, the Catskills still have a magical presence that defines a vast region of the mid-Hudson Valley and spreads westward across more than one million acres.

The highest peak in the Catskills is just 4,200 feet, so these are not the fierce guardians of the wilderness that challenge the mettle of mountaineers. Rather, the Catskills offer a quiet welcome and the promise of comfort and easy accessibility. Yet they have a beauty and variety disproportionate to their modest size.

"In no other American vacation land," writes T. Morris Longstreth in *The Catskills*, "can one find a more interesting alternation of forest tramping and village living, a richer background of subdued mountain and inviting valley. If the eternal isn't visible to you there it will never be in remoter lands."

One common theme of the Catskills is water. The name comes from the Dutch *Kaats Kill*, which means "wildcat stream." There is still something wild and untamed in the streams and rivers here as they tumble over rocky gorges and plunge from ledge to ledge. Some of the world's finest fly-fishing can be found in the Catskills' profusion of premier trout streams. Enthusiasts of all skill levels can enjoy just about any outdoor sport here, from camping to canoeing, hiking to bicycle touring, rock climbing to white-water kayaking. More leisurely pursuits beckon families with young children and those not athletically inclined.

Accommodations range from rustic inns to luxury hotels, offering peaceful surroundings, a refreshing dip in a pool, a good book, a cool drink, a fine meal, and a splendid view. Meandering country roads—there are no four-lane highways here—may lead motorists to the unexpected pleasures of a visit to an artisan's studio, a small museum, or a historic house.

The discoveries awaiting visitors are muted, delicate. The Catskills are the color of dusty blueberries just picked on a hazy morning, and their gentle hue and texture suggests undulating waves on a vast sea. A subtle romance lies waiting in their agreeable wilderness: the flash of a white-tailed deer bounding over a tangle of fallen birches, a pair of brook trout lying motionless as mossy stones in a limpid pool, a bald eagle perching on the highest branch of a pine upon a lofty limestone cliff.

This is the land of Rip Van Winkle, and it can still play tricks on one's sense of time and place. The mountains' enduring majesty continues to speak to scores of visitors each year in terms as poignant as those that inspired the landscape painter Thomas Cole, the naturalist John Burroughs, the writer Washington Irving, and countless other artists.

The Catskills are also full of paradoxes. They are settled but not overdeveloped, historic yet modern, used but not abused, and this careful balance of opposing forces gives the region its vitality. The Catskills, after all, are inextricably linked with New York City: Reservoirs in the Catskills supply the metropolitan area with award-winning drinking water. And untold thousands of city swellers seek solace here at the end of a hectic work week, as their parents and grandparents did before them.

The throngs escaping New York City created a lucrative market for resort complexes, whose regimented leisure activities have been immortalized in such movies as *Dirty Dancing*. But that was another era, another sensibility. What's left of the famous "borscht belt" lives on mostly in the memories of senior citizens. Today the region is known more for its open spaces than for gaudy ballrooms, for its wilderness opportunities rather than cornball theme nights. And those lured from New York as permanent residents are likely to be dedicated to the arts, crafts, and nature. The Catskills have, once again, become a mecca for artisans whose exquisite quilts, ceramics, stained glass, furniture, and hand-woven cloth are sought by collectors around the world. In crafts, more than anything else, the Catskills reclaim their roots in an electronic age and offer a living testament to the belief that what's past is a prologue of what's to come.

The major transportation route to the Catskills is the New York State Thruway (I–87), which links New York City and Albany and runs parallel to the Hudson River. In the northern Catskills, the Hudson River towns of Catskill and Kingston (Thruway exists 19 and 20, respectively) are good entry points for New York Routes 23, 23A, and 28 covering Greene and Ulster counties. In Delaware County, the principal access routes are New York Routes 23, 28, and 30. Sullivan County and the Upper Delaware River area can be reached via Route 17. The Shawangunk Mountain section, which draws rock climbers from around the country, can be reached by U.S. 209. Because of the region's vastness, each area will be described separately in detail.

Essential Information

Getting Around

By Plane The Albany County Airport, a one-hour drive from the heart of the Catskills, is served by **American** (tel. 800/433–7300), **Business Express/Delta Connection–Delta** (tel. 800/345–3400), **Eastern** (tel. 800/327–8376), **Northwest** (800/225–2525), **Precision-Northwest** (tel. 800/225–2525), **Pan Am Express** (tel. 800/221–2000), **United** (tel. 800/241–6522), **Midway** (tel. 800/621–5700), and **United** (tel. 800/241–65221).

The Oneonta Municipal Airport, located off I–88 in the northwest corner of the Catskill region, is served by **Catskill Airways** (tel. 607/432–8222; 800/252–2144 in New York State; 800/833–0196 in the Northeast), which offers daily flights from New York to LaGuardia, Newark, and Boston.

Stewart International Airport in Newburgh opened in May 1990 and is currently served by **American** (tel. 800/433–7300) and **United** (tel. 800/241–6522).

Sullivan Aircraft Services (tel. 914/583–5830) offers charter service to Sullivan County International Airport in White Lake, six miles west of Monticello.

Sidney Aviation (tel. 607/563–9727) offers charter service to Sidney Airport in Delaware County.

By Limo **Empire State Shuttle Service** (tel. 800/367–4732) offers only one trip a day in each direction between JFK and LaGuardia airports in New York City and Albany, via New Paltz, Kingston, Catskill, and Hudson.

By Train The fastest and most memorable way from New York City and Albany to the Catskills is by **Amtrak** (tel. 800/872–7245). It operates eight modern express trains a day on the Grand Central Terminal to Albany-Rensselaer run, many of them stopping at Poughkeepsie, Rhinebeck, and Hudson. The trip from New York City to Hudson, 15 miles east of the town of Catskill, takes only two hours. The best views of the Hudson River are on the left, heading north. The $8 surcharge for a reserved seat in first class is money well spent. All trains have buffet cars, serving snacks and cocktails; the evening New York–Chicago *Lake Shore Limited* has a refurbished Art Deco full-service dining car, but the food and wine list are uninspired.

By Bus **Greyhound** (tel. 800/528–0447) offers regular service to several Catskills communities from New York City and Albany.

Shortline (tel. 212/736–4700 or 800/631–8405) serves a half-dozen Sullivan County communities from New York City.

By Car The region is quite spread out, so the best way to get around is by car. Bring a bicycle, or rent one in any of several resort areas.

Important Addresses and Numbers

Information Centers Each of the four counties in the Catskills region maintains separate information centers to distribute materials about their respective areas.

The **Delaware County Chamber of Commerce** (56 Main St., Delhi, 13753; tel. 607/746–2281, 800/356–5615 within New York State; 800/642–4443 in the Northeast) is open weekdays 9–5.

The **Greene County Promotion Department** (Box 527, Catskill, 12414; tel. 518/943–3223 or 800/542–2414) maintains an information center at New York State Thruway Exit 21, Catskill, open daily 8–6.

The **Sullivan County Office of Public Information** (Sullivan County Government Center, Monticello, 12701; tel. 914/794–3000 or 800/882–CATS within New York State, 800/343–INFO elsewhere) maintains an information center at the Jamesway Mall, Route 42, Monticello. Open July and August, Monday–Thursday 10–6, Friday 11–7, Sunday 10–4; May, June, and September–October, weekends.

The **Ulster County Public Information Office** (Box 1800, Kingston, 12401; tel. 914/331–9300) operates tourism information counters located at New York State Thruway Exit 19, Kingston; on U.S. 9W, Highland; and on New York Route 28, Ellenville.

Contact the **Catskills Association for Tourism Services** (Box 449, Catskill, 12421; tel. 518/943–3223 or 800/542–2414).

Emergencies
Police and
Ambulance
The New York State Police maintains several substations in the region. Many of the larger towns also support their own police departments, along with emergency squads and rescue vehicles. The State Police, sheriff, or hospitals can direct you to the nearest emergency unit.

Sheriff. Delaware County, 607/746–2336; Greene County, 518/943–3300; Sullivan County, 914/794–7100; Ulster County, 914/338–3645.

State Police. Catskill, 518/622–8600; Ellenville, 914/626–2800; Ferndale, 914/292–6600; Highland, 914/691–2922; Kingston, 914/338–1702; and Margaretville, 914/586–2681.

Hospitals
Callicoon. Grover M. Herman Division of Community General Hospital of Sullivan County (Rte. 97, tel. 914/887–5530).
Catskill. Memorial Hospital of Greene County (Jefferson Heights, tel. 518/943–2000).
Delhi. O'Connor Hospital (Rte. 28, tel. 607/746–2371).
Harris. Community General Hospital of Sullivan County (Bushville Rd., tel. 914/794–3300).
Kingston. Benedictine Hospital (105 Mary's Ave., tel. 914/338–5590). Kingston Hospital (396 Broadway, tel. 914/331–3131). Medicenter (40 Hurley Ave., tel. 914/339–5285).
Margaretville. Community Memorial Hospital (Rte. 28, tel. 914/586–2631).
Stamford. Community Hospital (Rte. 23, tel. 607/652–7521).

Exploring the Catskills

Numbers in the margin correspond with points of interest on the Catskills map.

The High Peaks

From New York State Thruway (I–87) Exit 21, take Route 23A west from the Greene County village of Catskill (*see* Chapter 5) toward **Palenville,** home of Washington Irving's legendary sleeper, Rip Van Winkle. It's still a pretty quiet community, although a lively summer arts scene and the week-long **Festival of Circus Theater** (tel. 518/678–3332), spanning the last week of June and the first few days of July, get things rolling nicely with circus theater performances, clowning, storytelling, and masked plays.

In between, performances of classical and modern music, dance and theater, children's programs and workshops take place at the **Bond Street Theater Coalition** (tel. 518/678–3332), site of the Circus Theater, a colony of professional artists.

Palenville marks the start of one of the most spectacular drives in the Catskills: an eight-mile stretch of Route 23A that climbs past the cliffs and cataracts of Kaaterskill Clove to ski centers at Haines Falls and Hunter. Precipitous drops and hairpin turns offer wonderful views and challenging driving. Bastion (or Sabastian) Falls along this route is a popular stop for picnickers, waders (caution is advised), and camera buffs.

❶ At **Haines Falls, North–South Lake State Park** offers swimming, fishing, boating, and camping from May through October.

② Continue west on Rte. 23A to **Hunter** and **Hunter Mountain,** a famous ski center that, thanks to its location and tremendous snowmaking capabilities, is open 160 days a year. Hunter is also known for its summer festivals, including the Italian Festival (June–July), the three-week German Alps Festival (July), a country music festival featuring Nashville stars (July and Aug.), the National Polka Festival where Bobby Vinton reigns (early Aug.), and celebrations devoted to "Golden Oldies" (late Aug.), Celtic heritage (mid-Aug.), and Native American cultures (early Sept.). All festivals are held at the ski bowl. For schedule and ticket information contact *Exposition Planners, Bridge St., Hunter, 12422, tel. 518/263–3800.*

In summer, and particularly in fall when the mountains are ablaze with color, the **Hunter Mountain Sky Ride** (tel. 518/263–4223)—the longest and highest chair lift in the Catskills—offers breathtaking views of the region.

The Catskill slopes now enjoyed by skiers and hikers were once covered with thick stands of hemlock whose acidic bark generated a massive 19th-century tanning industry. Hunter, in fact, was once named "Edwardsville" after tanning mogul Colonel William Edwards, and the ski center is situated a short distance from Hunter Mountain on a peak known as Colonel's Chair.

③ Once the biggest tannery in the world—500 feet long and two stories high—was owned by Zadock Pratt in **Prattsville,** the community that now bears his name. His 1828 homestead in the center of town, 12 miles west of Hunter, now houses the **Zadock Pratt Museum** of local history. *Rte. 23, Prattsville, tel. 518/ 229–3395. Admission: $1 adults, 50¢ children. Open Memorial Day–Columbus Day, Wed.–Sun. 1–5.*

Picnickers might want to stop at nearby **Pratt Rocks,** a wooded park with a steep trail to rock ledges carved in the 1860s with likenesses of Pratt, his horse, and the venerable hemlock. Take Route 23 back east to **Windham,** a lively ski town.

Time Out   The drive from East Windham to Cairo is an eye-opening, ear-popping experience with Windham High Peak, Black Dome, and other mountains pushing in from the south, and expansive views of the valley below and New England beyond. Stop for a photo at the rest area halfway down the mountain.

④ Back on the valley floor just before Cairo, take Route 145 northwest to **East Durham.** Irish immigrants visiting the Catskills from New York City early in the century established vacation resorts in this green, stream-crossed area that so resembled the Old Sod. Now Irish pubs, hotels, and shops abound and an Irish-American heritage museum is being developed in this single-stoplight town. Summer is the busy season here, beginning with the Catskills Irish Festival (tel. 518/634–7100), which draws 20,000 people during Memorial Day weekend, and concluding with the traditional Irish dance competition for children in late August.

Need to cool off after all that merrymaking? Try the **Zoom Flume Aquamusement Park.** Two 300-foot water slides, a 2,600-foot "river" for tube floating, bumper boats, and something called the Thrill Hill provide lots of wet fun. *Shady Glen Rd., off Rte. 145, East Durham, tel. 518/239–4559. Admission:*

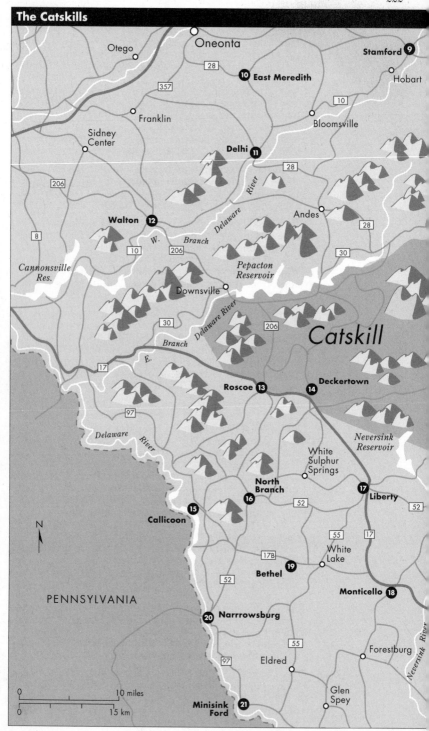

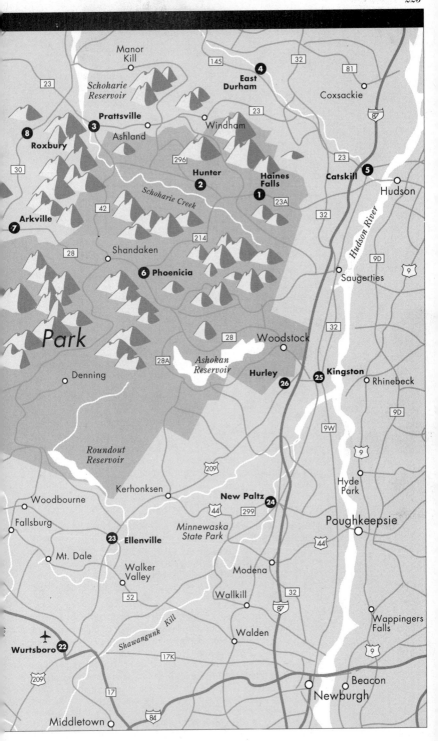

$10.95 adults, $8.95 children under 8. Open Memorial Day–Labor Day 10–7; June, weekends only.

Also on Route 145 and housed in an 1837 schoolhouse, the **Durham Center Museum** is packed with genealogical records, pioneer tools, fossils, minerals, and Native American artifacts. *Rte. 145, East Durham, tel. 518/239–6461. Admission free. Open June–Aug., Sat., Sun., Wed., Thurs. 1 to 4.*

If speed on the tarmac is more to your liking, head to the nearby **Supersonic Speedway & Fun Park** with its twisting Go-Kart track. There's also a championship miniature golf course, batting cages and kiddie rides. *Rte. 145, East Durham, tel. 518/622–9531 or 518/634–7200. Open May 1–Labor Day.*

❺ The shoot-outs and train robberies in **Catskill** at **Carson City** are a bit hokey, but children seem to love them. The set for several movies, Carson City has cancan dancers, prancing "Indians," and stagecoach holdups. *Rte. 32, Catskill, tel. 518/678–5518. Admission: $8.55 adults, $5.35 children 3–12, under 3 free. Open mid-May–June and Sept.–Nov., weekends; July and Aug., daily 9:30–6.*

The town of Catskill, eastern gateway to the Catskills, is the home of former world heavyweight boxing champ Mike Tyson and the host of professional national bass-fishing tournaments in summer. It also has its share of museums and quaint buildings.

The **Thomas Cole House** is a beautifully preserved home and studio of the founder of the Hudson River School of landscape painting. *218 Spring St., Catskill, tel. 518/943–6533. Admission free. Call for hours.*

Greene County Council on the Arts and the **GCCA Catskill Gallery** sponsor concerts, theater, literary readings, and shows by nationally known and local artists. *398 Main St., Catskill, tel. 518/943–3400. Open year-round.*

Also popular in town is the **Catskill Reptile Institute.** This unusual facility provides an up-close look at some of the world's most fascinating reptiles, from the playful garter snake to the exotic king cobra. *Rte. 32, Catskill, tel. 518/678–5590. Admission: $4 adults, $3 children 3–12 and senior citizens; children under 3 free. Open weekends noon–5.*

Somewhere in the 417,900 acres of Greene County lies a stone marker with RipVan Winkle's initials carved on it. It's here that he lost a precious ebony nine-pin he had spirited away from Hendrick Hudson's drunken crew of phantom revelers. A bit tipsy himself, Rip decided to take a nap in the woods, and when he awoke 20 years later, he couldn't remember where he had left it.

Today the nine-pin—studded with 68 diamonds, 21 moonstones, a 31-carat garnet and several ounces of pure gold, and insured for $100,000—is displayed in the Tanners branch of the Schenectady Trust Company on Main Street in Catskill. And it's yours—if you can find the stone marker. It's offered by The Kaaterskill Foundation, a group dedicated to preserving the natural beauty of Greene County. For clues and information about how to join this treasure hunt, send for a copy of *The Lost Treasures of Rip Van Winkle* ($5.95, plus $1.20 shipping), from the Kaaterskill Foundation (Box 551, Catskill, NY 12414).

Return to Route 23 and head south on Route 32 to the **Catskill Game Farm.** For more than 50 years the Lindemann family has operated this preserve, now home to 2,000 birds and animals including a large collection of rare hooved species. The petting zoo and playground are favorites with children. *Game Farm Rd., Catskill, tel. 518/678–9595. Admission: $10 adults, $6 children 3–12, under 3 free. Open mid-Apr.–Oct., daily 9–6.*

Follow Route 32 south to Saugerties in Ulster County and take Route 212 west to **Woodstock,** home to artists, craftspeople, and musicians of all sorts (*see* Chapter 5). Continue on through Bearsville, Lake Hill, and Willow to Mount Tremper; head ❻ north on Route 28 to **Phoenicia** on Esopus Creek. Long noted as an outstanding trout stream, the Esopus has in recent years developed a reputation for white-water kayaking in the spring and, in summer, the somewhat tamer sport of tubing—drifting along in inner tubes that can either be a relaxing pastime or a water-borne version of bumper cars. At least five outfitters rent tubes in Phoenicia and Mt. Pleasant.

Route 214 from Phoenicia north to Hunter winds through **Stoney Clove,** a spectacular mountain cleft that has inspired countless tales of witchcraft and the supernatural. Early entrepreneurs guided gullible tourists through rock formations they called the Devil's Kitchen, the Devil's Pulpit, and the Devil's Tombstone. The last—a six-by-seven-foot rounded sandstone slab—is the locale of Devil's Tombstone Public Campground. *Rte. 214, Hunter, tel. 914/688–7160 or 518/943–4030. Open May 15–Labor Day.*

Back at Phoenicia, cross the Esopus and drive south up lovely **Woodland Valley** to the well-marked trail to **Slide Mountain.** At 4,204 feet, this is the highest peak in the Catskills, and those who make the moderately strenuous six-mile climb are amply rewarded with glorious views from the summit. Be prepared to encounter lots of weekend trail traffic in summer.

As you continue the westward climb on Route 28, it's easy to understand why the Ulster & Delaware Railroad was nicknamed the "Up and Down." For many decades the U&D carried tourists to hotels and boarding houses in Pine Hill, Fleischmanns, and other resort towns along this route, and took milk and farm products back down to Kingston for shipment to New York City. The milk trains and the Friday night "husband trains," filled with men rejoining vacationing families after a work week in the city are long gone. But you can still get the flavor of this important era in Catskill history with a 12-mile ❼ round-trip excursion between **Arkville** and **Halcottsville** aboard the **Delaware & Ulster Rail Ride.** There are four hour-long trips daily along the East Branch of the Delaware River, with a turnaround stop at Lake Wawaka in Halcottsville. *Rte. 28, Arkville, tel. 607/652–2821. Fare: $6 adults, $5 senior citizens, $3 children 5–11. Open weekends June, Sept., and Oct.; Wed.–Sun. July–Labor Day.*

Another form of transport is spotlighted at the **Auto Memories Museum,** which displays 100 cars and trucks dating to 1906. Volunteers staff the museum and proceeds go to community improvement projects. *Cut-off Rd., Arkville. No phone. Admission: $2 adults, children under 12 free. Open July 1–Labor Day daily; Labor Day–Columbus Day, weekends 10:30–4:30.*

Delaware County

Newly discovered by big-city vacationers and second-home buyers, Delaware County is characterized by smaller peaks, shallower valleys called "hollows," and a generally gentler terrain than the abrupt "cloves" of the high peaks region. Traversed by the East and West branches of the Delaware River, the area is famous among anglers and hunters, who annually take bountiful numbers of trout, deer, and wild turkey.

With more than 500 family farms, Delaware County is a land of roadside stands full of honey, eggs, apple cider, and maple syrup. Its rural heritage is celebrated throughout the summer at country fairs, farm days, lumberjack festivals, ox pulls, and Saturday-night auctions.

The county contains more than 11,000 acres of reservoirs and 750 miles of streams and rivers packed with small-mouth bass, walleye, and trout. The Beaver Kill, birthplace of dry fly fishing in America, has a solid reputation for the best fishing in the Northeast.

In spring, it's hunting country. In summer, hiking and horseback riding on marked trails, particularly in the 64,000 acres of state-owned "forever wild" land, are the major attractions. Fall spells spectacular foliage. And in winter, it's back to the outdoors on the runs of five major downhill ski centers and hundreds of miles of cross-country and snowshoeing trails.

8 **Roxbury,** on Route 30 in northeast Delaware County, has a Norman Rockwell-like, picture-perfect Main Street of tidy homes with century-old maples on wide front lawns. A Main Street landmark is the **Jay Gould Memorial Reformed Church,** a magnificent limestone, oak, and stained-glass edifice erected in 1892 by the children of the Roxbury-born railroad tycoon. Visitors are welcome at Sunday morning services (9:30 July 4– Labor Day, 10:30 during the rest of the year).

Another native son is recalled at the more humble **Burroughs Memorial** off Hardscrabble Road just north of Roxbury. He was John Burroughs, the naturalist and author whose summer retreat, Woodchuck Lodge, is located on the farm where he was born in 1837 and buried in 1922. Although most of his adult life was spent at West Park (*see* Chapter 5), Burroughs wrote many of his 23 books and occasionally entertained influential friends such as Henry Ford and Thomas Edison at his Roxbury cabin. *Burroughs Memorial Rd., Roxbury, tel. 518/299–3498. Donation. Open weekends July 4–Labor Day 11–5.*

Go north from Roxbury on Route 30 to Grand Gorge, the headwaters of the East Branch of the Delaware, and take Route 23

9 west to **Stamford.** During the fall, the **Log Cabin Cider Mill,** three miles east of Stamford, offers apple-pressing demonstrations, tours, and free samples of fresh cider. *Blackberry St., Stamford, tel. 607/652–3384. Open Sept.–Nov. 9–5. Closed Tues.*

On the outskirts of Stamford, turn south on Mountain Avenue, opposite the red information booth. This will take you to the top of **Utsayantha Mountain,** now a favorite launch site for hang gliders.

Stamford also claims renowned storyteller Ned Buntline, king of the 19th-century dime novels and the discoverer of Buffalo Bill. Buntline was born in Stamford and spent his last years at **Eagle's Nest.** The house still stands on South Delaware Street but is not open to the public.

Time Out Quick, unpretentious, and folksy, **Nicole's Diner** (Main St., Stamford, no phone) dishes out big portions of diner staples and plenty of small-town talk at reasonable prices.

⑩ Continue west on Route 23 to Davenport Center and follow the sign to **East Meredith** and the **Hanford Mills Museum.** The sawmill, gristmill, and woodworking shop dating back to 1820 are powered by a 10-foot water wheel. The assemblage of wheels, belts, and pulleys churning along in continuous motion may resemble a Rube Goldberg arrangement but it works. The placid millpond is a lovely backdrop for a picnic. *Rtes. 10 and 12, East Meredith, tel. 607/278–5744. Admission: $3 adults, $1.50 children 6–12, under 6 free. Open May–Oct., daily 10–5.*

⑪ The nine-mile drive on Elk Creek Road south from east Meredith to **Delhi** is one of the least-known pleasures of Catskill touring. Lined with maples bearing sap buckets in the spring and blazing foliage in autumn, this classic country road winds past dairy farms and homesteads of amazing architectural variety.

Turn left (east) at Route 10 and travel a half-mile to the **Delaware County Historical Association.** The 1798 Gideon Frisbee house and tavern, an 1860s schoolhouse, and a 19th-century gun shop are open to visitors, as is a huge 200-year-old barn housing an extensive farming exhibit. A gift shop offers a good selection of books on local history. *Rte. 10, Delhi, tel. 607/746–3849. Admission: $1.50 adults, 75¢ children. Open Memorial Day–Oct., Tues.–Fri. 10–4:30, weekends 1–4:30.*

Route 10 west leads to Delhi, the county seat and home of the State University Agricultural and Technical College. Take Route 28 south for a scenic ride through Andes to Dunraven and the eastern end of the 22-mile Pepacton Reservoir, one of several regional sources of New York City water. The drive along the reservoir on Route 30 is beautiful, but be advised that there are no gas stations or rest areas.

⑫ As an alternative, continue west on Route 10 from Delhi to **Walton.** This is dairy country and the boulder-strewn pastures show why longtime residents claim the Catskills are made of "two rocks for every dirt." Route 206 south over Bear Spring Mountain leads to Downsville, where a **covered bridge** built in 1874 still carries traffic over the East Branch of the Delaware. Route 30 south between Downsville and the community of East Branch hugs the river, passing through hamlets like Shinhopple, which hosts the Peaceful Valley Bluegrass Festival each July. Call for information (tel. 607/363–2211).

Sullivan County and the Upper Delaware

⑬ The four-lane divided Route 17 neatly bisects Sullivan County and accesses most of the major resorts. Pick up Route 17 in Delaware County at the East Branch and head east to **Roscoe,** the self-styled "Trout Town, USA." In the mid-1800s, American fly-fishing was born east of Roscoe at Junction Pool, situated at the confluence of Willowemoc Creek and the Beaver Kill. On opening day of fishing season each April 1, it's lined shoulder-to-shoulder with hopeful anglers.

⑭ The **Catskill Flyfishing Center** at **Deckertown,** between Roscoe and Livingston Manor, consists of a seven-acre pond, casting pool, and 2,000 feet of stream frontage on Willowemoc Creek. A museum displays exhibits on rods, flies, and other paraphernalia used by the greats of the sport. Guest flytiers demonstrate their skills each Saturday during July and August. *Old Rte. 17, Deckertown, tel. 914/439–4810. Free. Open daily 10–5.*

Covered-bridge fanciers will find four such spans in this area: at Beaver Kill State Campground, in Hall's Mills over the Neversink River, and two over Willowemoc Creek, one near Livingston Manor, and another two miles west of the hamlet of Willowemoc.

⑮ Watch for the sign at the Roscoe exit on Route 17 for **Callicoon** and the **Apple Pond Farm.** Located about six miles south off Route 123, this organic, horse-powered farm offers two-hour tours and demonstrations of sheepherding, beekeeping, draft-horse driving, and other traditional rural skills. Along with lessons in local history and the environment, visitors get covered-wagon and sleigh rides. Breads, pies, meats, honey, and other homemade products are sold on the premises. *Hahn Rd., Callicoon Center, tel. 914/482–4764. Admission: $6. Reservations required. Open year-round.*

⑯ Just down the road, the Bernthal Brothers maintain another country tradition at the **North Branch Cider Mill**. Their turn-of-the-century press transforms apples into cider daily during spring and fall. Children can pet lambs, kids, ducks, and calves while adults sample a special hard cider. The adjacent Mill Store sells everything from pottery to pickles—cider, too. *Rte. 123, North Branch, tel. 914/482–4823. Free. Open Apr. 1–Dec. 24, daily 10–5:30.*

⑰ ⑱ **Liberty** and **Monticello** on Route 17 are jumping-off points for the legendary Catskill resorts. The cool, dry atmosphere of the region and its proximity to New York City attracted early sufferers of tuberculosis and other lung ailments. Later Russian and Eastern European Jews, who were not always welcome at hotels and boarding houses in other areas of the Catskills, escaped the heat and disease of the immigrant ghettos here. Over time, this network of resorts and vacation spots became known as the "borscht belt," and served as boot camp for innumerable entertainers who later gained national prominence. Resorts like the 1,250-room Concord in Kiamesha Lake, Kutsher's Country Club in Monticello, and Brown's Hotel in Loch Sheldrake still offer guests three gargantuan meals a day including entertainment, and sports in self-contained communities.

Over the past decade, however, the trend has been away from such large resort hotels, and the region is rapidly reverting to its earlier state as a refuge for the backwoods adventurer and the New York City intelligentsia. Today it's big on cabins, second homes, small hotels, and cozy, old-fashioned bed-and-breakfast lodgings.

Time Out   For close to 60 years, **Kaplan's,** the only authentic Kosher deli in the Catskills, has been serving overstuffed corned beef and pastrami sandwiches and stuffed cabbage. *319 Broadway, Monti-cello, tel. 914/794–6060.*

---

19 At Monticello, take Route 17B west nine miles to **Bethel,** site of the 1969 "Woodstock Music and Art Fair, an Aquarian Exposition," better known as **Woodstock.** When the fair's organizers were turned away from the original location in Woodstock, 50 miles northeast of Bethel, they used Max Yasgur's dairy farm for the gathering of a half-million folk and rock music fans. The event is commemorated by a monument located at the corner of Hurd and West Shore roads. (Take Hurd Road north from Route 17B.)

Stay on Route 17B until you reach Callicoon on the Delaware River. This is the midway point of the 73-mile National Park Service Upper Delaware Scenic and Recreational River.

20 Just north of **Narrowsburg** is **Fort Delaware,** a reconstruction of a stockade community inhabited by Connecticut Yankees from 1755 to 1785. Demonstrations of such crafts as candlemaking and musket-firing are conducted by staff in period dress. *Rte. 97, Narrowsburg, tel. 914/252–6660. Admission: $3 adults, $1.50 children 6–16, $8.50 families. Open weekends in June, daily July–Labor Day, 10–5:30.*

The **National Park Service Information Center** in Narrowsburg offers advice on fishing (eel, trout, walleye, bass, American shad), boating (canoe liveries along the Delaware do a roaring business in the summertime), and other matters of interest to travelers along the Delaware, which forms the boundary between New York and Pennsylvania. *Main St., Narrowsburg, tel. 914/252–3947. Open Memorial Day–Labor Day, daily 9–4:30.*

During the 1800s, the Upper Delaware River was a crucial route for gigantic rafts of Catskill Mountain logs bound for the shipyards and factories in Philadelphia and Trenton. In 1847, more than 30 years before he designed the Brooklyn Bridge, John A. Roebling built a span over the raft-crowded river. At
21 **Minisink Ford,** the one-lane **Roebling Suspension Bridge,** the oldest such structure in the United States, now carries pedestrians and vehicles between Lackawaxen, Pennsylvania, and Minisink Ford, New York. Free tours are available from park-service interpreters stationed at the former tollhouse on the New York end of the bridge. *Rte. 97, Minisink Ford, tel. 914/557–6363. Tollhouse open Memorial Day–Labor Day, daily 9:30–6.*

Route 97 meanders along the New York side of the Delaware. From October to April, this area is home to dozens of wintering bald eagles. For a great view of the river and the Pennsylvania woods to the west, stop at Hawk's Nest, a cliffside parking area some 400 feet above the water near Cherry Island, the southern terminus of the Upper Delaware Scenic and Recreational River.

Make your way back to Monticello via Route 52 and Route 17B from Narrowsburg, or Route 55 and Route 17B from Barryville four miles south of Minisink Ford. Route 17 will take you east to Wurtsboro and the Shawangunks.

You hear a lot of talk about ridge lifts, thermals, and waves in the Shawangunk Mountains (more familiarly, the 'Gunks). Airplane gliders and hang gliders are often seen soaring above the whitish cliffs that are a favorite of rock climbers. The family **②** that owns **Wurtsboro Airport** claims its facility is the oldest soaring site in the nation, going back to the 1920s. A glider ride costs $30, and instruction is available on Tuesdays. Pilot and passenger in an engineless sailplane are towed into the great beyond by a conventional craft and released to soar with the currents. Fridays, Saturdasy, and Sundays. Call ahead for reservations. *U.S. 209, Wurtsboro, tel. 914/888–2791. Airport open year-round daily 8:30–5, weather permitting.*

Between 40 and 60 hang gliders descend (or ascend) on **②** **Ellenville** (Ulster County) in June and October for Fun Fly-Ins from launch sites atop 1,000-foot Ellenville Mountain. Three parking areas along scenic Route 52 are the best spots from which to watch the gliders soar overhead and land in a field alongside the Nevele Hotel. The U.S. record for time aloft is 11 hours and 20 minutes, set by a pilot who took off from Ellenville. Several flights have gone nearly 100 miles to points along the Connecticut and Rhode Island coasts. Aerobatic demonstrations are held each July 4 in Ellenville, when the World Champion Aerobatics Pilot is joined by 25 other pilots for airborne maneuvers.

Ice Caves Mountain is another reason for coming to Ellenville. A registered national landmark, the Ellenville Fault Ice Caves are part of a privately held attraction that includes a mountain-top drive around Lake Maratanza, a self-guided one-mile walk to caves where ice clings to the rocks all year, and a spectacular view from 2,255-foot Sam's Point. *Six miles east of Rte. 52, Ellenville, tel. 914/647–7989. Admission: $6 adults, $4 children, under 6 free. Open daily Apr.–Nov.*

② In **New Paltz,** the **Minnewaska State Park,** northeast of Ellenville on U.S. 44, is an 11,600-acre undeveloped day-use area famous for two glacial lakes and fabulous 360-degree views. More than 90 miles of hiking trails (with 40 miles groomed for cross-country skiing) follow carriage roads that once led to two bygone hotels. Hike or bicycle 3½ miles to swim in Lake Awasting; or drive over to Lake Minnewaska and rent a boat. In early summer the park is filled with glorious displays of fragrant mountain laurel. *U.S. 44, New Paltz, tel. 914/255–0752. Admission: $3 per car on weekends, $5 per person for cross-country skiing in season.*

② Route 209 north to **Kingston** isn't especially noted for its natural scenery, but the proliferation of stone architecture en route is worthy of attention. The **Ulster County Historical Society Museum** in Stone Ridge is a particularly fine example. *Tel. 914/338–5614.*

② **Hurley,** a postcard-pretty little town just west of Kingston, boasts twenty-seven 200-year-old Dutch-built stone houses. Come on Stone House Day, the second Saturday in July, for guided tours of the privately owned homes. Follow the suggested walking tour—a map of the tour is mounted in a display case at the town offices on Main Street. Stroll down Main Street and through a grassy alley to a violet-strewn cemetery hidden among pines and birches. The stones, some inscribed in Dutch, date to 1713. Visitors are welcome until dusk each day.

More stone houses are found in New Paltz (*see* Chapter 5).

What to See and Do with Children

Children should enjoy the many outdoor recreation opportunities in the Catskills, but when the younger set craves its own kind of entertainment, they can find it here as well. Of particular amusement to children are the **Zoom Flume Aquamusement Park**, the **Catskill Game Farm, Catskill Reptile Institute, Carson City, Delaware & Ulster Rail Ride, Supersonic Speedway & Fun Park, Festival of Circus Theater, Hanford Mills Museum, Fort Delaware, Apple Pond Farm,** and the **Catskill Fish Hatchery.**

Off the Beaten Track

Catskill State Fish Hatchery. The New York State Department of Environmental Conservation Fish Hatchery in Debruce (Sullivan County) is home to 1.3 million trout (mostly German browns) in various stages of development. Kept in long concrete holding ponds, the fish are raised to stock lakes and streams in 11 surrounding counties. A separate set of runs contains the huge females (valued at $125 apiece) used as breeding stock. Feeding time is quite a spectacle. *Mongaup Rd., Debruce, tel. 914/439–4328. Open daily 8:30–4. Admission free.*

Shopping

Shopping is a major diversion in the Catskills. Malls, factory outlets, and shopping villages abound in the Lower Catskills. Treasure-hunting at festivals, auctions, flea markets, crafts fairs, antiques shops, and galleries is an all-season pastime throughout the region. Here are a few of the most intriguing and unusual shops:

Ethnic Gifts The **German Alps Festival Store** (Main St., Hunter, tel. 518/263–4114). Hummel figurines, Bonn wood carvings, Christmas ornaments, cuckoo clocks, and other European items. Open daily.

Guaranteed Irish (Rte. 145, East Durham, tel. 518/634–7409). The nation's largest collection of Irish goods including glassware, knits and tweeds, art, music, and books. Closed January and February.

St. John the Baptist Ukrainian Catholic Church (Rte. 23A, Jewett Center, tel. 518/263–3862). Imported items including embroidered clothing, inlaid wooden boxes, and hand-painted Easter eggs.

Regional Crafts **Craftspeople** (Spillway Rd., Hurley, tel. 914/331–3859). Glass, pottery, jewelry, leather, and other handmade items produced by 200 regional artisans, as well as some locally produced food items.

Candyman Chocolates in Catskill (tel. 518/943–2122) features hand-dipped chocolates, fresh creamery fudge, and regional specialties. Watch your chocolates being made.

Four Corners Studio in Freehold (tel. 518/634–7386) is the studio and gallery of Stanley Maltzman, who paints regional scenes and landscapes. Visitors are welcome, by appointment only.

Outlet Stores **Apollo Plaza** (East Broadway, Monticello, tel. 914/794–2010). An enclosed mall with 30 manufacturers' outlet stores selling everything from toys to furniture at discounts of up to 70%.

Participant Sports

Canoeing

The 79-mile Upper Delaware Scenic and Recreational River is one of the finest streams for paddling in the region. For a list of trip planners and rental firms, contact the **Sullivan County Office of Public Information** (*see* Important Addresses and Numbers, above).

Fishing

Some of the best trout streams in the world lie within the Catskills: Esopus, Willowemoc, Schoharie, Catskill, East Kill, and West Kill creeks; the Delaware and Neversink rivers; Beaver Kill and the Batavia Kill. In addition, smallmouth bass, walleye, and pickerel can be found in many lakes and in six reservoirs. To obtain the brochure "Catskill Fishing," which contains a map and information about streams and rivers, contact the **Catskill Association for Tourism Services (C.A.T.S.)** (Box 449, Catskill, NY 12414, tel. 800/542–2414), or any county tourism bureau (*see* Important Addresses and Numbers, above).

Golf

The Catskill region has 43 golf courses. Many, including "The Monster" at the Concord Hotel, which ranks among the nation's top 100 golf challenges, are located at the big resorts. Most courses have resident pros, instruction, and tournaments. Many resorts offer golfing vacation packages. To receive the "Golf Catskills" brochure, which lists public and private courses, rates, and packages, contact **C.A.T.S.** (*see* Fishing, above, or any county tourism bureau).

Hiking

The New York State Department of Environmental Conservation maintains more than 200 miles of marked hiking trails through the Catskill Forest Preserve. Twenty of the 34 peaks above 3,500 feet have trails to their summits. To receive the booklet "Catskill Trails," contact the DEC, 50 Wolf Rd., Albany, NY 12233.

Horseback Riding

The best way to see the woodlands and meadows and rushing mountain streams is from atop an English or Western saddle. Riding opportunities for urban cowboys and cowgirls range from rental stables to formal academies to dude ranches, with lessons and terrains for all abilities. For lessons and training, try **Bittersweet Knoll Stables** in Leeds (tel. 518/622–8799). And for short, by-the-hour rides, mosey down to **Silver Springs Ranch** on Route 16 in Tannersville (tel. 518/589–5559).

Hunting

Deer, bear, wild turkey, rabbit, pheasant, and grouse are among the game taken annually on public and private lands within the region. The Department of Environmental Conservation "Big and Small Game Season Guides," available at license-issuing offices, outline regulations and describe areas open for public hunting. Get more information in "Hunting the Northern Catskills" from the Greene County Promotion Department; "Ulster County Hunting" from the Ulster County Public Information Office; and "Hunting Bulletin 1989–90" from the Sullivan County Public Information Office (*see* Important Addresses and Numbers, above).

For inexperienced hunters who would like a shot at a pheasant dinner, there's the **JR Shooting Preserve** on Grove School Road in Catskill (tel. 518/943–2069). This licensed preserve is open to the public. Shotguns, hunting dogs, handlers, and instruction are provided.

Skiing

Downhill Area ski centers include Highmount (tel. 914/254–5265); Belleayre Mountain (the only state-run ski facility in the Catskills), Highmount (tel. 914/254–5600); Bobcat, Andes (tel. 607/832–4829); Cortina Valley, Haines Falls (tel. 518/589–6500); Deer Run, Stamford (tel. 607/652–7332); Holiday Mountain, Monticello (tel. 914/796–3161); Hunter Mountain, Hunter (tel. 518/263–4223); Plattekill, Roxbury (tel. 607/326–7547); Ski Windham, Windham (tel. 518/734–4300); Big Vanilla at Davos, Woodridge (tel. 914/434–1000). Details on most ski centers are included in the "Ski the Catskills" brochure available through county promotion departments (*see* Important Addresses and Numbers, above).

Ski Windham offers extensive ski programs for the blind, hearing-impaired, developmentally disabled, amputees, and those with lower-body disabilities. There's also a wheelchair run. Lessons are by appointment.

Cross-country Some of the finest cross-country trails are found at Minnewaska State Park near New Paltz, where 40 miles of carriage roads are groomed in the winter (tel. 914/255–0752). Other Nordic ski facilities are White Birches Ski Touring Center, Windham (tel. 518/734–3266); Hyer Meadows, Tannersville (tel. 518/589–5361); Hanofee Park, Liberty (tel. 914/292–7690 or 9358); Town of Thompson Park, Monticello (tel. 914/796–3161); Frost Valley YMCA Camp, Oliverea (tel. 914/985–7400); North Lake Public Campground (tel. 518/589–5058); and Belleayre Mountain, Highmount (tel. 800/942–6904 in NYS or 800/431–6012 outside NY).

Tennis

Most courts are not located at the hotels and resorts, but at public parks, colleges, and schools scattered throughout the region. Many are free; others charge a nominal hourly fee.

Spectator Sports

Hang Gliding

The Southern New York Hang Glider Pilots' Association maintains launch sites at five Catskill locations. The highest is on 2,300-foot Overlook Mountain near Woodstock. Others are on High Point near Samsonville, Mount Utsayantha near Stamford, and Little Mountain near West Shokan. The most accessible site for both pilots and spectators is on Ellenville Mountain, where several events are slated each year (*see* Exploring The Catskills, above). *For more information, contact Mountain Wings, 150 Canal St., Ellenville, 12428, tel. 914/647–3377.*

Horse Racing

Monticello Raceway is a half-mile harness track with pari-mutuel wagering on weekends year-round but most frequently in summer. Club Escoffier, a glass-enclosed restaurant, overlooks all the action. *Rtes. 17 and 17B, Monticello, tel. 914/794–4100. Admission: $1.50. Post time Tues.–Sat. 7:30, Sun. 1:30.*

Rodeo

Staff members and those who board horses at Roundup Ranch Resort participate in weekly rodeos at the resort. *Rte. 206, Downsville, tel. 607/363–7300. Admission free. Mid-May–Labor Day, Sat. 7:30.*

Dining and Lodging

Dining While there is some outstanding food in the region, the most inspiring aspect of Catskill restaurants is often their setting. Restaurants that don't serve chops, steaks, chicken, and other standard American fare generally run along ethnic lines, principally German/Austrian, Italian, and French. Shellfish and seafood are surprisingly abundant in this landlocked region: Some restaurateurs travel frequently to Boston, New York, and Maine for the freshest catch—and a number serve Catskill Mountain trout. Some will even fix your own catch any way you like it.

Since most visitors are here for the outdoor life, casual dress is generally acceptable. Correspondingly, the price of dinner at most Catskill establishments falls into the inexpensive-to-moderate price ranges.

Many area restaurants close down or have abbreviated hours for at least part of the year. Some are open only during the summer months; others reopen for the ski season. It's best to phone ahead. While reservations are usually not required, they are advisable on holidays and on weekends in both summer and winter. Highly recommended places are indicated by a star ★.

Category	Cost*
Very Expensive	over $35
Expensive	$25–$35
Moderate	$15–$25
Inexpensive	under $15

*per person, without tax, service, or drinks

Lodging The Catskill area is noted for its mammoth resorts—the kind with hundreds of rooms, where such amenities as pools, health clubs, child care, golf courses, and nightly entertainment are standard, and where watching the other guests is as much a part of the vacation as shuffleboard or tennis. These mega-resorts offer all-inclusive packages, but if you want to plan your own trip there are other options: personal-touch bed-and-breakfasts and country inns reminiscent of the era when Catskill boarding houses welcomed summer-long refugees from the city, ski-center condos for those who want to stay close to the action, and efficiency cabins in the woods for those who don't. Small hotels, inns, lodges, bungalows, dude ranches, "guest farms," and B&Bs are alternatives. County promotion offices (*see* Important Addresses and Numbers, above) are good sources of free information on them.

Some B&Bs and country inns are listed with **The American Country Collection of Bed & Breakfast Accommodations** (984 Gloucester Place Schenectady, NY 12309, tel. 518/370–4948).

Of course you could always pack the tent, sleeping bags, and Coleman stove and go camping. Area promotion offices (*see* Important Addresses and Numbers, above) can send you information on Catskill campgrounds.

Category	Cost*
Very Expensive	over $100
Expensive	$85–$100
Moderate	$45–$85
Inexpensive	under $45

*Rates are per person per night, double occupancy. Some resorts rent only by the week or weekend with meals included. Unless otherwise indicated, all hotels are open year-round and all rooms have private bath. Room rates for hotels on the American Plan (AP) include three meals per day; Modified American Plan (MAP) includes breakfast and dinner.

Big Indian (Ulster)

Dining **Rudi's Big Indian.** Established in the 1960s by students of a
★ nearby Buddhist ashram as a vegetarian sandwich shop and antiques store, Rudi's has evolved into a popular spot for sophisticated dining. Oriental rugs, antiques, and local artwork create the ambience. Entrees include medallions of pork with pear butter and vegetable ricotta pie. Filled with greenery, the Conservatory dining room is a pleasant place for a full meal or for a dessert stop—coffee-toffee pie is highly recommended.

Rte. 28, tel. 914/254-4005. Dress: informal. AE, DC, MC, V. Closed Nov. Moderate.

Bloomingburg (Sullivan)

Dining and
Lodging

Eagle's Nest Hotel. This is a Viennese-style establishment where modest rooms come with three meals and afternoon coffee. Most rooms have twin beds, some have terraces. The German chef prepares a Continental menu; *wienerschnitzel* is a popular item. The view from the glass-walled dining room includes three states. *Mountain Rd., 12721, tel. 914/733-4561. Motel: 67 rooms available Memorial Day–Labor Day only; AP. 3-night minimum stay. Restaurant: open to nonguests Wed.–Sun. in July and Aug., Fri.–Sun. in spring and fall. No credit cards. Closed Dec.–Mar. Moderate.*

Bovina Center (Delaware)

Dining and
Lodging

Mountainbrook Chalet. Ruffled curtains and bedspreads brighten up two-room housekeeping apartments in this off-the-beaten-track motel. The German restaurant, which specializes in 10-inch stuffed pancakes and is noted for its Saturday-night German buffet, is open to the public six days a week in summer, weekends the rest of the year. *County Rte. 6, 13740, tel. 607/832-4424. 8 units. Restaurant: dress casual. MC, V. Inexpensive.*

Callicoon (Sullivan)

Dining and
Lodging

Villa Roma Resort & Country Club. This Italian-American resort has its own ski slopes, 18-hole golf course, and indoor sports complex. The dining room is famous for its Caesar's Night Dinner, an 11-course Roman feast held on Friday evenings. *Beechwoods, 12723, tel. 914/887-4880, 800/553-6767 in NY, 800/621-5656 outside NY. Hotel: 225 rooms; AP. Facilities: indoor-outdoor pools, tennis, racquetball, health club, golf, disco. Restaurant: dress informal. Reservations required for nonguests. AE, MC, V. Expensive.*

Catskill (Greene)

Dining

La Rive. Tucked away on a wooded slope just above a trout stream, this laid-back French country retaurant is housed in a 150-year-old farmhouse. The fare is simple and straightforward—duck bigarade, rack of lamb, sweetbreads in pastry, steak au poivre, and rabbit stew. You'll start with a multitude of hors d'oeuvres, such as cod-potato mousse and lentils vinaigrette, and end with fresh fruit and aged goat cheese. The excellent wines and rich desserts are not to be missed. *Old Kings Rd., just off Rte. 23A, tel. 518/943-4888. Dress: smart casual. MC, V. No lunch. Closed mid-May–Thanksgiving and Wed. Moderate.*

Debruce (Sullivan)

Dining and
Lodging

Debruce Country Inn. Individually designed rooms feature Oriental rugs, silk drapes, and matching spreads. The restaurant serves a variety of vegetable and pasta dishes along with such fresh-fish specialties as Willowemoc Swimming Trout, baked local trout surrounded by rice and greens. *Debruce Rd., 12724,* *tel. 914/439-3900. Hotel: 15 rooms; bed-and-breakfast or MAP. Facilities: outdoor pool, sauna, exercise room. Restaurant: dress informal. MC, V. Moderate.*

Deposit (Broome)

Dining and Lodging **Scott's Oquaga Lake House.** A spring-fed lake is the focal point of this resort, best known for its family atmosphere and sing-along cruises on a 60-passenger showboat. Seven buildings, including an 1869 farmhouse, accommodate guests in simple surroundings. Rates include three home-cooked meals. *Oquaga Lake, 13754, tel. 607/467-3094. 140 rooms; AP. No credit cards. Restaurant: dress casual. Closed Oct.–May. Moderate.*

Downsville (Delaware)

Dining and Lodging ★ **Roundup Ranch Resort.** This is a place for horse lovers, with trail rides, lessons, indoor arena, sleigh rides, even a rodeo every Saturday night during summer. No two rooms are alike; the decor is contemporary. *Rte. 206, 13755, tel. 607/363-7300. 35 rooms (26 more under construction); AP. Facilities: 9-hole golf course, stocked trout pond, gift shop. Restaurant: dress casual. AE, MC, V. Open daily May–Oct., weekends rest of year. Moderate.*

Dining **Old Schoolhouse Restaurant.** Steaks, chops, chicken, and veal are now served where local children learned the three Rs from 1905 to 1937. Hung with moose heads, deer racks, and mounted fish, the Sportsmen's Bar used to be the first-grade classroom. The original tin ceiling, oak floors, and hemlock siding remain. *Main St., tel. 607/363-7814. Dress: informal. No credit cards. Inexpensive.*

East Branch (Delaware)

Dining and Lodging **Buck-Horn Lodge.** Period furnishings and family memorabilia adorn the rooms in this Victorian-era guest house. Seven simply furnished housekeeping cottages are nearby. The dining room features roast beef, fried chicken, fresh vegetables, and other home-style fare. *Rte. 30, 13756, tel. 607/363-7120. Hotel: 7 rooms, 7 cottages. Restaurant: dress informal. Reservations required. No credit cards. Closed Jan.–Apr. Inexpensive.*

East Durham (Greene)

Dining and Lodging **The Country Place.** Motel units, some with sitting rooms, take a back seat to the main attraction here—the Zoom Flume Aquamusement Park (*see* Exploring the Catskills, above). *Shady Glen Rd., 12423, tel. 518/239-4559. 20 rooms; MAP; 2-night minimum stay. Facilities: pool. MC, V. Open May–Oct. Moderate.*

Elka Park (Greene)

Dining and Lodging ★ **Redcoat's Return.** The ambience of an English country inn is offered in beautiful Platte Clove. Guest rooms are individually decorated. Dinner, served in a room with a view of surrounding mountains or in the cozy library, might include Yorkshire pudding or steak and kidney pie. *Dale La., 12427, tel. 518/589-6379. Hotel: 14 rooms, 5 with private bath; breakfast in-*

cluded. *Restaurant: dress informal. Reservations requested. AE, DC, MC, V. Open Memorial Day–Oct., Jan.–Mar. Moderate.*

Eldred (Sullivan)

Dining and
Lodging

Eldred Preserve. Hunting and fishing packages are offered on a 2,500-acre resort where deer, turkey, and trout flourish. Rooms are contemporary; many have recently been refurbished. Seven miles of nature trails are suitable for cross-country skiing. *Rte. 55, 12732, tel. 914/557–8316. 21 rooms. Facilities: pool, tennis, restaurant. AE, DC, MC, V. Moderate.*

Ellenville (Ulster)

Dining and
Lodging
★

Nevele Hotel. This is one of the most up-to-date of the legendary Catskill megaresorts. There are five buildings in this sprawling complex, ranging from two to six stories high. Most deluxe is the Empire Wing, with suites containing two double beds as well as a dressing area. The Towers building offers the best views, with vistas of the hotel's well-manicured grounds. The Art Deco lobby was refurbished two years ago. *Nevele Rd., 12428, tel. 914/647–6000 or 800/647–6000. 400 rooms; MAP. Facilities: 18-hole golf course, 15 tennis courts, 5 pools, ice rink, horseback riding, skiing, private lake, boating, fishing, nightly entertainment. AE, MC, V. Moderate–Expensive.*

Fleischmanns (Delaware)

Lodging

The Runaway Inn. A bowl of fresh fruit awaits guests in Victorian rooms furnished with highboard beds, oil paintings, and period antiques. Breakfast may include raspberry French toast, eggs Benedict, or fresh muffins. *Main St., tel. 914/254–5660. 5 rooms, 3 with private bath; bed-and-breakfast. MC, V. No children. Moderate.*

Freehold (Greene)

Dining and
Lodging

Pleasant View Lodge and Golf Club. The rooms in the 12 buildings here are modern; some suites have fireplaces and balconies. There's also a dining room and cozy fireplace bar. *Gayhead Rd., 12431, tel. 518/634–2523. 120 rooms. Facilities: 9-hole golf course, indoor-outdoor pools, tennis, sauna, ballroom. Restaurant: dress informal. Reservations requested. AE, MC, V. Moderate.*

Glenford (Ulster)

Dining

La Grillade. This charming French country restaurant spent 21 prosperous years in Manhattan before owners Albert and Lizette Deniel moved north to set up their kitchen in the Catskills. Now Manhattanites have to drive up here for the couple's memorable duck confit, leg of lamb, seafood, and French pastries. *Maverick Rd., Rte. 28, tel. 914/657–8630. Dress: smart casual. MC, V. Closed Tues. Moderate.*

Grand Gorge (Delaware)

Lodging

The Colonial Motel. You may stay in standard motel units or in one of the antique-furnished rooms in the 1832 main house. All rooms feature 19th-century photographs of local people taken by Anna Carroll. *Rtes. 23 and 30, 12434, tel. 607/588–6122 or 588–6495. 14 rooms. MC, V. Inexpensive.*

Greenville (Greene)

Dining and Lodging

Greenville Arms. Antiques decorate the rooms in the 1889 main house; contemporary furnishings outfit units in the former carriage house. *Rte. 32, 12083, tel. 518/966–5219. 19 rooms; meal plans available. Facilities: pool. AE, MC, V. Open May–Nov. Moderate.*

Pine Lake Manor. Landscaped lawns, putting greens, three well-stocked lakes, and a 19th-century main house complement this 150-acre resort. *Rte. 26, tel. 518/966–5745. 58 rooms. Facilities: handball/racquetball, tennis, pools. No credit cards. Open May–Oct. Moderate.*

Haines Falls (Greene)

Dining and Lodging

Hunter Mountain Resort Ranch. Bunk beds in some rooms indicate that this place caters to families. Wranglers lead rides on 20 acres of horse trails. Nightlife means square dances on Tuesdays and a country-western band on Thursdays. *Rte. 23A, 12436, tel. 518/589–6430. 24 rooms. Facilities: indoor-outdoor pools, tennis, volleyball, archery, shuffleboard, basketball, minigolf. No credit cards. Moderate.*

Villa Maria. This is a full-service resort during the summer and a bed-and-breakfast operation in the off-season and skiing months. Italian-American specialties are served at the adjacent Marianna Restaurant. *Rte. 23A, 12436, tel. 518/589–6200. 54 rooms. Facilities: indoor-outdoor minigolf. AE, MC, V. Moderate.*

Honsonville (Greene)

Dining

Vesuvio. The regional Italian menu here includes *ossobuco,* *pansotti* (homemade stuffed pasta with a walnut sauce), seafood specials, and desserts such as *zabaglione,* a hot custard prepared tableside and served over ice cream and fruit. A sophisticated wine list, candlelight, and fresh flowers contribute to an elegant atmosphere. *Goshen Rd., tel. 518/734–3663. Dress: casual (but no shorts). Reservations preferred. AE, DC, MC, V. Moderate.*

Seeley's. Seafood, steaks, and other American fare have been served here since 1911. The Friday night lobster and the Catskill Mountain Chicken (chicken breast on a bed of wild rice and spinach with a creamy cheese sauce) come highly recommended. *Rte. 296, tel. 518/734–9892. Dress: informal. AE, MC, V. Closed Tues. dinner. Inexpensive.*

Hunter (Greene)

Dining

Fireside. Chops, steaks, fish, and some Italian dishes are among the entrees at this no-frills eatery. A children's menu is available; a bar is not. *Main St., tel. 518/263–4216. Dress: informal. Reservations advised on weekends. AE, MC, V. Inexpensive–Moderate.*

Dining and Lodging ★ **Scribner Hollow Motor Lodge.** There are 16 fireplaces in this ultramodern lodge, plus theme rooms like Future World (sunken bath, waterfall, and an environmentally controlled bed chamber) and Hunting Lodge (Remington prints and sporty decor). The two-story Penthouse Suite (sunken living room, balcony, king-size bed) costs $220 per night. The restaurant overlooks the mountains. *Rte. 23A, 12442, tel. 518/263–4211. 38 rooms; extensively refurbished; MAP. Facilities: pool, Jacuzzi, sauna. AE, DC, MC, V. Expensive–Very Expensive.*

Sun-Land Farm Motel & Cabins. Motel, boardinghouse, and housekeeping cabins make up this eclectic establishment. The dining room has an American-Czechoslovakian menu that includes such entrees as roast pork with dumplings and sweet-and-sour cabbage. *Rte. 23A, 12442, tel. 518/263–4811. 15 rooms, 2 cabins. Facilities: pool. AE, DC, MC, V. Inexpensive–Moderate.*

Kerhonkson (Ulster)

Dining and Lodging **Granit Hotel and Country Club.** This is one of the big resorts, and the rooms here come with three (American-style) meals. Rooms range from "standard" to "ultra deluxe," but the difference is more in their size (and price) than in the amenities. *Kerhonkson, 12446, tel. 914/626–3141, 212/563–1881, or 800/431–7681. Facilities: pools, tennis, ice rink, golf, health club, nightclub. AE, MC, V. Moderate–Expensive.*

Kiamesha Lake (Sullivan)

Dining and Lodging ★ **Concord Resort Hotel.** This is one of the most enduring Catskill resorts. The Concord's 3,000 acres encompass three golf courses, 40 tennis courts, horseback-riding trails, an indoor-outdoor skating rink, volleyball, basketball, shuffleboard, and nearby skiing. The hotel annually serves more than 2.5 million strictly kosher meals in dining rooms that can seat more than 3,000 people at a time. *Kiamesha Lake, 12751, tel. 914/794–4000 or 800/431–3850. 1,200 rooms; AP. Facilities: ski slope, 3 nightclubs, 2 pools, men's and women's health clubs, toboggan run. AE, DC, MC, V. Moderate–Expensive.*

Lexington (Greene)

Dining and Lodging **Lexington Hotel.** If you don't mind sharing a bath, this 103-year-old hotel on the banks of Schoharie Creek is one of the best bargains around. An unpretentious restaurant featuring a Ukrainian buffet on Friday nights and serving three meals daily during July and August. *Rte. 42, 12452, tel. 518/989–9797. 24 rooms, no private baths. No credit cards. Inexpensive.*

Liberty (Sullivan)

Dining **Pursuit of Happiness.** Known for top-flight entertainment, this nightclub also has a passable dinner menu. Entrees include prime ribs and coq au vin; a cafe menu is available for light or late-night diners. The homey Victorian structure is filled with greenery, pottery, works by local artists, antique furniture, and a custom-built oak bar. *117 S. Main St., tel. 914/292–6760. Dress: informal. Reservations suggested on show nights. Open* *for dinner Tues.–Sat. in spring and summer; Sat. and show nights the rest of the year. DC, MC, V. Inexpensive.*

Dining and Lodging **Days Inn of Liberty.** The guest rooms are standard, but there's a game room and bar where a DJ entertains a 30-ish crowd. The Dynasty restaurant serves surf and turf and Oriental-style fare. *Sullivan Ave., 12754, tel. 914/292-7600. 120 rooms. Facilities: indoor-outdoor pools. AE, DC, MC, V. Inexpensive.*

Livingston Manor (Sullivan)

Dining and Lodging **Menges' Lakeside.** An informal family atmosphere, folk-dance weekends, and a beautiful location on Sand Lake distinguish this family-run resort. There's no air-conditioning and most baths are shared, but that doesn't deter the regular clientele from returning year after year. *Shandalee Rd., 12758, tel. 914/439-4569. 70 rooms, 40 with private bath; AP. Facilities: tennis, lake swimming, boating, fishing. No credit cards. Open daily July–Labor Day, weekends only May–June, Labor Day–mid-Oct. Moderate.*

Loch Sheldrake (Sullivan)

Dining and Lodging **Brown's Resort Hotel.** This family-oriented Catskill biggie underwent an expensive face-lift over the past couple of years. Its long list of amenities includes two golf courses, minigolf, tennis, a health club, disco, horseback riding, two pools and an indoor roller rink, top-name entertainment, and kosher food. *Loch Sheldrake, 12759, tel. 914/434-5151 or 800/3-BROWNS. 570 rooms; AP. AE, MC, V. Expensive.*

Maplecrest (Greene)

Dining and Lodging **Sugar Maples.** Taken over by a new owner in 1988, this traditional resort now has a Hellenic identity, with moussaka and lamb *kapama* in the dining room and Greek music in the nightclub. The rooms are modern, and rates include three meals. *Main St., 12454, tel. 518/734-4000. 150 rooms; AP. Facilities: pool, tennis, ice skating. MC, V. Moderate.*

Narrowsburg

Lodging **Wolfe's Pioneer Motel.** Located within the New York State National Scenic and Recreation Area near Skinners Falls on the Delaware River, this motel caters to canoeists and fishermen. *Rte. 97, 12764, tel. 914/252-3385. Facilities: pool, picnic area. MC, V. Inexpensive.*

Dining and Lodging **Narrowsburg Inn.** Sullivan County's oldest inn (and the third-oldest in the state) was built in 1840 as a stopover for Delaware River loggers and raftsmen. Photos of old Narrowsburg and the rough-and-tumble tree cutters who once worked here hang on the walls. The restaurant serves homemade soups, steak, seafood, and veal dishes. *Rte. 52, 12764, tel. 914/252-3998. 7 rooms with shared bath. Restaurant: casual dress. Reservations recommended on weekends. Open daily Apr.–Oct., closed Wed. rest of year. Inexpensive.*

Margaretville (Delaware)

Dining and Lodging
Kass Inn. About half of the summer guests here attend the Roland Stafford Golf School on the premises and practice at the nearby Hidden Waters Golf Course. Motel-type rooms come with two or three meals, served in the antiques-filled restaurant. Diners can choose from four or five daily specials in addition to regular offerings. Prime rib is a Saturday night tradition, as is the live music. *Rte. 30, 12455, tel. 914/586-9844. 68 rooms; MAP. Facilities: tennis, pool, fishing. Restaurant: casual dress. MC, V. Moderate.*

Lodging
Margaretville Mountain Inn. Once an elaborate Victorian boardinghouse, this bed-and-breakfast establishment offers rooms decorated with antiques, quilts, and cheery curtains. The ivory-and-oak bridal suite comes with a split of champagne. A wide veranda overlooks a long, sloping lawn. *Margaretville Mountain Rd., 12455, tel. 914/586-3933. 5 rooms, 3 with private bath. AE, MC, V. Moderate.*

Dining
Binnekill Square. The fare at this casual Swiss-French eatery ranges from Black Angus sirloin with blue-cheese butter and veal Provençale to imaginative pasta dishes and grilled breast of duckling with green peppercorns. If you prefer your duckling live, take a table on the deck overlooking Binnekill Creek and watch the mallards paddle under the building. *Main St., tel. 914/586-4884. Dress: casual. Reservations not accepted. No credit cards. Closed Mon. Moderate.*

Monticello (Sullivan)

Dining
Scalawags. If this restaurant reminds you of Houlihans in New York City, it's because they were both designed by the same firm. The menu ranges from hamburgers to lobster and duck. A DJ entertains most nights; live dance music is featured Saturdays starting at 11 PM. *358 Broadway, tel. 914/794-3131. Dress: casual. Reservations not accepted. AE, MC, V. Moderate.*

Lodging
Kutsher's Country Club. A grand Catskill resort where golf, tennis, and swimming are summer pastimes, and cross-country skiing, snowmobiling, snowshoeing, and ice skating are winter pursuits. Children's and teens' programs are offered. *Anawana Lake Rd., 12701, tel. 914/794-6000, 212/243-3112, or 800/431-1273. 450 rooms; AP. Facilities: golf, tennis, racquetball, pool, health club. AE, DC, MC, V. Moderate-Expensive.*

Mount Tremper (Ulster)

Dining
Catskill Rose. Imaginative entrees include curried mussels over pasta with peanut sauce and lamb chops with roasted red peppers. Art Deco surroundings feature pink flamingos on the tables, an oak-and-mahogany bar with frosted-glass windows illuminated by colored lights, and a periwinkle and gray color scheme. Classical, jazz, or contemporary piano music is featured Saturday nights. *Rte. 212, tel. 914/688-7100. Dress: casual. Reservations appreciated. DC, MC, V. Closed Mon. in winter. Moderate.*

Lodging
Mount Tremper Inn. This bed-and-breakfast inn has early-Victorian guest rooms and breakfasts featuring home-baked

breads. The common room sports red-velvet walls and a gold-leaf ceiling; shuffleboard and badminton are played on two acres of manicured lawn. One large suite contains two beds and two sitting rooms. *Rte. 212 and Wittenberg Rd., 12457, tel. 914/688–9938 or 914/688–5329. 12 rooms, 2 with private bath. MC, V. Moderate.*

Oliverea (Ulster)

Dining and Lodging **Slide Mountain Forest House.** This country inn in the woods caters to an outdoorsy crowd. With its mounted game, the sitting room resembles a hunting lodge. The rooms have contemporary furnishings, and the restaurant serves German-American family-style food. *Oliverea Rd., 12462, tel. 914/254–5365. 24 rooms. Facilities: pool, tennis, handball. No credit cards. Open Memorial Day–Dec. 1. Inexpensive.*

Palenville (Greene)

Dining and Lodging **Friar Tuck Inn.** A big, contemporary resort near the base of Kaaterskill Clove, Friar Tuck features architecture and furnishings with a touch of Camelot, but the cuisine in the Sherwood Dining Room is Italian-American. There is boating and fishing on a man-made private lake, bikes for rent, and organized activities. *Rte. 32, 12463, tel. 518/678–2271. 550 rooms; MAP. Facilities: tennis, nightclub, sauna, gym. Restaurant: casual dress. AE, DC, MC, V. Moderate–Expensive.*

Phoenicia (Ulster)

Dining **Margo's.** Sauerbraten with potato dumplings, veal goulash, and apple strudel are some of the Hungarian and German specialties here. There's a homey European atmosphere, with wood carvings of bears and birds throughout. *Rte. 28, tel. 914/688–7102. Dress: informal. MC, V. Open Fri.–Sun., mid-Apr.–Memorial Day; daily Memorial Day–mid-Nov. Inexpensive–Moderate.*

Yvonne's. Cassoulet and duck, especially smoked, and the confit are the specialties in this quaint eatery with a slight French accent. Yvonne's is best known for its unusual game—venison, antelope, moose and wild boar—all raised for the table at "game" farms. Quilts on the ceilings and mismatched chairs complete the country decor. *Rte. 28, tel. 914/688–7340. Dress: casual. Reservations suggested. No credit cards. Open weekends for dinner, Apr.–Oct., and at owner's discretion. Call ahead. Moderate–Expensive.*

Pine Hill (Ulster)

Dining and Lodging **Pine Hill Arms Hotel.** At this country inn with a family air, you may have to step over the owner's cats, dogs, and kids to reach the front desk. Continental fare, big steaks, and seafood are served in a greenhouse dining room. *Main St., 12465, tel. 914/254–9811. 30 rooms. Facilities: pool, game room, Jacuzzi. Restaurant: informal dress. Reservations recommended. MC, V. Moderate.*

Hideaway Hotel-Restaurant. There are motel units, cottages, and 14 rooms in the main inn situated on a quiet mountaintop. The German-American restaurant commands wide views from its picture windows. Room rates include two meals. *Hunt-*

ersfield Rd., 12465, tel. 518/299–3616. 14 rooms; MAP. No credit cards. Moderate.

Round Top (Greene)

Dining and Lodging **Winter Clove Inn.** Colonial architecture and decor (four-poster beds, wide-board pine floors, braided rugs) distinguish this 150-year-old inn. There are miles of foot trails on 400 acres adjoining the Catskill Forest Preserve. *Off Rte. 32, 12473, tel. 518/622–3267. 50 rooms. Facilities: pool, tennis, bowling, 9-hole golf course. DC, MC, V. Closed Dec. Moderate.*

Roxbury (Delaware)

Dining **Roxbury Run.** Lots of ornate woodwork and antiques highlight this rustic Swiss-style restaurant. Braised duckling, rack of lamb, veal cordon bleu, and chocolate fondue top the menu. *Denver Rd., tel. 607/326–7577. Dress: casual. Reservations required. Closed Mon.–Wed. MC, V. Moderate.*

Lodging **Scudder Hill House.** Home-grown, home-cooked food is the hallmark of this bed-and-breakfast inn located in a former farmhouse. Fresh eggs and bacon, pesto omelets, blueberry pancakes, and a variety of breads and cookies are served in the fireside dining room. Antiques, hand-stenciling, and attractive furnishings make it homey. *Rte. 30, 12474, tel. 607/326–4364. 5 rooms. MC, V. Moderate.*

Shandaken (Ulster)

Dining and Lodging
★ **Auberge des 4 Saisons.** The atmosphere of a European inn prevails here, with some of the rooms located in a chalet, others in the main house where baths are shared. The restaurant serves French country cuisine with specialties from different provinces featured on weekends. Goat cheeses and locally grown vegetables are also featured. *Rte. 41, 12480, tel. 914/688–2223 or 914/688–5480. 36 rooms, 19 with private bath. Restaurant: casual dress. Reservations requested. AE, DC, MC, V. Open daily Memorial Day–Labor Day, weekends rest of year. Moderate.*

Copper Hood Inn. Colonial print bedspreads and Priscilla curtains give an Early American look to the guest rooms here. It's quiet, too: no TVs or telephones, and you can play tennis on a private island. The Continental restaurant serves hotel guests only. *Rte. 28, 12480, tel. 914/688–9962 or 212/261–2341. 20 rooms. Facilities: indoor pool, Jacuzzi, sauna. MC, V. Moderate.*

South Kortright (Delaware)

Dining **The Hidden Inn.** The Friday night surf-and-turf smorgasbord (prime rib, shrimp, crab legs, clams) is a bargain here. Homemade rolls and desserts (cream puffs, chocolate mousse) are other favorites. Local artwork is exhibited in the Colonial dining room. *Main St., tel. 607/538–9359. Dress: casual. Reservations recommended. MC, V. Closed Mon. Inexpensive.*

Stamford (Delaware)

Dining and **Red Carpet Motor Inn.** Motel rooms, some with sitting areas,
Lodging refrigerators, and small decks, surround the pool. The restaurant prides itself on its "all-American" menu—steaks, chops, chicken, and porkchops. A pastry chef prepares mousses, tortes, and other specialties fresh daily. *Rtes. 10 and 23, 12167, tel. 607/652–7394. 37 rooms. Facilities: pool, lounge. AE, DC, MC, V. Moderate.*

Swan Lake (Sullivan)

Dining and **Stevensville Country Club.** One of the major Sullivan County
Lodging super-resorts. This place has 400 rooms, a kosher kitchen, and myriad activities for young and old. *Swan Lake, 12783, tel. 914/292–8000 or 800/431–3858. 400 rooms; AP. Facilities: pools, golf, tennis, racquetball, minigolf, health club, disco. AE, DC, MC, V. Moderate–Expensive.*

Tannersville (Greene)

Dining and **Eggery Inn.** This picturesque bed-and-breakfast inn has a
Lodging Franklin stove and player piano in the parlor lounge, a hand-crafted oak bar in the dining room, and comforters on brass beds in individually appointed rooms. *County Rte. 16, 12485, tel. 518/589–5363. 15 rooms, breakfast included. AE, MC, V. Moderate.*
Villa Vosilla Resort. A honeymoon suite with Jacuzzi and king-size bed, and a three-room family suite are among 100 motel and lodge units. The restaurant serves northern Italian fare. *Main St., 12485, tel. 518/589–5060 or 800/543–1450. 100 rooms. Facilities: pool, sauna/spa, exercise room, game room, nightly entertainment. AE, DC, MC, V. Moderate.*

Westkill (Greene)

Dining and **Schwarzenegger's Sunshine Valley House.** The German owners
Lodging call their location, situated in a wide valley surrounded by five mountains, "a small Bavaria." Rooms are available with breakfast only or with three German-American meals. *Spruceton Rd., 12492, tel. 518/989–9794. 18 rooms; bed-and-breakfast or AP. Facilities: pool. MC, V. Inexpensive.*

White Lake (Sullivan)

Dining **The Lighthouse.** The exterior doesn't look like a lighthouse, but there's a bit of a nautical theme in the dining room. Seafood, chops, steaks, and some Italian dishes are offered here, and the deck overlooks lovely White Lake. *Rte. 17B, tel. 914/583–9865. Dress: casual. MC, V. Inexpensive–Moderate.*

Windham (Greene)

Dining **La Griglia.** Elegant and intimate, this fine northern Italian and
★ Yugoslavian restaurant specializes in such items as scaloppini of pork sautéed with tomato, garlic, and fruit juices and layered with grilled apples; desserts include chocolate Frangelica mousse torte and apricot *spuma*. It also may have the best wine list in upstate New York. A brunch-type menu, taken pri-

marily from the appetizer list, is available at a cafe with out-door seating overlooking the golf course. *Rte. 296, tel. 518/734–4499. Dress: casual (no jeans). Reservations required. AE, MC, V. Expensive.*

Chalet Fondue. As the name implies, fondues are the specialty here—beef, veal, cheese, chocolate. German, Swiss, and Austrian dishes, such as *jagerschnitzel*—fresh veal with a creamy mushroom sauce—are served in an Alpine atmosphere. Dine in the wicker-and-glass greenhouse or in the rathskeller, where wine barrels line the walls. *Rte. 296, tel. 518/734–4650. Dress: casual. Reservations required. AE, DC, MC, V. Open Thurs.–Mon. summer; daily except Tues. winter; other times call. Moderate.*

Dining and Lodging
★
Thompson House. Guests are remembered by their first names at this resort that has been run by five generations of the same family for over a century. Guest rooms, including some Jacuzzi suites, are located in the 1860s-era main house, the Victorian Spruce Cottage, and several other buildings. *Rte. 296, 12496, tel. 518/734– 4510. 110 rooms. Facilities: pool, tennis, putting greens, recreation room. MC, V. Open May–Oct. and ski season. Inexpensive–Moderate.*

Wurtsboro (Sullivan)

Dining
★
The Repast. This is an elegant eatery in a country sort of way. Such entrees as salmon Dijon and *poulet portofino* (sautéed breast of chicken with a banana-liqueur sauce), seafood, and big lamb chops are served with Caesar salad and homemade desserts. Come for lunch and follow it up with a visit to the adjacent Canal Towne Emporium, a restored 1845 country store. *Sullivan St., tel. 914/888–4448. Dress: casual. Reservations suggested. MC, V. Open daily for lunch; Thurs.–Sun. for dinner. Moderate.*

Yulan (Sullivan)

Dining
YesterYears. Try the blackened fish, jambalaya, or the duck à l'orange at this rural restaurant that mingles French, New Orleans, and American cuisines. Red tablecloths covered with lace, red velvet drapes, and oak floors adorn the three dining rooms. Chocolate velvet cake is a favorite here. *Four Corners, tel. 914/557–6464. Dress: casual. Reservations suggested. MC, V. Open May–Oct. Moderate.*

The Arts and Nightlife

The Arts

For centuries artists have found their creative muse in the Catskills. The trend continues. Outstanding craftsmen are moving here from New York City and finding that without the pressures of city life, they can make a living by their craft.

Several well-established regional art and cultural organizations offer a full menu of performing and decorative arts year-round, although in summer the cultural calendar is especially busy. The wide array of performances embraces music, theater, and dance, as well as film and literary series and changing art exhibits. Contact the following groups for schedules of events and exhibits:

Art Awareness, Inc. Sponsors exhibits, experimental theater, dance, and musical events in and around a former Victorian hotel on Schoharie Creek. *Rte. 42, Lexington, tel. 518/989–6433.*

Bond Street Theater Coalition. Offers music, theater, dance, children's programs, and workshops during August. *Palenville Interarts Colony, Woodstock Ave., Palenville, tel. 518/678–3332.*

Catskill Mountain Theatre. Summer performances by professional and local talent at various outdoor locations and at the Halcottsville Creamery. *Tel. 914/586–4894 or 212/884–4230.*

Catskills' Dance Theater. Dance company and schedule of guest artists. *Athens Community Center, Athens, tel. 518/734–3807.*

Delaware Valley Arts Alliance. Sponsors art events and maintains a gallery with rotating exhibits. *Main St., Narrowsburg, tel. 914/252–7576.*

Erpf Catskill Cultural Center. Named after the late Armund Erpf, art patron and philanthropist, the center sponsors summer readings, a winter concert series, and regular exhibits. It is reconstructing a round barn in Halcottsville for use as a regional museum and folk-arts center. *Arkville, tel. 914/586–3326.*

Green County Council on the Arts. Maintains galleries at 398 Main Street in Catskill, and on Main Street in Windham; also sponsors special arts events throughout the year. *Box 463, Catskill, tel. 518/943–3400.*

Handcrafts at Clearbrook. Works by local artists. *Rte. 32, Cairo, tel. 518/622–9083.*

Roxbury Arts Group. Programs year-round arts events for Delaware County, including an annual Chamber Music Festival in July, an outdoor art show, a country fair, and changing gallery shows. *Main St., Roxbury, tel. 607/326–7908.*

Shadowland Theater. Professional stage company in residence year-round. *157 Canal St., Ellenville, tel. 914/647–5511.*

Silver Cloud Music Festivals. Wide-ranging musical offerings staged from June to September in a natural amphitheater at the Rondout Valley Country Club in Accord. *Box 346, High Falls, tel. 914/331–4183 or 914/687–9007.*

Stone House Gallery. Paintings, sculpture, furniture, jewelry. *Off Rte. 23A, 1 mi east of Lexington, tel. 518/989–6755.*

Sullivan County Museum, Art & Cultural Center. Shows, classes, lectures, and monthly exhibits at the headquarters of the Sullivan County Historical Society, the Catskill Art Society, and the Sullivan County Dramatic Workshop, all in Hurleyville. *Tel. 914/434–8044.*

Sullivan County Arts Council. Presents ballets, musicals, jazz, opera. *Sullivan County Community College, Loch Sheldrake, tel. 914/434–5750.*

Thornwood Center for the Performing Arts. Sponsors music and dance events and the annual Central New York Renaissance Fair in August. *Delhi, tel. 607/746–2910.*

West Kortright Centre. Storytelling, dance, community socials, and music held at an 1850s Greek Revival Church. *East Meredith, tel. 607/278–5454.*

Nightlife

Some of the spots with regular live entertainment include the **Hunter Village Inn** (Main St., Hunter, tel. 518/263–4788), catering to the skiing-singles crowd; **Mount Pleasant Lodge** (Rte. 28, Phoenicia, tel. 914/688–2278), with weekend dance music primarily for the under-30 set; **Pursuit of Happiness** (117 S. Main St., Liberty, tel. 914/292–6760), where you'll hear local and nationally known performers of everything from bluegrass to jazz; **Railz** (Rte. 28, Arkville, tel. 914/586–2992), a pizzeria and Italian-food restaurant where New York metropolitan-area bands draw a 20- to 40-year-old crowd; **The Square Restaurant** (Binnekill Square, Main St., Margaretville, tel. 914/586–4884), with a piano bar popular with the over-40 crowd.

7 Leatherstocking Country

Introduction

"Off the Beaten Track," a subheading in most travel listings, sums up Leatherstocking Country. Encompassing nine counties and 7,000 square miles, the region is roughly defined by three rivers: the Susquehanna, Chenango, and Mohawk. These historic waterways, with their romantic Indian names, are now traced by the concrete infrastructure of Routes 88, 90, and 81. Travelers accustomed to exhaust-choked commutes at home will marvel as the panorama of pastoral central New York State swirls by on wide-open Route 88 between Schenectady and Binghamton, a 2½-hour drive.

Visit Bleinheim's historic covered bridge in Schoharie County. Take a side trip to Cooperstown, home of the Farmers' Museum, the Baseball Hall of Fame, and the lakeside Glimmerglass Opera. Divert the car to Route 7, which parallels both the river and Route 88, and be on the lookout for out-of-the-way antiques shops and canoeing and fishing spots.

Binghamton, at the junction of Routes 88 and 81, is the largest city in the region, and has museums, theaters, a zoo, shopping centers, and a good variety of accommodations. State, municipal and county parks offer picnic spots, camping, and hiking. And, the Triple Cities—Binghamton, Johnson City, and Endicott—have five operating carousels.

Leatherstocking Country's diverse ethnic heritage is most evident in Binghamton. The early Yankees in their leather leggings gave the region its nickname, but the later waves of immigrants from Eastern Europe, attracted by the factory jobs in the "Parlor City" (so named for the Broome County cigar factories) have left a legacy of onion-domed churches, Lenten specialty feasts, and the Roberson-Kopernik Observatory, named for an early Polish astronomer.

Heading north, bypass I-81 for the slower pace of Route 12. The stately old villages along the way—Greene, Cazenovia, and Norwich among them—showcase small-town America. Take a walking tour down tree-lined avenues, past imposing, elegant houses and town halls; duck into an inn for lunch; then pause for a rest in the village square.

For a quintessential rural experience, check for signs announcing chicken barbecues. Firemen, both volunteer and paid squads, know the nuances of barbecueing chicken to perfection. And for the price of dessert at a big-city restaurant, you'll not only get a full dinner (perhaps with dessert), but an earful of suggestions of things to see and do from local residents sharing your table.

Where Route 12 meets the New York State Thruway (I-90), stands the city of Utica, at the far eastern edge of Oneida County. Take a brewery tour, visit the zoo or museums, or shop at Charlestown, the old munitions factory that's now a factory outlet center. Utica is rich with Italian restaurants. Just about anyone can direct you to the well-known ones, but save some time for the smaller, family operations in the city's Little Italy.

The Mohawk Valley's past as the site of Revolutionary War battles and, with the completion of the Erie Canal in 1825, the Industrial Revolution, is preserved in monuments, battlefields, and living museums such as Old Fort Johnson.

Follow Route 5, or drop down to Route 20, to explore the in̄ or of Leatherstocking Country. Take the unmarked side roads and the county routes along the way. Asking directions could lead you to another find—a bookstore stacked with out-of-print treasures, an auction, a dairy bar with the cows dotting the hills in the background. Take along bicycles, hiking boots, or a canoe—or cross-country skis and snowshoes in winter—to explore the quietness of the gently rolling rural setting with only your exercise-labored breathing to disturb the sounds of nature.

Essential Information

Getting Around

By Plane Leatherstocking Country has two airports. Utica–Rome is served by **Mohawk Airlines** (tel. 800/252–2144), while Binghamton's Link Field is served by **USAir** and **USAir Express** (both tel. 800/428–4253), **Continental Express** (tel. 800/525–0280), **TWA Express** (tel. 800/221–2000), and **United Express** (tel. 800/241–6522).

By Train **Amtrak** (tel. 800/872–7245) serves Amsterdam, Utica, and Rome.

By Bus **Greyhound** (tel. 800/528–0447) has regular service to several Leatherstocking communities from Buffalo, Scranton–Wilkes Barre, PA, Albany, and New York City.

By Car The region is 200–300 miles northeast of New York City via the New York State Thruway and Route 28 from Kingston. It can also be reached via I–81 from Scranton, about 70 miles south of Binghamton; I–90 from Boston to Buffalo, via Albany and Utica; and I–88 from Albany to Binghamton via Oneonta.

Guided Tours

Cooperstown Historic Tour (tel. 607/547–5134) is a 45-minute limousine tour that covers 200 years of local history and is available year-round. The cost is $10 per person, with a minimum of 4.

Important Addresses and Numbers

Tourist Information The Binghamton, Cooperstown, and Mohawk Valley–Utica tourist bureaus all publish a variety of free maps, booklets, and brochures with information about accommodations, restaurants, shopping, and entertainment. In areas without a tourist bureau, the local county or town chamber of commerce usually functions as the center for tourist information and referrals. Most offices are open weekdays 9–5.

Broome County Convention & Visitors Bureau (Security Mutual Building, 80 Exchange St., Box 995, Binghamton 13902, tel. 607/772–8860).

Cooperstown Chamber of Commerce (Chestnut Street, Box 46, Cooperstown 13326, tel. 607/547–9983).

Oneida County Convention & Visitors Bureau (Mohawk Valley–Utica, Box AA, Oriskany 13424, tel. toll-free in NY 800/237–0100).

Leatherstocking Country, NY (200 N. Prospect St., Herkimer 13350, tel. 315/866–1500).

Chenango County Chamber of Commerce (29 Lackawannna Ave., Box 249, Norwich 13815, tel. 607/334–3236).

Oneonta Chamber of Commerce (58 Market St., Oneonta 13820, tel. 607/432–4500).

Greater Utica Chamber of Commerce (258 Genesee St., Utica 13502, 315/724–3151).

Emergencies   Dial "0" for police or ambulance assistance.

Hospitals   Emergency rooms: **Binghamton General Hospital** (Mitchell Ave., tel. 607/770–6611), **The Mary Imogene Bassett Hospital** (Atwell Rd., Cooperstown, tel. 607/547–3355), **St. Elizabeth Hospital** (2209 Greene St., Utica, tel. 315/798–8111).

Exploring Leatherstocking Country

Numbers in the margin correspond with points of interest on the Leatherstocking Country map.

We'll start our tour at Cooperstown, then introduce you to the Mohawk Valley and Binghamton areas.

First made famous by James Fenimore Cooper's "Leather-stocking Tales," **Cooperstown** is now home to a number of museums and historic landmarks. Fans of the great American pastime make pilgrimages to the **National Baseball Hall of Fame** throughout the year, particularly in the summer. Even if you're not a fan, you'll enjoy seeing this temple of baseball: Babe Ruth dominates the entry area. Large displays, photographs, paintings, and audiovisual presentations trace the origin of the game and the development of the museum from a one-room exhibit to today's 50,000-square-foot display area. Savor the nostalgia of Abbott and Costello's engaging "Who's on First?" routine, as well as the radio broadcast from a 1950s World Series game. Baseball movies are shown periodically throughout the day in the National Baseball Library, and there's a gift shop with all manner of baseball mementos. Just down the street from the Hall of Fame is **Doubleday Field,** where baseball began back in 1839 and where the annual Hall-of-Fame Game takes place each summer when new members are inducted. *Main St., tel. 607/547–9988. Admission: $6 adults, $2.50 children 7–15. Open May 1–Oct. 31, daily 9–9; Nov. 1–Apr. 30, daily 9–5. Closed Thanksgiving, Christmas, and New Year's Day.*

Paramount among local landmarks is the **Farmers' Museum,** a historic farm complex with permanent exhibits and daily demonstrations of blacksmithing, food preparations, spinning, and weaving. Visitors can play 19th-century games, take a wagon ride, or sample the food cooked in the fireplace of the Lippitt Farmhouse. At the village crossroads, a group of 19th-century buildings draws you back into history. The Main Barn, once a working dairy, features an introductory exhibit, weaving loft, and woodworking areas. *Route 80, 1 mi north of Cooperstown. Lake Rd., tel. 607/547–2593. Admission: $6 adults; $2.50 children 7–15. Open May–Oct., 9–6. Call for winter schedule.*

Down the road from the Farmers' Museum is **Fenimore House,** headquarters of the New York State Historical Association and a museum of James Fenimore Cooper memorabilia. It is home to a fine collection of American folk art—billed as the extraordinary creations of ordinary people. The collection includes 19th- and 20th-century paintings, sculptures, textiles, ceramics, decoys, weather vanes, and other decorative objects. *Admission: $5 adults, $2 children 7–15. Open daily May–Oct., 9–6. Call for winter schedule. Combination tickets are available from the Farmers' Museum and the Baseball Hall of Fame. All three attractions, $13 adults, $5 children. For more information about the Farmers' Museum and the Fenimore House, contact the New York State Historical Association, Lake Rd., Box 800, Cooperstown 13326, tel. 607/547–2533.*

Time Out   **Pioneer's Patio** is a friendly German-style restaurant serving big sandwiches, wursts, beer, wine, and cold beverages. In summer there's alfresco dining on a flower-laden porch. *46 Pioneer Alley, tel. 607/547–5601. Open Oct.–Apr., 7 AM–3 PM; Apr.–Oct., 7 AM–9PM. No credit cards. Inexpensive.*

For a relaxing prelude to dinner, take an hour-long cruise on ❷ **Lake Otsego**—James Fenimore Cooper's Glimmerglass. Excursions on the *Chief Uncas*, and the *Narra Mattah*—two classic wooden luxury launches built at the turn of the century and refurbished in the '50s—depart from the Lake Front Marina Lighthouse at the foot of Fair Street. Operated by Lake Otsego Boat Tours of Cooperstown, both hour-long cruises take in historic and scenic sights halfway up the nine-mile-long lake. *Tel. 607/547–5295; charter information, tel. 607/547–8238. Fare: $8 adults, $5 children 3–12. Departures daily on the hour 10–6, mid-May–mid-Oct.*

❸ About a 1½-hour drive southwest of Cooperstown is **Binghamton,** a city of 64,000 whose civic pride centers on a bounty of attractions, including **The Roberson Center for the Arts and Sciences,** a complex of museums, galleries, ballet studios, a planetarium, and a 300-seat theater. The center's collections and exhibitions represent and interpret the region's history, art, and sciences. Exhibits range from ancient pottery to paintings by American masters. Both the center's headquarters and the Broome County Historical Society's museum are located in the restored Roberson Mansion, a handsome Renaissance Revival structure. Roberson offers classes in a variety of arts and crafts, sponsors an annual Holiday and Arts Festival in early September and a Christmas Forest each December, and publishes a monthly calendar of events. *30 Front St., Binghamton 13905, tel. 607/772–0660. Admission: $3 adults, $1.50 children 5–16, $2 senior citizens; free on first Tues. of the month. Some special activities or programs carry a nominal fee. Open Tues.–Thurs., Sat. 10–5, Fri. 10–9, Sun. noon–5.*

Ross Park Zoo opened in 1875, making it one of the country's oldest zoos. With its diverse terrain, rock hedges, and shale stratifications, the heavily wooded 25-acre compound displays animals in their natural habitat. The woodland waters exhibit provides a naturalistic setting for beaver, otter, native waterfowl, and fish. Recently completed was the cat-country exhibit, which has cougars, a white Bengal and an orange Siberian tiger. The visitors' area is glassed, and the cats are free to prowl

Leatherstocking Country

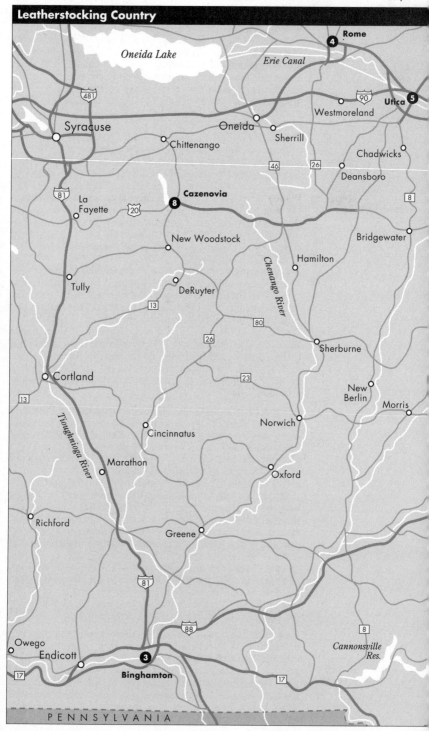

Oneida Lake

Erie Canal

Rome 4

481

90 **Utica** 5

Westmoreland

Syracuse

Oneida

Sherrill

Chittenango

Chadwicks

46 26

Deansboro

8

81

La Fayette

20

Cazenovia 8

New Woodstock

Bridgewater

Hamilton

Chenango River

Tully

DeRuyter

13

80

26

Sherburne

23

Cortland

New Berlin

Morris

13

Cincinnatus

Norwich

Tioughnioga River

Marathon

Oxford

Richford

Greene

81

88

8

Owego

Endicott

3

Cannonsville Res.

17

Binghamton

17

PENNSYLVANIA

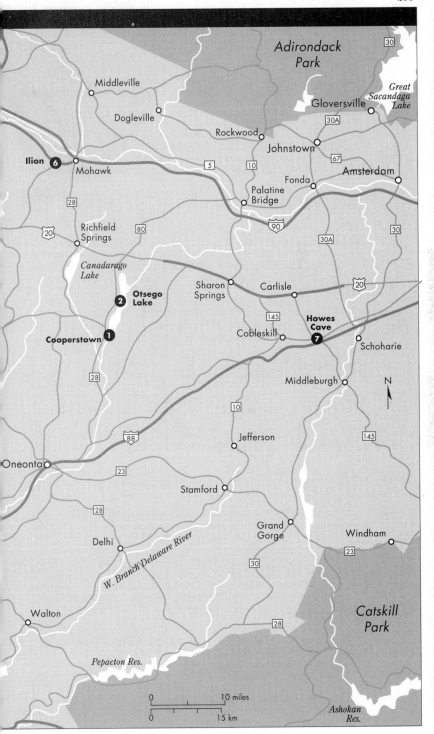

around among plants, rocks, and a pool. Special crowd-pleasers include the timberwolf pack, which thrives in the 2½-acre wolf compound, the children's petting zoo, and the free, recently restored carousel. There is also an education center, a waterfowl pond, a gift shop, an amphitheater, and picnic facilities. *185 Park Ave. and Morgan Rd., Binghamton 13903, tel. 607/724–5461. Admission: $2, 75¢ senior citizens, children under 2 free. Open Apr. 2–Nov. 15, 10–4:30.*

The $3 Ross Park Pass includes admission to the **Discovery Center,** a hands-on children's museum where the motto is "Nothing is ever complete." All exhibits are interactive, each spurring an idea that eventually turns into another exhibit. The Discovery Center was designed with children in mind, but adults can't seem to stay away. Climb into a real jet cockpit or "drive" the fire truck. Bubble trays, light arcades, and a zoo motel are a few of the attractions. *Tel. 607/773–8661. Admission: $2.50, children under 3 free. Open Tues.–Sat. 10–4, Sun. noon–5.*

Time Out   **Whole in the Wall** is a natural-food restaurant with the motto: "You are what you wheat." Try the locally famous cream of mushroom soup with some homemade whole-grain bread and butter. Also featured are lovely fresh salads and chicken and seafood entrees. *435 Washington St., tel. 607/722–0006. Open weekdays 11:30–2 and 5–8:30, Sat. 11:30–8:30. Inexpensive.*

Walter Edmonds made the Mohawk Valley famous in his Revolutionary War epic *Drums Along the Mohawk*. Here you'll find such historic monuments as Herkimer Home, Old Stone Fort, and Oriskany Battlefield, as well as at **Rome,** the **Fort Stanwix National Monument.** Originally a British post, Fort Stanwix was abandoned and later taken over by the Americans to defend the Mohawk Valley during the Revolutionary War. On Sunday, August 3, 1777, forces commanded by British General John Burgoyne and Colonel Barry St. Leger laid siege to the fort. Six days later, Colonel Peter Gansevoort wrote to St. Leger, "It is my Determined resolution with the Forces under my Command, to defend the Fort to the last Extremity. . . ." Fortunately, Gansevoort's "last extremity" was not required. After a 21-day siege, the British retreated in the face of the advancing relief troops of the Continental Army.

This Continental Army outpost is a faithful reconstruction of the original and includes barracks, storehouse, bastion, museum, Indian trade center, and officers' quarters. Self-guided walking tour. *Located in downtown Rome off Exit 33 of the New York State Thruway, at the intersections of Rtes. 365, 49, and 69; 112 E. Park St., 13440, tel. 315/336–2090. Admission: $1, children under 16 free. Open Apr. 1–Dec. 31, 9–5. Closed Thanksgiving and Christmas. Visitors may park at the city parking garage on N. James St.*

You can relive the days when the warning, "Low bridge— everybody down!" was commonplace at the **Erie Canal Village,** a circa-1840 village reconstructed near the spot where the first shovelful of dirt was turned for "Clinton's Folly," as the waterway was disparagingly known. Ride the 1840 horse-drawn passenger packet boat along a refurbished section of the original canal or take the narrow-gauge steam train ride and explore the village, a cluster of buildings typical of a 19th-century canal hamlet. These include Bennett's Tavern (still serving cold draft

beer or root beer), a church meeting house, a blac[...]
a weaving and spinning house, a schoolhouse, an[...]
cabin. Seasonal events take place at the village an[...]
There's the Visitors Reception Center, a gift shop, ...u a snack
bar. *Rte. 49W, Rome 13440, tel. 315/336–6000 ext. 250 or 315/
337–3999 (weekends). Open mid-May–Sept., daily 10–5. Admission: $6 adults, $5 children 12–17, $3 children 7–11, under
7 free.*

Port Rickey Discovery Zoo features exotic and native animals
and a large petting and feeding area. There are pony rides, a
gift shop, and a picnic area. *Rtes. 46/49W, 3 mi W., Rome, tel.
315/336–1930. Open mid-May–Sept. 30, 10–6. Admission:
$3.25 adults, $2.25 children 2–13.*

⑤ **Utica** lies just east of Rome. Here you'll find the **Utica Zoo,**
home to mammals, birds, reptiles, and a children's zoo with
petting area and picnic facilities. Located in Roscoe Conkling
Park—designed by Frederick Law Olmsted, who also planned
Central Park in New York City—the zoo has more than 300 animals, from polar bears and Siberian tigers to tropical birds and
primates. In Zoolab, children can explore the contents of 10
self-discovery boxes dealing with such subjects as animal
coverings, reptiles, and zoo-animal diets. The most popular exhibits are the big cats and the California sea lions. *Steel Hill
Rd., Utica, tel. 315/738–0472. Open year-round, 10–5. Children's zoo operates mid-May–Oct. Admission: $3 adults, $1.50
children 2–12.*

The **Children's Museum of History, Natural History, and Science** is a handsomely restored building that houses what's
billed as the finest children's museum between New York City
and Toronto. It features hands-on exhibits, educational programs, and creative crafts. There is free parking in the lot diagonally across from the museum. *311 Main St., Utica, tel. 315/
724–6128. Open July 5–Labor Day, Tues.–Sat. 10–4:30, Sun.
1:30–4:30. Closed Mon. and most major holidays. Admission:
$1.50, children under 3 free.*

For a refreshing change of pace, stop in for a tour of the **F. X.
Matt Brewery.** The staff—some in period dress—greet visitors
with a warm welcome; you can end the tour with beer (or root
beer). The brewery tour, trolley shuttle, and a visit to the 1888
tavern takes about an hour. *Court and Varick Sts., Utica, tel.
315/732–0022. Open June–Aug., weekdays 10–5. Closed weekends and July 4th. Open Sept.–May, weekdays by reservation
only. Admission: $2, children under 12 free.*

Annie Oakley wasn't called "Little Miss Sure Shot" for nothing;
she hit the mark every time with a Remington 22 rifle. At the
⑥ **Remington Firearms Museum,** in **Ilion,** you'll find a collection of
handguns, rifles, and shotguns including flintlocks, percussion
rifles, Civil War muzzle loaders, and "transition rifles" that led
to modern repeaters. The gallery features guns belonging to
the famous—and the infamous. *Catherine St. off Route 5S,
Ilion, tel. 315/894–9961. Open year-round. Self-guided tour
Mon.–Sat. 9–4. Plant tour 1 PM weekdays. Admission free.*

If you're looking for a cool spot on a hot summer day, drop in at
⑦ **Howes Cave** to check out **Howes Caverns,** Leatherstocking's underground natural wonder. Beneath the picturesque countryside is a prehistoric world. Guided tours through the underground caverns wind for nearly 1½ miles along paved walk-

ways and over man-made and natural bridges. Knowledgeable guides explain uncommon rock formations, such as the Titan's Temple with its Chinese Pagoda. The cavern tour includes a quarter-mile boat ride on an underground lake. *Rte. 7 between Central Bridge and Cobleskill, tel. 518/296–8990. Open year-round, 9–6. Admission: $8.50 adults, $4.25 children 7–12, $3.25 children 6 and under, but free when accompanied by parents.*

8 **Cazenovia,** on scenic Route 20, is one of the region's prettiest towns. "Situation superb, fine land" were the words of John Lincklaen, agent for the Holland Land Company when he first viewed the land at the foot of Cazenovia Lake, where he would build his home. Lincklaen's elegant Federal-style mansion, with 20 acres of lawns, formal gardens, and wooded groves, is known as **Lorenzo.** There's a collection of horse-drawn vehicles and a restored carriage house. Guided tours of the house are available, and picnicking and cross-country skiing are permitted on the grounds. Special events such as the Annual Driving Competition, Harvest Day, and Christmas Open House are held here. *Rte. 13 (¼ mi south of Rte. 20), tel. 315/655–3200. Admission free. Open May–Labor Day, Wed.–Sat. and Mon. holidays 10–5; Sun. 1–5. Grounds open year-round, 8–sunset.*

Time Out For a taste of the pioneering days and the true flavor of the backroads, head 25 miles south of Utica on Route 8 to the **Gates Hill Homestead** in Brookfield Valley. Donna Tunney wrote a children's book, *The Eternal Hills,* about the land her father settled and she and her husband, Charles, turned into a rambling 1700s-style pioneering homestead from the fieldstone and logs they found on their 64 acres of land. Today it's the Tunneys' restaurant and three-bedroom B&B. Guests are brought here—along the twisting road up the picturesque valley and over a covered bridge—by a four-horse stagecoach (sleigh ride in winter). Everyone feasts family-style, under candlelight chandeliers, on homemade breads and rolls, chicken breast with cranberry-orange relish or smoked ham with cranberry-raisin sauce, various salads and home-baked desserts. Overnight guests don't soon forget the breakfast either. *Gates Hill Homestead, Brookfield 13314, tel. 315/ 899–5837. Reservations required. MC, V. Dress: "respectably casual." Closed mid-Mar.–end of Apr. Inexpensive– Moderate.*

What to See and Do with Children

Leatherstocking Country is family-oriented. Although some attractions might be a bit esoteric for very young children, they, too, are usually allowed to participate. The **National Baseball Hall of Fame, Ross Park Zoo, The Discovery Center, Utica Zoo, Children's Museum of History, Erie Canal Village, Port Rickey Game Farm, Lake Otsego Cruise,** and **Howes Caverns** are all described above. Children will also enjoy the **Music Museum** (*see* Off the Beaten Track, below).

Rogers Environmental Center is a 571-acre preserve dedicated to teaching young people to appreciate and conserve natural resources. *Rte. 80W, Box 716, Sherburne 13460, tel. 607/674–4017. Admission free. Open weekdays 8:30–4:45, weekends 1–5; grounds open during daylight hours. Trails open 24 hrs a day.*

Off the Beaten Track

The "hands-on" policy of the **Musical Museum** in **Deansboro,** just south of Utica, invites you to crank, pump, and play restored music boxes, melodeons, nickelodeons, grind organs, and much more. Whether your musical tastes run to Paderewski's playing Chopin's rousing "Polonaise in A" or Elvis singing "You Ain't Nothin' But a Hound Dog," this museum will strike just the right note with any music fancier. There are 17 rooms (don't miss the giant calliope), a shop that stocks parts, special fabrics, information on repairing various music antiques, and a picnic area. The Old Lamplighter shop specializes in antique lamps, lamp parts, repairs, and restorations, and has an impressive variety of china shades. *Rte. 12B, Deansboro, tel. 315/841-8774. Open Apr. 1–Dec. 31, 10–4. Admission: $3.50 adults; $2.50 children 6–12, under 6 free; $3 senior citizens.*

Shopping

Auctions A dollar can go a long, long way here, and given the quaint and unusual items on the block, chances are you'll quickly become an auction junkie. It's fun and folksy, old-time Americana at its best, with a language all its own. Admission is free. A wealth of antiques—Civil War uniforms to toys, books to ornate furniture—are passed on in an amusing, mesmerizing blur. Snacks and homemade lunches can be hearty and downright cheap. Some auctions are held at the "estates" themselves; but most are at auction barns. For locations, look for posters at the local general store, churches, and in local newspapers.

Bazaars Churches, schools, and community centers, particularly on weekends in summer and fall, are good places to sniff out excellent, true values in the otherwise forgotten American art of handicrafts.

For a break from the usual malls and shopping districts (of which Leatherstocking Country has plenty), visit **Charlestown Factory Outlet Center,** which features about 25 name-brand and one-of-a-kind specialty shops. Though the prices are not particularly low, shopping in this converted munitions factory is fun. *311 Turner St., Utica, tel. 315/724-8175. Open Mon.– Thurs. 10–5, Fri. 10–9, Sat. 10–6, Sun. noon–5.*

The region abounds in 19th-century Americana. Almost every town has its antiques dealers, so be alert for the signs. Saturdays are best; many dealers do not have set hours and are open by inspiration or by appointment. In Binghamton, don't miss **Clinton Street's** antiques row, where deceptively derelict storefronts hide a multitude of treasures, including lots of oak furniture. There is also **General Clinton Antiques,** which offers period pieces and collectibles. *132 Clinton St., Binghamton, tel. 607/723-1596. Open Tues.–Sat. 10–5.*

A more upscale housewares outlet is the **Oneida Silversmith's Factory Store** in Sherrill, which features silver, stainless steel, pewter, silverplate, flatware, cutlery, hollowware, china, and glass. *Sherrill Rd. at Noyes Blvd., Sherrill, tel. 315/361-3661. Mon.–Sat. 9–4:30.*

Another good bet is the **China Factory Outlet** in Oneida, specializing in Noritake china and nationally advertised stoneware, along with Royal Doulton and Minton, at discount prices. *30 Genesee St., Rte. 5, Oneida, tel. 315/363–4231. Weekdays 9:30–5:30, Sat. 9:30–5.*

Participant Sports

The Leatherstocking region lures a broad spectrum of sports lovers. Almost every town has swimming pools and tennis courts open to the public either free or for a modest fee. The fishing is excellent, with public access areas along rivers and streams.

Beaches   Although firmly landlocked, there are several large, beautiful lakes at state parks, with excellent beaches, boat rentals, concession stands, and hot showers. Except for weekends, they're uncrowded. Fees range from nothing to $3.50. Four-mile-long **Sylvan Beach** (tel. 315/762–9934) is one of the best known. Contact county tourist offices (*see* Important Addresses and Numbers, above).

Horseback Riding   Hone your equestrian skills at **Fieldstone Farm** (lessons, English- and western-style) in Richfield Springs, tel. 315/858–0295.

Golf   Leatherstocking has many courses; those listed here are 18-hole courses: **Afton Golf Club** (Afton, tel. 607/639–2454), **Seven Oaks Golf Club** (Hamilton, tel. 315/824–1432), **Canasawacta Country Club** (Norwich, tel. 607/336–2685), and **En-Joie Golf Club** (Endicott, tel. 607/785–1661). Golfers with short attention spans should try **Hot Diggitty Dog Golf** (Rtes. 46/49, Rome, tel. 315/339–3333).

Skiing   Skiers can find downhill action at **Shu-maker Mountain** (Little Falls, tel. 315/823–1111), **Snow Ridge Ski Area** (Turin, tel. 315/348–8456 or 800/962–8419 in NY), or **Ironwood Ridge** (Cazenovia, tel. 315/655–9551).

Spectator Sports

Baseball   The **Oneonta Yankees** (a NY Yankees farm team) play Class-A ball at Damaschke Field in Oneonta, tel. 607/432–4500. Also, the National Baseball Hall of Fame's All-Star and Old Timers' games are played at Abner Doubleday Field in Cooperstown during August.

Horse Racing   Place your bets on spirited trotters and pacers competing for almost $5 million in purses at **Vernon Downs** (Vernon, tel. 315/829–2201), from mid-April through early November.

Motocross   In mid-July, the pace heats up with **U.S. Grand Prix Motocross** action at the Unadilla Valley Sports Center in New Berlin. For information, contact Ward Robinson (Box 5119F, Edmeston 13335, tel. 607/965–8784 or 607/847–8186).

Polo   Matches are played on Sundays at the **Village Farms Polo Club** (Gilbertsville, tel. 607/783–2764 or 607/783–2737). The season runs from early June through early September. Starting time is 3 PM. *Admission: $3 adults, children under 12 free. Call for schedule.*

Dining and Lodging

Dining From price to cuisine, eating out in Leatherstocking Country exemplifies middle-American dining. The region's only culinary claim to fame is the *spiedie*, which hails from the Binghamton area. Spiedies (originally lamb, but now often beef, pork, or chicken) are lean chunks of marinated meat grilled on a skewer and served on Italian bread. Spiedies appear in many of the local restaurants, but most Binghamtonians maintain a loyalty to their favorite spiedie spot.

One of the pleasures of a summer evening is driving into Endicott's Union District (near Binghamton) for a spiedie from Lupo's Deli and then backtracking to Pat Mitchell's on Main Street for a double dip of award-winning ice cream. To really be a part of the in crowd, you have to sit on the cemetery wall abutting Pat's store and eat a banana split while watching traffic pile up as half of Endicott stops in for their ice-cream fix.

Category	Cost*
Very Expensive	over $60
Expensive	$40–$60
Moderate	$20–$40
Inexpensive	under $20

per person without tax (6%–8%, depending on the county), service, or drinks

Lodging "You get what you pay for" is a good rule in Leatherstocking. With few exceptions, most accommodations fall within the inexpensive-to-moderate range. Keep in mind that Cooperstown is a summer resort; reservations should be made at least six weeks in advance. The area has a lot of colleges and universities, which makes it a bit difficult to get a room if you're visiting Binghamton, Oneonta, Cobleskill, or Hamilton during late August—parents' weekend—or mid-May—graduation.

Bed-and-Breakfast Accommodations range from sharing the family homestead to cozy rooms in refurbished barns, furnished with antiques from the local auction; from Victorian cottages to luxurious Colonial mansions set in manicured, lakeside estates. For those who can't bear to be away from urban necessities, many B&Bs come with Jacuzzis and VCRs. Prices range from $35 to $75 for two persons, $10–$20 for an additional bed; big, back-to-the-farm breakfasts are included.

Some B&Bs don't list at all, they merely hang up a sign when they feel like it. If you don't like taking chances—and don't, especially in summer and fall—compare properties listed with B&B collectives. For details and reservations, two good bets are: **The American Country Collection** (984 Gloucester Pl., Schenectady 12309, tel. 518/370–4948) and **Bed & Breakfast Leatherstocking** (389 Brockway Rd., Frankfort 13340, tel. 315/733–0040).

Highly recommended dining and lodging establishments are indicated by a star ★.

Category	Cost*
Very Expensive	over $120
Expensive	$90–$120
Moderate	$50–$90
Inexpensive	under $50

double room without tax (4%–7%, depending on the county) or service

Binghamton

Dining **Drovers Inn.** This lovely old mansion in Vestal (near Binghamton) has been converted into the most elegant inn in the area. A
★ beautiful lounge has tables for two; even more intimate is the Rose Room (it seats a maximum of four diners). Try the chateaubriand for two; for dessert, nothing but Chocolate Decadence will do. *2 N. Main St., Vestal, tel. 607/785–4199. Dress: informal. Reservations strongly recommended. Rose Room must be booked in advance. AE, DC, MC, V. Moderate–Expensive.*

Lodging **Best Western Hotel de Ville.** Located in the former City Hall in the heart of the downtown business district, this lovely hotel has 63 luxurious rooms and an American-cuisine restaurant, Dion's. An outstanding example of French Renaissance architecture in the late-Beaux Arts style, the building is listed on the National Register of Historic Places. *80 State St., 13901, tel. 607/722–0000. AE, DC, MC, V. Expensive–Very Expensive.*
Econo-Lodge. The 155 rooms in this centrally located motel are basic but pleasant. Some rooms have saunas, Jacuzzis, and waterbeds. There's an outdoor pool, a lounge with live music, and a daily "happy hour" from 3 to 7 PM. *Upper Court St., 13904, tel. 607/775–3443. AE, DC, MC, V. Moderate.*

Cazenovia

Dining and **The Brae Loch.** The staff wear kilts, and hosts Grey Barr and
Lodging his son Jim sport full Highland regalia. The menu features
★ Scotch steak (steak and kidney) pie, muckle sow (sugar-cured ham), cock o' the north (rock Cornish game hen), and Angus Dundee (beef fillet with crab and mustard sauce). There's a Scots import shop on the premises. Guest rooms include four-poster beds, imported antiques, and complimentary Continental breakfast. *5 Albany St., 13035, 315/655–3431. Dress: informal. AE, DC, MC, V. Moderate–Expensive.*

Cooperstown

Dining and **Otesaga Hotel.** A grand hotel circa 1909 on a smaller scale—135
Lodging rooms and suites—with a manicured garden right on Otsego Lake, this property has tennis courts, a heated pool, and an adjoining 18-hole golf course. It wears the frown of age and is a bit set in its ways—no pets, men must wear jackets in public rooms, and so on. All hotel guests are charged MAP—breakfast and dinner included in the rates. *Lake Rd., tel. 607/547–9931. AE, MC, V. Closed Nov.–mid-Apr. Expensive.*

Dining **Hickory Grove Inn.** This renovated stagecoach stop has been serving travelers since 1804. The new management now offers Italian and Continental specialties. *Rte. 80, tel. 607/547–8100. Dress: informal. AE, DC, MC, V. Closed end of Oct.–early Mar. Moderate.*

Lodging **Cooper Motor Inn.** This beautifully restored 1812 Federal mansion has 20 modern guest rooms. Guests are entitled to all privileges at the nearby Otesaga Hotel. Continental breakfast included in rates. *Main St., tel. 607/547–9931. Very Expensive.*

Hickory Grove Motor Inn. Situated six miles north of Cooperstown, this 12-unit, family-run motel offers a rare tranquillity in manicured gardens reflecting the management's New Zealand hospitality. The rooms are comfortable and decorated with fresh flowers. *Rte. 80, 13326, tel. 607/547–9874. 12 rooms. Complimentary coffee. AE, MC. V. Open May–Oct. Moderate.*

Coventry

Dining and Lodging **Silo Carriage House.** Built like a silo, in an old barn, this 166-acre landscaped estate has a winding staircase leading to a loft. There are spectacular views, especially at sunset, of Greene and the valley, six miles away. The food is straightforward American, with prime rib, big steaks and lamb chops, trout, lobster, and veal. *Moran Rd., 6½ miles east of Greene, tel. 607/656–4377. Reservations recommended. Dress: smart casual. AE, MC, V. Inexpensive–Moderate.*

Greene

Dining and Lodging ★ **Sherwood Hotel.** This refurbished 1838 hotel has a Victorian country flair. Its 34 beautifully appointed rooms and suites feature brass beds and modern conveniences. The cozy lounge has a fireplace and the cheery dining room (open to the public) seats 90. It serves country and Continental fare—seafood, veal dishes, and steaks. *25 Genesee St., tel. 607/656–4196. Reservations recommended. Jacket required. AE, MC, V. Moderate.*

Oneonta

Dining **Brooks House of Barbecues.** This establishment, with its 30-foot-long pit, claims to be the world's largest barbecue, and the aroma of barbecued ribs, chicken, pork chops, and seafood can be sensed a mile away. The place seats 300 and serves up to 1,500 meals a day—in addition to a roaring take-out business. *Rte. 7, East End, tel. 607/432–1782. No reservations or alcohol. Dress: casual. No credit cards. Closed Mon. and last week Dec.–mid-Jan. Inexpensive.*

Rome

Dining and Lodging **The Beeches-Paul Revere Lodge.** This 52-acre resort offers 75 rooms decorated in Early American style. The resort has a restaurant, breakfast room, pool, and par-3 golf course. *Rte. 26, Turin Rd. 13440, tel. 315/336–1776. Moderate.*

Utica

Dining **Grimaldi's.** Billed as one of Utica's oldest, largest, and finest restaurants and cocktail lounges, Grimaldi's serves a traditional Italian-American menu in a warm, friendly atmosphere. *418-428 Bleecker St., tel. 315/732-7011. Dress: informal. AE, MC, V. Open daily 11:30-11. Moderate.*

Lodging **Sheraton Utica Hotel & Conference Center.** The 156 rooms here are attractive and comfortable, and the lobby was redone in black Italian marble. The skylit dining room has a bamboo-jungle decor. There's live entertainment in the lounge Monday-Saturday. Facilities include indoor heated pool, whirlpool, and fitness center. Champagne brunch is served on Sunday. *200 Genesee St., 13502, tel. 315/797-8010. AE, MC, V. Moderate.*

The Arts

Leatherstocking Country has a thriving arts community; its two major performance centers are the **Anderson Center for the Performing Arts** at the State University of New York (Binghamton 13901, tel. 607/777-ARTS) and the **Stanley Performing Arts Center** (259 Genesee St, Utica 13501, tel. 315/724-4000). These facilities present a full range of artistic performances, including concerts, opera, and occasional ballets. Obtain tickets directly from the centers. For the most complete listing of regional arts events, check local newspapers.

Theater

Cider Mill Playhouse is the State University of New York's off-campus theater. Located at 2 S. Nanticoke Avenue in Binghamton, it's a 300-seat cabaret theater that presents a year-round bill of shows. Box office: weekdays noon-5:30, Room 133, Fine Arts Building, SUNY-Binghamton Campus (tel. 607/777-ARTS or 607/748-7363). Tickets go on sale at the Cider Mill one hour before each show.

Binghamton's **Broadway Theater League** stages its performances at The Forum, 228 Washington St., but sells its tickets at the Arena Box Office (tel. 607/723-6626).
Broadway Theater League of Utica presents five performances a season at the Stanley Performing Arts Center (259 Genesee St., Utica 13501. Box Office, tel. 315/724-7196).

Beck's Grove Dinner Theater (4286 Oswego Rd., Blossvale, tel. 315/336-7038). Twelve miles south of downtown Rome, this theater presents musical comedies and seasonal shows from mid-March through mid-January.

Music

There's a wealth of concerts, operas, and other musical presentations at major centers. In outlying areas, performances of regional bluegrass, country-western, and other grassroots bands are listed in local newspapers.

The Forum (228 Washington St., Binghamton, tel. 607/778-1369 or 607/778-6626) is the Center for the Broome County Performing Arts. A former vaudeville house, it is home to the B.C. Pops (country to classical), the Tri-Cities Opera, the Binghamton Symphony and Choral Society, and the Broadway Theater League.

Broome County Veterans Memorial Arena (Box 1146, Binghamton, 13902, tel. 607/778–6626) is the venue for a wide range of entertainment activities.

Opera

Glimmerglass Opera (Box 191, Cooperstown, 13326, tel. 607/547–2255). Summer festival performances are held at the Alice Busch Opera Theater on Route 80, eight miles north of Cooperstown and two miles south of the junction of Routes 20 and 80. This unusual, partially open-air theater features sidewall panels that dramatically roll back before performances and during intermissions to reveal the wooded landscape and admit the fresh mountain air. Bring a sweater and a blanket. Evening performances and matinees.

Earlville Opera House (16 E. Main St., Earlville, 13332, tel. 315/691–3550). The summer season here comprises musical performances ranging from opera and string quartets to bluegrass and vaudeville variety shows. Call for schedule.

Film

Although the occasional art or foreign film shows up in college campus theaters and local arts centers, film is not especially distinguished in Leatherstocking Country. A notable exception is **The Art Theatre** (1204 Vestal Ave., Binghamton, tel. 607/724–7900). If you're looking for a movie, check the entertainment pages of local newspapers.

Nightlife

The great outdoors can be invigorating—and blissfully exhausting. Folks still gather around the family hearth, walk by the lake, or turn in early with a good book and a fire at their feet. The little nightlife that exists is in the cities. Check with local sources of tourist information (*see* Important Addresses and Numbers, above) and local periodicals. Here are some of the most popular gathering spots:

Esprit. This is a major night spot, with dancing for the young professional set. Proper attire means no shorts or midriffs for ladies, dress jeans for men, and shoes, not sneakers. Tuesday–Friday there's a shrimp buffet during happy hour. *Ramada Inn, 65 Front St., Binghamton, tel. 607/773–8390. AE, MC, V. Closed Mon. and Tues.*

Lily Langtry's. There is live entertainment on Tuesday evenings and happy hour 5–7 daily. *700 Varick St., Utica, tel. 315/724–5219. AE, DC, MC, V. Open 11 AM–2 AM; no cover, no minimum.*

Number 5. Downstairs, have drinks in a trendy lounge reminiscent of television's *Cheers*, then retire upstairs to the supper club, where the menu offers satisfying Continental and American cuisine. *33 S. Washington St, Binghamton, tel. 607/723–0555. AE, DC, MC, V. Daily.*

Peper's Market Place. The restaurant features live jazz and big-band music during the summer until 10. *93 Main St., Cooperstown, tel. 607/547–5468. No credit cards.*

8 Saratoga Springs and the North Country

Introduction

by *Peter Oliver*

A New York writer who covers sports, travel, and the outdoors, Peter Oliver's articles have appeared in Backpacker, Signature, Skiing, Travel-Holiday, *and* USA Today.

George Meegan, an Englishman who made a seven-year, 19,000-mile journey on foot through the Americas, wrote in his account, *The Longest Walk*, "Upstate New York may be America's best kept secret." The "secret" world of the North Country of New York includes everything from refined civility to absolute wilderness. You might cross paths with the rich and famous, or you might cross paths with deer and bear; it just depends on how and where you choose to spend your time in the North Country.

Saratoga Springs, in the southeast corner, is one of America's oldest summer playgrounds of high society. Northwest of Saratoga, and in stark contrast, is Adirondack Park. With six million acres, 2.3 million of which have been declared "forever wild" by New York State, it is the largest park expanse in the United States outside of Alaska. Girding the entire region are lakes and rivers, principally Lake George and Lake Champlain to the east, the St. Lawrence River to the north, and Lake Ontario to the west.

The secret character of the North Country came about both through disregard and design. Early American settlers didn't show much interest in the region. The rugged land, inhospitable soil, and often unmerciful winter conditions sent them elsewhere in search of good land to clear for farms. Only the east, from Saratoga north to Lake Champlain, saw any significant settlements in the 1700s.

In the 1800s, wilderness lovers as disparate as Ralph Waldo Emerson and Teddy Roosevelt discovered the Adirondack wilds and returned extolling their virtues. Wealthy families from New York City built what came to be known as the "great camps"—large lodges in remote areas. Meanwhile, doctors were recommending that their patients partake of the benefits of the clean Adirondack air, and sanitoriums, most notably the Trudeau Sanitorium in Saranac Lake, were built. Doctors also recommended that their patients go to Saratoga for the healthy spa waters, but Saratoga also attracted visitors with its gambling casinos and horse racing. In any event, the North Country became one of the first regions in America to have tourism as a principal industry. Enormous hotels were built in Saratoga, and as the railroads reached as far north as the Thousand Islands area along the St. Lawrence River, enormous hotels were built there, too.

In the 1950s, the area declined as summer vacationers began to opt for seaside beach resorts rather than mountains and lakes. When gambling was outlawed about the same time, Saratoga lost much of its appeal.

Winter travelers seemed to prefer Vermont and the Rockies, where ski resorts were better developed. Farming, mining, and shipping kept economic life ambling along, but tourism played much less of a role.

During the past 20 years, however, interest in the North Country has regained momentum. The enduring attraction of horse racing, the growing appeal of the Saratoga Performing Arts Center, and the proximity for commuters to the capital area of Albany contributed significantly to Saratoga's comeback. The

1980 Winter Olympics in Lake Placid helped to renew interest in the Adirondacks in general and Lake Placid in particular as a winter and summer sports center.

Watertown, with a population of about 28,000, is the largest city in the North Country. The smaller cities of Massena and Odgensburg have grown modestly since 1959 and the opening of the St. Lawrence Seaway, connecting the Great Lakes and the Atlantic Ocean. Glens Falls and Plattsburgh were given a push with the opening of the Northway (I-87) during the 1960s. But none of these cities is a "big city" in any sense of the word. Except for Saratoga, North Country cities are not the attraction. The region is now, as it has been historically, a place of escape, a place to retreat to from the pressures of city life.

Even during the peak periods of summer, there is no bustle, no commotion, no crowds. To be sure, there are hives of tourist activity in Saratoga, Lake George, Lake Placid, and the Thousand Islands. But if you consider the size of the North Country —equal to the states of Massachusetts, Connecticut, and Rhode Island combined—that leaves plenty of quiet, uncrowded space.

And what visitors seem to enjoy most about the North Country is this lack of civilization. The vast, interconnected waterways and hiking trails of the Adirondacks cover one of the two areas of genuine wilderness left in the U.S. Northeast, the other being northern Maine. The abundance of lakes and rivers throughout the region offer plenty of opportunity to hop aboard a canoe or houseboat and explore, fish, or just separate yourself from landlocked civilization. In the fall, when the leaves change color, the great expanses of forested land make for one of nature's most dramatic and fleeting spectacles.

What the North Country lacks sometimes creates inconveniences. The region has no major airports. To reach the North Country generally means flying first into a peripheral city— Albany, Syracuse, Montreal, Burlington, or New York City. From there, you can get a connecting flight to one of the smaller airports in the region, but there are relatively few scheduled flights.

There are also just two interstate highways in the North Country, I-81 and I-87, both running north–south. There are no major east–west highways, except for the New York State Thruway, which runs just south of the North Country's southern rim. Although most roads in the region are in very good condition, traveling on two-lane highways through small towns can be slow.

The operative words throughout most of the North Country are simple and rustic rather than elegant and refined. That is as it should be in a region that makes its statement as a world of retreat and escape. Lodging is generally simple and comfortable, and food is generally simple and good. Except for one or two places in Saratoga and Lake Placid, haute cuisine is an unknown concept in the North Country. And save for a few hot spots in Saratoga, Lake Placid, Lake George, and Alexandria Bay, nightlife tends to fade with nightfall.

The North Country is also very much a seasonal world. Tourism is in high gear in June, July, and August, downshifts in September and October, and slows considerably thereafter. Such areas as Lake Placid and North Creek continue through the winter as active skiing centers, and snowmobilers, cross-country skiers, and ice fishermen throughout the region make what they can of the cold winter months. With sizeable winter populations, such cities as Saratoga, Watertown, Glens Falls, and Plattsburgh remain reasonably active during the off-seasons. Generally speaking, though, the North Country itself goes into something of a retreat from November through April.

Essential Information

Getting Around

The principal international gateways are New York City to the south and Montreal to the north. The New York City airports are about a four-hour drive from Saratoga Springs; Montreal's Dorval Airport is about a 1½ hours' drive from the city of Plattsburgh.

Some airlines serve the tri-city area of Albany–Troy–Schenectady, 25 miles south of Saratoga; Syracuse, 65 miles south of Watertown; and Burlington, Vermont, directly across Lake Champlain from the Adirondacks. To fly into these cities, however, usually requires an indirect or connecting flight through a major Eastern seaboard airport.

By Plane The principal carrier throughout the North Country is **TWA Commuter** (tel. 800/221–2000), which has scheduled flights from New York, Albany, and Burlington to Saranac Lake, Plattsburgh, and Watertown.

Charter air services make it possible to reach smaller airports or remote areas of the North Country. **Adirondack Flying Service** (tel. 518/523–2473) in Lake Placid, **Bird's Seaplane Service** (tel. 315/357–3631) in Inlet, and **Helms Aero Service** (tel. 518/624–3931) in Long Lake operate sightseeing trips into the Adirondack wilderness and are permitted to land on some lakes to provide access for fishermen or canoeists.

By Bus **Adirondack Trailways** (tel. 800/225–6815) provides bus service throughout the region. More than two dozen charter operators also offer sightseeing tours in the summer, foliage tours in the fall, and ski tours in the winter. Call *I Love New York* (tel. 800/225–5697) for information about operators and the tours they offer.

By Train **Amtrak's Adirondack** (tel. 800/872–7245) operates daily between New York and Montreal, with North Country stops in Saratoga Springs, Fort Edward—Glens Falls, Whitehall, Fort Ticonderoga, Port Henry, Westport, and Plattsburgh. The section of the route along Lake Champlain is particularly scenic.

By Car Most people drive to the North Country. The primary route through the region is the Northway (I–87), which links Albany and Montreal. The major north–south route in the west is I–81, which runs from Syracuse through Watertown and into Canada over the Thousand Islands International Bridge.

There is no major north–south highway through the central part of the North Country, nor is there any east–west highway. However, the main roads through the Adirondack region, including routes 3, 8, 28, and 9N, are all well maintained, with

55 mph speed limits for most sections. Keep in mind that considerable snow falls throughout the North Country in winter, so have your car ready for snow conditions.

The **Adirondack North Country Association** publishes a first-rate map of the region (although, curiously, mileages are not included). It is a big map, hard to open in the car, but it outlines several scenic and historic driving routes throughout the region, including the Seaway Trail along the St. Lawrence River, the Adirondack Trail, and the Underground Railroad Trail. The map is $1.25 and may be ordered from Adirondack North Country Association (ANCA, Box 148, Lake Placid 12946, tel. 518/523–9820).

Scenic Drives   Route 28N between North Creek and Long Lake and Route 73 between Lake Placid and Exit 30 of the Northway (I–87) offer some of the best views of the mountains, with numerous trailheads along the way, should you feel so inclined. For river scenery, routes 86 and 9N, from Lake Placid to Keeseville, and Route 9 toward Plattsburgh, follow the Ausable River and its West Branch much of the way.

Car campers and recreational-vehicle travelers might enjoy touring the Seaway Trail along the St. Lawrence River. State campgrounds near the river's edge and along the Lake Ontario shore between Massena and Oswego are generally large and well maintained, but you must make reservations ahead of time if you expect to get a space on summer weekends.

By Boat   A popular way to see the Thousand Islands and St. Lawrence Seaway area is by houseboat. **Remar Rentals** in Clayton (tel. 315/686–3579 or 315/686–4170) can set you up, but remember to reserve at least six months ahead for peak season, July and August.

Power boats for cruising, fishing, or waterskiing can be rented on a daily or weekly basis at marinas at Lake George, Lake Champlain, Lake Saratoga, and other lakes in the Adirondacks that permit power-boating. Summer boat traffic can be heavy, particularly on Lake George. It is less congested—and safer— at Bolton Landing or Dunham Bay, a few miles north of the town of Lake George.

On Foot   The New York State **Department of Environmental Conservation** (DEC) maintains more than 1,000 miles of hiking trails throughout the Adirondack region. Free trail maps for selected hiking regions in the Adirondacks are available from DEC Publications, 50 Wolf Rd., Albany 12233.

Guided Tours

Many charter-bus operators feature foliage tours in fall and ski tours in winter, leaving from a number of metropolitan areas in the northeast, including New York City, Philadelphia, and cities in western New York. *I Love New York* (tel. 800/225–5697) can provide a list of operators and the tours they offer. A more intimate, if more energetic, way to see the changing colors of fall is by bicycle. You can stick to the road with **Adirondack Bicycle Touring** (tel. 518/523–3764) in Lake Placid or go off-road with **Adirondack Wilderness Tours** (tel. 518/835–4193) at Caroga Lake. Operators of foliage tours tend to define the season as Labor Day through October, but the peak period—the time when you really want to be there—is considerably shorter, usually about a week and generally during the first two weeks of October. **Upstate Transit Tours** (tel. 518/584–5252), the **Saratoga Circuit Tour** (tel. 518/587–3656), and **Mike's Guided Tours** (tel. 518/885–2650) all feature tours of Saratoga Springs and its environs during the summer.

For a bird's-eye view of the North Country, **Adirondack Balloon Rides** (tel. 518/793–6342) offers flights of up to two hours long in the early morning and evening, when the winds are lightest. Flights are expensive—up to $150–$175 per person— and unpredictable, as they operate only when weather conditions are ideal. But champagne is a traditional perk on balloon flights. Sightseeing flights by airplane are offered by **Adirondack Flying Service** (tel. 518/523–2473) in Lake Placid, **Bird's Seaplane Service** (tel. 315/357–3631) in Inlet, and **Helms Aero Service** (tel. 518/624–3931) in Long Lake. The flights are the quickest way to get to see the deep wilderness areas of Adirondack Park.

If you are interested in the Adirondack backcountry, you can hire a canoe or fishing guide. For a list of licensed guides, contact the **New York State Guides Association** (Box 4337, Albany 12204) or the New York State **Department of Environmental Conservation** (50 Wolf Rd., Albany 12233). A private firm coordinating licensed guides is **Guides for All Seasons** (Box 855, Saranac Lake 12983, tel. 518/891–1176). If you are interested in an extended hiking or backcountry-skiing tour of the region, the **Adirondack Mountain Club** (*see* Important Addresses and Numbers, below) offers many backcountry trips, some of which include wilderness-skills training and ecology study.

Important Addresses and Numbers

Information Centers *I Love New York*, the public-information wing of the New York State Division of Tourism, is the best general source for most tourism materials, including maps, visitor guides, tour and package information, and events listings. The regional *I Love New York* office in Lake Placid (90 Main St., tel. 518/523–2412) also has information on all North Country regions except Saratoga. The best source for information on that city is the **Greater Saratoga Chamber of Commerce** (494 Broadway, Saratoga Springs 12886, tel. 518/584–3255).

For other specific North Country regions, the main contacts are: The **Thousand Islands International Council** (Box 400, Collins Landing, Alexandria Bay 13607, tel. 800/8–ISLAND or 800/5–ISLAND in New York), the **Central Adirondack Association** (Tourism Information Center, Old Forge 13420, tel. 315/369–6983), and the **Olympic Regional Development Authority** (Olympic Center, Lake Placid 12946, tel. 518/523–1655, or 800/462–6236 in New York).

Tourism information centers are located along the Northway (I –87) between exits 11 and 12 and between exits 17 and 18 northbound, and at Exit 32 and between exits 40 and 41 southbound. Information centers can be found for the Thousand Islands region off I–81 at Exit 45 at the Zayre Plaza booth in Watertown and at the Thousand Islands International Council office at the foot of International Bridge.

The **Adirondack Park Visitor Interpretive Center** (Paul Smiths 12970, tel. 518/327–3000) focuses on the Adirondacks' natural environment through exhibits, interactive displays, theater programs, and miles of nature trails through Adirondack terrain.

The **Adirondack Mountain Club** (RR 3, Box 3055, Lake George 12845, tel. 518/668–4447) is the best source of backcountry information throughout the region. The club is a good source for up-to-date information on trail conditions both for hiking as well as backcountry skiing in winter and for waterway conditions for canoeists. Alpine skiers can get current snow conditions by calling the toll-free *I Love New York* phone number: 800/225–5697.

Emergencies   Emergency phone numbers vary throughout the North Country. 911 is used in Lake George and Saratoga; consult a phone book or dial the operator for other areas.

Hospitals   The major hospitals in the region are **Saratoga Hospital** (Church St., Saratoga Springs, tel. 518/584–6000), **Glens Falls Hospital** (Park St., Glens Falls, tel. 518/792–3151; 518/761–5261 for the emergency room), **Champlain Physicians Hospital** (in Plattsburgh, tel. 518/561–2000), **Saranac Lake General Hospital** (tel. 518/891–4141), and **Mercy Hospital** (in Watertown, tel. 315/782–7400).

Late-Night   There are no 24-hour pharmacies in this region, but **Grant's**
Pharmacies   **Drugs** at 101 Public Square, Watertown (tel. 315/788–1291) is open until 9:45 weeknights and Saturday. **Fay's** at Holbrook Plaza in Lake Placid (tel. 518/523–2011) and **Kinney Drugs** at 188 Broadway in Saranac Lake (tel. 518/891–3132) are open until 9:30 weeknights and Saturday.

Exploring the North Country

Saratoga

Saratoga County stretches south to the Mohawk River and east to the Hudson, west to Great Sacandaga Lake and north to Glens Falls. But most people who visit the area come to spend most of their time in Saratoga Springs, a historic spa resort (also referred to simply as Saratoga). Beautiful Victorian homes, historic sites, horse racing, cultural events, and mineral waters—not necessarily in that order—are the town's primary attractions.

Saratoga in August, when the racing fraternity is in residence, is quintessential Saratoga. With owners, breeders, and trainers on hand for the races, the socializing, and the wheeling and dealing of the yearling auction during the second week of the race meet, the old town takes on a bit of the glamour it had in the days when wealthy families came to take the waters and high-stakes gamblers peopled its fancy casinos. A spin down Broadway will give you a glimpse of bygone days when members of the upper crust kept a little mansion in Saratoga as part of the roving social scene of summer.

The crush of visitors drawn by the thoroughbred-racing session provides many businesses in the community with the wherewithal to make it through the other 11 months of the year. The track itself is open for just 24 racing days, yet it manages to turn enough of a profit in that time to be able to maintain the rambling, big-roofed grandstand, the grounds, and the barns (all listed on the Register of Historic Places) in impeccable condition throughout the year.

Those who visit Saratoga in August should expect crowds and premium prices as well. Hotel-room rates typically double and triple for the month. Although restaurant prices remain about the same, extravagant specials such as Beluga caviar tend to show up on the menus of such Saratoga institutions as the Union Coach House. August visitors tend to be more indulgent than the year-round crowd. Dinner reservations must be made well in advance.

So, too, must lodging reservations. The Greater Saratoga Chamber of Commerce can scrounge up a room for you somewhere should you come into town unannounced on, say, a Saturday in August. Such lodging arrangements may fall below your normal standards and above your normal price range and will probably be several miles from the center of town. You should book accommodations for the peak season at least six months in advance.

After the racing meeting, Saratoga reverts to its true self—a compact city of historical, cultural, and architectural significance, a community experiencing something of a renaissance. The tri-city area (Albany–Schenectady–Troy) 25 miles to the south seems to have adopted Saratoga in the last decade as a distant suburb, and about half of Saratoga's population today is made up of commuters.

June and September are especially good months to visit. It's best to avoid the crowds of August and fall, when countless foliage tours roll through town.

Saratoga Springs

Numbers in the margin correspond with points of interest on the Saratoga Springs map.

Most people come into Saratoga from the Northway (I–87), taking exits 13, 14, or 15. Turning north on Route 9 from Exit 13, on your left you'll pass the 2,000-acre **Saratoga State Park** and its performing arts center, some monolithic spa buildings constructed under the Work Projects Administration of the 1930s, two golf courses, tennis courts, and other facilities. On your right is the back entrance to Saratoga's harness-racing track which, unlike its more renowned thoroughbred-racing cousin, is open for close to 11 months of the year. A bit farther along on your left is the **National Museum of Dance**, housed in a handsome, low-slung building that was once a public spa facility. A mile or so farther, Route 9 turns into Broadway, the main drag that runs through the center of the city.

❶ If you take Exit 14, you'll enter town on Union Avenue. **Yaddo,** a highly regarded retreat for artists and writers, is on your left; its 400-acre grounds and its rose garden are open to the public. Closer to town on the left is Saratoga Raceway, partially obscured by cultivated stands of shade trees.

❷ A few blocks west on Union Avenue is the **National Museum of Racing,** just across Union Avenue from the race track. A $6 million upgrading of the museum was completed in June of 1988. A

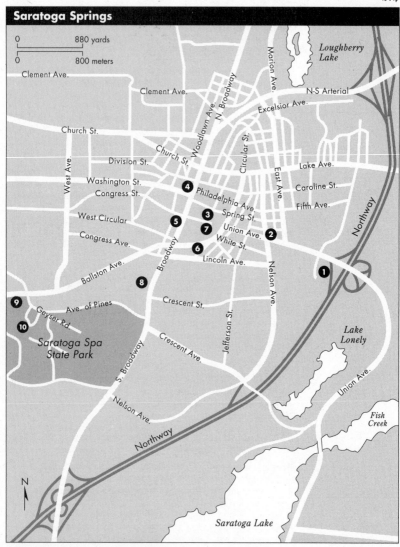

Saratoga Springs

0 — 880 yards
0 — 800 meters

Loughberry Lake

Clement Ave.
Clement Ave.
N-S Arterial
Excelsior Ave.
Church St.
Division St.
Church St.
Washington St.
Congress St.
Lake Ave.
Caroline St.
Philadelphia Ave.
Fifth Ave.
West Circular
Spring St.
Congress Ave.
Union Ave.
White St.
Lincoln Ave.
West Ave.
Woodlawn Ave.
N. Broadway
Marion Ave.
Circular St.
East Ave.
Broadway
Nelson Ave.
Ballston Ave.
Crescent St.
Jefferson St.
Ave. of Pines
Geyser Rd.
Crescent Ave.
S. Broadway
Nelson Ave.
Northway
Northway
Union Ave.

Saratoga Spa State Park

Lake Lonely

Fish Creek

Saratoga Lake

N

Adelphi Hotel, **4**
Batchellor Mansion, **6**
Canfield Casino, **7**
Congress Park, **3**
National Museum of Dance, **8**

National Museum of Racing, **2**
Roosevelt Bath House, **10**
Saratoga Performing Arts Center, **9**
Saratoga Springs Urban Cultural Visitor Center, **5**
Yaddo, **1**

highlight of the museum is its Hall of Fame, with video clips of races of the horses and jockeys who have been enshrined. *Tel. 518/584–0400. Admission: $3 adults, $2 students and senior citizens, children under 5 free. Open Mon.–Sat. 10–4:30, Sun. 12–4:30; during Aug., daily 9–5.*

3 Union Avenue leads into Circular Street, which forms the back border of **Congress Park,** the small patch of greenery that marks the center of town. Turn left, and the street winds back to south Broadway. Turn right, and you will be heading north, passing on your left the narrow passageways of Spring, Phila, and Caroline streets, where several of the city's best restaurants are located. Phila and Caroline streets are one-way, and you must turn left on Lake Avenue and left again on Broadway, heading south, if you intend to give these streets a look-see. The blocks of Broadway between Lake Avenue and Spring Street is where you will find many of Saratoga's better boutiques.

4 In the summer, especially during the racing session, people-watching in Saratoga is a finely honed art, and one of the best places to get started is on the balcony of the **Adelphi Hotel** (*see* Lodging, below), overlooking Broadway, at breakfast time.

The Adelphi is also an excellent introduction to Saratoga's Victorian past. Furnished with authentic period pieces—everything from swayback love seats to a century-old cash register in the lobby—the hotel is in the process of being restored, a few rooms a year, to its original grandeur. The small balcony opens off of a second-floor parlor, from which coffee and pastries are served in the morning. The Adelphi is a last vestige of great hotels of the 1800s, when such luminaries as Andrew Jackson and Washington Irving came to Saratoga and Ballston to partake of the spa waters.

5 In July and August, guided walking tours of the city are offered from the **Saratoga Springs Urban Cultural Visitor Center** (on Broadway across from Congress Park), but, armed with literature from the visitor center, you can get around on your own reasonably well. *Tel. 518/587–3241. Open July–Aug., daily 9–4; guided tours $2, leave 10:30 AM Mon.–Sat., 2 PM Sun. By reservation only Sept.–June.*

There are more than two dozen active springs in and around the city, and you can drink or fill containers free of charge. Each spring has water of varying mineral content and effervescence; taste carefully—the water from some springs, such as the notoriously noxious stuff that comes from Hathorn No. 1 off Spring Street, may take some getting used to.

More than 700 structures in Saratoga are listed on the National Register of Historic Places, and about 400 of them are ornate homes dating to the Victorian era. Ten years ago, most of these homes were in disrepair and even decay, but private initiative, along with various forms of public support, has spearheaded a citywide restoration effort.

6 Many of the most impressive Victorian houses are behind Congress Park, along Union and Circular avenues. Especially noteworthy is the **Batchellor Mansion,** on Circular Avenue two blocks from Broadway, with its turrets and multiangled facade restored to mint condition. Unfortunately, like most of the Victorian structures, the Batchellor Mansion is a private home and is not open to the public for tours.

❼ Canfield Casino, the lone building in Congress Park, is now a museum devoted to Saratoga's colorful history as a gambling center, beginning in 1842. Gambling was a thriving enterprise in Saratoga for more than 100 years until the 1950s, when a U.S. Senate commission headed by Estes Kefauver cracked down on unlawful betting. In fact, until its demise, gambling was a bigger drawing card in Saratoga than horse racing or the spa waters. Bettors stayed at the gargantuan hotels of the time, such as the United States Hotel and the Grand Union, whose dining rooms could seat up to 1,000 people. Among the frequent visitors to Saratoga were such infamous gamesmen as Bet-A-Million Gates and Diamond Jim Brady. Brady, never short on showmanship, arrived in Saratoga in 1896 with 27 houseboys and daily changes of jewelry. Lillian Russell, Brady's companion, entertained herself about town on a goldplated bicycle.

After a few brushes with the law, the casinos finally closed for good in the 1950s. It touched off an immediate and severe tourism decline in Saratoga, which had little other economic activity to support itself. Yet Saratoga's gambling legacy was kept alive with the Canfield Casino museum as well as two notable contributions to American culture. The Canfield Casino is reputed to be where the card game was invented and the first place where a club sandwich was served. *Tel. 518/584–6920. Admission: $2 adults, $1.50 students and senior citizens, 25¢ children under 7. Open Nov.–late May, Wed.–Sun. 1–4; June, Sept., and Oct., Mon.–Sat. 10–4, Sun. 1–4; July and Aug., daily 9:30–4:30.*

On your way to the **Saratoga State Park,** make a point of stop-
❽ ping in at the **National Museum of Dance.** Opened in 1987, the museum features rotating exhibits on the history and development of dance. The gallery that houses the dance hall of fame honors dance luminaries such as Fred Astaire and Martha Graham. Small television monitors show five- to 10-minute video vignettes of each inductee, and there are terrific photos of dancers and choreographers in action. *Rte. 9S, tel. 518/584–2225. Admission: $3 adults, $2 senior citizens and students, $1 children under 12. Open Tues.–Sat. 10–5, Sun. noon–5.*

Saratoga State Park has more activities packed into one open space during the summer than any place in New York north of New York City's Central Park. From June to September, the New York City Opera, the Philadelphia Orchestra, the New York City Ballet, and acclaimed dance companies make the
❾ Saratoga Performing Arts Center (tel. 518/584–9330 and box office, 518/587–3330), in Saratoga State Park, their home away from home. Of course, the events that really pack the house— or the open-air amphitheater and surrounding grounds—are pop performances by the likes of the Grateful Dead and Linda Ronstadt. During the off-season, local and regional performing groups keep the stage of the park's Little Theater alive.

The park itself has two golf courses (18-hole and 9-hole), eight tennis courts (free), two swimming pools, and cross-country skiing and ice skating in winter. The **Crystal Spa** (92 S. Broadway, tel. 518/584–2556) is a privately owned spa with mineral baths, though at $17 the mineral bath, wrapped-towel rest, and

🔟 massage special at the **Roosevelt Bath House** is one of the best deals in town. There are also several picnic areas in the park, for which a small per-car fee is charged during the summer months. *Tel. 518/584–2011. No admission charge. Park closes at dusk daily.*

Excursions from Saratoga Springs

Numbers in the margin correspond with points of interest on the North Country map.

❶ The requisite excursion from **Saratoga Springs** is to the **National Historic Park,** site of an important battlefield of the American Revolution and nine miles from the center city. Take Route 9 south beyond I–87 to Route 9P east, to Route 423 east, and Route 32 north. The way is well marked. A loop back to the city can be made by heading north on Route 32 to Schuylerville (the original Saratoga of the 1700s) and turning left on Route 29 west.

British general John Burgoyne had planned to move south from Canada with his troops, take command of the waterways between Montreal and New York, and eventually consolidate with the forces of William Howe in New York City. Instead, American generals Horatio Gates and Benedict Arnold engaged him in two fierce battles here in the fall of 1777 and eventually forced him to surrender.

The battlefield tour starts at the visitor center, which houses a few artifacts—small cannon, infantry gear, and other battle materials recovered at the site—as well as maps and history books. The most compelling reason to drop by the visitor center (other than paying the park fee) is to watch the 21-minute film about the two battles. It is a good primer since there is really not much to *see* at the battlefield other than some fine views of the Hudson River farming country. Designated stopping points along the way are equipped with audio recordings to explain what you would be seeing if you were there in 1777. But there are few structures or archaeological remnants. *Rtes. 4 and 3 at Schuylerville, tel. 518/664–9821. Admission: $3 per vehicle or $1 per person. Open 9–5 daily; visitor center open year-round, battlefield closed to vehicles Dec.—Mar.*

On your way to or from the battlefield, you might want to make a stop at **Saratoga Village,** a few miles south on Route 9 past the turn-off for Route 9P. This mall, built like a neo–New England village, houses 60 stores, mostly factory outlets.

❷ Another worthwhile excursion is south on Route 50 to **Ballston Spa,** if for no other reason than to visit the **National Bottle Museum,** with its antique bottles, jars, stoneware, and related items. *Verbeck House, 20 Church Ave., tel. 518/885–7589. Donations. Open June–Labor Day, daily 10–4. Closed weekends Oct.–Apr.*

The Adirondacks

Adirondack Park is a place of big numbers. The official boundaries of the park encompass 6 million acres (9,375 square miles), almost three times the land area of Yellowstone National Park. There are 1,000 miles of rivers, 30,000 miles of brooks and streams, and more than 2,500 lakes and ponds. At an esti-

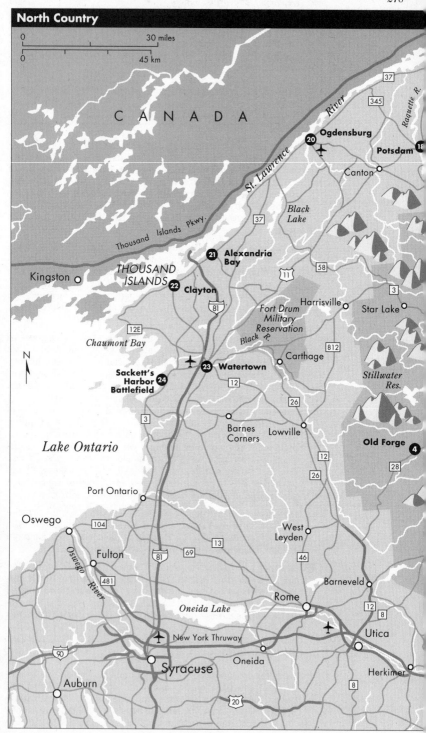

North Country

0 _____ 30 miles
0 _____ 45 km

CANADA

Ogdensburg 20 ✈

37

345

Raquette R.

Potsdam 1

Canton

St. Lawrence River

Thousand Islands Pkwy.

Black Lake

37

Alexandria Bay 21

THOUSAND ISLANDS

Clayton 22

Kingston

81

12E

Chaumont Bay

58

11

Harrisville

Star Lake

3

Fort Drum Military Reservation

Black R.

812

Carthage

Stillwater Res.

✈ 23 **Watertown**

Sackett's Harbor Battlefield 24

12

26

3

Barnes Corners

Lowville

12

Old Forge 4

28

Lake Ontario

26

N

Port Ontario

West Leyden

Oswego

104

Oswego River

Fulton

481

81

69

13

46

Barneveld

12

8

Oneida Lake

Rome

90

✈ New York Thruway

Oneida

✈

Utica

Syracuse

Auburn

20

Herkimer

8

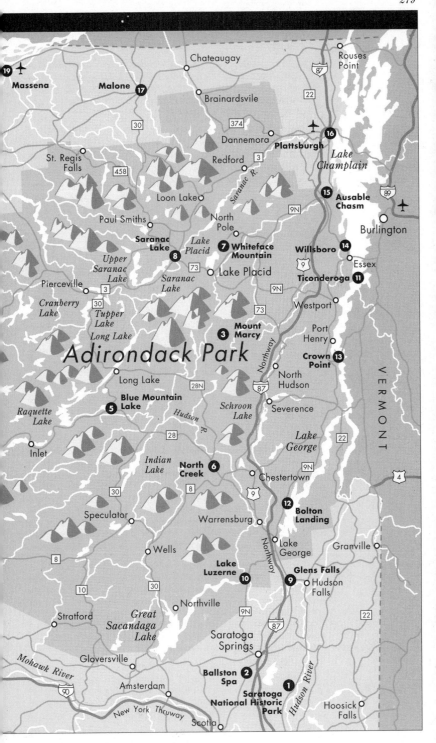

mated 1.2 billion years old, its mountains are "the survivors of the most ancient geologic formation in North America," according to the Adirondack Park Association.

The numbers impress, but they are just by way of introduction to the Adirondacks. Understanding the Adirondacks is a matter of sensory perception rather than number crunching. It is a place not only to be seen but also to be heard and smelled and, during winters that are often harsh, felt as well.

From spring through fall, every lake view or mountain vista or walk in the woods comes with the fragrance of hemlock and spruce and musty soil and the sounds of songbirds, woodpeckers, loons, or any of the 220 species of birds in the region.

By and large, the Adirondacks were so ignored by early American settlers that it wasn't until 1837 that the first white man, Ebenezer Emmons, on assignment from the New York State legislature to catalog the region, reached the top of **Mt. Marcy.** Mt. Washington in New Hampshire, by comparison, had been climbed almost 200 years earlier in 1642.

This extended lack of interest in the Adirondacks proved, in the long run, a boon for wilderness lovers. By the 1800s, the idea that there was value in the wilderness itself began to gain popular support. Ralph Waldo Emerson became an Adirondacks admirer after his 1858 stay at "Philosophers' Camp" with a group of Boston intellectuals. (Originally named Camp Maple by James Lowell Russell, it was given the nickname Philosophers' Camp by guides for the group). After publication in 1869 of William H. H. Murray's classic *Adventures in the Wilderness,* extolling the freshness and purity of the Adirondack air, the region became recognized as a place of recuperation. The famous Trudeau Sanitorium in Saranac Lake was visited by many notables of the late 1800s, among them Robert Louis Stevenson, who apparently didn't care much for the cold winter air, no matter how pure it was.

Wealthy families discovered the Adirondacks toward the latter part of the 19th century, giving rise to a concept of rustic elegance that became known as the "great camps." These camps were generally built of native materials—wood and stone—and had a rough-hewn look to them, but were otherwise spacious and luxurious. **Camp Sagamore,** four miles south of Route 28 at Racquette Lake Village (tel. 315/354–5311), one of the great camps built in 1897 and now open to tours in the summer months, is a good example of what it means to rough it, uppercrust style.

The wilderness was also protected by law very early; Adirondack Park was created by the state in 1892, and two years later all state-owned forest land was designated as "forever wild," prohibiting future development; today 2.3 million acres in the park are so classified. However, the Adirondacks is not a complete wilderness area; almost 58% of the land within the park boundaries is privately owned.

Trails for hiking, snowmobiling, or cross-country skiing are generally well cleared and well marked, as are water accesses. Campgrounds are well maintained. As a state-managed park, regulations are somewhat different from those at national parks; for example, fire regulations in the park are somewhat less restrictive.

Also, the checkerboard of public and private lands gives the Adirondacks a character that is different from that of most national parks. Motels, lodges, and restaurants can be found throughout the park region on private land and are privately owned and operated. Canoe rentals, seaplane (or lake plane) services, and guide services are all private enterprises, while most campgrounds, trails, and waterways are maintained on public land by the state, through the Department of Environmental Conservation (DEC).

For the most part, the public-private union has been harmonious, although environmentalists occasionally express concern about potential development of private lands within the park, and private landowners occasionally complain about trespassing. One area of dispute, for example, is the right of free passage through private waters—a right that canoeists and fishermen claim, but one that many landowners refuse to recognize.

Keep in mind the substantial distances between settlements with lodging and services when exploring the region. Stretches of 30 or more miles between settlements are common, especially in the central Adirondacks and the far north. Keep an eye on the gas gauge.

Life in much of the Adirondacks is seasonal. Lakeside lodges and motels tend to close between November and April. Although interest in winter activities such as backcountry skiing, snowshoeing, snowmobiling, and ice fishing is on the rise, many places aren't properly winterized. If you are traveling through the Adirondacks in winter, you may have to travel a long way before finding a place to bed down, except in the Lake Placid area, which has a rich and established winter tradition.

Southern and Central Adirondacks The two main roads—virtually the only roads at all—through the southern and central Adirondacks are routes 28 and 30. Route 28 forms an east–west crescent from Warrensburg through Old Forge to Woodgate. Route 30 reaches north from Gloversville to Tupper Lake. The two routes run together for about 10 miles between Indian Lake and Blue Mountain Lake, the approximate geographical center of the Adirondacks. Route 28N makes a northerly swing from Route 28 at North Creek before turning west and joining Route 30 at Long Lake, 11 miles north of Blue Mountain Lake. Route 8, which runs along West Canada Creek and Piseco Lake and Lake Pleasant, joins Route 30 in Specaculator and is the major road in the southwestern part of the park. (The Lake George region, as well as the Lake Champlain region, is technically within the park boundaries. *See* Lake George and Lake Champlain, below.)

Even in the peak season of July and August, peace and tranquility are the underlying themes of the southern and central Adirondacks. This is early-to-bed, early-to-rise country. Lodges often serve dinner at 6 PM; dinner at 8 is considered late. Gigantic breakfasts tend to be the order of the morning: Oatmeal, eggs, bacon, pancakes, toast, juice, coffee, and morning indigestion are de rigueur. The big-breakfast tradition probably has its roots in the logging days, but a big-breakfast, light-lunch formula makes sense, since most people are on the go in the middle of the day, hiking, fishing, exploring, or touring by car.

Although most people associate "Adirondacks" with high mountains, the southern and central landscape is primarily one of lakes, rivers, and rolling hills. The notable exception is Blue Mountain, which stands 3,828 feet above everything that surrounds it. Its summit lookout tower affords a sweeping 360° view that includes the chain of lakes that reach toward Inlet, but the price of that view is a fairly steep scramble of about a mile.

4 The center of tourist activity in the southern and central Adirondacks is **Old Forge,** but even its amusements and lakeside activities are low-key in comparison to Lake George. In fact, one of its most popular spots is the Old Forge Hardware store on the main drag, which sells exotic gifts, paintings, sculpture, pottery, and books, in addition to the usual camping equipment and tools.

5 **Blue Mountain Lake,** the cultural center of the region, is home of the **Adirondack Museum,** the best museum about the Adirondacks. The museum covers the entire cultural and historical spectrum of the region. It is easily possible to spend two full days exploring the museum, but if you don't have that kind of time, the canoes and guideboats, Adirondack furniture, and outdoor sporting-paraphernalia displays are the most fascinating. *Rte. 28N, tel. 518/352–7311. Admission: $8 adults, $5 children. Open Memorial Day–mid-Oct. 9:30–5:30.*

Blue Mountain Lake is also home of the **Adirondack Lakes Center for the Arts** (tel. 518/352–7715), a working retreat for artists, writers, and musicians. The center also stages musical performances, craft demonstrations, and other cultural activities open to the public during the summer. Crafts, incidentally, are a vital part of the central Adirondacks character, and many artists, furniture builders, weavers, and boat builders live in the area around Long Lake and Blue Mountain Lake. A few tend to be reclusive, but others welcome visitors interested in their craftsmanship. The **Adirondack North Country Association** (Box 148, Lake Placid 12946, tel. 518/523–2062) or the Adirondack Lakes Center for the Arts in Blue Mountain Lake can provide lists of local craftspeople and those who welcome visitors at their workplaces.

6 Route 28 east from Blue Mountain Lake leads to **North Creek,** which could be considered the sporting capital of the central Adirondacks. Gore Mountain, with a 2,150-foot vertical rise, is the second-largest ski area in the state (after Whiteface), but is something of a secret among skiers in the know in New York. Gore doesn't have as severe a climate as Whiteface to the north, nor does it have the crowds of Hunter Mountain in the Catskills. Nonskiers can get in on the view from the top of Gore in the summer and fall when the gondola operates for sightseers; there is also a road leading up the mountain. *Tel. 518/251–2411. Gondola ride is $4.*

Skiing isn't the only athletic activity in North Creek. The town is also the white-water hub of the Adirondacks and site of the annual **Whitewater Derby** during the first full weekend in May (*see* Spectator Sports, below). Spring is the time when the real white-water daredevils like to put their kayaks and canoes into the river because the water is highest after the run-off from the snow melt. The most popular runs are along the Indian River from Indian Lake and then on to the Hudson River leading to

North Creek. If you want to give the river a go—by raft, inner tube, or kayak—Hudson River Rafting Company (Main St., North Creek 12853, tel. 518/251-3215), a leading white-water outfitter, operates out of North Creek.

If you have the time, the drive between Long Lake and North Creek on Route 28N is one of the prettiest in the Adirondacks and less traveled than Route 28 to the south. While the trip along Route 28N is worthwhile for the mountain and lake views alone, there are also a few points of interest along the way. A historic marker between Minerva and Newcomb commemorates the estimated point where, in 1901, Teddy Roosevelt became President after the assassination of William McKinley. Roosevelt had been climbing in the High Peaks at the time, and it took considerable effort to get word to him of McKinley's death. A small road leading north from Route 28N between Newcomb and Minerva provides southern access for hikers going into the High Peaks region, and the road follows the Hudson River along its northernmost extreme. If the out-of-the-way world of Route 28N really captivates you, try the 90-site Lake Harris Campground, three miles north of Newcomb off Route 28N, on the shores of Lake Harris (tel. 518/582-2503).

For the most part, the tranquility of the southern and central Adirondacks turns to dormancy in winter. However, because the terrain is gentler than the High Peaks region to the north—and nearer the population centers of the south—snowmobiling and cross-country skiing are popular winter activities. The substantial snowfall and the interconnected lake and trail systems form an extensive snowmobile network. Old Forge, Schroon Lake, and Speculator are towns where snowmobilers tend to congregate.

Lake Placid If there is an aortal link between the southern, central, and northern Adirondacks, it is the **Northville–Placid Trail.** The trail meanders along 130 miles of generally rolling terrain from Northville, past Great Sacandaga Lake, then on to Lake Placid. The full trip is made by serious backpackers in summer—and *very* serious backcountry skiers in winter—although the northern section of the trail, from Long Lake to Lake Placid through the High Peaks area, is the more traveled.

Lake Placid is unquestionably the hub of the northern Adirondacks. Most Lake Placid visitors come in from the east, off Exit 30 on the Northway (I-87). From Exit 30, follow Route 73 as it climbs past Chapel Pond, descends through Keene and Keene Valley, then climbs again past the birch-lined Cascade Lakes. In summer, world-class cyclists can be seen making the climb as part of regular training rides; in winter, you might spot ice climbers on the cliffs above Cascade Pond. From here Route 73 descends six miles to Lake Placid.

From Exit 34, Route 9N follows the Ausable River to Jay; from there, Route 86 forks right and leads through Wilmington to Lake Placid. No matter which route you take into Lake Placid, there are early indications that you are coming into Olympic country. Along Route 73, you pass **Mt. Van Hoevenberg,** site of the luge and bobsled runs, as well as the cross-country ski tracks. Soon, the towers of the 70- and 90-meter ski jumps loom on your left. The jumps are stark and exposed and seem out of place, but the view from the top of the 90-meter jump is dramatic. You get a bird's-eye view of the entire lay of the land and the High Peaks around Lake Placid. You also get a stomach-gripping view of what the jumpers see while preparing to take flight.

❼ If you come into Lake Placid on Route 86, **Whiteface Mountain,** New York's largest ski area, will be on your right. On spring and summer mornings, you are apt to see fly fishermen in hip boots casting their lines out onto the waters of the Ausable River.

Lake Placid's mile-long Main Street, from the intersection of routes 73 and 86 to the swing left onto Saranac Avenue, is a tight cluster of hotels, restaurants, and shops, not to mention the Olympic Ice Arena and the speed-skating oval. For that reason, traffic is often backed up in summer; the best way to enjoy Lake Placid is to park—if you can find a parking space—and walk around. An alternate way to get around is via Holly the Trolley, a 75¢ bus ride making a 21-stop tour of Lake Placid from Memorial Day to Labor Day. Main Street is great for browsing; if you're looking for books about the life and history of the Adirondacks, drop in at With Pipe and Book (91 Main St., tel. 518/523–9096).

Take one of the boat tours that leave from the marina at the end of Main Street; guides point out all the summer homes (or "camps") of the well-to-do along the lake shores. Unless you're well acquainted with New York State's social register, though, the tour is most enjoyable as a nice, easy spin around the lake on a hot summer day. You can also take a guided tour of Olympic sites. Contact the Olympic Regional Development Authority (tel. 518/523–1655).

Self-guided tours can be made of the **John Brown Farm** (tel. 518/523–3900), home and burial place of the famed abolitionist who operated the farm for runaway slaves. Located off Route 73 just past the Olympic ski jumps, the farm is open from early May to late October.

During the summer, you can reach the top of Whiteface either by chairlift or by car on Veterans Memorial Highway, and the short walk to the summit provides a superb view—Lake Placid in one direction, Lake Champlain in another, and the High Peaks to the south. Go on a clear day if possible.

There isn't much to do at Mt. Van Hoevenberg in summer, except to ride to the top of the bobsled run, but in winter you can try bobsledding—as a passenger with an experienced driver—or luge. On the luge run you are on your own, although you only have to maneuver through the last few turns of the course. Still, it's not for the timid.

❽ Ten miles west of Lake Placid is **Saranac Lake,** where, more than a century ago, the **Trudeau Sanitorium** opened, establishing forever the healthy-air reputation of the Adirondacks. In February, Saranac Lake hosts the most celebrated winter carnival in the Adirondacks. Revelers seem to enjoy wreaking havoc on the ice sculptures on Flower Lake as much as they do creating them; the storming of the Ice Palace, complete with fireworks, is the traditional carnival finale. (For information, tel. 518/891–1990).

From Saranac Lake, Route 3 leads west through Tupper Lake and Cranberry Lake on its way to Watertown. The mountains gradually give way to more rolling forest land as you make your way westward. You are entering prime canoe country, as the **St. Regis Canoe Area's** multiple lakes, ponds, and primitive forest is off-limits to power boats. Tupper Lake and Raquette Pond are also great for exploring by canoe, and the reedy nooks of Raquette Pond provide some of the best black-bass fishing grounds in the North Country. The lakes and ponds of this area are part of a vast network of interconnected waterways, linked primarily by the Raquette and Saranac rivers. You could hire a guide (Guides for All Seasons, Saranac Lake, tel. 518/891–1176) or spend months trying to cover just a fraction of the network by canoe.

Cranberry Lake is the largest body of water in the relatively unexplored northwestern corner of the park. Several long and gentle hiking trails wind through the area around the lake, and the quick and easy hike to a lookout from Bear Mountain provides a sweeping view of the lake and the unspoiled countryside beyond. The hike can be combined with a swim and picnic at the 173-site Cranberry Lake Campground, off Route 3, from which the trail up Bear Mountain leads (Cranberry Lake Village, tel. 315/848–2315).

Lake George and Lake Champlain

Just 40 miles north of Saratoga, the village of Lake George is altogether another world. If Saratoga is culture and sophistication, with a little snobbishness thrown in, Lake George is unabashed kitsch. That's what makes it fun, especially for families with young children; there are endless pop-culture activities to keep them amused. Saratoga and Lake George have one common denominator: large crowds in July and August. Even more than Saratoga, Lake George is a summer community. About 90% of the community shuts down after Labor Day and doesn't reopen until May.

You may feel as if you're entering a time warp as you drive north along Route 9 into the village of Lake George, at the southern end of the lake. The clusters of small motels, amusement parks, miniature golf courses, and stores selling ersatz Indian artifacts seem drawn from American Vacationland, circa 1958. You get the feeling that at any time, you might see Ricky, Lucy, little Ricky, and the Mertzes zip by in the old Rambler, on their way to some place like Magic Forest, a funland with a 30-foot statue of Uncle Sam out front. This kind of thing might be a bit dated, but it certainly isn't run-down. The continuing popularity of Lake George as a moderately priced weekend or summer-vacation resort ensures that the attractions are well maintained.

❾ The road to Lake George really begins in **Glens Falls,** about halfway between Saratoga and Lake George. The city of 19,000 is home to a minor-league hockey team in winter. A good reason to visit Glens Falls is the **Hyde Collection.** Housed in the former residence of a prominent Glens Falls family, the collection features a broad and exemplary group of works by artists ranging from Rembrandt to Whistler. *161 Warren St., tel. 518/792–1761. Admission charge. Open year-round.*

Heading north on Route 9, you'll know you're entering Lake George country when you pass **Great Escape** (tel. 518/792–6508; open Memorial Day–Labor Day 9–6 PM), the North Country's largest amusement park, and the motels begin to appear fast and furiously. Just before the village of Lake George, you'll find the **Adirondack Mountain Club** headquarters (*see* Important Addresses and Numbers, above) which can provide all sorts of valuable information if you're planning to continue north into the park. Also here, Route 9N branches left from

⑩ Route 9 and leads to **Lake Luzerne,** a smaller and quieter vacation community 10 miles away. Lake Luzerne is known for its dude ranches and is sometimes called "Big Hat" country, as in 10-gallon hat. It is the southern Adirondack center for horseback riding, pony riding, or extended trail rides into the park. At Hadley, the little village neighboring Lake Luzerne, you can rent a houseboat and explore Great Sacandaga Lake, equal in size to Lake George but less trafficked.

Another road branching off Route 9 just before you get to Lake George leads up **Prospect Mountain,** to its ballyhooed 100-mile view. You can drive it or hike it—the trip is fairly short either way—but there are other short climbs around that are more enjoyable and far less congested. The three-mile hike up Buck Mountain, beginning near Pilot Knob, offers a terrific view of the lake with the Adirondacks as a backdrop.

Route 9 through Lake George village is tightly packed with motels, moderately priced and inexpensive restaurants, and a few stores. The road that branches right around the southern extreme of the lake leads past the boat docks and the beach, with a small public park for walking, picknicking, and bicycling across the way.

Boat cruises from the town dock are extremely popular from May through October. The Lake George Steamboat Company operates three cruise ships for one- , two- , and 4½-hour sight-

⑪ seeing tours on the lake to **Ticonderoga,** as well as dinner cruises complete with Dixieland band. (Tel. 518/668–5777. Cruises cost $5.95–$11.50 adults and $3–$4.50 children.) Boats can be rented at the dock, although congestion in the summer in recent years has raised increasing concerns about safety at the southern end of the lake. If you want to rent a boat, it is worth driving the few miles up the east side of the lake to Dunham Bay or 10 miles on Route 9N to Bolton Landing.

⑫ **Bolton Landing** is best known as the home of **Sagamore,** a sprawling and luxurious year-round resort on its own small island. The centerpiece of the Sagamore is the old hotel, built in 1883 and recently restored. The resort features seven outlying lodges, several restaurants, myriad recreational facilities, and a slate of activities that include theater productions and "murder-mystery weekends" during the quiet winter months (*see* Lodging, below).

One worthwhile excursion from Lake George village is to **Warrensburg,** a low-key clapboard village eight miles north on Route 9. Several antiques stores here can make for a pleasant day or afternoon of browsing.

The Champlain Valley In addition to the Northway, there are two ways to reach Ticonderoga from Glens Falls: Route 4 to Route 22 and Route 9 to 9N. Route 4, which can be reached from Glens Falls by taking 32 west, is worth following for two reasons. Between Fort Ann and Whitehall, it runs along the Champlain Canal, which connects Lake Champlain and the Hudson River. If your timing is good, a barge or boat will be passing through the lock five miles north of Fort Ann. Take the time to pull over and watch the intricate maneuvering. The other reason is to pass through Whitehall, which claims "the birthplace of the American Navy": There Benedict Arnold launched America's first fleet in 1776 to do battle with the British on Lake Champlain. The Skenesborough Museum in Whitehall commemorates this historic event.

Fort Ticonderoga (Rte. 74, tel. 518/585–2821) was built by the French in 1756 to take control of the southern extreme of Lake Champlain—and, in effect, the entire water route between Montreal and Albany. It was strategically important—a position that was fought for dearly. It was held by the French, captured by the British (during the French and Indian Wars), and later by the Americans during the Revolution. The fort has been beautifully restored, and its museum, with uniforms and weaponry, is an excellent primer in 18th-century military history. The Revolutionary hoopla that takes place in the summer months—dress parades, cannon firings, and the like—tends toward hokiness, but it is the sort of stuff that is close enough to living history to be of interest to children. The fort is open from Memorial Day to mid-October.

⓭ Farther north is a state historic site at **Crown Point** (Rtes. 9 and 22, tel. 518/597–3666), where another French fort was built in 1734, but it is an archaeological site, not a restored site like Fort Ticonderoga. Plan to spend a few hours at the lakeside village of Essex, which has several 18th- and 19th-century buildings in fine condition, good shops for browsing, and an active marina. There is also a ferry that runs during the summer months from Essex to Vermont, if you have time.

Route 22 angles away from the lake after Essex, and the next
⓮ stop worth making is the **fish ladder in Willsboro,** especially in the fall when the landlocked salmon make their most concerted rush north; there's a viewing window here that allows you to view the action.

⓯ Just after Keeseville is the **Ausable Chasm.** The Ausable River has carved a seemingly impossible path through deep layers of sandstone, leaving cliffs that reach well over 100 feet high in places. This geological spectacle is often overrun during summer months—it is a stop on every tour-bus romp through the region.

North of the chasm are some interesting wetlands—the **Ausable Marsh State Wildlife Management Area**—where birdwatchers might want to pull in, especially during the fall migration. There is a state campground just beyond the wildlife
⓰ management area. The small city of **Plattsburgh,** six miles to the north, is more likely to be a supply stop in your travels through the North Country than a destination. It was, however, a city of strategic importance during the War of 1812, when the U.S.-Canadian border was an issue of dispute. Stop at the Kent-Delord House (17 Cumberland Ave., tel. 518/561–1035), which was seized by the British in 1814 and affords a good capsule look at family life in the 19th-century. It has a fine collection of portrait paintings.

Two things to keep in mind as you tour the Champlain Valley. Legend persists that a Loch Ness–like monster makes its home in the lake. Even Samuel Champlain claimed he saw some unusual creature during his original exploration of the lake in 1609. If you think you see something, report your sighting to a local town clerk or harbormaster. Your sighting will be laughed at and duly filed away as part of the legend.

More important, the Champlain Valley is a productive farming region in the North Country. If you are visiting the area during the late summer or early fall, be sure to sample the regional produce at farm stands, farmers' markets, or local restaurants. And if you are in the area in October, apple-picking is a popular activity. Many orchards allow visitors to pick their own. New York cheeses are famous and available any time of year.

The Thousand Islands—Seaway

The name "Thousand Islands" is less than accurate; there are, in fact, nearly twice that number, depending on who is doing the counting and what you consider an island. Any clump of land that could support two trees was the definition used by the National Geographic Society when it counted "1,800 or so islands" a few years ago. But that doesn't quite have the proper ring to it.

There is also much more to the region than the island-studded area of the St. Lawrence River called the Thousand Islands. The name usually refers to an area defined by the Adirondacks to the east, the St. Lawrence River to the north, and Lake Ontario to the west. Its largest city, Watertown, is more than 30 miles south of the Thousand Islands and is itself something of a misnomer, since it is not on any water at all.

Most of the region is flat or rolling farmland, but the economy is heavily dependent on the St. Lawrence Seaway. The river defines a coastline running for more than 100 miles southwest from Massena to Cape Vincent, where the river meets Lake Ontario. The St. Lawrence is the throat of a waterway that leads through the Great Lakes and which, with the completion of its lock system in 1959, formed the longest navigable inland passage—more than 2,300 miles—in the world.

The main roadways of the Thousand Islands area are I–81, which runs north from Syracuse through Watertown, and the Seaway Trail, a combination of Routes 37, 12, and 12E, which follows the river and the Lake Ontario shore. The two main roadways intersect at the Thousand Islands International Bridge, leading into Canada. The juncture of the two roads is the geographic nexus of the region, and the two riverside towns of Alexandria Bay and Clayton see a considerable amount of summer traffic. The small cities to the northeast, Odgensburg and Massena, are more shipping than tourism towns, although they are not without their attractions. The locks at Massena, in fact, are the best place to see the shipping industry of the Seaway in action.

An inland road that parallels the Seaway Trail for much of the way is Route 11, which runs from Lake Champlain through the cities of Malone, Potsdam, and Canton to Watertown. There are a couple of points of interest along this route. Ballard Mill **(17)** (tel. 518/483–5190), a converted woolen mill in **Malone,** is an arts and crafts center with demonstrations and theater presentations in the summer. Route 11 is also the college route, to a branch of the State University of New York in Potsdam and St. Lawrence University in Canton. The Crane School of Music **(18)** (tel. 315/265–3070), affiliated with the university in **Potsdam,** stages excellent music-theater presentations in summer. Don't be surprised to see horse-drawn carriages along the route, as there are pockets of Amish settlements in this part of the region. Route 11 for the most part, however, is the east–west route of expedience through the north rim of the North Country. The more scenic route is the Seaway Trail following the river.

The Seaway Trail The thing to see in **Massena** is the **Eisenhower Lock,** through
⑲ which huge cargo vessels pass on their way to and from the Atlantic and the industrial heartland of America. To be sure you'll see the lock in action, call ahead (tel. 315/769–2422) to find out what time a ship is scheduled to pass through. During the nine months of the shipping season (the Seaway freezes in winter), traffic is fairly steady.

The procedure of getting a ship through the lock takes about 45 minutes, and the statistics are amazing: Raising or lowering a ship by more than 40 feet requires the displacement of 22 million gallons of water in the lock, and that amount can be flooded or drained in just 10 minutes. The statistics at the nearby St. Lawrence–Franklin D. Roosevelt Project, one of the largest hydroelectric stations in the United States, are also awesome: 150 million gallons a minute pass through the dam, propelled by the force of all the water stored in the Great Lakes. The power project can be reached by continuing through the tunnel beneath the Eisenhower Lock for three miles.

From Massena, the Seaway Trail follows Route 37 southwest to
⑳ **Ogdensburg,** the oldest settlement in the region. Its custom house, built in 1809, is the oldest active federal building in the United States. But the main reason to stop in Ogdensburg is the **Remington Museum** (303 Washington St., tel. 315/393–2425). Although Frederic Remington gained fame as a painter of the American West, he was born just to the south in Canton. The museum houses more than 200 of his works, the largest collection in the United States.

The Seaway Trail joins Route 12 in Ogdensburg, and state campgrounds begin to appear at regular intervals of 15 miles or so along the route. One bears the name of Jacques Cartier, the Frenchman who first explored the St. Lawrence in 1535 and who gave the river its name. Making nightly stopovers in the campgrounds is a popular way to tour the Seaway during the summer. The campgrounds are well maintained, with plenty of room for picnicking or recreational sports. For example, the state park at Wellesley Island, just below the International Bridge, has a golf course and a nature preserve in which to explore. But the real appeal of the campgrounds is the fascination of the Seaway traffic, from small sailboats to large tankers, passing before your campsite. For summer weekends, campsites must be booked well ahead of time, especially if you have a vehicle that requires hookups.

Alexandria Bay and Clayton are the focal points for summer visitors to the Thousand Islands. They are the ports from which most of the island owners make their way to their secluded summer homes. Both are good walking towns, since they are well away from the highway traffic and are fairly compact. They are also the dining and lodging centers of the region. Lunching dockside or at one of the restaurants with outdoor patios is one of the great pleasures of the Thousand Islands on a summer day.

㉑ **Alexandria Bay** is the place from which tour boats leave to explore the Thousand Islands; unless you have your own boat, taking a cruise tour is one of the obligatory things to do in the Thousand Islands. The trip includes the option of stopping at **Boldt Castle,** the signature structure of the islands. The 120-room replica of a stone castle was built by George Boldt, developer of the Waldorf-Astoria Hotel in New York City. The castle was to be a gift from Boldt to his wife. In the spirit of romanticism, he even had the island reshaped in the configuration of a heart, and hearts are integrated as design elements throughout the house. Boldt's wife died in 1904 before construction was finished, and he never visited the island again. The castle has a dark and ponderous character, but it is definitely worth a visit. In summer, Uncle Sam Boat Tours (tel. 315/482–2611) and Empire Boat Tours (tel. 315/482–9511) offer guided cruises of one to two hours from the dock at Alexandria Bay. Empire also features a "Late Night Love Boat" cruise, departing at 11 PM.

㉒ **Clayton** is a compact copy of Alexandria Bay in its shingled, clapboard character. The **Thousand Islands Shipyard Museum** houses everything from a small launch that is believed to have belonged to Ulysses S. Grant to a collection of outboard motors dating to the first one that was mass produced. *750 Mary St., tel. 315/686–4104. Admission: $4 adults, $3 senior citizens, $2 children 7–17. Open mid-May–mid-Oct.*

The other point of note in Clayton is the children's playground, a wonderful jumble of turrets and wood planks to climb and crawl over. If you have children under 10, expect them to be entertained for hours at a time.

The Seaway Trail from Clayton then follows Route 12E to Cape Vincent. As Route 12E hooks back to the southeast after Cape Vincent, you enter the breadbasket of the Thousand Islands region. This is the world of silos and pastureland, with occasional glimpses of Lake Ontario in the distance off to the right. This **㉓** interior nook of the North Country, bounded by **Watertown,** Lake Ontario, and the St. Lawrence Seaway, is active farming country, although the harsh winter conditions that charge off of Lake Ontario make for a short growing season. If you are interested in the farming life of the region, you might want to make a short detour to the **Agricultural Historical Museum** at Stone Mills, in the middle of the Thousand Islands–Cape Vincent–Watertown triangle. The museum, with its cheese factory and farm kitchen and demonstrations of farming activities, provides a good feel for farming in the region a century ago. *Box 108, Rte. 180, La Fargeville 13656, tel. 315/658–2353. Open June–Aug., 11–4.*

The history of settlement in this part of the North Country does not reach back much more than a century and a half. The **㉔** one historical site worth visiting is **Sackets Harbor Battlefield** (tel. 315/646–3634), which you reach by following the curl of the Seaway Trail along the lake on Route 180 and then Route 3. Sackets Harbor was the headquarters of U.S. naval operations in the St. Lawrence–Lake Ontario region for much of the 19th century. During the War of 1812, when the border between the United States and Canada was under dispute, Sackets Harbor was the scene of heavy fighting between American and British troops. The battlefield holds a position of prominence overlooking the harbor and Lake Ontario, and the breezes that come off the lake make for welcome relief in the heat of summer; it is open from mid-May through October. A reenactment of the battle is held every July, with participants from around the world sleeping out in tents on the battlefield and donning period costumes. What is most interesting about Sackets Harbor is the number of its well-preserved 19th-century structures. A particularly appealing stop is the quirky **Pickering-Beach Museum,** a small house built in 1817 that hardly feels like a museum. Instead, with its furnishings and trinkets from the 19th century, it gives more of a sense of stepping into someone's home of a previous era (tel. 315/646–2052; open June–Labor Day, 11–5).

Keep in mind that following the Seaway Trail by car is not the only way to explore the Seaway. Many summer visitors enjoy meandering through the Thousand Islands and the lake by boat —some just poking around, others with rod and reel in hand. The St. Lawrence is known as one of the best bass and muskellunge rivers in North America, and you can hire a guide service in Alexandria Bay or Clayton to get to the best fishing spots. (Fishing is not just a summertime pursuit in the Thousand Islands. Ice fishing also has its adherents during the winter-weekend derbies.) For those who want to spend just a few days exploring the islands, houseboat rentals are available in Clayton in summer, and there are many campgrounds and marinas where boats are welcome to pull in for the night. During July and August, houseboats must be booked several months in advance.

What to See and Do with Children

The Adirondacks have long been summer-camp country, and the many activities that keep campers occupied in the summer are activities that families can enjoy together: camping, hiking, canoeing, fishing, white-water rafting, etc. Keep in mind, of course, the physical capabilities of your children. Many hikes, particularly in the High Peaks region, can be rugged, with long, steep sections, and might be difficult for smaller children. Both alpine and cross-country skiing, as well as skating, are popular activities in winter throughout the North Country (*see* Participant Sports, below).

Less strenuous access to the beauty of the Adirondack region is possible at **Ausable Chasm** on Route 9, just north of Keeseville; High Falls Gorge off Route 86 near Wilmington; and **Natural Stone Bridge and Caves** near Potterville. The chasm, where the Ausable River, flowing down from the High Peaks, cuts through sandstone cliffs, is especially dramatic. Guided boat rides take visitors through parts of the chasm. The chasm is one of the oldest organized tourist attractions in the United States, dating to 1870.

For a good look back at New York's farming past, the **Agricultural Museum at Stone Mills** (Box 108, LaFargeville 13656, tel. 315/658–2353) is open from June through August. Cheese-making demonstrations, crafts fairs, and horse pulls are among the museum's demonstrations. Family farms and farm-product markets throughout the region, in cooperation with the **Adirondack North Country Association** (ANCA) offer tours and demonstrations of milking, wool-shearing, maple-syrup making, and other activities. Contact ANCA, Box 148, Lake Placid 12946, tel. 518/523–9820, for information.

The 12 county fairs scheduled throughout the region in late July and August feature various amusements and musical performances, in addition to the traditional livestock and produce competitions. The three-day Warren Youth Fair in Warrensburg in August is specifically geared toward the young farmers of the future. For fair dates, contact the **Agricultural Farm Liaison** (NYS Dept. of Agriculture and Markets, 1 Winners Circle, Albany 12235, tel. 518/457–3412).

Younger children will also enjoy the **Thousand Islands Zoo and Game Farm** in Redwood (tel. 315/628–5821), which includes a petting zoo, and the fish hatcheries at Saranac Inn (north of Saranac Lake), Cape Vincent, Crown Point, and Warrensburg.

To learn more about local ecology and wildlife, visit the **Adirondack Park Interpretive Centers,** one on Route 30 in Paul Smiths and the other, scheduled to open in autumn of 1990, on Route 28N in Newcomb. For more information, contact the Adirondack Park Interpretive Center (Box 3000, Paul Smiths 12970, tel. 518/327–3000).

Lake George has several amusement parks. **Great Escape,** with 100 rides, minishows (short performances by clowns and magicians) and activities, is about five miles south of Lake George on Route 9. **Gaslight Village,** in the village of Lake George, offers 45 rides, along with magic shows, musical jamborees, and so on. For information about both theme parks, tel. 518/668–5459 or 518/792–6568.

Other amusement/theme parks in the North Country include **Waterfun,** just off the International Bridge in the Thousand Islands area, **Enchanted Forest** in Old Forge, and **Santa's Workshop** in North Pole, off Veterans Memorial Highway leading up Whiteface Mountain.

For more cultural and educational activities, the **Adirondack Museum** in Blue Mountain Lake, the **National Museum of Racing** in Saratoga, the **Six Nations Indian Museum** in Onchionta north of Saranac Lake, and the **Thousand Islands Shipyard Museum** in Clayton hold the greatest appeal for children. **Fort Ticonderoga** and the battlefields at Saratoga and Sackets Harbor are the primary historic spots to hit (*see* Exploring the North Country, above).

Children-only backstage tours are available before and after each New York City Ballet matinee at the **Saratoga Performing Arts Center;** you must make arrangements in advance by contacting the National Museum of Dance (tel. 518/584–2225).

Puppet shows are part of the schedule of the **Adirondack Lakes Center for the Arts** (tel. 518/352–7715) in Blue Mountain Lake. The center also features crafts demonstrations and art classes for children 5 to 14.

Off the Beaten Track

Off-track diversions are the very essence of traveling through the North Country. With most of the driving in the region on two-lane roads rather than interstate highways, there is plenty of opportunity to pull over for a good view, an interesting shop, a yard sale, or a place for a picnic. Here are a few interesting alternatives:

The Mansion (tel. 518/885–1607) in Rocky City Falls, about seven miles west of Saratoga Springs on Route 29, is a good place to be close to the action but away from all the commotion of the summer scene. The stately Victorian home, with its 14-foot ceilings and eight-foot windows, is now a bed-and-breakfast. It exudes a quality of time-honored civility: Fresh flowers adorn the five bedrooms, and home-baked breads and fresh fruit are served at breakfast. The Mansion even has its own little barn stuffed with antiques if you want to poke around in the morning before heading off to the horse races.

Heading into the Adirondacks, you may want to stop by the **Barton Mines** off Route 28 in North River. Producing 90% of the world's industrial garnet (a deep-red mineral), the mine is a last vestige of the previous, and relatively unproductive, era of mining in the Adirondacks. There are tours of the mines as well as a gift shop with garnet jewelry.

Visiting a garbage dump might not seem the sort of thing you would want to do on a vacation, but taking dinner leftovers to the town dump is something of an evening ritual in the central Adirondacks. Bears, relatively tame and very responsive to the idea of a free meal, also tend to make it their presunset ritual to visit the dumps for an evening snack. The town dump at **Long Lake** is especially well known as a place for feeding the bears. In 1991, however, environmental regulations will begin closing many treasured Adirondack dumps, leaving the bears to fend for themselves. Until then, keep in mind that although most of the bears aren't aggressive, it is still a good idea to maintain a reasonable distance.

In the Thousand Islands area, the **Muskie Hall of Fame** (403 Riverside Dr., Clayton, tel. 315/686–1823), in the Old Town Hall at Clayton, honors one of the world's most neolithic-looking species of fish and the anglers who have become legends in pursuing it. The hall of fame is worth visiting less for what is there than for the peculiar thing that it is.

Shopping

Gift Ideas

The North Country is generally not the place for a shopping binge, but there are a few local items, such as maple syrup and cheeses—pungent, sharp cheddar in particular—that are widely available and make good gifts. You'll get a better feel for the character of the region—and save a dollar or two—by buying directly from the producer. Farmers' markets in the North Country and especially in the Champlain Valley and Thousand Islands areas are held most regularly in the late summer and early fall. You may also notice roadside signs near farmhouses advertising maple syrup, usually the proprietor's own reserve. Don't hesitate to stop, as passersby are usually offered a sample. Both the syrup and the cheese (if it is tightly sealed in heavy black wax) keep well for shipping.

Crafts

Crafts are another integral part of North Country life, with pottery, furniture, woolen products, wood carvings, and quilts among the products that might catch your eye. "Craft Trails in the Adirondack North Country," published by the **Adirondack North Country Craft Center** (Box 148, Lake Placid 12946, tel. 518/523–2062), is an excellent guide to shops, galleries, dealers, and individual craftspeople in the North Country. Among the places to find good crafts are the **Adirondack Lakes Center for the Arts** and **Blue Mountain Designs**, both in Blue Mountain Lake; the **Arts & Crafts Loft** in Lake George; the **Adirondack North Country Crafts Center** in Lake Placid; and **Ballard Mill Center for the Arts** in Malone. Many crafts shops and galleries keep irregular hours during the off-season, so you may have to call ahead for an appointment out of season.

Outlets

There are a number of factory outlets worth a visit. Most notable is **Saratoga Village**, a 58-shop complex in Malta about five miles south of Saratoga Springs on Route 9.

Sporting Goods

There are numerous places for sporting equipment—outfitters, tackle shops, bait shops, etc. A good place for fishing gear is **Francis Betters** on Route 86 in Wilmington; good places for canoes and canoe gear are **Moose River Outfitters** (tel. 315/369–3682) in Old Forge and **All Season's Outfitters** (tel. 518/891–6159) in Saranac Lake.

Participant Sports

It is hard to imagine coming to the North Country and not getting involved in some kind of physical activity. Hiking, canoeing, fishing, climbing, and white-water rafting are popular spring through fall, as are golf and tennis. Hunting is the sport in fall, and winter is the time for skiing (alpine and cross-country), as well as skating and ice fishing.

A guide can make your trip far more enjoyable, especially if you're taking your first trip to the Adirondacks. They not only know the best routes and are well versed in the proper safety precautions, but they can also make light work of the cumbersome preparations and logistics necessary for any outing.

Guides are licensed by New York State. A list can be obtained from the **New York State Guides Association** (Box 4337, Albany 12204), the **New York State Department of Environmental Conservation** (DEC) (50 Wolf Rd., Albany 12233), or DEC regional headquarters in Ray Brook (12977, tel. 518/891–1370), Warrensburg (12885, tel. 518/623–3671), or Watertown (13601, tel. 315/785–2261).

If you are interested in improving your wilderness skills, the **Adirondack Mountain Club** (RR 3, Box 3055, Lake George 12845, tel. 518/668–4447) runs regular training programs. Group outings are also open to members through the club, and the nominal cost of membership may be a worthwhile investment if you are planning an extended visit to the Adirondack backcountry areas. **Sagamore Lodge and Conference Center** (Raquette Lake 13436, tel. 315/354–5311) also offers seminars in wilderness-skills development.

Pesky black flies and mosquitoes take over later in the summer. An effective bug repellent is essential equipment if you are planning to spend time in the outdoors. Black bears have made a strong comeback in the Adirondacks in recent years, primarily as scavengers, so if you plan on camping out, be sure to have enough rope to suspend your food from a tree limb at least 12 feet above the ground. Even if you aren't deep in the wilderness, you might still be susceptible to the probing ways of the ever-resourceful, ever-hungry black bear. Roadside sightings are common. So you should stow your food in your car or out of reach even at roadside campsites.

Bicycling

There are several designated bicycling routes throughout the North Country that are marked by roadside signs. The marked bicycling route on Route 28 covers some pretty mountainous terrain, but the Seaway Trail between Alexandria Bay and Cape Vincent runs through generally flat or rolling farmland. The **Warren County Bikeway** meanders through wooded areas, with glimpses of the mountains, on its eight-mile trail between Lake George and Glens Falls. A map of bike routes in the Saranac Lake region is available from the **Saranac Lake Chamber of Commerce** (30 Main St., Saranac Lake 12983, tel. 518/891–1990).

Canoeing

The vast network of rivers and lakes in the North Country makes canoeing one of the best ways to experience the outdoors. Trips of 100 miles or more are possible with little or no portage required: The 170-mile Raquette River is the second-longest river in New York State. One of the best areas for canoeing in the Adirondacks is the St. Regis Canoe Area, east of Saranac Lake, where power boats are prohibited in more than 100 miles of navigable waters.

Canoe rentals are available at most lakes in the Adirondack region, both on a daily and an extended basis. For extended trips, hiring a guide service is strongly recommended. Located close by, **Adirondack Canoe Tours** (Box 291, Lake Clear 12945, tel. 518/891–1080) offers week-long sessions during the summer and fall (autumn is the best time for Adirondack canoeing). Guests enjoy lakeside log cabins and hearty meals, and each session consists of daily guided canoe trips, side hikes, and guest speakers. You might also find it advisable or necessary to hire a lake-plane service for pickup at the end of your trip, to avoid backtracking or car shuttling. **Bird's Seaplane Service** in Inlet (tel. 315/357–3631) and **Helms Aero Service** in Long Lake (tel. 518/624–3931) offer pickup service for canoe trips or fishing trips.

Fishing

Fishing is a year-round sport in the North Country. The St. Lawrence River offers some of the best bass fishing in the country. Muskellunges ("muskies," for short), averaging about 17 pounds, are also a common catch between Ogdensburg and Cape Vincent. Ice-fishing tournaments give Thousand Islanders a little sport on weekends in January and February.

Many lakes, ponds, and streams in the Adirondack area are stocked with trout and salmon. Brook trout and lake trout traditionally do well in Adirondack waters, although in recent years fishermen report catching landlocked salmon with increasing regularity. The Raquette River and Lake Champlain are reputed to be excellent waters for catching walleyed pike.

Anglers over the age of 16 are required to get licenses, which can be obtained at regional DEC offices, at town or county clerk offices, and at many sporting-goods stores, bait shops, and outfitters. The DEC maintains fishing hotlines to help steer you toward the best fishing; the number for the southeastern areas of the North Country is tel. 518/623–3682 and for the northeastern areas, tel. 315/782–2663. Again, hiring a guide is highly recommended, especially if you are interested in an extended backcountry fishing trip. Contact the New York State Guides Association or the DEC (*see* Canoeing, above).

Golf

There are 35 18-hole golf courses in the North Country open to the public and numerous other nine-hole courses. The courses at the **Whiteface Resort** (tel. 518/523–2551) in Lake Placid; the **Sagamore** (tel. 518/644–9400) in Bolton Landing; the **Saranac Inn Golf Club** (tel. 518/891–1402) on Upper Saranac Lake; and the **Westport Country Club** (tel. 518/962–4470) on Lake Champlain are especially challenging.

Hiking

Hiking is the simplest and one of the best ways to experience the North Country outdoors. Most trails are well maintained and marked by the DEC, and many trailheads are along the major routes through the Adirondack area. Look for wood signs with yellow lettering.

The most popular area for hiking is the High Peaks region, accessible from the Lake Placid area in the north, Keene in the east, and Newcomb in the south. Much ado is made of Adirondack "46ers"—the people who have ascended the 46 highest peaks in the region (most over 4,000 feet high). The **Adirondack Loj,** seven miles south of Lake Placid, off Route 73, is an excellent place to stay for climbers; it is right at the main trailhead to Mt. Marcy, Algonquin, and the rest of the High Peaks core. This lodge is accessible by car; the **John Brooks Lodge,** operated by ADK, is accessible only by a 3½-mile hike. For more information, contact **ADK Lodges** (Box 867, Lake Placid 12946, tel. 518/523–3441).

Although the High Peaks region tends to draw the most attention, it has the most rugged hiking. Many less strenuous climbs and hikes offer rewarding views and backwoods experiences, whether for half-day hikes, full-day outings, or multiday backpacking trips. There is good hiking with minimal climbing around Cranberry Lake and Schroon Lake.

Horseback Riding

There are a number of dude ranches in the Warrensburg–Lake Luzerne area. Their season generally runs from May to November. Among the best is the **Roaring Brook Ranch & Tennis Resort** (Box 671, Rte. 9 NS, Lake George 12845, tel. 518/668–5767). For North Country bridle path and trail maps, contact the DEC.

Ice Skating

People who like their ice skating with a touch of history should enjoy the public skating sessions at the **Olympic Center Ice Arena** in Lake Placid (tel. 518/523–3325), where the U.S. hockey team pulled off the "Miracle on Ice" against the Soviet Union in 1980. There are also ice rinks at Glens Falls, Plattsburgh, Saranac Lake, Potsdam, and Canton. Speed-skating enthusiasts can get in their workouts on the ovals in Lake Placid and at Saratoga State Park.

Rafting

The best month for white-water rafting and tubing is June, when the rivers swell with waters from the mountain snow run-off. However, damming along many rivers in the region, particularly the upper Hudson, maintains a fairly steady flow of water throughout the year. The Hudson River Gorge and the Moose River have rapids consistently rated up to Class V, which is pretty bracing stuff. The waters of the Sacandaga River, another favored rafting route, are generally less fierce. The top rafting companies in the region are **Adirondack River Outfitters** in Watertown (tel. 315/369–3536) and **Hudson River Rafting Co.**, with offices in North Creek (tel. 518/251–3215), in Lake Luzerne (tel. 518/696–2964), and in Watertown (tel. 315/782–7881).

Skiing

Alpine   The largest alpine skiing resort in the North Country is **Whiteface Mountain** in Wilmington, eight miles east of Lake Placid and site of the 1980 Winter Olympic alpine events. Four other North Country areas have vertical rises of more than 1,000 feet. They are (in descending order of size): **Gore Mountain** in North Creek, **Hickory Ski Center** in Warrensburg, **Big Tupper** in Tupper Lake, and **West Mountain** near Glens Falls. Smaller areas with good skiing are **Oak Mountain** near Speculator and **Snow Ridge** near Turin. **Mt. Pisgah Ski Area** in Saranac Lake recently became one of the few community-operated ski centers in the country with both snowmaking facilities and night skiing.

Backcountry   Backcountry skiing has become increasingly popular in the North Country. There are several trails to ski up and down Mt. Marcy, with access from Keene and from the Adirondak Loj (tel. 518/523–3441). It is rugged work, and backcountry skiers, especially in the High Peaks area, should be well versed in the potential hazards of winter in the backcountry.

Cross-country   With 50 kilometers of groomed tracks, **Mt. Van Hoevenberg,** the site of the 1980 Winter Olympic cross-country events, seven miles south of Lake Placid on Route 73, has the most extensive track system in the North Country. The tracks are often used for races and training. These trails now link with the **Jackrabbit Trail,** an ever-growing network of ski trails connecting Keene Valley, Lake Placid, Saranac Lake, and the High Peaks region (Adirondack Ski Touring Council, Box 843, Lake Placid 12946, tel. 518/523–1365). There are several first-rate ski centers in the North Creek–Gore Mountain area. Most private ski centers charge a trail fee of between $4 and $7; tracks in state parks, such as at **Saratoga State Park** and **Wellesley Island State Park** near Alexandria Bay, are free, as are the Dewey Mt. trails in Saranac Lake (tel. 518/891–2697).

Sledding

For those looking for a different sort of winter thrill, there are the bobsled and luge runs at **Mt. Van Hoevenberg.** If you give bobsledding a shot, it will be as a passenger with an experienced driver; on the luge, you're on your own the last few turns of the course.

Snowmobiling

Trails cover many of the summer hiking trails, especially in the southern and western reaches of the Adirondacks and throughout the Thousand Islands area. Trail maps are available from the Department of Environmental Conservation, 50 Wolf Rd., Albany 12233.

Spectator Sports

The Lake Placid area has been designated an official training site by the U.S. Olympic Committee, so at any time of year you may see Olympic-caliber athletes in a variety of sports, either in training or in competition. Summer athletic competitions are held in boxing, cycling, figure skating, and ski jumping on plastic mats on the 70-meter jump just south of town. This is also where freestyle skiers practice and perform "aerials"—the twisting and somersaulting jumps that are part of the growing sport of freestyle skiing. Aerialists can be seen training at the site for much of July and August, and a major competition is held at the end of August. Lake Placid is also the site of the *I Love New York* Horse Show that is held in mid-July and features some of the top show jumpers in the country.

The athletic competition picks up in winter at Lake Placid, with national and international competitions in bobsledding and luge at Mt. Van Hoevenberg, alpine racing and freestyle competition at Whiteface, and speed skating at the Olympic oval in the center of town. Hockey and figure-skating competitions are held in the Olympic ice arena, right next door to the speed-skating oval. For information on Lake Placid athletic events, contact the **Olympic Regional Development Authority** (tel. 518/523–1655 or 800/462–6236).

Boating

Sailing regattas are held during summer weekends on Lake Champlain, Lake George, and in the Thousand Islands region. Yacht racing can be visually dramatic, but the competition (unless you are well versed in the subtleties of the sport) can be less than enthralling. A more thrill-packed combination of vessel and water are the canoe and kayak races during the **Hudson River White Water Derby** (tel. 518/251–3465) in North Creek the first weekend in May.

Horse Racing

The 24-day thoroughbred-racing session at **Saratoga Raceway** (tel. 518/584–6200) each August is a major social as well as sporting event. The highlight of the season is the Travers Stakes, but the 100-year-old flat track attracts high-quality thoroughbreds for all its races. Post time for the first race is 1:30 PM, but true racing fans come for breakfast, served between 7 and 9:30, and spend the morning soaking up all the atmosphere in the barn and paddock areas.

Saratoga Harness (tel. 518/584–2110), about a mile from the thoroughbred track, is open throughout the year except for periods in April and December. Post time for the first race is 7:45 PM, and the glass-enclosed grandstand provides welcome comfort during the winter months. The trackside restaurant is excellent.

Dining

Saratoga is indisputably the culinary champion of the North Country in quantity, variety, and, generally speaking, quality. Saratoga has the advantage of having a sizable, relatively affluent year-round population that restaurants can bank on for business. This is not to say that the North Country north of Saratoga is a dining wasteland; the Olympic region in particular has a number of fine eateries, primarily in Lake Placid. Alexandria Bay and Clayton have the largest clusters of good restaurants in the Thousand Islands–Seaway area.

Throughout much of the Adirondack region, however, restaurant dining is a limited concept. Meals at traditional lodges tend to be tied to accommodations, although many establishments will accept nonguests for dinner. The emphasis tends to be on large portions and on home cooking, meaning that freshbaked breads and rolls are a common treat. Surprisingly, with all the fishing in the North Country, truly fresh fish is not an easy find. New York food inspection regulations require fish, by and large, to go through a food inspection center before it is okayed for consumption. There are, however, restaurants that will cook up your fresh catch for you. Just be sure to call ahead before walking through the door with your stuffed creel.

Highly recommended restaurants are indicated by a star ★.

Category	Cost*
Expensive	over $25
Moderate	$15–$25
Inexpensive	under $15

*per person without sales tax (7%), service, or drinks

Central Adirondacks

Expensive **Big Moose Inn.** A lot of Adirondack flavor is found in this off-the-beaten track, chef-owned restaurant and cocktail lounge overlooking the lake. A fireplace warms things up if needed, and there is outdoor dining when weather permits. Homemade breads, soups, and desserts as well as the prime rib, veal, and lamb dishes are the draws at this inn. Daily specials attract the budget-conscious; those who want a special lunch or evening treat come for the vintage wines and ambience. *5 mi from Rte. 28 at Eagle Bay, tel. 315/357–2042. Dress: casual. AE, MC, V. Open mid-May–Oct. 20 and Christmas Day. Expensive.*

Friends Lake Inn. This restored 1860s country inn emphasizes sophisticated dining, although rooms and cottages also are available. The "regional imaginative" label doesn't begin to describe the range of choices on the menu. From appetizers to dessert, everything is fresh and flavorful. The distinctive dining room features low tin ceilings, slender columns, and wainscoting of chestnut wood. The cocktail lounge in the front has the best lake view and a respectable wine list. In winter, a free skiing package is arranged at nearby Gore Mountain. *Friends Lake Rd., Chestertown, tel. 518/494–4751. Dress: casual. Reservations preferred. MC, V.*

Rene's. A remarkable place that proves distance should be no hindrance when it comes to finding first-rate dining. Rene's sits on a high ridge between the Northway and Route 9, not far from Lake George, with a view of the mountains that is forgotten once the food appears. Continental cuisine and luscious French dessert concoctions make a meal here a feast to remember. The decor, kept deliberately low-key, is enhanced by candlelight and elegant touches. The lounge area is limited and subdued. *White Schoolhouse Rd., Chestertown, tel. 518/494–2904. Dress: informal. Reservations suggested. MC, V. Closed Mon.–Tues. during the off-season.*

Moderate **Eckerson's.** Long lines in summer testify to the popularity of this roadside restaurant. The building has little to distinguish it, inside or out, which is not an uncommon trait in the Adirondacks. However, the evident pleasure of people enjoying good food, also made and served without frills, is unmistakable. *Rte. 28, Eagle Bay, tel. 315/357–4641. Dress: casual. MC, V. Closed Tues. in June and Sept. Hours and days open vary during the off-season.*

Long View Lodge. Many generations of travelers have found good food and shelter at this roadside inn, which sits on a low bluff looking down Long Lake. Area residents drive miles for the bountiful meals (breakfast and dinner only). The accommodations are not fancy, but the care of the fourth-generation owners makes up for any deficiencies. The Lodge has 15 rooms, most with private bath, plus two cottages located near the beachfront. The food is bountiful and well prepared. *Rt. 28N, Long Lake, tel. 518/624–2862. Closed Dec. 2–Apr. 30. MC, V.*

Old Mill Restaurant. A huge mill wheel, a remnant of this building's former function, decorates the front of this restaurant on Old Forge's main street. The interior may seem dark and gloomy, but no one cares once the food is served. It is substantial and thoroughly American: steaks, seafood, and homebaked bread. The bar is designed for no-nonsense drinking, not sitting about all evening. In summer, outdoor dining can be very relaxed. *Rte. 28, Old Forge, tel. 315/369–3661. Dress: casual. AE, MC, V.*

Van Auken's Inn. This inn is a restored historic building fronted by large white columns and two levels of porches. The original bar, left from the old lumbering days, will never lose its aura. A family dedicated to producing good food has made it a place much sought after, especially since it serves throughout the day. *Off Rte. 28, Old Forge, tel. 315/369–3033. Dress: casual. MC, V. Check hours during the off-season.*

Inexpensive **Cobbletone.** This longtime restaurant has an Adirondack ambience: a big, airy room with carpeting, nice lighting, and service bar. The service is generally good, and the menu can extend from chicken wings and pizza to standard steak and seafood dishes. *Rte. 30, Long Lake, tel. 518/624–6331. Dress: casual. AE, DC, MC, V.*

Farm Restaurant. The big, open interior decorated with antiques and old farm implements is popular with families who really pay more attention to the liberal helpings of food. Adirondack-style breakfasts have real lasting power. Burgers, good soups, sandwichs, and omelets make up the lunch menu. This is a good place to stock up for the outdoor activities prevalent in the area. *Rte. 28, Old Forge. No phone. Dress: come as you are. No credit cards.*

Lake George Area

Expensive **The Algonquin.** "One if by land and two if by sea" might be the watchword; those who live or vacation on the lake arrive at this Sagamore restaurant by boat as often as by car. Two generations and 30 years' tradition account for its steady expansion. The downstairs Pub Room is more casual and stresses a burger-sandwich menu and light meals. The upper level Topside offers gourmet entrees featuring veal and seafood. Dockside activity provides entertainment for bar guests and front tables. *Lake Shore Dr., Bolton Landing, tel. 518/644–9442 or 518/644–9440. Dress: informal. Reservations requested for Topside. AE, DC, MC, V. Closed Nov. 15–Apr.*

The Grist Mill. Trappings of the original mill that literally overhangs the bubbling waters of the Schroon River are part of the Grist Mill's decor. A split-level interior hugs the bank; timbered ceilings, interesting woodwork, and strategic window placement add to the visual enjoyment. The preparation and presentation of the food, labeled American regional, are equally attractive. *River St., Warrensburg, tel. 518/623–3949. Dress: casual. Reservations advised. AE, CB, MC, V.*

The Log Jam. A new greenhouse has expanded the luncheon crowds. Steak and prime rib plus creative seafood selections keep up with changing American tastes. *Rtes. 9 and 149, Lake George, tel. 518/798–1155. Dress: informal. AE, CB, DC, MC, V.*

★ **The Sagamore.** Each of the three dining rooms at this island resort has its own atmosphere and cuisine. **Trillium** features formal gourmet dining with a hint of nouvelle; **Sagamore Dining Room** features Continental and American fare (grilled seafood and veal are specialties) and a great Sunday brunch buffet; **Club Grill** re-creates a Tudor atmosphere and serves up steaks, burgers, and other grilled items. *Bolton Landing, tel. 518/644–9400. Reservations required. AE, DC, MC, V. Lunch and dinner in all but Trillium, which has dinner only.*

Shoreline Restaurant and Marina. A large, canopied deck puts visitors right in the middle of the action surrounding the Lake George public docks. Cajun and mesquite-grilled dishes and fresh seafood in some tantalizing combinations are among the specialties. The menu is less extensive than imaginative—just reading it makes the mouth water. *4 James St., Lake George, tel. 518/668–2875. Dress: casual. Reservations advised. AE, MC, V.*

Moderate   **Bavarian House.** The solid look of this big, square brown building that sits above the highway is lightened inside by plenty of wide windows and welcoming service at any time of day. In warm weather, the terrace is used. German specialties at very reasonable prices and standard American offerings are featured on the dinner menu. *Lake Shore Dr., Lake George, tel. 518/668–2476. Dress: casual. AE, MC, V.*

Garden in the Park. The Queensbury Hotel in Glens Falls faces a small, neat park, hence the name of its restaurant. American cuisine—steaks and seafood—is featured. The Sunday brunch attracts locals as well as hotel guests. *Queensbury Hotel, 99 Ridge St., Glens Falls, tel. 518/792–1121. Reservations advised. AE, CB, D, DC, MC, V.*

Mario's. Many call this the best Italian restaurant between Albany and Montreal. This interior of this sizable, white-clapboard building of no particular distinction resembles an Italian villa with red-velvet trim and all the appropriate aromas. Fresh seafood and veal dishes are featured. *469 Canada St., Lake George, tel. 518/668–2665. Dress: casual. Reservations requested Sun., holidays. AE, DC, MC, V.*

The Coachman. An imposing building constructed of huge logs, this restaurant has a reputation for fine food that is as solid as its fieldstone foundation. Inside, the veneered logs, heavy beams, wrought-iron fixtures, judicious lighting, and fireplaces continue the rustic atmosphere. Traditional American fare is highlighted by prime rib and seafood specialties. A salad bar, tasty soup concoctions, and homemade bread and pastries can make a meal simple or lush. *Lake George Rd., Rte. 9, Glens Falls, tel. 518/793–4455. Dress: casual. Reservations advised. Valet parking evenings in summer. AE, DC, MC, V.*

Olympic Region

Expensive   **Charcoal Pit.** The main dining room has high ceilings, a fireplace, hanging plants, paintings on the walls, and big windows on two sides. All entrees have a Continental touch by the chef-owner, with a combination of Greek, French and Italian specialties; the veal and seafood are particularly well done, as are the beef and chops. A small bar and cocktail lounge and other rooms of varying size accommodate overflow during busy times. The wine vault is visible at the entrance. *Rte. 86 near Cold Brook Plaza, Lake Placid, tel. 518/523–3050. Reservations accepted. AE, DC, V.*

★   **Lake Placid Manor.** One of the private "great camps" built before the turn of the century, this small, personal hotel stands as a prime example of the rustic architecture for which the Adirondacks are famous. Sumptuous and sophisticated meals with a Continental flair have become a tradition. During good weather, cocktails on the porch are enhanced by magnificent views of Lake Placid and Whiteface Mountain. *Whiteface Inn Rd., Lake Placid, tel. 518/523–2573. Reservations preferred. AE, MC, V.*

Lindsay's at the Woodshed. Upstairs at the rear of a more conventional, streetside restaurant is a candlelit setting that gives the feeling of having stepped momentarily onto a movie set. Gourmet entrees with primarily French antecedents, coddled with wines, herbs, and sauces are featured. There are simpler dishes, too, and at least a sampling of most meat and seafood choices. Espresso and cappuccino generally suffice for the finishing touch. *237 Main St., Lake Placid, tel. 518/523–9470. Reservations advised. DC, V.*

Steak and Stinger. Genuine Tiffany lamps and barnsiding interiors were installed here before the style was imitated. These touches, along with a collection of paintings of uneven quality, contribute to a country setting. Cocktails are served in the greenhouse, and in high season, summer and winter, munchies can be ordered there if the wait is long. Daily specials lean toward fresh seafood, and several exceptional appetizers are offered. Beef and veal are the headliners; soups are prepared in-house. *Rte. 73, Cascade Rd., Lake Placid, tel. 518/523–9927. DC, MC, V.*

Moderate   **Alpine Cellar.** A modest motel occupies the main level, but a large downstairs room with high windows facing the mountains is the real draw. A cocktail lounge on a small balcony overlooks the dining tables and sets the atmosphere with its big steins for beer. Traditional German food is served. *Rte. 86, Wilmington Rd., Lake Placid, tel. 518/523–2180. Reservations advised. No lunch. AE, MC, V.*

Cascade Inn. A pleasant, homey atmosphere is presented with simple decor and low-ceilinged rooms. On one side, the bar and some tables share a fireside setting that encourages before and after dinner chatting if traffic permits. A straightforward American style offers few frills, but high quality. Nightly specials are highlighted on Saturdays by prime rib. The inn is the kind of place travelers are delighted to find after a hard day of driving or outdoor activities. A motel is attached. *Rte. 73, Cascade Rd., Lake Placid, tel. 518/523–2130. Reservations advised. AE, DC, MC, V.*

Great Adirondack Steak and Seafood. "Sophisticated rustic" might describe this interior warmed by real wood and a judicious number of antiques. The street and sidewalk scene visible from the front windows may prove diverting. Imagination goes into the treatment given to a basically American menu, with some lively regional twists, such as Cajun cooking. A small room keeps the bar activity separate from the dining area. The movie theater is next door and the public park, with weekly summer concerts, is across the street. *Main St., Lake Placid, tel. 518/523–1629. AE, DC, MC, V.*

Red Fox. The setting of this restaurant is less important than a reputation that is built on consistently good food, prepared with care, and generous libations. The interior, divided into four long, narrow rooms that make it intimate, is made comfortable with carpeting (except for a small dance floor), wood paneling, and subdued lighting. The bar shares the space at one end of the building but is not obtrusive; a cozier corner with fireplace is an alternative. The cuisine is basically American, with plenty of choice and good specials. It's one of the first places the locals will recommend. *Rte. 3, Tupper Lake Rd., Saranac Lake, tel. 518/891–2127. DC, MC, V.*

Villa Vespa. An unpretentious atmosphere pervades this restaurant. In addition to the expected offerings, there are several good meatless dishes and fresh-baked breads. Daily specials include fresh seafood, and everything comes in generous proportions. It's a place favored by athletes taking part in the year-round cross-country skiing and running events. There is outside service on the patio during the summer. *Rte. 86, Saranac Ave., Lake Placid, tel. 518/523–9959. Reservations advised. AE, DC, MC, V.*

Inexpensive **Artist's Cafe.** This popular spot on Lake Placid's Main Street has an enclosed lakeside deck and a coziness to its dining room and bar. Hearty soup, omelets, and imaginative sandwich combinations make up the lunch menu. Dinner entrees are known for quality rather than quantity and carry the label "new American." Seafood dishes are particularly good, but standard fare is given distinctive treatment. *Main St., Lake Placid, tel. 518/523–9493. AE, DC, MC, V.*

★ **Casa del Sol.** Travelers who know the Southwest will be surprised to find this bright and funky Mexican outpost so far from its origins. The food's spiciness is restrained, but the authenticity should not be questioned. Casa del Sol is an Adirondack legend, and its popularity can be measured by the size of the crowd in the tiny bar on Friday nights off-season and anytime in summer. *Rte. 86, Lake Flower Ave., Saranac Lake, tel. 518/891–0977. No credit cards.*

Saratoga Area

Expensive **Cock N' Bull.** The smallest incorporated village in New York State (Galway) is the site of this barn-cum-restaurant featuring chalkboard specials of pheasant, quail, and game (in season); otherwise a Continental menu—prime rib and seafood—prevails. *Parkis Mills Rd., off Rte. 147, Galway, tel. 518/882–6962. Reservations accepted. No credit cards. Dinner only.*

The Elms. Homemade pastas—including such novelties as redpepper pasta—and veal scallopine are the specialties of this house, operated by the Viggiani family with lots of Italian-style warmth. *Rte. 9, Malta, tel. 518/587–2277. Reservations advised. No credit cards. Dinner only.*

Moderate **Eartha's Kitchen.** This small country kitchen is a local favorite,
★ especially for the mesquite-grilled seafood dishes chosen from an outstanding chalkboard menu. *60 Court St., Saratoga Springs, tel. 518/583–0602. Reservations are a must. AE, DC, MC, V. Dinner only.*

Gaffney's. This restaurant is many miles from Buffalo, yet that city's culinary claim to fame is featured on the menu: Buffalo wings. If that doesn't satisfy you, there's an ample selection of salads, burgers, pasta, and veal. The garden bar out back helps take care of the spillover. *16 Caroline St., Saratoga Springs, tel. 518/587–7359. No reservations. AE, DC, MC, V. Lunch and dinner.*

★ **Sperry's.** A new and somewhat Art Deco bistro, Sperry's is already highly regarded for its individualized care. The fresh fish, pasta, and veal are all good, and the soft-shell crab and malt sole are outstanding. The barroom is quite pleasant. *30½ Caroline St., Saratoga Springs, tel. 518/584–9618. No reservations. MC, V. Lunch and dinner.*

Springwater Inn. Big windows overlook Union Avenue from this dining room, which mixes the casual decor typical of the Adirondacks with Victorian charm. There is often a piano player featured in the Bucktrout Taproom. Try the Adirondack platter, which includes grilled brook trout, rabbit, and venison, or Chicken Hopkins, a boneless breast of chicken along with jumbo shrimp. *139 Union Ave., Saratoga Springs, tel. 518/584–6440. AE, DC, MC, V. Lunch and dinner.*

Wheatfields. This recent addition to the Saratoga scene has locals lining up for the more than two dozen pasta dishes. All pasta and breads are made on the premises. *440 Broadway, Saratoga Springs, tel. 518/587–0534. Reservations not accepted. AE, D, DC, MC, V. Lunch and dinner.*

Inexpensive **Bruno's.** A pizza parlor circa 1955 is the best way to describe this eatery where the menus are printed on album jackets and the pies come with such unlikely toppings as zucchini and barbecued chicken. Yes, you can order mushrooms and sausage if you care to be so mundane. *237 Union Ave., Saratoga Springs, tel. 518/583–3333. Reservations not accepted. MC, V.*

★ **Hattie's Chicken Shack.** The house special, surprise surprise, is fried chicken. But the rest of the southern fare, as served up by Hattie and husband Bill Austin, an older couple with ties to the Deep South, is just as tempting. *45 Phila St., Saratoga Springs, tel. 518/584–4790. Reservations a must in summer. No credit cards. Breakfast, lunch, and dinner.*

Lodging

Luxurious accommodations are hard to come by in the North Country, although good, comfortable lodging is plentiful. A few of the places listed are technically bed-and-breakfasts but feature enough hotel or motel amenities—private baths or privacy in general—to be included. Quite a few lodges offer meal plans, which are a recommended option, especially in the Central Adirondacks, where there are relatively few restaurants.

Room price and availability vary with the season. The highest rates coincide with the tightest room squeeze during Saratoga's racing season (the month of August), when rates more than double. Make reservations at least six months ahead. Throughout the North Country expect to pay more during July and August, the fall foliage season, and during the Christmas holidays. Many places offer special rates for children (sharing a room with their parents) and senior citizens. Be sure to inquire. In areas of the Adirondacks you might find it harder to come up with a room in the winter than in the summer, since many places close between November and May. Lodgings that are closed in the off-season are so noted in the listings.

Though B&Bs are common in this region of New York State, their character and quality varies considerably. You can stay in a farmhouse for less than $15 a night or opt for suitelike accommodations in a Victorian mansion for close to $100 a night.

Meals vary as well, since they are generally prepared by the proprietor rather than by a chef. Many B&Bs are open only during the peak summer season, especially in the Adirondacks. Shared baths are common, in-room television or phones are rare, and warm hospitality is the norm. One advantage of a B&B over a hotel: The proprietors are often more willing to provide useful inside information on the best places to fish, shop, and eat.

For further information, contact **North Country B&B Reservations Service** (Box 238, Lake Placid 12946, tel. 518/523–9474). In the Lake George area, contact the **Warren County Tourism Office** (Municipal Center, Lake George Village 12845, tel. 518/ 761–6366). In Saratoga, contact the **Saratoga Chamber of Commerce** (494 Broadway, Saratoga Springs 12866, tel. 518/584– 3255). And in the Thousand Islands, contact the **1000 Islands International Council** (Box 400, Alexandria Bay 13607, tel. 800/8– ISLAND or 800/5–ISLAND in New York).

Highly recommended hotels are indicated by a star ★.

Category	Cost*
Very Expensive	over $80
Expensive	$60–$80
Moderate	$40–$60
Inexpensive	under $40

per double room without meals, tax (8%), or service

Central Adirondacks

Expensive ★ **Balsam House Inn and Restaurant.** This elegantly restored inn located on a bluff overlooking Friends Lake dates to 1860. A spiral staircase, lots of wicker, and charming bedrooms all help to connote the past. Balsam House has a bar, cocktail lounge, patio, and windows that look out upon the beachfront. The dining room is a regional favorite for the candlelight, classical music ambience, and the exceptional French country cuisine. Specialties include rack of lamb, sweetbreads, and Adirondack trout. Sunset cocktail cruises on the lake can be arranged. *Friends Lake, Atateka Dr., Box 365, Chestertown 12817, tel. 518/494–2828 or 518/494–4431. 20 rooms. Reservations preferred; recommended in high season. AE, CB, DC, MC, V.*

Elk Lake Lodge. This 12,000-acre private preserve at the southern edge of the High Peaks has its own and public hiking trails, trout and salmon fishing in the lake and surrounding streams, and designated hunting areas. The spacious common rooms in the main lodge have the ambience of an old Adirondack camp, which it once was; the fare generally is hearty American. Quiet places for picnicking, swimming, or even a little reading can be found along the shore. *Blue Ridge Rd., North Hudson 12855, tel. 518/532–7616. 6 rooms in main lodge, 7 sleeping cabins. No credit cards. Closed Dec.–Apr.*

Hemlock Hall. The complex lies at the end of the only public road that reaches the farther shores of Blue Mountain Lake, which gives guests great privacy. The main lodge feels old without looking old and has the more intimate rooms of a private home. Modern cottages are set about the woodsy shore. The meals are the most favored in the area, but space for outside diners is limited. Tennis court, beach with boats and canoes, and box lunches for day trips are alternatives to a good workout in a front porch rocker. *Hemlock Hall Rd., Blue Mountain Lake 12812, tel. 518/352–7706. 13 lodge rooms, 12 cottages. No credit cards. Closed Nov.–Apr.*

Wood's Lodge. The main-street bustle is only a few blocks from this lovely old inn with cottages overlooking Schroon Lake, one of the few survivors of its kind in the region. Big maple trees dominate the scene; boats are provided on the private beach. Wood's Lodge is a change of pace from the usual frenetic activity evident elsewhere on the summer scene. *East St., Schroon Lake 12870, tel. 518/532–7529. 20 rooms. Kitchen apartments and cottages. No credit cards. Closed Oct.–Apr.*

Moderate   **Cold River Ranch.** The ranch is well off the beaten path and little known, which adds to its appeal. You can gain access on horseback or cross-country skis to the western side of the High Peaks Wilderness area, and the major canoe route through the region is also not far away. Ice fishing and snowshoeing are alternatives in winter, and guides and instruction are available. Fishermen and hunters find the ranch an ideal haven. *Corey's, Rte. 3, Tupper Lake 12986, tel. 518/359–7559. 6 rooms; shared baths. No credit cards.*

Country Club Motel. A perfectly standard motel operation that might be found anywhere, this location has the advantage of space and snow in winter so snowmobilers can head off from home base for their cross-country forays. Some connected units, some refrigerators, and extended-stay discounts encourage family groups in summer and long-weekend visits in winter. The motel is near the golf course and has a heated outdoor pool on its ample grounds for summer enjoyment. *Rte. 28, Box 419, Old Forge 13420, tel. 315/369–6340. 27 units. AE, D, MC, V.*

Dun Roamin Cabins. Although this cabin/cottage complex may look like a relic of the '30s from the outside pine paneling, carpeting, and up-to-date furnishings have an entirely different effect inside. This property is hooked into one of the region's snowmobiling networks, and public hiking and cross-country ski trails are literally next door. Ice fishing is another sport option. In summer, boats are maintained at a nearby marina, and an outdoor pool, a variety of lawn games, grills, and picnic tables are available on the grounds. *Rte. 9, Box 535, Schroon Lake 12870, tel. 518/532–7277. 9 rooms: 3 cabins, 6 cottages (efficiencies). MC, V.*

Garnet Hill Lodge. The main lodge, a former private camp, has a big common room replete with a striking fireplace made from stone quarried nearby. The kitchen, one of the best in the region, serves American cuisine and a magnificent Saturday night buffet. Dining is also available on the porch, with a wonderful view. Except for one vintage summer cottage, outlying buildings and the lodge sleeping rooms are done in modern style. Wilderness, including nearby Thirteenth Lake, and the most extensive private cross-country ski trails in the region, is very much part of the scheme. Garnet Hill Lodge also features tennis courts. *13th Lake Rd., North River 12856, tel. 518/251–2444. 25 rooms, 9 cottages. No credit cards.*

The Hedges. The main inn of this sprawling complex has a Victorian look and a dining room serving guests only, and the cottages might be found along almost any beachfront. The current owners are updating their property but retaining the Adirondack rustic touches. The docks and beach are replete with boats and canoes; tennis courts are closer to the highway, but everything is screened from traffic and noise by trees. Picnic lunches can be arranged. *Rte. 28, Blue Mountain Lake 12812, tel. 518/352–7325. 13 rooms, 13 cabins. No credit cards. Closed Dec.–Apr.*

Inexpensive   **Blue Spruce Motel.** A compact, crisp facility, this small motel near the center of the village does indeed have big spruces standing guard over the outdoor heated pool. It also sits next door to one of the best restaurants in Old Forge. Some units are connected, and one is an efficiency. Additional parking for snowmobile and boat trailers is available. *Main St., Box 604, Old Forge 13420, tel. 315/369–3817. 13 rooms. MC, V.*

Inn on Gore Mountain. This resort is often overlooked because it lies just beyond the ski-center entrance. The main lodge has a rustic interior, big beams overhead, and stone fireplaces. The restaurant, which serves dinner only, has a loft overlooking the main floor and a cocktail lounge downstairs. Skiing, an outdoor pool for summer use, river-running, hunting, and fishing are all available. *Peaceful Valley Rd., North Creek 12853, tel. 518/251 –2111. 16 rooms. AE, V. Restaurant closed Aug.–Oct.*

Red Top Inn. This bright, well-kept inn has a desirable lake view. Like other area inns, it shares the shoreline with the highway, but the beachfront is nevertheless enjoyable. In winter it has the advantage of proximity to Big Tupper Ski Center, which also operates chairlift rides in summer. An outdoor pool sheltered by the buildings is an alternative in case the lake water is cool or the breeze is strong. A picnic area with fireplaces is provided. *Moody Rd., Tupper Lake 12986, tel. 518/359–9209. 15 rooms, 4 cabins, 4 efficiencies. AE, DC, V.*

Sunset Park Motel. This motel provides idyllic settings—a broad expanse of lake with low mountains on the far horizon—and activity at the village outdoor recreation center next door—everything from ballgames to annual lumberjack contests. Boats, motors, and canoes can be rented. Some of the units have kitchenettes, but shopping and fast-food services are close by. *Demars Blvd., Rte. 3, Tupper Lake 12986, tel. 518/359 –3995. 11 rooms. AE, MC, V.*

Valhaus Motel. Large rooms and comfortable furnishings can be found in this alpine-design motel with appropriate wood trim and diamond-paned windows. There is little in the way of extras except for complimentary coffee in the rooms, but the motel is located on the road to Gore Mt. Ski Center and not far from the Hudson River. *Peaceful Valley Rd., North Creek 12853, tel. 518/251–2700. 12 rooms. DC, V.*

Lake George Area

Expensive
★
Canoe Island Lodge. The island facing the main lodge and cottages provides an escape for shoreside activities. It also lends privacy and intimacy to one of the widest spots in 30-mile-long Lake George. This lodge is a carefully preserved former private retreat with an air of understated elegance. A leisurely attitude overtakes even the pursuit of water sports and tennis. A restaurant, coffee shop, and cocktail lounge cover all needs. Box lunches are provided for excursions. Guests may bring their own boats. *Lake Shore Dr., Box 144, Diamond Point 12824, tel. 518/668–5592. 72 rooms. No credit cards. Closed mid-Oct.–mid-May.*

Dunham's Bay Lodge. This resort motel is located on the quieter side of Lake George, the main lodge has a rustic old-inn feeling, with a large, inviting fireplace and spacious grounds. The indoor/outdoor pool and beach are the focal points, as viewed from sun terraces around the pool. A heated indoor pool, tennis courts, playground, and picnic area round out the recreational facilities. A coffee shop, snack bar, and cocktail lounge are also available. *Rte. 9L, RR1, Box 1179, Lake George 12845, tel. 518/ 656–9242. 55 rooms, 10 cottages. AE, MC, V.*

Georgian Motel. Part of Lake George's largest and glitziest motel stretches alongside the village's main street and the remainder reaches to the waterside. Its elegant restaurant features French-American cuisine and a view of the lake. The night scene at the Terrace Lounge is about the liveliest in town, featuring entertainment and music for dancing. Leisure time can be divided between the 75-foot heated outdoor pool with patio and the lakefront. *384 Canada Street, Lake George 12845, tel. 518/668-5401. 167 rooms. AE, MC, V.*

Hidden Valley Mountainside Resort. Gemlike Lake Vanare and wooded hills give this complete resort a hidden air. It features tennis and other racquet games, archery, horseback riding, plus indoor and outdoor heated pools and a beach. Excellent food is served in several settings, with separate spaces for cocktail lounges, entertainment, and dancing. Special theme weekends, including mystery-solving, go on throughout the year. In winter, on-premises skiing with chairlift and instruction, snowmobiling and sleigh rides are offered. *Hidden Valley Rd., RR2, Box 228, Lake Luzerne 12846, tel. 518/696-2431 or NYS 800-HIDDENV. 105 rooms. AE, DC, V.*

Melody Manor Resort Motel. Spaciousness distinguishes this lakeside resort. Motel units are on broad lawns that slope gently to the private beach. Small boats are available, plus tennis, lawn games, outdoor pool, a playground, and a picnic area. In the highly recommended Manor Inn Restaurant, which serves breakfast and dinner, pine paneling and a large fireplace impart a welcoming atmosphere; there is also a cocktail lounge with entertainment. *Lake Shore Dr., Box 366, Bolton Landing 12814, tel. 518/644-9750. 40 rooms. No credit cards. Closed Nov.-Apr.*

Merrill Magee House. A narrow lane leads from the street to the rear of this restored 19th-century house, which has wide lawns, gardens, and big maple trees. Antiques are perfectly at home in the small, low-ceilinged rooms. A remodeled former carriage house attached at the rear has a cathedral ceiling and high windows that add charm to the main dining room. The Continental cuisine, with many choices in each course, has a well-deserved reputation for excellence; reservations are preferred. *Hudson St., Warrensburg 12885, tel. 518/623-2449. 13 rooms. AE, DC.*

Roaring Brook Ranch and Tennis Resort. This is a superb resort only a short drive into the mountains west of Lake George. The main building houses a rustic pub, coffee shop, sitting and game room with fireplace, and a spacious dining room with wide windows that face Prospect Mountain. Large, strategically placed motel units vary in style but blend well because of exterior woodwork. Three pools, one indoors, five lighted tennis courts, and horseback riding fill the day. Entertainment, dancing, and summer cookouts provide evening diversion. *Luzerne Rd., Lake George 12845, tel. 518/668-5767. 141 rooms. MC, V.*

Tahoe Beach Club and Resort. Multilevel, deluxe motel units with private balconies or terraces extend down the steep slope between the highway and the lakefront. The Tahoe Beach Club has a restaurant, bar, and cafe for breakfast and lunch. Service is available at the heated outdoor pool. The waterfront has a beach, boats, and dock space for rent. *Lake Shore Dr., Lake George 12845, tel. 518/668-5711. 73 rooms. AE, DC, V. Closed Nov.-Apr.*

Moderate **Colonial Manor Inn.** The trim and tended appearance of the buildings plus the convenient location make the Colonial Manor appealing. It features both cottages and motel units, where children under age 12 stay free. The pool faces the street, but pleasant lawns, trees, and a playground offer alternative space at the rear. *Canada St., Box 528, Lake George 12845, tel. 518/ 668–4884. 35 motel rooms, 20 cottages. AE, MC, V.*

Juliana Motel. Seclusion is provided by big trees that screen out both highway and neighbors. But the sloped setting allows for a clear view of the lake. The motel is set between the outdoor pool, with a sun deck and the beachfront with its boats and aquabikes. Cottages, efficiencies, and connected units in the motel make for flexible arrangements. There is also a playground and picnic area with fireplaces. *Lake Shore Dr., Rte. 9N, Box 63, Diamond Point 12824, tel. 518/668–5191. 26 rooms. No credit cards. Closed Sept.–May.*

Split Rail Motel and Cottages. This series of well-kept motel, efficiency, and cottage combinations, some with fireplaces, are stepped down in close proximity from the highway to the water's edge. Accommodations can be adjusted to the size of the party. Games and a playground are available, as well as an outdoor pool, picnic area, and full range of activities on the waterfront. This Split Rail appeals to families. *Lake Shore Dr., Rte. 9N, Box 63, Diamond Point 12824, tel. 518/668–2259. 26 rooms. No credit cards. Closed Sept. 15–May 15.*

Victorian Village Resort. A handsome brick-and-stone mansion set back from the highway behind a circular drive lined by huge pines and spruces serves as this resort's main lodge. The motel units slope toward the lake. Swimming, waterskiing, boats, canoes, and dockage are available. The grounds of this former private estate include a tennis court and space for organized ball games. Breakfast is served in a dining room overlooking the lake. *Lake Shore Dr., Box 12, Bolton Landing 12814, tel. 518/644–9401. 30 rooms. No credit cards. Closed Nov.–Apr.*

Inexpensive **Briar Dell Motel.** This is one of the smaller resorts on the steep shoreline along Lake George. Pleasant motel rooms and cabins are located on the lakefront. It is rare to find private beach facilities, boats, and dockage at such modest prices so close to Lake George village. A picnic area with fireplaces is also available. *Shore Dr., Box 123, Lake George 12845, tel. 518/668–4819. 22 rooms. No credit cards. Closed mid-Oct.–Memorial Day.*

King George Motor Inn. The front units of this inn have one of the area's premier views—north down the length of Lake George. Rear units view the outdoor pool, playground, picnic area, and Prospect Mountain. Lawn games and an indoor arcade supplement the activities for youngsters. Breakfast is served in the coffee shop, which also has a view. *Rte. 9, Lake George 12845, tel. 518/668–2507 or 800/342–9504. 54 rooms. AE, DC, V. Closed mid-Oct.–mid-Apr.*

Olympic Region

Very Expensive **The Point.** One-time home of William Avery Rockefeller, this elegantly rustic inn is the most exclusive retreat in the Adirondacks. It is operated in the manner of a sophisticated private home with no commercial overtones. It has only 11 rooms, but each has its own bath and most have stone fireplaces. Guests are required to dress for dinner. Member of Relais et Châteaux. *Star Rte., Upper Saranac Lake 12983, tel. 518/891–5674. 11 rooms. Facilities: restaurant, lounge, open bar, game room, swimming, sailing, and cross-country skiing on premises. AE.*

Expensive **Adirondack Inn.** A dark wood and stone construction gives the exterior of this hotel an imposing look that is carried inside to public rooms decorated with fireplaces, heavy furniture, and such rustic touches as wrought-iron fixtures and chandeliers. Found opposite the Olympic Center, the hotel overlooks the refrigerated outdoor skating oval, while at the rear is the heated outdoor pool and Mirror Lake's public beach and tennis courts. Rooms are well appointed and the dining room, which serves three meals a day in-season, features German cuisine. *217 Main St., Lake Placid 12946, tel. 518/523–2424. 50 rooms. Facilities: indoor pool, sauna, solarium, game rooms, color TV. Open year-round. AE, DC, MC, V.*

★ **Lake Placid Manor.** One of the only hotels found directly on Lake Placid, this rustic, European-style inn has several outlying cottages and lodges aside from the rooms in the main inn. Its Continental restaurant is considered by many to be the best in the region. *Whiteface Inn Rd., Lake Placid 12946, tel. 518/523–2573. 31 rooms. Facilities: beach, restaurant, lounge, nearby 18-hole golf course. AE, MC, V. Closed Nov.*

Whiteface Resort. This historic facility has kept up with the times with a versatile combination of condominiums, town houses, and small lodges. Guest rooms can include fireplaces, kitchens, balconies, and patios, and there is an 18-hole golf course that can be used for cross-country skiing in winter. *Whiteface Inn Rd., Lake Placid 12946, tel. 518/523–2551. 75 rooms. Facilities: restaurant, cocktail lounge, pool, tennis courts, recreation center, golf course. AE, MC, V. Open year-round.*

Moderate **Hotel Saranac of Paul Smith's College.** An unexpected oasis in the Adirondack "wilderness," this full-service hotel is operated as a training ground for Paul Smith's college's students of hotel management. The ornate Italian palazzo-style main lobby is an unexpected find in this location, and most rooms have been refurbished. The pleasant dining rooms, serving three meals daily, is a social hub of Saranac Lake, and a lighter menu is offered in the Boathouse Lounge. *110 Main St., Saranac Lake 12983, tel. 518/891–2200. 92 rooms. AE, DC, MC, V. Open year-round.*

Interlaken Inn. The scalloped trim and patterned woodwork outside hint at the Victorian decor found inside: lace, flowers in baskets, tin ceilings, four-poster beds, and crackling fires. Located on a hill between Mirror Lake and Lake Placid, the house is conveniently situated—even if you aren't staying here, you'll want to seek out the sophisticated "country fare" of its dining room. *15 Interlaken Ave., Lake Placid 12946, tel. 518/523–3180. 12 rooms. Facilities: restaurant. AE, MC, V. Closed Apr. and Nov.*

Whiteface Chalet. A few rustic touches persist at this otherwise modern hotel, such as handsome fireplaces and big beams in the common rooms. Whiteface Mountain Ski Center is visible from the dining room, 15 wooded acres of hiking and cross-country trails can be found in the rear, and the Ausable River is nearby. *Springfield Rd., Wilmington 12997, tel. 518/946–2207. 17 rooms. Facilities: outdoor pool, tennis, lawn games. MC, V. Open year-round.*

Inexpensive **Deer's Head Inn.** A cozy atmosphere pervades this pleasant 19th-century inn. The dining room, a string of connected small rooms, serves Swiss-German cuisine and is a gathering place for village residents, local politicians, and sportsmen. *Court St., Rt. 9, Elizabethtown 12932, tel. 518/873–9903. 6 rooms. Facilities: restaurant, bar. MC, V. Open year-round.*

Schulte's Motor Inn. Alpine-style stucco-and-wood buildings with peaked roofs and balconies make this compact motel very attractive. Country fabrics, bright colors, and modern appointments carry the cheerful theme indoors. *Cascade Rd., Rte. 73, Lake Placid 12946, tel. 518/523–3532. 30 rooms, 15 cottages. Facilities: restaurant, lounge, picnic area, playground, outdoor pool. MC, V. Open year-round.*

Saratoga Area

Very Expensive **Gideon Putnam Hotel and Conference Center.** A sumptuous, high ceiling graces the interior of this Victorian grande dame located on the grounds of Saratoga State park. It is within walking distance of the Saratoga Performing Arts Center (SPAC) and mineral baths, and is the site of much social activity when SPAC is in session. *Saratoga State Park, Saratoga Springs 12866, tel. 518/584–3000. 132 rooms, including 22 suites. Faciities: dining room, 3 pools, health club, golf and tennis nearby, cross-country skiing and skating in winter. AE, DC, MC, V.*

Expensive **Adelphi Hotel.** This refurbished Victorian property dates to 1877 and is one block from Congress Park in downtown Saratoga Springs. The sloping floors and Victorian furnishings in the lobby give it a true 19th-century feel. Many of its 28 rooms have been restored. *365 Broadway, Saratoga Springs 12866, tel. 518/587–4688. 28 rooms, all with shower/bath, air conditioning, phone, and TV. Facilities: Continental breakfast, restaurant (open July and Aug.), bar, cafe. AE, MC, V. Open Apr.–Nov.*

Ramada Renaissance. Adjacent to the Civic Center, this elegantly furnished brick-and-mahogany hotel, inside an office-building exterior, is for those who love to be pampered. All rooms feature color cable TVs, and there's fine dining (Sandalwood Restaurant) and entertainment on the premises. *534 Broadway, Saratoga Springs 12866, tel. 518/584–4000. 190 rooms and suites. Facilities: indoor pool, gift shop, newsstand, valet service. AE, DC, MC, V.*

Moderate **Carriage House.** A comfortable place on Saratoga's main street, this accommodation is especially welcoming to families and senior citizens. It features 10 air-conditioned kitchen units with refrigerators, cable TVs and free cribs. *178 Broadway, Saratoga Springs 12866, tel. 518/584–4220. Family, weekly, senior citizen, and ski packages available. AE, M.*

Inn at Ash Grove Farm. On Church Street near downtown Saratoga Springs, this small, country-style place has several bedrooms with fireplaces and offers a full American breakfast. *Rte. 9N on Church St., Saratoga Springs 12866, tel. 518/584–1445. AE, V.*

Inexpensive **Empress Motel.** All 12 of these neat units have air-conditioning and cable TV. There's a coffee shop on the premises. *Rtes. 4 and 29, 177 Broadway, Schuylerville 12871, tel. 518/695–3231. No credit cards.*

The Arts

Arts Centers The **Adirondack Lakes Center for the Arts** in Blue Mountain Lake (tel. 518/352–7715) features concerts, dramatic presentations, films, and demonstrations of arts and crafts throughout the summer.

The **Lake Placid Center for the Arts** (tel. 518/523–2512) is another hub of cultural activity in the Adirondacks, with films, concerts, and theater presentations during the summer. Jazz and classical-music concerts are part of the winter schedule.

The **Saratoga Performing Arts Center** (tel. 518/587–3330) makes Saratoga the performing arts capital of the North Country. The New York City Opera comes to SPAC in June, the New York City Ballet performs here in July, and the Philadelphia Orchestra is in residence in August. In addition, well-known pop performers are featured attractions in the summer, and dance and theater performances are staged in the Little Theater, next to the main open-air amphitheater. The amphitheater is closed from fall through spring, but drama presentations keep the Little Theater going throughout the year.

Music The **Lake George Opera Festival** (tel. 518/793–3858), highlighted by evening lake-cruise performances, is held in July and August.

In July and August some of the Philadelphia Orchestra members performing at Saratoga moonlight at the **Lake Luzerne Chamber Music Festival** (tel. 518/696–2771) just up the road.

Theater A professional repertory company, **Pendragon Theatre** (tel. 518/891–1854), in Saranac Lake, performs June–September, November–December, and February–March.

9 The Finger Lakes Region

Introduction

Cayuga, Canandaigua, Keuka, Hemlock, Honeoye, Otisco, Owasco, Canadice, Conesus, Skaneateles, and Seneca sound like a roll call for the Indians of the Iroquois Confederacy who dominated this area for more than two centuries. But they are also the names of the Finger Lakes in central New York State.

Iroquois legend has it that the Finger Lakes region was formed when the Great Spirit placed his hand in blessing on this favored land. Geologists have a more prosaic explanation: The lakes were created when Ice Age glaciers retreated about a million years ago. The intense pressure of those ice masses created the long, narrow lakes lying side by side, the deep gorges with rushing falls, and the wide fertile valleys that extend south for miles. These features are found nowhere else in the world.

The area is bounded on the west by Rochester and on the east by Syracuse. The glacial lakes run north and south, bordered by Lake Ontario and the Erie Canal to the north, the Chemung and Susquehanna rivers to the south.

The mercurial landscape is notched with gorges and more than 1,000 waterfalls. The highest is Taughannock, at 215 feet—higher than Niagara Falls. It is also one of 20 state parks in the region. Letchworth State Park, with a deep gorge and three waterfalls, has been aptly dubbed the "Grand Canyon of the East." At Watkins Glen State Park you can walk under a waterfall and sit spellbound while being whisked 4.5 billion years into the past with lasers and special sound effects in "Timespell," a twice-nightly sound-and-light show explaining the birth and life of the famous glen.

The Finger Lakes is the land of dreamers—dreamers who founded a religion, began the women's rights movement, invented the camera, were early pioneers in motion pictures, and created great schools and universities. Diversity is the keynote of the region, not only in the variety of natural landscapes but also in the plethora of recreational, educational, and cultural facilities. The area's numerous museums are devoted to such varied subjects as agriculture, auto racing, aviation, dolls, electronics, the Erie Canal, glass, Indians, the 19th century, photography, salt, soaring (or airplane gliding), and winemaking. The region has played a significant role in American social, economic, and political history as the home of statesmen, inventors, industrialists, and writers.

Mark Twain wrote most of his classics, including *The Adventures of Huckleberry Finn*, from his summer home in Elmira. Glenn H. Curtiss put Hammondsport on the aviation map. In 1908 his *June Bug* flew just under a mile—the longest distance of a preannounced flight. Harris Hill is considered the birthplace of soaring, and its National Soaring Museum has the country's largest display of classic and contemporary sailplanes.

Seneca Falls is the home of the women's rights movement, and the National Women's Hall of Fame is on the site of the first Women's Rights Convention, held in 1848. Palmyra was the early home of Joseph Smith, whose vision led to the founding in 1830 of the Church of Jesus Christ of Latter-Day Saints, the

Mormons. Every summer in late July this event is commemorated with the Hill Cumorah Pageant, the oldest and largest religious pageant in the United States. Residents of Waterloo dreamed up the idea of Memorial Day in honor of the dead of the Civil War, and the country's first Memorial Day was celebrated on May 5, 1866.

Rochester is the birthplace of the Kodak camera and film and the Xerox copy machine. Corning is famous for the Corning Glass Works and its Steuben Glass division, which produces fine works of art. Steuben masterpieces have been presented as gifts to foreign heads of state and are in museums around the world.

Viniculture is another of the Finger Lakes' many offerings. Not only did the retreating glaciers create the Finger Lakes, they also created ideal conditions for grape growing by depositing a shallow layer of topsoil on sloping shale beds above the lakes. The deep lakes also provide protection from the climate by moderating temperatures along their shores.

It all began in 1829 when the Reverend William Bostwick transplanted a few grapevines from the Hudson Valley to the shore of Keuka Lake in Hammondsport to make sacramental wine for his parishioners at St. James Episcopal Church. The grapes grew well, and within a few years grapevines could be found around Keuka, Canadaigua, and Seneca lakes. In 1860, 13 Hammondsport businessmen resolved to form a company "for the production and manufacture of native wine," and created the Hammondsport and Pleasant Valley Wine Company, the first commercial winery to open in the region. It became known as Great Western and later merged with the giant Taylor Wine Company.

The success of the vineyards and wines created new jobs. Young carpenter Walter Taylor arrived in the late 1870s to make barrels for the wineries and began planting grapevines and making wines himself; in time, his winery became the region's largest. Since 1976, when the state legislature eased regulations on the establishment of wineries producing 50,000 gallons a year or less, some 20 small farm wineries have opened in the region, and new techniques and grapes are earning medals for the area's wines at international and national competitions. The federal government has designated the area the official "Finger Lakes Wine District."

Essential Information

Getting Around

By Plane   **American, United, USAir, Continental, Delta,** and **TWA** all serve the Rochester and Syracuse airports. **USAir** serves airports at Ithaca and Elmira/Corning.

By Train   **Amtrak** (tel. 800/USA–RAIL) serves both Rochester and Syracuse.

By Bus   **Greyhound** (tel. 716/454–3450 in Rochester; 315/471–7171 in Syracuse) provides service to cities and towns in the region. The Rochester-Genesee Regional Transportation Authority and Syracuse & Oswego Motor Lines (tel. 315/422–9087) provide service within their regions.

By Car Most visitors tour the Finger Lakes area by car. From east to west use Route 17, the Southern Tier Expressway; I–90, the New York State Thruway; or the northern Trail of Route 104. Major north–south highways are I–81, and Route 15, and I–390. All major car-rental agencies operate in Rochester and Syracuse.

Scenic Drives Just about every road in the Finger Lakes area provides views of blue lakes, rolling hills, vineyards, and farmhouses. The following are a few drives of particular interest:

Route 14 from Geneva to Watkins Glen. Route 14 borders the western side of Seneca Lake, affording vistas of the lake vineyards, stately 19th-century mansions, and farmhouses.

Route 89 along the western shore of Cayuga Lake. Start the drive in Ithaca, home of Cornell University and Ithaca College, and head north to Taughannock Falls. This route is especially splendid in autumn when the multicolored foliage reflect in the blue lake.

Route 54 and 54A around Keuka Lake. This route around the lake is studded with vineyards, and the trip can be broken up a half-dozen times for winery tours and tastings.

Guided Tours

Bus Tours Escorted bus tours of the region are provided by **Regional Transit Service** (1372 E. Main St., Rochester 14609, tel. 716/654–0200, operates weekdays 7:45–4:30) and **K-Ventures Minicoach** (Box 522, Penn Yan, tel. 315/536–7559). City tours of Rochester and surrounding area are offered by **Personal Tours of Rochester** (Box 18055, Rochester 14618, tel. 716/442–9365).

Boat Tours **Capt. Bill's Lake Ride** (1 N. Franklin St., Watkins Glen, tel. 607/535–4541) offers 10-mile cruises leaving every hour. Luxury dinner cruises are available, and there are individual and group rates. **Capt. Gray's Lake Tours** operates one-hour lecture tours of Canadaigua Lake leaving from the Canadaigua Sheraton at 770 S. Main Street. Contact C. Gray Hoffman, 92 Park Avenue, tel. 716/394–5270. **Mid Lakes Navigation Company** (Box 61, Skaneateles, tel. 315/685–8500) offers morning mail delivery, luncheon and dinner, and cruises on Skaneateles Lake and on the Erie Canal.

Important Addresses and Numbers

Tourist Information **The Finger Lakes Association** (309 Lake St., Penn Yan 14527, tel. 315/536–7488 or 800/KIT–4–FUN) has free brochures, booklets, and maps. **Rochester Convention & Visitors Bureau** (126 Andrews St., Rochester 14604, tel. 716/546–3070) and **Syracuse Convention & Visitors Bureau** (100 E. Onondaga St., Syracuse 13202, tel. 315/470–1343 or 800/234–4SYR) also have information, brochures, and maps of their areas. In Rochester, call 716/546–6810 for a listing of daily events. In addition, Canandaigua, Elmira, Geneva, Waterloo, Watkins Glen, and Camillus operate information centers year-round, and 25 smaller communities staff centers during the summer.

Emergencies Police and ambulance, tel. 911.

Exploring the Finger Lakes

The Finger Lakes Region encompasses counties in the center of New York State. Midway between New York City and Niagara Falls, it is anchored on the west by the state's third-largest city—Rochester—and on the east by the fourth-largest city—Syracuse.

The area attracts more than 7 million visitors a year, but because it is so vast it rarely seems crowded. And though it has special appeal for outdoors lovers—anglers, hunters, boaters, sailors, campers, and hikers—it also boasts elegant castles and inns, fine wining and dining, first-rate museums, concerts, and art galleries.

The crop that put the Finger Lakes on the tourist as well as the economic map is the grape, and the most popular time to visit is May–October, when the wineries are open for tours, generally on a daily basis. The 11 lakes, from Conesus Lake due south of Rochester to Otisco Lake near Syracuse, offer lush, scenic vistas from every turn in the road. They cover 9,000 square miles, and their collective shoreline covers nearly 600 miles.

Rochester

Numbers in the margin correspond with points of interest on the Rochester map.

The largest city in, and a good starting point from which to tour, the Finger Lakes is **Rochester.** Although they are not nearly as large or dramatic as Niagara Falls, there are two 100-foot waterfalls in the middle of the city, which is well situated on the Genesee River. Lake Ontario serves as the city's northern boundary. In the early 19th century Rochester was considered the flour capital of the nation. But as the sources of grain moved westward, Rochester became a nursery and seed capital and acquired the nickname "Flower City," which has stuck to this day.

❶ **Highland Park,** between S. Goodman Street and Mt. Hope Avenue, a few blocks from the river, is the site of the annual 10-day Lilac Festival in late May, which draws thousands to see and smell the 22 fragrant lilac varieties. There are also gardens filled with magnolias, azaleas, crab apples, hawthorns, peonies, and other blossoms. A spectacular pansy bed holds more than 5,000 plants. The park's **Lamberton Conservatory** hosts five major displays throughout the year.

❷ **The Stone-Tolan House** is believed to be the oldest surviving building in the county, with one wing dating to 1792. Its four-acre site has vegetable and herb gardens and orchards. *2370 East Ave., tel. 716/442–4606. Admission: $1.50 adults, 75¢ senior citizens, 50¢ students, 25¢ children under 14, children under 6 free. Open Mar.–Dec., Fri.–Sun. noon–4 PM.*

Rochester is often called The Picture City, and with good reason. It is the birthplace and home of the Kodak Company. Head north on Goodman Street and turn right on East Avenue to ❸ reach the **International Museum of Photography** at the **George Eastman House,** which houses the world's largest collection of photographic art and technology.

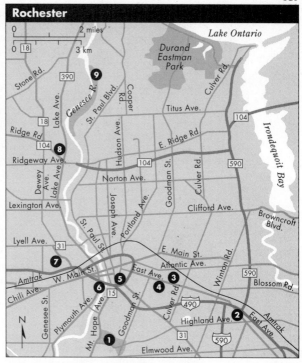

The new archives building houses a collection of over 600,000 photographic prints and negatives and nearly 6,000 films. In addition to viewing some of the best photography of the 19th and 20th centuries here, movie fans and researchers may rent booths and watch individual movies. Eastman's 50–room mansion has recently been renovated. Using photographs that Eastman had taken in order to document his house, restorers were able to reproduce the details of the house, right down to the light fixtures. Ninety-five percent of the original furnishings were returned to the house through donation and purchase. It was in his bedroom at age 78 that Eastman committed suicide, writing in a note: "My work is done—why wait?" During his lifetime he gave away about $100 million. *900 East Ave., tel. 716/271–3361. Admission: $3 adults, $2.50 senior citizens and students, $1 children under 12. Open Tues.–Sat. 10–4:30, Sun. 1–5.*

❹ **The Rochester Museum and Science Center** presents exhibits on regional history as well as natural science, anthropology, and human biology, and has Iroquois artifacts and period rooms that depict 19th-century life in the city. The Strasenburgh Planetarium has daily star shows under a 60-foot dome. *657 East Ave., tel. 716/271–1880 (museum), tel. 716/442–7171 (planetarium). Admission: $3.50 adults, $3 senior citizens, $2 students, children under 4 free. Planetarium fee varies with show. Museum open Mon.–Sat. 9–5, Sun. 1–5. Planetarium shows nightly; weekend and summer matinees.*

Margaret Woodbury Strong, who was the largest single Kodak shareholder when she died in 1969, contributed her considerable fortune and her lifetime collections to a museum named in her honor. Opened in 1982, the **Strong Museum** houses nearly 500,000 artifacts from the 19th and early 20th centuries, including the country's foremost collection of Victorian furniture, glassware, ceramics, miniatures, toys, and 20,000 antique dolls. The museum uses these resources to mount periodic exhibits on the drama of everyday life in the industrial era. Recent displays include a history of advertising in America and a survey of a century of substance abuse. *1 Manhattan Sq., tel. 716/263–2700. Admission: $2 adults, $1.50 senior citizens, 75¢ children 4–16. Open Mon.–Sat. 10–5, Sun. 1–5.*

The Campbell-Whittlesey House in the city's historic Third Ward is one of America's finest examples of Greek Revival architecture. Today it is operated by the Landmark Society of Western New York. *123 S. Fitzhugh St., tel. 716/546–7028. Admission: $1.50 adults, 75¢ senior citizens, 50¢ students, 10¢ children under 17. Open Feb.–Dec., Fri.–Sun. noon–4.*

Susan B. Anthony House was home to the 19th-century advocate of women's rights, and it was here that Anthony wrote *The History of Woman Suffrage*. The home is furnished in the style of the mid-1800s. *17 Madison St., tel. 716/235–6124. Admission: $1 adults, 50¢ children under 12. Open Wed.–Sat. 1–4.*

Film manufacturing tours of **Eastman Kodak,** the company that George Eastman founded, are unfortunately no longer available. (Kodak, by the way, is a nonsense word conceived by Eastman because he wanted a name that could not be translated into another language.) You may, however, want to view their corporate headquarters at 343 State Street (downtown); or make a photo expedition to their 2,000-acre facility to see where all those black-and-yellow boxes come from.

Rochester's **Seneca Park** has hiking trails along the east side of the Genesee River; its zoo features an aviary with uncaged birds, a polar bear enclosure, and an elephant exhibit. *2222 St. Paul St., tel. 716/266–6846. Admission: $2 adults, $1.50 children 10–15, children under 10 and senior citizens over 62 free. Open daily 10–5, summer weekends and holidays until 7 PM.*

Fairport, Mumford, and Castile

Numbers in the margin correspond with points of interest on the Finger Lakes Area map.

For an introduction to the area's wines, visit **Fairport** and the **Casa Larga Vineyards,** just 12 miles east of Rochester. This is a small farm winery, opened in 1978, that bottles primarily varietal wines made from vinifera grapes. *2287 Turk Hill Rd., off Rte. 31 or Rte. 96, Fairport, tel. 716/223–4210. Open Tues.–Sat. 10–6, Sun. noon–6.*

Twenty miles southwest of Rochester via routes 383 and 36 in the town of **Mumford** is the **Genesee Country Village and Museum,** where you can step back into the 19th century. This is a village of 57 buildings gathered from throughout the region and reconstructed here. Highlights include an elegant 1870 octagonal house and a two-story log house, circa 1814. You can watch guides cook, work in gardens, spin yarn, weave, and make baskets, and the country's largest collection of wildlife art can be seen in the **Gallery of Sporting Art.** *Flint Hill Rd., Mumford, tel. 716/538-2887. Admission: $8 adults, $5.50 students, $4 children 6-12, under 6 free; $7.50 senior citizens on weekdays. Open Sat. before Mother's Day-3rd Sun. in Oct., daily 10-5; closed Mon. except July and Aug.*

3 Aviation buffs will want to go to **Geneseo,** a bit farther south in the heart of the hunt country, to see the **National Warplane Museum.** It is home to one of the nine B-17s still flying in the country, as well as such aircraft as the Curtis P-40 Warhawk and C-46 Curtis Cargo plane, the PT-17, the Fairchild PT-19 and PT-26, the Vultee BT-13, and Boeing B-17G used by generals Eisenhower and MacArthur. *Big Tree La., off Rte. 63, Geneseo, tel. 716/243-0690. Open weekdays 9-5, weekends 10-5. Admission: $3 adults, $1 children under 12. Call first as planes may be away for air shows.*

4 About five miles farther south in **Castile** is **Letchworth State Park,** dubbed the "Grand Canyon of the East." It comprises 14,350 acres along the Genesee River and has few rivals in the east for spectacular beauty. It includes dramatic cliffs, some nearly 600 feet high; three waterfalls, one of which is 107 feet high; lush woods; and the **Glen Iris Inn,** once the country home of the park's donor, William Pryor Letchworth, and now a popular hotel and restaurant (*see* Dining and Lodging, below). Fall weekends are usually booked years in advance at Glen Iris because of the special seasonal beauty of the park and gorge. The park has extensive camping facilities, fishing, hunting, swimming, and cross-country skiing. The park's **William Prior Letchworth Museum** tells the story of the early days of the area with artifacts, books, and displays. There is also an original **Iroquois Council House,** which was moved here from a nearby location. *For information and reservations on camping facilities, contact Letchworth State Park, Castile 14427, tel. 716/493-2611, and for the Glen Iris Inn, tel. 716/493-2622, or write to the inn at the park address.*

Canandaigua Lake Area

Heading south from Rochester the first of the Finger Lakes is **5** **Canandaigua,** which can be reached by following I-390 north to U.S. 20 west to the town of Canandaigua, a bustling tourist city especially popular in the summer; its Seneca name means "the chosen place." One of the city's prime attractions is the **Sonnenberg Gardens and Mansion,** a 50-acre estate recognized by the Smithsonian Institution as having "one of the most magnificent late-Victorian gardens in America." Nine gardens, including rose, Japanese, Italian, rock, and Colonial, surround the mansion, which has restored period rooms with some original furnishings. The **Canandaigua Wine Company Tasting Room** located here offers wine tastings. *151 Charlotte St., tel. 716/394-4922. Admission: $5 adults, $2 children 6-16, $4 senior citizens. Open mid-May-mid-Oct., daily 9:30-5:30.*

Another area attraction is the **Granger Homestead and Carriage Museum.** It includes the restored 1816 Federal mansion of Gideon Granger, U.S. Postmaster General under Presidents

Finger Lakes Area

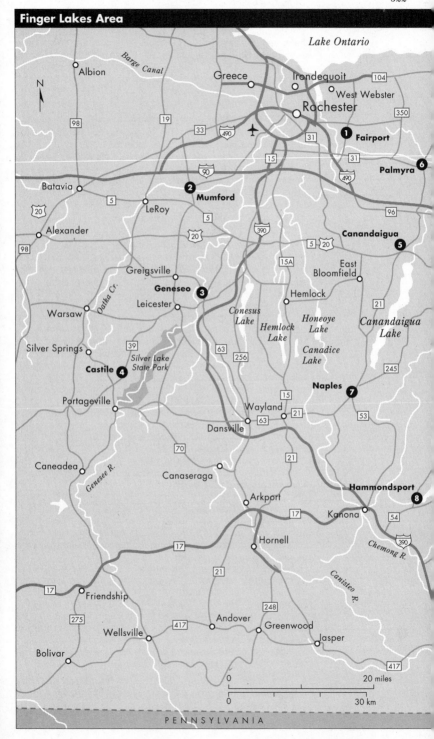

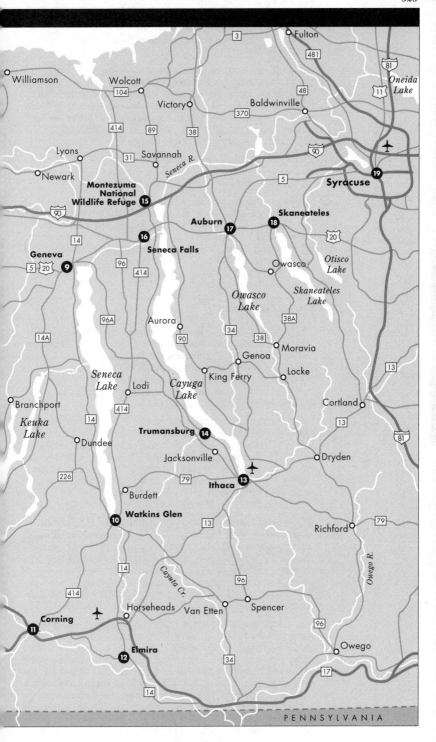

Jefferson and Madison and a collection of 40 horse-drawn vehicles dating from 1820–1930. *295 N. Main St., tel. 716/394–1472. Admission: $2.50 adults; $1 children 7–16, children under 7 free. Open May–Oct., Tues.–Sat. 10–5, Sun. 1–5.*

❻ About 15 miles north of Canadaigua is **Palmyra,** birthplace of the Mormon religion. Here you can visit the Mormon Historic Sites, including the repository of historic records translated by Joseph Smith into the *Book of Mormon* and a monument to the Angel Moroni, Smith's spiritual guide. *Visitor Center, movies, guided tours. Rte. 21, north of NYS Thruway Exit 43, tel. 315/ 597–5851. Admission free. Open daily 9–6.*

The Joseph Smith House is the restored farmstead of the Mormon church founder Joseph Smith. *Stafford Rd., tel. 315/597– 4387. Admission free. Open 9–6, in summer 9–9.*

❼ The next stop is the village of **Naples** at the southern end of Canandaigua Lake. Many buildings on Main Street date to the early 1800s. Naples is home to the century-old **Widmer's Wine Cellars,** which has daily tours and tastings during the season. Widmer's is the only winery in the region that ages sherry and port in barrels on the roof. *Rte. 21, Naples 14512; tel. 716/374– 6311. Tours and tastings June–Oct., Mon.–Sat. 10–4, Sun. 1–4. Other times, call ahead.*

Keuka Lake Area

The next lake—one of the loveliest in the area—is the 22-mile-long **Keuka Lake,** southeast of Canandaigua via routes 247 and **❽** 364. The village of **Hammondsport** at the southern end of the lake is the birthplace of the Finger Lakes wine industry and is a good base for a concentrated wine tour. The streets are lined with Victorian homes, and a park with an old-fashioned bandstand is in the center of the village.

To relive the early history of aviation, stop in at the **Glenn H. Curtiss Museum of Local History.** It displays the accomplishments of native son Curtiss, a pioneer in aviation and other fields. The famous *June Bug* and *Curtiss Jenny* planes, and other local memorabilia are on display in this jumbled but fascinating museum. *Lake and Main Sts., tel. 607/569–2160. Admission: $3 adults, $2 students, $1 children 7–12, $7 family. Open Apr. 15–June, Mon.–Sat. 9–5; July–Oct. daily.*

The area's largest winery is two miles outside of Hammondsport. **Taylor Wine Co.** is operated by **Vintner's International.** Anyone who stops at the Taylor Wine Visitors Center can see a film on the winery and its history—the theater was built in a former wine tank—and take the hour-long tour that is one of the most comprehensive in the area, in which tastings are offered. *Lake St., Hammondsport, tel. 607/569–2111. Admission free. May–Oct., daily 10–4; Nov.–Apr., Mon.–Sat. 11–4.*

Just a mile north of town is **Bully Hill,** the most talked-about winery in the region. It is presided over by Walter S. Taylor, a grandson of the founder of the Taylor Wine Co. and the closest thing the wine world has to a folk hero. The protracted court fight over the use of the Taylor name (he lost) helped put his winery on the map. **Greyton H. Taylor Museum,** adjacent to the vineyards, is housed in a 100-year-old wood and stone building and displays antique equipment used in tending the vineyards and making wines. *Greyton H. Taylor Memorial Dr., Ham-*

mondsport, tel. 607/868–3610. Tours and tastings free. Open Mon.–Sat. 9–5, Sun. noon–4:30.

Time Out The **Champagne Country Cafe** is next door and serves fresh pasta dishes and other light fare along with wine.

Other Keuka Lake wineries include **Chateau De Rheimes** (8319 Pleasant Valley Rd., Hammondsport, tel. 607/569–2040); **Hunt Country Vineyards** (4021 Italy Hill Rd., Branchport, tel. 315/595–2812); **Heron Hill** (Middle Rd., Hammondsport, tel. 607/868–4241); and **McGregor Vineyard Winery** (5503 Dutch St., Dundee, tel. 607/292–3999).

Seneca Lake Area

East of Keuka Lake is **Seneca Lake,** the deepest (650 feet) of the Finger Lakes and home to the National Lake Trout Derby. The stately city of **Geneva** is at the northern end of the lake. South Main Street has been acclaimed as "the most beautiful street in America." It is lined with 19th-century homes and century-old trees. The scenic campus of **Hobart** and **William Smith colleges** is here, too.

Three miles east of Geneva, overlooking the lake, is **Rose Hill Mansion.** Built in 1839, it is a handsome Greek Revival restoration and National Historic Landmark. Decorated in elegant Empire style, it has 24 rooms open to the public, a carriage house, slide show, and boxwood gardens. *Rte. 96A, tel. 315/789–3848. Admission: $2 adults; $1 children 10–18, under 10 free. Guided tours only. Open May 1–Oct. 31, Mon.–Sat. 10–4, Sun. 1–5.*

Wineries surround the southern half of the 36-mile-long lake. The following are open for tours and tastings: **Glenora Wine Cellars** (RD 4 Route 14, Dundee, tel. 607/243–5511); **Hazlitt 1852 Vineyards** (Rte. 414, Hector, tel. 607/546–5812); **Four Chimneys Vineyards** (RD 1, Hall Rd., Himrod, tel. 607/243–7502), the only organic winery in the Northeast; **Poplar Ridge** (RD 1, Valois, tel. 607/582–6421); **Rolling Vineyards** (Rte. 414, Hector, tel. 607/546–9302); and **Wagner Vineyards and Ginney Lee Cafe** (Rte. 414,Lodi, tel. 607/546–9302); and **Hermann J. Wiemer** (Rte. 14, Dundee, tel. 607/243–7971).

The village of **Watkins Glen** is at the southern end of Seneca Lake adjoining the 669-acre **Watkins Glen State Park** (Rte. 14, tel. 607/535–4511). The glen drops about 700 feet in two miles and is highlighted by rock formations and 18 waterfalls. Cliffs rise 200 feet above the stream; a 165-foot-high bridge spans the glen, which is lit at night. **Timespell,** a 45-minute dramatic sound and laser-light show, traces the natural and human history in the gorge. The stirring voice of the narrator says, "We are about to leave human time altogether and go far, far back into the geologic past . . . to a time when the earth was young— over 4½ billion years ago." *The show is presented twice nightly in season and once nightly off-season, beginning at dusk, May 15–Oct. 15. Admission: $4.75. Tel. 607/535–4960.*

Corning and Elmira

Watkins Glen is a good place to break from lake touring. Travel south along Route 414 to **Corning,** famous as the home of Corning Glass Works and its Steuben Glass division.

The Corning Glass Center houses the **Corning Museum of Glass,** which contains the world's foremost glass collection. The present building, designed by architect Gunnar Birkerts, opened in 1980. The center also includes the Hall of Science and Industry with push-button exhibits, live demonstrations, and films. The exhibits show how glass is made and used in science, industry, and the home. Steuben Glass Factory allows visitors to watch craftsmen create works of art. There are gift shops, including the Steuben shop and a separate shop for Corning products with a large selection of discount items. *Off Rte. 17, tel. 607/974–8271. Admission: $5 adults, $3 children 6–17, children under 6 free, $4 senior citizens, $13 family. Open daily 9–5.*

The **Rockwell Museum** has more glass art, including Carder Steuben glass and the largest collection of western American art in the East. There is also a grand assortment of antique toys on display. The exhibits are housed in the restored 1893 Old City Hall. *Denison Pkwy. and Cedar St., tel. 607/937–5386. Admission: $3 adults, $2.50 senior citizens. Open Mon.–Sat. 9–5, Sun. noon–5; July and Aug. until 7.*

Corning's downtown Market Street has been restored to its 19th-century glory and is listed on the National Register of Historic Places. Free English-style double-decker buses provide transportation to the glass center and down Market Street.

The 1796 **Benjamin Patterson "Inn" Museum** consists of a restored furnished inn and former stagecoach stop, a 1784 log cabin, a 1878 one-room schoolhouse, and a restored barn with an early agricultural exhibit dating from 1850 to 1860. The museum is filled with furnishings, crafts, and costumes of the area dating to 1784. *59 W. Pulteney St., tel. 607/937–5281. Admission: $2 adults, $1 children 6–18. Open weekdays 10–4.*

The **Wine Center & Market** provides an introduction to winemaking history and lore. Tastings are held in what was once the Baron Steuben Hotel ballroom. *Baron Steuben Pl., tel. 607/272–2125.*

Traveling southeast along scenic Route 17, the next stop is **Elmira,** site of an important Revolutionary War battle. The **Newtown Battlefield Reservation** marks the location of the battle won by Major General John Sullivan over a large force of Indians and Tories.

Elmira is also where Samuel Clemens, better known as Mark Twain, spent more than 20 summers and wrote many of his classics, including *The Adventures of Huckleberry Finn*. His wife, Olivia Langdon, grew up here, and Clemens loved the Chemung Valley area, which he called "a foretaste of heaven." Clemens and his family are buried in Woodlawn Cemetery. His famous octagonal study, with some original furniture, a replica of his typewriter (he was one of the first writers to submit a typed manuscript to a publisher), photos, and memorabilia may be visited on the Elmira College campus. Nearby Quarry

Farm, Clemens's residence, has been turned into a center for Twain scholars. It offers lectures and theater productions on Monday evenings. *Mark Twain Study, Elmira College, tel. 607/732-0993. Admission free. Open weekdays in summer 10-4, weekends 10-5.*

The Elmira area is known as the "Soaring Capital of America," and the area's hills and valleys present ideal airplane soaring and gliding conditions. The **National Soaring Museum** displays more than a dozen fully assembled historic gliders and sailplanes as well as artifacts pertaining to motorless flight. You can sit in a simulator cockpit to experience the soaring sensation. For the real thing, take a sailplane ride at the adjacent glider field or just watch the sailplanes perform (*see* Participant Sports, below). *Harris Hill, tel. 607/734-3128. Admission: $3 adults, $2 senior citizens and students, children under 10 free. Open daily 10-5.*

Cayuga Lake Area

⑬ **Ithaca,** best known as the home of **Cornell University,** is north of Elmira at the southern tip of Cayuga Lake, the longest of the Finger Lakes at 38.1 miles. The town is more spectacular than most in the Finger Lakes because of the deep gorges and more than 100 waterfalls that run throughout it, and it was a favorite location for movies during the silent era. Ithaca is also the birthplace of the ice-cream sundae.

Cornell University, founded by Ezra Cornell in 1865, is situated on 750 acres overlooking Cayuga and Ithaca. The **Herbert F. Johnson Museum of Art,** at the northern edge of campus, was designed by I. M. Pei. The museum is as well known for its collection of contemporary and Asian art as for the spectacular views it offers of the sprawling campus and surrounding countryside. *Tel. 607/255-6464. Admission free. Open Tues.-Sun. 10-5.*

Cornell Plantations lie along the gorges bordering the campus. The 2,800 acres include beds of azaleas, lilacs, peonies, wildflowers, rhododendrons, and viburnums. There are lakes, ponds, streams, bogs, swampland, wooded areas, and an arboretum, as well as a magnificent collection of Japanese tree peonies. Of special interest is the **Walter C. Muenscher Poisonous Plants Garden.** The **Robison York State Herb Garden** has more than 800 herbs. There's a gift shop, and guided tours are available by prior arrangement. *1 Plantation Rd. near Rte. 366, tel. 607/255-3020.*

⑭ Just northwest of Ithaca is **Trumansburg** and the **Taughannock Falls State Park** (Rte. 89, tel. 607/387-6739). The 215-foot-high falls in a rock amphitheater with 400-foot walls is the highest straight-drop falls in the Northeast. The 783-acre park has complete camping facilities and offers swimming, fishing, boat launching, hiking trails, and cross-country skiing.

Ithaca is also the starting point for the **Cayuga Wine Trail.** The lake's wineries offering tours and tastings include: **Americana Vineyards** (4367 E. Covert Rd., Interlaken, tel. 607/387-6801), **Knapp Vineyards** (2770 County Road 128, Romulus, tel. 315/549-8865), **Lakeshore Winery** (5132 Rte. 89, Romulus, tel. 315/549-8461), **Lucas Winery** (RD 2, County Road 150, Interlaken, tel. 607/532–4825), and **Plane's Cayuga Vineyard** (6800 Rte. 89 at Elm Beach, Ovid, tel. 607/869–5158).

🔟 The **Montezuma National Wildlife Refuge,** at the north end of Cayuga Lake, gives migrating birds a protected rest and feeding area and serves as a nesting ground for numerous others. There are more than 6,300 acres of cattail-covered marshland, swampwoods, and fields with easy access from Exits 40 and 41 of the Thruway.

🔟 About five miles west of the north end of Cayuga Lake is **Seneca Falls,** birthplace of the women's rights movement in America. On July 18, 1848, the first women's rights convention brought 300 people to the Wesleyan Methodist Chapel at 126 Falls Street. Famous former residents include Amelia Bloomer, who popularized the undergarment bearing her name, and Elizabeth Cady Stanton, organizer of the first women's rights convention.

The **Women's Rights National Historical Park** includes a visitor center and the restored **Elizabeth Cady Stanton Home** at 32 Washington Street. The center chronicles the development of the women's movement through changing exhibits, slide programs, and interpretive talks. *116 Fall St., Seneca Falls, tel. 315/568–2991. Admission free. Park: open daily 9–5. Stanton Home: June–Sept., daily 9–5; Oct.–May, Wed.–Sun. noon–4.*

Just down the street is home of the **National Women's Hall of Fame.** The hall honors famous American women, past and present, such as humanists Jane Addams and Eleanor Roosevelt, painter Mary Cassatt, and recently inducted tennis player Billie Jean King. The stories of these famous American women are told through portraits, photographs, biographies, and memorabilia. *76 Fall St., Seneca Falls, tel. 315/568–8060. Donations accepted. Open May–Oct., daily 10–4; Nov.–Apr., Wed.–Sat. 10–4, Sun. noon–4.*

🔟 Heading east on Route 20, we come to **Auburn** at the northern end of Owasco Lake. Here in a parklike setting is the last remaining building of the Auburn Theological Seminary, the **Willard Memorial Chapel.** This small treasure is the only structure in America completely designed by Charles L. Tiffany, best known for the lamps that bear his name. Not only the ornate and brightly colored stained glass but even the pews and benches display his distinct fanciful touch. *17 Nelson St., Auburn, tel. 315/252–0339. Donations accepted. Open Tues.–Fri. 1–4.*

Auburn was the home of William Henry Seward, New York governor, U.S. senator, and secretary of state for presidents Lincoln and Johnson. He was a leading figure in the founding of the Republican party and in the Alaska purchase. Alaska's banks and schools are closed every year on the last Monday in May in his honor. The **Seward House** has original furnishings, and most of the 15 rooms open to the public are filled with Seward's personal possessions. The second-floor gallery contains Seward's collection of 132 prints and photographs of world leaders he met on diplomatic missions around the globe. *33 South St., tel. 315/252–1283. Admission: $3 adults, $2.50 senior citizens and children 12–18, children under 12 free. Open Apr.–Dec., Tues.–Sat. 1–4.*

Auburn was also the home of Harriet Tubman, who used it as an "underground railroad" station for the more than 300 slaves she led to freedom. During the Civil War she served as a Union Army spy and scout. Special tours of the **Harriet Tubman Home** are available by appointment. *180 South St., tel. 315/255-3863.*

Skaneateles Lake Area

Though it is one of the smallest of the Finger Lakes, **Skaneateles Lake,** seven miles east of Auburn on U.S. 20, is one of the loveliest. (Skaneateles is Indian for "beautiful squaw.") Today tasteful storefronts housed in 19th-century brick buildings line the main streets of **Skaneateles.** The Sherwood Inn (*see* Dining and Lodging, below), overlooking the lake, has been welcoming travelers since 1809. This is a town of wealth and elegance. Sunday afternoons are reserved for polo games during the summer. You can tour the lake while the mail is being delivered on a unique morning mail ride operated by Mid-Lakes Navigation Sailboat Co.; there are also luncheon and dinner cruises (*see* Guided Tours, above).

Syracuse

The final stop on our Finger Lakes tour is **Syracuse,** known as "Salt City." The Indian chief Hiawatha chose this location as the capital of the Iroquois Confederacy during the 16th century. The **Onondaga Indian Reservation** at Nedrow is now the seat of the Indian Confederacy. Salt brought the Indians, the French, and subsequent settlers to Syracuse and, for many years, Syracuse was the source of most American salt.

The **Salt Museum** has exhibits and a reconstructed 1856 salt factory where salt processing is demonstrated. The museum, built during the Depression as a work-relief project, is housed in a replica of an early salt block and focuses primarily on the salt industry during the Industrial Revolution. *Onondaga Lake Park, Liverpool, tel. 315/451-7275. Admission prices undetermined at press time. Open May–Oct., 10–5.*

The state's fourth-largest city, Syracuse has played host to the New York State Fair since 1841 and is also home to one of the country's largest private educational institutions—Syracuse University.

The Erie Canal no longer runs through Syracuse, but the era is recalled at the **Erie Canal Museum,** the last of seven weighlock buildings in the state through which canal boats passed. It is a National Register Landmark building with indoor and outdoor exhibits that explore the construction and operation of the canal. Visitors board a 65-foot reconstructed canal boat to view the exhibits. *318 Erie Blvd. at Montgomery St., tel. 315/471-0593. Open Tues.–Sun. 10–5. Tuesday free. Wed.–Sun. $1 adults, 50¢ children 5–12.*

The **Discovery Center of Science & Technology** offers hands-on displays dealing with gravity, perception, chemistry, light, sound, electricity, optics, magnetism, mechanics, space, and the human body. There is also a planetarium and a museum shop. *321 S. Clinton St., tel. 315/425-9068. Admission: $2 adults, $1 children under 12. Planetary show 50¢. Open Tues.–Sat. 10–5, Sun. noon–5.*

The county's **Burnet Park Zoo** has recently undergone a $10 million renovation. There are more than 1,000 animals in nine separate complexes that re-create natural habitats—from arctic tundra and arid desert to tropical rain forest. *S. Wilbur Ave., tel. 315/478-8516. Admission: $3 adults, $1.50 children 5–14, children under 5 free, $1.25 senior citizens, $9 family. Open daily 10–4:30; Memorial Day–Labor Day until 7.*

Sainte Marie de Gannentaha or **French Fort** is a re-creation of a French Jesuit Colonial settlement established on the shore of Onondaga Lake in 1656. Authentically costumed interpreters perform traditional crafts demonstrations. The fort was being renovated at press time but is scheduled to reopen in the summer of 1991. *Onondaga Lake Pkwy., Liverpool, tel. 315/451-7275. New admission prices and hours undetermined at press time.*

What to See and Do with Children

Children usually enjoy the **wine tours,** and all of the wineries that offer tours and tastings provide grape juice for children and nondrinkers. Some even provide hayrides during the fall harvest season (*see* Exploring the Finger Lakes, above).

Genesee Country Museum (*see* Exploring the Finger Lakes, above).

Margaret Woodbury Strong Museum (*see* Exploring the Finger Lakes, above).

The **Victorian Doll Museum** has more than 2,000 identified collector dolls, a toy circus, a puppet show, a doll hospital, and a gift shop. *4332 Buffalo Rd., North Chili, 10 miles west of Rochester, tel. 716/247-0130. Admission: $1.50 adults, 75¢ children. Open Tues.–Sat. 10–4:30, Sun. 1–4:30. Closed holidays and Jan.*

Wild Winds Farms and Village has gardens, a log fort, a petting zoo, a nature center, a maple-sugar house, and a restaurant.

Discovery Center of Science & Technology (*see* Exploring the Finger Lakes, above).

Off the Beaten Track

Visitors to **Gates-Rockwell Department Store** in Corning who expect a typical small-town department store will be surprised to find a wealth of art treasures, Carder-Steuben glass, antique guns, toys hanging on the walls, and displays amid the regular items for sale (display items are not for sale). This store houses some of the overflow from the Rockwell Museum. *23 W. Market St., Corning, tel. 607/962-2441. Open Mon.–Wed. and Sat. 9–5:30, Thurs. and Fri. 9–9.*

The town of **Waterloo** calls itself the birthplace of Memorial Day, and the **Memorial Day Museum** is a 20-room mansion filled with items about that holiday, the Civil War, the two world wars, and the Korean conflict. The museum contains photographs and displays of newspapers, clothes, and knickknacks of the time when Waterloo first established the day to honor its fallen soldiers. *35 E. Main St., Waterloo, tel. 315/539-2474. Admission free. Open Memorial Day–Labor Day, Tues.–Fri. 1:30–4.*

Misty Meadow Hog Farm is the place for anyone who has ever wanted to pet a pig. This is a working family farm with piglets and the full cycle of production. There are haywagon rides, crafts, and a farm kitchen restaurant. The farm sells its own frozen meat. *Vineyard Rd., off Rte. 89, Romulus, tel. 607/869–9243. Tours June–Aug., Tues.–Sat. 11 AM, 1 and 2 PM.*

Millions of fish eggs are hatched and cared for at the **New York State Fish Hatchery,** which started in 1865 and is the oldest fish hatchery in North America. It raises rainbow trout, and chinook and coho salmon. *Rte. 36, 16 North St., Caledonia, tel. 716/538–6300. Admission free. Open daily 8–4:30.*

The **Norton Chapel of Keuka College** near Penn Yan is on a lovely spot at the edge of Keuka Lake. It was modeled after a Latin cross. Artist-craftsman Gabriel Loire of Chartres, France, designed the mosaic glass windows.

Participant Sports

Boating

In addition to the Finger Lakes, there are boating opportunities on Lake Ontario and the Barge Canal. There are numerous boat-launching sites throughout the area. The two longest lakes, Seneca and Cayuga, are connected by a canal that, in turn, is connected to the Erie Canal, thereby linking them all to the waterways of the world.

Fishing

The area has long attracted fishing enthusiasts, who are drawn here by the record-breaking brown trout, rainbow trout, bass, pike, pickerel, salmon, and panfish. The area is also known for its large lake trout. Opportunities include deep trolling in lakes, off-shore spincasting, stream fishing, smelting, and ice fishing in winter. Lake Ontario has been successful with a restocking program for chinook and coho salmon. Be sure to check the latest Health Department advisory on eating fish from Lake Ontario; there are restrictions because of chemical contamination. Call Lake Ontario Hotline, tel. 716/875–9725 or 315/587–9508, for latest fishing update. *For information on licenses, seasons, and limits contact the Department of Environmental Conservation, 6274 E. Avon-Lima Rd., Avon 14414, tel. 716/226–2466.*

Golf

Nearly 30 golf courses in the region welcome visitors. In Elmira, there's the 18-hole Chemung Valley and 18-hole Mark Twain. In Ithaca, Cornell University has an 18-hole golf club and there's the 9-hole Newman Course. In Rochester, there is a new 18-hole Genesee Valley course and an old 18-hole course. In Syracuse, there's the 18-hole Tanner Valley, and there are 9-hole courses in Geneva, Cayuga, and Watkins Glen.

Hunting

Some of the state's best hunting takes place in the Finger Lakes. Steuben County, where Corning is located, has one of the largest deer harvests in the state. The ruffed grouse is considered "king of the game birds" in the southern Finger Lakes. Wild turkey, which has made a fantastic comeback in the region, is also a much sought-after game bird. To the north there is excellent goose hunting adjacent to federal and state game refuges. The area is part of the Eastern Flyway for migratory birds. *For information on licenses, seasons, and bag limits, contact the Department of Environmental Conservation, 6274 E. Avon-Lima Rd., Avon 14414, tel. 716/226-2466.*

Skiing

Cross-country skiing is available in state and local parks, as well as in the Green Mountain National Forest. The largest downhill ski centers are Bristol Mountain (Rte. 64, Canandaigua, tel. 716/374-6000) and Greek Peak (Rte. 90, Cortland, tel. 607/835-6111). Both offer lessons and rentals.

Soaring

The Elmira area's hills and valleys present ideal soaring and gliding conditions. For rides and instruction, contact Harris Hill Gliderport (RD 3, Elmira 14903, tel. 607/734-3128) or Schweizer Soaring School (Chemung County Airport, Rte. 17 between Elmira and Corning, tel. 607/739-3821). In Syracuse, contact Thermal Ridge Soaring (115 Kittell Rd., Fayetteville 13066, tel. 315/446-4545).

Spectator Sports

Auto Racing

Watkins Glen International has major professional road racing June–September. Events include Camel Continental, Trans-Am Nationals, Supervee, Vintage Cup, and 24-hour Firestone Firehawk. *For schedules, contact Watkins Glen International, Box 500, Watkins Glen 14891, tel. 607/535-2481.*

Baseball

The Rochester Red Wings—an International League farm club of the Baltimore Orioles—plays at Silver Stadium from April through October. The Syracuse Chefs AAA baseball team plays from April to September at MacArthur Stadium.

Basketball

The highly rated Syracuse University basketball team plays at the university's Carrier Dome November–March.

Horseracing

Thoroughbreds run at the Finger Lakes Race Track, Thruway Exit 44 and Rte. 96, April–November, tel. 716/924-3232. Harness racing takes place at Batavia Downs in Batavia and the Syracuse Mile in Syracuse.

Dining and Lodging

Dining   Restaurants in the Finger Lakes are as varied as the lakes and communities. Rochester and Syracuse boast some fine dining rooms, as do several smaller cities and towns. Ithaca on Cayuga Lake has a surprisingly large assortment of top restaurants, in part due to the large university community and the university's hotel-management school.

Highly recommended restaurants are indicated by a star ★.

Category	Cost*
Very Expensive	over $25
Expensive	$18–$25
Moderate	$10–$17
Inexpensive	under $10

per person, not including beverage, tax, or tip

Lodging   The region's hotels, motels, and inns cater to a wide range of tastes and pocketbooks. Country inns have been a tradition in the area since the early 19th century, but lately they have been "rediscovered." Many lakeside motels have lower rates off-season; some close after November 1 and do not reopen until May. The peak season is summer.

Bed-and-breakfast inns have been growing in this region recently. Most are in historic homes and farmhouses. Some accept major credit cards, but many do not; be sure to inquire in advance when making reservations. Rates range from budget to expensive. **Cherry Valley Ventures,** tel. 315/677–9723, handles reservations for a number of B&B establishments.

Category	Cost*
Very Expensive	over $90
Expensive	$70–$90
Moderate	$50–$70
Inexpensive	under $50

Sales tax throughout the region is 7%. In Monroe County (Rochester) there is an additional 2% occupancy tax on room charges, while Onondaga County adds a 3% occupancy tax. Rates are based on double occupancy.

Canandaigua Lake Area

Dining   **Crickett's of Canandaigua.** Rochester residents consider it worth the drive to experience this gourmet Continental restaurant in a century-old building in downtown Canandaigua. Specialties include beef Wellington and champagne chicken with raspberry sauce. On the second floor is the new Burke's Tavern and Raw Bar, offering live entertainment in a casual atmosphere. Crickett's has a well-stocked wine cellar featuring many local vintages. *169 Main St., Canandaigua, tel. 716/394–7990.*

Jacket suggested for Crickett's. Reservations advised. MC, V. Expensive.

Gay 90s Tap Room. A local favorite since 1895, the Gay 90s Tap Room in the Naples Hotel serves traditional American fare with an emphasis on steak, prime rib, and seafood. *Main St., Naples, tel. 716/374–5630. Dress: informal. Reservations advised in summer. MC, V. Expensive.*

Bob's and Ruth's. Reminiscent of an old-fashioned diner, Bob's and Ruth's features chicken hot off the spit and homemade soup and pies. One entire wall is stocked with wine bottles, many of them from the area. The Vineyard Room, connected to the main restaurant, offers more sophisticated fare. *Rtes. 21 and 245, Naples, tel. 716/374–5122. Dress: informal. MC, V. Moderate.*

★ **Wild Winds Farms & Village.** This working farm features all natural foods: fresh-baked breads, pastries, crepes, quiches, and vegetables grown on the grounds. The flowers on your plate are edible. There are a country store, sugarhouse, nature trail, greenhouses, and gardens. *Clark St., 3 mi west of Naples, tel. 716/374–5523. Dress: informal. Open Memorial Day–Oct., lunch daily and dinner, Fri. and Sat. AE, MC, V. Moderate.*

Lodging **Sheraton Canandaigua Inn.** This is a large and busy resort, the most complete one in the area. It occupies a prime lakefront site. The rooms were recently renovated and some have balconies and private patios. It's popular with families because of the family plan and facilities. *770 S. Main St., Canandaigua 14424, tel. 716/394–7800. 147 rooms with bath. Facilities: pool, dining room, cocktail lounge, conference facilities for 300, sauna, playground, laundry, game room, recreation room, docks. AE, CB, DC, MC, V. Expensive.*

Maxfield Inn. This historic mansion dates from 1841. The front part of the inn dates from the 1860s. The first bottled wine and sherry in the area came from the inn. Many of the old bottles are still in the cellar. High tea is served Tuesday–Sunday. *105 N. Main St., Naples 14512, tel. 716/374–2510. 6 rooms. Facilities: 3,200-bottle wine cellar; includes breakfast with fresh sticky buns and fruit salad. No credit cards. Moderate.*

The Vagabond. This inn is located high on a secluded hill. The rooms are elegantly furnished; there is one suite with a Jacuzzi. *330 Slitor Rd., Naples 14512, tel. 716/554–6271. 10 rooms with bath. Facilities: pool, full breakfast included. MC, V. Moderate.*

Kellogg's Pan-Tree Inn. This is an economical but comfortable motel on the lake, opposite the park, a swimming beach, and the marina. The rooms are simply furnished. *130 Lake Shore Dr., Canandaigua 14424, tel. 716/394–3909. 15 rooms with bath. Facilities: restaurant, private patios. Open late Apr.–Oct. MC, V. Inexpensive.*

Cayuga Lake Area

Dining **L'Auberge Du Cochon Rouge Restaurant.** This award-winning
★ restaurant in a restored 1840 farmhouse is presided over with the utmost attention to detail and imagination by owner-chef Etienne Merle. The dining rooms have fireplaces and planked floors, and there is even a private dining room for romantic occasions. Friday nights mean lobster festivals, and a fixed-price menu is offered on Mondays and Tuesdays. The extensive wine list boasts reserve ports and 17 French reds. Specialties in-

clude rack of lamb, magret of duck, sweetbreads, and salmon prepared with caviar. The dessert trolley consists of specialties made by the pastry chef and is hard to resist. *1152 Danby Rd., Ithaca, tel. 607/273–3464. Reservations recommended. AE, D, V. Dinner and Sun. brunch only. Very Expensive.*

Aurora Inn. Nineteen eighty-eight marked the 155th year of this landmark inn overlooking Cayuga Lake. The menu features fresh seafood, chicken, steaks, and pork chops. *Main St., Aurora, tel. 315/364–8842. Dress: informal. Closed Jan. and Feb. MC, V. Expensive.*

Oldport Harbour. Ask for one of the dockside tables and dine by the water on seafood flown in daily from Boston. Lunch and dinner cruise boat leaves from dock from spring to early fall. *702 W. Buffalo St., Ithaca, tel. 607/272–4868. Dress: informal. Reservations recommended. AE, DC, MC, V. Expensive.*

The Station Restaurant. This restaurant is a National Historic Landmark. Dine in the reconstructed Lehigh Valley Railroad Passenger Station or on board a real train car. Specialties include prime rib, fresh seafood, and veal. *806 W. Buffalo St., Ithaca, tel. 607/272–2609. Dress: casual. Reservations recommended. Closed Mon. AE, D, MC, V. Dinner only. Expensive.*

Taughannock Farms Inn. There are three dining rooms in this 1873 Victorian mansion, which overlooks the park and Cayuga Lake. Dinners include such all-American fare as roast turkey, duckling, lamb, prime rib, shrimp, and fresh fish. The inn has five guest rooms and serves breakfast to its guests. *State Rd. 89/Gorge Rd., Taughannock Falls State Park, Trumansburg, tel. 607/387–7711. Reservations required. Closed Dec.–Mar. AE, MC. Dinner only. Expensive.*

Turback's. This long-established restaurant—a converted 19th-century mansion filled with Tiffany lamps—is considered the "grande dame of Ithaca." It features regional New York State food, and there are always one or two imaginative vegetarian entrees on the menu. There is a wine shop on the premises. *Rte. 13, Ithaca, tel. 607/272–6484. Reservations recommended. AE, D, MC, V. Dinner only. Expensive.*

Abby's Restaurant. No other restaurant in central New York exemplifies the movement to nouvelle American cuisine better than Abby's. The atmosphere is simple but elegant: black and silver decor brightened by Impressionist paintings. Specialties include filet mignon with multicolored peppers, lamb with mint pesto, and Norwegian salmon prepared on a mesquite grill. *309 Third St., Ithaca, tel. 607/273–1999. Reservations recommended. AE, DC, MC, V. Dinner only. Moderate.*

Lodging **Rose Inn.** This country inn rests on an estate among mature apple, spruce, and maple trees. The owners have individually decorated each room with antiques, flowered quilts, and an occasional eclectic touch, such as Egyptian headpieces. The mahogany circular staircase is the focal point; it took two years for a master craftsman to complete it. Gourmet dinners are served by reservation only, but breakfast is included in the room cost. *Auburn Rd., Ithaca 14850, tel. 607/533–7905. 16 rooms with bath. AE, MC, V. Very Expensive.*

La Tourelle. This Mediterranean–style inn provides the amenities, efficiency, and romance expected from a European luxury hotel. Try the circular tower suite, complete with Jacuzzi, or one of the more traditional doubles with excellent hilltop views and plenty of sunlight. Walking trails behind the hotel lead to a nearby state park. *1150 Danby Rd., Ithaca 14850, tel. 607/273–*

2734. 35 rooms with bath. Facilities: conference room, ballroom. AE, MC, V. Very Expensive.

The Statler Hotel. This hotel on the Cornell campus was recently renovated, exchanging worn charm for bustling professionalism. Hotel guests have full use of all university facilities, including golf course, swimming pool, weight rooms, and sauna. *Cornell University Campus, Ithaca 14853, tel. 800/541–2501 or 607/257–2500. 150 rooms with bath. Facilities: conference center, 3 restaurants, cocktail lounge. AE, MC, V. Closed Dec. 22–Jan. 2. Expensive.*

Aurora Inn. This 1833 landmark on the lake is just down the road from Wells College; guests may use the college's golf course and tennis courts. Some rooms have four-poster beds and antique furnishings. There is a large porch, and the ground-floor sitting rooms feature portraits of early innkeepers and the early days of Wells College. *Main St., Aurora 13026, tel. 315/364–8842. 17 rooms with bath. Facilities: dining room, Continental breakfast included. AE, MC, V. Closed Jan.–mid-Feb. Moderate–Expensive.*

Corning–Elmira Area

Dining **Pierce's 1894 Restaurant.** This award-winning family-owned
★ restaurant is located in a big, rambling brick building with Victorian parlors. Fresh flowers grace every table, enhanced by linens, fine silver, and china. The wine list features wines of the region. Specialties include blackened Norwegian salmon and veal steak with asparagus. *228 Oakwood Ave., Elmira Heights 14903, tel. 607/734–2022. Reservations recommended. AE, D, MC, V. Closed Mon. Dinner and Sun. brunch only. Expensive.*

Rojo's & The Greenhouse. Rojo's offers such casual fare as quiche, burgers, and onion soup. The dining room is decorated with antiques, and there's an outdoor cafe. The adjacent and more formal Greenhouse is a real greenhouse and serves up American fare, including veal, seafood, and beef. It's just two blocks from the Glass Center and Market Street. *36 Bridge St., Corning 14830, tel. 607/936–9683 or 607/962–6243. Dress: informal. AE, MC, V. Closed Sun. Moderate–Expensive.*

Sorge's Restaurant. This old-fashioned Italian restaurant, complete with red-and-white-checkered tablecloths, dark-wood paneling, and comfortable atmosphere, serves ample portions of good food. There are daily specials, Friday fish fries, and a pasta buffet. The prices are quite economical. *66–68 Market St., Corning, tel. 607/937–5422. Dress: informal. Reservations recommended. AE. Moderate.*

Taste of China. This popular Corning restaurant is well known in the Southern Tier. There is an extensive Cantonese/Szechuan/Hunan menu, and the walls are decorated with Chinese lanterns and murals. *84 E. Market St., Corning, tel. 607/962–6176. Dress: informal. AE, DC, MC, V. Moderate.*

Turf Club. This restaurant's specialties include chateaubriand, steak Diane, and prime rib. Desserts are baked on the premises. *131 E. Corning Rd., Corning, tel. 607/936–3900. Dress: informal. Reservations recommended. AE, D, DC, MC, V. Closed Sun. Dinner only. Moderate.*

Lodging **Corning Hilton Inn.** Within a short walk of historic Market Street attractions, the Hilton is a focal point of renovated Corning. The rooms are large and comfortable with subdued decor;

some are quite elegant. *Denison Pkwy. E, Corning 14830, tel. 607/962–5000. 180 rooms with bath. Facilities: indoor pool, cafe, bar, entertainment. AE, CB, DC, MC, V. Expensive.*

Best Western Lodge on the Green. This is an attractive motor inn about three miles outside of Corning. It's popular with families. There are studio rooms. *Rte. 417 W, Painted Post 14870, tel. 607/962–2456. 135 rooms with bath. Facilities: pool, cafe, bar, meeting rooms. AE, CB, DC, MC, V. Moderate.*

Holiday Inn. About three miles outside of Corning in Painted Post, this property caters largely to families during the summer and school breaks. *304 S. Hamilton St., Painted Post 14870, tel. 607/962–5021. 105 rooms with bath. Facilities: pool, wading pool, cafe, bar, laundry, shop, barber, beauty shop. AE, CB, DC, MC, V. Moderate.*

Rosewood Inn. Each of the seven antiques-filled rooms in this 1860 three-story Tudor inn is named for and furnished after a famous person. The Herman Melville room contains whaling memorabilia, while early railroading is the focus of the George Pullman suite. The inn is just two blocks from Market Street and the Rockwell Museum. *134 E. First St., Corning 14830, tel. 607/962–3253. 7 rooms, 5 with bath. Facilities: TV in common room, full breakfast. AE, DC, MC, V. Moderate.*

Huck Finn Motel. Despite its name, this is a basic modern motel, which started operating long after the tales of Huck Finn were written in the region. The rooms were recently renovated. *Rtes. 14 and 17, Horseheads 14845, tel. 607/739–3807. 40 rooms with bath. Facilities: pool, coffee shop. AE, D, MC, V. Inexpensive.*

Keuka Lake Area

Dining **Pleasant Valley Inn.** The formal dining rooms in this 19th-century Victorian inn are surrounded by vineyards and the imaginative menu makes full use of local produce and wines. Fresh flowers decorate every table and many corners of the inn. Lunch and dinner are served. *Rte. 54, Bath-Hammondsport Rd., Hammondsport, tel. 607/569–2282. Dress: casual but neat. Reservations advised. AE, CB, MC, V. Expensive.*

The Vintage. The large picture windows here provide a panorama of the bluff and Keuka Lake; specialties are beef and fresh seafood. There are private docks for diners arriving by boat. This is a particularly popular spot during the summer season. *Rte. 54A between Hammondsport and Branchport 14840, tel. 607/868–3455. Dress: informal. AE, DC, MC, V. Open May–Oct. Expensive.*

Lakeside. Located in an 1881 homestead overlooking Keuka Lake, this is a popular spot with area residents and cottagers, with many a diner arriving by boat. There is an outside dining and cocktail patio. Specialties include seafood, prime rib, and chicken dishes. *Rte. 54A, 7 mi north of Hammondsport, tel. 607/868–3636. Dress: informal. No reservations. AE, CB, DC, MC, V. Moderate.*

Snug Harbor. This restaurant has a Victorian look both indoors and outdoors. In the summer you can dine outdoors with a view of the lake. Specialties include seafood and prime rib. *Rte. 54A, 1½ mi north of Hammondsport, tel. 607/868–3488. Dress: informal. Reservations for parties of more than 8. AE, MC, V. Moderate.*

Lodging **Pleasant Valley Inn.** This large, rambling Victorian inn with a vineyard just outside the front door has antiques-filled rooms and a large elegant dining room. A bottle of wine awaits every guest. *Rte. 54, Bath-Hammondsport Rd., Hammondsport 14840, tel. 607/569–2282. 2 rooms with shared bath. Facilities: full breakfast included. AE, DC, MC, V. Moderate.*

Viking Resort Apartment Motel. The range of accommodations makes this resort appealing to families: apartments, housekeeping cottages, and studio units with kitchens. Many rooms have wood paneling and a rustic feeling. A large yacht gives cruises on the lake for a small fee. There are free rowboats, and waterskiing and sailing are also available. *680 E. Lake Rd., Penn Yan 14527, tel. 315/536–7061. 38 units with bath, including apartments and cottages. Facilities: pool, sauna, hot tub. No credit cards. Open Apr.–Oct. Moderate.*

Colonial Motel. This quiet motel is just down the road from Keuka College and is near swimming facilities. Some of the rooms have kitchenettes. *175 Lower Lake Rd., Penn Yan 14527, tel. 315/536–3056. 16 rooms with bath. Facilities: kitchens. AE, MC, V. Weekly rates available. Inexpensive.*

Vinehurst Motel. An otherwise basic motel, the Vinehurst has a distinguishing feature—it's surrounded by vineyards. The effect can be quite heady in the fall when the grapes hang heavy on the vines. *Rte. 54, Hammondsport 14840, tel. 607/569–2300. 32 rooms with bath. MC, V. Inexpensive.*

Letchworth State Park Area

Dining and Lodging **Genesee Falls Inn.** This 1870 inn a half-mile from the south entrance of Letchworth State Park was recently renovated. The guest rooms are done up in old-fashioned flowered wallpaper and antiques. There are also five modern rooms in an adjoining motel unit. The public areas and bar are filled with 19th-century memorabilia. The fare in the Victorian-style dining room is all-American: roast duckling, steak, chicken, and ham. There's also an informal coffee shop for breakfast and lunch. Bread and desserts are made on the premises. *Rte. 436, Portageville 14536, tel. 716/493–2484. 10 rooms with bath, 2 with shared bath. 5 in inn and 5 in motel. Facilities: bar, coffee shop, dining room. Restaurant: dress informal. Reservations advised. No credit cards. Closed Tues. and mid-Nov.–Apr. 1. Moderate.*

★ **Glen Iris Inn.** This inn was home of Buffalo industrialist and philanthropist William Pryor Letchworth, who donated the lands that became Letchworth State Park in 1910. The rooms, each named for one of the species of trees that abound in the park, are simply furnished. The library on the third floor offers many regional books and provides a good view of the Middle Falls. Rooms here are often fully booked several years in advance during the fall foliage season. The dining room features such specialties as chicken Chesapeake (breast filled with crab and spinach), prime rib, and veal. Finger Lakes wines are featured. *Letchworth State Park, Castile 14427, tel. 716/493–2622. 21 rooms with bath, 15 in inn and 6 in nearby motel. Facilities: dining room, gift shop, organized park activities including nature hikes, pools, fishing, hunting in season. Dress: casual. Reservations advised, especially in fall. AE, MC, V. Moderate.*

Rochester Area

Dining **Chapels.** The former criminal detention pen in the Rochester
★ City Hall has been transformed into an ultrasophisticated restaurant where diners are greeted by liveried waiters and a
wine steward. There are three rooms with vaulted brick ceilings and walls. The menu is based on whatever is fresh at the
market that day and changes with the seasons. Among the specialties: lobster *chapina*, rack of lamb with rosemary, and roast
wild guinea hen. The extensive wine list includes area wines.
The newly opened sidewalk cafe offers a more casual atmosphere with similar fare. *30 W. Broad St., Rochester, tel. 716/
232–2300. Jacket required. Reservations recommended. AE,
DC, MC, V. Closed Sun. and Mon. Dinner only Sat. Very Expensive.*

Edwards Restaurant. There are leaded-glass windows from a
synagogue, tapestries from a Presbyterian church, oak paneling from a Catholic seminary, and George Eastman's hunting
trophies in this Victorian-style edifice, which was built in 1873
as the Rochester Free Academy. Dining areas include the Hunt
Room, Pontchartrain Room, Tapestry Room, English Library
Room and the crimson and black Oriental Room. The menu includes such imaginative dishes as scallops Parisienne, shrimp
stuffed with dill and feta, grilled muscovy duck, stuffed quail,
chicken veronique, and beef Wellington with mushroom pâté.
*13 S. Fitzhugh St., Rochester, tel. 716/423–0140. Jacket sug-
gested. Reservations recommended. Dinner only Sat. AE, CB,
D, DC, MC, V. Closed Sun. Expensive.*

Richardson's Canal House. This restored original Erie Canal
tavern (on the national register), has a patio where you can dine
outdoors for lunch in warm weather. Fixed-price selections include duckling, seafood, and beef tenderloin. There's folk music on Friday nights. *1474 Marsh Rd., Pittsford, tel. 716/248–
5000. Jacket requested. Reservations recommended. AE, CB,
DC, MC, V. Closed Sun. Dinner only Sat. Expensive.*

Oliver Loud's Inn, also run by the Canal House, is an old restored stagecoach inn on the canal with eight rooms, each with
a private bath and telephone. Full cable television is available
upon request. *1474 Marsh Rd., Pittsford, tel. 716/248–5200.*

Spring House. This four-story brick house in Southern Colonial
style was once an Erie Canal inn and has been serving food to
hungry travelers since 1822. The house specials include prime
rib, steaks, and seafood, and all pastries and breads are baked
on the premises. *3001 Monroe Ave., Rochester, tel. 716/586–
2300. Jacket requested. Reservations recommended. AE, DC,
MC, V. Closed Mon. Lunch Tues.–Sat., dinner Tues.–Sun.
Expensive.*

Victor Milling Company. Housed in an old mill, this restaurant
is a favorite dining spot for people in the Rochester area. The
cozy atmosphere is accentuated by an open hearth. Specialties
include lamb chops, seafood bisque, chicken dishes, and salads.
*75 Coville St., Victor, tel. 716/924–4049. Reservations recom-
mended. MC, V. Moderate.*

Crescent Beach Hotel. This replica of a Victorian hotel boasts a
lovely garden and a patio overlooking the lake. Specialties include seafood and prime rib. There's dancing here on Friday
and Saturday. *1372 Edgemere Dr., Rochester, tel. 716/227–
3600. Dress: informal. Reservations recommended. AE, MC,
V. Closed Jan. and Feb. Moderate.*

Daisy Flour Mill. A restored mill, dating from 1848, alongside a stream, this restaurant is filled with old mill artifacts and antiques. It specializes in veal, game, and fresh seafood. *1880 Blossom Rd., Rochester, tel. 716/381–1880. Jackets required. Reservations recommended. AE, CB, DC, MC, V. Dinner only. Moderate.*

Lodging   **Holiday Inn-Genesee Plaza.** This large, luxurious Holiday Inn is connected to the new Riverside Convention Center, shops, and restaurants. The top floors have a good view of the Genesee River and the falls. *120 Main St., Rochester, 14604, tel. 716/ 546–6400. 467 rooms with bath. Facilities: pool, airport transportation, restaurant, bar, in-house theater, laundry. AE, CB, DC, MC, V. Very Expensive.*

Stouffer Rochester Plaza. This large, luxury hotel is centrally located on a city park along the Genesee River. The rooms are also large and well designed. *70 State St., Rochester 14616, tel. 716/546–3450. 364 rooms with bath. Facilities: pool, restaurant, bars, meeting rooms, airport transportation, fitness center, luxury level with private lounge, complimentary breakfast. AE, CB, DC, MC, V. Very Expensive.*

Strathallan. Located in the center of Rochester's museum district, this hotel started life as an apartment house; there are one- and two-bedroom suites as well as one room that converts to a three-bedroom suite. The rooms are large and nicely furnished, many with balconies. *550 East Ave., Rochester 14607, tel. 716/461–5010. 152 rooms with bath. Facilities: bar, restaurant, meeting rooms, entertainment, airport transportation, sauna, activities room, solarium. AE, CB, DC, MC, V. Very Expensive.*

Genesee Country Inn. Once a mill, dating from 1830, with two-foot-thick walls, this inn is about a 20-minute drive from Rochester and about a half-mile from the Genesee Country Village and Museum (*see* Exploring the Finger Lakes, above). It's located on six acres of woods, waterfalls, and ponds with resident ducks and trout. Antiques and period reproductions give guest rooms an authentic touch, and many of the rooms also feature hand stencils. A guest book in each room invites comments, and they are uniformly enthusiastic. Afternoon teas are served. *948 George St., Mumford, 14511, tel. 716/538–2500. 10 rooms with bath. Facilities: small meeting rooms, full breakfast included. AE, DC, MC, V. Moderate.*

Rose Mansion and Gardens. A country inn in the middle of the city, this property is set behind a stone wall on five acres of gardens and orchards. In 1867, the horticulturist George Ellwanger enlarged what was originally a simple farmstead and gave it its present-day Tudor style. There are five fireplaces, a grand piano, oak paneling, book-filled cases, and a most imposing, working Hooks & Hasting pipe organ (circa 1883) on the staircase landing. Each room is named after a rose and has Victorian-era antiques; three have working fireplaces. Most of the bathrooms, though modernized, contain original fixtures. *625 Mt. Hope Ave., Rochester 14616, tel. 716/546–5426. 10 rooms with bath. Facilities: Continental breakfast included. AE, MC, V. Expensive.*

Seneca Lake Area

Dining   **Belhurst Castle.** This elegant 100-year-old Romanesque mansion is located on the shores of Seneca Lake. Some of the dining rooms have fireplaces, and all are trimmed with intricately carved woodwork. During the summer months the terrace is open for dining. The chef is an avid hunter who prepares such game dishes as venison and pheasant in season. Other specialties include veal Oscar, rack of lamb, and veal piccata. *Box 609, Geneva, tel. 315/781–0201. Jacket requested. Reservations recommended. AE, CB, DC, MC, V. Expensive.*

The Dresden. Located near the lake in the heart of fishing country, this local favorite has a wood-paneled dining room and large picture windows. Specialties include seafood and prime rib. *Rtes. 14 and 54, Dresden, tel. 315/536–9023. Dress: informal. MC, V. Closed Mon. Moderate.*

Wing Tai Oriental Restaurant. The dining rooms are decorated with Chinese murals. The extensive menu features Cantonese, Hunan, and Szechuan dishes, and there's a large selection of Finger Lakes wines. *Castle and Main Sts., Geneva, tel. 315/ 789–8892. Dress: informal. AE, DC, MC, V. Closed Sun. Moderate.*

Pumpernickel. This friendly, casual dining spot features homestyle cooking: fried chicken, fried fish, homemade breads and desserts. The food's good and a bargain, too. *825 Canandaigua Rd., Geneva, tel. 315/789–9655. Dress: informal. No credit cards. Closed Wed. Inexpensive.*

Lodging **Belhurst Castle.** This unique, well established inn where the
★ guests are transported back into a gilded age was built by noted architect Albert W. Fuller—it took 50 workmen, laboring six days a week, four years (1885 to 1889) to complete this fantasy for the original owner, Carrie Harron Collins. Though some of the rooms are beginning to show signs of wear, the Belhurst still offers such luxuries as a spigot on the second floor that dispenses local wines—free to guests. One suite, a former Victorian dancing room, has an 18-foot-high ceiling, a sauna with a window overlooking the lake, a porch, a spiral staircase leading to a turret, a large living room, and equally enormous bedrooms. All the rooms have modern bathrooms, TVs, and telephones; many have working fireplaces. Throughout, there are intricately carved oak, cherry, and mahogany, and more stained glass than is found in many churches. *Box 609, Geneva 14456, tel. 315/781–0201. 12 rooms with bath. Facilities: dining room, swimming and boating in lake, 25 acres landscaped grounds. AE, CB, DC, MC, V. Very Expensive.*

Historic James Russell Webster Inn. Hosts Leonard and Barbara Cohen welcome the discriminating traveler to their home. The inn, an 1845 Georgian mansion filled with antiques, has two suites, one in the Palladian and one in the Italianate style. The dining room resembles a private art gallery, filled with original sculpture and painting. The menus often feature duck, lobster, veal, and salmon. Those coming to dinner are requested to make reservations several days in advance, since every meal is personally planned and designed. *115 East Main St., Waterloo 13165, tel. 315/539–3032. Reservations required. CB, DC, MC, V. Very Expensive.*

★ **Geneva-on-the-Lake.** This three-story lakeside mansion, listed on the National Registry of Historic Places, was built in 1911 by malt tycoon Byron Nester after a 16th-century villa in Frascati, near Rome. Since then it has been a Capuchin monastery, an apartment complex, and now an elegant, all-suite resort. Each suite is decorated distinctively and stocked with local wine, coffee, and fresh fruit. Several suites have working fireplaces. There are 10 acres of formal gardens and a large pool lined with classic statuary, pillars, and urns. The elegant Lancellotti dining room serves up fine Continental dinners while violinists and singers provide background musical entertainment. A variety of weekend specials are offered throughout the year. Friday night wine-and-cheese parties are included in the weekend plans. *1001 Lochland Rd., Geneva 14456, tel. 315/789–7190. 29 suites with bath and kitchens. Facilities: Continental breakfast included, pool, dock with marina nearby, dining room. AE, D, MC, V. Very Expensive.*

Rainbow Cove Motel. This attractive motel's chief asset is its lakeside location. Though the rooms are standard, there are a gently sloping bathing beach, docks, and marina. There's even a diving school. The restaurant serves home-style cooking and has large picture windows with views of the lake. *Rte. 14, Himrod, tel. 607/243–7535. 24 rooms with bath. Facilities: game room, recreation and meeting hall, pool, docks, marina, scuba school, dining room. AE, MC, V. Open May–Oct. Inexpensive.*

Skaneateles Lake Area

Dining **Krebs.** This 1899 landmark is operated by the third generation of the founding family. The seven-course dinners are what made Krebs famous, but there are lighter meals for those with smaller appetites. Specialties include prime rib, lobster Newburg, and pan-fried chicken. Bread and desserts are baked on the premises. There's a formal English garden and Early American decor with antiques throughout. *53 W. Genesee St., Skaneateles, tel. 315/685–5714. Jacket suggested. Reservations recommended. AE, CB, DC, MC, V. Open May–Oct. Dinner daily, brunch Sun. Expensive.*

★ **Sherwood Inn.** Originally a stagecoach stop (in 1807) this inn overlooks the lake, and the tables on the porch are a must on hot summer nights, since the inn has no air-conditioning. The decor in each of the several dining rooms is Early American, and there are plants, fresh flowers, white linens, and candles all about. Specialties include seafood stew and prime rib, though the menu changes frequently. *26 W. Genesee St., Skaneateles, tel. 315/685–3405. Dress: casual but neat. Reservations recommended. AE, CB, DC, MC, V. Expensive.*

Doug's Fish Fry. People come here from miles around for fresh seafood—trucked in daily from Boston. The fish fries are a real bargain, and the chowder is legendary. *8 Jordan St., Skaneateles, tel. 315/685–3288. Dress: informal. No credit cards. Moderate.*

Syracuse Area

Dining **Pascale Wine Bar & Restaurant.** This historic Victorian town house, dating from 1875, is graced with period decor and antiques. There's an extensive wine list that includes Finger Lakes wines, available by the glass. The equally imaginative menu features saddle of venison, duckling, fingerling trout, and crab sautée à la Provençale. Everything is baked on the premises. *304 Hawley Ave., Syracuse, tel. 315/471–3040. Jackets suggested. Reservations recommended. AE, CB, DC, MC, V. Closed Sun. Dinner only. Very Expensive.*

Glen Loch Mill. A converted feed mill (1870) set in a glen next to a waterwheel provides the setting for this special restaurant.

There's entertainment on Friday and Saturday nights and outdoor dining during the warm weather. Specialties include Norwegian *caulviac* and prime rib. All baking is done on the premises. *4626 North St., Jamesville, 10 mi south of Syracuse, tel. 315/469–6969. Jacket required. Reservations recommended. AE, DC, MC, V. Expensive.*

Poseidon. This restaurant has the atmosphere and decor of a Mediterranean island cafe. Dishes are prepared at tableside and include souvlaki, red snapper, and veal. All baking is done on the premises. There's also a pianist. *770 St. James St., Syracuse, tel. 315/472–4474. Jackets required. Reservations recommended. AE, CB, DC, MC, V. Closed Sun. Expensive.*

Coleman's Authentic Irish Pub & Restaurant. Situated in the heart of a firmly entrenched Irish neighborhood, this pub is like a bit of the Old Sod: Menu items are written in both English and Gaelic, and green is the regulation color. The menu, however, includes Continental fare in addition to the mandatory soda bread and cabbage soup. *100 S. Lowell Ave., Syracuse, tel. 315/476–1933. Dress: informal. AE, DC, MC, V. Moderate.*

Ichiban. Dinner at the Ichiban is both a meal and entertainment. Every dish is prepared tableside by a master chef on a hibachi. There is a traditional sushi bar. *302 Old Liverpool Rd., Liverpool, tel. 315/457–0000. Reservations recommended. AE, D, DC, MC, V. Dinner only. Moderate.*

Sterio's Landmark. Housed in the historic Gridley Building, dating from 1869, this restaurant features fin-de-siècle decor; there's also an outdoor dining area. Specialties include rack of lamb, chateaubriand, and fresh seafood. Open for dinner and breakfast. *103 E. Water St., Syracuse, tel. 315/472–8883. Dress: casual but neat. Reservations recommended. AE, CB, D, DC, MC, V. Closed Sun. Moderate.*

Lodging **Sheraton University Inn & Conference Center.** If you want to be in the center of university life, this is the place to stay. Rates often go up during special university events. There are conference facilities here, so it's a popular meeting spot, particularly the lobby. Rooms are large and attractive. *801 University Ave., Syracuse 13210, tel. 315/475–3000. 232 rooms with bath. Facilities: indoor pool, bar, dining room, entertainment, gift shop, health club, tennis and golf privileges. AE, CB, DC, MC, V. Very Expensive.*

Hilton at Syracuse Square. This large, modern property in the center of the city attracts a meetings-and-conventions crowd. It is connected to, and shares facilities with, the older Hotel Syracuse. The plant-filled lobby is bright and bustling. Rooms are spacious. *500 S. Warren St., Syracuse 13202, tel. 315/422–5121. 201 rooms with bath. Facilities: dining room, garage, bar, nightclub, shopping arcade, barber, beauty shop, game room, indoor tennis, and health club privileges. AE, CB, D, DC, MC, V. Expensive.*

Holiday Inn–University Area. Downtown and close to Syracuse University, this hotel is popular for conferences and for those attending sports events at the university's Carrier Dome. *701 E. Genesee St., Syracuse 13210, tel. 315/474–7251. 290 rooms with bath. Facilities: indoor pool, sauna, restaurant, bar. AE, D, DC, MC, V. Moderate.*

Hotel Syracuse at Syracuse Square. This is an older, traditional center-city hotel that connects to the adjacent Hilton. Together, they serve as a focal point in downtown Syracuse. All public areas have been renovated and outfitted with comfortable chairs, plants, and a restaurant that spills out into the lobby. The simply furnished rooms are on the smallish side. *500 S. Warren St., Syracuse 13202, tel. 315/422–5121. 525 rooms with bath. Facilities: dining room, nightclub, entertainment, garage, 5 two-bedroom units. AE, D, DC, MC, V. Moderate.*

★ **Sherwood Inn.** An inn has stood on this spot overlooking the lake since 1807, and the present property, named after the first innkeeper, dates back 100 years. The rooms, many of which have lake views, have been renovated and are decorated with antiques. Television is available for guests in the library, and all the baths are modern. The bridal suite has a large canopy bed and a sitting room. Several rooms are doubles with a connecting bathroom. *26 W. Genesee St., Skaneateles 13152, 315/685–3405. 17 rooms with bath. Facilities: dining room, bar, Continental breakfast included, public beach opposite. AE, CB, DC, MC, V. Moderate.*

Bird's Nest. This economical motel near the lake is popular with families. There are outdoor picnic tables and grills, and some rooms have refrigerators. The rooms are decorated simply. There are some honeymoon suites. *1601 E. Genesee Rd., Skaneateles 13152, tel. 315/685–5641. 28 rooms with bath, 3 with kitchens. Facilities: pool, playground, duck pond. Open year-round. AE, CB, D, DC, MC, V. Inexpensive.*

Red Roof Inn. This motel delivers just what it promises: a clean, economical place to spend the night. *6614 N. Thompson Rd., Syracuse 13206, (Thruway Exit 35 at Carrier Circle), tel. 315/437–3309. 115 rooms with bath. Facilities: adjacent restaurant. AE, D, DC, MC, V. Inexpensive.*

Campgrounds Because of the traditionally cold winters, camping facilities generally are open only from April or May until October. However, several are open year-round. A number of state and county parks have camping facilities, and there are also some private campgrounds. There is a toll-free number for making reservations throughout the state (800/456–CAMP), but if you want additional information, it is more helpful to call the individual sites. The selected campgrounds listed below offer full hookup, laundry, and sanitary facilities:

Canandaigua KOA, 5374 Farmington Rd., Canandaigua, tel. 716/398–3582. 120 sites. Facilities: swimming, fishing, children's area, recreation building, restaurant, store. Open Apr.–Nov.

Cayuga Lake State Park, 2664 Lower Lake Rd., Seneca Falls, tel. 315/568–5163. 286 sites. Facilities: swimming, fishing, launching ramp, recreation building, children's area. Open May–Oct.

Hamlin Beach State Park, 2 miles west of Rte. 19, Hamlin, tel. 716/964–2121. 264 sites. Facilities: swimming, fishing, boat launching ramp, camp store, recreation building, children's area. $12 (plus $1 entry fee). Open Apr.–Oct.

Keuka Lake State Park, Rte. 54A, Bluffpoint, tel. 315/536–3666. 150 sites. Facilities: swimming, fishing, boat launching area, children's area. $10. Open May–Sept.

Letchworth State Park, Rte. 19A, Castile, tel. 716/493–2611. 270 sites. Facilities: swimming, fishing, children's area, recreation building. $12. Open May–Oct.

Watkins Glen State Park, Rte. 14, Watkins Glen, tel. 607/535–4511. 303 sites. Facilities: swimming, fishing, children's area. $10. Open Jun.–Sept.

The Arts

Except for the colleges and universities with on-campus music and theater programs, the arts scene is largely centered in Rochester and Syracuse during the winter season.

Music

Rochester Philharmonic Orchestra (100 East Ave., tel. 716/222–5000) is one of the country's major orchestras and plays at the Eastman Theatre. During the summer the orchestra's home is Finger Lakes Performing Arts Center in Canandaigua.
Eastman School of Music (Gibbs and E. Main Sts., Rochester, tel. 716/274–1100) also performs at the Eastman Theatre (above). Part of the University of Rochester, it is one of the nation's most prestigious schools of music.
Syracuse Symphony Orchestra (Civic Center of Onondaga County, tel. 315/424–8222) is a major symphony orchestra that performs in the Civic Center of Onondaga County, an unusual building complex that combines a performing arts center with government offices.

Theater

Several theaters in the area present entertainment from plays to concerts, some of which are geared for the tourist season.

GeVa Theatre (Woodbury Blvd. & Clinton Ave., Rochester, tel. 716/232–1363) is Rochester's only resident professional theater. It stages eight productions a year in a renovated historic building that also houses a cabaret.
Masonic Temple & Auditorium Theater (875 E. Main St., Rochester, tel. 716/454–7743) offers touring Broadway productions, concerts, and solo artists.
Rochester Community Theater. There are five local companies that offer frequent performances. Call the Visitor Information Center (tel. 716/546–3070) for schedules.
Salt City for the Performing Arts (601 S. Crouse Ave., Syracuse, tel. 315/474–1122) presents drama, comedy, and musicals.
The **Syracuse Area Landmark Theater** (362 S. Salina St., Syracuse, tel. 315/475–7979) provides facilities for concerts, plays, dances, and classic movies in a National Historic Landmark building (circa 1928) filled with carvings, gold leaf, and ornate decorations.
Syracuse Stage (820 E. Genesee St., Regent Theater Complex, Syracuse, tel. 315/443–3275) is Syracuse's professional theater company.
Samuel L. Clemens Performing Arts Center (Clemens Center Pkwy. and Gray St., Elmira, tel. 607/562–3211) presents theater, dance, jazz, and classical artists year-round.
Smith Opera House for the Performing Arts (82 Seneca St., Geneva, tel. 315/781–LIVE) presents year-round professional and amateur productions and films in a historic 1,500-seat theater.
Corning Summer Theater (Glass Center, Corning, tel. 607/936–4634) presents professional companies during July and August in the Center's auditorium.

10 Niagara Falls, Buffalo, and Chautauqua

Introduction

Cynics have had a field day with Niagara Falls, calling it every-thing from "water on the rocks" to "the second major dis-appointment of American married life" (Oscar Wilde).

Others have been more positive. Missionary and explorer Louis Hennepin, whose books were widely read across Europe, first described the falls in 1678 as "an incredible Cataract or Water-fall which has no equal." Nearly two centuries later, novelist Charles Dickens wrote: "I seemed to be lifted from the earth and to be looking into Heaven. Niagara was at once stamped upon my heart, an image of beauty, to remain there changeless and indelible."

Part of the longest unfortified border in the world, the falls are actually three cataracts: the American and Bridal Veil Falls, in New York State, and the Horseshoe Falls in Ontario. The falls are responsible for the invention of alternating electric cur-rent, and they drive one of the world's largest hydroelectric de-velopments. And it really is all that water (more than 700,000 gallons per second in the summer) on its way from four of the Great Lakes—Superior, Michigan, Huron, and Erie—to the fifth, Ontario, that makes Niagara what it is: the most accessi-ble and famous waterfall in the world. There may be taller cata-racts in Africa, South America, and even elsewhere in New York State, but the sheer size and tremendous volume of Niag-ara are unsurpassed.

As with many other geographic features, Niagara's origins are glacial. More than 10,000 years before the first inscription, "My Parents Visited Niagara Falls and All They Got Me Was This Lousy T-Shirt," the glaciers receded, diverting the wa-ters of Lake Erie northward into Lake Ontario. (Before that, they had drained south; such are the fickle ways of nature.)

There has been considerable erosion since, more than seven miles in all, as the soft shale and sandstone of the escarpment have been washed away. Wisely, there have been major water diversions for a generating station (1954) and other machina-tions (1954–1963), which have spread the flow more evenly over the entire crestline of Horseshoe Falls. The erosion is now down to as little as one foot every decade. At that rate it will be some 130,000 years before the majestic cascade is reduced to an impressive rapids somewhere near present-day Buffalo, 20 miles to the south.

For many Americans, Buffalo has an unjust reputation as the Blizzard Capital of the United States. At least once a year it seems to crop up on television news spots about winter whiteouts and wicked windchill factors. Despite the fact that the heaviest snowfall is where the people want it—in ski coun-try south of Buffalo—and that recent winters have been re-markably mild (snow had to be imported for the city's winter festival in 1987 and 1988; the festival was postponed and then canceled in 1989), Buffalo's snowy image persists. The snows are caused in part by the city's location on Lake Erie, but the lake also acts as a giant air conditioner in the summer. Days are warm, but seldom excessively so. Once a depressed, industrial city, Buffalo is now undergoing a major regeneration. Buffalo is home to the nation's only inland naval park and has a splendid new baseball stadium in the heart of a rebuilding downtown. The waterfront has been undergoing a renewal, and the acres of undeveloped lake frontage hold the promise of a transformation on a grand scale.

Buffalo is a city of Victorian and turn-of-the-century elegance, a city of taverns and churches, a place with a strong ethnic tradition. It has the largest St. Patrick's Day Parade west of New York City and the biggest Pulaski Day Parade, a celebration of Polish heritage, east of Chicago.

Though Buffalo is the state's second-largest city, it is definitely "small town" when compared with its glamorous downstate sister. Friendliness and affordability are its selling points. Distances aren't great, and it's easy to get around. The city has a distinct style, a product of its rich ethnic, cultural, and architectural heritage.

The focal point for most visitors to Chautauqua County, which follows the shores of Lake Erie south of Buffalo to the border of Pennsylvania, is the Chautauqua Institution. The center for arts, education, religion, and recreation, founded in 1874, today has a full complement of schools and day camps, a lecture series, and performances in its 6,000-seat amphitheater. At nearby Cassadaga Lake is the Lily Dale Assembly, a spiritualist center begun in 1879, which still attracts mediums and the psychically curious. Other highlights of a visit to the region include the Amish community in the Conewango Valley; the ski resorts of Ellicottville; tours and tastings at area wineries; Fredonia, one-time Seed Capital of the United States; and Westfield, the self-proclaimed Grape Juice Capital of the world and home to Welch's Foods.

The county takes its name from its largest lake, which is 22 miles long and was called "Jad-dah-gwah" by the Indians. French explorers landed on the Lake Erie shores of the Chautauqua area in 1679. Their quest was for a southward passage to the Ohio and Mississippi rivers, and the route connecting Lake Erie with Chautauqua Lake, known as the Portage Trail, offered an answer. Indeed, the dispute between France and England over possession of this trail led to the French and Indian War.

In 1874 John Heyl Vincent, a Methodist minister, and Lewis Miller, an industrialist, established a training center for Sunday-school teachers on the shores of Chautauqua Lake. The Chautauqua Institution rapidly grew into a summer-long cultural encampment, and tent-show proprietors crisscrossed the country with their own versions of Chautauqua's lectures, drama, and music. The Chautauqua circuit faded into history, but the institution is now well into its second century.

The institution offers an unusual mix of arts, education, religion, and recreation during the nine-week summer season. Nine U.S. presidents, from Ulysses S. Grant to Gerald Ford, have delivered addresses here. Other notables have included Leo Tolstoy, William Jennings Bryan, and Amelia Earhart. In 1985 the institution hosted the first in a series of conferences on U.S.–Soviet relations. Two years later, more than 200 Soviet citizens came to Chautauqua and lived with American families for a week.

Chautauqua County is the largest American grape-growing area outside of California; its vineyards produce more Concord grapes than any other area in the country. The 50-mile drive from Silver Creek to Ripley, along the shores of Lake Erie, is known as the Chautauqua Wine Trail. Along the route are five wineries, roadside fruit and produce stands, and antiques shops.

Essential Information

Arriving and Departing

By Plane Greater Buffalo International Airport is the primary point of entry by air for the Buffalo–Niagara Falls area. The Niagara Falls Airport, which failed to make a go of regularly scheduled service, currently handles military and charter planes. Buffalo's airport is served by USAir, American, United, Northwest, Continental, Pan Am Express, TW Express, Eastern, Mall, and Delta. In the Chautauqua area, USAir serves the Jamestown airport, which is 16 miles from Chautauqua. With advance reservations, limousines meet planes in Buffalo for the $50 round-trip ride to the Chautauqua Institution. Contact **Chautauqua Limousine** (tel. 716/753–7010) or **Care-Van** (tel. 716/665–6535 or 716/688–1162).

Between the Airport Shuttle buses between the Buffalo airport and major hotels in
and Niagara Falls Niagara Falls are operated by **Niagara Scenic Bus Lines, Inc.**
and Buffalo (tel. 716/648–1500 or 716/282–7755). The one-hour shuttle runs from 7:30 AM to 5:30 PM; fare $8 each way. Taxi service to Niagara Falls is also available; fares are between $30 and $35. It is about 10 miles from the airport to downtown Buffalo, and average taxi fares are $15. Many hotels have their own shuttle buses, with free phones by the baggage area in both the airport's terminals. The **Niagara Frontier Transportation Authority** (NFTA) MetroBus also provides bus service with a fare of $1.20.

By Train **Amtrak** has two connecting stations in Buffalo: 75 Exchange St., downtown (tel. 716/856–2075) and 55 Dick Rd., Cheektowaga, south of the airport (tel. 716/683–8440). The Amtrak station in Niagara Falls is at Hyde Park Boulevard and Lockport Road (tel. 716/285–4224 or 800/877–7245).

By Bus **Greyhound** (181 Ellicott St., tel. 716/855–7511) operates from the Ellicott Street Bus Terminal in Buffalo and the Niagara Falls Transportation Center, 4th and Niagara Streets in Niagara Falls.

In the Chautauqua area, Jamestown and Fredonia are served by **Greyhound** (tel. 716/485–7541), **Blue Bird Coach Lines** (tel. 716/484–1900), and **D&F Transit** (tel. 716/485–7541). Limousine and taxi service is available to the Chautauqua Institution via **City Air Bus Ltd.** (tel. 716/489–3470).

Chautauqua Area Regional Transit System (CARTS) operates two round-trip buses daily between Jamestown and Westfield. The system may be used for shopping trips or to make travel connections. Call collect, tel. 716/665–6466. The Institution provides free shuttle-bus service from 9 AM to 9 PM. **Jamestown Area Regional Transit System** (JARTS) (tel. 716/664–2805) buses leave Jamestown hourly, starting at 9 AM. Buses circle the lake, stopping at various points, including the institution.

By Car   Access from the east, west, and south is primarily via I–90, the New York State Thruway. The expressway spur, I–190, leads from I–90 at Buffalo, across Grand Island to the Robert Moses Parkway into Niagara Falls. Approaches from the west and north are via a number of highways in Canada, including the Queen Elizabeth Way, with three bridges funneling traffic stateside. Highways leading to Buffalo from the south are U.S. 219 from Ellicottville and Route 400 from South Wales, both of which connect with I–90.

Getting Around

The major sights in Niagara Falls can easily be reached on foot. Although most people arrive by car, it is best to park the car and just walk.

By Subway   NFTA MetroRail provides light rail rapid-transit service in Buffalo. The system is above and belowground. The aboveground portion is free; the fare to go underground is $1, and tickets must be purchased at the stations. Bus-to-train or train-to-bus transfers are free. Each station is decorated with original paintings, photography, or sculpture. For information, tel. 716/855–7211.

By Bus   NFTA provides bus service within the Buffalo area, including Niagara Falls. The fare is $1 within both cities; $1.35 between cities; 40¢ children 5–12, under 5 free. Bus-to-bus transfers are 5¢; exact fare is required. Buses generally operate 5 AM–12:30 AM. For information, tel. 716/855–7211.

By Taxi   Taxi rates in Buffalo are $2.25 to start and $1 for each additional mile. Taxi rates in Niagara Falls are $1 for the first tenth of a mile and 10¢ for each tenth of a mile thereafter.

Scenic Drives

Niagara Parkway   Thirty-five miles of perfectly maintained parkland, this highway follows the Niagara River from Ft. Erie, Ontario (across from Buffalo) to Niagara Falls and on to Niagara-on-the-Lake. The stretch from Queenston to Niagara-on-the-Lake is particularly agreeable, with lovely homes and farms, vineyards, and orchards along the riverbank.

Robert Moses Parkway   This is the most scenic route to Niagara Falls from Grand Island. Continue on the parkway to Lewiston and Youngstown along the Niagara River.

Route 20A from East Aurora   Heading east through rolling hills and charming dairy farms, this drive is especially worthwhile in the fall.

Routes 430 and 394   The drive around Chautauqua Lake is particularly beautiful during the early fall, but spring and summer also offer splendid views of the lake, hills, and boats across the water.

Route 62   Drivers who follow this route through the Conewango Valley near Jamestown are likely to be slowed down by the numerous horse-drawn carriages, the mode of transportation for the Amish people who live in the valley; but this will afford you more opportunity to relish the scenery.

Important Addresses and Numbers

Tourist
Information

The **Niagara Falls Tourism Information Center** (4th and Niagara Sts., tel. 716/284–2000) is open daily 9 AM–7 PM; during the Festival of Lights, 4–10 PM.

The **Niagara Falls Convention & Visitors Bureau** (345 Third St., Niagara Falls, tel. 716/278–8010) has guides, maps, and brochures. Its 24-hour recorded message (tel. 716/278–8112) summarizes the day's events and gives suggestions on sights and activities. The **Greater Buffalo Chamber of Commerce** (107 Delaware Ave., tel. 716/852–7100) is open weekdays 9–5.

The **Chautauqua County Vacationlands Association** (2 N. Erie St., Mayville 14757, tel. 716/753–4304) is open weekdays 9–5. The association also operates an information center on the New York Thruway at Ripley. Open daily. Brochures and information also are available at **Northern Chautauqua Chamber of Commerce** (212 Lake Shore Dr. W, Dunkirk 14048, tel. 716/366–6200); **Lakewood Area Chamber of Commerce** (Box 51, Lakewood 14750, tel. 716/763–8557); and **Southwestern Gateway Tourist & Visitors Bureau** (101 W. 5th St., Jamestown 14701, tel. 716/484–1101). **Chautauqua Institution** (Chautauqua 14722, tel. 716/357–6200) provides brochures on its events, concerts, the summer school, and accommodations.

Emergencies

Dial 911 for police and ambulance. Hospitals in Buffalo closest to downtown hotels are **Buffalo General Hospital** (100 High St., tel. 716/845–5600) and **Millard Fillmore Hospital** (50 Gates Circle, tel. 716/887–4600); in Niagara Falls, the **Niagara Falls Medical Center** (621 10th St., tel. 716/278–4000) is just a five-minute drive from the falls; and in the Chautauqua area is **WCA Hospital** (207 Foote Ave., Jamestown, tel. 716/487–0141). Hospital emergency rooms are open all night.

Guided Tours

Orientation Tours

Boat 'n Bus Tours (tel. 716/285–2211) offers a 3½- to 4-hour comprehensive tour of the U.S. and Canadian sides of the falls plus a trip across the Rainbow Bridge and a ride up the Skylon Tower for a high-elevation view of Niagara Falls. **Bridal Veil Tours** (tel. 716/297–0329) gives a four-hour tour of the falls with pickup at area hotels, motels, and campgrounds. It also runs custom and special-events tours.

Gray Line of Niagara Falls (tel. 716/694–3600) has daily sightseeing tours of both Niagaras.

Special-Interest
Tours

Buffalo Guide Service (tel. 716/852–5201) operates personalized tours of the Buffalo area in small vans. **Silent Partners** (tel. 716/854–4434) custom-designs tours of Buffalo and Niagara daily year-round.

Exploring

The Niagara Falls Area

Numbers in the margin correspond with points of interest on the Niagara Falls map.

There are two cities called Niagara Falls—one in the United States and the other in Canada. Beyond the famous waterfall, viewable from both sides of the border, from the water in the *Maid of the Mist* boat, from above in towers, helicopters, or planes, the main attractions are easily reached on foot from the cataract.

The Niagara River forms the Canadian–U.S. border. The area north of the falls on both sides of the river is primarily orchards and vineyards. Stateside, the historic community of Lewiston is the site of Artpark, the only state park in the nation devoted to the arts. Farther north, where the river opens into Lake Ontario, are the scenic villages of Youngstown on the U.S. side and Niagara-on-the-Lake on the Canadian side, about a 20-minute drive from the falls. The latter is replete with many inns, restaurants, and shops, and is the site of the famous Shaw Festival every summer.

A 20-minute drive in the other direction is Buffalo, another waterfront community. Attractions here are more diverse and spread out, and a car can really be helpful, especially if you are interested in water sports, skiing, hunting, or some of the area's spectator sports.

Any tour of Niagara Falls begins at the falls themselves. For a good orientation of the falls, stop at the Niagara Visitor Center in the **Niagara Reservation State Park,** the oldest state park in the nation. The center has an information booth, displays, a snack bar, and daily screenings of *Niagara Wonders*, which captures the falls from every possible vantage point in 70mm and six-channel sound, and provides a brief look at the area before the modern-day tourist invasion. *Admission to the Visitor Center free; admission to film: $2 adults, $1 children 3–12, $1.50 senior citizens. Open daily 10–9.*

❶ **Goat Island**—part of the state park—offers the closest possible views of the American Falls and the upper rapids. Niagara Viewmobiles sightseeing trains can be boarded at several locations on Goat Island and at Prospect Point near the **Observation Tower.** The 40-minute tour includes a close-up view of the falls; stopovers are permitted at Goat Island Heliport, Cave of the Winds, Terrapin Point, Schoellkopf Museum, Aquarium, and Three Sisters Islands. *Goat Island, tel. 716/278–1796. Admission: $2.50 adults, $1 children 5–11. Hours vary seasonally.*

Queen Victoria Park (tel. 416/356–4699), on the Canadian side, is the best place for viewing **Horseshoe Falls.** To fully appreciate the power of the falls, many visitors take a ride on the *Maid of the Mist*, which can be boarded on either the American or Canadian side. In operation more or less continually since 1846, this trip has become as much a symbol of Niagara as the falls themselves. Just about every celebrity and head of state who has ever visited the falls has taken a ride on the boat. Theodore Roosevelt called it "the only way to fully realize the Grandeur of the Great Falls of Niagara."

Everyone is provided with heavy black or blue rubber slickers with hoods. On warm summer days some riders enjoy the feeling of the heavy spray without the slickers, but even with them, you will definitely get wet. The captain expertly guides **❷** the boat past the base of the **American** and **Bridal Veil Falls** and almost into the thunderous deluge of the Horseshoe Falls. Spray stings the face and hands and blurs vision. Of course, it is

Niagara Falls

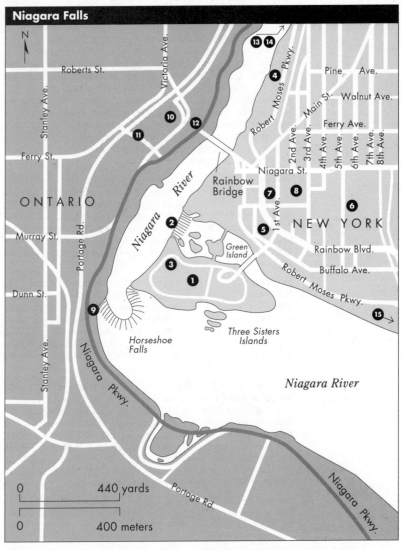

American and Bridal
Veil Falls, **2**

Cave of the Winds
Trip, **3**

Clifton Hill, **11**

Falls Street Station, **8**

Goat Island, **1**

Grand Island, **15**

Lewiston, **13**

Maple Leaf Village, **10**

Native American
Center for the Living
Arts, **5**

Niagara Falls
Museum, **12**

Niagara Splash Water
Park, **6**

Schoellkopf Geological
Museum, **4**

Table Rock Scenic
Tunnels, **9**

Wintergarden, **7**

Youngstown, **14**

all perfectly safe, and only once has one of the *Maid of the Mist*'s cork life preservers been used. Back in the summer of 1960, seven-year-old Roger Woodward was swept over the falls after a boat he was in stalled and broke up on rocks near the brink. He was wearing an orange life jacket, so passengers spotted the child quickly and threw him the preserver. Plucked from the turbulent waters, he became the only person in history to survive a plunge over the falls without a protective device. He returned 20 years later on his honeymoon. *Niagara River at base of falls, tel. 716/284–8897. Admission: $5.25 adults, $3.15 children 6–12; plus 75¢ on Canadian side for incline railway or 50¢ on American side for Observation Tower. Open daily 9–7, mid-May–late-Oct.*

3 The **Cave of the Winds** trip is one way to almost touch the falls by following wooden walkways to within 25 feet of the base. In 1984 a Korean visitor was hit by a 15-pound chinook salmon trying to swim up the great cataract. He wasn't hurt, but he was definitely surprised. *Rain slickers and foot coverings are provided. Trip starts on Goat Island, tel. 716/278–1730. Admission: $3.50 adults, $3 children 5–11. Open daily Memorial Day–mid-Oct. Hours vary.*

4 For insight into the geological history of the falls, visit the **Schoellkopf Geological Museum** in Niagara Reservation State Park. A geological garden and nature trail are on the grounds; tours of the park area are scheduled regularly. *Main St. near Rainbow Bridge, tel. 716/278–1780. Admission: 50¢; children under 5 free. Open daily 9:30–7, Memorial Day–Labor Day; daily 10–5, Labor Day–Nov. 1; Wed.–Sun. 10–5 the rest of the year.*

5 Just a few steps from the Niagara Reservation Park is the **Native American Center for the Living Arts,** or "The Turtle," because of its turtlelike look. It houses a museum and art gallery focusing on American Indian heritage, culture, symbols, and art. Iroquois dance performances are held during the summer season, and it has a gift shop and restaurant. *25 Rainbow Mall, tel. 716/284–2427. Admission: $3 adults, $1.50 children 6–12, $2 senior citizens. Open May 1–Sept. 30, daily 9–6; Oct. 1–Apr. 30, Tues.–Fri. 9–5, weekends noon–5.*

6 **Niagara Splash Water Park,** behind the convention center, offers waterlovers a variety of ways to experience water directly. The park features a five-story water flume, six-story speed slides, a lazy river ride, year-round wave pool, activity pool, remote-control boats, cruiser, and a sand beach. *700 Rainbow Blvd., tel. 716/284–3555. Admission: $11.95 adults, $9.95 children 3–12; after 5 PM, $6.95 for everyone. Open daily 11–8 AM, early summer–Labor Day.*

7 On the other side of the Convention Center and connected to the Radisson Inn is **Wintergarden.** This seven-story, indoor tropical garden is free and open daily. (In the spring and summer it is a popular site for weddings, especially on Saturdays.) During the Festival of Lights—late-November to mid-January— the garden is decorated with thousands of multicolored lights.

8 Between the Convention Center and Wintergarden is the new **Falls Street Station,** a complex of shops and restaurants with the theme of turn-of-the-century Niagara Falls. Adjacent to the station is the **Falls Street Faire,** an indoor entertainment center featuring amusement rides and fast-food restaurants.

To sample the falls from another country, cross the Rainbow Bridge into Canada. **Niagara Falls, Ontario,** is a real contrast in atmosphere and style, from the perfectly manicured gardens along the Niagara Parkway and Queen Victoria Park to the garish and somewhat tacky souvenir shops and mélange of museums along Clifton Hill.

Parking can be quite difficult, especially on summer weekends, so hop aboard the **Niagara Parks People Mover,** a loop bus system that allows you to get off and on as many times as you wish for one price: $1 adults, 50¢ children. It operates mid-May–mid-Oct., daily 9–11.

❾ At **Table Rock Scenic Tunnels,** you don a weatherproof coat and boots, and an elevator takes you down to a fish-eye view of the Canadian Horseshoe Falls and the Niagara River and a walk through three tunnels cut into the rock. *Open mid-June–Labor Day, 9 AM–11 PM; 9–5 the rest of the year. Tours begin at Table Rock House, in Queen Victoria Park. Tel. 416/358–3268. Cost: $3.75 adults, $1.90 children 6–12. Closed Christmas and New Year's Day.*

If you want to see the falls from on high, you can take a helicopter ride over the falls or an elevator up the three towers on the Canadian side. **Niagara Helicopters** allows you to see the falls at an unforgettable angle. Yes, they do accept major credit cards, so you won't feel the cost for weeks. *Victoria Ave. at River, tel. 416/357–5672. Departures year-round except first 2 wks in Feb., 9 AM–sunset. AE, DC, MC, V.*

❿ The **Skylon Tower** and the **Minolta Tower** have restaurants and observation areas. The **Kodak Tower** is in the **Maple Leaf Village,** a complex of shops, museums, and rides, including the world's second-largest Ferris wheel.

The **Elvis Presley Museum,** in Maple Leaf Village, has the King's cars, jewelry, clothing, and furnishings from his Graceland and Hollywood homes. *5705 Falls Ave., tel. 416/357–0008. Admission: $3.95 adults, $2.75 children 6–12. Open year-round 9 AM–10 PM, Jan.–Mar. weekends only.*

⓫ A variety of museums are located on the walk up **Clifton Hill.** They also offer some good rainy day diversions and are usually open in the evening. **Circus World Display** has an array of circus-related shops, an arcade, and an old-fashioned fun house. *4848 Clifton Hill, tel. 416/356–5588. Admission: $2 adults, $1.50 children 6–12. Open daily 9 AM–midnight.*

Louis Tussaud's Waxworks features life-size reproductions of the most famous and infamous people in historically accurate costumes and settings. *4915 Clifton Hill, tel. 416/374–6601. Admission: $6.05 adults, $2.95 children 6–12, $4 senior citizens. Open daily 9 AM–midnight.*

For views of the record breakers of history, visit the **Guinness Museum of World Records,** containing hundreds of exhibits that made it into the Guinness record book. *4943 Clifton Hill, tel. 416/356–2299. Admission: $6 adults, $3.95 students, $2.95 children 6–12. Open daily 9 AM–10 PM.*

For another perspective on the strange and wonderful, visit **Ripley's Believe It or Not Museum,** with its 500-odd exhibits of strange, surprising, but true happenings and facts. *4960 Clifton Hill, tel. 416/356–2238. Admission: $6.55 adults, $2.95 children 6–12, $4 senior citizens. Open daily 9 AM–11 PM.*

If you enjoy a good scare, stop at the **House of Frankenstein.** The museum warns foolish mortals to beware, because once you walk up the 13 stairs you are on your own. Exhibits in blood and gore abound. *4967 Clifton Hill, tel. 416/356–8522. Admission: $3.95 adults, $2 children 6–12. Open daily 10–10.*

⓬ Niagara Falls Museum, at the Rainbow Bridge, includes everything from shlock to quality. Here you'll find the Daredevil Hall of Fame, dinosaurs, and a very solid collection of Egyptian mummies dating from before the Exodus from Egypt. There are also Indian artifacts and zoological and geological exhibits. *5651 River Rd., tel. 416/356–2151. Admission: $5 adults, $4 students and senior citizens, $2 children 6–12. Open June–early Oct., 9 AM–midnight; Nov.–May, weekdays 10–5, weekends 11–5.*

Flower lovers should not miss the **Niagara Falls School of Horticulture,** six miles north of the Horseshoe Falls. Students in the school maintain all the gardens along the 35-mile Niagara Parkway, which runs from Fort Erie to Niagara-on-the-Lake. The school contains 100 acres of gardens, including a magnificent rose garden that is at its most glorious in June.

The **Floral Clock** is less than six miles north of the falls, along River Road. Nearly 20,000 plants that bloom from earliest spring to late autumn make up one of the world's biggest, bloomin' clocks. Chimes ring every quarter-hour, and it actually keeps the right time. Adjacent to the clock are the Centennial Lilac Gardens, with 256 varieties of lilacs and more than 1,500 bushes that bloom during May.

⓭ Just north of the clock is the village of Queenston. From here you can take the Lewiston–Queenston Bridge across the river to the United States and the historic village of **Lewiston,** seven miles north of the falls. It's best known as the home of **Artpark.** The only state park in the nation devoted to the visual and performing arts, Artpark encompasses 200 acres along the Niagara River. You can sit at the feet of a storyteller in the woods, don a mask and join a company of actors, watch your child create a puppet, or try your hand at Oriental brush painting. Nightly concerts and plays are staged by the Buffalo Philharmonic Orchestra, touring companies, and big-name entertainers. *Artpark, Lewiston, 14092, tel. 716/694–8191. Park is free, but concerts and plays run from $4 to $24. Parking: $2.50. Open daily June 28–Sept. 11.*

⓮ Continue north to **Youngstown,** home of **Old Fort Niagara,** about 15 minutes from Artpark. Occupied by the French, British, and Americans, the fort's original stone buildings have been preserved in their pre-Revolutionary state. French Castle, the oldest building in the Great Lakes area, was built in 1726. Military reenactments, battles, grand reviews, tent camps, fifes and drums, crafts, and archaeological digs are scheduled throughout the year. *Youngstown 14174, tel. 716/745–7611. Admission $4.75 adults, $2.75 children 6–12. Open July 1–Labor Day, daily 9 AM–7:30 PM; closing hours vary at other times.*

(15) South of Niagara Falls, there are 19 islands in the Niagara River. By far the largest is **Grand Island,** which is about five square miles larger than Manhattan. If you have children, take in its **Fantasy Island Park,** with more than 100 rides, shows, and attractions. Diving, musical, and stunt shows are held daily. There are five theme areas; picnic areas; and rides, including a log flume, waterslide, and dragon coaster. *2400 Grand Island Blvd., tel. 716/773-7591. Admission: $14.95 adults, $10.95 children 3-11, $9.95 senior citizens. Open daily 11:30 AM-8:30 PM, mid-June-Labor Day.*

On the southern tip of Grand Island is **Beaver Island State Park,** which has a fine beach, marina, and golf course. Back in 1825, Major Mordecai Manuel Noah, a lawyer and judge, founded Ararat on Grand Island as a refuge city for Jews who were being persecuted in Europe. The plan failed due to lack of support, but the cornerstone is on display in the Grand Island Town Hall.

Buffalo

Numbers in the margin correspond with points of interest on the Buffalo map.

(1) The best place to begin touring Buffalo is at its **City Hall,** considered one of the finest examples of Art Deco architecture in the country. The 28th-floor observation deck offers views of Lake Erie and the surrounding city, its radiating street plan modeled after Washington, DC. Louis Sullivan's 1895 Guaranty Building is acknowledged to be one of the most influential skyscrapers ever built and a prime example of Sullivan's ideas of functional design and terra-cotta ornament.

The nearby **Hyatt Regency Buffalo** is an elegant hotel with an atrium spanning an entire city block. The hotel started life as an office building designed by architect E. B. Green, who masterminded a number of the city's most stately mansions; its transformation into a hotel won several awards. The walls throughout the hotel's public areas are covered with original artwork by area artists. On a clear day, the 38th-floor restaurant in the **Marine Midland Center** (open for lunch only on weekdays) offers impressive views of the area, including the spray from Niagara Falls, some 20 miles away.

(2) Just beyond the Marine Center is the **Naval and Servicemen's Park,** the country's only inland naval park. It is home to the destroyer USS *The Sullivans,* the cruiser *Little Rock,* and the submarine *The Croaker,* all of which are permanently berthed in the Buffalo River and are open for exploration. There is also a PT boat, aircraft, guided missiles, and Servicemen's Museum. *1 Naval Park Cove, tel. 716/847-1773. Admission: $5 adults, $3.50 children 5-16 and senior citizens, $10 family. Open Apr. 1-Nov. 30, daily 10-5.*

Hop on the city's Light Rapid Rail System, partially underground, whose stations are decorated with original art and sculptures commissioned for the project. Stop on Allen St. in **(3)** the heart of **Allentown,** one of the nation's largest historic preservation districts. It is filled with 19th-century Victorian homes, boutiques, restaurants, and art galleries. The Allentown Art Festival, held the second weekend in June, is one of the largest outdoor art shows in the country.

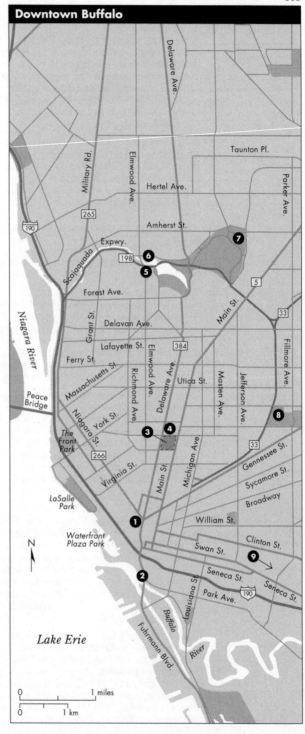

Albright-Knox Art Gallery, **5**

Allentown, **3**

Buffalo and Erie County Historical Society, **6**

Buffalo Museum of Science, **8**

Buffalo Zoo, **7**

City Hall, **1**

East Aurora, **9**

Naval and Servicemen's Park, **2**

Theodore Roosevelt Inaugural Site, **4**

Downtown Buffalo

North on Delaware Avenue, within a block of Allen Street, is
❹ the **Theodore Roosevelt Inaugural National Historic Site,** a
Greek Revival structure dating from 1838, when it served as
headquarters for military officers. The library where Theodore
Roosevelt was sworn in as the 26th president has been restored. Displays cover Roosevelt's inauguration and the assassination of President McKinley in Buffalo in 1901. An art
gallery on the second floor has changing exhibits. *641 Delaware
Ave., tel. 716/884–0095. Donation: $1–$2. Open Mon.–Fri.
9–5; Jan., noon–5.*

Head north on Delaware, which turns into Chapin then Lincoln
Parkway, for a total of two miles; at the entrance to the
❺ Scajaquada Expressway you'll find the **Albright-Knox Art
Gallery,** which has brought worldwide acclaim to Buffalo,
largely through the efforts of industrialist Seymour Knox. It
houses one of the most superb collections of contemporary art
in the world, as well as a comprehensive general collection, and
was the first U.S. museum to buy works by Picasso and Matisse. Alternatively, parallel Delaware by taking Elmwood Avenue, one block west, to the Albright-Knox. Elmwood is a
cheery, bustling street of shops, bars, and eateries. *Museum
shop and restaurant. 1285 Elmwood Ave., tel. 716/882–8700.
Donation. Open Tues.–Sun. 10–5.*

❻ Just across Scajaquada Creek is **Buffalo and Erie County Historical Society,** the only remaining building from the Pan
American Exposition of 1901. The emphasis is on area history
and Indian culture with a variety of imaginative, changing exhibits. *25 Nottingham Ct., tel. 716/873–9644. Admission: $2.50
adults, $1 children under 12, 90¢ senior citizens, $5 family.
Open Tues.–Sat. 10–5, Sun. noon–5.*

Head east on Nottingham Road along the northern edge of Delaware Park for a mile and turn left on Amherst Street to the
❼ **Buffalo Zoo,** one of the country's oldest. Highlights include a
tropical rain forest, a gorilla habitat, and a simulated Asian forest. There's a new $2 million habitat for tigers and lions. The
children's petting zoo is popular and includes camel and elephant rides. *Delaware Park, tel. 716/837–3900. Admission: $3
adults, $1 children 11–16, 50¢ children 4–10, $7 family; admission free several days a month. Open daily 10–5.*

Leave the zoo in the opposite direction, continuing less than a
block on Amherst, turning right (south) on Parkside Drive to
the Scajaquada Parkway (Rte. 198). Go east for two miles to
❽ Martin Luther King Jr. Park, where you'll find the **Buffalo Museum of Science.** It features exhibits on anthropology, archae-
ology, astronomy, botany, geology, and zoology, including
gigantic insect models and a children's discovery room. *Humboldt Pkwy. at Northampton St., tel. 716/896–5200. Admission: $2.50 adults; $1 children 3–17, students, senior citizens.
Open daily 10–5. Kellogg Observatory open Sept. 1–May 31,
Fri. 7–9:45 PM, weather permitting.*

Twenty miles southeast of Buffalo, via Route 400, is the pictur-
❾ esque village of **East Aurora,** home of the Roycroft Movement.
Elbert Hubbard, "the sage of East Aurora" and a successful
soap company executive turned philosopher and writer,
founded the movement in 1895. At its height, more than 500
Roycrofters were working as printers, coppersmiths, furniture
makers, silversmiths, potters, artists, and innkeepers. The

historic **Roycroft Inn,** filled with Roycroft furniture, is under renovation. The 14 buildings in the Roycroft Campus have been designated a National Landmark and transformed into shops, art galleries, a museum, town offices, and the County Extension Service.

During the third quarter of the 19th century, East Aurora was known as "the world's trotting nursery." Racehorses were raised and trained here on large farms, and the "world's only one-mile covered racetrack" was nationally known. The village's racing history is celebrated during the last weekend in July, when horse-drawn carriages parade down Main Street. Stop in to see the 17 stained-glass Tiffany windows in Baker Memorial Church, four of which were signed by Louis Tiffany.

Millard Fillmore practiced law in East Aurora before moving on to Buffalo and later to the White House as the nation's 13th president. The **Millard Fillmore House** (24 Shearer St., tel. 716/ 652–5362) is open to the public.

The Chautauqua Area

Numbers in the margin correspond with points of interest on the Chautauqua Area map.

The Chautauqua Institution, about 70 miles southwest of Buffalo, is the magnet that draws visitors to the shores of the 22-mile-long Chautauqua Lake. The institution is a walking town (no cars are allowed except to load or unload), a perfect Victorian village with contemporary amenities. It is a self-contained community with a full range of summer sports and endless opportunities to exercise the mind.

For exploring outside the institution, a car is recommended. The region can truly be said to appeal to myriad tastes and interests, from boating to hunting and fishing, from antiquing to wine tasting, and from the arts to world affairs.

① A tour of the Chautauqua area begins at **Silver Creek,** southwest of Buffalo on the shores of Lake Erie. From there you can follow the so-called Chautauqua Wine Trail, via the New York State Thruway, Route 20, which is preferred, or Route 5, along Erie's vineyard-dotted south shore. Several of the wineries along this route offer free tours and tastings: **Woodbury Vineyards Winery,** *S. Roberts Rd., off Rte. 20, 3 mi south of Dunkirk, tel. 716/679–WINE. Mon.–Sat. 10–5, Sun. 1–5.* **Chadwick Bay Wine Co.,** *10001 Rte. 60, 1½ mi south of Exit 59, off the NYS Thruway, tel. 716/672–5000. Mon.–Sat. 10–5, Sun. noon–5.* **Merritt Estate Winery,** *King Rd., off Rte. 20, tel. 716/ 965–4800. Mon.–Sat. 10–5, Sun. 1–5.*

② **Dunkirk,** the largest community on the south shore of Lake Erie, was so named because of its resemblance to the harbor at Dunkerque, France. This is a typical lakeshore community, where boating and water sports are essential elements of the lifestyle. **The Historic Dunkirk Lighthouse and Veteran's Park** at Point Gratiot is the chief tourist attraction. Visitors may climb the 95-foot lighthouse for a bird's-eye view of the area or visit the museum dedicated to the armed forces; there is a separate room for each branch of the service. *Off Rte. 15, tel. 716/ 366–5050. Apr.–June, daily 9–4; July and Aug., daily 9–9; Sept.–Nov., weekdays 9–2.*

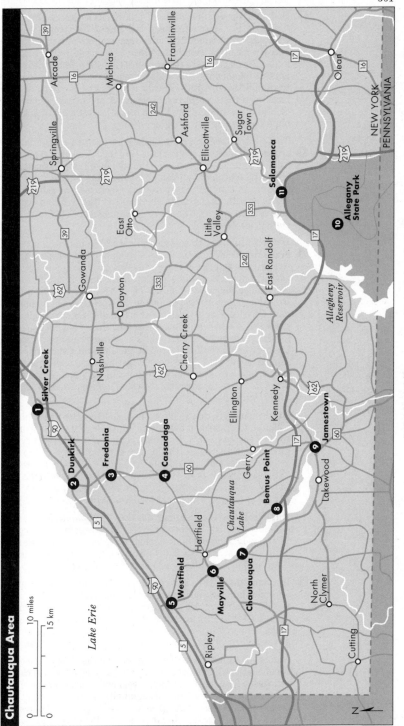

Chautauqua Area

❸ Fredonia, three miles south of Dunkirk on Central Avenue, was the site of America's first gas well (1821); the streets were lit with gas lamps when Lafayette stopped here on his American tour. Ironically, given the number of vineyards in the area, this is also the place where the Women's Christian Temperance Union was founded in 1873. Today Fredonia is a charming college town of attractive 19th-century buildings, a number of which have been restored in recent years. A prime example of successful renovation is **The White Inn;** stop for lunch or stay the night (*see* Dining and Lodging, below).

Those interested in spiritualism may want to take Route 60 **❹** south to **Cassadaga,** home of the **Lily Dale Assembly.** This spiritualist center, established on the shores of Lake Cassadaga in 1879, attracts mediums from throughout the United States and Canada. In summer, there are daily lectures, workshops, and sessions with clairvoyants. Private spiritual readings can be arranged. *1 mi off Rte. 60 at Cassadaga, tel. 716/595–8721. Open June 27–Sept. 1.*

If you continue southwest along Route 20 from Fredonia, you'll **❺** reach **Westfield,** home of Welch's Foods and the self-proclaimed Grape Juice Capital of the world. Westfield is also an antiques center; some 20 dealers display their finds in 19th-century homes (*see* Shopping, below). The 1928 lighthouse at nearby Barcelona Harbor was the first in the world to be lit by natural gas. Charles Edgar Welch, who founded the town and the grape-juice business, always asserted that "God did not mean for the grape to be fermented." Those who prefer to decide for themselves may want to stop at the **Johnson Estate Wines** to sample some that have been. Tastings are available year-round, but are even more frequent in July and August. *W. Main Rd., 3 mi southwest of Westfield, off Rte. 20, tel. 716/326–2191. Daily 10–6.*

Head inland off Route 20, on Route 394 to the north end of **❻** Chautauqua Lake and the town of **Mayville.** This is the home of the 90-ton *Sea Lion,* a hand-built replica of a 16th-century English merchant vessel. During the summer, tours of the ship are available, and a 90-minute cruise on the lake is offered on Saturdays; reservations are essential. *Chautauqua Lake Historic Vessels Co., 15 Water St., Mayville 14757, tel. 716/753–7823. Cruise cost: $25. Tours available June 1–Sept. 30.*

Mayville is also the home port for the *Chautauqua Belle,* a Mississippi River–style steamboat that does regular lake cruises as well as brunch and dinner cruises. In summer, the *Belle* sails Tues.–Sun. at 11, 1:15, 3, 4:45, and cruises cost $9 per person. *Chautauqua Lake Historic Vessels Co. (see above).*

❼ In **Chautauqua,** the 856-acre **Chautauqua Institution** is just a few miles farther south along the lake on Route 394. Here a visitor can fish for record-breaking muskellunge in the morning, attend a lecture by an internationally known speaker before lunch, play golf in the afternoon, study music or a foreign language before dinner, and attend an opera or concert at night.

Admission to the institution grounds and the wide range of accommodations and restaurants is by gate ticket, which can be purchased for periods of a day, a weekend, a week, or the eight-week summer season. The ticket admits you to the amphitheater and most events on the grounds except operas and plays, for which separate tickets are sold. A gate ticket is required for anyone 13 years and older. In keeping with the institution's religious origins, admission is free on Sunday. *Chautauqua Institution, Chautauqua 14722, tel. 716/357-6200. Gate admission ranges from $16.50 for Mon.–Wed. after 5 PM to $1,170 for the 8-week season. Weekend rates: $35.*

8 **Bemus Point,** a good spot for fishing enthusiasts, can be reached by taking Route 394 south to Stow, then following U.S. 17 across the lake via a bridge. There are several boat liveries in the town, and fishing guides can be arranged here. The Casino at the ferry landing has a small steamboat museum and refreshments. Next to the casino is a small beach and good swimming. During the summer you can ride the Bemus Point–Stow Ferry (tel. 716/753-2403) across the narrows of the lake. The cable-drawn ferry, in operation for more than 170 years, carries cars ($2.50 each way) as well as individual passengers ($1) and livestock (50¢).

9 **Jamestown,** with a large population of Swedish derivation, is at the southern tip of Chautauqua Lake. In 1988 the city celebrated 350 years of Swedish settlement in America. It has two areas of architectural interest where buildings span the 75 years from Gothic Revival to Art Deco styles. The **Old Northside and Southside Walking Tours** (tel. 716/483-7521) start at the **Penton Historical Center,** a museum housed in a Civil War-era mansion built for New York Governor Reuben E. Penton. The building is on the National Register of Historic Places. The museum has Italian and Swedish heritage rooms and is a good resource for genealogical material. *67 Washington St., tel. 716/483-7521. Open Mon.–Sat. 10-4.*

10 Outdoors lovers and anyone interested in Indian culture should head east on Route 17 to the 65,000-acre **Allegany State Park** (tel. 716/354-2535) and Salamanca, the only city on an American Indian reservation. The park, the largest in the state parks, has 75 miles of hiking trails and offers fishing, swimming, and hunting for deer, small game, and turkey in season, and camping year-round. The Seneca Iroquois National Museum on the Allegany Indian Reservation, adjacent to the state park, has exhibits on the history and contemporary culture of the Seneca Nation of Indians. *Rte. 17, tel. 716/945-1738. Open May 1–Oct. 1, Mon.–Sat. 10-5, Sun. noon-5.*

11 In the town of **Salamanca, the Salamanca Rail Museum,** housed in a restored 1912 passenger depot, has exhibits and operates rail excursions during the summer and fall. *170 Main St., tel. 716/945-3133. Open Mon.–Sat. 10-5, Sun. 12-5.*

What to See and Do with Children

Niagara Falls Exploring the falls can be exciting for children and adults alike, whether viewed from the deck of the *Maid of the Mist,* the Niagara Viewmobile, the Cave of the Winds trip, or from a tower or railing.

Aquarium of Niagara Falls. The performing dolphins, sea lions, and electric eels are only a few of the aquatic creatures from around the world on display here. *Whirlpool St. at Pine Ave., tel. 716/285-3575. Admission: $5.50 adults, $3.50 children, $3 senior citizens. Open Memorial Day–Labor Day, daily 9-7; the rest of year 9-5.*

Marineland. Killer whales, dolphins, and sea lions are big attractions here. On the grounds are an aquarium and a game farm with bear, deer, elk, and buffalo. The Hot Air Fantasy Show has 20 animated singing characters. There are a few rides for adults and children. Plan on spending at least half a day here if you want to see everything. *7657 Portage Rd. on the Canadian side, tel. 416/356–8250. Admission varies with season: summer, $14.50 adults, $9.95 over 59 and children 4–9; spring and fall, $12.95 adults, $6.95 over 59 and children 4–9; winter, $5.95 adults, $4.25 over 59 and children 4–9.*

Mahoney Silver Jubilee Dolls' House Gallery. The 140 dollhouses here, decorated and furnished in the style of houses built between 1780 and 1985, are worth more than $1 million. This large collection is in Ft. Erie, Ontario, just across the Peace Bridge from Buffalo. Ft. Erie marks the beginning of the Niagara Parkway, which ends in Niagara-on-the-Lake. *657 Niagara Blvd., Fort Erie, Ont., tel. 416/871–5833. Admission: $2 adults, $1.50 children 5–15. Open daily 10 AM–4 PM.*

Maple Leaf Village. This amusement complex sports a 350-foot observation tower, one of the largest Ferris wheels on the continent, and a huge IMAX theater. There are also rides, musical shows, shops, boutiques, and restaurants. *5685 Falls Ave., Niagara Falls, Ont., tel. 416/374–4444. Admission to the village is free. Outdoor rides are open June 15–Sept. 15. Visiting the observation tower costs 99¢. Combination price of $9.95 includes unlimited use of rides and a number of attractions.*

Buffalo **Buffalo Museum of Science** has a hands-on exhibit room for children 6–12. Children and their parents may handle prehistoric stone tools, touch a stuffed alligator, learn about snakes, play musical instruments, and try on African clothing. *Humboldt Pkwy. at Northampton St., tel. 716/896–5200. Admission: $2.50 adults, $1 students, senior citizens, and children 3–17, and $5 per family. Open daily 10–5.*

The **Children's Zoo,** part of the Buffalo Zoo, has animals for petting and riding. *Delaware Park, tel. 716/837–3900. Admission: $3 adults, $1 children 11–16, 50¢ children 4–10, $7 per family. Open daily 10–5:30.*

Theater of Youth (TOY) Company (Center Theater, 691 Main St., Buffalo) stages several major children's shows each year. Tel. 716/856–4410 for schedules and ticket information.

Chautauqua **Chautauqua Institution** has a complete program of activities for young people from 2½ years to college age. There is a children's school for those up to six years old and a summer day camp for children 6–15. Both programs run weekdays during the season. The Youth Activities Center (tel. 716/357–6200) plans and coordinates activities for high school and college-age youth.

Gadfly III, a cruise boat, sails from the institution's bell tower daily except Monday during the season (tel. 716/753–3528).

Sea Lion Project Ltd. (RD 1, Sea Lion Dr., Mayville, tel. 716/753–2403) has boat rides on three craft that are popular with children—the Bemus Point–Stow Ferry, the steamer *Chautauqua Belle,* and the *Sea Lion,* a replica of a 16th-century English ship.

Off the Beaten Track

Back of the Beyond. This is a bed-and-breakfast establishment with self-guided tours through organic herb, flower, and vegetable gardens with samples included. It is about 20 miles southeast of Buffalo. *7233 Lower E. Hill Rd., Colden, tel. 716/652–0427. Open daily.*

Broadway Market. Head to this store at 999 Broadway, in the heart of Buffalo's Polish neighborhood, to sample Polish kielbasa and other ethnic specialties.

Forest Lawn Cemetery. The resting place of President Millard Fillmore and Seneca Indian chief Red Jacket is at 1411 Delaware Ave., in the middle of Buffalo.

Griffis Sculpture Park in Ashford Hollow is the creation of Buffalo artist Larry Griffis, who turned 400 acres of meadow and woods into a sculpture garden. His metal figures—"Dancing Lady," "Round Man," and "Poet" add an artistic aura for hiking or cross-country skiing. *Rte. 219. Open daily.*

Kazoo Museum. Visit the world's only metal kazoo manufacturer. *8703 S. Main St., Eden, tel. 716/992–3960. Admission free. Open Tues.–Sat. 10–5, Sun. noon–5.*

Panama Rocks, just off Route 474 and eight miles southwest of Chautauqua Lake, is a private park with self-guided walking tours of caves, cliffs, crevices, and passages formed more than 300 million years ago. The Indians used these rocks and caves for shelter long before the arrival of French explorers in the mid-1600s. For a time in the early 1800s, outlaws used the rocks to hide their loot, and local legend has it that a cache of gold is buried here. *Panama, tel. 716/728–2845. Admission: $5 adults, $2 children under 12. Open May 1–Oct. 26, 9 AM–sunset.*

QRS Music Rolls, along the river in Buffalo, is the world's oldest and largest player-piano roll manufacturer. *1026 Niagara St., tel. 716/885–4600. Admission free. Tours weekdays only at 10 AM and 2 PM.*

Vidler's (690-694 Main St., East Aurora) is one of the last of a vanishing breed: a real five-and-dime. It has fresh popped popcorn for 5¢, slanted wooden floors, aisle after aisle of items including some for 5¢ or 10¢, and a large collection of Fisher-Price toys (East Aurora, the home of the giant toy company, is about 20 minutes southeast of Buffalo).

Shopping

Most Buffalo and Niagara Falls area stores are open weekdays 9–5:30 and Sat. 9–5:30 except in the suburbs, where stores are open until 9. Downtown stores are closed on Sunday but usually open noon–5 on Sundays in the suburbs. The sales tax is 7% in Niagara County (Niagara Falls) and 8% in Erie County (Buffalo). The **Factory Outlet Mall** at 1900 Military Road in Niagara Falls (tel. 716/773–1797) has more than 100 manufacturer outlets offering savings of 20%–70%. The **Factory Outlet Mall** at 1881 Ridge Road in West Seneca (tel. 716/674–8920) has more than 30 manufacturer outlets. Both are open Monday–Saturday 10–9 , Sunday 10–5.

Antiques

The village of Westfield in Chautauqua County has 20 antiques dealers. **Stockton Sales Antiques & Collectibles** (6 Mill St.,

Stockton, tel. 716/595–3516) has 30,000 square feet of barn space packed with antiques, collectibles, furniture, and reproductions. The **Lock Stock & Barrel Country Store** (Rte. 62, Ellington, tel. 716/287–3675) is a country grocery and antiques store. **Good Morning Farm** (Rte. 394, Stow, tel. 716/763–1507) is a 19th-century farm with seven shops featuring local arts and crafts, as well as a restaurant and bar.

Participant Sports

Boating

With the region's ample supply of lakes and rivers, waterborne recreation is a definite diversion. **Seven Seas Sailing School** (Erie Basin Marina, Buffalo, tel. 716/856–4109) and **Serendipity Sailing Services** (2493 Garrison Rd., Ridgeway, Ont., tel. 416/894–0696) provide sailboat rental and instruction. **Bouquard's Boat Livery** (1581 Fuhrmann Blvd., Buffalo, tel. 716/826–6189) and **Wolf's Boat House** (327 S. Ellicott Creek Rd., Tonawanda, tel. 716/691–8740) rents motor boats.

Fishing

After years of negative publicity regarding pollution in the area, conditions have improved and lake trout and other freshwater fish have returned to Lake Erie, Niagara River, and Lake Ontario. **John M. Sander's Fishing Guide** is a detailed guide to area fishing, available in sporting-goods stores and bookstores. There is still a health advisory against eating fish from Lake Ontario and the Niagara River below the falls. Consult the New York State Department of Environmental Conservation (DEC) (tel. 716/847–4600) for health and license information. Write or call DEC (50 Wolf Rd., Albany 12233, tel. 518/457–5400) for booklets on Great Lakes fishing and state boat launching sites. Bass, trout, muskie, salmon, and northern pike are being caught in large numbers. There are a number of charter fishing operators in the Buffalo, Lake Erie, and Niagara River area, and at Lake Ontario in Niagara County. They include **Great Lakes Fishing Charters** (8255 West Point Dr., Amherst, tel. 716/741–3453), **Olcott Charter Service** (6460 Hope La., Lockport tel. 716/434–9902), and **Downrigger Charters** (2683 Grace Ave., Newfane, tel. 716/778–7518).

Chautauqua Lake attracts serious anglers who come to challenge the native muskellunge, or "muskie," that is famous for its fight and size. Minnie Methuselah III has haunted Chautauqua since 1974. A "tiger" muskellunge, she weighed 44 pounds and stretched 52 inches that year when she was tagged with the number 2C-2963. Whoever catches her will have boated a record catch—and a $1,000 reward. Muskies often live to the age of 30.

Good-size walleyed pike, bass, and panfish are also caught in Chautauqua Lake. Lake Erie and Cassadaga and Findley lakes also provide good fishing. Ice fishing is popular during the winter. Some selected charter sportfishing outfits are:

Chautauqua Lake Charters, Box 1187, Chautauqua 14722, tel. 716/753–5255.

The Frenchman Boat, Box 231, Ashville 14710, tel. 716/763–8296.
J&C Charters, 4976 Webster Rd., Fredonia 14063, tel. 716/672–5674.
Pequod II Charters, 33 Newton St., Fredonia 14063, tel. 716/673–1117.
Salmon Tracker Charters, 6 Pennington Pl., Cassadaga 14752, tel. 716/595–3917.

Horseback Riding

Chautauqua-area stables give lessons, rent horses, and provide well-marked trails for riding at about $10 an hour. They include **Crackerjack Farms** (Bemus-Ellery Center Rd., Bemus Point, tel. 716/386–5054), **Danero Riding Stable** (Hewes Rd., Mayville, tel. 716/789–4600), and **Double D.A.B. Riding Stable** (Welch Hill Rd., Ripley, tel. 716/736–4418).

Hunting

Excellent hunting opportunities for whitetail deer, wild turkey, upland birds, waterfowl, and small game abound within an hour's drive of Buffalo. For information on licenses, seasons, bag limits, permissible weapons, public hunting grounds, and private preserves, write Department of Environmental Conservation (DEC) (50 Wolf Rd., Albany 12233 or tel. 716/457–5400).

Skiing

Kissing Bridge (Rte. 240, Glenwood, tel. 716/592–4963), the closest ski center to Buffalo and also one of the largest in the area, is only a 45-minute drive from downtown. **Holiday Valley** (Rte. 219, Ellicottville, tel. 716/699–2644) is the most extensive ski center in the area. Cross-country skiing is allowed in the city's parks. For ski conditions, tel. 800/CALL–NYS.

The Chautauqua area's other ski resorts for both downhill and cross-country skiing are **Cockaigne,** Cherry Creek (tel. 716/287–3223) and **Peek 'n Peak,** Clymer (tel. 716/355–4141).

Tennis and Golf

There are more than 100 public tennis courts and a number of public golf courses in the Niagara Falls–Buffalo area. Contact the Buffalo Parks Department (tel. 716/855–4200) or Erie County Department of Parks and Recreation (tel. 716/846–8352).

Windsurfing

For equipment rentals and lessons in windsurfing, parasailing, and waterskiing contact **Windsurfing Chautauqua** (Chautauqua 14722, tel. 716/789–2675).

Spectator Sports

Baseball The **Buffalo Bisons** AAA baseball team plays at gleaming new Pilot Field in the heart of downtown (tel. 716/878–8055).

Football The National Football League **Buffalo Bills** play at Rich Stadium (Orchard Park, tel. 716/649–0015).

Hockey The **Buffalo Sabres** professional hockey team plays at War Memorial Auditorium (tel. 716/856–3111).

Horse Racing **Buffalo Raceway** (Erie County Fairgrounds, Hamburg, tel. 716/649–1280) has harness racing. **Ft. Erie Raceway** (Bertie St., off Hwy. 3 just one-half mile from the Peace Bridge in Ft. Erie, tel. 416/871–3200) has thoroughbred racing.

Dining

Buffalo has given the world two classics—Buffalo chicken wings and beef on weck. The former is served mild, medium, or spicy hot, alongside blue-cheese dressing and celery; the latter consists of roast beef—carved on the spot—and heaped on a fresh, flaky kimmelweck roll that has been sprinkled with coarse salt. Buffalo, however, abounds in casual, rather inexpensive restaurants, many of which reveal surprising flourishes.

The emphasis in the Chautauqua area is on seafood and American-style menus. Reservations are necessary in the summer, especially if you plan a pretheater meal at the institution.

Highly recommended restaurants are indicated by a star ★.

Category	Cost*
Very Expensive	over $25
Expensive	$18–$25
Moderate	$10–$18
Inexpensive	under $10

per person, without sales tax, service, or drinks

Buffalo

Very Expensive **Rue Franklin West.** This French restaurant is housed in a 100-
★ year-old Victorian brick house. Every dish is extra-fresh and prepared from scratch. The menu changes seasonally but is imaginative year-round. Its specialties include chocolate desserts. There is an extensive wine cellar. *341 Franklin St., Buffalo, tel. 716/852–4416. Jacket required. Reservations advised. AE, MC, V. Dinner. Closed Sun., Mon.*

Expensive **Asa Ransom House.** This dining establishment-cum-inn (four rooms) is in a picture-perfect country setting. It is a historic house, parts of which date to the 18th century, and is appropriately crammed with antiques. The friendly waitresses are dressed in Early American costumes. Two of the house dishes are corned beef with apple-raisin sauce and salmon pond pie (salmon in a deep dish with tomatoes, topped with a cheese pastry). *10529 Main St., Clarence, tel. 716/759–2315. Jacket re-*

quired. *Reservations advised. MC, V. Dinner; lunch only on
Wed. Closed Fri. and Sat.*

Lord Chumley's. This is a venerable, dependable restaurant in
a rather elegant brownstone in Buffalo's trendy Allentown District. The menu is extensive, offering both American standards
and a few Continental dishes. Order the Caesar salad. *481 Delaware Ave., tel. 716/886–9159. Jacket required. Reservations
advised. AE, CB, DC, MC, V.*

★ **Old Orchard Inn.** This charming restaurant originated as a
farmhouse in the 1860s and was later a hunting lodge and tearoom. Large stone fireplaces burn warmly in the winter. The
expansive grounds feature a duck pond and sweeping views of
the countryside. Specialties include chicken fricassee with biscuits, chicken pot pie, and fresh fish. Old-fashioned dinners on
Sundays feature turkey, ham, roast pork, and prime rib.
Crustless-lemon angel pie is also a specialty. *2095 Blakely Rd.,
East Aurora (about 20 mi southeast of Buffalo), tel. 716/652–
4664. Jacket required. Reservations advised. AE, MC, V. Dinner.*

Billy Ogden's. This delightfully offbeat place serves superb
food. On the outside it looks like one of Buffalo's many indigenous taverns, which is what it once was. On the inside it still
looks like a tavern—but today it offers the freshest and most
delicately seasoned broiled fish imaginable. *1834 William St.,
Buffalo, tel. 716/896–8018. Dress: informal. AE. Closed Mon.*

Salvatore's Italian Gardens. Salvatore's would be at home on
the Las Vegas strip. It's an extravaganza with life-size statuary, fountains, and colored lights. The dining rooms are equally
ornate; new ones appear constantly at the owner's whim. There
is a wide selection of Italian dishes, but the house specialty is
steak à la Russell, tenderloin prepared at tableside. *6461 Transit Rd., Cheektowaga, tel. 716/683–7990. Jacket required. Reservations advised. AE, CB, DC, MC, V.*

Moderate **Anchor Bar.** Buffalo chicken wings were invented here in 1964
by the late owner, Dominic Bellissimo, and tons are served up
every week, accompanied by celery and blue-cheese dressing.
Anchor wings have been flown all over the country by former
residents homesick for this delicacy. Other traditional Italian
dishes are also in demand. *1047 Main St., Buffalo, tel. 716/886–
8920. Dress: informal. No credit cards. Lunch and dinner.*

Brick Alley Bistro. A small and charming place with a diverse
menu, running from standard lunch fare to rather ambitious
dinner undertakings, served with casual elegance. As the
name suggests, both the dining room and the alley-entrance
bar are brick-walled. In the summer the sidewalk cafe opens.
1375 Delaware Ave., tel. 716/881–1151. Dress: informal. Reservations advised. AE, MC, V. Lunch and dinner.

★ **Chef's Restaurant.** This spot has long been praised by politicians, media folk, and just about everyone who works or visits
downtown. It is especially busy on hockey and baseball nights.
Owner Louis Billittier personally oversees the kitchen, which
serves traditional southern Italian dishes. *291 Seneca St.,
Buffalo, tel. 716/856–9187. Dress: informal. Reservations advised. AE, MC, V. Lunch and dinner. Closed Sun.*

Eckl's Beef & Weck Restaurant. This dining establishment
serves beef on weck supreme. It is housed in a renovated 100-
year-old house not far from Rich Stadium, where the Buffalo
Bills play. Owner Dale Eckl personally carves the beef to order, dipping the weck roll deftly into the roast beef juices to re-

tain the roll's flaky texture. Fish fries are also popular. *4936 Ellicott Rd., Orchard Park, tel. 716/662-2262. Dress: informal. No credit cards. Lunch and dinner.*

Harbour Marine. A favorite restaurant especially in the summer, primarily because of its location at a busy marina on the Niagara River. It offers a fine view of the Canadian shore. White fish Oscar and fish fries are specialties. *2191 Niagara St., Buffalo, tel. 716/877-9349. Dress: informal. Reservations advised, especially during the summer. AE, MC, V. Lunch and dinner.*

Pettibones Grille. This elegant restaurant is in the Pilot Field baseball stadium in downtown Buffalo. A game ticket is required for buffets at game time, but the restaurant is open year-round. The decor matches that of the baseball park outside—red chairs, green walls, and a deep green carpet. But the menu is a far cry from peanuts and Crackerjacks, favoring such items as grilled steaks and chops; grilled, broiled, or baked red snapper; swordfish or shrimp en brochette; and Manicotti Antoinetta (with lamb and artichokes). The desserts include a selection of Rich products (the Rich family owns the Buffalo Bisons baseball team as well as the restaurant and made some of its millions with Coffee Rich creamer). *Pilot Field. Enter on Washington St. and take the elevator to the mezzanine level, tel. 716/846-2000. Dress: informal. No reservations accepted. AE, CB, DC, MC, V. Lunch and dinner.*

Shooters. The newest place on Buffalo's rapidly developing waterfront and the one that seems most to capture the recreational spirit of things. In addition to its wide-ranging casual menu, it offers boat docking with valet service, sun decks, patio eating and drinking, a swimming pool, and pervasive festivity. *325 Fuhrmann Blvd., tel. 716/854-0416. Dress: informal. AE, MC. Lunch and dinner.*

Inexpensive **Towne Restaurant.** In the heart of Allentown, this restaurant was once just a hot-dog stand specializing in dogs with spicy hot sauce. It just grew and grew and now resembles a Greek taverna, complete with stucco walls covered with scenes of Greece. The owner hails from Rhodes and knows the meaning of Greek hospitality. Lemon chicken and moussaka are specialties, as is rice pudding. *186 Allen St., tel. 716/884-5128. Dress: informal. AE, MC, V. Breakfast, lunch, and dinner.*

Chautauqua Area

Expensive **Athenaeum Hotel.** The large dining room in this Victorian hotel
★ is the most venerable dining establishment at the institution. There is a prix-fixe menu. The food is simple but good and makes use of the fresh local produce. The two-dessert dinner is an Athenaeum tradition, designed, perhaps, to make up for the firm policy of no alcohol. Ask to see Thomas A. Edison's table by the window that overlooks the huge front porch. A shy man, Edison used to enter and leave the dining room by the window. The porch, with its rows of wicker rockers, is the spot for predinner socializing. *Chautauqua Institution, tel. 716/357-4444. Jacket required for dinner. Reservations required. No credit cards. Open only during 8-week summer season. Breakfast, lunch, and dinner.*

Galley. This popular restaurant and tavern has a nautical decor and overlooks Dunkirk harbor. There is outdoor dining as well as a private dock for those who arrive by boat. Specialties include quiche and seafood spinach soufflé. *2 Mullet St., Dun-kirk, tel. 716/366-3775. Dress: informal. Reservations advised in summer. MC, V. Lunch and dinner.*

Inn at the Peak. The elegant Tudor-style restaurant at this ski and golf resort specializes in roast beef and has an extensive wine list. During the winter, the fireplaces burn brightly and warmly. *Ye Olde Rd., Clymer, tel. 716/355-4141. Jacket required. AE, DC, MC, V. Lunch and dinner.*

★ **The White Inn.** A charter member of the elite Duncan Hines Family of Fine Restaurants, the White Inn now has new owners who are striving to reestablish its national reputation. The large dining room has a garden decor: linen cloths and fresh flowers on the tables. Winning entries from the Culinary Olympics on the menu include Lamb Wyoming, seafood sausage, and seafood symphony—fresh clams, shrimp, crabmeat, oysters, scallops, and garden vegetables served in an open pastry shell. Local wines are featured. For dessert the chocolate mousse cake is a chocolate lover's dream. *52 E. Main St., Fredonia, tel. 716/672-2103. Jacket required. Reservations advised. AE, MC, V. Lunch and dinner.*

Moderate **Good Morning Farm.** This 150-year-old farmhouse, embellished with antiques, baskets, and large wood beams, serves country-style meals; everything is made from scratch. Specialties include stuffed chicken, a seafood sampler called Anchor's Away, and homemade breads, muffins, and desserts. The chef, an artist, has her works on display. *Rte. 394, tel. 716/763-1507. Dress: informal. AE, MC, V. Open Memorial Day–Labor Day.*

The Tally-Ho. Another favorite at the institution is this restaurant that has been operated by the Streeter Family for more than 50 seasons. There are two dining rooms, one specializing in charcoal-broiled steaks and the other a family-style dining room. The decor is Victorian. *Chautauqua Institution, tel. 716/357-3325. Jacket required for dinner. Reservations required. No credit cards. Open summer season only. Breakfast, lunch, and dinner.*

★ **Ye Hare'N'Hounds Inn.** This charming old English-style inn on the lake is noted for fresh seafood, beef, and veal. There is a private dock for guests arriving by boat. On fine days ask for a table outside. *Rte. 430, Bemus Point, tel. 716/386-2181. Dress: informal. AE, MC, V. Open year-round. Lunch and dinner.*

Niagara Falls

Expensive **Clarkson House.** An 1818 landmark, this place is especially popular during the Artpark summer theater season. Lobster is flown in daily from Maine, and steaks are a favorite. *810 Center St., Lewiston, tel. 716/754-4544. Dress: informal. Reservations advised in summer. AE, DC, MC, V. Lunch and dinner.*

★ **John's Flaming Hearth.** Although the menu was recently expanded, this Niagara Falls standby is still justifiably famous for its charcoal-broiled steak. Beef cattle are raised on a ranch in Colorado and must pass a tenderizer test. Seafood, chicken, and veal are also on the menu. Pumpkin ice-cream pie is a dessert specialty. *1965 Military Rd., Niagara Falls (across from Factory Outlet Mall), tel. 716/297-1414. Jacket required. Reservations advised. AE, CB, MC, V. Lunch and dinner.*

The Red Coach Inn. With a spectacular view of the upper rapids of the falls, this 1923 inn has an old English atmosphere, with wood-burning fireplaces and an outdoor patio that is terrific for summer dining. Prime rib is one specialty. Others include Boston scrod and seafood sausage mornay. *2 Buffalo Ave., Niagara Falls, tel. 716/282–1459. Dress: informal. Reservations advised in summer and on weekends. AE, DC, MC, V. Lunch and dinner.*

Skylon Tower. Ride the outside elevator high up the tower for some of the best views of the falls, then dine in the revolving dining room on lobster, fresh fish, beef, and veal. *5200 Robinson Rd., Niagara Falls, Canada, tel. 416/856–5788. Jacket required. Reservations advised. AE, MC, V. Lunch and dinner.*

Wintergarden Restaurant. The restaurant, part of the Radisson Inn, sits within the towering tropical gardens of the Wintergarden and has a distinctly tropical feeling, particularly striking in winter. It is just a three-minute walk from the brink of the falls. Special dishes include pasta primavera, Cornish hen, and chicken florentine. *240 Rainbow Blvd., Niagara Falls, tel. 716/282–1212. Dress: informal. Reservations advised. AE, MC, V. Lunch and dinner.*

Moderate **Fortuna's.** Since 1945 this place has attracted area residents.
★ The Italian home cooking includes such favorites as lasagna and ravioli. *827 19th St., Niagara Falls, tel. 716/282–2252. AE, MC, V. Closed Mon. and Tues. Dinner.*

Pete's Market House. All the restaurant basics—steak, lobster, veal—are here in a warm, bustling environment. The lines are long, the portions are huge, and the prices are low. *1701 Pine Ave., tel. 716/282–7225. Dress: informal. No reservations. No credit cards. Lunch and dinner.*

Top of the Falls. This is the place for lunch at the falls if you like the feeling of being on top of them. The restaurant serves the usual luncheon fare, such as hamburgers, chicken, and hot roast beef. *Goat Island, Niagara Falls, tel. 716/285–3316. Dress: informal. AE, MC, V. Lunch only, except for groups of 50 or more.*

Lodging

Hotels and motels in the Niagara Falls–Buffalo area fall primarily into two categories: major chains and lower priced budget properties. In Niagara Falls, high-season rates apply from Memorial Day through Labor Day. Prices are highest in the immediate vicinity of the falls; elsewhere they remain the same year-round. Most of the area's hotels and motels tend to be moderately priced.

On the Chautauqua Institution grounds you can stay in stately Victorian hotels, guest houses, apartments, modern condominiums, or rooms in denominational houses operated by various religious groups. Some condos are available on a weekly basis, although most apartments are available only during the eight-week season. Since many people return year after year, reservations are essential. **Chautauqua Accommodations Referral** (Chautauqua 14722, tel. 716/357–6204) can help in locating lodgings at the institution.

Bed-and-Breakfast Reservations for the entire western New York/Chautauqua area can be made with **Rainbow Hospitality** (466 Amherst St., Buffalo, tel. 716/874–8797). The accommodations vary from historic homes to Victorian mansions to working farms in the country. Prices average $50–$85 for a double. Some B&Bs welcome children, but others do not; inquire in advance.

Highly recommended hotels are indicated by a star ★.

Category	Cost*
Very Expensive	over $90
Expensive	$70–$90
Moderate	$50–$70
Inexpensive	under $50

per double without sales tax or service

Buffalo

Very Expensive **Hyatt Regency Buffalo.** This converted office building has a three-story glass atrium overlooking Main Street, and combines the best of the new and the old. The rooms are individually decorated with original works of art. Because many rooms were once offices, they have interesting, irregular shapes. *2 Fountain Plaza, Buffalo 14202, tel. 716/856–1234. 400 rooms with bath. Facilities: in-room movies, indoor pool, hot tub, 2 restaurants, bar, entertainment, drugstore, beauty shop, concierge, free airport transportation, tennis, golf, racquetball privileges, health club. Regency Club with private lounge. AE, CB, DC, MC, V.*

Expensive **Asa Ransom House.** Parts of this exquisite country inn date to the early 19th century. In 1799, the Holland Land Company offered lots here to "any proper man who would build and operate a tavern upon it." The first to accept was Ransom, a young silversmith. There are four bedrooms in the new section of the building, each furnished with antiques and period reproductions. The Green Room has two double beds and a view of the herb garden. No smoking allowed in the bedrooms. *10529 Main St., Clarence 14031, tel. 716/759–2315. Breakfast included. MC, V. Closed Fri. and Sat.*

Buffalo Hilton at the Waterfront. The best rooms at this luxury property overlook both the Niagara River and Lake Erie. It features an expansive health club with a pool, tennis courts, and indoor jogging track. The waterfall in the lobby restaurant creates a tropical feeling. *Church and Terrace Sts., Buffalo 14202, tel. 716/845–5100. 475 rooms with bath, including suites and studio rooms. Facilities: in-room movies, indoor pool, 3 restaurants, 3 bars, entertainment, gift shop, drugstore, free garage, free airport transportation, 6 indoor tennis courts, 4 racquetball courts, handball, squash, health club, game room, sauna in some suites, refrigerators available. Executive Level with private lounge. Children free. AE, CB, DC, MC, V.*

Moderate **Lenox.** In the historic Allentown District, this hotel is venerable but still comfortable. Many suites have permanent guests and most of them are senior citizens. *140 North St., Buffalo 14201, tel. 716/ 884–1700. 50 rooms with bath. Facilities: restaurant, bar, free airport transportation. AE, CB, DC, MC, V.*

Inexpensive **Best Western Inn Downtown.** This is an economical but pleasant hotel located along stately Delaware Avenue in downtown Buffalo. The rooms are standard motel fare. *510 Delaware Ave., Buffalo 14202, tel. 716/886–8333. Facilities: wet bar in suites, children free, health club privileges. AE, CB, DC, MC, V.*

Chautauqua

Very Expensive
★

Hotel Athenaeum. This "grande dame" of Chautauqua hotels was built in 1881 and at one time was reputedly the largest wooden hotel in the country. Many visitors have been returning for generations. It is a National Historic Site that has hosted all manner of presidents and celebrities over the years. The hotel was recently restored. The restoration was painstaking and precise—paints were matched exactly to conform to the original. The result is a spruced-up and most comfortable Victorian hotel. All guest rooms have new paint, bedspreads, and carpeting, but no TVs. *Chautauqua Institution 14722, tel. 800/862–1881, in NYS 800/821–1881. 160 rooms with bath. Facilities: dining room and all the facilities of the Institution. Summer only. American plan only with breakfast, lunch, and dinner included. No credit cards.*

St. Elmo Hotel. This hotel-and-condo complex opened in June 1988 on the site of a razed hotel of the same name. It was built in traditional Victorian style to blend in with the surrounding hotels, homes, and cottages. All standard rooms and the one- and two-bedroom condos have furnished kitchens, telephones, cable TVs; most have private porches. *1 Pratt Ave. 14722, tel. 716/357– ELMO. 64 rooms with kitchen and bath; Facilities: dining room, health club, shop, laundry room. American plan on request. Open year-round. AE, MC, V.*

Moderate

Cary Hotel. This Victorian hotel has an excellent location—one block from the amphitheater. Although the rooms were recently remodeled, they are all furnished in Victorian style—some even have the original flowered wallpaper. There are no phones or TVs in the rooms; the only ones are in the lobby. There are two large porches filled with rocking chairs. The atmosphere is friendly and homey. *9 Bowman Ave. 14722, tel. 716/357–2245. 28 rooms with bath; 2 also have kitchens. Facilities: dining room. No credit cards.*

Hotel Lenhart. This old-fashioned hotel on the lake has been operating since 1881, and has been under one family's management for three generations: Formal family portraits line the stairway. Rooms are simply furnished and have neither telephones nor TVs. Brightly painted blue, red, green, and yellow rocking chairs beckon from the front porch. There is a beach, park, and marina next door. MAP (breakfast and dinner) is mandatory in the summer. The dining room is rather formal, with starched linen tablecloths, fresh flowers, and home-style meals (choice of three entrees.) *Rte. 17, Bemus Point 14712, tel. 716/386–2715. 53 rooms, 43 with bath. Facilities: dining room. No credit cards. Open Memorial Day–Sept. 15. Off-season rates June and Sept.*

★ **Webb's Resort and Marina.** This Chautauqua Lake resort strives to offer something for just about every interest, from a marina and bowling alleys to a goat-milk fudge factory with tours and tastings. The average motel-type rooms have recently been refurbished. *Rte. 394, Mayville 14757, tel. 716/753–2161. 26 rooms with bath. Facilities: 5 dining rooms, marina, cable TV, game room, restaurant, pool, gift shop, bowling alleys, fudge factory. AE, MC, V. Open all year.*

★ **The White Inn.** Chautauqua County's oldest continuously operating hotel was named for Dr. Squire White, the "father of Fredonia," who first built a small house on this site in 1811. His son's home, built on the same site, was turned into an inn in 1919. Currently owned by two philosophy professors who renovated all the rooms and public areas, the inn is furnished with antiques and fine furniture reproductions from nearby Jamestown. (Some of the antiques are for sale.) The rooms are large and comfortable, individually decorated, and all have new plumbing. *52 E. Main St., Fredonia 14063, tel. 716/672–2103. 20 rooms with bath. Facilities: dining room, bar, Continental breakfast included daily except Sun. AE, MC, V.*

The William Seward Inn. This inn, overlooking Lake Erie, was built in 1821 as the home of Secretary of State William Seward, who served under President Lincoln and was responsible for the purchase of Alaska. Totally renovated and filled with antiques, it has a homey, comfortable feeling. *S. Portage Rd., Westfield 14787, tel. 716/326–4151. 10 rooms with bath. Facilities: gourmet breakfast included, skiing nearby. MC, V.*

Niagara Falls

Expensive **Holiday Inn Resort & Conference Center.** Located about a 15-minute drive from the falls, this is a true resort with just about every type of facility—golf, ice skating, indoor and outdoor pools, fishing, boat dock, bikes, exercise rooms, and saunas. *100 Whitehaven Dr., Grand Island 14072, tel. 716/773–1111. 265 rooms with bath. Facilities: dining room, cocktail lounge, coffee shop, rental bikes, and 2 pools. AE, CB, MC, V.*

Days Inn Falls View. A longtime landmark at the falls, this bustling property has recently undergone a much-needed renovation: Ask for one of the renovated rooms. The top floors with a view of the Upper Rapids are best. The rooms are compact but attractive. The hotel has the same owner as John's Flaming Hearth Restaurant; the dining room is better than typical hotel fare. *201 Rainbow Blvd., Niagara 14301, tel. 716/ 285–9321. 200 rooms with bath. Facilities: dining room, cocktail lounge. AE, CB, MC, V.*

Inexpensive **Bit-O-Paris Motel.** This is not quite Paris, but it is a comfortable and economical motel along Niagara Falls Boulevard, the city's motel row. There are several two-bedroom units, which are handy for families. *9890 Niagara Falls Blvd. 14304, tel. 716/ 297–1710. 25 rooms with bath. Facilities: pool, refrigerator, whirlpool bath. AE, MC, V.*

Coachman Motel. This motel represents one of the best values near the falls. It is just three blocks from the Convention Center and the falls. *523 Third St. 14301, tel. 716/285–2295. 19 rooms with bath. Facilities: refrigerator. AE, MC, V.*

Campgrounds

Campgrounds are open from May to October. Exact opening and closing dates vary. Following are some area camping facilities:

Niagara–Buffalo **Darien Lakes State Park** (10289 Harlow Rd., Darien Center, tel. 716/547–9242). *158 sites. Facilities: fireplace, flush toilets, swimming, fishing, children's area, recreation building. $10. Open June–Sept.*

Niagara Falls KOA (2570 Grand Island Blvd., Grand Island, tel. 716/773–7583). *350 sites. Facilities: fireplaces, flush toilets, hot showers, swimming, fishing, boat rentals, store, laundry facility, children's area. $16.95–32.95. Open May–Oct.*
Niagara Falls North KOA (1250 Pletcher Rd., Lewiston, tel. 716/754–8013). *100 sites. Facilities: fireplaces, flush toilets, hot showers, swimming, children's area, store, laundry. $16.95–$32.95. Open Apr.–Oct.*

Chautauqua/ Cattaraugus Camping facilities in the area include state and private campgrounds ranging from rustic woodland sites for tents to those with all utilities and programs of entertainment and recreation. The premier camping area is **Allegany State Park,** which comprises a substantial portion of the southwest corner of the state. It offers a diverse variety of cabin rentals, but no tent camping. **Lake Erie State Park,** a 318-acre woodland park along Lake Erie, has campsites, some with electrical hookup, as well as cabins. Reservations for both state parks can be made through 1–800–456–CAMP in New York State. Commercial campgrounds listed below offer full hookup, laundry, and sanitary facilities:

Camp Chautauqua (Rte. 394, Stow, tel. 716/789–3435). *450 sites. Facilities: on lake, swimming, fishing, boat rentals, children's area, store, recreation building. $18. Open year-round.*
Chautauqua Family (Dinsbier Rd., Mayville, tel. 716/753–2212). *35 sites. Facilities: swimming, fishing, children's area, store. $10. Open May–Sept.*
Forest Haven Campground (Page Rd., Kennedy, tel. 716/267–5902). *106 sites. Facilities: pool, store, recreation building, children's area. $10. Open May–Oct.*
KOA Lake Erie/Westfield Kampground (1 E. Lake Rd., Barcalona, tel. 716/326–3573). *116 sites. Facilities: 2 pools, fishing, children's area, recreation building, store. Open Apr.–Oct.*
Safari Camp Chautauqua Lake (Rte. 17 and Thumb Rd., Dewittville, tel. 716/386–3804). *100 sites. Facilities: pool, children's area, recreation building, store. Open year-round.*

The Arts

The Buffalo–Niagara Falls area is surprisingly rich in the arts, from Artpark—the country's only state park devoted to the performing arts—to a renowned art museum and the Buffalo Philharmonic Orchestra, which enjoyed a triumphant European tour in 1988. Opera, theater, dance, and film are all on the program at the Chautauqua Institution during its eight-week summer season. *For tickets and information, contact Chautauqua Institution, Chautauqua, 14722, tel. 716/357–5635.*

Theater

Buffalo has long been respected for its theater. Actress Katherine Cornell was born and played here. The theater district on Main Street between Virginia and Chippewa streets has undergone a renaissance. A lane in the district is named after native son Michael Bennett of *Chorus Line* fame.

The **Alleyway Theatre** is an intimate theater in the heart of the Theater District. *One Curtain Up Alley, Buffalo, tel. 716/852–2600.*

Kavinoky Theatre is a professional theater on the D'Youville College campus. *320 Porter Ave., Buffalo, tel. 716/881–7668.*

Lancaster Opera House is an elegantly restored 19th-century opera house now used for plays and operettas. *21 Central Ave., Lancaster, tel. 716/683–1776.*

Pfeifer Theatre is home to the State University of New York at Buffalo's Department of Theater and Dance. Performances Oct.–Dec. and Feb.–May. *681 Main St., Buffalo, tel. 716/831–3742.*

Shaw Festival in nearby Niagara-on-the-Lake, Ontario, is a world-renowned theater festival featuring the works of Shaw and his contemporaries in three theaters. *Open May–Oct., tel. 416/468–2172 for ticket and accommodations information.*

Shea's Buffalo Theater is the showplace of the district. It is an ornate crystal palace that has been restored to its original grandeur. It boasts one of the largest Wurlitzer organs ever built. Theater, dance, opera and music, national touring companies. *646 Main St., Buffalo, tel. 716/847–0050.*

Studio Arena Theater is the city's resident theater, with live performances September to May. World premieres and pre-Broadway productions are staged here. *710 Main St., Buffalo, tel. 716/856–5650.*

Concerts

Buffalo has had a long tradition as an important music town, both classical and jazz. Although he doesn't play often in Buffalo, funk star Rick James was born in Buffalo and lives in nearby East Aurora. The Arts Council of Buffalo and Erie County (700 Main St., tel. 716/856–7520) provides information about all area arts and music events on **ARTSline**, a 24-hour hotline (716/847–1444). The renowned 87-member **Buffalo Philharmonic Orchestra** (tel. 716/885–5000) celebrated its 50th anniversary season during 1985–86. The orchestra performs in Kleinhans Music Hall, Symphony Circle, acclaimed as being acoustically perfect.

Michael D. Rockefeller Arts Center, State University of New York College at Fredonia (tel. 716/673–3217). Concerts are given during the school year by Fredonia Chamber Players, student orchestras, and such professional orchestras as the Buffalo Philharmonic Orchestra. In addition, nationally known musicians perform here.

Film

A new theater complex in the heart of the Buffalo Theater District—decorated with huge photos of Buffalo theaters from an earlier age—has been attracting crowds. Art films and repertory films are shown regularly at area colleges and universities and the Albright-Knox Art Gallery (tel. ARTSline 716/847–1444).

Nightlife

Cabaret

Canterbury, *2250 Niagara Falls Blvd., Tonawanda, tel. 716/ 695–3557.*
Forks Hotel. Magicians perform here every weekend. *Broadway and Union Rd., Cheektowaga, tel. 716/683–6545.*
Red Jacket Inn, *7001 Buffalo Ave., Niagara Falls, tel. 716/ 283–7612.*
Daffodil's is a lush restaurant with weekend entertainment. *930 Maple Rd., Williamsville, tel. 716/688–5413.*

Jazz

Anchor Bar, birthplace of Buffalo chicken wings, with jazz on the weekends. *1047 Main St., Buffalo, tel. 716/886–8920.*
Blue Note features regular jazz combos nightly, as well as occasional national artists. *1677 Main St., Buffalo, tel. 716/883– 5826.*
Colored Musicians Club. The name refers to the club's origins in the 1930s as the union local for black musicians. It's now a cherished institution for all jazz lovers. *145 Broadway, Buffalo, tel. 716/855–9383.*
Marshall's. Nothing but the blues—this friendly hole-in-the-wall books name acts. *1678 Main St. Buffalo, tel. 716/881–4185.*
Tralfamadore Cafe. The largest and best-known jazz club in the area. It books not only headlining jazz groups, but also national-level comedy, folk, blues, and rock. *Theater Pl. off Pearl St., tel. 716/854–1415.*

Rock

Alibi Lounge. A popular swinging rock club on the falls. *7121 Niagara Falls Blvd., Niagara Falls, tel. 716/283–9896.*
Bachmann's Surfside. Especially popular with the young crowd during the summer. *4471 Lake Shore Rd., Hamburg, tel. 716/ 627–7960.*
Nietzsche's. An affably bohemian place, as likely to feature reggae, blues, or folk. In the heart of Allentown. *248 Allen St., Buffalo, tel. 716/886–8539.*
Surf Club. Chautauqua's premier party bar. *Bemus Point, tel. 716/386–5088.*

Country-Western

Al-E-Oops. *5389 Genesee St., Lancaster, tel. 716/681–0200.*
Country Club. *2186 Seneca St., Buffalo, tel. 716/824–8448.*
Golden Nugget. *2464 Seneca St., West Seneca, tel. 716/825– 9013.*
Hello Dolly's Lounge. *481 Niagara Falls Blvd., Tonawanda, tel. 716/836–9357.*
Wagon Wheel. *7201 Niagara Falls Blvd., Niagara Falls, tel. 716/283–9861.*

Comedy

The Comedy Line. National artists and open mike. Fridays. *Holiday Inn, Fredonia, tel. 716/673–1351.*
The Comedy Trap. National acts and open mike. *1180 Hertel Ave., Buffalo, tel. 716/874–LAFF.*
Stuffed Mushroom. National acts and open mike. *2580 Main St., Buffalo, tel. 716/835–7971.*

Folk

Belle Watling's Eating and Drinking Establishment. Folk groups on weekends. *1449 Abbott Rd., Lackawanna, tel. 716/ 826–8838.*
Buffalo Irish Center. Mostly Irish music, of course. *245 Abbott Rd., tel. 716/825–9535.*
Paddy O's Restaurant. Again, lots of Irish music and singers, especially on weekends. *4000 Bailey Ave., Amherst, tel. 716/ 835–4000.*
Network of Light. Coffeehouse series on weekends. *224 Lexington Ave., Buffalo, tel. 716/882–1205.*

Index

Personal Itinerary

Departure *Date*

Time

Transportation

Arrival *Date*   *Time*

Departure *Date*   *Time*

Transportation

Accommodations

Arrival *Date*   *Time*

Departure *Date*   *Time*

Transportation

Accommodations

Arrival *Date*   *Time*

Departure *Date*   *Time*

Transportation

Accommodations

Addresses

Name	*Name*
Address	*Address*
Telephone	*Telephone*
Name	*Name*
Address	*Address*
Telephone	*Telephone*
Name	*Name*
Address	*Address*
Telephone	*Telephone*
Name	*Name*
Address	*Address*
Telephone	*Telephone*
Name	*Name*
Address	*Address*
Telephone	*Telephone*
Name	*Name*
Address	*Address*
Telephone	*Telephone*
Name	*Name*
Address	*Address*
Telephone	*Telephone*
Name	*Name*
Address	*Address*
Telephone	*Telephone*

Fodor's Travel Guides

U.S. Guides

Alaska	Florida	New York State	The Upper Great
Arizona	Hawaii	Pacific North Coast	Lakes Region
Boston	Las Vegas	Philadelphia	Vacations on the
California	Los Angeles	Puerto Rico	Jersey Shore
Cape Cod	Maui	(Pocket Guide)	Virgin Islands
The Carolinas & the	Miami & the	The Rockies	Virginia & Maryland
Georgia Coast	Keys	San Diego	Waikiki
The Chesapeake	New England	San Francisco	Washington, D.C.
Region	New Mexico	San Francisco	
Chicago	New Orleans	(Pocket Guide)	
Colorado	New York City	The South	
Disney World & the	New York City	Texas	
Orlando Area	(Pocket Guide)	USA	

Foreign Guides

Acapulco	Egypt	London	Spain
Amsterdam	Europe	(Pocket Guide)	Sweden
Australia	Europe's Great	Madrid & Barcelona	Switzerland
Austria	Cities	Mexico	Thailand
The Bahamas	France	Montreal &	Tokyo
The Bahamas	Germany	Quebec City	Toronto
(Pocket Guide)	Great Britain	Morocco	Turkey
Baja & the Pacific	Greece	Munich	Vienna
Coast Resorts	The Himalayan	New Zealand	Yugoslavia
Barbados	Countries	Paris	
Belgium &	Holland	Paris (Pocket Guide)	
Luxembourg	Hong Kong	Portugal	
Bermuda	India	Rio de Janeiro	
Brazil	Ireland	Rome	
Budget Europe	Israel	Saint Martin/	
Canada	Italy	Sint Maarten	
Canada's Atlantic	Italy 's Great Cities	Scandinavia	
Provinces	Jamaica	Scandinavian Cities	
Cancun, Cozumel,	Japan	Scotland	
Yucatan Peninsula	Kenya, Tanzania,	Singapore	
Caribbean	Seychelles	South America	
Central America	Korea	South Pacific	
China	London	Southeast Asia	
Eastern Europe	London Companion	Soviet Union	

Special-Interest Guides

Cruises and Ports	Smart Shopper's	Shopping in Europe
of Call	Guide to London	Skiing in North
	Healthy Escapes	America